JEWS AND JEWISH LIFE IN RUSSIA
AND THE SOVIET UNION

The Cummings Center for Russian and East European Studies
The Cummings Center Series

Jews and Jewish Life in Russia and the Soviet Union

Yaacov Ro'i, Editor

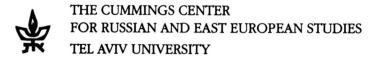

THE CUMMINGS CENTER
FOR RUSSIAN AND EAST EUROPEAN STUDIES
TEL AVIV UNIVERSITY

The Cummings Center is Tel Aviv University's main framework for research, study, documentation and publication relating to the history and current affairs of Russia, the former Soviet republics and Eastern Europe. Its current projects include Fundamentalism and Secularism in the Muslim Republics of the Soviet Union; the Establishment of Political Parties and the Process of Democratization in Russia; Religion and Society in Russia; the Creation of New Historical Narratives in Contemporary Russia; and Soviet Military Theory and History.

In addition, the Center seeks to establish a bridge between the Russian and Western academic communities, promoting a dialogue with Russian academic circles through joint projects, seminars, roundtables and publications.

THE CUMMINGS CENTER SERIES

The titles published in this series are the product of original research by the Center's faculty, research staff and associated fellows. The Cummings Center Series also serves as a forum for publishing declassified Russian archival material of interest to scholars in the fields of history and political science.

Managing Editor – Deena Leventer

JEWS AND JEWISH LIFE IN RUSSIA AND THE SOVIET UNION

EDITED BY
YAACOV RO'I

Routledge
Taylor & Francis Group

LONDON AND NEW YORK

First published in 1995 in Great Britain by
Routledge
2 Park Square, Milton Park, Abingdon, Oxon, OX14 4RN
270 Madison Ave, New York NY 10016

Transferred to Digital Printing 2006

Copyright © 1995

British Library Cataloguing in Publication Data

Jews and Jewish Life in Russia and the Soviet Union. - (Cummings
Center Series)
I. Ro'i, Yaacov II. Series
947.004924

ISBN 0–7146–4619–9 (cloth)
ISBN 0–7146–4149–9 (paper)

Library of Congress Cataloging in Publication Data

Jews and Jewish life in Russia and the Soviet Union / edited by Yaacov
Ro'i
       p. cm. - (The Cummings Center Series)
       Includes index.
       ISBN 0–7146–4619–9 (cloth) - ISBN 0–7146–4149–9 (paper) :

1. Jews - Soviet Union - History. 2. Antisemitism - Soviet Union. 3. Soviet Union
- Emigration and immigration. 4. Jews - Russia - History. 5. Soviet Union - Ethnic
relations. I. Ro'i, Yaacov. II. Series
DS135.R92J46/ 1995
947', 004924–dc20

                                             94–33683
                                            CIP

*All rights reserved. No part of this publication may be reproduced in any form or
by any means, electronic, mechanical, photocopying, recording or otherwise,
without the prior permission of Routledge and Company Limited.*

Typeset by University Publishing Projects, Tel Aviv, Israel

Publisher's Note
The publisher has gone to great lengths to ensure the quality of this reprint
but points out that some imperfections in the original may be apparent

To the memory of

SHMUEL ETTINGER

who taught so many of us so much

Contents

Acknowledgements

The Cummings Center for Russian and East European Studies is grateful to Beatrice Cummings Mayer, for her inspiration and dedicated support of the Center's activities.

Jews and Jewish Life in Russia and the Soviet Union evolved from an international conference held in Moscow in April 1993 by the Cummings Center for Russian Studies of Tel Aviv University, the Graduate School and City College of the City University of New York and the Department of History of the Russian Academy of Sciences. The conference was made possible through a generous grant from the Nathan Cummings Foundation. It was also sponsored by the Jewish Agency and the American Jewish Joint Distribution Committee.

Prof. Aleksandr Oganovich Tchoubarian was an instrumental partner in organizing the conference. Drs. Mikhail Narinsky and Boris Morozov made every effort to ensure its success.

Finally, thanks are due to Deena Leventer and Beryl Belsky for their professionalism and perseverance in editing the manuscript.

Introduction

The story of Russian and Soviet Jewry is basically that of the interrelationship between a number of factors which transcended transformations in the country's political order. One of these factors is, paradoxically, regime policy; another, the attitude of the surrounding population to the Jews; and a third, the Jews' socio-economic conditions, which were largely a function of the first two. Indeed, it often seems as though external factors, rather than developments and trends intrinsic to the Jews' own existence, determined the *sui generis* nature of the Russian and Soviet Jewish community, to the extent that one wonders whether it is appropriate to use the term community, which implies a certain homogeneity.

The four chapters which address themselves to the pre-Soviet era are singularly salient to this issue. While they necessarily touch upon only a few aspects of Russian Jewish existence prior to the October Revolution, each of these features is a significant one. Indeed, the question posed by Eli Lederhendler, whether one can legitimately speak of a Russian Jewry in the 19th century, goes directly to the heart of the matter. Lederhendler's basic contention is that a priori, upon their initial inclusion in the Russian empire, the Jews of Poland, Ukraine, Belorussia and Lithuania were split ideologically, structurally and culturally. It was their common experience with tsarist policy that gradually began to weld them together. Only at the very end of the tsarist period does Lederhendler discern a Russian Jewry in the sense that one speaks of Western national Jewries, namely one that begins to associate with the non-Jewish populations around it, to identify with some of their problems and to aspire to take part in their culture.

Shaul Stampfer dwells on domestic migration within the tsarist empire: its dimensions, quality and significance for Jewish society. Because of the very large Russian Jewish emigration to the United States in the thirty or so years preceding World War I and its relevance for American Jewish historians in particular, local migratory trends have been generally downplayed. Certainly, this migration demonstrated some of the central strengths and weaknesses of the Russian Jewish community: on the one hand, a solidarity that enabled Jews to change their places of residence with a greater feeling of confidence than could other sectors in the population; on the other, a basic volatility and uncertainty that made Jews especially prone to

1

move, on the assumption that almost anywhere living conditions would be better than those they were enduring. The most important point, surely, that emerges from Stampfer's essay is that this *perpetuum mobile* began to erode the traditional stability of the Jewish communal structure and the Jews' individual existence before 1917.

The chapters by Ascher and Klier address themselves more directly to political issues. Ascher's topic, the anti-Jewish pogroms in the period of the 1905 revolution and the involvement of the tsarist government in inciting them, has remained a deeply controversial question up to the present day. Ascher contends that the top level of government had a definite and conscious interest in preventing the pogroms, which they feared might further destablize an already mercurial situation and jeopardize the entire system. Yet, the interaction between official and social anti-Semitism, that is the traditional Russian Judaeophobia that was manifest both from above and from below, was undoubtedly a main factor in unleashing the pogroms. It, too, continued to be one of the key characteristics of Jewish life in the Soviet period.

Klier analyzes Jewish participation in the revolutionary movement in the generation prior to 1917. He takes as his point of departure Igor' Shafarevich's avowedly anti-Semitic condemnation of the Jews as an isolated, offish group in Russian society that had at heart its own interests and not those of the country and the general population, and was, therefore, by definition disloyal. Klier then examines the socio-economic and political conditions in which the Jews lived under the tsars and claims that these basically explain the Jews' attraction to radicalism, combined, he agrees, with a certain 'inner Jewish drive'. As the Soviet regime 'reverts to type', almost, as it were, consciously following in the footsteps of the tsars, both regarding the Jews, against which it discriminates, and on a general plane, as it becomes increasingly corrupt, bureaucratic and inefficient, all three elements that characterized the Jewish situation re-appear under communism. The first of these is the gap between the Jews and Russian society, although in the Soviet period this rift is infinitely more nebulous than before. The second is the uniquely disadvantageous situation of the Jews in an environment in which the vast majority of the population at large endures considerable hardship and suffering. Thirdly, we find again a peculiar Jewish intellectualism-cum-romanticism that makes Jews somehow different and suspect. Shafarevich is, after all, a product of Soviet education, even if his criteria, parameters and values are those of nineteenth-century Russian nationalism.

The ideology upon which the Bolsheviks posited their policy

regarding the Jewish question was, in fact, new, different and, naturally, peculiar to their regime. Naomi Blank examines the Bolshevik/Soviet position on the level of principle — at the various stages of the party's lifetime — regarding the Jewish question, the issue of the existence of such a question and possible solutions to it. Since Lenin and Stalin saw the Jews as destined to assimilate, and since the Jews did not fulfil the conditions laid down for nationhood, their continued existence as a minority in the Soviet Union was solely provisory and did not obligate their receipt of national rights as a collective. Until the mid-thirties recognition of the prevalence of anti-Semitism, however, did dictate acceptance of at least the possibility of a Jewish question. From that time on, the party itself initiated an ideological campaign designed to eradicate Jewish distinctiveness. This, however, was not limited to Jews who maintained a specifically Jewish identity, but included those who had acculturated totally. In fact, the latter were sometimes viewed as the more dangerous enemy in that they had ingratiated themselves into Soviet society and culture. By the late Stalin period the regime claimed that the Jewish question had disappeared. Future expressions of Jewish identity and even blatant nationalism in the USSR were to be met by 'anti-Zionist' propaganda that, despite its manifest anti-Semitic overtones, purported to draw a distinction between Zionism and Judaism.

Ideology notwithstanding, policy was rooted rather on pragmatic considerations and political constraints. Robert Weinberg's treatise on Birobidzhan illustrates once more the continuity between the Jewish policy of the tsars and that of the RCP(b) — the Russian Communist Party (of Bolsheviks) — in the 1920s and 1930s. The Birobidzhan project was intended to 'productivize' Jews, a slogan that had been used by one school at least within tsarist officialdom. In particular, it aimed to settle them on the land — a goal that not a few nineteenth century officials had contemplated for Jews, notably in the southern part of the Pale of Settlement, in 'New Russia'. The failure of Birobidzhan to 'solve' the Jewish question was due to a series of factors that had led to the similar outcome of earlier plans to colonize Jews, namely the socio-economic characteristics of the Jews' own background and such extraneous influences as the dysfunctional link between government planning and implementation.

In contrast, Fishman's essay focuses on new trends that pertained explicitly to Bolshevik policy. True, Jewish education had suffered under the tsars, but it had never been actually suppressed, let alone threatened with extinction. In the 1920s, the Bolshevik regime, committed to 'socialist construction' on the foundations laid by Marxist dialectical materialism, sought to rid the country of the trappings of religion, which it viewed as a relic of a class-based society. One of its first edicts — even prior to the separation of church from state and school from church — had decreed the complete control of educational matters and institutions by the Commissariat of Education. Education became a crucial instrument in mobilizing the population as a whole to participate in the building of communism. All education had perforce to come under the aegis of the Soviet party and state. Fishman describes the rearguard action of Jewish religious functionaries throughout the 1920s to maintain surreptitiously the traditional institutions of Jewish religious education, the *heder* and the *yeshiva*. It included the formation and operation of an underground organization that supervised this educational activity, with the material assistance of US Jewry through the American Jewish Joint Distribution Committee (the JDC). Not surprisingly, even the resilience of Jewish communal activists and the cooperation between them and world Jewry were unable to withstand the renewed and virulent campaign launched against all religions following the new anti-religious legislation of 1929.

Yet, not all was the outcome of Bolshevik policy. Here and there, groups of Jews, or even individual Jews, played an autonomous role. Such were the Jewish writers who returned to the Soviet Union during the 1920s because they believed that the communist regime was fulfilling their own dreams. They thought that they would, or even should, devote their talents to participate in creating the new society, in bringing to the Jewish masses the message of what they perceived as the new utopia. Der Nister, as David Roskies shows, hoped to find a niche for his anti-bourgeois art in the USSR, only to find himself, by the end of the 1920s, severely curtailed by its increasingly rigorous constraints. With all his wealth of associations — Jewish, Christian and European — Der Nister sought to enrich the new Soviet Yiddish culture. But his offering was rejected and he was personally consumed by the regime, at first silenced artistically and eventually, over twenty years later, tried and executed.

In the interwar period, then, the forecast of Lenin and Stalin seemed to be materializing. Soviet policy, on the one hand, and the desire of Jews themselves to integrate into the new society and take advantage of the demographic, educational and professional opportunities now open to them, on the other, propelled them in the direction of assimilation. World War II transformed this trend radically. The annexation of the 'Western territories' in conjunction with the Molotov-Ribbentrop Pact, the influx of several hundreds of thousands of refugees from those parts of Poland overrun by the Germans in

INTRODUCTION

1939, the Nazi occupation of large areas of the Soviet Union including all of Belorussia and the Ukraine, and the Holocaust reawakened Jewish consciousness and clarified for Jew and non-Jew alike that the Jews had remained a distinct people. Paradoxically, the physical annihilation of two million or so Jews (the exact number has not yet been finally resolved), made Soviet Jewry a distinct nationality in the Soviet Union, perhaps for the first time. The collaboration of non-Jewish Soviet citizens with the Nazis in anti-Jewish 'actions', the resonance enjoyed by Nazi propaganda among large sections of the population and, toward the end of the war, the beginnings of a virulent official anti-Semitism on the part of the top party leadership also served to bring home this point. Altshuler, in his analysis of the singular features of the Holocaust in the Soviet Union, dwells on these issues in detail, demonstrating that the Nazis' identification of bolshevism with the Jews, the specifics of the Soviet regime and the Jews' position within Soviet society led to different tactics in the Nazi treatment of the Jews in that country and dictated the nature of the attitude thereto of the non-Jewish population and of Jewish resistance.

Nowhere, perhaps, was the new situation created by the war more evident than in the writings of one of the leading Soviet Jewish literary figures, Vasilii Grossman. The fact that Grossman wrote in Russian and was, indeed, a product of Russian culture made this all the more poignant. John Garrard in his chapter on Grossman's contribution to the literature on the war — as distinct from his journalism (Grossman was a war correspondent for the army newspaper *Krasnaia zvezda*) and his work on *The Black Book* — depicts colourfully the writer's new Jewish consciousness and awareness of his Jewish roots. He shows how, in the precarious conditions in which artists lived and worked in the Soviet Union at the time, Grossman sought to circumvent the constraints of censorship to bring to subsequent generations the individual and collective message of the Holocaust precisely in the *genre* of belletristics.

The period immediately following the liberation of the USSR's western areas from the Nazi occupation seemed in many ways to be a harbinger of a new era of conciliation toward the USSR's Jewish population, according to Allan Kagedan. Hundreds of thousands of Jews who had fled into the country's interior in the face of the Nazi invader, began returning to the Ukraine, Belorussia, the European parts of the USSR and the Baltic republics. In this apparently positive atmosphere a group of Jewish public figures linked with the Jewish Anti-fascist Committee proposed the establishment of a Jewish autonomous region in the Crimea. It soon became clear, however, that while the Soviet leadership was prepared to enable Jews to try to return to a normal existence as individuals, it was not willing to condone, let alone encourage, any collective normalization of Jewish existence.

The Jewish community, for its part, continued to display what appeared to the authorities unduly nationalistic inclinations. One of the spheres in which this atmsophere was particularly prevalent was the synagogue, where the various religious communities that renewed their existence and function after the war resorted to a spate of activities that in no way corresponded to what the party and government believed compatible with their *raison d'être*, that is, the conduct of religious worship in the strictest and narrowest meaning of the word. The chapter by Ro'i tries to give a sense of the scope of this new dynamism that seemed to encompass Jewish communities in a large number of towns. Had it not been for the very close control of the powers-that-be, which were not averse to taking severe punitive measures, such as the removal of rabbis and even the closing of synagogues, it is more than likely that the atmosphere that prevailed among certain sectors of the Jewish community might well have taken on significant dimensions.

The situation in Georgia, where there were a disproportionately large number of synagogues, deserves special attention. Lili Baazova shows the basically traditional way of life of the Georgian Jewish community and the importance of the synagogue for Jews in that republic from the immediate postwar period to the 1970s. It was the emigration to Israel of large numbers of Georgian Jews in that decade that terminated the existence of not a few communities, especially in the villages and smaller townships. Even in Georgia, however, already prior to this emigration, the authorities had taken repressive measures against certain synagogues, although in some instances, uncharacteristically, these had been totally unavailing and the authorities had been compelled by the virulence of the Jewish reaction to retract them.

The constraints and restrictions practised against Jewish religious and cultural life in the late 1940s–early 1950s were not sufficient. The regime in the late Stalin years, which was one of the most ideologically stringent, politically harsh and internationally isolationist of all periods from 1917 to 1991, was determined to make the Jews the latest example of a 'punished people', which would be uprooted from their homes like the peoples deported toward the end of the war. The *mise-en-scène* was to be provided by the Doctors' Plot, the basic postulate of which was the treachery and constant subversion of the Jews as a group. Preparations for this drama, as Iakov Etinger, the son of one of the arrested doctors shows, had been going on for over two years before the actual announcement of the 'plot' by TASS on 13 January 1953.

One of the many interesting aspects of the Doctors' Plot was the reverberations it evoked among the non-Jewish population. Many Jews who lived through this period, including Il'ia Erenburg in *Ottepel'* (*The Thaw*) published in 1956, have given testimony to the tribulations suffered by Jews in general and Jewish scientists and doctors in particular at the hands of the population during the weeks prior to Stalin's death on 5 March 1953. Alexander Lokshin describes the reaction of non-Jews to the statement published by the new leadership that the entire plot had been a fabrication. He gives us a fascinating insight into the variegated viewpoints held by different sectors of the population, both regarding the Soviet leadership as such and its manipulations and machinations of public opinion and the atmosphere in society, and regarding the Jews themselves. An interesting slant on his story is the significance the party élite attributed to the attitude of the population and the implications of this for the study of the interaction between official and social anti-Semitism, between the deliberate, political anti-Semitism from above and the spontaneous anti-Semitism from below.

The post-Stalin period never reverted to the viciousness of the Black Years of Soviet Jewry, yet anti-Semitism and anti-Jewish discrimination remained the order of the day. Nevertheless, as a result of pressures from both within and without, there was a certain erosion in the official Soviet position. This was made evident in the field of Yiddish culture, which, although never fully rehabilitated and legitimized, did, little by little, gain minimal recognition, with all the limitations that this entailed in an authoritarian regime. One of the people who participated in Yiddish cultural activity in the last decade or so of the USSR's existence, Velvl Chernin, records its scope and content, not in its *samizdat* and clandestine, but in its official and open form.

The attitude to Yiddish cultural activity was but a single component in what Igor Krupnik calls 'post-totalitarian manipulation'. He insists that there was no consistent, carefully thought out and strictly implemented Jewish policy. There was no consistency, uniformity or strategy in the post-Stalin regime's treatment of its Jewish population. On the whole, the Jews were dealt with within the terms of reference of Soviet nationalities theory and policy in this period as in the pre-World War II years. Furthermore, the post-Stalin leadership introduced few, if any, new elements into policy toward the Jews as an ethnic group and toward Jewish culture in its transition from the 'ardent restructuring' and 'blunt annihilation' that had characterized the earlier and later Stalin era respectively, to ad hoc maneouvering. Its lack of initiative, however, was more than countered by the Jews' own drive toward social mobility — large numbers of Jews figuring in certain professional and social fields (science, technology, culture and the arts). A challenge seemed in fact to be presented by the Jews' very existence and characteristic features within Soviet society, which contested and contradicted Soviet theory regarding nationality in both its political and ethnic aspects. As a result, the establishment moved erratically from totally ignoring the Jews and Jewish history, including their contribution to the evolution of the Soviet experiment, to lashing out at Jewish nationalism, the reactionary nature of Judaism and the Jews' links to the capitalist, imperialist order. Its failure was practically predetermined by both the lack of consecutive thinking and the anachronistc nature of Yiddish and Birobidzhan, which were the only two existing channels for recognizing and allowing concessions to the Jews as an ethnic group and were a priori incapable of competing with Hebrew and Israeli culture that began seeping through to Soviet Jews as of the late 1950s. The final blow was probably dealt by the *aliya* activists in the 1970s who raised general issues of Jewish identity and survival as part of their struggle to opt out of the system totally.

The vicissitudes of Soviet policy toward the Jews were perhaps no match for Jewish cultural activism and the emigration movement. At the same time, they seem in some ways to have triumphed, especially when one analyzes the Jews' demographic pattern from World War II until the final disintegration of the Soviet Union, and, indeed, even afterwards. This trend, which has been entirely consistent and indicates a dwindling of the Jewish population beyond the point of potential revival, is underscored in its stark reality by Mark Tolts. The processes of modernization and assimilation that had begun to manifest themselves in the pre-war years — urbanization, a falling birth rate, mixed marriages — were accelerated by the concomitants of the war itself, its tremendous losses and the new mobility of the surviving population. The Jews became one of the most elderly populations in the country, intermarriage became the order of the day, the birth rate continued to fall. All these factors were predominant in determining a persistent shrinking of the Jewish population even before emigration began taking its toll in the 1970s, and continued to account for most of the diminution of the Jewish group inhabiting the USSR until the mass exodus of the late 1980s–early 1990s made emigration the prominent factor in this decline.

The story of Soviet Jewry affected not only the Soviet domestic arena. One of the interesting aspects of Soviet policy toward Israel from the time of its establishment, as appears in the chapter by Sementchenko and Mirokhin, is the Soviet leadership's attitude toward the connection between its own Jewish citizens and the new Jewish state. While officially denying the existence of any such link, it was clear to the USSR's decision-making bodies that this was not an entirely realistic position. Strizhov gives us the official explanation for Soviet support of Israel's establishment and the context in which that support unfolded. Using Soviet foreign ministry documentation, he demonstrates that Moscow's main motivation was the desire to be included in the solution of a pressing international problem that was giving rise to a major local conflict. Its strategy was to take advantage of differences of opinion between the US and Britain, as well as of the obviously partial position of the former, given its exposure to Jewish pressure, and the complex situation of the latter as a directly interested party, to make its mark in the international arena as the debate over Palestine's future unravelled. Yet, the global and regional points of view are clearly not the entire picture. Sementchenko and Mirokhin, basing themselves on the same documentation, give us an insight into the Soviet ruling élite's deliberations concerning immigration to Palestine (until May 1948) and Israel (after that date), including in the latter instance that of Jews from the USSR itself. Despite continued caution in relating directly to this issue, reports from the Soviet legation in Israel in the very first period dwell upon Israeli interest in Soviet Jewish emigration. By 1951 it was being suggested that this might well become the criterion for relations between the two countries.

Israel necessarily felt its relevance for Soviet Jewry. At first, it kept the issue low key in its relationship with Moscow, focusing instead on other, less controversial points of contact, including *aliya* from the East European people's democracies. However, the extreme manifestation of official anti-Semitism in both Eastern Europe and the USSR, as given expression at the end of the Stalin period in the Slansky Trial and the Doctors' Plot, brought things to a head, and Israel, as Govrin points out, became the spearhead of a worldwide campaign directed toward aiding Soviet Jews. This aid was to have two main aims — improving the Jews' situation within the Soviet Union and facilitating the emigration to Israel of those among them who wished to opt out of a socialist society committed to the disappearance of the Jews as a nation. By the 1960s these endeavours were beginning to have effect.

Soviet Jewry also played a significant role in Soviet-US relations. Minton Goldman shows some of the intricacies of the interconnection between, on the one hand, the US' general, including strategic, interests and its desire to ameliorate emigration conditions for Soviet Jews, and, on the other, the different perceptions of the Administration and Congress as to how pressures could and should be exerted on the Soviet Union. The results may perhaps not always have been to the best and immediate interests of Soviet Jewish would-be emigrants, although Soviet Jews did find considerable moral support in the Jackson-Vanik amendment and in the knowledge that their fate was discussed at the top-level of superpower politics. Moreover, in the long run the US did make its forceful contribution to the final freedom of emigration enacted toward the end of the Gorbachev period, even if, at the same time, it in practice severely limited its own role as a destination for that emigration by refusing refugee status to more than a core number of Soviet Jewish emigrants.

Eventually, then, as a result of domestic and external pressures, Soviet Jews did begin leaving the Soviet Union in large numbers to Israel and the US, and some to other countries. Prior to the era of large-scale emigration in the 1970s, there persisted a more or less monolithic image of the Soviet Jew, although admittedly it differed somewhat outside and inside the Soviet Union. The very process of large-scale emigration, Markowitz points out, broke down the old stereotypes, which, in any case, did not correspond to reality. In addition, the Russian Jewish émigré adopted certain characteristics of his new country of residence. Simultaneously, he retained specific features of his earlier self-identification, including the imprint of his Soviet experience and of the Russian culture to which most Jews assimilated. Perhaps, more surprisingly, the contact with former friends and relatives and the changing circumstances in their own country have led to transformations in identity among those who have stayed behind. In this way a new 'trans-national' Russian Jewish community has been formed. If, during most of the nineteenth century, there was as yet no meaningful Russian Jewish community even in Russia, by the end of the twentieth century, this community was straddling three continents.

Another channel of mutual influence between Russian Jews who have emigrated to Israel and those who have remained behind is that of literature. Dimitri Segal discusses the mutual reflections of Russian and Hebrew literature, the culminating point of which is the adoption of Russian literary models and values, both traditional and modernistic, by emergent modern Hebrew writers and the effect of Israeli and Hebrew patterns on the literature of olim who continue to produce in Russian. In this way, perhaps the Russian Jew whether in Israel, or even in Russia (through his new acquaintanceship with Hebrew literature and his earlier familiarity with Jewish literature written originally in Russian), may bridge the gap and correct the asymmetry that exists between the two cultures as a result of the dearth of reference in Russian culture to the world of Hebrew culture.

Our story, thus, does not end with the disintegration and disappearance of the Soviet Union. On the one hand, the Soviet or Russian Jew has survived with his own specific identity and features that are the outcome of a lifelong education and experience. On the other hand, just as the Soviet regime inherited a Jewish question from its tsarist predecessor, so did it in turn bequeath to its successor states most of the ingredients of that same anomalous situation that had characterized Soviet Jewish existence. The Jews had indeed largely assimilated, or, at least, acculturated. They had intermarried, perhaps more than any other ethnic minority in the Soviet Union. Yet, they remained distinct, and as the new states sought and seek their identity — political, social, ethnic — the position of the Jews remains a sensitive issue, a barometer, as it were, of both their political orientation and social stability. True, one of the last enactments of the Soviet Union had been legislation recognizing the right of its citizens to leave and return to the country of their free will. And while large numbers of Jews availed themselves of this opportunity (over 400,000 emigrating in the two single years 1990–91), many Jews found themselves in a major quandary. Rosefielde analyzes the economic considerations that might have helped and might continue to help Jews decide one way or the other whether to throw in their lot with the country of their residence or risk the costs of emigration. Unquestionably, the economic factor is a significant, if not the predominant, one in reaching such a decision for large numbers of Jews. It would appear that, except for a relatively small group of entrepreneurs, if material considerations are going to be determinant, the outlook for Russia is such that most Jews will choose to leave.

Ryvkina looks at three major issues in the lives of Jews in the three Slavic countries of the CIS — their national self-identification and attitude to Jewish culture, their professional status and opportunities, and their attitude to emigration. Significantly, in all three fields she finds basic contradictions, which seem to indicate that today, as in the Soviet period, the position of the Jewish population is fundamentally anomalous, characterized by inherent conflict and unpredictability. Neither the Jews themselves nor the society surrounding them appear to be able to decide what the nature of the Jewish existence in the CIS should be, either on the collective or on the individual level.

As Ryvkina points out, only the future will tell how this dual dilemma will be solved. Although today Jews have the possibility to leave at will, many are reluctant to do so for a variety of reasons. To judge by history, specifically, the accommodation of the Jews to the Soviet regime and of both the authorities and society in that period to the new conditions of co-existence with the Jews, resolution of the dual dilemma may take a long time and may develop along different, even conflicting, lines as circumstances change within the country.

Yaacov Ro'i
Tel Aviv
July 1994

I

THE TSARIST LEGACY: SOCIO-ECONOMIC TRENDS

1

Did Russian Jewry Exist prior to 1917?

ELI LEDERHENDLER

Was there, properly speaking, a Russian Jewry prior to 1917? It is, of course, incontestable that there were Jews living in the Russian empire; but were these indeed *Russian* Jews, and did they constitute an identifiable *Jewry*? In other words, was there anything Russian about them, and did they form a single collective community?

These questions are not raised facetiously. The existence of a Jewry that was 'Russian' is not self-evident: it requires explication; the explication, in turn, ought to tell us something about the historical legacy of that Jewry. This issue will be addressed briefly, and on two levels. First, to what extent are we able to discern a recognizable internal unity that might legitimate a collective label? Second, does the designation 'Russian' bear real historical significance in terms of the life of that Jewry? The thesis of this chapter is that the first two generations that lived under Romanov rule remained divided and heterogeneous and that these Jews' links to Russia were attenuated. But, by the middle decades of the nineteenth century, we may discern processes that led to the emergence of a Russian Jewry, properly designated as such. Those processes accelerated at the end of the nineteenth century and in the first decade and a half of the twentieth, achieving a definitive character after 1917. Further, the proposition shall be put forth here that it was the *Russian state* that played the key role in creating Russian Jewry as a historical entity.

* * *

What's in a name? The labels that we use to designate Jewish populations have (or should have) inherent and demonstrable historical significance. Thus, we use such general labels as 'East

European', 'Sephardi', and 'West European' Jewry - terms that are meant to stand for a certain set of distinctions that have cultural, social, political, and economic relevance. They indicate that each such Jewry possesses its own characteristic historical experience and historical profile, gained through exposure to different socio-political circumstances. Such terms are useful, for example, when we generalize about historical processes affecting particular Jewish populations in a distinctive way, as we do when we talk about 'emancipation' — Jewish integration into Western societies in the nineteenth century — or when we focus on East European Jewish emigration as a phenomenon that is different from other Jewish migration streams.

We also speak conventionally of Jewish communities as individual geo-political entities: 'German Jewry', 'French Jewry', 'Italian Jewry', 'Anglo-Jewry', 'Hungarian Jewry', and so on. That is, we identify historically distinct Jewish communities with their native lands. This kind of designation is neither arbitrary nor a simplified shorthand. It goes beyond the level of mere scholarly convention because there are valid historical reasons for employing these labels. By the nineteenth century, the Jews living in the countries mentioned were citizens who identified with the nationality of their land; they had adopted the native language as their mother tongue; and they had created Jewish cultural, educational, religious and communal institutions that fully reflected the encounter between them and the wider national society and that set them apart from Jewries elsewhere.

Can we speak in the same way of a 'Russian Jewry'? Jews were not native to Russia in the way that they were native to other lands: it was Russia that came to the Jews, not the other way around. Relatively few Jews spoke Russian. A Russian-language Jewish press hardly existed until the 1870s, one hundred years after the first annexations of lands from the Polish Commonwealth. In terms of civil status, although the Jews were classified according to existing Russian social estates, they were also segregated within the Russian legal system. Eventually, they were segregated geographically, as well, in areas that were not preponderantly Russian, ethnically speaking. The Jews' cultural, educational and communal institutions were formed well before the onset of Russian rule and continued to reflect Jewish segregation from, rather than integration into, the society around them.

What is crucial, however, is that the Jews who came under Russian rule in the period from 1772 to 1815 were not the members of one definable society. No simple transfer took place, then, from a 'Polish' to a 'Russian' Jewry when Russian imperial rule replaced that of the Polish Commonwealth.

In actual fact, no Jewry is ever quite monolithic. Factional, doctrinal and cultural variations always exist (as they do in any large society). Nations are divided along lines of social class, political faction, religious views, regional variation and allegiance, and so on. A seamless homogeneity is not a requirement here: we know that we are dealing with one definable national society when factors are present that neutralize the divisive forces. Overall territorial and linguistic unity, common literary traditions, the introduction of universal compulsory education, a shared governmental system, and shared experiences in times of war or other crises — all of these can create unity out of diversity or hold an otherwise diverse society together.

Modern European Jewish communities were formed in just this way out of diverse elements. They emerged from the late Middle Ages with strong local traditions and certain attributes of a dispersed world communion. But their identification with the nation-state and their struggle to integrate themselves socially and economically into the national society endowed them with separate and distinctive identities and different political interests. The question is, can the same be said for Russia's Jews, or were they subdivided into too many separate groups and jurisdictions to be considered a national community? To what extent did they possess an underlying affinity and solidarity with one another?

For a century before the advent of Russian rule, there had been two separate Jewries on the territory of the Polish Commonwealth. The Jewish communities of Poland had been loosely joined in a confederation, the *Va'ad arba' aratsot*, and the Jewish communities of Lithuania had had their own separate national council, *Va'ad medinat Lita*. These communal bodies existed formally until 1764 (less than a decade before the first partition of Poland) and endowed the Jewish communities in Poland with whatever collective structure that they possessed. The historical separation between the two national confederations was itself a feature of strong regional and divergent local factors that continued to play an important role in East European Jewish society.

From the start, then, we are dealing here with a population that was not a single entity. Regional differentiation was most distinct in the development of religious life in the eighteenth century: the growth of Hasidism in the Ukraine and in Polish areas was pronounced, while White Russia and particularly Lithuania were areas which presented obstacles to Hasidic influence. Compounding these different patterns of communal leadership and religious experience were differences of local custom, dialect or accent in Yiddish pronunciation, and different stereotypes of temperament and mentality that were enshrined in folklore and literature.

The piecemeal annexations that made this population subject to Russian imperial rule — a process that lasted forty-three years from the first partition of Poland to the Congress of Vienna, and even then Poland remained legally separate — also militated against the formation of one national Jewish entity. Jewish political leadership in the first few decades of Russian rule bore a pronounced regional rather than national character.[1] The Russian state, for its part, did not encourage Jewish communities to unite in a national *kahal*, synod or consistory, on the French or Hungarian model, and in fact the Russian authorities obstructed the formation of a national Jewish leadership.[2]

Strong local and regional influences are clear in the case of the Jews in Congress Poland, home to the largest part of the Jewish population in the Russian empire.[3] Over the course of the nineteenth century, Jews in the Polish provinces developed closer associations with Polish culture and the Polish language. Some Jews also sympathized with, or even supported, the cause of Polish independence, and far-reaching civil reforms, culminating in 1862, improved the Jews' economic and legal status there, in contrast to the case in the rest of the empire.[4]

Similarly, we can point to important local variations in the social and cultural spheres in other Jewish communities in imperial Russia, outside Poland. In Riga, the dominant non-Jewish cultural influence was German. In Odessa, a modern, urban commercial community was developing in close association with Habsburg Galicia. In Vilna, a thriving publishing trade, a non-Hasidic élite rabbinic establishment, and a polyglot culture based on Hebrew, Yiddish, Polish, Russian and German helped to make that city a major Jewish literary and scholarly centre. In Bessarabia, still other conditions and cultural influences were dominant.

Thus, as we survey the map of the major Jewish communities in Russia, we are struck with the salience of local and regional differentiation. Prior to the annexations that expanded the tsarist empire in Eastern Europe, the Jews who lived there were divided amongst themselves, and after the advent of Russian rule those divisions and variations continued to obtain. There was as yet no single entity that could accurately bear the label, 'Russian Jewry'. Instead, there were Jews of Poland, Lithuania, White Russia and the Ukraine, Hasidic Jews and non-Hasidic Jews. To these we have to add the Jews of the Caucasus and Central Asia who shared little of the cultural and social experience characteristic of the Jews in the Pale of

Settlement. Circumstance had brought them all together under the Russian crown. One might compare them, by way of analogy, to the native peoples of North America, who became 'American Indians' only by virtue of the fact that the continent was colonized by 'Americans'.

The Jews of Russia, it is true, shared kinship ties and a common religious heritage. But these ties they shared with other Jews elsewhere as well: other Ashkenazi Jews throughout Europe, in the first instance, and Sephardi Jews of the Levant in the second. What is suggested here is that there was little beyond that minimal similarity that bound the Jews of Russia to each other as a *national community* at the turn of the nineteenth century.

Most historians have, nevertheless, favoured a collective approach in defining this population and its history, and it is well worth considering why that is so. Dubnow, for example, viewed all Jewish inhabitants of the Russian empire, including the Polish provinces, as a society with common characteristics. He discussed developments in Poland in their own local context, but he saw little historical validity in actually severing the Polish-Jewish experience from that of the rest of the Jews in tsarist Russia.[5] Iulii Gessen, too, included sections on Poland as part and parcel of his history of the Jews of Russia.[6]

One is led to the supposition that Jewish historians who wrote prior to 1917 took this inclusive approach at least in part because the early history of the Jews in 'Russia' was in fact the history of the Jews in the Polish Commonwealth — and, thus, susceptible to a collective definition. Yet, one may also surmise that this approach was also dictated by the political and social realities created by the nature of Russia itself: an empire with a distinctive autocratic system of government under which the Jews were assigned a special status, and therefore experienced a common historical development beginning in 1772. In other words, writing at the turn of the twentieth century, modern Jewish historians viewed the Russian political framework as a compelling, defining attribute for the Jewry that lived under the tsarist sceptre, fully analogous to the manner in which German, French, English and Italian Jews were defined by their respective citizenships.

An analogous issue has been recently addressed by William McCagg, with reference to the question of Habsburg Jewry. Here, too, a Jewish population, highly diverse geographically and culturally speaking, but ruled by one imperial house and increasingly affected by national, political and economic trends, began to exhibit aspects of a 'national' Jewry over a period of time. McCagg argues that, despite the breakup of this Jewry with the disintegration of the Habsburg empire, a distinctive Habsburg Jewry did exist prior to 1918, and his conclusions are relevant to our problem: 'Habsburg Jewry never had the clarity of identity of Anglo-Jewry or French Jewry. But, in the sharing of a vast though amorphous cultural-political experience, it was as much there as the Habsburg state itself.'[7] The prominence of the political influence — the power of the state and state-controlled bodies — makes for a consolidating process of historically separate Jewish communities that ultimately can create a national Jewry. The analogy with the case of Russian Jewry is quite close. The difference, of course, lies in the fact that the Habsburg state indeed disintegrated following the First World War, leaving in its wake a variety of smaller national entities, including a series of smaller national Jewries; while the Russian empire was replaced by the Soviet state, in which earlier trends toward the crystallization of a national Jewry were, if anything, magnified. But of this, more will be said in the conclusion.

Another theoretical justification for treating Russian Jewry as a single entity was offered by Ben-Zion Dinur, but for reasons not directly related to Russian rule per se.[8] Dinur focused on factors internal to Jewish society that shaped this largest of all Jewish populations and distinguished it from other Jewish societies:
- the sheer size and the high degree of concentration and segregation of the Jewish population, living for the most part in towns and cities where they formed either a majority or else a significant minority of 25 per cent or more;
- the relative social and cultural stability and solidarity, in terms of language, educational institutions, creative cultural output and family life, that characterized the life of this Jewry, at least until the end of the nineteenth century;
- the exceptionally high degree to which this Jewry remained attached to traditional religious values and lifestyles, compared to Western Jewries.

Dinur argued that Russian Jewry retained and developed a tremendous vitality in cultural, demographic and economic terms that clearly differentiated it from Jewish societies elsewhere in Europe. The internal distinctions between Poland and White Russia, the Ukraine and Lithuania, north and south, Hasidic and non-Hasidic (as noted above) were not as significant, Dinur implied, as were the more fundamental distinctions that divided Russian Jewry from other Jewries. Hence, he could speak of Russian Jewry as a collective entity by virtue of its 'otherness'. Indeed, his willingness to overlook internal distinctions within Russian Jewry allowed him also to view post-traditional groups and political movements (socialists, Yiddishists, Hebraists, Zionists, and even mass emigration to the West) as aspects or products of internal Jewish cohesion in Russia, rather than as evidence of break-up, dissent and contention. All such phenomena could be bracketed, as he argued, within a collective Jewish 'revolt' against Russian imperial rule, or, put differently, a collective defence, in various forms, of vital Jewish interests.[9]

The underlying concept which most of these historians (and many of their contemporaries) shared and used throughout their works was that of 'national character', or *Volksgeist*, a national-cultural unity that Russian Jewry possessed. This is particularly evident in the cases of Dubnow and Dinur, both of whom were committed Jewish nationalists and were predisposed, therefore, to think in terms of 'organic' or corporate national entities. Armed with their definition of a Jewish national character, they were able to fit social reality and ideological concept into one framework and thus to emphasize the importance of a collective Jewish consciousness, despite internal cleavages. Moreover, in their dichotomous view of the contemporary Jewish world, they emphasized the *national* character of East European Jewry as against the *assimilatory* character of Western Jewries[10] — once again highlighting the distinctive nature of the East European experience. They assumed that distinctive experience was based on a distinctive, historically-rooted identity.

It is the contention here, nonetheless, that this common identity did not exist a priori, and was not inherent in Jewish society as such. This much is suggested by the lack of overarching structures (political or cultural) that we have noted earlier. Rather, the common identity that Dubnow and Dinur discerned was forged over time and it was gradually nurtured by significant social and political forces. Thus, internal migration (especially from north to south) helped to promote greater internal homogeneity in Jewish society in Russia. The processes of urbanization that brought more and more Jews to live in fewer individual locations also contributed to the transcending of local distinctions. The coming of the railroad and the telegraph and other forms of improved transportation and communication certainly facilitated these processes. The alliance that took shape among traditionalists — Hasidic and non-Hasidic alike — prompting the formation of a new Orthodoxy, arrayed against anti-traditionalist forces in the Jewish community, also promoted new bonds of solidarity in place of earlier divisiveness.[11] These elements began to fall into place by the middle of the nineteenth century, basically altering previous social and cultural realities.

The policies pursued by the government, from promotion of Jewish agricultural colonies to military conscription; from the establishment of state-sponsored schools for Jews and rabbinical seminaries to the abolition of the *kahal*; from a retention of the Pale of Settlement to expulsions from rural areas and (in 1891) from Moscow — all these were indispensable elements in determining how Jews lived and how they would respond, over time, as an emerging collective Jewry. In this way, it may be said, that Russian Jewry was partly, if unintentionally, a creation of the Russian state.

Finally, conscious efforts were made by the rabbinic élite and the liberal intelligentsia alike, from the 1860s on, to reconstruct the basis of a Jewish national community. That goal was clearly expressed in the Jewish press that arose in the second half of the nineteenth century and it may also be discerned in the rise of new, trans-regional organizations and, finally, political parties that emerged by the turn of the century.[12]

Thus, in the final decades of Romanov rule, though significant internal distinctions remained (especially in the sphere of social-class stratification), it became increasingly valid to consider the Jewish inhabitants of the Russian empire as one 'Jewry'.

• • •

But in what sense, if at all, was this Jewry 'Russian'? The overwhelming majority — 96.5 per cent — stated in 1897 that their mother tongue was Yiddish. The twenty-five *gubernii* comprising the Jewish Pale of Settlement (including the Polish *gubernii*) accounted for 95 per cent of the Jewish population. In most of that area, ethnic Russians accounted for only one to five per cent of the urban population.[13] Clearly, Jews were not living in an environment naturally conducive to russification. Of those Jews who reported a mother tongue other than Yiddish, 29 per cent were Polish speakers, 17 per cent were German speakers, and 10 per cent spoke Georgian, Crimean Tatar, Judaeo-Tadzhik and Judaeo-Tat. Only 67,000 Jews, or less than half of the tiny non-Yiddish-speaking minority, were native Russian speakers, and of those, 24,000 resided outside the Jewish Pale of Settlement. Another 14,000 lived in Odessa and 10,500 in major regional centres like Kiev, Warsaw, Vilna, Minsk and Vitebsk.[14] In 1898, 54 per cent of all Jewish children in the empire still attended traditional Jewish elementary schools rather than Russian schools — but that figure rose much higher within the Pale itself, so that in Kiev Guberniia over 70 per cent attended traditional Jewish schools.[15]

Such figures support the argument of historians who maintain that Jews in the Russian empire formed a stable, cohesive ethnic mass, endowed with a common culture, mentality and lifestyle; but at the same time, they beg the question: was this Jewry in any way Russian? Or was it merely that part of a larger East European Jewry that happened to be living under a Russian government?

Clearly, there is a semantic difficulty here that is related to the multinational character of the Russian empire itself. The situation of the Jews there was not analogous to that of the Jews in, say, France or Germany. Jews in the tsarist empire lived largely in areas that were ethnically non-Russian. By what justification, then, can we call them 'Russian'?

For that matter, 'Russia' itself lacked clear boundaries or a defined national identity during the first half of our period. That was due to the expansion of the tsarist state into non-Russian territories, making the empire a multinational one, as well as to the country's social structure and cultural development. At the beginning of the nineteenth century, when the Jews of Poland and Lithuania were only beginning their encounter with the land of the tsars, the literary culture of Russia was still in the process of being discovered and crystallized. As for the Russian nation itself, it would take decades before the social and political élites would 'discover' their common links with the enserfed peasantry. Service to the tsar and service to God in the Orthodox church, colonizing expeditions into Central Asia and the Far East, the campaign to repel Napoleon's invasion, peasant revolts and the Decembrist conspiracy, the controversy over 'westernization' — all these were elements in an ongoing and lengthy process of state-formation and national development. They reflect the preliminary stages of a Russian national consciousness. Indeed, even at the turn of the twentieth century, some issues of national definition remained unresolved, given the fluidity of national designations in such places as Warsaw, Kiev and Vilna.[16]

Nevertheless, we do find some aspects of 'russianization' among Jews as early as the 1820s, mainly among groups of acculturated merchants, writers, army veterans, professionals and students that grew in relative importance in the second half of the nineteenth century.[17] A growing Jewish presence in Moscow and St. Petersburg (and elsewhere outside the Pale) tended to underscore the significance of this process, if it were continued and expanded — something that would occur after 1917.

Moreover, the self-descriptive use of the term 'Russian' by Jews from within the Pale, at the end of the nineteenth century, indicates that the label had significance beyond the small minority of Jews who lived outside the Pale. Thus, Jewish expatriate students in Western Europe at the turn of the century were clearly identified as 'Russian'.[18]

An Orthodox rabbi from the Ukraine, living in central Poland, could describe himself in a letter to another Polish rabbi as having been born 'a native of Russia', and he could refer to Warsaw Jewry as 'the biggest Jewish community in Russia'.[19] And in 1905, Jews were granted the right to cast their ballots in elections to the new State Duma, the first unequivocal act recognizing the Jews' political rights as Russian subjects.[20]

While these examples should not lead us to conclude that national affiliation in the *ethnic* sense was being expressed, the reality of an 'all-Russian' (*rossiiskoi*) empire was compelling enough to make the label 'Russian' relevant — perhaps even self-evident — to Jews living under the Russian crown, in a way that was not at all the case at the turn of the nineteenth century. The political 'nation' of Russia was being defined by territorial unity and unitary government. Jews 'belonging' to Russia were, in that sense, Russian.

Literary expression was given to these trends by various Jewish writers. Possibly one of the most direct examples is the novel *Goriachee vremia*, by Lev Levanda. Published in the early 1870s, the novel revolves around a protagonist, Arkadii Sorin, who declares: 'Our plan is to make the Jews into Russians. We live in Russia, and so we must be Russians.'[21] Clearly, once again, the outstanding argument for adopting a Russian label was geo-political: 'we live in Russia'. To Levanda, such political realities deserved to be recognized by the Jewish population: Jews ought to consider Russia their homeland in the national sense. (The fact that the idea required substantiation by this kind of propaganda in the 1870s is illuminating. It testifies to the unresolved status of the issue.)

Among those who had resolved the issue for themselves, the idea of Russian Jewry appeared already self-evident. Looking back in retrospect to before the turn of the twentieth century, Jewish political activist Genrykh Sliozberg recalled:

> Since my childhood I have been accustomed to think of myself first of all as a Jew. But from the very start of my conscious life, I felt myself also to be a son of Russia...To be a good Jew did not mean one could not be a Russian citizen, and vice versa. To be a good Russian citizen was no obstacle to being a good Jew, believing in national Jewish culture and being loyal to one's people and helping them as best one could. The affinity to Russian culture, which in the course of my conscious life, grew in giant strides, was in consonance with my loyalty to national Jewish culture.[22]

Sliozberg articulated a rationale for a dual identity, combining Jewish ethnic affiliation with Russian civic and cultural affinity:

> It was not difficult for us to reconcile Jewish nationality with Russian citizenship and to make Russian culture our own as much as our own

> Jewish culture...A Russian Jew could easily consider himself a Jew by nationality and a Russian by civic affiliation [*gosudarstvennosti*].[23]

The distinction between nationality and citizenship — one that was logical enough to assert in a multinational empire — is made somewhat fuzzy by the 'cultural' character that Sliozberg assigned to both affiliations. Russian culture, perhaps much more than Russian citizenship, was highly prized. It conferred a sense of belonging that could be compared to a sense of nationality along lines familiar from the experience of Western Jewries. Such, however, was the case only for the most acculturated among the Jews, for whom Sliozberg was an able spokesman. Unlike Western Jews, however, who considered themselves to be Jews by religion only (and unlike even those Polish Jews who claimed to be Poles of the Mosaic faith), Sliozberg's formulation managed to hold onto both national identities at once: 'We were not a foreign element, for Russia had many nationalities, all of whom were united as citizens of the Russian state.'[24] In this formulation, then, 'russianness' became the common property of all the empire's nationality groups, even though the 'Russians', narrowly defined, remained nationally distinct.

We have here a definition of Russian nationhood that was obviously identified with Russian nationality in the cultural sense, but beyond that, was also a political concept, rooted in the existence of the Russian empire, and transcending the sum of its individual parts. Such a definition reflected the penetration of Russian administration, with all its powerful centralism and autocratic symbolism, into all walks of life. In fact, the Russian state created and fostered this sense of 'Russia', and in so doing, it also created a Russian Jewry. Given the figures that we reviewed before on the minimal extent (among Jews) of Russian education, Russian as mother tongue, and even residence in ethnic Russia; given what is known about the continued separateness of Polish Jewry in a social, cultural and civil sense; and given the second-class citizenship endured by Jews in Russia at the turn of the twentieth century, Russian Jewry could *only* be characterized as 'Russian' insofar as it was a Jewry that *pertained to Russia as a geopolitical entity.*

The distinction between political and cultural loyalty, on the one hand, and ethnic affiliation on the other, is familiar to us from other multi-ethnic societies: those, like the United States, where ethnicity has no legal or territorial, or even linguistic ramifications; as well as those, like Canada, India, or even the United Kingdom, where territorial, linguistic and other distinctions are formally recognized, without thereby denying Canadian, Indian, or British nationhood.

Had Russia evolved democratically, following the February revolution of 1917, some version of that system might have developed there as well. The regime that took power at that time promulgated full civil equality for Jews, opening the way to a wider civic 'belonging'; to the possibility of feeling oneself to be not merely 'in' Russia or subject 'to' Russia, but to actually be 'of' Russia. The earlier historical trends toward a national Russian Jewry were undoubtedly escalated in the wake of this political change. Even under sovietization, these trends continued and were reinforced. By 1926, large numbers of Jews had moved out of the former Pale of Settlement, many of them settling in Russia itself.[25] Subsequently, the Soviet-German war and the accompanying slaughter of Jews in the German-occupied zones accelerated the demographic shift of the Jewish population toward central and northwestern Russia. The demographic changes were accompanied by an important linguistic shift, so that by the post-1945 period, Russian had taken the place of Yiddish as the most widespread vernacular of Jews. Thus, by the mid-twentieth century, the question of whether or not a 'Russian' Jewry existed, was definitively resolved. But, of course, this new 'Russian Jewry' lies beyond the purview of this chapter, and deserves to be addressed in its own historical and political context.

Suffice it to say, that the issue, seemingly settled, would be reopened in the 1990s, when the breakup of the Soviet Union led to the introduction of separate political citizenships and, in consequence, the designation of separate national Jewries.

NOTES

1. On Jewish leadership in Russia in the nineteenth century, see Eli Lederhendler, *The Road to Modern Jewish Politics: Political Tradition and Political Reconstruction in the Jewish Community of Tsarist Russia* (New York: Oxford University Press, 1989), pp. 52–7, 68–81, 133–46.
2. Ibid., pp. 52–7.
3. Population figures from the census of 1897 are cited from Ben-Zion Dinur, 'Dmuta ha-historit shel ha-yahadut ha-rusit u-ve'ayot ha-heker ba', *Zion* 22, 2/3 (1957), p. 96.
4. See Artur Eisenbach, *The Emancipation of the Jews in Poland, 1780–1870* (Oxford: Blackwell, 1991); cf. Ezra Mendelsohn, 'A Note on Jewish Assimilation in the Polish Lands', in Bela Vago (ed.), *Jewish Assimilation in Modern Times* (Boulder: Westview, 1981), pp. 141–9.
5. Simon Dubnow, *History of the Jews in Russia and Poland*, 2 vols. (Philadelphia: Jewish Publication Society, 1916); cf. the historiographical summary in Binyamin Pinkus, *Yehudei Rusia u-Vrit ha-Mo'atsot, toledot mi'ut leumi* (Jerusalem/Beersheva: Ben-Gurion University, 1986), pp. 4–12, 19–20.
6. Iulii Gessen, *Istoriia evreiskogo naroda v Rossii*. 2 vols. Vol. 1 (Petrograd, 1916); Vol. 2 (Petrograd, 1925); cf. Pinkus, *Yehudei Rusia*, p. 20.
7. William O. McCagg, Jr., *A History of Habsburg Jews, 1670–1918* (Bloomington: Indiana University Press, 1989), p. 223.
8. Dinur, 'Dmuta ha-historit', pp. 93–4.

9. Ibid., pp. 98, 101, 110–11, 114–5.
10. On the dichotomous or dualistic view of modern Jewish history, see Jonathan Frankel, 'Assimilation and the Jews in Nineteenth-Century Europe: Towards a New Historiography?' in Jonathan Frankel and Steven Zipperstein (eds.), *Assimilation and Community, The Jews in Nineteenth-Century Europe* (Cambridge: Cambridge University Press, 1992), pp. 1–31.
11. Michael Stanislawski, *Tsar Nicholas I and the Jews: The Transformation of Jewish Society in Russia, 1825–1855* (Philadelphia: Jewish Publication Society, 1983), pp. 133–7.
12. Lederhendler, *Road to Modern Jewish Politics*, Ch. 5.
13. Robert A. Lewis, Richard H. Rowland and Ralph S. Clem, *Nationality and Population Change in Russia and the USSR: An Evaluation of Census Data, 1897–1970* (New York: Praeger, 1976), pp. 239, 415 (Appendix E.14).
14. Yehuda Slutzky, *Ha-itonut ha-yehudit-rusit ba-mea ha-tesha'-esre* (Jerusalem: Mosad Bialik, 1970), p. 35.
15. As late as 1912, figures on Jewish students enroled at municipal and elementary schools in the Russian educational system throughout the empire show a total of only 67,000 — see Steven S. Zipperstein, *The Jews of Odessa, A Cultural History, 1794–1881* (Stanford: Stanford University Press, 1985), p. 130; Yehuda Slutzky, *Ha-itonut ha-yehudit-rusit be-reishit ha-mea ha-esrim* (Tel Aviv: Tel Aviv University, Diaspora Research Institute, 1978), p. 12.
16. On the confusion of national identities in Warsaw, see Stephen D. Corrsin, *Warsaw Before the First World War: Poles and Jews in the Third City of the Russian Empire, 1880–1914* (New York: Columbia University Press, 1989), pp. 9, 11–12, 20, 28, 78, 107–8.
17. See Slutzky, *Ha-itonut ha-yehudit-rusit ba-mea ha-tesha'-esre*, pp. 13–36; Slutzky, *Ha-itonut ha-yehudit-rusit be-reishit ha-mea ha-esrim*, pp. 9–13.
18. Slutzky, *Ha-itonut ha-yehudit-rusit be-reishit ha-mea ha-esrim*, p. 12; Jehuda Reinharz, Chaim Weizmann, *The Making of a Zionist Leader* (New York: Oxford University Press, 1985), pp. 31–6; Jack Wertheimer, 'Between Tsar and Kaiser: The Radicalization of Russian-Jewish University Students in Germany', *Leo Baeck Institute Year Book* 28 (1983), pp. 329–49.
19. Moshe Nahum Yerusalimsky, undated letter, ca. 1911: see Eli Lederhendler, *Jewish Responses to Modernity: New Voices in America and Eastern Europe* (New York: NYU Press, 1994), pp. 100, 101 (doc. 15).
20. On Jewish political activity in preparation for the first Duma, see Alexander Orbach, 'The Jewish People's Group and Jewish Politics in Tsarist Russia, 1906–1914', *Modern Judaism* 10, 1 (1990), pp. 1–15.
21. Lev Levanda, 'Goriachee vremia', in *Evreiskaia biblioteka* 1 (1871), p. 347; also cited by Slutzky (1970), p. 100.
22. Genrykh Sliozberg, *Dela minuvshikh dnei. Zapiski russkogo evreia*, (Paris, [S. N.], 1933), Vol. 1, pp. 1–5; Vol. 2, pp. 42–67. Quoted in Lucy S. Dawidowicz, *The Golden Tradition: Jewish Life and Thought in Eastern Europe* (New York: Holt, Rinehart, Winston, 1967), p. 471.
23. Sliozberg, *Dela minuvshikh dnei*, Vol. 2, pp. 297, 302, 306.
24. Ibid., p. 302.
25. Lewis, *et al.*, *Nationality and Population Change*, pp. 199, 238ff.

2

Patterns of Internal Jewish Migration in the Russian Empire

SHAUL STAMPFER

The phenomenon of migration of East European Jews in the modern period before World War I is by no means a neglected area of research.* The attention given to migration is justified because large-scale population movements constitute one of the outstanding characteristics of the modern period — in general history as well as in Jewish history. However, in order to understand the role and dynamics of migration among Jews in the Russian Empire in the late nineteenth century, one must consider not only international and long-distance migration but also internal migration among Jews, including the distinctive features of Jewish migration as compared with migration in other populations. Once the scope and features of migration among Jews are understood, it will be possible to examine some of its consequences. Important studies have been devoted to the mass migration of East European Jews to the United States,[1] and a few to large-scale movements of Jews within the tsarist empire, as well as to Poland.[2] Yet, to the best of this author's knowledge, there is no comprehensive study of migration by Jews within the Russian empire.[3]

It is difficult to determine the degree and pattern of internal mobility of East European Jews before the end of the nineteenth century. One could point, of course, to dramatic events in the past, particularly persecutions and wars, which led to significant population movements. The most notable of these were the massacres of 1648

* The author is grateful to Gershon Bacon for his assistance and encouragement in the preparation of this study. Appreciation is due also to Yossi Goldstein and Gershon Zin for their comments and Mark Tolts for his stimulating suggestions.

which drastically depopulated many Jewish communities of the Polish Commonwealth and led to the flight of refugees to destinations as far away as Amsterdam. There were similar events, albeit on a smaller scale, during the eighteenth and nineteenth centuries. However, they do not seem to have involved anything close to a majority of the Jewish population.[4] Large-scale internal migration over long distances would have blurred regional distinctiveness. However, the persistence of regional dialects of Yiddish up to the twentieth century, as well as local foods, customs and other cultural elements, suggest that such a migration did not take place.[5] The long-distance migrations in the Middle Ages, which created what would be the Jewish communities of the Russian Empire,[6] were apparently not followed by continued inter-regional migration, though there were, of course, innumerable cases of individuals who moved from region to region and there might have been high levels of internal migration within regions.

The first half of the nineteenth century saw a significant population flow. Tens of thousands of Jews moved from the Pale to southern Russia and to southern Ukraine, either out of a desire to take advantage of opportunities in an expanding economy or to settle on the land in the framework of a government plan to turn the Jews into farmers. By World War I close to one million Jews lived in the southern *gubernii*, in which perhaps 100,000 had lived in the mid-nineteenth century.[7] Significantly, these migrants formed the basis for important Jewish communities in the south, such as Odessa and Ekaterinoslav. New patterns of behaviour, culture and education which developed in these communities, such as russification and Zionism, influenced other Jewish communities of the Russian empire. Though large, the numbers involved in this movement were limited and a general redistribution of the Jewish population was not taking place at the beginning of the nineteenth century.

However, by the end of the nineteenth century large numbers of Jews were clearly on the move (see Tables 2-1 and 2-2). Not all were long-distance migrants (see Tables 2-3 and 2-4). Many moved from small towns to regional centres and between neighbouring cities. Published Russian statistical reports do not provide direct sources for following these movements because data on migration was not reported by religion, nationality or language, all of which would have provided a gauge for Jewish migration. However, a careful reading of the 1897 census material gives a rough picture of the scope of internal Jewish migration.[8]

Among the various population characteristics described in the volumes of the census are the numbers of residents by social status and by geographic origin (same *uezd* or *guberniia*, different *uezd* or *guberniia*). These data shed no direct light on the geographic background of the Jews in question. However, analysis of the data can be enlightening. Jews fell almost entirely in the ranks of one social class, the *meshchane*,[9] and constituted over half of the *meshchane* in most of the locations where they lived. Therefore, data on the movements of the *meshchane* should give a very good indication of the geographic patterns of migration of the Jews. It can be assumed that geographical mobility among Jews was certainly not less than geographical mobility of non-Jews among the *meshchane*. In fact, Jews were probably more mobile than non-Jews, so this is a conservative working hypothesis. Tables 2-1 and 2-2 present data on the percentage of *meshchane* born in the *uezd* in which they were living. The lower the percentage, the greater the role of migrants in the *meshchane* population. The *guberniia* at the top of the list are those in which the greatest proportion of the population were migrants. Figures 2-1 and 2-2 compare male and female patterns, and they are clearly highly correlated. It should be noted that at that time in the Russian empire (excluding Congress Poland), about 1.7 million Jews were recorded as urban, and another 0.8 million in Poland. The population of rural[10] Jews was about 2.1 million in the Russian empire and 0.5 million in Poland. The figures were more or less even with a growing trend toward urbanization.

Tables 2-1 and 2-2 present the share of locally born among the Jewish *meschane*. The data allow us to distinguish between different types of migrants by the distance they travelled. Presumably, the dynamics of moving a short distance from home are very different from those involved in moving far away. The census data do not provide exact details about distance travelled but they do divide migrants into three categories: those who were born in the same *guberniia* but in a different *uezd*; those who were born in a different *guberniia*; and those who were born abroad. The numbers born abroad were insignificant enough to justify concentrating on the first two. The difference between migration within a *guberniia* and between *gubernii* is not always one of distance. There were undoubtedly, many cases where, in fact, inter-*guberniia* migrants moved short distances between two nearby points located on opposite sides of an artificial administrative border. Nonetheless, generally speaking, inter-*guberniia* travel tended to involve longer journeys than moves within a *guberniia*. Thus comparing the relative size of the two groups can give us a rough indication of the types of migrants within a pool of newcomers.

30

TABLE 2-1 Percentage of local-born Jewish *meshchane* among urban Jewish *meschchane* in 1897 by *guberniia*

	Male			Male	
guberniia	% local born	w/20% correction	*guberniia*	% local born	w/20% correction
Ekaterinoslav	50	40	Piotrkov	54	43
Piotrokov	54	43	Ekaterinoslav	55	44
Kurland	56	45	Kurland	58	46
Tauride	60	48	Tauride	65	52
Kharkov	61	49	Warsaw	65	52
Kherson	61	49	Kherson	66	53
Kiev	63	50	Kharkov	66	53
Warsaw	63	50	Kiev	67	54
Vilna	65	52	Vilna	69	55
Kovna	67	54	Vitebsk	72	58
Plock	68	54	Poltava	73	58
Poltava	70	56	Kovna	73	58
Lomza	70	56	Grodno	74	59
Mogilev	71	57	Minsk	75	60
Grodno	71	57	Plock	76	61
Volhynia	72	58	Kalisz	76	61
Vitebsk	72	58	Volhynia	77	62
Minsk	72	58	Lublin	78	62
Bessarabia	75	60	Bessarabia	78	62
Suwalki	75	60	Podolia	78	62
Podolia	75	60	Lomza	79	63
Kalisz	76	61	Mogilev	79	63
Lublin	76	61	Kielce	79	63
Kielce	77	62	Chernigov	80	64
Radom	77	62	Radom	80	64
Chernigov	79	63	Suwalki	80	64
Siedlece	83	66	Siedlece	86	69

TABLE 2-2 Percentage of local born Jewish *meshchane* among rural Jewish *meschchane* in 1897 by *guberniia*

guberniia	Male		guberniia	Male	
	% local born	w/20% correction		% local born	w/20% correction
Ekaterinoslav	48	38	Ekaterinoslav	55	44
Warsaw	54	43	Warsaw	59	47
Tauride	57	46	Tauride	66	53
Kurland	64	51	Kurland	68	54
Piotrkov	65	52	Kharkov	70	56
Kharkov	66	53	Piotrkov	74	59
Suwalki	70	56	Lublin	75	60
Plock	72	58	Bessarabia	75	60
Bessarabia	72	58	Podolia	76	61
Lublin	73	58	Suwalki	76	61
Kherson	74	59	Plock	76	61
Podolia	75	60	Kherson	77	62
Lomza	75	60	Vitebsk	77	62
Vitebsk	76	61	Mogilev	78	62
Chernigov	77	62	Siedlece	79	63
Poltava	78	62	Chernigov	79	63
Kalisz	78	62	Kiev	79	63
Kiev	79	63	Kalisz	79	63
Siedlece	79	63	Volhynia	80	64
Mogilev	79	63	Poltava	80	64
Kovna	79	63	Lomza	81	65
Kielce	79	63	Kielce	81	65
Volhynia	80	64	Radom	82	66
Radom	81	65	Vilna	84	67
Grodno	82	66	Minsk	85	68
Vilna	83	66	Grodno	86	69
Minsk	84	67	Kovna	87	70

FIGURE 2-1 Relation between levels of local born among male and female urban Jewish *meschane* in 1897 in the western provinces of the tsarist empire by *guberniia*

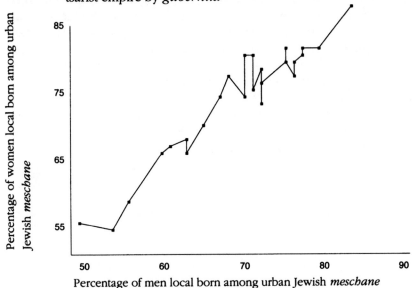

FIGURE 2-2 Relation between levels of local born among male and female rural Jewish *meschane* in 1897 in the western provinces of the tsarist empire by *guberniia*

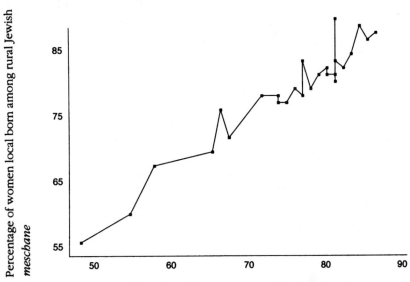

Table 2-3 is a calculation of the ratio, in urban populations, of migrants from other districts within the *guberniia* to the number from outside the *guberniia*. In other words, the smaller the figure, the larger the proportion of long-distance migrants among total migrants. A high figure indicates that most migrants were local. Not surprisingly, new communities such as Odessa or Ekaterinoslav, which were far from the traditional centres of Jewish population, attracted many migrants from afar while veteran ones in *gubernii* which were relatively stagnant economically, such as Podolia and Minsk, attracted few outside migrants. Furthermore, Table 2-4 clearly shows that fewer long-distance migrants moved to rural areas than short-distance ones. Figure 2-3 (urban) shows greater differences between male and female patterns than does Figure 2-4 (rural). This probably reflects greater variations in employment opportunities in cities than in villages.

The high levels of short-range migration have been noted in recent studies on Jews of Polish cities. Corrsin[11] raises questions about the scale of immigration of Lithuanian Jews to Warsaw (the 'Litvak Invasion') and in a recent study, Scott Ury[12] found that in the late nineteenth century, most of the immigration of Jews to Lodz was apparently from nearby regions.

The data presented probably underestimate significantly the role of migration in urban populations. A large percentage of the Jews in almost every locality were children. In fact, about half of the Jewish population of the empire was less than 20 years old in 1897, and more than half of these were nine years old or less. If a family consisted of a father and mother who migrated to a city (as often was the case) and a number of young, locally-born children, the parents would be counted as migrants and the children as locals. However, from the functional viewpoint, the whole family should be regarded as migrants since both parents and children were open to all the special influences and behaviour patterns of people new to a region. Evidence from studies in other societies suggests that a disproportionate number of migrants were young single adults who married after settling down in a city. If this was also the case with regard to internal migration of Jews in the Russian empire, then the figures for migrants should be concentrated more in the adult groups than among children.[13] If we discount the percentage of local born by 0.2 as a corrective for the age imbalance among migrants,[14] a conservative correction, we derive the second column in Tables 2-1 and 2-2.

TABLE 2-3 Ratio of urban migrants from within the *guberniia* to migrants from outside the *guberniia* (= other *uezdy*/other *gubernii*)

Urban	Male	Female
Ekaterinoslav	0.22	0.28
Kherson	0.31	0.39
Kharkov	0.35	0.46
Warsaw	0.44	0.54
Tauride	0.45	0.60
Piotrkov	0.51	0.56
Bessarabia	0.53	0.66
Poltava	0.55	0.64
Kiev	0.55	0.63
Vitebsk	0.62	0.73
Lomza	0.65	1.67
Suwalki	0.69	1.90
Siedlece	0.72	0.98
Vilna	0.80	0.96
Plock	0.80	1.13
Kovna	0.81	1.39
Kurland	0.99	1.18
Radom	1.01	1.21
Volhynia	1.02	2.00
Chernigov	1.05	1.22
Lublin	1.12	2.11
Kalisz	1.16	1.62
Grodno	1.26	1.74
Mogilev	1.28	0.98
Minsk	1.32	1.43
Kielce	1.35	1.39
Podolia	1.41	1.85

TABLE 2-4 Ratio of rural migrants from within the *guberniia* to
migrants from outside the *guberniia* (= other *uezdy*/other *gubernii*)

Rural	Male	Female
Ekaterinoslav	0.36	0.45
Suwalki	0.48	0.94
Piotrkov	0.54	0.56
Kherson	0.71	0.81
Tauride	0.74	0.72
Kharkov	0.75	1.00
Kurland	0.77	0.90
Lomza	0.80	1.18
Radom	0.85	0.94
Siedlece	0.91	0.91
Vilna	0.93	0.98
Chernigov	1.01	1.09
Volhynia	1.02	1.12
Poltava	1.02	1.16
Grodno	1.03	1.80
Plock	1.03	1.38
Vitebsk	1.09	1.13
Warsaw	1.17	1.55
Mogilev	1.19	1.37
Kalisz	1.23	1.47
Bessarabia	1.25	1.37
Lublin	1.27	1.67
Minsk	1.30	1.34
Kielce	1.44	1.52
Podolia	1.46	1.77
Kiev	1.50	1.70
Kovna	1.87	1.77

It is clear that there were considerable regional variations and that some regions and cities had many more migrants than others. However, even more notable is the fact that migration was a significant phenomenon everywhere, and that even in the most stable regions, about one-third of the Jewish population were apparently not born locally. It is inconceivable that the character of Jewish life could remain unaffected by this; in the conclusion to this chapter, some of the consequences of the pervasiveness of migration will be discussed.

The proportion of migrants among Jews was far greater than that of migrants among non-Jews of the Russian empire. However, Jewish migration was distinctive not only quantitatively but qualitatively as well.

International Jewish migration was characterized by the larger proportion of women, children and older dependents among the migrants than was the case among most other migrant groups.[15] Figures 2-1 and 2-2 (for internal migration) suggest that both Jewish men and Jewish women tended to migrate in similar numbers in the late nineteenth century. In this respect internal migration was similar to international migration. Whether women, children and older dependents also constituted a greater share with regard to internal migration is not determinable on the basis of available published sources. The reasons for this distinctive pattern are complex. A disproportionately large number of Jewish migrants to the United States came from areas that were typified by economic depression along with a low level of anti-Semitic violence. This indicates that economic hardship consititued the main impetus for East European Jews to migrate abroad.[16] In this respect Jewish immigrants to America were similar to immigrants of other nationalities. However, having made the decision to emigrate, Jews tended, as noted above, to bring over families more than other groups did. The reason for this seems to lie in their concern about possible anti-Semitism, which convinced them to make the decision to leave permanently, with their families, rather than to go on a temporary basis for the purposes of 'making good'. The decision on whether to take family or not was influenced by living conditions and by perceptions of anti-Semitism in the old country and the new. The relationship between bringing family members and the decision to migrate permanently, as opposed to temporarily, is underscored by the tendency of non-Jewish immigrants to the United States who came to be farmers, to bring over more family members than immigrants to cities who often came with the intention of returning home.[17]

37

• • •

The question that must be asked is whether Jewish migration in general was distinct in other ways. As a starting point for comparing Jewish and non-Jewish migration it is worth considering Ravenstein's 'laws' of migration which attempt to describe general characteristics of migrations, and which are often cited in the literature on this topic.[18] Grigg formulated Ravenstein's laws essentially as follows:

1. The majority of migrants go only a short distance.
2. Migration proceeds step by step.
3. Long-distance migrants generally prefer to go to one of the great centres of commerce or industry.
4. Each current of migration produces a compensating counter-current.
5. Town natives are less migratory than natives of rural areas.
6. Females are more migratory than males within the region of their birth, but males more frequently venture beyond.
7. Most migrants are adults; families rarely migrate great distances.
8. Large towns grow more by migration than by natural increase.
9. Migration increases in volume as industries and commerce develop and transport improves.
10. The major direction of migration is from the agricultural areas to the centres of industry and commerce.
11. The major causes of migration are economic.

Considering these laws one by one, we find that not all of them applied to the Jews of the Pale and that the socio-economic character of the Jewish community was the major cause of the distinctive pattern of Jewish migration.

1. If we take the very rough estimates for the number of short-distance and long-distance migrants, we find that the ratio at point of destination varies wildly (Figures 2-3 and 2-4). There were apparently large numbers of long-distance migrants — especially if one adds the figures for international migration.
2. It is impossible, using the current data, to determine if Jewish migration proceeded step by step. One possible avenue of research is a prosopographic study which would be based on a variety of population groups. Unfortunately, most biographies deal with members of élite groups so that it is difficult to generalize from them for the population as a whole.
3. The large-scale migration of Jews to Odessa and Warsaw in particular, regions of economic growth, is in line with Ravenstein's

FIGURE 2-3 Relation between male and female Jewish urban migrants from within the *guberniia* to Jewish urban migrants from outside the *guberniia* in the western provinces of the tsarist empire in 1897, by province

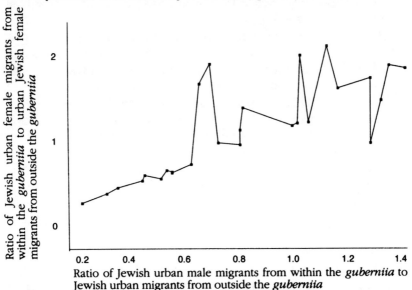

Ratio of Jewish urban male migrants from within the *guberniia* to Jewish urban migrants from outside the *guberniia*

FIGURE 2-4 Relation between male and female Jewish rural migrants from within the *guberniia* to Jewish rural migrants from outside the *guberniia* in the western provinces of the tsarist empire in 1897, by province

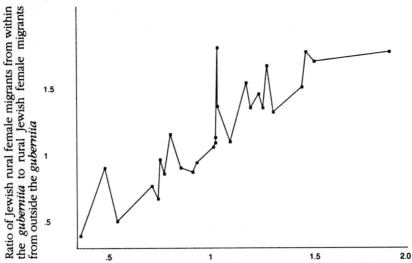

Ratio of Jewish rural male migrants from within the *guberniia* to Jewish rural migrants from outside the *guberniia*

Note: Levels are estimated and not absolute

39

observation.[19] In this respect, Jewish internal migration complies with Ravenstein's laws more than the long-distance internal migration of non-Jews, such as the migration to Siberia which was often motivated by land hunger.

4. A compensating counter-current of Jewish internal migration is not to be found.[20] However, this observation cannot be dismissed out of hand. One reason which contributed to the migration of the Jews at the end of the nineteenth century was the emancipation of the serfs and the consequent move of many former peasants to the cities, which led to occupational changes in the rural population. Indeed, one might wonder whether Jewish migration was compensation for peasant urbanization, or vice versa.

5. It is difficult to determine whether urban Jews were more or less migratory than rural Jews. However, it does not appear that a disproportionately large number of immigrants to the United States were from the very big urban centres. If we take the list of *landsmannschaften* (hometown societies) in New York City in 1931, it is possible to identify migrants from big cities. Their percentage in the total *landsmannschaften* approximates the percentage of big-city Jews in the Jewish population of the tsarist empire in 1897. These urban centres had grown after 1897 so that big-city migrants were probably underrepresented among the migrants to the US. Perhaps migrants from big cities were less likely to join *landsmannschaften* than people from small towns but it is just as likely that people from small towns joined big-city *landsmannschaften* for the benefits that they promised. In many of the *landsmannschaften*, up to half of the members were not born in the community (not *landsleit*). Unfortunately, there appears to be no study of immigrant Jewish life that attempts to measure the number and role of migrants from major cities.[21]

6. The many cases of *agunot* (abandoned wives) in rabbinic literature fit this observation, since they suggest different patterns of migration of men and women. However, the sex ratio of males to females among Jews in 1897 does not bear out Ravenstein's observations. In the southern *gubernii* there was generally an oversupply of men but the differences were not drastic. Therefore it seems that both Jewish women and men migrated, and in similar patterns. One key reason for this similarity would appear to lie in the fact that young Jewish women did not have a tradition of going to cities to work as domestic help as was common among peasants. Religion and tradition precluded them from serving in the houses of non-Jews.

TABLE 2-5 Estimated number of migrant Jewish *meshchane* in 1897 by *guberniia*

	Urban		Rural		Urban	Rural
	Male	Female	Male	Female	M/F	M/F
Bessarabia	20500	20200	22900	22400	1.01	1.02
Chernigov	9000	9800	10500	10800	0.92	0.97
Ekaterinoslav	17900	16000	8400	7100	1.12	1.18
Grodno	29800	30600	21200	34100	0.97	0.62
Kalisz	6900	7400	4900	5100	0.93	0.96
Kharkov	3000	2300	200	200	1.30	1.00
Kherson	53300	50100	14700	14300	1.06	1.03
Kiev	32100	31700	51000	53700	1.01	0.95
Kielce	6700	6900	6900	6800	0.97	1.01
Kovna	13000	13300	25200	23400	0.98	1.08
Kurland	5400	6200	3600	1600	0.87	2.25
Lomza	7500	6600	10400	9500	1.14	1.09
Lublin	13500	13800	12000	16400	0.98	0.73
Minsk	25900	26900	32900	33800	0.96	0.97
Mogilev	15200	14200	21200	23400	1.07	0.91
Piotrkov	42800	44200	11700	10800	0.97	1.08
Plock	6400	7700	3700	3700	0.83	1.00
Podolia	19000	19000	49300	50900	1.00	0.97
Poltava	16200	15800	5100	5200	1.03	0.98
Radom	9300	9200	9100	9300	1.01	0.98
Siedlece	10000	10100	9200	9900	0.99	0.93
Suwalki	5500	5300	4500	4200	1.04	1.07
Tauride	8700	7200	5000	4300	1.21	1.16
Vilna	18900	19500	18400	19200	0.97	0.96
Vitebsk	21100	24100	11200	12000	0.88	0.93
Volhynia	24000	22700	47200	49900	1.06	0.95
Warsaw	59700	60900	16800	15600	0.98	1.08
% of total Jewish *meshchane*	46%	43%	39%	38%		

7. As noted above, Jewish international migration involved the family far more than among non-Jews. However, in a sense, Jews were no different from non-Jews. It was customary among Jews for a male to set off alone, get established and then to bring over his family. It was less common for families to set off together to cross the ocean and begin the process of settling down together.[22]

8. The impact of migration on the growth of large towns is difficult to determine with regard to the Jewish population. However, the very high percentages of migrants in urban areas would conform with Ravenstein's thesis. Unfortunately, data on the population of cities before 1897 are patchy as is information on rates of population growth so that a clear conclusion is impossible.[23]

9. The literature on the period seems to confirm that industrial and commercial development brings with it an increase in migration. However, the absence of statistical material from different periods makes it difficult to check.

10. It is generally agreed that in the late nineteenth century, the countryside in the Pale of Settlement was in decline and that population flowed to the urban centres, both in the Pale and without, and not in the reverse direction. The rapid growth of cities during this period would seem to reinforce this view.[24]

11. It certainly appears to have been the case with regard to Jews, that the main motivation for migration was economic. It is worth noting that despite the pogroms in the south of Russia, the region continued to attract migrants. They apparently felt that the economic opportunities the region offered outweighed the risk of violence. Indeed, even in retrospect this assessment appears reasonable. The number of casualties from pogroms was minimal relative to the size of the Jewish population. Of course, head or body counts have nothing to do with perceptions of threat or danger nor do they guarantee logical responses.

The differences between Jewish and general patterns of migration were related to the fact that most Jews in the Russian empire, including those who lived in rural areas, were employed either in commerce or in trade, and their migration involved a change in setting and not in occupation. Therefore, it is not surprising that rural Jews should behave differently from rural non-Jews. For example, a peasant going to the city had to change his entire way of life and to earn a livelihood in a way his father never did. A Jewish migrant, however, often continued an occupation, and hence lifestyle, similar in many ways to that in his place of origin.[25]

A decision to migrate is affected by factors besides the attractiveness of the potential new place of residence. Relocation involves a variable degree of risk with regard to the improvement of living conditions: the migrant may find himself in the same conditions as in his place of origin. It also involves leaving a familiar social setting and seeking to re-establish social frameworks. Given that this is the case, it is clear that selection of a target location is dependent not only on the relative difficulty of reaching it, but also on the degree of information available about conditions there and the possible frameworks for assistance on arrival. Due to their involvement in commerce and contacts with traders as well as family networks, Jews had more access to information than peasants did and could anticipate with confidence the risks involved in moving. They often could rely on the assistance of relatives or the anticipated help of the established Jewish community. Hence, it was much easier for a rural Jew to contemplate migration than for a rural peasant — anywhere.

As we have shown, migration was a widespread phenomenon among Jews in the tsarist empire. They migrated not only to America and Odessa, but to many less known places as well. If we sum up the figures for internal migration, we find that by the end of the nineteenth century, many of the Jews in the tsarist empire could regard themselves as newcomers. The data we have derived enables us to estimate the numbers of internal Jewish immigrants within the tsarist empire. During the years 1881–97, 465,000 Jews also migrated to the United States and these were of course a majority of the Jews who emigrated from the tsarist empire.[26]

One of the most important developments in East European Jewish history in the nineteenth century was the great transformation of values.[27] This became manifest, particularly among the younger generation, at the turn of the century. Much of the study of Jewish history — whether of political movements, assimilation, new modes of cultural expression, etc., — is concerned with different aspects of this transformation. In contrast to the similar phenomenon in Central Europe, it cannot simply be explained as a product of exposure of small communities to an overpowering culture or government intervention. Explaining how traditional values can be drastically altered in a relatively short time frame is not simple. However, if we bear in mind that a large proportion of the Jewish community was made up of migrants, and especially the population of leading communities which set patterns for smaller ones, then it will be clear that extraordinarily propitious conditions existed for behavioural and value change.[28] This is because migrants are more open to

behavioural change and to new values than they would be, if they
were to remain in their birthplace; and in their new homes they in turn
influence the local born population. Hence the importance of the
evidence on the scope of migration. To be sure, not all communities
attracted the same numbers of migrants, and change is rarely the
product of one variable. Disparities between the numbers of migrants
in different cities can at one and the same time be an indication of
variations between the appeal of the communities and also of the
potential for behavioural and value change. At the same time, the
ubiquitousness of migration — and of value change — should not be
overlooked.

NOTES

1. The most useful introduction to this topic is S. Kuznets, 'Immigration of Russian Jews
   to the United States: Background and Structure', *Perspectives in American History* 9
   (1975) pp. 35–124.
2. See notably Yehuda Slutsky, 'Migration as a Factor in the History of the Jews in Eastern
   Europe Before 1881', in *Lectures at History Conferences* (Hartsaot bi-knasei ha-iyyun
   be-historiya) Jerusalem, 1973, pp. 67–79 and most recently, Gershon Bacon 'Jewish
   Society in the Polish Congress Kingdom 1860–1914', in S. Trigano (ed.), *La société
   juive à travers l'histoire* (Paris: Fayard, 1992); also see Barbara Anderson cited below.
   The precise number of internal migrants has never been calculated.
3. For the only study, which has major limitations, see the article by Rubinstein
   (Rubstein) cited below in n. 23. B. Tikhonov wrote a book, *Pereselenie v Rossii*
   (Moskva: Nauka, 1978), devoted to internal migration but the Jews got no attention.
   The author is grateful to Mark Tolts for making his personal copy of this book
   available. The more recent S. I. Bruk and V. M. Kabuzan, *Migratsionnyi protessy v
   Rossii i SSSR* (Moscow: Nauka, 1991), does pay significant attention to Jewish migra-
   tion but concentrates almost entirely on international migration. Barbara Anderson in
   her book *Internal Migration during Modernization in Late Nineteenth-Century Russia*
   (Princeton: Princeton University Press, 1980), devotes a chapter (No. 7 'Modern
   Destinations in the Pale', pp. 167–78) to migration to Odessa and Kiev but does not
   deal with Jewish internal migration in general. L. Hersch, *Le juif errant d'aujourd'hui*
   (Paris: Giard & Brière, 1913) devotes a chapter (Part II, Ch. 8, pp. 248–53) to internal
   migration but deals with causes and not volume. The most detailed study of Jewish
   migration to Odessa is in Peter Shaw, 'The Odessa Jewish Community 1855–1900',
   unpublished Ph.D. thesis, Jerusalem, 1988, pp. 142–6, 163. Of related interest is also
   Moses Shulvass *From East to West* (Detroit: Wayne State University Press, 1971); H.
   Avni, *Mi-bitul ha-inkvisitsiya ve-ad hok ha-shvut: Toldot ha-hagira ha-yehudit le-
   Argentina 1810–1950* (Jerusalem: Magnes, 1982); J. S. Kirshenbaum, 'Ha-hagira ha-
   yehudit mi-Rusiya ve-Polin le-Germaniya, Tsarfat ve-Angliya be-reva ha-aharon shel
   ha-meah ha-yud-tet ve-hit'arutah be-artsot eile', unpublished Ph.D. thesis, Jerusalem,
   1950; B. Z. Dinur, *Ktavim historiim*, Vol. IV, *Dorot ve-reshumot* (Jerusalem: Bialik,
   1978), pp. 208–9, esp. note 17 on pp. 208 and 226–8. Arcadius Kahan's *Essays in
   Jewish Social and Economic History* (Chicago: University of Chicago Press, 1986) can
   be read with profit in this context. See especially pp. 33, 122.
4. A useful overview of some of these issues may be found in Salo Baron, *The Russian
   Jews under Tsars and Soviets* (New York: Schocken, 1987), Ch. 5, pp. 63–74, and of
   course in the standard bibliographic guide to East European Jewish Studies, G.
   Hundert and G. Bacon, *The Jews in Poland and Russia* (Bloomington: Indiana
   University Press, 1984), pp. 42–3, 49–50, 133–4, 153–8.

44

5. See M. Herzog, (ed.) *Language and Cultural Atlas of Ashkenazic Jewry* (Tübingen: Max Niemeyer, 1992); V. Bavisker *et al.*, *Yiddish Language in Northern Poland* (The Hague: Mouton, 1965); M. Weinreich, *History of Yiddish Language* (Chicago: University of Chicago Press, 1980), esp. pp. 15–20, 578–9. Of course, since dialects can be learned, dialectical differences alone cannot prove that migration was limited.
6. For sources on settlement in Eastern Europe, see Hundert and Bacon, *The Jews in Poland and Russia*, Chs. II and V.
7. How many Jews moved to the south in the 19th century is unclear. A feeling for the scale can be gained by the following comparison made by Jacob Leshchinsky, *Yidishe folk in tsifern* (Berlin: Klal Verlag, 1922). He notes (p. 35) that in Bessarabia, Kherson, Ekaterinoslav and Tavrig (Tauride) *gubernii* there were reportedly about 100,000 Jews in 1844 and almost 750,000 in 1897.
8. N. A. Troinitskii (ed.), *Pervaia vseobshchaia perepis' naseleniia Rossiiskoi imperii, 1897 god* (Moscow: Central Statistical Committee/Interior Ministry), Vols. 1–89 (1899–1905). The best introduction to the 1897 census is Henning Bauer, Andreas Kappeler, and Brigitte Roth (eds.), *Die Nationalitäten des russischen Reiches in der Volkszahlung von 1897/Quellen und Studien zur Geschichte der ostlichen Europa* 32, A–B (Stuttgart: Franz Steiner Verlag, 1991). In the tables above Tables VI and XXIV of the census were used.
9. Seton-Watson had the following to say about *meshchane*: it was 'roughly equivalent to "small burgher" — covered a multitude of persons of whom little could be said except that they were not capitalists and that they were not artisans registered in a corporation'. H. Seton-Watson, *The Russian Empire 1801–1917* (Oxford: Clarendon Press, 1967) p. 28. It goes without saying that they were also not peasants or farmers.
10. Rural here means of course not living in locations defined for govermental and census purposes as urban. The Jewish rural population was not made up of peasants.
11. Stephen D. Corrsin, *Warsaw before the First World War* (Boulder: East European Monographs, 1989). However, data from 1897 says, of course, nothing about subsequent developments. For more discussion and references on the 'Litvak invasion' see Bina Garncarska-Kadow, *Helkam shel ha-yehudim be-hitpathut ha-ta'asia shel Varsha ba-shanim 1816/20–1914*, (Tel Aviv: Tel Aviv University, 1985), p. 292. The author is grateful to G. Bacon for pointing this out.
12. Scott Ury in an unpublished research paper, Hebrew University, 1994 on the Lodz Jewish community.
13. Among Jewish migrants to the USA in 1899–1914, about 24 per cent were less than 14 years old — Kuznets, 'Immigration of Russian Jews', p. 96, Table X, lines 12, 13, 14, while in the Russian empire in 1897 the same age group comprised slightly less than 40 per cent of the population — ibid., line 10. In other words, children were under-represented among migrants to America. If we posit the same underrepresentation of children in internal migration in the empire, then the share of adults among migrant Jews was greater than their share in the total Jewish population. Hence, in a Jewish population of a given location, migrants were not equally represented in all age groups but were concentrated among adults, and locally born were 'over-represented' among the younger age groups. Therefore, if we want to consider the percentage of locally born among adults, we have to correct our data. A 20 per cent correction, more or less the difference between age patterns of migrants to the USA and those of the Jews of Russia, is a conservative correction.
14. This is a conservative figure. The new communities in the south were functionally migrant communities even though statistically many were recorded as locally born. Of these locally-born Jews, few were second generation locally born.
15. Kuznets, 'Immigration of Russian Jews', pp. 94–100.
16. This was discussed in Shaul Stampfer, 'The Geographic Background of East European Jewish Migration to the United States before World War I', in I. Glazier and L. De Rosa, (ed.) *Migration across Time and Nations* (New York: Holmes & Meier Press, 1986), pp. 220–30.
17. Samuel Joseph, *Jewish Immigration to the United States*, Columbia University Studies in History, Economics and Public Law, Vol. LIX, No. 4 (New York: Columbia University Press, 1914), Tables XXXVIII aand XXXIX.

18. The following articles proved very useful and serve as a basis for argumentation here: Lee Everett, 'A Theory of Migration', *Demography* III (1966), pp.47–57; D. B. Grigg, 'E. G. Ravenstein and the "Laws of Migration"', *Journal of Historical Geography* 1 (1977), pp. 41–54.
19. This was not always the case in Eastern Europe. The settlement of the Ukraine by Jews was apparently a case of de-urbanization. See S. Ettinger, 'Helkkam shel ha-yehudim ba-kolonizatsia shel Ukraina, 1569–1648' *Zion* 21 (1956), pp. 107–42.
20. But see J. Sarna, 'The Myth of No Return', *American Jewish History* LXXI, 2 (Dec. 1981), pp. 256–68.
21. See G. Kingman, (ed.), *The Jewish Landsmannschaften of New York* (New York: Yiddish Writers' Union, 1938). The list of organizations is on pages 247–361. It can be calculated — see Shaul Stampfer, 'The Geographic Background of East European Jewish Migration' — that about 145,000 *landsmannschaft* members were from the tsarist empire (including Poland and taking into account unidentified *landsmannschaften*). This would be about 2.8 per cent of the total *1897* population. On this basis the following table was constructed:

Landsmannschaft membership

City	Members	% of total membership in NY	% of 1897 Jewish pop. in empire
Warsaw	5521	3.8	4.0
Odessa	2030	1.4	2.7
Lodz	5194	3.6	1.9
Vilna	3010	2.1	1.2
Ekaterinoslav	1146	0.8	2.9

Note the underrepresentation of Odessa and Ekaterinoslav. Unfortunately, we do not have full population data for the early twentieth century. There are data for individual cities but without data on the size of the total Jewish population, calculations based on them could be misleading.
22. 'Young men sent steamship tickets to their wives, children and fellow townsmen' — Moses Rischin, *The Promised City* (Cambridge, MA: Harvard University Press, 1962), p. 20. This pattern of delayed migration of family members also fits the claim mentioned above that the main impetus among Jews to migrate was economic and not fear of violence. If there had been a concern for imminent danger, it would not have been so common for men to travel and leave women and children behind.
23. This is discussed by B. Rubstein (printed as Rubinstein) in his article 'Di idishe innerlikhe ibervanderung in Russland' in *Das naye lebn* (New York), Vol. II, 2 (1910). This seems to be the only study devoted to Jewish internal migration. There are many typographical errors in the article. Printing Rubstein's name as Rubinstein was only one of them. Rubstein extrapolates from 1881 urban population on the basis of expected natural population growth and explains the difference between the population in 1897 and the expected result of natural population growth as the product of migration. However, the true level of migration was probably higher than his figures. There was also out-migration from cities, which was replaced by incoming migration. For a short biography, see Berl Kagan *et al.* (eds.), *Biographical Dictionary of Modern Yiddish Literature*, Vol. VIII (New York: Congress for Jewish Culture, 1981), pp. 426–7.
24. See Leshchinsky, *Yidishe folk in tsifern*, for a discussion. This is a very valuable book though Leshchinsky does not always cite his sources and it is clear that many of them have to be used with great caution. However, his conclusions are usually correct.
25. Zvi Halevy pointed out that the proportion of skilled labourers among Jewish immigrants to the USA was higher than that of skilled workers among the Jews of Russia. Many of the immigrants, if not most, found their first employment in the USA in the clothing industry. In other words, they were employed in the same occupations in the US as in Russia — Zvi Halevy, 'Were the Jewish Immigrants to the United States Representative of Russian Jews?', *International Migration* (Geneva) 16, 3 (1979), pp. 66–73.
26. Calculated on the basis of Table XXXI in Joseph, *Jewish Immigration*.

27. Israel Hazani pointed out to the author in a conversation that even patterns of halachic behaviour are tied to migration. Mixed communities often adopt the stringencies of each component while well-rooted communities often have traditional sanctions for lenient halachic decisions (*kulot*).
28. For a fascinating study of the impact of migration on the Russian city see David Brower, *The Russian City Between Tradition and Modernity* (Berkeley: University of California Press, 1990); a useful introduction to the problematics of urbanization in modern Jewish history in Europe is Steve Zipperstein, 'Jewish Historiography and the Modern City', *Jewish History* Vol. II (1987), pp. 73–89. More specifically related to East European Jewry is his article 'Russian Maskilim and the City', in D. Berger, *Legacy of Jewish Migration* (Boulder: East European Monographs, 1983), pp. 31–45.

II

THE BOLSHEVIK/SOVIET APPROACH
TO THE JEWISH QUESTION

3

Redefining the Jewish Question from Lenin to Gorbachev: Terminology or Ideology?

NAOMI BLANK

The existence of a Jewish question in the USSR was denied throughout the Soviet era. Yet, this 'non-existent question' was perpetually being redefined and at times, even stood at the centre of public discussion. The purpose of this chapter is to examine whether the various definitions of the Jewish question formulated during the Soviet period mirrored ideological changes in the perceptions of the Soviet regime, or whether they were solely terminological variations. Given the dialectical basis of Marxism, terminological modifications have an ideological connotation in any case.

Before concentrating on the Soviet period, we shall take a look at the pre-October 1917 era and the initial Bolshevik attempts to define the problem, in order to examine possible differences between the years prior to the seizing of power, when a theoretical-ideological foundation for the issue was formed, and the period following the October Revolution, when Bolshevik doctrine was applied.

The Russian Social-Democratic Party, and especially its Bolshevik leader, Vladimir Lenin, were the most active opponents of Jewish nationalism as a solution to the Jewish question. Although Leninist theory, which served as the basis for communist ideology during Soviet rule, did not offer an exclusive and comprehensive view of the Jewish question in the country, it was ideologically consistent in its characterization of and solutions to the problem. In his definition, Lenin avoided a materialist, class-conscious interpretation, and focused on the uniquely Jewish-nationalist aspects as the dominant components of the Jewish question.

The Leninist solution focused on the total assimilation of the Jews in their surroundings in Russia and all over the world. This was to be 'the important contribution of the Jewish race to the world'.[1] Lenin made a distinction between a Jewish minority enjoying equal rights, in an assimilation process which would turn it gradually into an integral part of Russian society, and elements within that minority, which aspired to develop nationalist uniqueness, or in other words, 'Jewish nationalism'.[2]

In this connection, Lenin opposed Jewish nationalist manifestations, on the one hand, and anti-Semitic demonstrations, on the other, as activities which underscored Jewish distinctiveness and delayed the inevitable process of assimilation.[3]

Lenin's solution appeared in several versions, with varying degrees of radicalism, according to the changing requirements of the revolutionary party. It was sometimes supported by socialist philosophers, such as Karl Kautsky, the leader of the Social-Democratic Party in Germany, and the Austrian socialist theoreticians Otto Bauer and Karl Renner, or by Lenin's own attempts at a 'scientific' analysis of Jewish reality in Russia and countries in Western and Eastern Europe; at other times, he combined his doctrine with party and national considerations. But the conclusions, regardless of the ideological framework, did not change.

From early 1913 on, Lenin returned several times to the Jewish question in the framework of the ongoing debate over the nationality question in Russia as a whole. The change in his general approach, however, did not lead to an essential modification of his basic perception of the Jewish question, but rather stressed its distinctiveness, despite the attempt to correlate the two problems. As early as 1903, Lenin had already 'scientifically' refuted the idea that the Jews constituted a separate nation.[4] The Jews, Lenin summed up, 'are a sect and not a nation'.[5]

This 'scientific' statement served as a supplement to the political solution of the nationality question proposed by Lenin, which defined a nation as a creation of the capitalist stage of development and as a group inhabiting a specific territory. He completely rejected any federative or autonomous solutions in post-revolutionary socialist society.[6]

The Leninist concept was supported by Stalin's definition, of 1913, which stated that 'a nation is a historically constituted, stable community of people, formed on the basis of a common language, territory, economic life and psychological make-up manifested in a common culture'.[7]

These three definitions, while acknowledging the temporary existence of a Jewish national minority in Russian society, disallowed any recognition of Jewish nationalism or of specific rights for the Jewish nation.

According to Lenin, the Jewish people, lacking territory and not conforming to the 'scientific' Marxist-Leninist definition of a nation, had skipped the 'national' stage in their historical development. This stage, comprising a national awakening, which characterizes each and every nation on its path to socialism, is essential in the struggle against oppression since it ultimately leads to the creation of a national state. Thus, the Jews, who did not win national recognition, turned into the 'pioneers of socialism' and moved on directly to the stage of assimilation. National consciousness and national equality, which Marxism-Leninism classify as essential stages, were non-existent in Jewish development, whose sole direction was towards total national and cultural assimilation. The Jewish people were chosen by the Bolsheviks to serve as a model for extra-territorial ethnic groups which were intended to assimilate into dominant nations. In this framework, Lenin did recognize the existence of some kind of Jewish history, but the Jewish present was 'doubtful' and the future, of course, did not promise any Jewish existence as such.

The Leninist dichotomy, which on the one hand regarded the Jews living in the Russian empire as a minority in advanced stages of assimilation, deserving of equal rights and protection against anti-Semitic persecution, while on the other, denying them any right to national recognition, served as the theoretical foundation for the policy of the Soviet regime towards the Jewish question. Throughout the years, this policy assumed various forms, especially as regards the living conditions of the Jewish nation, and it created a complicated theoretical and practical problem for the Jews. In fact, it dictated the destiny of the Jewish minority for more than 70 years.

The Bolshevik Revolution shifted the discussion of the Jewish question from the theoretical to the intra-party level. The Bolsheviks, headed by Lenin, vehemently denounced all manifestations of anti-Semitism which accompanied the transitional period, especially during the Civil War in Russia, and permitted limited Jewish representation in party organizations.[8] This representation constituted a deviation from the Marxist-Leninist line, which negated the existence of a Jewish nation. However, the deviation was temporary and stemmed from the needs of the hour.

Despite the abolition of restrictions against them and the party's denunciation of all anti-Semitic manifestations, the Jews won only temporary and limited recognition of their representational and cultural claims, while their difficult existential problems were ignored. One newly created Jewish body was the Jewish commissariat — *evkom* (which operated in 1918–24) in the framework of Narkomnats — the Commissariat for Nationality Affairs. Its main function was to fight the Jewish socialist Zionist parties, abolish them and help implement the government's policy among the Jewish public. Another Jewish body, founded in 1918, was the Jewish section of the Central Committee — *evsektsiia*, which operated alongside additional national sections — German, Polish, Yugoslav, Lithuanian, Estonian, Czech and Hungarian. It was not granted an autonomous organizational status, remaining a sub-unit of the Central Committee's Propaganda Department.

Limited recognition of a Jewish national existence was granted in the 1920s, providing it conformed to the communist 'format'. However, when the Soviet Union was founded in 1924 it abolished, ideologically and practically, all nationalist tendencies by liquidating the Narkomnats and transferring its main functions to the new government institutions. Thus, the national minorities lost their only representation in the central government institutions, and all that remained were the national representatives on the local level. In January 1930, a decision was reached to disband the national sections in the party as well, despite the fact that they existed in accordance with Soviet regulations; in the early 1930s, the regime went as far as physically liquidating its former representatives among the Jewish masses.[9] Nevertheless, at this stage, the destruction of the Jewish cadres must not be regarded as relating specifically to this national minority, since Ukrainian, Uzbek, Georgian and other national cadres were also eliminated, under the guise of a general reorganization of the party. Two factors seem to have led to the ultimate liquidation of the national sections: Stalin's increasing power and the fact that there was no longer any need to make concessions to the national minorities. We should add to this, of course, the ideological claim of 'socialism in one country', with its significant domestic repercussions on Stalin's nationality policy. In the 1920s, when the Soviet Union was growing and stabilizing, there was no specifically Jewish national policy to speak of, with one exception — the Soviet attempt to establish a national-territorial entity which would grant the Jews legal status and provide them with certain national rights.

In this connection, the Birobidzhan solution is of special note, since it best reflected the Soviet regime's contortions *vis-à-vis* the Jewish question. On the one hand, the autonomous Jewish district, which was supposed to attract a large number of Jews, granted them national representation and territory — as a sign of nationhood.[10] Birobidzhan supplied a concrete alternative to Palestine, while seeking to prove the increasingly popular claim that an autonomous national Jewish culture could exist in the Soviet Union.

On the other hand, this solution of the Jewish question was limited, since the proposed territory was situated as far as possible from the large population centres where an increasing number of Jews were concentrating. Moreover, outside the borders of Birobidzhan, Jewish culture had received limited recognition as an expression of a Jewish nationality. This contradiction reached its ironic and tragic climax when Stalinist purges penetrated the very territory which the Soviets defined as 'destined' for Jewish existence, executing important public figures among the Jewish community in Birobidzhan.[11]

The Birobidzhan solution to the Jewish question, which served specific Soviet interests during the period under discussion, was not mentioned in one of the most important authoritative sources of the Soviet regime, namely the *Bol'shaia Sovetskaia Entsiklopediia* (*The Great Soviet Encyclopedia*).[12] In its first edition, the encyclopedia devoted a large entry to the worldwide historical development of the Jews, alongside social and anthropological aspects. This was to be the only scientific entry dealing with the Jewish question during Soviet rule in all three editions that were published.

The author of the entry, M. Vol'fson, defined the Jewish question as an 'issue focusing on the relations between the Jews and the ruling classes, and between the Jews and the population among whom they live'.[13] He examined the topic throughout the historical periods of the Marxist model: the feudal, bourgeois and proletarian periods, and determined that Jewish assimilation had not been possible during the first two periods due to religious and economic factors which characterized Jewish existence at the time.[14]

Apart from his historical survey, the author also wrote an extensive and quite detailed ideological study which analyzed the various views held by Jews, as well as by East and West European theoreticians, regarding the essence and solution to the Jewish question. He argued that the various options for a solution were not feasible and that the only genuine solution was included in the platform of the Russian Social Democratic Workers' Party and concerned the 'national program' devised by Lenin. According to this program, 'a gradual solution to the Jewish question will be found through a revolutionary process, wherein society will convert from a capitalist to a communist society'.[15] The author added:

> The solution to the problem lies in unprecedented implementation in the Soviet Union. Anti-Semitism and Judaeophobia, which were so deeply rooted in tsarist Russia have begun to disappear...due to the decisive struggle of the party against such prejudices and manifestations.

Finally, he stated:

> The Jews in the Soviet Union maintain, together with all the other nationalities in the Soviet Union, an international culture which is above nationalism...socialist in content and nationalist in form...the Jews together with other nations are drawing close to the realization of a sober socialism which will eliminate the national question.[16]

To the universality of the Jewish question, as emphasized by the entry in the Soviet encyclopedia, was added an anthropological dimension.[17] On the one hand, a uniquely Jewish stereotype was constructed from an anthropological point of view, using detailed physical descriptions; at the same time, the entry stressed that time had created physical similarities between the Jews and the nations among which they lived; namely, there had been physiological assimilation in addition to the national and environmental assimilation of the Jews in their surroundings.

The entry underlined the existence of an ancient Jewish question which traversed geographical and historical boundaries and demanded the application of an assimilationist solution in a socialist society, as proposed by the Marxist-Leninist model.

However, the significance of the entry did not lie in the ideas it presented (since they did not include anything new), but rather in its very existence. In discussing the Jewish question, it revealed that there was still some willingness on the part of the authorities to recognize a specific Jewish problem and to solve it in an all-national context. Such a definition, as we shall see, was to disappear completely from Soviet rhetoric, as the objective situation of the Jews deteriorated.

Starting from the second half of the 1930s, the Soviet regime initiated an anti-Jewish campaign with explicitly anti-Semitic overtones. It ignored the differences between the Jews who had assimilated into Soviet society and those who maintained their Jewish identity. The regime presented its decision to put an end to Jewish national and cultural existence, in the form of an ideological struggle against bourgeois nationalism and cosmopolitanism.

The campaign escalated with the awakening of nationalism among Soviet Jews during the period following the Holocaust and the establishment of the new Jewish state.[18] For Soviet Jews, the State of

Israel constituted a real and attractive solution to the Jewish question. The Zionist alternative to the Soviet solution of the Jewish question revived discussion of the issue in various Soviet publications. One of the first contributions to this polemic was the response in *Pravda*, the press organ of the Communist party, over the signature of the writer Il'ia Erenburg, to the question posed by a Jew in Munich: 'Does the establishment of the State of Israel constitute a solution to what is usually referred to as the Jewish question?' Erenburg declared that anti-Semitism was the factor which brought about the establishment of the State of Israel. The Jews, said Erenburg, are loyal and attached to the place where they were born and raised. Wherever anti-Semitism and racial prejudice were prevalent, this loyalty ceased to exist and Jews set out for Israel, not 'in order to seek happiness, but rather to regain their right to human respect'. The solution to the Jewish question should be found in their place of residence, and not by gathering Jews who have nothing in common from all over the world in the State of Israel. In particular, said Erenburg, the bourgeois-capitalist character of the State of Israel is unattractive to a member of a socialist society who has liberated himself from the capitalist burden.[19]

The second edition of the *Great Soviet Encyclopedia*, begun in Stalin's last years and completed under Khrushchev, supplied an official confirmation of the solution of the Jewish question in the Soviet Union. Twenty years after the issue was widely discussed in the first edition, and in the midst of some of the worst anti-Semitic persecutions in Soviet history, the author of the entry 'Jews' stated that 'Lenin's and Stalin's policy of nationalities, which granted equal rights to all nations, has caused the Jewish question to disappear'.[20] The Jews were not included in the list of Soviet nationalities since they did not constitute a historical community which developed on the basis of a common language, territory, economic and cultural life. The author claimed that the Jews shared these elements with the peoples among whom they lived, rather than with the Jews themselves. By adding an anthropological justification to his views, the author stressed that the assimilation of the Jews was physiological, and not only cultural and national. Moreover, he stated, the assimilation process of the Jews in the socialist states was very rapid, while in capitalist states it was slow, due to the class war raging there in general and in the Jewish community in particular, and also because of the fascist and racist attitude towards national minorities, especially Jews.[21]

During the first years of the Stalin regime, there was some discussion of the Jewish question, and even an extensive campaign against anti-Semitism. The Birobidzhan solution was proposed, reflecting a certain readiness on the part of the Soviet government to recognize the existence of a Jewish question. However, towards the end of the Stalinist era, while persecution intensified, official discussion of the Jewish question ceased altogether, and it was explicitly stated that the issue had already been fully resolved within the boundaries of the Soviet Union and in the states of the People's Democracies. Not only were there no official utterances relating to the Jewish question, but there were also no publications about Jewish matters — symptoms of an official line which attempted to ignore Jewish existence.[22]

It is notable that during the Stalinist period, there was a strong correlation between recognition of Jewish existence and recognition of a Jewish question. As long as the Soviet regime discussed the existence of a specific Jewish question, and in this framework also denounced anti-Semitic manifestations, recognition of the existence of a Jewish entity in the Soviet Union, albeit temporary and limited, was implied. However, as soon as official Soviet declarations stated that the Jewish question had been fully resolved, the issue disappeared from the agenda, since the Jews had been allegedly assimilated into Soviet society, which was supposed to grant them full and equal rights and help them find their place among the peoples with whom they lived.

With the disappearance of the Jewish question, by definition anti-Semitic phenomena were precluded from occurring, since as Stalin stated, they 'characterize a cannibalistic fascism'.[23] He also asserted:

> Our fraternal feelings towards the Jewish people spring from the fact that the Jewish people gave birth to the creator of genius of the ideas of the communist liberation of mankind — Karl Marx.[24]

The 'return to Lenin' or the 'de-Stalinization' of the Khrushchev period secured a degree of liberalism towards Jewish culture, but not towards the Jews or towards the Jewish question. Thus, a certain level of cultural activity was allowed. On the other hand, the economic trials of the 1960s were clearly anti-Jewish in character.[25] The doctrinaire changes which highlighted the Khrushchev era made it possible to engage in ideological and ethnographic discussions of the issue of nationality in general, and the Jewish question in particular.[26] These discussions, based on the classical Stalinist-Leninist-Marxist perception, did not generate a new ideological doctrine. Instead, they emphasized the rigidity of existing attitudes and were aimed primarily at finding 'scientific' justification for the regime's ideology — including its refusal to recognize the existence of a Jewish nation.[27]

Though the 'Jewish question' and 'anti-Semitism', were officially declared non-existent, and were removed from Soviet polemics, they were used by the very same Khrushchev regime in the struggle against clericalism and nationalism in general, and against the Jewish religion in particular.[28]

The Soviet avoidance of a discussion of the Jewish question and the negation of the existence of anti-Semitism in Soviet society were blatantly expressed following the publication of Evgenii Evtushenko's poem 'Babii Iar' in September 1961 by the periodical *Literaturnaia gazeta*.[29]

Evtushenko, who wrote about the existence of the Jewish nation, which had suffered so much for so long, and who exposed in an unequivocal manner the scope of anti-Semitism in Soviet society, was violently attacked by the Soviet authorities and nationalist and conservative Russian circles. They denounced him for focusing on Jewish suffering while completely ignoring the afflictions of other nationalities. The references to the Jewish question in the Soviet Union, as expressed in the poem, were ignored by the critics. The poem became the focus of public discussion not because of the Jewish issue, but rather because it exposed the anti-patriotic tendencies of its author.[30]

An anti-Israeli and anti-Zionist attitude, born in 1957 and increasing by 1958, was added to the general trend. It focused on the Middle East conflict, and gradually developed into an all-out attack against the Jews.[31]

Thus, towards the end of the Stalinist period, the Jewish question disappeared from the political and public lexicon. Those who used the term were considered to be anti-Soviet elements who stressed anti-socialist national alternatives as a solution to the problem. From then on, the Soviet regime 'transferred' the Jewish question to states beyond the Iron Curtain, providing tragic descriptions of the Jews downtrodden by oppressive and exploitive capitalist-bourgeois rule.[32]

Any official reference by the Soviet regime to the existence of a Jewish question within the boundaries of the Soviet Union was only in retaliation to the accusations of anti-communist elements who tried to undermine the USSR's achievements in solving national problems in general, and the Jewish question in particular, regardless of the existential reality in the Soviet Union.[33] The discussion of the definition and significance of the Jewish question in the Soviet context was henceforth replaced by a discussion of the nature of the elements using it. The phrase 'what is customarily called the Jewish question' was frequently used to indicate the non-existence of the problem on the one hand, and the use made of it by foreign elements, on the other hand.

Israel's sweeping 1967 victory over the USSR's Arab partners and the enthusiastic Jewish reaction to it, which recalled the national awakening in the USSR in 1948, forced the Soviet authorities to contend with rising Jewish nationalism and the revival of Zionist inclinations among Soviet Jews.

The Soviet reaction was an anti-Israeli and anti-Zionist propaganda campaign exposing the internal inconsistency which characterized Soviet policy towards the Jewish question: the simultaneous denial of anti-Semitism and its propagation.

The anti-Zionist campaign concentrated on two complementary issues: rejection of the 'Zionist option' and its demonic ramifications as a solution to the Jewish question, and the use of anti-Zionism as an expression of governmental anti-Semitism, while abolishing any differentiation between the terms 'Zionist' and 'Jew'.

The discussion of the Jewish question which re-emerged in 1968, concentrated in part on the 'Zionist option' and its national expressions. The extensive literature published in the late 1960s and 1970s purported to be a 'scientific' examination of the State of Israel and its economic, social, ideological, political and geographical aspects, and constituted a denial of the Zionist solution to the Jewish question, by exposing the capitalist, imperialist, anti-class and corrupt aspects of Zionism.[34]

The repeated conclusion stated that 'as experience shows, the State of Israel and Zionism are incapable of solving what is called the Jewish question'.[35] Moreover:

> Jewish self-isolation serves hostile propaganda and activities aimed against the Soviet Union and the socialist states, where Jews enjoy equal rights. The Zionist leaders intervene in the internal affairs of the Soviet Union and attempt to revive the non-existent Jewish question. They strive to isolate and detach the Jewish working citizen from the structure of socialism, proposing the charms of capitalism instead.[36]

The Soviet Union proved that 'the "Jewish question" has been radically solved and has been removed from the agenda not by means of Zionism but on the basis of the victory of socialism'.[37] This declaration was accompanied by a detailed description of the Soviet vision of Jewish 'revival' in the Soviet Union:

> In resolving the national question, including the Jewish question, the Communist Party of the Soviet Union has consistently realized the principle of political, economic and social equality. The revolution has ultimately destroyed all traces of national oppression, uprooted all anti-Semitic excesses...and changed the social, political and moral image of the Jewish population...The establishment of the Jewish Autonomous Oblast in Birobidzhan turned the right of self-determination into a reality: territorial concentration in a Soviet national unit, or the rapprochement and merging into other nations wherever they live...Jewish classics and

> the works of Soviet Jewish authors are published in Yiddish...Lack of economic security has disappeared...Unquestionably, the concomitant of this is the assimilation of large groups of the Jewish population...Intermarriage, the mastery of Russian, Ukrainian, Belorussian, Georgian and other tongues as native languages, the elimination of religious and nationalist prejudices have contributed to the fact that the process of merging which is taking place, absolutely voluntarily...has taken on a mass character.[38]

In Soviet publications, the Jewish question was replaced by the 'Zionist question'. The issue of the existence of a Jewish nation was discussed again not in the framework of the national problem, but rather in the 'Zionist connection'. Soviet propagandists went on to attack Zionist nationalism, which attempted to create a fictitious worldwide 'Jewish nation'.[39]

Anti-Semitism was no longer the weapon of reactionaries in the Soviet Union, but rather it was encouraged and fostered by Zionism, in its attempt to rally the Jews around the international centre of fascism and racism, namely — the State of Israel.[40]

The anti-Zionist campaign was epitomized by the outright anti-Semitic attitude of the regime, which equated the terms 'Jewish' and 'Zionist'. According to Soviet propaganda, Zionism was rooted in the historical, cultural and religious nature and characteristics of Judaism, which has always striven to gain control of the world, and was the later expression of this age-old aspiration. This international conspiracy was depicted in monstrous dimensions, endangering the existence of the Soviet Union. Thus, the Jewish question was turning into an all-Soviet problem 'due to the Jews living there'. In this context, anti-Semitism served as a legitimate and even essential means of defence, employed by the peoples of the Soviet Union in their struggle against Jewish (or Zionist) imperialist plots. The use of terms such as 'Nazi-Zionist anti-Semitism' further legitimized these notions. These explanations were based on a historical survey of Judaism and its place in Russia and later in the Soviet Union. They warned the Russian people of the 'Russophobia of the Zionists'.[41]

Thus, beginning in the post-Khrushchev period, and especially from 1967 until the second half of the 1980s, while the Soviet leaders did not deal much with the Jewish question officially, the issue did acquire two characteristics, which complemented each other ideologically and found expression in the Soviet regime's policy towards the Jews in the Soviet Union: unrestrained anti-Zionism, which ultimately acquired an explicitly anti-Semitic dimension. During this long period, there was not only terminological or ideological change, but rather a kind of synthesis between the two. The Jewish question, which until the end of the Khrushchev period had been presented officially as having reached an assimilationist solution by a merger of the nations under the new socialist society, was removed from the public agenda in the Soviet Union, and transformed into a problem pertaining to the capitalist part of the world. However, it returned in full force to the borders of Eastern Europe as a Soviet and mainly Russian problem, and anti-Semitism constituted the only legitimate and even essential means of combating this 'Jewish-Zionist threat'.

Until 1967, the Soviet regime had vacillated between de-emphasizing Jewish exclusivity and the Jewish question, on the one hand, and stressing them by means of anti-Jewish and anti-Zionist publications, on the other hand. It recognized their right to live as citizens with equal rights and then rejected any recognition of their national existence and denied them adequate and equal social status. The Soviet propagandists and scientists were forced to manoeuvre between these two attitudes. From the early 1970s on, the regime adopted a party ideology devoid of internal conflict, abolishing the ambivalent assessment of Jewish existence.

The first years of the Gorbachev period reflected continuity, rather than a change in the attitude towards the Jewish question and the Zionist alternative. The traditional anti-Zionist trend found expression in the research literature and in the Soviet press.[42] Simultaneously, the Soviet regime denied any persecution of the Jews and continued to assert, as before, that the status of the Jews in the Soviet Union was equal to that of the other nationalities.

Thus, responding to questions posed by the French newspaper *l'Humanité* about the persecution of Jews, Gorbachev declared:

> This question has become part of an inflated anti-Soviet campaign, and a psychological attack against the USSR...Jews here are as free as people of any other nationality, possessing equal rights...and to my mind, the attention of anti-communist and Zionist propaganda to the fate of the Jews in the USSR is nothing other than hypocrisy.[43]

Nevertheless, despite the continuity regarding the main issues, there were gradual changes in the manner of expression and their content. It is notable that under Gorbachev, attention to the Jewish issue was kept at a minimum relative to former periods. Anti-Semitic publications with racist overtones, common until then, gradually disappeared from the media and there was also some 'matter-of-fact' criticism of this kind of literature.[44] The attitude towards anti-Semitism had altered and its denunciation no longer heralded increased anti-Jewish persecution.

Outright anti-Semitic publications reflected in the main, the position of opposition and conservative groups, who had been represented previously in official party policy. Freedom of discussion, which was one of the signs of glasnost, increased gradually and exposed the basic attitude of Soviet society, and not only the Soviet regime, to the Jewish question. While there was no specific official discussion of the Jewish question during the Gorbachev period, the use of racist, anti-Zionist and anti-Semitic terms was still common in public debates, exposing more than ever the deep-rooted anti-Semitism which characterized Soviet society and parts of the Soviet regime; the latter, by partly ignoring these manifestations, granted them a certain legitimacy. The essential differences in the attitude of the Soviet regime to the Jewish question were in the spheres of propaganda and publications, as well as in daily life.

Soviet Jews were gradually permitted to conduct Jewish cultural activity within the Soviet Union and to make contact with the outside world, in particular with Jews from other countries, including Israel.[45] Most important of all, as of 1989 almost any Jew who wished to do so was permitted to emigrate. This open-door policy was accompanied by efforts to dissuade Soviet Jews from emigrating from the Soviet Union. The Soviets emphasized both the unhappiness of those 'trapped' abroad and the joy of those permitted to return to their Soviet homeland. The Gorbachev era was characterized by a process of de-ideologizing Marxist-Leninist theory and Soviet ideology. As long as the regime was a communist one, based on ideology and ruled by the communist party, terminology and ideology were inseparable and even indistinguishable. Glasnost and perestroika enabled the policy-makers to refer, for the first time, not only to various ideological options, but primarily to new political ones. The practical and theoretical separation between ideology and politics finally brought about a split between ideology and terminology as a tool of propaganda in explaining the regime's policy.

Thus the Gorbachev period, for the first time, offered a different option for the Jewish question in the Soviet Union. This option, which was unthinkable during years of Soviet rule, was the departure of the Jews from the 'socialist garden of Eden'. Based on a pragmatic domestic and foreign policy, which dispensed with the need for ideological justifications, the Gorbachev option made it possible for Soviet Jews, as an ethnic group, to defend their national interests. Recognition of the existence of a Jewish nation, with specific national and cultural characteristics, of the existence of a Jewish question and of a solution which differed from the traditional Soviet one — indicated for the first time in the history of Russia and the Soviet Union

that there was an ideological, and not merely terminological, change
in the practical and theoretical approach to the Jewish question.

NOTES

1. V. I. Lenin, 'The Position of the Bund in the Party' (22 Oct. 1903), in *Selected Works*
   (Moscow: Progress, 1961–70), Vol. 7, p. 101.
2. Ibid.
3. Ibid. During the pre-revolutionary era, Lenin regarded anti-Semitic manifestations in
   Russian society as marginal. He denounced such phenomena as characterizing a
   reactionary regime and reiterated that the only way to prevent them was the merger of
   the Jewish proletariat with its Russian counterpart, for the sake of their joint struggle.
   'In Russia the workers of all nationalities, especially those of non-Russian nationality,
   endure economic and political oppression such as exists in no other country. The
   Jewish workers, as a disenfranchised nationality, not only suffer general economic and
   political oppression, but they also suffer under the yoke which deprives them of
   elementary civic rights. The heavier this yoke, the greater the need for the closest
   possible unity among the proletarians of the different nationalities; for without such
   unity a victorious struggle against the general oppression is impossible. The more the
   predatory tsarist autocracy strives to sow the seeds of discord, distrust and enmity
   among the nationalities it oppresses, the more abominable its policy of inciting the
   ignorant masses to savage pogroms becomes, the more does the duty devolve upon
   us, the Social-Democrats, to rally the isolated Social-Democratic parties of the different
   nationalities into a single Russian Social-Democratic Labour Party' — Lenin, 'To the
   Jewish Workers' (June 1905), in *Selected Works*, Vol. 8, pp. 495–6. See also, 'Draft
   Resolution on the Place of the Bund in the Party' (June–July 1903), in *Selected Works*,
   Vol. 6, p. 470; 'National Equality Bill' (March 1914), in *Selected Works*, Vol. 20, pp.
   172–3; 'Anti-Jewish Pogroms' (no date), in *Selected Works*, Vol. 29, p. 252.
4. Lenin, 'The Position of the Bund', Vol. 2, p. 100.
5. Lenin, 'Draft Platform for the Fourth Congress of Social Democratics of the Latvian
   Area' (May, 1913), in *Selected Works*, Vol. 19, p. 117.
6. Lenin , 'Critical Remarks on the National Question' (December 1913), in *Selected
   Works*, Vol. 20, pp. 26–7.
7. J. Stalin, *Marxism and The National and Colonial Question* (London: Martin
   Lawrence, n.d.) p. 8.
8. 'People's Commissariat [for Nationality Affairs] Decree on Uprooting the Anti-Semitic
   Movement', *Izvestiia VTsIK*, as quoted in H. Sloves, *Mamlachtiut yehudit bi-Vrit ha-
   Mo'atsot* (Tel Aviv: Am Oved, 1980), p. 211.
9. Zvi Gitelman, *Jewish Nationality and Soviet Politics. The Jewish Section of the CPSU
   1917–1930* (New Jersey: Princeton University Press, 1972), pp. 513–24.
10. Excerpts from the contradictory speech of Mikhail Kalinin, the President of the Soviet
    Union, which promises recognition of Jewish nationality through territorial settlement,
    as in Mordechai Altshuler, *Ha-yevsektsia bi-Vrit ha-Mo'atsot, 1918–1930. Bein
    leumiut le-komunizm* (Tel Aviv: Moreshet and the Institute of Contemporary Jewry,
    1980), pp. 200–2.
11. For the Birobidzhan program, its aims and means of realization, see Y. Levavi, *Ha-
    hityashvut ha-yehudit be-Birobijan* (Jerusalem: The Historical Society of Israel, 1965)
    and Sloves, *Mamlakhtiut yehudit bi-vrit ha-Mo'atsot*. See also Robert Weinberg, 'Jews
    into Peasants? Solving the Jewish Question in Birobidzhan', in this volume.
12. The *Bol'shaia Sovetskaia Entsiklopediia* not only supplied the reader with information,
    it also served as a genuine mirror of the changing policy of the Soviet regime, and
    even more so — of its ideological concepts. The publication process of the three
    editions of the encyclopedia relates to the main periods in Soviet history. A

comparison of the various editions provides the possibility of determining political values at a given time and examining the transmutations which these values underwent, in accordance with the changing ideology.

13. 'Evreiskii vopros', *Bol'shaia Sovetskaia Entsiklopediia* 24 (1932), p. 149. The author of the entry 'The Jewish Question', M. B. Vol'fson (1880–1932), was a member of the editorial board and served as assistant to the editor-in-chief of the encyclopedia. Additional entries referring to the Jews in this edition were written by prominent figures among the Jewish community in the Soviet Union. For example, Semen Dimanshtein, who wrote the entry 'Jews', had served in important government posts during the twenties and thirties and was one of the leaders of the *evsektsiia* and chairman of the central committee of Ozet. Also, he served as editor of important newspapers, such as *Der Emes* and *Tribuna*. The entry 'Jews in the Soviet Union' was written by G. Mindlin, a correspondent of the *Eynikeyt* newspaper, while the entry 'Hebrew Literature' was written by Isak Nusinov, a Jewish literature researcher who was the focus of government attacks during the forties.

14. Ibid.

15. Ibid., p. 157.

16. Ibid.

17. 'Evrei — Antropologicheskii', *Bol'shaia Sovetskaia Entsiklopediia*, pp. 13–14.

18. For the Jewish national awakening following the Holocaust and the establishment of the State of Israel and its repercussions see Y. Ro'i, *Soviet Decision Making in Practice. The USSR and Israel, 1947–1954* (New Brunswick: Transaction, 1988), pp. 186–206; Ro'i, *The Struggle for Soviet Jewish Emigration 1948–1967* (Cambridge: Cambridge University Press, 1991), pp. 23–32.

19. I. Erenburg,'Po povodu odnogo pis'ma', *Pravda*, 21 Sept. 1948.

20. 'Everei', in *Bol'shaia sovetskaia entsiklopediia* (Second edition) 15 (1952), p. 378.

21. Ibid., pp. 377–8.

22. Mordechai Altshuler (ed.), *Pirsumim russiim bi-Vrit ha-Mo'atsot al yehudim ve-yahadut 1917–1967* (Jerusalem: Society for Research on Jewish Communities and the History Society of Israel, 1970), Introduction by M. Altshuler, pp. 41–6.

23. I. Stalin, *Sochineniia* (Moscow: Gosudarstvennoe izdatel'stvo politicheskoi literatury, 1951), Vol. 13, p. 28.

24. Stalin's words were cited in Molotov's speech at the 8th Congress of the Soviets on the new constitution in *Pravda*, 30 Nov. 1936, as quoted in Solomon M. Schwarz, *The Jews in the Soviet Union* (Syracuse: Syracuse University Press, 1951), p. 296.

25. On the economic trials of the Khrushchev era, see G. Kline, 'Economic Crimes and Punishment', *Survey* 57 (1965), pp. 67–72. See also Benjamin Pinkus, *The Soviet Government and the Jews 1948–1967. A Documentary Study* (Cambridge: Cambridge Univ. Press, 1984), pp. 201–7.

26. Soviet periodicals like *Voprosy filosofii*, *Voprosy istorii*, and *Sovetskaia etnografiia* included articles by Soviet ethnographers such as S. Tokarev and V. Kozlov which provided interesting discussions and contradictory approaches to the Jewish question — S. A. Tokarev, 'Problema tipov etnicheskikh obshchnostei', *Voprosy filosofii* 11 (1964), pp. 43–53; V. I. Kozlov, 'O poniatii etnicheskoi obshchnosti' *Sovetskaia etnografiia* 2 (1967), pp. 100–101.

27. V. I. Kozlov, 'Sovremennye etnicheskie protsessy v SSSR', *Sovetskaia etnografiia* 2 (1969), p. 72.

28. For the place occupied by the Jews in anti-religious publications during the Khrushchev period, see Altshuler, *Pirsummim russiim*, pp. 46–50, as well as the following books: M. S. Belen'kii, *Chto takoe talmud?* (Moscow: Nauka, 1963), pp. 83–93, 139–41; M. I. Shakhnovich, *Reaktsionnaia sushchnost' iudaizma. Kratki ocherk proiskhozhdeniia i klassovoi sushchnost' iudeiskoi religii* (Moscow: Nauka, 1960).

29. E. Evtushenko, 'Babii Iar', *Literaturnaia gazeta*, 19 Sept. 1961.

30. 'What kind of real Russian are you, when you have forgotten your own people?' asked the Russian poet, Aleksei Iakovlevich Markov in his reply to Evtushenko — A. I. Markov, 'Moi otvet', *Literatura i zhizn'*, 24 Sept. 1961. See also Dmitrii Viktorovich Starikov's article: 'Ob odnom stikhotvorenii', *Literatura i zhizn'*, 27 Sept. 1961.

31. The first book attacking the State of Israel and Zionism was published in 1958 — K. Ivanov, Z. Sheinis, Z. Savel'evich, *Gosudarstvo Izrail', ego polozhenie i politika* (Moscow: Gospolitizdat, 1958). Another book including attacks on Zionism, Israel and the Jewish religion is G. S. Ziskin, *Iudaizm i sionizm. Komu i kak oni sluzhat* (Kuibyshev, 1963).
32. 'Evrei', in *Bol'shaia Sovetskaia Entsiklopediia* (1952), Vol. 15, pp. 378–9.
33. 'Obmen pis'mami mezhdu B. Rasselom i N. S. Khrushchevym', *Pravda*, 1 March 1963.
34. Many books about the State of Israel and Zionism were written starting in the late 1960s. For example, see G. S. Nikitina, *Gosudarstvo Izrail'. Osobennosti ekonomicheskogo i politicheskogo razvitiia* (Moscow: Nauka, 1968); B. I. Kiselev and N. P. Oleinikov, *Protiv sionizma i izrail'skoi agressii* (Sbornik materialov progressivnoi pechati) (Moscow, 1974); I. I. Mints *et al.*, *Sionizm: teoriia i praktika* (Moscow, 1973).
35. Nikitina, *Gosudarstvo Izrail'*, p. 34.
36. Ibid., p. 366.
37. Ibid., p. 108.
38. I. Braginskii, 'Klassovaia sushchnost' sionizma', *Kommunist* 9 (1970), pp. 108–9.
39. E. Evseev, *Fashizm pod goluboi zvezdoi* (Moscow: Molodaia gvardiia, 1977), pp. 27–35. V. V. Benevolenskii *et al.*, *Gosudarstvo Izrail'* (Moscow: Nauka, 1986), pp. 26–30.
40. Benevolenskii *et al.*, *Gosudarstvo Izrail'*, p. 29.
41. L. A. Korneev, *Klassovaia sushchnost' sionizma* (Kiev: Politizdat Ukrainy, 1982), p. 212; for the 'contribution' of Korneev and Ivanov to the Soviet anti-Semitic genre in the 1970s and 1980s, see L. Dymerskaya-Tsigelman, 'L. Korneev as a Phenomenon of the Soviet Anti-Semitism in the 1970's–1980's', *Jews and Jewish Topics in the Soviet Union and East Europe* (Bulletin of the Center for Research and Documentation of European Jewry), 2–3 (June 1986); I. Ivanov, *Ostorozhno: Sionizm! Ocherki po ideologii, organizatsii i praktike sionizma* (Moscow: Politizidat, 1971), pp. 11–21.
42. I. D. Zviagel'skaia and A. G. Ivanov, *Sionizm v sisteme imperializma* (Moscow: Nauka, 1988). *Komsomol'skaia pravda* published a 'Zionism is Racism' series with articles on the Jewish Defense League. For example, see the articles of V. Bashkin, 'Liga provokatorov', 22 Jan. 1987, p. 3; A. Zhukov, 'Rozhdennye nenavist'iu', 29 Oct. 1986, p.3; Tsezar' Solodar', 'Sionizm-agressiia-lozh' ', 18 July 1986, p. 3.
43. 'Otvet M. S. Gorbacheva na voprosy gazety *Humanité*', *Pravda*, 8 Feb. 1986.
44. To gain a perspective on this phenomenon, see L. Dymerskaya-Tsigelman, 'Party Criticism of the Racist Interpretation of Zionism: What It Refuted, What It Maintains and What It Fails to Mention', *Jews and Jewish Topics* 5 (1987).
45. On the growth of Jewish cultural activity across the Soviet Union, see L. Hirszowicz, 'Breaking the Mould: Jewish Culture under Gorbachev', *Soviet Jewish Affairs* 18, 3 (1988).

4

Soviet Cultural and Ethnic Policies towards Jews: A Legacy Reassessed

IGOR KRUPNIK

In the wake of recent transitions in the former Soviet Union and its successor states, the study of Soviet Jewish history is undergoing a rapid transformation from being mainly a saga of political oppression and discrimination to a more balanced academic discipline.* Accumulated data and resources will eventually necessitate a new approach, structured along the scholarly lines adopted to survey Jewish communities elsewhere in the modern world. With few exceptions, the paradigms of modernization, ethnicity, generational cultural change and social mobilization are but marginal issues, although these and other research tools of modern sociology are fully relevant to the study of Soviet Jewish history.

The purpose of this chapter is to examine the experience of Soviet Jewry in the broader context of general Soviet history. It will be argued here that the main transition of the communist regime was its transformation, during the mid and late 1950s, from a vigorous

* Several ideas on the fate of Soviet Jewry expressed in this chapter were formulated in discussions with Yurii Rodnyi (a former Jewish refusenik from Moscow now living in Palo Alta, CA). His contribution to this text deserves special gratitude. Another major intellectual stimulus was provided in the 1980s by Moscow-based economist Vitalii Naishul', with his theory on the post-Stalin transformation of the Soviet economic system. Any faults in the interpretation of both sources are the author's. Research was conducted under the Skirball Fellowship at the Oxford Centre for Postgraduate Hebrew Studies in 1993.

totalitarian regime to a decrepit post-totalitarian one. The previous regime was distinctly characterized by an unprecedented level of authoritarian oppression and terror. Publicly, however, it professed a creed of 'social engineering', that is, of a state-induced reconstruction of the social environment, including the status and basic features of the Soviet peoples and their ethnic cultures. The post-totalitarian state lost both its initial fervour and the resources of its predecessor. Therefore, it resorted to a series of social manipulations in order to sustain entrenched dogmas and political stability.

A similar distinction may be applied to the Soviet state's attitude towards Jews. The 'Jewish policy' of the regime was never more than a small fragment of its prevailing doctrine and, as such, it was strictly subordinate to the priorities and political zigzags of official ideology. This chapter challenges the perspective that seeks unbroken continuity in the general contempt or even open hostility that characterized Soviet treatment of its Jewish population. In its place, it introduces a fundamental dichotomy, stemming from two different creeds — totalitarian and post-totalitarian. The former was a 'builder', by self-definition (either a 'class-destroyer' or a 'new-life-builder'), while the latter was no more than a 'legacy-keeper'. As such, its policy towards Soviet Jews illustrates a strategy aimed primarily at maintaining the status quo and even at bare bureaucratic survival.

ONE POLICY OR MANY?

A student of Russian Jewry could easily trace a certain historiographic tradition in addressing Soviet Jewish history. This tradition has produced, so far, a framework of established phases that includes: the time of the Bolshevik Revolution and the Civil War (1917–22); the period of Yiddish-based *korenizatsiia* (nativization), from the mid 1920s to late 1930s; the Second World War and the Holocaust; postwar destruction; the post-Stalin years of the 1950s and 1960s; the *aliya* movement in the late 1960s, and so forth.[1]

The first point which should be noted is that Jews neither constituted an isolated enclave nor were they the main target of Soviet nationalities policy. Aside from a few short-term and highly orchestrated anti-Jewish onslaughts (such as the campaign against 'cosmopolitanism' in 1948, the Doctors' Plot of 1953, public attacks on Zionism after the Six-Day War, etc.), Jewish policy was a fairly integrated component of Soviet nationalities policy. Several other peoples were purged and promoted in roughly the same way, while a few had a far more tragic record of persecution by the communist state. Whereas Jews liked to demonstrate the uniqueness of their path, they normally had no other choice but to follow the general course undertaken by the Soviet regime.

This chapter questions whether the Soviet state, during its seventy years of existence, really had a uniform nationalities policy rather than a variety of shifting policies. John Armstrong argues that after an initial period of Marxist 'universalism', the regime tended more and more to rely on the 'imperial' component of its core, that is, its major ethnic population, the Russians.[2] In a somewhat similar fashion, William Orbach sees the Soviet policy towards Jews as a series of alternations between the so-called 'communist' and 'Russian' perspectives.

> When the pendulum has swung to the 'communist' side, [Jewish] religion has been persecuted, but as far as education and economic opportunities were concerned, the situation was good...and Jewish culture and language have been permitted to exist...On the other hand, under the Russian 'perspective', anti-Semitism has been rampant,...but emigration, although limited, has at times been permitted,...[and] Jewish culture and language have been subject to Russianization.[3]

In this framework, Orbach records a few alternating periods in Soviet policy towards the Jews, although he recognizes its gradual transition from 'liberal communism', through 'Sovietism', to dominating 'Russianism'.

TOTALITARIAN VERSUS POST-TOTALITARIAN STATE

Using the idea of a non-linear evolution of the communist regime and of its nationalities policy, a line of progression could be drawn in a different direction. Indeed, the key metamorphosis, occurred when the Soviet state changed from a completely totalitarian system to a more subtle post-totalitarian one. The death of Stalin in 1953 was a genuine turning point, though the transition actually continued into the 1960s.

The level and universality of coercion is a standard characteristic of any totalitarian regime.[4] Equally important is the degree of enthusiasm for building, which is embedded in the dominant ideology and public mood alike. The totalitarian system (or its ruling party) normally comes to power as a 'builder of a new life' and a 'social engineer' on behalf of the nation.

As such, social engineering becomes the overtly declared, if not the exclusively accepted policy. The totalitarian state commits itself to a whole set of impressive construction programs for reshaping the social, cultural and ethnic composition of society. This fervour for 'construction' was a crucial feature of the early Soviet regime, as new nations and social classes were invented; ancient towns were renamed and capital cities changed; republics were established and nullified; and millions of citizens were purged or relocated to participate in mammoth economic endeavours. Culture became a new 'construction site' as well.[5] Whole areas of former cultural tradition were condemned; pre-1917 (that is, 'bourgeois') literature and art were invalidated; religion was oppressed; and alphabets were replaced in the process of building a new 'socialist' culture for the Soviet nations. All ethnic groups of the Soviet Union, large and small alike, passed through the same orgy of totalitarian reconstruction.

The era of 'social engineering' in the Soviet Union ended with the death of Stalin in 1953 or soon after; and that was the close of the totalitarian regime itself.[6] By 1960, the transition was obvious. The old totalitarianism was gone, and a new society emerged via post-totalitarian mutation.

The core of the post-totalitarian system was entirely different from its predecessor, as the formerly monolithic power structure split into a number of bureaucratic fragments. A unified state machine became gradually transformed into a set of individual 'social projects' that pursued different and sometimes conflicting goals. Coordination among agencies became increasingly difficult, so that it was impossible to carry out state-wide, all-union constructive efforts and social engineering. Soviet 'newspeak' revealed this trend in a remarkable way. Whereas the old regime had one overall state policy, the new government began pursuing various policies: 'party policy', 'economic policy', 'agrarian policy', 'sports policy', 'editorial policy', 'theatre policy', and so forth. As factions and agencies fought for privileges of their own, the post-totalitarian regime was forced to resort to constant manoeuvring and social manipulation.[7]

In terms of its ethnic policy, the post-totalitarian regime adhered to a consistently conservative approach. A few cosmetic modifications in the Soviet federal system were all but completed by the late 1950s.[8] Not a single new ethnic unit was created, or territory up- or downgraded in its administrative status, in the three subsequent decades. The claims of a few exiled peoples that did not succeed in attaining their right of return by the late 1950s, were shelved for decades. The Soviet power and military élite became extremely monolithic in ethnic composition, due to its growing xenophobia towards all non-Slavic nationals.[9]

On the other hand, the transition to a post-totalitarian society triggered impressive modernization in the state economy and in the lifestyle of Soviet citizens. Although the main vehicle for post-Stalin economic growth was a boom in the military and related industries, immense resources were channeled into new technologies, academic research and social infrastructure. Employment in science, technology and management skyrocketed, as new research and academic centres mushroomed all over the country. The number of state-employed research scientists grew seven-fold between the years 1950 and 1973: from 162,500 to 1,108,000.[10] To meet the demand, the system of college and university education was upgraded. Within a decade, the number of college students in the USSR roughly doubled, from 2,395,500 in 1960 to 4,580,600 in 1970.[11]

The modernization of the 1960s coincided with the inception of Khrushchev's program for constructing inexpensive housing. As millions of Soviet citizens moved from inner-city communal residences to family apartments in suburbia, they tasted the Soviet version of consumerism. They also acquired notions of privacy and individualism they had lacked over decades of building communism. The emerging Soviet 'middle-class', while fully loyal to the system, was anxious to create stability for itself through education, professionalism and economic wealth.

The decade of the 1960s was remarkable for several other breaches in a formerly stiff control system built by the Stalin regime. Some, like the boom in fine arts, film and theatre-production and literature, were the fruits of greater intellectual freedom. Others were mainly the outcome of modern technology, such as the accessibility of the tape recorder, which enabled the spread of uncensored political songs and folk music. A burgeoning post-totalitarian 'counter-culture' produced an electrifying alternative to official 'socialist' art. Created in Russian, by Russian-speaking intellectuals of various ethnic origins, it boosted the role of the Russian language and its status as the dominant cultural medium for the Soviet urban population and, in particular, its educated élite.

Obviously, the communist rulers were far from enthusiastic in the face of this new level of cultural and social expression. They tried to regain control through censorship and suppression or by outlawing the forms they could not command, such as modern art and *samizdat* literature. That policy was both inefficient and inadequate. It produced a flourishing network of double-standards and overt and cynical double-thinking that was so typical of Soviet society in the 1960s and 1970s. In a striking deviation from the early totalitarian models *à la* Joseph Stalin or George Orwell, different value systems and behaviour coexisted in a commonly accepted pattern, across all spectrums of post-totalitarian Soviet life.

71

COMPONENTS OF SOCIAL MANIPULATION

The general framework presented above, is fully relevant to the history of Soviet Jewry. It was Zvi Gitelman who pioneered this approach in the 1970s, when he viewed Jewish national life in the first decade of Soviet rule as 'a history of the modernization and secularization of an ethnic and religious minority resulting from attempts to integrate this minority into a modernizing state'.[12] For the purposes of this chapter on Soviet Jewry in the post-Stalin years, one has to acknowledge the enormous efforts made by the communist regime in its so-called 'policy of construction', that is, in the social engineering of its Jewish population during the initial period.[13]

By the late 1930s, the 'era of building' was over. Most of the state-engineered innovations introduced previously to Jewish social and cultural life, such as Yiddish schools, Yiddish-language courts, Jewish agricultural communes and local autonomous districts were gone or effectively destroyed. In this respect, however, Jews did not differ from several other Soviet minority groups. They all suffered a similar fate, as their ethnic districts were liquidated, schooling and publishing in native languages were halted and the native cultural élite were purged all over the Soviet Union.

The Jews became a specific target for communist repression only in the late 1940s. The regime then proceeded vigorously to dismantle the last remaining vestiges of Jewish life. This drive included public harassment of Jews through 'anti-cosmopolitan' and anti-Zionist campaigns and the physical execution of the Jewish cultural élite. The last act in Stalinist 'engineering of destruction' was to have been the mass deportation of Soviet Jews to Siberia scheduled for early 1953.[14] Here again, the pattern of totalitarian deportation was not introduced especially for Jews since it was an accepted Soviet practice in the 1930s and 1940s.[15]

Immediately after the death of Stalin in 1953, any sort of totalitarian programs targeting Soviet Jews ceased altogether. It seemed as if the state had given up its former attempts to transform Soviet Jewry according to any imposed design. In their approach toward Jews, the new rulers mainly followed the strategies developed by the late-Stalin regime, although their actions were hesitant, at best. Before the outbreak of mass Jewish emigration in the early 1970s, the post-totalitarian state had barely introduced a single innovation in its Jewish policy — either in ideology or in governmental practice.[16]

While direct governmental actions were modest by all standards, the spontaneous transformation of Soviet Jewry progressed on a remarkable scale. Jews as a population made great strides socially, due to the post-Stalin wave of modernization. Their educational level soared and stayed by far the highest among all Soviet nations.[17] The number of Jews concentrated in large urban centres of the Soviet Union continued to grow,[18] as did the Jewish presence in key sectors of the Soviet economy and culture.

As an illustration of the ongoing social mobility of Soviet Jews, in 1935 there were 74,900 Jewish students in Soviet colleges and universities out of a population of some 2,700,000, that is 27.7 per every 1,000 Jews. In 1956 the ratio was about 38 per 1,000, and in 1968 it peaked at 112,000 Jewish students for barely 2,000,000 Soviet Jews, that is, 56 per 1,000.[19] The number of Jewish 'scientific workers', that is, those working at colleges and universities, industrial research centres, and institutions of the Academy of Sciences, soared even more dramatically. Their number nearly doubled in just one decade (from 33,500 in 1960 to 64,400 in 1970).[20] This means that in the 1960s alone more than 30,000 Jews entered prestigious fields of academic research and teaching. In Moscow, which has the largest concentration of Soviet academic work force, Jews constituted more than 10 per cent of all research personnel and 19.7 per cent of its academic élite (*doktora nauk*), as of the early 1970s.[21]

This account of social achievement could hardly pass for a testimony of oppression and ongoing discrimination. By 1979, the educational level of Soviet Jews was twice as high as that of the Israeli Jewish population.[22] In some areas, that is, in the large Russian urban centres, Soviet Jews even surpassed American Jews in their educational status.[23] According to Theodore Friedgut, this remarkable upward social mobility of Soviet Jewry, based on the acquisition of higher education, is 'a success story which rivals, and perhaps overshadows, the economic and social achievements of North American Jewry'.[24]

As mainly second-generation urban-dwellers and educated professionals, Jews made a disproportionally high contribution to the new Soviet urban middle-class of the 1960s and 1970s. Friedgut termed this mainstream middle-class Soviet Jewry the 'silent majority', in reference to its progressive assimilation and abandonment of Jewish values.[25] The pattern of transformation is, actually, better portrayed as a post-totalitarian Soviet modification of Jewish *embourgeoisement.*[26] Although in the communist environment, Soviet Jews missed out on the ritual and political aspects of the transition to *embourgeoisement,* they followed its main behavioural trend, in terms of adapting to liberal middle-class values and standards of living.[27]

The Soviet Jewish drive towards social mobility and middle-class status was, however, persistently thwarted by the communist state through its practice of discrimination in employment and education. These humiliating practices are revealed in detail in numerous publications and memoirs of Soviet Jewish émigrés.[28] On the one hand, the regime still regarded its Jews as a skilled and valuable work force, first and foremost for defence research and industry. As such, thousands of Jews continued to work in medium and high-ranking positions throughout the 1960s and 1970s. On the other hand, Stalin's heirs pursued a policy aimed at curbing the 'Jewish presence' at the top of the system, mainly in governmental, party, military and other vital institutions. These conflicting policies produced an intriguing combination of social niches available to Jews. Those 'open niches', were, moreover, constantly reshaped by the closing of old and the opening of new opportunities, mostly at the lower and middle echelons. While by 1950 Jews maintained only a token presence in the top state bureaucracy, they continued to be widely represented in the Soviet academic, cultural and artistic élite.[29] In the 1970s, when access to top research institutions was restricted, Jews poured into the burgeoning fields of computer science and information services.[30]

The Jewish movement for emigration, first to Israel and then to the US, was the only new component that the post-totalitarian Soviet government had to deal with in its policy towards Jews in the late 1960s. The regime, however, failed to find a successful response to the new challenge or even to demonstrate a consistent approach towards mass emigration. It never formulated a clear-cut policy regarding the new movement nor did it address the issue at any general level. Instead, it occupied itself with specific issues, such as reunification of families, refuseniks, *aliya* activists, individual applicant and so on, but never with the Jewish population as a whole.

Although considerable efforts have been invested in analyzing the twists and turns in Soviet policy toward Jewish emigration, the simplest answer is probably that there was no policy whatsoever; instead, there was a totally unpredictable manipulative 'game', with no fixed rules and no visible strategies.[31] The same model could well explain the shifts in the Soviet treatment of Jews as an ethnic group and of Jewish culture, in the transition from ardent restructuring to blunt annihilation, and then to decades of *ad hoc* manipulation.

JEWS AS A 'PEOPLE' AND THE SOVIET ATTITUDE TOWARD THEM

Although every single essay on Jewish history in the Soviet Union starts with an analysis of Lenin's and Stalin's attitudes towards Jews and Jewish identity, Marxist dogma turned out to be far from relevant to Bolshevik *realpolitik*.[32] Before 1917, both leaders asserted that Jews did not constitute a nation, as they lacked a defined ethnic territory and were doomed to assimilation. Nevertheless, immediately after the 1917 Revolution, the Jews were labeled a 'nationality', along with other ethnic minorities of Russia. As such, they were treated officially as an ethnic group.

A Jewish Commissariat (*evkom*) was established in 1918 within the Commissariat of Nationality Affairs, Narkomnats, along with other ethnic-based commissariats, such as Polish, Latvian, Belorussian, Lithuanian, Armenian, and 'Muslim'. Special 'Jewish sections', *evsektsii*, were introduced to the Communist party in the same year.[33] By these and other actions, the Bolsheviks actually created a Jewish 'nationality' in Russia. They reclassified Russian Jewry as a 'people', rather than its previous status as a religious group in the Romanov empire.

Although both the Jewish Commissariat and the *evsektsii* were soon abolished (in 1924 and 1930, respectively), the status of Jews as one of the minority 'peoples' of the Soviet Union was not challenged. Jews were recorded as such in official publications and, beginning in 1932, in the internal Soviet passport.

In the late 1920s, some Jewish communists and high-ranking Soviet officials, including the first President of the USSR, Mikhail Kalinin, were anxious to upgrade the status of Jews as a minority nation. The issue was addressed through programs in agricultural resettlement and territorial autonomy. Even the option of an autonomous Jewish republic, either in Birobidzhan or in Crimea, was debated.[34] The latter motion, if accepted, would have transformed Soviet Jewry into a 'normal' territorial nation within the Soviet federal system. Such plans, however, were abandoned by the late 1930s, leaving the Jewish autonomous *oblast'* in Birobidzhan as the sole relic of the abortive attempt at Jewish nation-building in the USSR.

Failing to get more than an autonomous *oblast'* meant that Jews were condemned to a second-rate status in Soviet society, even without an anti-Semitic stance on the part of the regime. The Soviet federal state was designed as an openly hierarchical system built upon the unequal ranking of its component nations.[35] The peoples of the USSR were often recorded in a strange hierarchical order which had nothing in common with their population numbers or alphabetical order of their names. The Russians were invariably the first to be listed, followed by the 14 titular nations of the other union republics, then the 29 nations with autonomous republics, and penultimately, smaller ethnic groups with autonomous provinces and areas. Minorities lacking any territorial unit of their own, were always placed at the very bottom of the list.

It was this ranking that determined the political role of the nation under Soviet federalism. It held the key to a nation's public and legislative representation, its designated share in state resources, the power assigned to its élite, and even to the amount of data available in the press, in census records, encyclopedias and handbooks, etc. The fifteen nations with union republic status normally received the fullest coverage, while those of the lower ranks were rarely mentioned outside their designated ethnic areas.[36]

The Jews, according to this categorization, were ranked along with other peoples of autonomous provinces somewhere between the 44th and 50th position, among some hundred Soviet nations. When judged by their population share, Jews formed the seventh largest Soviet nation in 1926 and 1939, eleventh in 1959, and sixteenth in 1979. In fact, the Jewish presence was even more prominent since Jews constituted the third largest urban population, after the Russians and Ukrainians. By placing them among the tiny peoples of 'autonomous provinces', the state deliberately downplayed the status and economic role of its Jewish population.

This deception, implemented with sophistication by post-totalitarian statistical jugglers, opened the way for all sorts of data manipulation.[37] Published data on Soviet Jews were censored or restricted, and comparative studies were downgraded, as Jews were routinely eliminated from the list of 'major' Soviet nations. Jews, however, did not constitute the only target in this pattern of manipulation. Census and/or sociological data on Soviet Germans or Poles were even less accessible, as these ethnic groups were not granted any autonomy of their own. The most extreme cases were those of true outcasts such as the Crimean Tatars, who were not even listed as a separate nation in postwar Soviet records. Thus, no statistical data whatsoever — even on Crimean Tatar overall population numbers — were published between 1945 and 1989.

While statistical data on and mention of Soviet Jews were manipulated according to the low rank designated them by the system, several other factors reduced Jewish representation vis-à-vis the other Soviet nations. Since Soviet federalism was based on territorial ethnic autonomy, nations had to be located mainly within their designated ethnic 'homes'. If, for some historical reasons, certain nations crossed those boundaries or even spread all over the country, this, naturally, raised questions about the legitimacy of the 'home territories' granted them by the regime. Jews were the worst 'trouble-makers' in this regard since 99 per cent of them lived outside their appointed autonomous region in Birobidzhan. For this reason alone, Jews were normally not included in showcase exhibitions of state nationalities policy.[38]

Another factor was the continuous decline of Soviet Jewry registered by all population censuses after 1959. Under communist doctrine, numerical growth was a sign of progress, social fitness and the success of the Soviet system, while decline was equated with failure. Jews were the largest Soviet nation with a steady population decline, thus they openly contested the communist obsession with progress and growth. This, too, made Jews unmentionable in any discussion of nationalities policy.

Last but not least, was an ambiguity in the general ethnic status of Jews created by shortcomings in Marxist social theory. While Jews remained on the list of Soviet peoples, the very existence of a 'Jewish people', that is, the ethnic unity of world Jewry, was first questioned and then bluntly repudiated by the communist regime. The most decisive negation was published in the *Great Soviet Encyclopedia* of 1952, in which the word 'Jews' was defined as merely 'a [common] name given to different populations having a common origin in the ancient Hebrews that inhabited Palestine, from the middle of the second millennium BCE until the first to second centuries AD'.[39] This degrading definition of Jews, as a plethora of unrelated and rootless populations, was recycled in numerous Soviet encyclopedias and official handbooks until the late 1980s.[40]

As a result of their equivocal status, Jews created confusion in Soviet ethnic and political theories. For various reasons it was deemed safer to avoid mentioning them altogether or to leave the issue to a few appointed ideologists.[41] As scholars opted out of the discussion, the image of Jews in Soviet social science was further manipulated by slurs which conjured up a 'world Jewish conspiracy' or the 'non-nation' status of Soviet Jewry.

Beyond those general factors, manipulation was based on dozens of hidden reasons and local conditions. There was not a single reference to Jews in the official history of the Ukrainian SSR (1982), nor were Jews listed among Soviet partisans, war heroes or Nazi victims in Belorussia.[42] In contrast, Jews and Jewish issues were cited more openly in publications printed in Georgia, Armenia and the

Baltic republics. In fact, regions and union republics, industries and academic fields, colleges and periodicals, even the neighbouring departments within one agency might differ greatly in their acceptance and treatment of Jews. A Jew had no choice but to master the intricate map created by these overlapping layers of manipulation.

THE POLICY TOWARDS JEWISH CULTURE

The post-totalitarian, post-Stalin, Soviet state is often perceived as consistently malicious toward Jews because of its hostility toward Jewish culture. This perspective is only partly true, since discussions of Jewish cultural life in the USSR rarely placed it in the context of the Soviet approach to other ethnic cultures. This was modeled upon two principles: a perception of culture as a combination of 'positive' and 'pernicious' elements which were easy to identify and which had to be treated individually; and a hierarchical format in cultural policy depending upon the administrative ranking of each nation within the Soviet federal system.

Jewish culture in the USSR was badly traumatized by both of these political tenets. Zvi Gitelman has defined four types of Jewish culture in Russia and the Soviet Union: religious, secular Yiddishist, secular Hebraic and secular Russian variants.[43] The Bolsheviks had an entirely different perspective since they never recognized religion as 'culture' and virtually eliminated both the Hebraic and Russian-Jewish secular variants as pernicious 'bourgeois legacies'. It was only the secular Yiddishist stream that was actively promoted by the Soviet state during the 1920s and 1930s. Its content, however, was completely revised according to communist cultural doctrine.

Analysis of the 'Jewish' curriculum at Soviet Yiddish schools and educational institutions in the 1930s indicates an extremely narrow concept of the Jewish cultural and historical legacy. As Gitelman notes: 'The very concept of "Jewish history" was excluded from the school. In a second-grade curriculum the only "Jewish" content consisted of warnings against "non-hygienic customs" such as kissing the Torah.'[44] The new 'Soviet Jewish culture' dismembered the history of ancient and medieval Jewry and dwarfed Jewish roots to Sholem Aleichem, the *shtetl* legacy and class-struggle.[45] In comparison to other ethnic cultures, however, Soviet Jewish culture neither occupied a unique position nor was it distorted according to a unique scenario.

If this version of Jewish culture had survived the purges of the late 1940s, it would have been an ideal tool for later propaganda attacks against Israel and American Jews. In the case of Soviet Jews, however, whatever new 'socialist culture' had been created for them was all but ruined by the same totalitarian regime. When a tiny offshoot of the former Soviet Yiddishism was rehabilitated in the late 1950s,[46] it was characterized by national longings, nostalgia and Soviet parochialism. As such, it was too weak to fight any new contenders.

A brand of modern secular Hebraism in the form of Israeli popular culture had trickled through to Soviet Jews from the late 1950s. During the 1960s and 1970s, the *aliya* movement succeeded in transforming this esoteric stream into an appealing alternative for cultural survival. From the late 1970s, the international book fairs in Moscow made available to thousands of Soviet Jews a powerful display of both the Israeli and American versions of modern Jewish culture. Enormous lines that formed in front of Israeli and American Jewish book stalls revealed the bankruptcy of Soviet Yiddishism in favour of more captivating forms of Jewish ethnicity.

It is doubtful whether Soviet officials ever addressed this trend as a cultural challenge rather than a political threat. If they did, they still reacted according to established Soviet policy, which bound every nation's cultural activity to its 'native' language and the appointed rank of its territorial autonomy. For Soviet Jews it was the same old 'package' of Yiddish as the prescribed ethnic language and the Jewish Autonomous Oblast in Birobidzhan as the designated ethnic 'homeland'. To Soviet officials, then, the game was simple: in response to international pressure on behalf of the cultural rights of Soviet Jewry, the state established a Jewish musical theatre in Birobidzhan (in 1978), instituted a few Yiddish classes at local schools and kindergartens in the Jewish Autonomous Oblast (1980), printed a Yiddish primer for Birobidzhan schools (1982) and a Russian-Yiddish dictionary (1984) and made promises to re-establish a college in Birobidzhan, with scientific and editorial programs (in the mid 1980s).[47]

Both Yiddish and Birobidzhan were 'dead horses', unable to compete with the appeal of Israel and the ethnic awakening of a highly educated and acculturated Soviet Jewry. But the failure of any official response was predictable. Apparently, the post-totalitarian state never formulated a strategy to deal with any contemporary ethnic culture beyond the bounds of their ranked territorial autonomies and the old paradigm of 'socialist in form and national in content'. The latter was nothing but the very same combination of schools, literature, official media, theatres and broadcasting in native languages, introduced in the 1920s and 1930s. In the case of other Soviet nations, it was the task of their political élites to lobby in favour of more resources to be devoted to local cultural institutions or for greater tolerance toward native religion and cultural legacies.

After the purges of the late 1940s, Soviet Jews lacked any recognized establishment to channel their cultural aspirations. Nor could Jews found any 'partner' agency within the Soviet state system which would be willing to deal with a dispersed urban minority outside its assigned territorial autonomy. As a result, post-totalitarian Jewish culture in the USSR was more an offspring of various types of manipulation than of a centralized policy of strangulation or vicious state anti-Semitism. While reducing public Jewish activities to a bare minimum, the state neither followed any standard pattern nor demonstrated any persistent guidelines in its policy. It was nothing but a muddle of 'post-totalitarian geography' that created two Jewish theatres in Moscow and none in Kiev or Leningrad[48]; Jewish concert tours in Gomel' and Bobruisk and none in Minsk.

A few Western observers have tried to discern some kind of logic in this intrinsic geography of officially permitted Jewish culture in the former USSR.[49] Others have just stressed its striking inconsistency comparable to the official handling of Jewish emigration.[50] A similar lack of uniformity and deep inner contradictions have been reported elsewhere for the Soviet approach to the Nazi Holocaust, the role of Jews during the Second World War, and the course taken by the anti-Zionist campaign.[51] Therefore, the depiction of a well-oiled, tightly controlled policy, was hardly applicable to post-totalitarian Soviet society. Rather, it was a myth perpetuated by the system in order to stay afloat under the increasing pressure of new challenges. When the pressure finally became unbearable, the system collapsed, with its former 'Jewish' policy, as well as several other practices in social manipulation, being buried in the rubble.

CONCLUSIONS

This chapter introduces a new turning point in the history of relations between Soviet Jews and the communist regime, that of a transition from 'totalitarian engineering' to 'post-totalitarian manipulation'. The implications of this distinction transcend pure taxonomy and enter a broader realm. It is generally accepted that every single totalitarian program in 'social engineering' targeting Soviet Jews in the 1920s and 1930s, turned out to be a failure.[52] That covers a variety of initiatives, such as Birobidzhan and other resettlement projects, the creation of Jewish autonomies as alternatives to Palestine, Yiddish schooling, Yiddish-language courts, the suppression of the Jewish religion and the transformation of Jews into a 'socialist nation'.

Despite the bankruptcy of particular projects, communist engineering was, on the whole, highly successful. It succeeded in transforming Russian Jewry into a loyal and devoted component of the new system, so-called 'Soviet citizens of the Jewish nationality'. The social composition of Russian Jewry was entirely reorganized; its élite was annihilated; its former ethnic values were repudiated and its institutions of cultural continuity were crushed by purges and strangulation.

In this regard, the record of Soviet Jewry was quite similar to the experience of other Soviet ethnic groups dragged into the same engineering policy of the totalitarian regime. Some nations, such as the Germans, Crimean Tatars, Chechens and Kalmyks suffered even greater losses in the totalitarian ethnic mill. Their entire populations were stigmatized and exiled as social outlaws, their 'ethnic homes' abolished, even their names eradicated among the list of 'peoples of the USSR'. That tragedy never happened to the Jews.

The post-totalitarian regime, on the other hand, devised a more selective approach. While pressure on other Soviet nations mostly abated, Jews were specially targeted by the state propaganda machine. Virulent public campaigns against Judaism, Zionism and Israel were more intensive than was warranted by any reasonable impact the Jewish people could have had upon Soviet politics.[53] By the late 1960s, the humiliating pressure on everything labeled 'Jewish' increased dramatically, though it extended unevenly across the various spheres of Soviet public life.

Despite these efforts, post-totalitarian manipulation failed to reach its two major targets, namely, to halt Jewish emigration and to accelerate the erosion of the few remaining vestiges of Jewish life. The true outcome of the 'manipulation era' was the half million Soviet Jews who had fled the country by the early 1990s and the thousands more who recaptured their ethnic identity which had been impaired or lost during the previous totalitarian decades.

What, then, was the role of the 'manipulation era' in Soviet Jewish history? In a certain sense, the years after Stalin's death served as a time for the recuperation of Soviet Jewry. That gradual recovery was painful, indeed. Loyalty to the communist system constituted but a fraction of the legacy left by Stalin's social engineering. Its major contribution was an ideologically motivated openness to (or, at least, acceptance of) broad assimilation, that is, rejection of former ethnic values in favour of modernization and the doctrine of 'communist universalism'. The latter was packaged under the appealing labels of 'internationalism' and 'joining the human race' through the adoption of Russian culture and language.[54] That electrifying blend was further enriched by a legacy of heroic sacrifices in building the new socialist society and/or in fighting nazism during the Second World War. It produced a powerful and highly emotional mixture — one that could not be overcome easily. For most of the Soviet people, including Jews, it took about forty years to debunk this legacy.

The image of a crippled Jewish identity engrained by totalitarian engineering, was another component of that same legacy. Soviet Jewish ethnicity, beyond the burden of dubious loyalty and discrimination, was reduced to parochial *shtetl* memories, to Yiddish as a dying language, and to the ambivalent status of a 'non-nation' within the family of thriving Soviet ethnic groups. The post-totalitarian Jewish identity was, then, characterized by overt pessimism and bitterness, since it was doomed to vanish.

As it turned out, the decades of the 'manipulation era' saw a fundamental transition in Soviet Jewry. These years were spent beyond impressive modernization and social mobility — in nurturing new channels of affiliation since the post-totalitarian state system ceased to be the only arbiter of ethnic and cultural identity. The onset of a mass *aliya* movement in the 1970s was a major breakthrough in that gradual process. To thousands of Soviet Jews, it suddenly offered the option of an alternative ethnicity which was free of any Soviet legacy and state affiliation. By raising general issues of Jewish survival and by their own Zionist stand, the *aliya* activists reintroduced the pluralism of modern Jewish identities eradicated by the Stalin regime in the 1920s and 1930s. The very option of being a Jew (or a non-Jew), with positive and non-ambiguous modern ethnicity — in its Israeli, American, or any other variant — triggered the demise of the old Soviet legacy.

The post-totalitarian system responded to the challenge of emigration with a set of manipulations and an overdose of anti-Zionism. By virtue of this choice, it lost all control whatsoever over the Soviet Jewish ethnic revival. For Jews, it took another twenty years of wandering across the 'desert of manipulation', before they could test a new brand of their identity as a post-communist reality.

NOTES

1. See Yelena Luckert, *Soviet Jewish History, 1917–1991. An Annotated Bibliography* (New York: Garland, 1992); Salo W. Baron, *The Russian Jew under Tsars and Soviets* (New York: Macmillan, 1987); Alfred Low, *Soviet Jewry and Soviet Policy* (New York, 1990); Zvi Gitelman, *A Century of Ambivalence. The Jews of Russia and the Soviet Union, 1881 to the Present* (New York: Schocken, 1988). For more detailed versions, see Benjamin Pinkus, *The Jews of the Soviet Union. The History of a National Minority* (Cambridge: Cambridge University Press, 1987), pp. XVIII, 49, 138, 209; Nora Levin, *The Jews in the Soviet Union since 1917. Paradox of Survival* (New York: NYU Press, 1990).

2. John A. Armstrong, 'Soviet Nationalities Policies', *Soviet Jewish Affairs* 15, 1 (1985), p. 59.
3. William Orbach, 'A Periodization of Soviet Policy Towards the Jews', *Soviet Jewish Affairs* 12, 3 (1982), p. 62.
4. For example, the pyramid-like power structure topped by the charismatic leader; the commitment to a single ideological doctrine; the large-scale role of the secret police, etc. — see Hannah Arendt, *The Origins of Totalitarianism* (New York: Harcourt, Brace and World, 1973), pp. 395–410; Herbert J. Spiro, 'Totalitarianism', in D. L. Sills (ed.), *International Encyclopedia of the Social Sciences* (London: Macmillan, 1968), Vol. 16, pp.108–11; A. Kara-Murza and A. Voskresenskii (eds.), *Totalitarizm kak istoricheskii fenomen* (Moscow, 1989), pp. 10, 97.
5. That perspective is exposed in dozens of Soviet publications, with titles such as 'cultural construction' (*stroitel'stvo*), 'language-construction', 'writing-construction', etc. — see, e.g., references in Magomet Isaev, *Iazykovoe stroitel'stvo v SSSR* (Moscow: Nauka, 1979); *Kul'turnoe stroitel'stvo v SSSR* (Moscow, 1940); I. K. Beloded, *Leninskaia teoriia natsional'no-iazykovogo stroitel'stva v sotsialisticheskom obshchestve* (Moscow, 1972).
6. On the unequivocal termination of the Soviet totalitarian regime with the death of Joseph Stalin in 1953, see Arendt, *The Origins of Totalitarianism*, pp. XXV, XXIV–XXXV.
7. One may define the practice of 'social manipulation' as a set of actions that lacks any established long-term goal, or a declared strategy which is induced by *ad hoc* interests or for purely pragmatic reasons. In a more general sense, manipulation is defined as 'management with use of unfair, scheming, or underhanded methods especially for one's own advantage' — see *Webster's Third International Dictionary of the English Language* (Springfield: Merriam, 1986), p. 1376.
8. Those were: the transfer of the Crimean Peninsula, formerly the Crimean Autonomous Republic, from the Russian Federation to the Ukrainian Republic (1954); downgrading the status of the Karelian (Karelo-Finnish) Union Republic to autonomous republic (in 1956) and upgrading Tuvin Okrug to autonomous republic (in 1961); restoration of the ethnic territories of some North Caucasian nations that had been exiled in 1943–44 (the Kalmyks, Chechen-Ingush, Karachai-Cherkess, etc., 1956–58).
9. See Armstrong, 'Soviet Nationalities Policies', p. 66.
10. Mordechai Altshuler, *Soviet Jewry since the Second World War. Population and Social Structure* (New York: Greenwood Press, 1987), p. 175; Alec Nove and J. N. Newth, 'The Jewish Population: Demographic Trends and Occupational Patterns', in L. Kochan (ed.), *The Jews in Soviet Russia since 1917* (London: Oxford University Press, 1978), p. 164; Thomas E. Sawyer, *The Jewish Minority in the Soviet Union* (Boulder: Westview Press, 1979), p. 50.
11. Michael Checinski, 'Soviet Jews and Higher Education', *Soviet Jewish Affairs* 3, 2 (1973), p. 14.
12. Gitelman, *Jewish Nationality and Soviet Politics. The Jewish Sections of the CPSU, 1917–1930* (Princeton: Princeton University Press, 1972), pp. 8–9.
13. Cf. Pinkus, *The Jews of the Soviet Union. The History of a National Minority* (Cambridge: Cambridge University Press, 1987), pp. XVI–XVII. See also, Gitelman, 'Formirovaniia evreiskoi kul'tury i samosoznaniia v SSSR: gosudarstvo v kachestve sotsial'nogo inzhenera', *Sovetskaia etnografiia*, 1991, pp. 40–2.
14. On the prepared deportation of Soviet Jews in 1953, see Levin, *The Jews in the Soviet Union since 1917. Paradox of Survival*, Vol. 2, pp. 548–50. Estimates run up to some 600,000 Jews that were to be removed from the urban centres of European Russia to Birobidzhan and other parts of Siberia. The official explanation for the action was, nonetheless, submitted as a 'reconstruction': 'After the war, the NKVD revealed too many Jews as being renegades, saboteurs, spies, and economic criminals. The objective causes of this phenomenon were that the Jews lacked their own working class and socialist peasantry. The Soviet government wished to help the Jews correct their mistakes and create appropriate conditions for them to build [sic] their own working class and collective peasantry in Siberia' — Levin, *The Jews in the Soviet Union*, p. 549.

15. More than a dozen Soviet nations — Germans, Koreans, Kalmyks, Crimean Tatars, Chechens, Ingushes, Finns, Meskhetian Turks, etc. — were exiled during the late 1930s and 1940s to Siberia and Central Asia, with their entire administrative and cultural infrastructure being eliminated altogether — see N. F. Bugai, 'K voprosu o deportatsii narodov SSSR v 30–40kh godakh', *Istoriia SSSR* 6 (1989), pp. 135–44; V.N. Zemskov, 'Massovoe osvobozhdenie spetsposelentsev i ssyl'nykh (1954–1960 gg.)', *Sotsiologicheskie issledovaniia* 1 (1991), pp. 5–26.

16. See reviews of the official Jewish activities in cultural and public spheres during the 1950s and 1960s in Pinkus, *The Jews of the Soviet Union*, pp. 271–83; Lucasz Hirszowicz, 'Jewish Cultural Life in the USSR — a Survey', *Soviet Jewish Affairs* 7, 2 (1977), pp. 12–20.

17. In 1939 for every 1,000 Jews aged ten and over there were 330 people with more than seven years of schooling, compared to 83 per 1,000 in the general Soviet population. In 1959, the similar figure for Jews increased to 556 per 1,000; and in 1970, it was already 760 for every 1,000 — Pinkus, *The Jews of the Soviet Union*, pp. 266–7. By 1979, 56.7 per cent of Jews of working age in the RSFSR and 38.4 per cent in the Ukraine were graduates from colleges and universities (an additional 2.6 per cent had between three and five years of college studies), compared to 10.8 per cent among the Russians — Viacheslav Konstantinov, 'Jewish Population of the USSR on the Eve of the great Exodus', *Jews and Jewish Topics in the Soviet Union and Eastern Europe* 3, 16 (1991), pp. 15–16.

18. By any demographic criteria, Soviet Jewry is the highest urbanized ethnic group in the country and maybe among the most urbanized people in the world — see Robert Lewis, Richard Rowland and Ralph Clem, *Nationality and Population Change in Russia and the USSR. An Evaluation of Census Data, 1897–1970* (New York: Praeger, 1976), p. 173.

19. On the fluctuations in the number of Jewish students, see Altshuler, *Soviet Jewry since the Second World War*, pp. 118-9, 135; Pinkus, *The Jews of the Soviet Union*, p. 267; Sawyer, *The Jewish Minority in the Soviet Union*, p. 46.

20. The peak of 69,400 was reached by 1975. Of these about 25,000 were Ph.D. graduates (*kandidaty nauk*) and about 4,300 had post-doctoral degrees (*doktora nauk*) — see Altshuler, 'Some Statistical Data on the Jews among the Scientific Elite of the Soviet Union', *Journal of Jewish Sociology* 15, 1 (1973), pp. 46–7; Konstantinov, 'Jewish Population of the USSR on the Eve of the Great Exodus', p. 20.

21. Altshuler, 'Some Statistical Data', p. 49.

22. In 1979, 26.4 per cent of working Israeli Jews had higher education; cf. figures for Jews in the RSFSR and Ukraine in note 17.

23. According to the 1990 National Jewish Population Survey, 53.1 per cent of American 'core' Jews aged 25 and over had graduated from college. The figure for Jews in Moscow, as of 1989, was 64.7 per cent. For 1979 figures, see note 17; see Altshuler, 'Socio-Demographic Profile of Moscow Jews', *Jews and Jewish Topics in the Soviet Union and Eastern Europe* 3, 16 (1991), pp. 33, 39; Sidney Goldstein, 'Profile of American Jewry: Insights from the 1990 National Jewish Population Survey', *American Jewish Year Book, 1992*, Vol. 92, p. 159.

24. Theodore H. Friedgut, 'Soviet Jewry: The Silent Majority', *Soviet Jewish Affairs* 10, 2 (1980), p. 6.

25. Ibid., pp. 4–8.

26. On the concept of Jewish *embourgeoisement*, as a modern cultural adaptation, see, Jonathan Webber, 'Modern Jewish Ethnicities: The Ethnographic Complexities', *Journal of Jewish Studies*, 48, 2 (1992), pp. 255–6.

27. On Soviet Jews, as predominantly middle and high-level earners, see Pinkus, *The Jews of the Soviet Union*. p. 271.

28. On the Soviet patterns of anti-Jewish discrimination, see Lukasz Hirszowicz, 'Anti-Jewish Discrimination in Education and Employment', *Soviet Jewish Affairs* 15, 1 (1985), pp. 25–30; Harry G. Shaffer, *The Soviet Treatment of Jews* (New York: Praeger, 1974), pp. 45–55. For memoirs, see Mark Azbel, *Refusenik. Trapped in the Soviet Union* (Boston: Houghton Mifflin, 1981), pp. 181–5; and Yossi Goldstein, 'The Jewish National Movement in the Soviet Union: A Profile', in Y. Ro'i and A. Beker (eds.), *Jew-*

ish Culture and Identity in the Soviet Union (New York: NYU Press, 1991), pp. 31, 38.

29. Claiming barely 1 per cent of the Soviet population, Jews contributed 8.5 per cent of Soviet writers and journalists, 7.7 per cent of actors and artists, 10 per cent of legal professions, and 11 per cent of the membership of the USSR Academy of Sciences (all figures are for the 1960s and early 1970s) — see Altshuler, *Soviet Jewry since the Second World War*, pp. 118–9, 135; Pinkus, *The Jews of the Soviet Union*, pp. 269–70; Sawyer, *The Jewish Minority in the Soviet Union*, p. 48.

30. By 1989, when the regime legitimized some sort of private entrepreneurship, the Jewish share among new businessmen in Moscow was four times higher than the average for the city population — see Altshuler, 'Socio-Demographic Profile of Moscow Jews', p. 39.

31. See Igor Birman, 'Jewish Emigration from the USSR: Some Observations', *Soviet Jewish Affairs* 9, 2 (1979), p. 55.

32. For some of the mutual influences of Marxist-Leninist ideology and Soviet policy-making regarding the country's Jewish population, see Blank's 'Redefining the Jewish Question from Lenin to Gorbachev: Terminology or Ideology' in this volume.

33. See Gitelman, *Jewish Nationality and Soviet Politics*, pp. 119–22; Galina Makarova, *Osushchestvlenie leninskoi natsional'noi politiki v pervye gody sovetskoi vlasti* (Moscow, 1969), pp. 77–9

34. On the Jewish Autonomous Region, as a means to upgrade the status of Jews, see Gitelman, *Jewish Nationality and Soviet Politics*, pp. 423–36; Pinkus, *The Jews of the Soviet Union*, pp. 71–3; Pinkus 'The Extra-Territorial National Minorities in the Soviet Union, 1917–1939: Jews, Germans, and Poles', *Studies in Contemporary Jewry* 3 (1987), p. 83.

35. On inequalities in the Soviet federal system, see Ian Bremmer, 'Reassessing Soviet Nationalities Theory', in I. Bremmer and R. Taras (eds.), *Nation and Politics in the Soviet Successor States* (Cambridge, Cambridge University Press, 1993), pp. 5–15.

36. The published proceedings of the Soviet population census of 1970 and 1979 provide complete sets of data on distribution, education, marital status and language proficiency for the 15 union republics. Nations with autonomous republics and provinces have the same set of data for the RSFSR only; other minorities are either covered irregularly or have no data whatsoever — see *Itogi vsesoiuznoi perepisi naseleniia 1970 goda* (Moscow: Statistika, 1973), Vol. 4 — 'Natsional'nyi sostav naseleniia SSSR'; *Itogi vsesoiuznoi perepisi naseleniia 1979 goda* (Moscow, 1989), Vol. 4 — 'Natsional'nyi sostav naseleniia SSSR', Parts 1–5.

37. The data of the Soviet population census of 1926 were processed identically for all the ethnic groups recorded by the census. During the 1920s and 1930s, statistical surveys targeted Soviet nations more or less indiscriminately, and Jews were covered by several focused and/or comparative studies — see *Evrei v SSSR* (Moscow, 1929); L. Zinger, *Evreiskoe naselenie v Sovetskom Soiuze. Statistiko-ekonomicheskii obzor* (Moscow and Leningrad, 1932); S. Dimanshtein (ed.), *Itogi razresheniia natsional'nogo voprosa v SSSR* (Moscow, 1936).

38. For example, Solomon I. Bruk and Mikail N. Guboglo, 'Razvitie i vzaimodeistvie etnodemograficheskikh i etnolingvisticheskikh protsessov v sovetskom obshchestve na sovremennom etape', *Istoriia SSSR* 4 (1974), p. 38.

39. 'Evrei', in *Bol'shaia Sovetskaia Entsiklopediia* (Moscow: Sovetskaia entsiklopediia, 1952), Vol. 15, p. 377.

40. See *Bol'shaia Sovetskaia Entsiklopediia*, 3rd ed. (Moscow: Sovetskaia entsiklopediia, 1972), Vol. 9, p. 10; *Sovetskaia Istoricheskaia Entsiklopediia* (Moscow: Sovetskaia entsiklopediia, 1964), Vol. 5, p. 444; *Malaia Sovetskaia Entsiklopediia* (Moscow: Sovetskaia entsiklopediia, 1959), Vol. 3, p. 773; *Sovetskii Entsiklopedicheskii Slovar'* (Moscow: Sovetskaia entsiklopediia, 1983), p. 422.

41. For more, see Jacob Miller, 'Soviet Theory on the Jews', in Kochan, *The Jews in Soviet Russia*, pp. 60–2.

42. Gitelman, 'History, Memory, and Politics: The Holocaust in the Soviet Union', *Holocaust and Genocide Studies* 5, 1 (1990), pp. 25–6; Daniel Fish (Ruth Okuneva), 'The Jews in Syllabuses of World and Russian History: What Soviet School Children Read about Jewish History', *Soviet Jewish Affairs* 8, 1 (1978), p. 13.

43. Gitelman, 'What Future for Jewish Culture in the Soviet Union?', *Soviet Jewish Affairs* 9, 1 (1979), pp. 21–2.
44. Gitelman, *Jewish Nationality and Soviet Politics*, pp. 339–43. On Yiddish school curricula, see also, Elias Schulman, *A History of Jewish Education in the Soviet Union* (New York: KTAV, 1971), pp. 123–45.
45. That approach climaxed in the famous Soviet exhibit 'Jews in Tsarist Russia and in the USSR' (1939). The exhibit devoted one-fourth of its space to the Jewish Autonomous Region in Birobidzhan and did not even mention the Jewish legacy beyond the Russian empire of the 1800s — see *Kratkii putevoditel' vystavki 'Evrei v Tsarskoi Rossii i SSSR'* (Leningrad, 1939).
46. For official Yiddish culture in the Soviet Union as of this period, see Velvel Chernin, 'Institutionalized Jewish Culture in the Soviet Union from the 1960s to the mid-1980s', in this volume.
47. See more data in Hirszowicz, 'Breaking the Mould: The Changing Face of Jewish Culture under Gorbachev', *Soviet Jewish Affairs* 18, 3 (1988), p. 36; 'Jewish Culture in the USSR Today', in Ro'i and Beker (eds.), *Jewish Culture and Identity in the Soviet Union*, pp. 281–2; 'Jewish Culture in the USSR Today', *Institute of Jewish Affairs Research Report*, 10 (1985), p. 8; When the Siberian branch of the Soviet Academy of Sciences started a multi-volume encyclopedia project on the folklore of the Siberian native peoples, Jews were granted a volume of their own, because of their autonomous province in Siberia.
48. There was a short-lived amateur troupe in Leningrad from 1957–61 — see Ro'i, *The Struggle for Jewish Emigration, 1948–1967* (Cambridge: Cambridge University Press, 1991), pp. 275–6.
49. See Hirszowicz, 'Jewish Cultural Life in the USSR — a Survey', pp. 17–18; Hirszowicz, 'The Soviet-Jewish Problem: Internal and International Developments', in Kochan (ed.), *Jews in Soviet Russia since 1917*, p. 388; Levin, *The Jews in the Soviet Union since 1917*, p. 770; Yaacov Ro'i, 'Nehama Lifshitz: Symbol of the Jewish National Awakening', in Ro'i and Beker (eds.), *Jewish Culture and Identity in the Soviet Union*, pp. 173–4.
50. 'As one cannot be absolutely sure of the causes of the dips and rises in emigration, one cannot be sure why there have been occasional, official concessions to Jewish cultural activity. They may be signals to the West, bargaining chips, or ways of deflecting criticism and charges of Soviet Anti-Semitism...Groups are formed and closed down and permissions are granted and withdrawn in an uncertain, teasing, carrot-and-stick manner, but Soviet offcials seem eager to publicize these programs' — Levin, *The Jews in the Soviet Union since 1917*, p. 767.
51. See Gitelman, 'History, Memory and Politics', pp. 35–6; Bernard Weinryb, 'Antisemitism in Soviet Russia', in Kochan (ed.), *Jews in Soviet Russia since 1917*, p. 329; Jonathan Frankel, 'The Anti-Zionist Press Campaigns in the USSR, 1969–1971: An Internal Dialogue?', *Soviet Jewish Affairs* 3 (1972), p. 25.
52. Gitelman, 'Formirovanie evreiskoi kul'tury i samosoznaniia v SSSR', pp. 41–2; Gitelman, 'The Evolution of Jewish Culture and Identity in the Soviet Union', in Ro'i and Beker (eds.), *Jewish Culture and Identity in the Soviet Union*, pp. 11–13; Gitelman, *Jewish Nationality and Soviet Politics*, pp. 493–9; Chimen Abramsky, 'The Biro-Bidzhan Project, 1927–1959', in Kochan (ed.), *The Jews in Soviet Russia since 1917*, pp. 74–7; Pinkus, 'Yiddish-Language Courts and Nationality Policy in the Soviet Union', *Soviet Jewish Affairs* 1, 2 (1971) pp. 57–8.
53. Between 1958 and 1967, that is, even before the Six-Day War, the number of copies of books attacking Judaism was seven times as great as that of books attacking Islam and twice as great as that of books attacking Christianity — William Korey, 'Soviet Law on Religious Associations: Implications for Judaism', *Soviet Jewish Affairs* 2, 2 (1972), p. 42.
54. The exchange was highly valuable, as Soviet Jews used their commitment to Russian culture to spur their social mobility — see Igor Krupnik, 'Constructing New Identities in the Former Soviet Union: The Challenges to Jews', in J. Webber (ed.), *Jewish Identities in the New Europe* (London: Littmann Library of Jewish Civilization, 1994), pp. 143–4.

5

Jews into Peasants?
Solving the Jewish Question
in Birobidzhan

ROBERT WEINBERG

> But those who would attempt to convert Jews into
> peasants are committing a truly astonishing error.
>
> Theodor Herzl, *The Jewish State*

In their effort to analyze the transformation of the social and economic landscape of the Soviet Union in the 1930s, historians generally focus on the tumultuous upheaval of Soviet society, which was hurled pell-mell into the twentieth century by a government committed to rapid industrialization and urbanization. The years of the first three five-year-plans were ones of unprecedented flux, mobility and dislocation as millions of peasants were either forcibly dispossessed or collectivized, while millions of other rural dwellers, seeking refuge from the state's savage policies in the countryside, migrated to cities and newly emerging industrial regions scattered across the vast expanses of the Soviet Union. For urban inhabitants, the uprooting might be no less dramatic, nor traumatic, given the efforts of the state to mobilize labour through coercion and enticement in the name of economic development and the building of socialism.[1] In contrast, historians have tended to ignore one aspect of these socio-economic changes, namely the effort of economic planners and policy makers to settle people on the land. This affected particularly the Soviet Far East, an underpopulated area which possessed untapped economic potential and geo-strategic significance due to the fear of Chinese and Japanese expansionism in the 1920s and 1930s.

The 1934 decision to establish the Jewish Autonomous Region

(JAR), a territory the size of Belgium and located some five thousand miles east of Moscow along the Chinese border in Khabarovsk Krai, stemmed from a variety of concerns. First, the creation of a Jewish national territory within the borders of the Soviet Union signified the government's recognition of Soviet Jewry as a full-fledged nation. In the context of Soviet nationalities policy as formulated by Lenin and Stalin, the Jews were an anomaly since they lacked a territorial homeland. Thus, the establishment of the JAR was designed to normalize the status of Soviet Jews, thereby facilitating the development of a secular, Yiddishist culture and a Jewish society rooted in socialist principles.[2] The government also hoped that territorialization would resolve a variety of problems besetting those Jews who continued to live in the area of traditional Jewish habitation, the former Pale of Settlement. Grinding impoverishment, unemployment, over-population and resurgent popular anti-Semitism during the 1920s prompted both Jewish and non-Jewish government and party leaders to address these concerns. Finally, government officials intended the colonization of the JAR by Jews — including those from foreign countries — to help solve the Jewish question via the agrarianization of Jews. This chapter focuses on the Bolshevik experiment to settle Jews on the land and how Soviet policy makers set out to deal with it.

Certain features of government attitudes and policies toward Jews during the first two decades of communist rule in the Soviet Union owed much to the preceding century and a half of tsarist policies. The roots of the Bolsheviks' Jewish policy can be traced back to the late eighteenth century, when the Russian empire absorbed a substantial Jewish population as a result of the partitions of Poland.[3] The basic outlines of government policies toward the Jews had been contradictory in nature, since they combined attempts to integrate Jews into Russian society with efforts to keep them segregated from the mainstream. These policies, such as enforced Jewish residence within the Pale of Settlement, conscription of Jewish youths into the military and enrolment in secular schools, worked at cross purposes and characterized tsarist treatment of the Jews until the collapse of the Romanov dynasty in 1917.

One aspect of the Jewish question, as defined by tsarist officials, was the perceived unproductive nature of Jewish economic life. As a group of people heavily involved in leaseholding, commerce, money-lending, and the sale of vodka, Russian Jews were regarded as parasites who exploited the defenceless peasantry. Some tsarist policies, particularly during the reign of Alexander I, consequently strove to 'normalize' the socio-economic profile of Russian Jewry by encouraging Jews to become agricultural colonists and small-scale manufacturers. The solution of the Jewish question therefore depended on transforming the Jews from a harmful and retrograde community to one which was incapable of causing social and economic damage.

This experiment in social engineering never achieved its desired ends, in part because Russian Jews preferred economic pursuits with which they had experience and familiarity. In addition, the government's commitment to agricultural colonization was half-hearted and never received serious financial and other material backing. More importantly, other policies designed to isolate the Jews countered the policy of land resettlement and dominated the government's Jewish policy at the end of the imperial era. Indeed, Jews were prohibited from settling on the land in the wake of the assassination of Alexander II in 1881. Nevertheless, slightly more than 50,000 Jews (or 3 per cent of the total Jewish population in the Russian empire), including the family of Leon Trotsky, tilled land as agricultural colonists on the eve of World War I.[4]

The effort to render Jews harmless by making them more like the peasantry and thereby promoting their assimilation into Russian society also shaped government policy toward Jews during the 1920s. Just as tsarist bureaucrats hoped to refashion the occupational profile of Russian Jewry, so too did Soviet policy makers hope that the settlement of Jews on the land as agricultural colonists and in factories as industrial workers would reduce the number of Jews involved in commerce, retail sales and handicraft production during the years of the New Economic Policy. This 'normalization' or 'productivization' of Soviet Jewry would in turn weaken the basis of popular anti-Semitism as well as promote the integration of Jews into an emerging socialist economy and society. Given the devastated condition of Soviet industry after the war and the lack of consensus regarding the appropriate path of economic development, government officials focused on agrarianization as a realistic strategy. The publication by Ozet (Association for the Settlement of Jewish Toilers on the Land) of two issues of the journal *Evreiskii krest'ianin* (The Jewish Peasant) in 1925 and 1926 underscores this official interest in Jewish land resettlement. Thus, beginning in the mid-1920s the Soviet government established Komzet (Commission for the Settlement of Jewish Toilers on the Land)[5] and charged it with overseeing the promotion and organization of Jewish resettlement on available farm land in Ukraine, White Russia and the Crimea. The organized settlement of *shtetl* Jews on the land supplemented the spontaneous drift of Jews into agriculture that had occurred during the severe economic dislocations caused by world war, revolution and civil war.[6] By 1930, 46,560 Jewish families, or approximately 231,000 persons, were engaged in agricultural activities throughout the Soviet Union.[7]

The 1928 decision to designate the Biro-Bidzhanskii Raion, commonly known as Birobidzhan and which became the JAR six years later, as the official territory for Jewish land colonization should be seen in the context of this commitment of both tsarist and communist officials to alter the occupational make-up of the Jews. With an eye toward establishing a strong presence in the Soviet Far East and the national and cultural consolidation of Soviet Jewry, the Soviet leadership, prompted by USSR President Mikhail Kalinin (chairman of VTsIK) who had adopted the territorialization of the Jews as a pet project, intended Birobidzhan to transform *shtetl* Jews from petty bourgeois shopkeepers and unemployed, unskilled labourers into productive Soviet citizens contributing to the building of socialism. The guiding principle behind the colonization of Birobidzhan by Jews was the effort to 'normalize' the occupational profile of Soviet Jewry along the lines of agricultural work by attracting unskilled Jews unsuitable for industrial employment.

In his perceptive analysis of the origins of Birobidzhan, Solomon Schwarz argues that 'any settlement of Birobidzhan that was not for the purpose of cultivating the land was to play a subordinate role'.[8] At a September 1928 meeting of Komzet regarding the settlement of Birobidzhan, an official stated that 'the aim of Jewish settlement is not to convert skilled workers into peasant labour'. He appealed to Komzet officials who were responsible for the recruitment and selection of the Jewish colonists in the European part of the Soviet Union to send to Birobidzhan 'those who are engaged in unproductive labour at home. It is clear that urban workers do not want to and should not have to become peasants.'[9]

No less an authority than Semen Dimanshtein, one of the heads of the *evsektsiia* and chairman of Ozet, wrote that the organized settlement of Birobidzhan would 'strengthen the tempo of the productivization of the Jewish poor'.[10] As Iurii Shpolianskii, chairman of Birbobidzhan's Royter Oktober Collective Farm, asserted, the activities of his collective belied the 'narrow-minded, bourgeois lie about the impossibility of Jews to master agricultural labour'.[11] His comments paralleled those made over a decade earlier by another supporter of Jewish agrarianization who noted that agricultural labour would lead to the 'physical rebirth and renewal' of Soviet Jewry.[12] Or as one of the first Jewish settlers in the region stated, 'I thank you, comrades, for sending me here. Here I am getting settled and will stop living life like a "Jew", that is as a *luftmensh*.'[13]

Thus, the 2,500 of the projected 3,000 Jewish families which were to settle the land in Birobidzhan in 1929 were to be unskilled and unemployed inhabitants of the former Pale of Settlement who were not involved in industry or manufacturing.[14] Incomplete figures regarding the background of Jewish migrants to Birobidzhan in 1931 underscore the commitment to attracting the most down-and-out *shtetl* Jews to agriculture. Of the 1,261 settlers to Birobidzhan for whom Komzet, whose chief responsibility now comprised the supervision of Jewish migration to the region, had information about their livelihoods before resettling in Birobidzhan, 623, or 49 per cent, characterized themselves as lacking any job skills. In addition, a complete list of the 3,320 Jews who moved to Birobidzhan in 1931 reveals that 2,472, or 77 per cent, found work at either state or collective farms. Only a miniscule number – 116 – found employment in industrial enterprises and 557 engaged in small-scale handicraft production (*kustarnichestvo*), with the remaining migrants working in the service sector, government offices and construction.[15] These figures are in keeping with the intentions of the government to 'send to Birobidzhan only those who at home have actually lost their means of support, that is, non-workers and handicraft workers not earning a living'.[16]

In order to attract impoverished Jews to Birobidzhan, the government provided migrants and members of their families with either free or significantly discounted travel and food subsidies and also extended credit, tax exemptions, and other material benefits to those who engaged in agriculture. And in accord with the state's desire to productivize Soviet Jewry, Jews who had been categorized as 'non-labourers' (*netrudovye*) would not be deprived of their electoral rights if they engaged in 'agricultural and other forms of productive and socially useful work' once they arrived in the region. Moreover, Jews deprived of their electoral rights would be permitted to enter vocational education programs in order to retrain, and persons in tax arrears, particularly those engaged in private enterprise and commerce, would not be prevented from migrating to Birobidzhan.[17]

The original intention of both government and party officials and migrants to settle the land is also revealed by the following incident. According to the minutes of a Komzet meeting held on 15 September 1928, about 125 of the first 642 Jews to arrive in Birobidzhan by late summer 1928 were directed to rice plantations located along the Amur River in the south-western area of the territory. These plantations had presumably been cultivated by either Koreans or Cossacks who inhabited the region before the decision to promote Jewish land settlement. The government evidently dispossessed these earlier settlers, giving control of the plantations to Komzet, which then directed contingents of Jewish migrants there. Conditions at the plantations were harsh and primitive; due to the short notice given to personnel at the plantations, they were ill-prepared to handle the influx of several dozen new settlers, many of whom had to sleep out-of-doors until tents arrived from Khabarovsk and barracks had been erected. The closest medical facilities were located some twenty miles away and lacked even basic medical equipment and supplies. Not surprisingly, the Jewish settlers, all of whom had made the arduous journey by train from the western reaches of the Soviet Union, lodged complaints about the lack of proper housing, food and other amenities. They also decried the poor leadership, drunkenness and high salaries of the *apparatchiki* responsible for taking care of them and accused the plantations' manager, L. G. Baskin, of mistreating and exploiting them. Baskin reportedly withheld the bread ration of a group of workers who had asked for a rest. When the workers complained about their low pay, he dismissed them as Zionists more interested in 'earning money' than in building socialism.[18]

Such descriptions of the poor working and living conditions reveal to us the lack of preparation by Komzet and other government agencies for the unexpected influx of Jewish settlers. The comments of one aggrieved Jewish migrant reflect the motivation of these early settlers. This man, evidently speaking for other settlers, responded to the offer of a job at a sawmill as an alternative to the rice plantations with these words: 'I don't want any other work...The work and pay at a sawmill are not bad, but this is not our goal. We came here to become peasants!'[19] Or, as another Jewish settler complained, 'Komzet must see to it that settlers don't return to the small shop (*lavochka*)'.[20]

However, in 1932 this focus on settling the bulk of newcomers on the land began to shift as government planners moved away from the heavy emphasis on land colonization to stress Birobidzhan's industrial development. This change in policy occurred in accordance with a decision taken in the second half of 1931 to grant Birobidzhan status as an autonomous administrative region for Soviet Jews by late 1933. It reinforced a trend already apparent in the early 1930s, namely, that the total number of Jews and gentiles working on collective and state farms in the region were becoming a minority of all workers engaged in agriculture and industry.[21] The specifically agricultural aim of Jewish settlement in Birobidzhan was being diluted by the government's decision to step up the diverse and broadly based economic development of the region, a policy that had been argued by some proponents of Birobidzhan from its inception. Manufacturing, construction and the extraction and processing of the region's natural resources were never entirely ignored by government planners. The promotion of well-rounded economic growth was necessary in order to develop the region's infrastructure and satisfy the diverse needs of the populace; it was essential that some of the colonists engage in skilled labour and construction in order to make a living as well as provide support services to those engaged in agriculture.[22]

The economic plan for Birobidzhan in 1932 and 1933 recognized that the 'Birobidzhan district cannot be considered a specifically agricultural region'.[23] In the words of one official involved in the implementation of the government's economic plan for 1932:

> Earlier settlers were recruited exclusively for agriculture, but this year the industrial enterprises of Birobidzhan which need skilled workers for various trades predominate.[24]

As Dimanshtein wrote in late 1931:

> The most important peculiarity of Birobidzhan is that it is not only an agricultural region but also possesses the necessary preconditions for being an industrial centre of the Far Eastern District, especially along the lines of heavy industry.[25]

Data for 1932 and 1933 testify to this shift. Economic planners projected that for these years the industrial sector of Birobidzhan required 29,935 additional workers, while agriculture needed 18,882. Statistics for the first six months of 1932 reveal that of the 4,531 Jews who found work in agriculture and industry, 1,982 or 44 per cent were living on collective or state farms and 2,549 or 56 per cent were employed in industrial enterprises.[26] A report preserved in the archives paints a similar picture: as of July 1932, 62 per cent of all Jewish settlers were directed to the industrial and manufacturing sectors, while only 38 per cent found work in agriculture, a significant turn-around given the original priority toward settling Jews on the land.[27] Moreover, the Second Five-Year Plan, which went into effect in 1933, envisioned 300,000 inhabitants by 1937, with only 77,000 or 26 per cent intended for agricultural work.[28] This trend continued for the remainder of the 1930s. During 1933, for example, 1,061 or 37 per cent of the 2,876 new Jewish residents of Birobidzhan for whom information exists found work in agriculture, with the rest settling into jobs in the industrial and service sectors and the burgeoning bureaucracy. Finally, an October 1934 resolution of the Council of

People's Commissars (*Sovnarkom*) stated that only 500 families out of a planned 4,000 which were projected to arrive in Birobidzhan during the second half of 1934 and 1935 would be directed to collective farms. The resolution does not specify whether all the prospective settlers were to be Jewish, but since it was issued upon the heels of the granting of autonomous status to Birobidzhan, it is reasonable to conclude that the government intended Jews to comprise a majority of these new settlers.[29]

Along with this focus on industrial development went a policy of recruiting Jews already engaged in agricultural and industrial work, thereby superseding the original aim of making Birobidzhan, in the words of Solomon Schwarz, a 'colonizing centre...for unemployed perishing Jewish paupers'.[30] Officials for several years had been aware of problems associated with attracting unskilled, inexperienced migrants. As one observer commented in 1930, 'the most important problem in the construction of Birobidzhan is undoubtedly that of cadres' who lacked the skills, training and preparation for life and work in Birobidzhan.[31] Although Birobidzhan officials tried to address this problem by providing training to migrants who had already arrived, they also noted that local vocational programs would have to be supplemented by similar programs of study before migrants set off for Birobidzhan. Organized recruitment of settlers had been part of the Birobidzhan experiment from the beginning, since the *raison d'être* of both Komzet and its non-governmental counterpart Ozet, until their disbandment in early 1938, was to seek out, select and provide financial assistance to potential migrants. This policy was reinforced by a 1930 Komzet decree to its regional organizations and a directive of the People's Commissariat of Labour to personnel in White Russia and Ukraine to redouble efforts to select migrants on the basis of the projected labour needs for agriculture, construction and industry in Birobidzhan.[32] There is no denying the shift away from a policy designed to siphon off the unskilled, downtrodden *shtetl* Jews toward one that tried to identify and recruit potential migrants with the skills and job experiences needed for the well-rounded development of Birobidzhan. As one observer of the economic development of the JAR stated in 1936:

> Previously, the recruitment of settlers was concerned with helping the poorest Jews who could not make a go of it; now we must not think about the needs of the settlers, but about satisfying the needs of industry in Birobidzhan.[33]

Notwithstanding this emphasis on industrial development and recruitment of workers for specific industrial jobs, government planners did not entirely ignore agricultural colonization and kept setting targets for the establishment of new collective and state farms. The Third Five-Year Plan, for example, set the ambitious target of attracting approximately 130,000 settlers between 1936 and the early 1940s, with some 30,000 intended for jobs on collective farms and the remaining headed for other sectors of the economy.[34] Still, by the end of the 1930s the orginal dream of settling large numbers of Jews on the land had not been realized. According to the census of 1939, 4,404 Jews or almost 25 per cent of the total Jewish population in the JAR lived in rural settlements, with not all of them engaged in agricultural pursuits.[35]

Virtually all non-Soviet observers of the JAR have noted that it never lived up to the goals of its proponents to become a centre of Soviet Jewry embodying the aspirations of a secular, Yiddishist culture. Another reason the Birobidzhan experiment was a failure was that very few Jews chose to start new lives engaged in agriculture. It is hard to see how the designation of a remote territory, a good portion of which was unsuitable for agriculture given the abundance of swamps, marshes and mountains, could have ever served as a magnet for the impoverished. Indeed, one could argue that the plan to resettle large numbers of Jews on the land as a way to alleviate the intense poverty of *shtetl* Jews was stillborn or at least destined to fail due to a variety of long-range and short-term reasons.

Most importantly, Jews had no historical roots in the region and were wary of starting life anew in an unknown and forbidding part of the Soviet Union. They were understandably reluctant to pick up and move several thousand miles in order to endure a harsh and arduous existence as agricultural colonists. Many Jews who may have desired to work the land were undoubtedly discouraged by the substandard living and working conditions they encountered on the collective and state farms and sought alternative, more comfortable and more familiar forms of employment. Victor Fink, an American who traveled to Birobidzhan in 1929 as a member of a fundraising organization, wrote a scathing account of the horrendous conditions he encountered. In Tikhonka, the railway station at which the vast major of newly-arrived migrants disembarked and which grew rapidly into the major city of Birobidzhan in a few short years, settlers lived in makeshift barracks which 'would put prisons to shame'. Even though the barracks were designed as temporary lodging — no more than three days — before the migrants were sent off to work the land, many settlers found themselves stuck in Tikhonka for two or three months because their intended place of destination was not ready or there was no way to traverse the swamps and marshes. Others returned to Tikhonka after venturing into the countryside to their designated place of settlement and being appalled by the substandard living and working conditions. In one instance, settlers arrived at a piece of land some 30 miles from Tikhonka, only to learn to their dismay that no one had bothered to survey the land, which had no potable water. Many families quickly went through their meagre food allocations and loans and were reduced to a state of penury. Begging proliferated and some women turned to prostitution in order to make ends meet. Fink concluded that the cause of these problems was the absence of any planning on how to absorb the sudden influx of hundreds of newcomers. In his words, 'the colonization of Birobidzhan was begun and executed without preparation, planning and study. All the misfortunes are due to the hasty manner' in which the Birobidzhan project was carried out.[36]

Other accounts testify to the trials and tribulations of many of the first settlers to the region; wagons became mired in impassable, muddy roads and the colonists had to haggle with officials over their land allotments, contend with mosquitoes and flies until the land was drained, and make due with livestock which fell victim to a variety of diseases. And to make matters worse, Birobidzhan fell victim to massive flooding in 1928 and 1932, destroying crops and forcing some collective and state farms to start from scratch.[37]

Even though rural life in the JAR gradually improved from the time the first settlers arrived in 1928, in the mid-1930s the collective and state farms still suffered from serious problems and shortcomings, not the least of which were insufficient housing and food, inadequate medical and sanitary facilities, the absence of social welfare and retail services, and land unsuitable for cultivation because it had not been drained. Frequently, land was neither surveyed nor cleared before being turned over to inexperienced Jewish farm-hands who had no idea how to drain it. The fledgling collective and state farms, which were chronically mismanaged and poorly organized, often lacked the basic necessities such as barns, livestock, tools and equipment.[38] Moreover, the overwhelming majority of Jews who came to Birobidzhan in its early years had little or no first-hand knowledge of farming and many were unprepared psychologically and physically for the rigorous demands of pioneer life. Indeed, in 1928 no Jewish colonists had agricultural experience. According to a 1932 Komzet report on Birobidzhan, of the 6,200 Jews who had come to the region during the first six months of that year, most had lived in large towns and cities in Belorussia and Ukraine and had worked as blacksmiths, carpenters, tinsmiths, woodworkers, and tailors before moving.[39]

Given these circumstances, it is no surprise that the population of the JAR remained highly mobile, continually searching for viable niches outside agriculture. The dismal state of affairs throughout the JAR contributed to a high drop-out rate for Jewish settlers. The yearly drop-out rate could reach 50 per cent and even higher during the first several years of settlement. For example, of the 19,635 Jews reported to have moved to Birobidzhan from 1928 through 1933, some 11,450, or almost 60 per cent, had returned home or gone to other parts of the Soviet Far East by 1933.[40] They either left the countryside for town life in the capital city Birobidzhan, or in one of the larger cities of the Soviet Far East such as Khabarovsk or Vladivostok, or returned to their native homes.

Those Jews who did choose to remain were more likely to gravitate to those occupations with which they had experience rather than plough the land. As Solomon Schwarz writes of the Jewish community in the JAR at the end of the 1930s:

> The bulk of the Jewish population had of necessity resumed their 'petty-bourgeois' or semibureaucratic occupations in the service trades, government offices and stores, public services, and small-scale artisan production.[41]

That Jews were attracted to non-agricultural employment should be understood in the context of the priorities of the planned economy which emphasized industrial development and the modernization of agriculture through the creation of an agrarian wage labour force. Many Jews who settled the land may have been disappointed that they were treated by the state as proletarians or farm labourers employed on state farms rather than given the opportunity to become individual farmers tilling their own land.

Jewish settlers also had to compete for work and housing with non-Jews, who also found their way to the region via channels not under the supervision of Komzet. The issue of populating the Soviet Far East had been the subject of intense discussion during the 1920s, and the government had decided to promote the development of the region through planned resettlement, primarily on the land. Appeals went out throughout the Soviet Union, claiming that the Soviet Far East was a land of opportunity for those willing to take the risk. With the decision in the late 1920s to pursue a course of rapid economic development centred on industry, the Soviet Far East witnessed a swift and steady rise in its population; in Khabarovsk Krai alone, the number of inhabitants jumped from 188,300 in 1926 to 1,140,600 by 1940. Most of the increase was due to the in-migration of settlers, though it is impossible to ascertain who came voluntarily or under duress as political exiles and inmates of the burgeoning prison camp system.[42] Not unexpectedly, large numbers of non-Jews found their way to Birobidzhan from its inception in 1928, especially since local officials, ever aware of the acute labour shortage, were eager to populate the region with able-bodied persons regardless of ethnic, national or religious background.[43] Indeed, the Second Five-Year Plan set an overly ambitious population target of 300,000, only half of whom were to be Jews.[44]

Thus, it is not surprising that gentiles outnumbered Jews in the purported national homeland of Soviet Jewry. By 1939 Jews accounted for 17,695 of the some 109,000 of the JAR's total population; most Jews (some 75 per cent) lived in the towns and cities of the region.[45] The borders of the JAR were porous and non-Jews willing to settle there without government assistance were expected and welcome. As Dimanshtein, in a realistic assessment of the Jewish presence in the JAR, wrote in 1934:

> We do not set ourselves the goal of establishing quickly a Jewish majority in the Jewish Autonomous Region; we are confident that this will come about as a natural consequence of migration. But this is not our fundamental aim, which would be inconsistent with our internationalism. Our first task is the expansion and strengthening of socialist construction in the Far Eastern krai and the Jewish Autonomous Region. Therefore, we shall welcome assistance from abroad and non-Jewish cadres as the most important and vital form of help.[46]

The building of socialism required labour, and given the flux and upheaval generated by the first two five-year plans, which led to a highly mobile work force, many non-Jews ended up in the JAR, just as many Jewish drop-outs from Birobidzhan ended up in both the established and newly emerging cities of the Soviet Far East. So dismal was the outcome of the campaign to settle Soviet Jewry in the JAR that the number of Jews in the JAR at the end of the 1930s was far less than the some 32,250 Russians, Koreans, Cossacks and indigenous peoples living in the region prior to its designation as a Jewish territory.[47] Even the 1937 decision to entrust the transfer and settlement of migrants to the JAR to the Department of Resettlement (*Pereselencheskoe upravlenie*), which sometime in the mid-1930s came under the administrative control of the NKVD, failed to achieve the desired result of increased Jewish resettlement, though it did lead to overall population growth.[48]

Finally, Jews seeking escape from the impoverished, dead-end world of the *shtetl* had other avenues for social and economic advancement than migration to the JAR. Ever since the abolition of the Pale of Settlement and the establishment of communist rule, hundreds of thousands of *shtetl* Jews had been flocking to the cities of the Russian heartland, a process that was accelerated after 1928 as opportunities continued to abound in education, government employment, technical and vocational training and factory work throughout the Soviet Union.

In sum, a combination of factors rooted in certain of the social and cultural characteristics of the Jewish population as a whole and of the Jewish settlers of the JAR in particular, the specific circumstances of life and work in the region during its early years, and shifting government priorities worked against the successful settlement of large numbers of Jews on the land. Just as Birobidzhan never became the national-cultural centre of Soviet Jewry, neither did it fulfil its promise to transform the socio-economic profile of *shtetl* Jewry by creating a *evreiskii krest'ianin* or more appropriately a *yidisher poyer*. The efforts of both tsarist and communist officials to settle Jews on the land fell way short of their objectives. The problem of productivizing and normalizing the occupational structure of Soviet Jewry was instead more effectively addressed through the assimilatory and integrating impact of general economic development, secularization and urbanization as well as the unexpected and tragic destruction of *shtetl* life in the wake of the Nazi occupation.

NOTES

1. For a recent discussion of these themes, see Sheila Fitzpatrick, 'The Great Departure: Rural-Urban Migration in the Soviet Union, 1929–33', pp. 15–40 and Stephen Kotkin, 'Peopling Magnitostroi: The Politics of Demography', in William Rosenberg and Lewis Siegelbaum (eds.), *Social Dimensions of Soviet Industrialization* (Bloomington: Indiana University Press, 1993), pp. 63–104.
2. The literature on Soviet nationalities policy toward the Jews is extensive and the following are recommended to interested readers: Hyman Lumer (ed.), *Lenin on the Jewish Question* (New York: International Publishers, 1974); Zvi Gitelman, *Jewish Nationality and Soviet Politics: The Jewish Sections of the CPSU, 1917–1930* (Princeton: Princeton University Press, 1972); Lionel Kochan (ed.), *The Jews in Soviet Russia since 1917*, (Oxford: Oxford University Press, 1978); Benjamin Pinkus, *The Jews of the Soviet Union: The History of a National Minority* (Cambridge: Cambridge University Press, 1988); Solomon M. Schwarz, *The Jews in the Soviet Union* (Syracuse: Syracuse University Press, 1951); see also Naomi Blank, 'Redefining the Jewish Question from Lenin to Gorbachev: Terminology or Ideology', in this volume.
3. For an extended discussion, see John Klier, *Russia Gathers Her Jews: The Origins of the 'Jewish Question' in Russia, 1772–1825* (Dekalb, IL: Northern Illinois University Press, 1986); see also Eli Lederhendler, 'Did Russian Jewry Exist prior to 1917?', in this volume.

4. Iu. L. Gol'de, *Zemel'noe ustroistvo trudiashchikhsia evreev* (Moscow: Tsentral'noe izdatel'stvo narodov Soiuza SSR, 1925), pp. 8, 57.
5. Komzet and Ozet were acronyms for Komitet po zemel'nomu ustroistvu trudiashchikhsia evreev and Obshchestvo po zemel'nomu ustroistvu trudiashchikhsia evreev. In Yiddish Kozmet was known as Komerd and Ozet as Gezerd.
6. Allan Kagedan, 'The Formation of Soviet Jewish Territorial Units, 1924–1937', unpublished Ph.D. diss., Columbia University, 1985; Schwarz, *The Jews in the Soviet Union*, Ch. 12; Nora Levin, *The Jews in the Soviet Union Since 1917: Paradox of Survival* (New York: NYU Press, 1988), Vol. 1, Chaps. 6, 7 and 10.
7. Gosudarstvennyi arkhiv evreiskoi avtonomnoi oblasti (GAEAO), fond (f.) 3, opis (op.) 1, delo (d.) 131, p. 2.
8. Solomon Schwarz, 'Birobidzhan: An Experiment in Jewish Colonization', in Gregor Aronson, Jacob Frumkin, Alexis Goldenweiser, *et al.* (eds.), *Russian Jewry, 1917–1967* (London: Thomas Yoseloff, 1969), p. 354.
9. GAEAO, f. 3, op. 1, d. 13, p. 18.
10. *Tribuna evreiskoi sovetskoi obshchestvennosti (TESO)*, 1 Oct. 1928, p. 1.
11. Ibid., 15 Nov. 1936, p. 20.
12. A. Fabrikant, 'Agrikul'turnye cherty evreiskogo zemledeliia v SSSR', *Evreiskii krest'ianin* 1 (1925), p. 24.
13. *TESO*, 1 Sept. 1928, p. 21. Another early settler stated that she moved to Birobidzhan with her husband because she was tired of being called a 'market-woman' (*torgovka*) which was a term of opprobrium — B. Koblents, *Wal'dgeim* (Moscow: Emes, 1934), p. 7. And still another Jewish colonist, a former shopkeeper who had settled the land in the Crimea in the 1920s, asserted that he 'envied' Russian peasants because 'they have land' (*oni imeiut zemliu*) — F. Veitkov and B. Polishchuk, *Evrei na zemle* (Moscow: Gosizdat, 1934), p. 15.
14. *TESO*, 15 Aug. 1928, p. 3.
15. GAEAO, f. 3, op. 1, d. 133, pp. 1–2. These figures include all settlers, even those under age 16.
16. *TESO*, 1 Feb. 1929, p. 7. See also the 1 March 1929, p. 25, issue which reiterated that migrants should be found among impoverished Jews who have no 'economic means of support (petty traders, the unemployed, handicraft workers, and persons without professions)'.
17. E. Zaslavskii, *Prava i l'goty pereseliaiushchimsia v Birobidzhan* (Moscow: Tsentral'noe Pravlenie OZET, 1930).
18. GAEAO, f. 3, op. 1, d. 13, pp. 1–18; *TESO*, 1 Sept. 1928, p. 1 and 1 Oct. 1928, p. 17.
19. GAEAO, f. 3, op. 1, d. 13, pp. 4–5.
20. Ibid., p. 2.
21. A. Kantorovich, *Perspektivy Biro-Bidzhana* (Moscow, Emes, 1932), p. 80.
22. A. Merezhin, *O Birobidzhane* (Moscow, Izdanie Komzeta, 1929), pp. 46–9.
23. *TESO*, 30 Dec. 1931, p. 8.
24. *TESO*, 30 Sept. 30, 1932, p. 4.
25. See *TESO*, 20 Dec. 1931, p. 5. In addition, Iankel Levin, party chief in Birobidzhan, stated in 1931 that the development of the region would not be 'purely agricultural...Our region will develop mainly as an industrial district'. Ia. Levin, 'God raboty v Birobidzhane', in S. Dimanshtein (ed.), *Birobidzhan* (Moscow, 1932), pp. 30–1. See the issues of *Tribuna* from 15 Aug. 1928, pp. 8–11, 1 Aug. 1930, pp. 6–7 and 15 Aug. 1932, p. 10 for other articles supporting the industrial as well as the agricultural development of the region.
26. Kantorovich, *Perspektivy Birobidzhana*, p. 79; *TESO*, 15 Aug. 1932, p. 8.
27. GAEAO, f. 3, op. 1, d. 156, p. 5.
28. *TESO*, 15 Aug. 1932, pp. 8, 12.
29. *TESO*, 15 Jan. 1934, p. 10 and 15 Oct. 1934, p. 1. Similarly, the plan for 1936 projected 10,000 migrants; only 16 per cent (compared with 75 per cent for industry, construction, transportation, and communications) were intended for agriculture. See B. Trotskii, *Stroitel'stvo evreiskoi avtonomnoi oblasti v 1935 i 1936 godakh* (Moscow: Emes, 1936), p. 33. Trotskii also notes that only 1,000 of the some 6,500 Jews who settled in the JAR in 1935 were directed to collective and state farms (pp. 18, 29).

30. Schwarz, 'Birobidzhan', p. 364. One official, mistakenly attributing changes in the socio-economic profile of Soviet Jewry to the establishment of the JAR rather than to the cumulative impact of two decades of Soviet rule, asserted in 1936 that since the JAR had taken care of the 'economic problem of Jewish poverty', then the task before it was the attraction of 'skilled cadres' in order to build socialism — *TESO*, 15 April 1936, p. 20. See also an article in *TESO*, 15 Jan. 1937, pp. 3–5, which emphasized the need to recruit Jews with prior experience on collectives and factories.
31. *TESO*, 10 March 1930, p. 8. See also the article on pages 19–20 in the 20 June 1930 issue.
32. *TESO*, 20 May 1930, p. 21.
33. S. Gorfinkel', 'K itogam plenuma OZET', *Revoliutsiia i natsional'nosti* 3, 73 (March 1936), p. 36. One visitor to the JAR wrote that the region occupied an 'honorary place' in the industrialization of the Soviet Far East — see 'Rastet industrial'nyi Birobidzhan', *TESO*, 30 April 1936, pp. 12–14.
34. On the target figure of the Third Five-Year Plan, see S. Dimanshtein, 'Evreiskaia avtonomnaia oblast' na novom etape', *Revoliutsiia i natsional'nostii* 6–7, 88–89 (June–July 1937), p. 64. On the continued importance of agriculture in the development of the JAR, see 'O sovetskom, khoziaistvennom i kul'turnom stroitel'stve Evreiskoi avtonomnoi oblasti', *Revoliutsiia i natsional'nosti*, 11, 81 (Nov. 1936), pp. 146–8 and S. Dimanshtein, 'Prezidium TsIK SSSR o Evreiskoi avtonomnoi oblasti', *Revoliutsiia i natsional'nosti* 10, 80 (Oct. 1936), pp. 50–6. In this latter article (p. 55), Dimanshtein writes that the Third Five-Year Plan had set the ambitious target of attracting at least 150,000 new settlers, with some 40 to 50 per cent intended for work in agriculture.
35. The author would like to thank Professor Mordechai Altshuler of the Hebrew University of Jerusalem, who has had access to the 1939 census, for providing these figures.
36. Victor Fink, 'Birobidzhan', *Sovetskoe stroitel'stvo* (May 1930), pp. 117–23. A mid-1932 description of conditions in Tikhonka noted that the barracks, which still existed, were 'filthy and overcrowded' and sanitary conditions in the town left much to be desired. — *TESO*, 15 Aug. 1932, p. 5. A later account of Tikhonka in 1937 — now known as Birobidzhan with a population of over 10,000 by 1936 — reported that the city lacked a sewage system and had no public lighting — *TESO*, 30 June 1937, p. 9. See GAEAO, f. 138, op. 1, d. 5, p. 6 for the population of Birobidzhan.
37. Koblents, *Wal'dgeim*, pp. 12–14; A. Korshunov, *Evrei-zemledel'tsy* (Moscow: Bezbozhnik, 1929), pp. 24–7; A. Merezhin, *Chto takoe Birobidzhan* (Moscow: Tsentral'noe Pravlenie OZET, 1929); *TESO*, 1 Aug. 1928, p. 6; 15 Aug. 1928, p. 18; 1 Nov. 1928, p. 16, and 1 Feb. 1929, pp. 6–11.
38. For a sampling of criticisms, see *Otdel rukovodiashchikh partiinykh organov* of the Central Committee at the Rossiiskii tsentr khraneniia i izucheniia dokumentov noveishei istorii (RTsKhIDNI), f. 17, op. 21, d. 5541, pp. 6–7, 42–5; D. Barshchevskii, 'Zemel'noe ustroistvo trudiashchikhsia evreev', *Sovetskoe stroitel'stvo* 1, 90 (Jan. 1934), pp. 86–93; I. Kamenetskii, 'Ocherednye narodnokhoziaistvennye zadachi evreiskoi oblasti', *Revoliutsiia i natsional'nosti*, 10, 68 (Oct. 1935), pp. 8–16; *TESO*, 1 Feb. 1929, pp. 6–11, 30 Dec. 1932, pp. 2–4 and 7–8, 15 Oct. 1933, pp. 10–13, 15 Sept. 1935, pp. 12–14 and 15 Nov. 1936, pp. 22–3; GAEAO, f. 75, op. 1, d. 52, pp. 29–30; Trotskii, *Stroitel'stvo evreiskoi avtonomnoi oblasti*, pp. 31–4.
39. *IX Dal'nevostochnaia kraevaia partiinaia konferentsiia, 22 fevralia – 1 marta 1929 goda. Stenograficheskii otchet* (Khabarovsk, 1929), p. 301; GAEAO, f. 3, op. 1, d. 156, p. 5; *TESO*, Nov. 7, 1929, p. 10.
40. GAEAO, f. 3, op. 1, d. 156, p. 14; Ia. Kantor, *Natsional'noe stroitel'stvo sredi evreev v SSSR* (Moscow: 1934), pp. 118–9.
41. Schwarz, *The Jews in the Soviet Union*, p. 184.
42. L. L. Rybakovskii, *Naselenie Dal'nego Vostoka za 150 let* (Moscow, 1990), pp. 105, 107, 110. On the concerted effort to populate the Soviet Far East, especially along agricultural lines, see A. M. Iarmosh, 'Dvizhenie naseleniia DVK na desiatiletie 1926–36 goda', *Ekonomicheskaia zhizn' Dal'nego Vostoka* 1–2 (Jan.–Feb. 1927), pp. 84–101 and Iarmosh, 'Plan kolonizatsii Dal'ne-Vostochnogo Kraia v period 1927–1936 gg.',

Ekonomicheskaia zhizn' Dal'nego Vostoka 1–2 (Jan. 1927), pp. 104–36; M. Tselishchev, 'K voprosu o kharaktere kolonizatsii DVKraia', *Ekonomicheskaia zhizn' Dal'nego Vostoka* 4 (April 1926), pp. 5–28; *Stoiat na Amure russkie sela* (Blagoveshchensk, 1978); G. Samarin and V. Antonovich, *Dal'nii Vostok zhdet pereselentsev*, (Moscow, 1940).

43. See Merezhin, *Chto takoe Birobidzhan*, p. 57 and Merezhin, *O Birobidzhane*, p. 66 for references to gentile settlers in the region.

44. *TESO*, 7 Nov. 1932, p. 8.

45. Once again, these figures are from Professor Altshuler.

46. S. D., 'Evreiskaia avtonomnaia oblast' — detishche oktiabr'skoi revoliutsii', *Revoliutsiia i natsional'nosti* 6, 52 (June 1934), p. 21.

47. Yaacov Levavi (Babitsky), *Ha-hityashvut ha-yehudit be-Birobijan* (Jerusalem: Ha-hevra ha-historit ha-yisraelit, 5728), p. 16.

48. In what might be the understatement of the time, Dimanshtein, who was discussing the agreement between Komzet and the Department of Resettlement, noted that the NKVD had 'a lot of experience…in carrying out the mass resettlement' of people. *TESO*, 30 June 1937, p. 3.

6

The Doctors' Plot:
Stalin's Solution to the Jewish Question

IAKOV ETINGER

The year 1993 marks the 40th anniversary of the Doctors' Plot, a major anti-Semitic provocation engineered by the Stalinist leadership. Fraught with the genocide of the Soviet Jews and their deportation to the country's remote regions, it is one of the darkest pages in the modern history of the Jewish people.

The Doctors' Plot was the natural outcome and apotheosis of the policy of state anti-Semitism pursued over the years by Stalin's totalitarian regime. The ground had been prepared by numerous anti-Jewish actions (some of them carefully camouflaged) on the part of the Stalinist leadership in the preceding decades, and it was by no means a chance occurrence.

The first symptoms of Stalin's anti-Semitic policy are rooted in his personality and may be traced to the pre-revolutionary period. Many people who knew him well, such as Khrushchev, suggested that his Judaeophobia was pathological.

Stalin's struggle against Trotsky and his numerous Jewish supporters fuelled the anti-Semitic trends in the Kremlin dictator's policy. 'Anti-Semitism and anti-Trotskyism reared their heads simultaneously', Trotsky wrote.[1] This is not to say, however, that Stalin had not been an anti-Semite well before that period. To all intents and purposes, this was his reaction to the disproportionately high participation of Jews in Russia's political life before the revolution and to their active role in political movements, except in ultra-right organizations such as the Union of the Russian People. Stalin's secretary, Boris Bazhanov, recollects that Stalin had crude anti-Semitic outbursts even when Lenin was still alive. In 1907 Stalin wrote a letter in which he referred to the

Mensheviks as a 'Jewish faction' and to the Bolsheviks as a 'truly Russian' one. 'It would do no harm to us Bolsheviks if we staged a pogrom inside the party', he suggested.[2]

The major landmarks of Soviet state anti-Semitism were the massive purges of the 1930s, in which, together with Russians, tens of thousands of Jews belonging to anti-Stalinist opposition groups were victimized; the Ribbentrop-Molotov pact of 1939, followed by the purge of Soviet foreign-policy institutions, the ousting of Litvinov and other high-ranking diplomats of Jewish descent; and the anti-Semitic 'actions' of 1942–43, when many Jewish cultural figures and editors of leading newspapers were sacked.

Toward the end of the war the party's anti-Semitic policy became more intense. Stalin is reported to have said in closed circles in 1946 that 'every Jew is a potential spy'. Jewish enrolment in many institutions of higher learning was restricted. In January 1948, acting on Stalin's direct instructions, State Security Ministry (MGB) agents killed the famous Jewish actor Solomon Mikhoels and in 1949, the Moscow Jewish Theatre was closed. Toward the end of 1948, the Jewish Anti-fascist Committee (JAC) was abolished and many prominent Jewish public figures who were its members — writers, poets, journalists — were put behind bars in the Lubianka and Lefortovo prisons. The so-called anti-cosmopolitan drive launched in 1949 was patently anti-Semitic. Eminent writers, scientists and cultural figures were castigated, accused of being 'unpatriotic', and labelled 'rootless cosmopolitans'.

On 12 August 1952, a group of former JAC members, convicted by the Military Collegium of the USSR Supreme Court, were put before a firing squad. Many other people of Jewish nationality — 110 in all — were arrested in connection with the JAC case on charges of 'espionage' and 'anti-Soviet Jewish nationalist activity'.[3]

At the time of the trial of the JAC members, preparation of the Doctors' Plot reached its final stage. Work at State Security headquarters on Lubianka Street continued around the clock. New lists of Jews to be arrested were constantly being compiled.[4] The MGB leadership was on the alert, waiting for a signal from Stalin. It was not long in coming.

On 13 January 1953, all leading Soviet newspapers carried the notorious TASS communiqué entitled 'The Arrest of a Group of Saboteur Doctors', which accused a number of Jewish doctors of plotting to murder leading Soviet figures using harmful methods of medical treatment. These doctors had allegedly caused the death of Central Committee Secretaries Aleksandr Shcherbakov and Andrei Zhdanov.

The provocation was part of a far-reaching plan to link the JAC case with the doctors' 'crimes'. This was alluded to in the following phrase from the TASS statement: 'Vovsi [one of the accused physicians] told the investigation that he had gotten orders to kill leading cadres in the USSR from the US-based Joint [the American Jewish Joint Distribution Committee] via a Moscow doctor, one Shimeliovich, and the prominent Jewish bourgeois-nationalist Mikhoels.'

The investigation committee wanted Shimeliovich, who had been a member of the JAC Presidium and had already been shot, and Professor Vovsi, Mikhoels's cousin, to play the role of the connecting link between the JAC and the arrested Jewish doctors. In other words, the upcoming trial was meant to 'demonstrate' that the JAC were the ideologues of a ramified and deeply entrenched 'Jewish plot' that was to be carried out by Jewish 'doctor killers'.

Of those mentioned in the TASS announcement, my father, Professor Iakov Giliarievich Etinger, was the first to be arrested. It happened on 18 November 1950, over two years before the TASS announcement of the 'plot'. A large group of State Security men headed by Lt.-Col. M. D. Riumin took part in his arrest. It is clear from the classified documents now available that approximately a year before his arrest Etinger had been relieved of his position as department head at Moscow Medical Institute No. 2 and then sacked, on Stalin's direct orders.

My father was born in 1887. He studied medicine in Germany before the revolution. From 1914 to 1918 he served as a doctor in the Russian Army, and then in the Red Army as head of a large hospital. After demobilization he worked at the Medical Faculty of Moscow University and in 1932–49 was department head at Moscow Medical Institute No 2. The USSR People's Commissariat of Public Health sent him on an assignment to Japan in 1923 and to Germany and the US in 1926. For many years Ia. G. Etinger was consultant to the Kremlin's special medical department. Among his patients were top army officers, prominent scientists and artists. He had for many years been the doctor of two members of the Soviet leadership — Kirov and Ordzhonikidze. On more than one occassion he expressed his doubts as to the official causes of their death. In particular, he was certain that Kirov had been killed on Stalin's orders.

Comintern leaders Palmiro Togliatti, Wilhelm Pieck, Georgi Dimitrov, and José Díaz as well as many of Poland's leading communists were also his patients. Many of them perished in the Stalin purges of the 1930s. I remember my father saying that José Díaz, leader of the Spanish Communist Party, had not committed suicide in

Tbilisi in 1942 because of a grave illness, as had been officially announced, but had been killed by State Security agents. Recently I was in Spain and met some of the country's politicians and they confirmed this version of events.

My father was an outspoken person, and very incautious, for that time. He was never a party member and did not take the trouble to conceal his negative attitude to the Stalin regime. The materials connected with his case, which I have read recently, show that my father and our family first came into the State Security's field of vision as far back as the late 1940s.

Shortly before my father's arrest, I myself was arrested. I was 21 and an external student at Moscow University's history department. As a teenager during the war, I had been in the Minsk Ghetto from 12 August 1941 to 7 May 1942. My nurse, Maria Petrovna Kharetskaia, and other anti-fascists helped me to escape and live in hiding in Nazi-occupied Minsk for two years, until 3 July 1944, when the city was liberated by the Soviet Army. Kharetskaia, who had lived with our family for several decades, was also detained in the summer of 1951, but was soon released, having made a written promise 'not to leave Moscow'. She died in 1961.

On 16 July 1951, my mother, R. K. Viktorova, was arrested. She was also a doctor, but by that time she had already retired. Later, the Special Conference of the USSR Ministry of State Security sentenced her to ten years in prison under Article 58-10 (anti-Soviet propaganda). My mother was incarcerated for more than three years, while I spent over four years in prison and prison camp. My father died in prison some months after his arrest, but I shall speak about this below.

Ia. G. Etinger was charged with 'intent to commit treason', Jewish nationalism and sympathy for Israel, 'slanderous allegations' about Stalin, comparing the Soviet regime with Hitler's fascism, condemning the struggle against cosmopolitanism and describing this struggle and many other social phenomena of the time as manifestations of state anti-Semitism engendered by Stalin. He was also accused of publicly criticizing 'Academician' T. D. Lysenko after the August 1948 session of the All-Union Academy of Agriculture, and of asserting that all the political trials of the 1930s in the USSR were frame-ups, just like the trials in Eastern Europe in the late 1940s.

Judging by the investigation materials of the Ia. G. Etinger case, no mention was made at the interrogations of the 'criminal treatment' of party and state leaders, in particular of A. S. Shcherbakov, Central Committee Secretary and RCP(b) Politburo Candidate Member. However, other classified documents of the CPSU Central Committee and the KGB, which are available today, indicate that at the very first interrogation, on 20 November 1950, Lt.-Col M. D. Riumin, Senior investigating officer of the MGB Section for Investigating High Priority Cases, who was in charge of my father's case, brought this charge too, although no records of the interrogation were kept. Riumin laboured to get a 'confession' out of my father.

My father had angina pectoris and the interrogations were an ordeal for him. The materials of the investigation recorded that he had 29 attacks of angina during the investigation, 10 in Riumin's room and the rest in his cell. The severest bouts were on 17 and 18 February 1951. The medical unit of Lefortovo Prison subsequently issued a certificate stating that 'in the future, any attack of angina pectoris attended by heart weakness may lead to unfavourable consequences'. This, however, did not deter Riumin. On 2 March 1951, at 5 p.m., my father returned to his cell after yet another interrogation. 'He went up to the table, had a bite of bread, took several steps to the door and fell unconscious', the investigation report said. Death was caused by heart failure. The autopsy was performed on 6 March 1951, at the Butyrskaia Prison medical unit and the pertinent papers were signed by P. I. Semenovskii, forensic pathologist of the City of Moscow.

There is no mention in the case whether my father was cremated or not, or where he was buried. His grave is unknown, like the graves of millions of other victims of communist rule in this country. For decades I have been trying to find some clues, but so far my attempts have been fruitless.

My mother and I faced the same charges as my father. At the beginning of 1949, the MGB clandestinely installed a bugging device in the phone at our apartment. For almost two years the State Security Ministry could hear and record all we were saying at home. It has become clear from recently declassified documents that the records went to Col.-Gen. V. S. Abakumov, Minister of State Security from 1946–51, who then reported on them to the party Central Committee and to Stalin himself. The charges brought against my father, my mother and myself in the course of the investigation were based on the records of our conversations.

Russian researcher Kirill Stoliarov summed up the results of his painstaking and profound study of the materials in the case of State Security Minister Abakumov in his book *Golgofa* (*Calvary*).[5] He writes there:

> Riumin investigated the Ia. G. Etinger case. He claimed that Abakumov, first, did not permit him to interrogate Etinger as a participant in the heinous murder of A. Shcherbakov...and, secondly, ordered Etinger...

transferred from the inner prison [of the Lubianka] to the Lefortovo Prison, where he suddenly died and thus priceless information on an extensive terrorist plot was buried. This calls for some explanation. In June 1951 [Abakumov] was expelled from the party, relieved from his post on 4 July and arrested on 12 July. A large group of high-ranking State Security Ministry officials were also arrested. All of them were detained on the strength of the information submitted to the party Central Committee.

M. D. Riumin informed the Central Committee that his superiors were 'glossing over' the terrorist plans of Etinger and 'enemy agents' spearheaded against Politburo members and Stalin personally; they deliberately neglected to record Etinger's interrogations which made it possible adroitly to conceal [from Stalin] mistakes 'in the struggle against the schemes of international imperialism...'

Sending such a letter to Stalin was doubtless a risky undertaking. The chances that it would reach him were very slim. 'But the miracle did occur', Stoliarov writes, 'and in defiance of common sense and chance...Stalin got the signal and after carefully thinking the matter over ordered that Abakumov be arrested.'

The Abakumov case was investigated by K. Mokichev, First Deputy Prosecutor-General. Stoliarov notes that Mokichev began the interrogations 'with facts cited by Riumin, namely, that the terrorist aims of the Jewish nationalist Etinger were being "glossed over" '. Stoliarov goes on to say:

This is what Abakumov testified about Etinger:

Question: Why did you delay Etinger's arrest and subsequently forbid interrogating him about terrorism, telling Riumin that Etinger would get him 'bogged down'?

Answer: The leadership of the Second Directorate reported to me that Etinger was hostile. I told them to prepare a memorandum for the Central Committee. The memorandum cited facts proving that Etinger was a dirty swine. (Abakumov was referring to the anti-Stalin views Professor Etinger expressed when speaking to his son, which constituted a counter-revolutionary crime punishable under Art. 58-10 of the RSFSR Criminal Code. Father and son were having a private conversation, which was tape-recorded — K. Stoliarov).

That was in the first half of 1950, I do not remember in which month. However, at that juncture we had no orders to arrest him. After the order from the higher authorities came, I had him brought to me because I knew that he was an active Jewish nationalist and vehemently anti-Soviet. 'You better tell the whole truth, without beating about the bush,' I said to Etinger. In reply to my questions he promptly answered that there were no grounds for his arrest and the truth was that Jews were being suppressed in this country. When I pressed further, he said he was an honest man, he was treating high-ranking people and mentioned my deputy, Selivanovskii, and then Shcherbakov. At this moment I said he would have to describe what exactly he had done to cause his death. He began speaking in great detail about Shcherbakov's serious condition and said he had been doomed. In the course of the interrogation it had become clear to me that all of this had nothing to do with terrorism, absolutely nothing. Later it was reported to me that nothing new or interesting had been gotten out of Etinger.

According to declassified documents of the CPSU Central Committee and the KGB, after another regular interrogation of Etinger in December 1950, Abakumov 'came to the conclusion' that there were no facts pointing to 'criminal medical treatment'. On 28–29 January 1951, Abakumov issued instructions 'to discontinue working with Etinger', that is, to stop trying to make him confess to 'criminal treatment' and only stick to the charges of anti-Soviet activity and Jewish nationalism. In the course of Etinger's interrogations, differences regarding his treatment of Shcherbakov arose between Riumin and Abakumov. Incidentally, Aleksandr Solzhenitsyn describes these differences in detail in his *Gulag Archipelago*, but unfortunately he says it happened in late 1952, which is incorrect.[6] But let us return to the verbatim records of Abakumov's interrogation.

> Question: Are you aware that Etinger was transferred to the Lefortovo prison and that conditions there were new to him?
>
> Answer: This is not correct. The inner [Lubianka] and Lefortovo prisons do not differ from one another.
>
> Question: Did you issue orders that Etinger be kept in special conditions, jeopardizing his health?
>
> Answer: What do you mean by special?
>
> Question: Harder than for the other inmates. Etinger was placed in a damp and cold cell.
>
> Answer: There is nothing extraordinary about that because he was the enemy. We are allowed to beat the inmates — I and my first deputy Ogol'tsov were repeatedly reminded at the RCP(b) Central Committee that whenever necessary our *chekisty* should not be afraid to use physical force against spies and other people who had committed crimes against the state. An inmate is an inmate, and prison is prison. There are no such things as warm and cold cells there. There was talk about a stone floor, but as far as I know all cells have stone floors. I told the investigating officer that we must get the truth from the inmate and I may have said that I did not want him to get us bogged down.

From the 'Matrosskaia tishina' Prison, Abakumov wrote a letter to Stalin, trying to prove that he was innocent and infinitely loyal to him. The letter said:

> Riumin's statement about my alleged hint to Etinger that he should refuse to testify regarding terrorism [the reference is to charges of causing Shcherbakov's death] is all wrong. There was nothing of the kind and could never be. Had we had any concrete facts to act upon we would have skinned him alive in order not to miss a case like that.

Abakumov's letter reached Stalin and he kept it. Three weeks later, the following note came to the USSR Prosecutor's Office:

> Comrade Mokichev, at 3 a.m. there was a phone call from Malenkov. He has gotten instructions to send the records of Abakumov's interrogation to Comrade Stalin tomorrow.

The note was dated 19 August 1951, 3:10 a.m. and signed by S. Ignat'ev, the new Minister of State Security.

At that time Riumin was doing his best to be put in charge of investigating the Abakumov case. According to Stoliarov, Riumin succeeded in getting what he wanted when Col. M. Likhachev, former deputy head of the USSR State Security Ministry investigating high priority cases, arrested shortly after Abakumov,

> obediently confirmed that before his death Professor Etinger had confessed to causing Shcherbakov's death. It was a stroke of unbelievably good luck opening vast prospects to Riumin: the late Etinger had been just a consultant, while Professor Vinogradov, Stalin's personal physician of long standing, had been treating Shcherbakov. Etinger could not have worked to kill Shcherbakov without Vinogradov's consent. Hence, it had been a joint operation.

Here Stoliarov must be corrected: Prof. Etinger and Professor V. N. Vinogradov took an equal part in Schcherbakov's treatment. In 1951, Riumin had written a report on the hostile intentions of S. A. Lozovskii, I. S. Fefer, L. S. Shtern, B. A. Shimeliovich — 14 people in all. The report said that 'the evidence has established that during their visit to America in 1943, former JAC leaders Mikhoels and Fefer were given an assignment by Jewish reactionaries to get the Crimea settled by Jews and have an independent republic established there to be used by the Americans as a bridgehead against the USSR at an opportune moment'.

In late 1951 Colonel Riumin was appointed Deputy Minister of State Security and was made responsible for the ministry's investigation. On 22 February 1952 State Security bodies were put in charge of the investigation of the case of Abakumov and his subordinates and the suspects were transferred from the 'Matrosskaia tishina' Prison to Lefortovo. As noted above, by that time Professor Etinger was already dead.

On the basis of my own personal experience as an inmate of Stalin's dungeons, I have formulated particular notions about when the plan and scenario of the Doctors' Plot originated.

After I was arrested I was kept in Lefortovo Prison. For about six months I was in solitary confinement. Riumin was often present at the regular nocturnal interrogations lasting from the autumn of 1950 to the late spring of 1951, but the participation of my father and other professors of medicine in any activities aimed at the 'criminal treatment' of leading Soviet cadres was never mentioned. The interrogations centred on Jewish nationalism and my statements to the effect that state anti-Semitism existed in the USSR and that Stalin was the architect of this policy. I remember Riumin well. From time to time he would rush into the investigator's room during interrogations and start swearing at me and threatening me with all and sundry punishment in between such expressions as 'Kike face, we'll strangle all of you Jews'. I do not remember him ever taking a seat. He paced the room endlessly, shouting abuse. It all created a forbidding impression.

In my case, with the documentation of which I also recently became acquainted, I found the investigator's ruling dated 23 April 1951:

> The investigation has established that for several years Ia. Ia. Etinger was engaged in hostile activities, speaking with particular viciousness about the leader of the Soviet people. Proceeding from the above and taking account of the fact that Etinger is a very dangerous criminal, Ia. Ia. Etinger shall serve his term at a special State Security Ministry camp.

On 17 May 1951 I was summoned to the commandant's office of Lefortovo Prison to hear the ruling of the MGB Special Hearing (*Osoboe soveshchanie*) of 5 May 1951. I was given a ten-year term under Art. 58-10. I stayed in Lefortovo for several more weeks and on 5 June 1951, was sent in stages to Kolyma. It took them more than a month to bring me to the Vanino transit camp on the shore of the Gulf of Tatar.

In early August 1951, all of a sudden, I was set apart from the rest of the prisoners and put in the camp's isolation ward, a kind of 'microprison'. From there I was sent back to Moscow via almost the same route, but instead of transit prisons, I was 'held' in internal prisons of MGB *oblast'* administrations and kept in strict isolation.

On 1 September 1951 I was returned to Lefortovo Prison and the interrogations resumed. At the first of these, the investigating officer said something to the effect that my father, acting jointly with Vinogradov, Vovsi, Gel'shtein and Zelenin had all confessed to being engaged in criminal medical treatment of many prominent Soviet personalities. He argued that many of the professors used to visit our house, that my father must certainly have discussed things with me and that I therefore could not have been unaware of the facts relating to the criminal medical treatment. He urged me to 'come clean'.

As has already been said, among other things, Ia. G. Etinger was charged with the 'criminal medical treatment' of Shcherbakov. From late 1944 to 10 May 1945, the day Shcherbakov died, he and Professor V. N. Vinogradov had been treating him. They had visited Shcherbakov twice a day and compiled morning and evening reports about his condition, which went to Stalin personally. Both of them were first-rate cardiologists and they did their best to save Shcherbakov who had been suffering from an incurable heart disease. I knew all about it and firmly rejected the investigator's assertions that my father and Vinogradov had been 'responsible' for Shcherbakov's death. Although I was subjected to all kinds of psychological and physical pressure, I did not sign a single document containing even a hint about the 'criminal medical treatment' of Shcherbakov.

Some ten MGB investigating officers on high priority matters took turns interrogating me. All of them held the rank of colonel. Each questioned me about a specific professor: one about B. Kogan, another about M. Vovsi, and so on. The interrogations went on for six months. All this led me to the conclusion that a large-scale operation was in the offing and the doctors in whom the investigators were 'interested' had already been arrested. (In fact, they were still free and utterly unsuspecting of what was in store for them. Most of the figures in the Doctors' Plot were arrested in November 1952.) The interrogations were not limited to the doctors. They wanted to 'know in detail' all about my father's relations with the poet S. Ia. Marshak as they were collecting evidence against him, as well.

I was kept in Lefortovo Prison up to mid-March 1952 and then transported to a camp in Kirov Oblast. Thus, the subject of the 'criminal medical treatment' of Soviet leaders by my father and other professors did not figure in my interrogations until the autumn of 1951. Had this subject been 'pursued' at the MGB earlier there would have been no sense in transporting me to Kolyma on 5 June 1951, 'wasting time' and then bringing me back to Moscow. Or they could have sent me back to Moscow from any point en route, without waiting for my arrival in Vanino. All this suggests that no detailed scenario of the Doctors' Plot existed until mid-summer of 1951. My mother also subscribed to the view that its fabrication began at about that time.

We believe that a detailed scenario of the Doctors' Plot, to which the arrest of Ia. G. Etinger was undoubtedly a prelude, was formulated in late July 1951, when my father was already dead. The scenario was set into motion after Abakumov's arrest as, it will be remembered, he thought there were no sufficient grounds for concocting such a case.

There is another circumstance that supports this. My mother was arrested four days after Abakumov's arrest and she was immediately questioned about 'facts regarding Ia. G. Etinger's malicious activities as a medical practitioner'.

As has already been noted, the main participants in the Doctors' Plot were arrested in November 1952. Simultaneously the anti-Semitic drive in the socialist countries of Eastern Europe was being stepped up. The trial of the 'anti-government conspirators' took place in Czechoslovakia in late November 1952.[7] The crusade against 'Jewish bourgeois nationalism' was gaining momentum and an unprecedented anti-Jewish purge was being prepared throughout the socialist camp with the main developments unfolding in Moscow.

In December, subsequent to the CPSU Central Committee Presidium[8] decree of 4 December 1952 'On the Situation in the Ministry of State Security and on Subversive Activities in Medical Treatment', the Central Committee issued instructions to party organizations concerning organs of the MGB.

N. A. Bulganin, then a member of the Presidium, told me that the instructions contained a passage about 'established facts regarding subversive activities in medicine' and the comments to the instructions stressed the 'key role' of Jewish professors 'closely linked with international Zionism and American intelligence'. There was another event that occurred at about this time, though it is hard to say if it happened before or after the decree was issued. Col.-Gen. of the Medical Service, E. I. Smirnov, then USSR Minister of Public Health, recalled:

> Shortly before 13 January 1953, I was Stalin's guest at his residence near Sochi. We were walking in the garden and talking. Stalin pointed to lemon and orange trees and described how they must be tended. And then abruptly changed the subject.
>
> – Comrade Smirnov, do you happen to know which of the doctors was treating Dimitrov and Zhdanov?
>
> – I do, I said, and named the person.
>
> – Isn't it odd? They were treated by one and the same doctor and both died.
>
> – Comrade Stalin, the doctor is not to blame for it.
>
> – What do you mean he 'is not to blame'?
>
> – I studied Dimitrov's case history and I know the results of the autopsy. I assure you it couldn't be helped. I know that Dimitrov himself recommended this doctor to Zhdanov. He thought he was a highly educated and tactful person and a good specialist.

Smirnov had in mind Boris Borisovich Kogan, a well-known Moscow internist, who, according to his son, L. B. Kogan, had at one point been responsible for the health of leading Comintern figures.

The preparatory phase in the Doctors' Plot was completed by late 1952. On 13 January 1953, the TASS statement announced the arrest of 'saboteur doctors'. On the same day *Pravda* carried a front-page editorial under the heading 'Despicable Spies and Murderers Disguised as Professors of Medicine'. I heard from Khrushchev that some claimed that it had been written by Stalin himself. After giving the gist of the TASS announcement about the 'arrest of the saboteur doctors', the article said:

> US tycoons and their British 'junior partners' know that it is impossible to impose their domination on other nations by peaceful means. Their frenzied preparations for a new world war include planting spies in the Soviet rear and the People's Democracies in an attempt to succeed where the Hitlerites failed: to create their subversive 'fifth column' in the USSR.

In other words, a clear hint was being made, that the 'Jewish bourgeois nationalists' were this 'fifth column'.

Unbridled anti-Semitic propaganda was unleashed in the country. The press was rife with Jewish names. The greatest 'zeal' was displayed by *Pravda, Izvestiia, Meditsinskaia gazeta.* Jewish doctors were accused of negligence, sloppiness, nepotism and malpractice. *Meditsinskaia gazeta* made a point to mention names like Rabinovich, Aizenshtein, Grinberg, Blokh and Gofman. Arrests of doctors continued. Besides those mentioned in the TASS statement, Academician B. I. Zbarskii, Professors V. E. Nezlin, S. E. Nezlin, E. M. Gel'shtein, N. A. Shereshevskii, M. Ia. Sereiskii, M. Ia. Temkin and Assistant Professor N. L. Vil'k were also arrested. Dr. S. E. Karpai, Dr. E. F. Livshits and many other excellent experts in their fields had been arrested earlier, in 1951. It is hard to establish the number of those arrested with any degree of accuracy, but beyond any doubt the investigating bodies were out to create the impression that there existed a widely ramified plot with agents in many cities. In the Gulag for Jewish prisoners, conditions worsened. In January 1953 I was in the Viatlag camp in Kirov Oblast. Right after the 13 January announcement I was put in the cooler and kept there until mid-April 1953, that is, until after the doctors were rehabilitated.

A campaign against Israel got under way at the same time. The Israeli government and people were shocked by the arrest of Jewish doctors and the fanning of anti-Semitism in the USSR. Soviet propaganda tried to create the impression that there was a correlation between the Doctors' Plot and the bombing of the Soviet mission in Tel Aviv in February 1953. Iurii Zhukov, one of the most venal and unscrupulous Soviet journalists, wrote in a *Pravda* article:

The anti-Soviet campaign in Israel became more frenzied than ever before after state security organs in the USSR and the People's Democracies cut off the blood-stained tentacles of the Joint, an international Jewish bourgeois nationalist organization, established by American intelligence to conduct espionage, subversive and terrorist activities against peace-loving states.[9]

On 21 January 1953, the newspapers published the Decree of the USSR Supreme Soviet Presidium awarding Doctor L. F. Timashuk the Order of Lenin 'for assistance rendered to the government in exposing the murderous doctors'. In order to understand the role of this woman in the Doctors' Plot we must return to the events which took place five years earlier, in 1948. It is now known from recently discovered classified KGB and CPSU Central Committee documents that on 29 August 1948, Timashuk, head of the electrocardiography laboratory at the Kremlin Hospital, sent a confidential letter to General N. S. Vlasik, chief of MGB security. It was a political denunciation asserting that on 28 August 1948, the head of the Kremlin's special medical department, Professor P. I. Egorov, summoned her to take an ECG of Politburo Member A. A. Zhdanov.[10] On that same day she and Professor Egorov, Academician Vinogradov and Professor V. Kh. Vasilenko flew from Moscow to Valdai where Zhdanov was at the time. She took his electrocardiogram and diagnosed coronary thrombosis. She immediately told the professors who had come with her about it. But, she went on, Professor Egorov and the physician in charge, Dr. Maiorov, said that the diagnosis was incorrect, that this was not a case of coronary thrombosis but of functional disorders caused by sclerosis and hypertension. They proposed that she, 'alter' the diagnosis and write 'caution' without mentioning coronary thrombosis as Dr. Karpai had done on the previous electrocardiograms.[11] Further on Timashuk said in her letter to Vlasik that on 29 August 1948 Zhdanov had had another acute heart attack and she was summoned from Moscow for the second time. However, on orders from Vinogradov and Egorov the electrocardiogram was not taken on 29 August but postponed until the following day. 'It was again proposed in a categorical fashion that I alter the diagnosis, and that myocardial infarction should not be mentioned. I notified Comrade A. M. Belov about it.' Belov was an MGB official responsible for Zhdanov's safety and Timashuk's turning to him was a piece of informing pure and simple, for he had nothing to do with methods of treatment of his charge. In conclusion, Timashuk pointed out that the consultants and the doctor in charge of the case 'clearly underestimated Zhdanov's grave condition, for they allowed him to get up and take a walk in the park'. In her opinion 'in future that could lead to fatal consequences'. Timashuk did not mention a single Jewish name, and still her letter was to play a key role in trumping up the Doctors' Plot; presumably this explains why three non-Jewish doctors were included in the Doctors' Plot.

On 30 August the letter was on the desk of the State Security Minister V. S. Abakumov. On that same day he sent a top-secret memorandum to Stalin:

> To Comrade Stalin, I. V., I am sending you a statement by Dr. L. F. Timashuk, head of the electrocardiography laboratory, about the condition of Comrade Zhdanov. As is evident from Dr. Timashuk's statement, she insists that Comrade Zhdanov had a myocardial infarction in the area of the anterior wall of the left ventricle and of the intraventricular septum. Head of the Kremlin medical department Egorov and Academician Vinogradov suggested that she alter the diagnosis omitting any mention of myocardial infarction.
>
> Enclosed: Statement by Comrade Timashuk and the ECG of Comrade Zhdanov.

Zhdanov died on 30 August 1948. After his death Timashuk sent several letters to the Central Committee, setting forth her opinion about Zhdanov's diagnosis and treatment.

At that point the case was shelved. But Stalin returned to it in the summer of 1952, when preparations for the Doctors' Plot were in full swing.

A letter Timashuk sent to the Presidium of the 23rd Congress of the CPSU in 1966 has recently been discovered in the Central Committee archives. It said:

> In the summer of 1952 I was suddenly summoned to investigator Novikov in the MGB investigation department on matters of highest importance and after some time to investigator Eliseev in connection with the case of the late A. A. Zhdanov. I again confirmed everything I had written to A. A. Kuznetsov, in the Central Committee . Six months later, on 20 January 1953, A. N. Poskrebyshev [head of the Central Committee's Special Sector, Stalin's personal secretariat] summoned me by phone and I was invited to the Kremlin. There G. M. Malenkov told me that a Council of Ministers meeting and Comrade Stalin personally had just thanked me for my personal courage displayed (that is, four and a half years ago) when I adhered to my professional opinion in the dispute with a prominent professor, and officially commended me and decorated me with the Order of Lenin. I was dumbfounded, for I could not believe that the doctors treating Zhdanov would turn out to be saboteurs. I told Malenkov that I did not deserve such a high award because I had done nothing special and any Soviet doctor would have acted in the same way under the circumstances. On the following day, 21 January 1953, the Order of Lenin was awarded to me and on 4 April 1953 [the day the doctors were rehabilitated] the USSR Supreme Soviet Presidium repealed the decision on my decoration as erroneous. When I returned the Order of Lenin to

the Supreme Soviet, A. F. Gorkin and N. M. Pegov [prominent party and Soviet functionaries] were present. They assured me that the government considered me an honest Soviet doctor and the repeal of the decree on my decoration would not affect my professional prestige or position. I continued working in the Kremlin Hospital as head of the functional diagnosis department. Three years later, in 1956, N. S. Khrushchev sent a secret letter dealing with Stalin's personality cult to the CPSU Central Committee and mentioned my name there in connection with the Doctors' Plot.

Timashuk was referring to Khrushchev's words describing her as a state security agent. It appears Khrushchev was right. This is confirmed by Timashuk's letter, mentioned above, to the head of the MGB security guards. Had the Doctors' Plot reached court trial stage, Timashuk might have been the main 'witness' for the prosecution.

After the decree on decorating Timashuk with the Order of Lenin was published, the press launched a powerful campaign to glorify her. She was presented as a Russian national heroine who had saved the country from 'a gang of Jewish murderers'. *Pravda* carried an article by Olga Chechetkina entitled 'The Mail of Lidiia Timashuk', extolling Timashuk's 'feat' and telling about the heaps of letters of gratitude she was receiving for her 'patriotic deed'. The article read in part:

> Just a while ago we knew nothing about this woman, and now the name of Doctor Lidiia Feodos'evna Timashuk has become a symbol of Soviet patriotism, extreme vigilance, an unrelenting, courageous struggle against the enemies of our Motherland. She helped to unmask the American hirelings, monsters who used their white doctors' smocks to murder Soviet people.

The article cited the verse written by pupils from the city of Sochi and dedicated to Timashuk: 'Shame on you, scum of the earth, for your grisly deeds, and eternal praise for the valourous Russian patriot.'

The arrest of doctors continued in January and February. Preparations were being made for a grandiose show trial which was to make the Beilis trial look like child's play. The Jewish population was in a state of shock. Everyone was expecting mass anti-Jewish repressions, a Holocaust — Soviet style. It was rumoured that after the trial and the doctors' public executions in the country's major cities, the Jews would be deported to remote regions of the Far East. These rumours later proved to be well-founded. It is now known that Malenkov and Suslov sent instructions to the Central Committee apparatus demanding capital punishment for the doctors and in general 'certain anti-Jewish actions'. Documents were drafted on exiling Soviet Jews to Siberia. It has been established further that new camps and barracks were being put up at the time to house the deported Jews.[12]

According to Stalin's plan, the trial would be accompanied by spontaneous pogroms instigated by the authorities. Il'ia Erenburg heard from Khrushchev that Stalin had told him openly about schemes for 'popular outbursts' against the Jews during their deportation to Siberia, attacks on trains carrying Jews in order to massacre them, so that only part of them would reach their destination. As Bulganin told me in 1970,[13] a series of train crashes was also to be devised. He also recounted to me that a plan was formulated to hang the doctors before huge crowds in big squares in Moscow, Leningrad, Kiev, Minsk, Sverdlovsk and other major cities. Everything was thought out in detail: it was specified in advance in which city this or that professor would be hanged. Bulganin believed that Stalin, Malenkov and Suslov were the main figures in the frame-up and were aided by executives of lower ranks. When I asked him who these people were, Bulganin smiled and said: 'You want me to name some of the country's present leaders. Many of the 1953 people are holding key posts today. I do not want to die before my time. I want to die peacefully.' It is difficult to say, of course, to what extent Bulganin had been involved in the Doctors' Plot. After several talks with him I am inclined to believe that he had very little to do with it. Once I asked Bulganin about Khrushchev's role and despite the fact that he had good reasons to bear a grudge against the former First Secretary, he said firmly: 'No. Nikita had nothing to do with it.'

The 'theoretical foundations' for deporting the Jews were elaborated by 'Professor-Philosopher' Dmitrii Chesnokov, elected to the Party Presidium at the 19th Party Congress. They hinged on the 'thesis' that Jews had proved to be 'unreceptive' to socialism. Chesnokov wrote a book on the subject which was to be published in a mass edition and circulated all over the country during the deportation.[14]

In parallel with the preparations for the doctors' trial, a signature collection campaign was launched among Jewish cultural figures and scientists. They were asked to sign a statement branding the arrested doctors as monsters and demanding the most severe punishment. In order to substantiate the need for resettling the Jews in outlying areas, the letter said it must be done to 'save them from popular anger' and 'to introduce them to useful physical labour and to the soil'. This letter was written by several Stalinist henchmen of Jewish origin — including Ia. S. Khavinson, who during the war headed TASS and later was a *Pravda* columnist under the pen-name M. Marinin.

A. N. Iakovlev, former Central Committee Secretary, who at one time headed the Politburo commission for rehabilitation and was well acquainted with many major political 'cases' of the postwar years, said that the letter was devised and put into circulation by Chesnokov.[15]

Iakovlev recalls that another 'philosopher', Mark Mitin, and 'historian', Isak Mints, collected the required signatures of Jewish scientists and cultural figures. We know that several people to whom the trio turned refused to sign — Il'ia Erenburg, People's Artist of the USSR, Mark Reizen, Hero of the Soviet Union, Colonel-General Ia. G. Kreizer, and composer I. O. Dunaevskii. Among those who did sign was M. I. Blanter, the author of the famous song 'Katiusha'.[16] The full list of those who signed this document is unknown.

Meanwhile the investigation of the Doctors' Plot was going on in the Lubianka. But, in the latter half of February, signs of change appeared in the investigators' behaviour. I had the opportunity to talk with almost all the physicians arrested in connection with the case, and they all recalled that at the end of February the interrogations practically stopped or were conducted quite 'peacefully'. They had no idea what this signified. Today we can assume that it was probably caused either by Stalin's illness, and his virtual removal from power, or the bitter struggle in the Kremlin leadership around the Doctors' Plot. The well-known historian A. Avtorkhanov believes that the Doctors' Plot precipitated Stalin's death. He writes:

> Stalin had only just managed to censure the 'toadies', execute the 'Zionists'(1952)[17] and put the saboteur doctors behind bars when he was helped to die by his closest Russian associates — Malenkov, Khrushchev, Bulganin and his compatriot Beria who betrayed him.[18]

On 5 March, if we are to believe the official version of events, Stalin died. It later came to light that in the last days of the dictator's life, the CPSU leadership was in session around the clock. On that same day, a joint session of the Central Committee Plenum, the Council of Ministers and the Supreme Soviet Presidium was held. The session adopted a resolution on the reorganization of the country's party and state leadership. A major decision adopted there was the merger of the Ministry of State Security (MGB) and the Ministry of Internal Affairs (MVD) into a single Ministry of the Interior headed by Beria, who was also appointed first deputy chairman of the USSR Council of Ministers. Having taken over the state security bodies, Beria began an extremely ingenious political game.[19] He began calling Stalin a tyrant and suggested that Central Committee members get acquainted with numerous facts showing his cruelty, abuse of power and political terrorism.[20]

The country's new leadership was extremely worried by the fact that Beria had attained full control of the state security organs and could make use of their archives to suit his own purposes — primarily to expose the entire group of Stalin's successors as accomplices and perpetrators of the massive repressions in the 1930s. Therefore, the elimination of Beria was a matter of vital importance for the new Kremlin leaders. With his penchant for adventurism, Beria was increasingly becoming the main contender in the struggle for power.

Beria used the Doctors' Plot as his trump card in this struggle for power and demanded that the doctors be immediately released. It is worth recalling Kaganovich's statement at the July 1953 Central Committee plenum in which he went out of his way to deny that the Doctors' Plot had any anti-Semitic overtones. He also stressed that Beria used the Doctors' Plot in order to consolidate his position in the country and to curry favour with world public opinion as the man who denounced the provocation and had the framed victims released. Kaganovich stated:

> Let us, for example, take the Doctors' Plot, which some elements have erroneously linked with Jewry as a whole. The party was right in releasing the doctors, but Beria sensationalized it out of all proportion, resorted to his usual method of patting himself on the back and alleging that it was he who had done it and not the Central Committee, that it was he who had set things right and not the government.

Undoubtedly Beria did try to use the Doctors' Plot to suit his own political purposes. And it naturally worried his political rivals who feared that this would bring him dividends not only within the country but also in the international arena.

Throughout March 1953 the debate over the Doctors' Plot continued among the country's leaders. The new Kremlin bosses were convinced they had to put an end to the Doctors' Plot and release the doctors. In March, the interrogations essentially ceased. The Kremlin strategists were feverishly looking for a formula to justify the release of the 'doctor murderers'.

Meanwhile Beria made another move. On 2 April 1953 he sent a letter to the party Presidium addressed to Malenkov stating:

> An examination of the materials in the Mikhoels case has revealed that in February 1948, in Minsk, former USSR MGB Deputy Minister Ogol'tsov and former Belorussian MGB Minister Tsanava carried out an illegal operation to liquidate Mikhoels on orders from USSR MGB Minister Abakumov...In this connection Abakumov has been interrogated at the MVD and explanations have been received from Ogol'tsov and Tsanava. Abakumov gave the following evidence...'As far as I can remember, in 1948, the head of the Soviet government I. V. Stalin gave me an urgent assignment — to promptly organize the liquidation of Mikhoels by MGB personnel and charge specially selected people with the task. Then it came to our knowledge that Mikhoels and his friend, whose name I do not remember, had gone to Minsk. When this was reported to Stalin he

immediately ordered us to carry out the liquidation in Minsk...After
Mikhoels was liquidated Stalin highly praised the operation and ordered
that the people who had performed it be decorated, which was carried
out.'[21]

The letter goes on to describe in detail how Mikhoels was
'liquidated'. There were several options for eliminating Mikhoels: a) a
car accident, b) running him over with a lorry in a deserted street.
Since neither gave a 100 per cent guarantee the following course was
decided upon: to invite Mikhoels, through one of our agents, to visit
an acquaintance of his late at night, provide a car from the hotel he
was staying in, allegedly to drive him there, take him to Tsanava's
dacha and liquidate him. Then the body was to be put in an out-of-
the-way deserted street and run over by a lorry. And that is how it was
done. To keep the matter secret, agent Golubov, who accompanied
Mikhoels on this fatal visit, was also done away with (they were run
over by a lorry near the dacha). At the end of the letter Beria declared:

> The MVD deems it necessary a) to arrest and initiate proceedings against
> former USSR Deputy MGB Minister S. I. Ogol'tsov and former State
> Security Minister of Belorussia L. F. Tsanava, b) to repeal the Supreme
> Soviet decree conferring honours on the participants in the murder of
> Mikhoels and Golubov.

Beria insisted on the immediate release of the arrested physicians.
Finally, on 3 April 1953 at 12 noon, the CPSU Presidium adopted a
decision to set free 37 doctors and the members of their families being
held for investigation in the Lubianka and Lefortovo prisons. The
decision was to be published in the central press and broadcast over
the radio on 4 April. At this juncture Beria made a brilliant political
move. During the night he called the *Pravda* editorial offices and
demanded that the title of the communiqué on setting the doctors free
be altered. The heading now read 'Communiqué of the USSR MVD'
instead of 'Decree of the CPSU Central Committee Presidium'.[22]

Naturally, people reading this communiqué on the physicians'
rehabilitation got the impression that Beria's rise to power in the MVD
led to his investigation of the Doctors' Plot and the release of the
innocent victims. Beria was scoring points in the struggle for power
not only within the country but also abroad, for world public opinion
was greatly concerned about the outburst of anti-Semitism in the
USSR.[23]

Two days after the publication of the MVD communiqué, a *Pravda*
article revealed that the doctors' investigation had been headed by
Riumin, who was 'now under arrest'.[24]

More than 15 months later, from 2–7 July 1954, the Military

Collegium of the USSR Supreme Court heard the case of Riumin, who was accused of crimes specified in Articles 5–7 of the RSFSR Criminal Code.

It is noteworthy that in the announcement of the USSR Supreme Court there was no mention whatsoever that the Doctors' Plot had any Jewish aspect. The clique of Stalin's successors that had come to power in the country was out to erase recollections of the anti-Semitic character of this provocation. This is quite understandable, since many leading representatives of this upper crust were directly involved in the Doctors' Plot and continued to harbour anti-Semitic plans. Naturally, they hastened to get rid of Riumin who had been the immediate perpetrator of these schemes and knew too much to be left alive. Riumin was shot, the doctors resumed their work, but everything was done to make people try and forget the Doctors' Plot. It did not surface again until the 20th CPSU Congress, when Khrushchev delivered his report 'On the Stalin Personality Cult and Its Consequences'.

In it there is not the slightest hint about the anti-Semitic nature of the Doctors' Plot. Was it fortuitous or not? Beyond all doubt it was done deliberately. Khrushchev did not want to draw attention to the anti-Jewish character of the Doctors' Plot. It is well known that the country's leaders continued to pursue the policy of state anti-Semitism after Stalin's death. By 1955-56, sufficiently strong links with Egypt, Syria and other Arab states had been established, and Soviet weapons were being supplied to their regimes solely for their struggle against Israel and the destruction of the Jews. The new Kremlin rulers did not want to condemn political actions directed against the Jews because of the anti-Semitic attitudes of a great part of the Soviet population and the interests of their allies in the Arab East. Hence the 'neutral' explanation of the Doctors' Plot at the 20th Congress.

Some time after Khrushchev's removal from power I had a conversation with him concerning the Doctors' Plot. When I asked him why he had treated the Doctors' Plot the way he had, he said: 'I did not want to emphasize the national composition of those arrested in the Doctors' Plot. This could have been misunderstood by the party leadership.' To my remark that had he underscored the anti-Semitic character of the Doctors' Plot, it would have gotten a favourable response in the West, he snapped: 'In 1956 it was more important to me to have good relations with Nasser than with such supporters of Israel as John Foster Dulles, Anthony Eden and Guy Mollet.'

It is absolutely obvious that, in closing the Doctors' case, the Soviet leadership was by no means discontinuing the policy of state anti-Semitism that was continuing to thrive. An anti-Israel campaign of an overtly anti-Semitic character was launched during the rule of Khrushchev and vigorously continued under Brezhnev and Andropov. These decades saw the emergence of political forces which in the past few years have openly engaged in building a Nazi movement in Russia. Their mouthpieces, for instance the newspaper *Russkoe voskresen'ie*, are trying to revive the Doctors' Plot. This fascist publication is packed with monstrous insults and sallies against the Jews who are referred to as 'kikes'. It bears a photograph of Hitler, who is described as a 'highly moral' person 'of great integrity'. One of its articles stated the following: 'After the mass death of newborn babies in maternity homes in 1952 Stalin himself responded to the people's supplications. The rascals killed him during the Jewish holiday of Purim.' Or again, 'After Stalin died, the Jewish people, and with it the Yids were immediately rehabilitated and the Doctors' Case was closed.'

Forty years have passed since the Doctors' Plot, but it has remained the subject of political speculations of Russian fascists striving to stage another Holocaust on Russian soil. The exposure of this major anti-Jewish provocation is, therefore, still topical.

NOTES

1. V. Solov'ev, E. Klepikov, *Zagovorshchiki v Kremle* (Moscow, 1991) p. 216.
2. Ibid.
3. Thirteen of them were sentenced to death, the rest were given various prison terms: twenty people — 25 years, three — 20 years, eleven — 15 years, fifty — 10 years, and so on. See Shimon Redlich, *Tehiya al tnai. Ha-va'ad ha-yehudi ha-anti-fashisti ha-sovyetit. Aliyato ve-shki'ato*, (Tel Aviv: Massada, 1990).
4. From the author's personal discussions with former Prime Minister Nikolai Bulganin.
5. Kirill Stolerov, *Golgofa. N. A. Shchelokov, V. S. Abakumov. Dokumental'naia povest'* (Moscow: Fizkul'tura i sport, 1991), p. 28.
6. Aleksandr Solzhenitsyn, 'Arkhipelag GULAG', *Novyi Mir* 1 (1990), p. 153.
7. For the so-called Slánský Trial, see, e.g., Jiri Pelikan (ed.), *The Czechoslovak Political Trials, 1950–1954. The Suppressed Report of the Dubček Government's Commission of Inquiry, 1968* (London: Macdonald, 1971).
8. The name of the Politburo had been changed to *Presidium* at the 19th Party Congress in October.
9. *Pravda* 14 Feb. 1953.
10. The author expresses his deep acknowledgement to *Novoe vremia* columnist, A. Iu. Dubnov for acquainting him with material concerning L. F. Timashuk's letters regarding the Doctors' Plot.
11. Sof'ia Efimovna Karpai was one of the best electrocardiography specialists in the country. From 1942 to March 1950 she worked at the Department of Internal Medicine of the Kremlin Hospital. Her monograph 'Analysis and Clinical Assessment of Electrocardiography', written together with Professor V. E. Nezlin and published in 1948, was used for years by thousands of medical practitioners in their daily work. She was arrested on 16 July 1951. Professor Nezlin was arrested at the end of 1952.

12. From personal discussions with Bulganin after his retirement; see also Redlich, *Tehiya al tnai*.
13. From a conversation the author had with him in the autumn of that year.
14. The author was told about this 'work' in detail by the prominent journalist Ernst Henri in the summer of 1957.
15. Chesnokov was removed from the Party Presidium on 6 March 1953 when, following Stalin's death, there was a reshuffle in the top party and state leadership.
16. Blanter informed the author of this in a discussion he had with him in 1955.
17. A reference to the Slánský Trial.
18. A. Avtorkhanov, *Imperiia Kremlia. Sovetskii tip kolonializma* (Vilnius, 1990) p. 209; the author's hypothesis is confirmed in Konstantin Simonov's memoirs 'The Mystery of Stalin's Death'. He believes that Stalin might have died as a result of a plot by Beria — cf. *Znamia* 4 (1988).
19. Its details can be discerned by scrutinizing the minutes of the CPSU Central Committee plenum held on 2–7 July 1953 and published in *Izvestiia TsK KPSS*, 1–2 (1991). As is known, this plenum was devoted exclusively to 'Beria's criminal anti-party and anti-state activities'.
20. From personal discussions with Khrushchev and Bulganin.
21. *Argumenty i fakty* 2 (1992).
22. The author was informed about this in discussions with Khrushchev in 1966 and Bulganin in 1970. Both said it had come as a complete surprise to them. 'We were shocked by such perfidy on Beria's part', Bulganin said.
23. During the last few years I had the opportunity to visit several Western European countries and to talk with some people who had occupied responsible positions at the time, and they all spoke about the shock felt in the Western capitals in connection with the Doctors' Plot. One prominent Dutch politician who preferred to remain anonymous said that NATO leaders were holding continuous consultations during the Doctors' Plot. For the relation to the Doctors' Plot in Israel and the West, see also Yosef Govrin, 'The Beginnings of the Struggle for Soviet Jewish Emigration and Its Impact on Israel-Soviet Relations', in this volume.
24. On 14 November 1952 he was relieved of his responsibilities as Deputy Minister of State Security and appointed senior superviser of the Party Control Committee. It is interesting to note that the arrest of doctors continued even after this date. One of the incriminated doctors, Iakov Rapoport, was arrested only on 3 Feb. 1953. Rapoport has left us his own fascinating account of his arrest, investigation and release. On many issues his story tallies with that of Etinger — see Yakov Rapoport, *The Doctors' Plot of 1953* (Cambridge, MA: Harvard University Press, 1991). One important point that Rapaport makes is that initially, the Doctors' Plot had no nationalistic colouring; both Russian and Jewish doctors were implicated. But before long it was given an anti-Semitic slant. Riumin of the MGB was responsible for turning it into a Jewish conspiracy — Rapoport, p. 221.

III

THE INTERACTION BETWEEN POPULAR
AND OFFICIAL ANTI-SEMITISM

7

Anti-Jewish Pogroms
in the First Russian Revolution,
1905–1907

ABRAHAM ASCHER

The anti-Jewish pogroms during the first Russian Revolution, and in particular the two major waves of violence in October 1905 and in the early summer of 1906, shocked the enlightened sectors of the Russian public.[*] The outrages against the Jews seemed to be yet another sign of the Tsar's and his ministers' depravity, adding urgency to the calls for the abolition of the old order. But close study of the pogroms suggests that the highest authorities in St. Petersburg did not play nearly as critical a role in unleashing the violence as was widely assumed. The pogroms were, to a very large extent, spontaneous actions by ordinary people who objected to the presence of Jews in their midst. Resentments that had been contained turned into violence during a period of revolutionary turbulence.

Contrary to popular perception, Russian autocrats and their governments did not deliberately and systematically instigate pogroms to deflect the widespread hostility toward the prevailing political and social order. In fact, quite a few men in high positions of authority realized that it was in their interest to prevent such outbreaks of mass violence. Even Tsar Alexander III, a notorious reactionary, disapproved of the anti-Jewish pogroms of 1881–82 and let his

---

[*] This chapter is based on accounts in the author's previously published works, *The Revolution of 1905: Russia in Disarray* (Stanford: Stanford University Press, 1988) and *The Revolution of 1905: Authority Restored* (Stanford: Stanford University Press, 1992).

subordinates know that he wanted them to put a stop to the violence. If, during the tumultuous years from 1905 to 1907, Tsar Nicholas II did not express similar sentiments, there is also scant evidence that he or his chief ministers played a central role in organizing pogroms.[1]

This is not to suggest that the monarchs in late Imperial Russia were well disposed toward Jews. On the contrary, they and most of their ministers harboured deep prejudices against Jews and maintained numerous restrictive measures against them. And they often voiced anti-Semitic views that appeared to give an aura of legitimacy to bands such as the Black Hundreds, which specialized in physical attacks on Jews. But at the same time many political leaders feared lawlessness even when directed only at Jews because it might serve as a prelude to attacks on Christian property owners, the nobility, and ultimately the authorities themselves. That this fear was not far-fetched became evident during the anti-Jewish unrest in 1905. In an exhaustive study of peasant disorders in the autumn of that year, it emerged that in several provinces — Tambov, Kharkov, Poltava, Chernigov, Kursk, Orel, Riazan', Tula, and Voronezh — peasants interpreted the indifference of local authorities to the attacks on the Jews as an invitation to 'rob landlords' estates'. As one observer of the peasant disorders put it:

> The agrarian movement was caused by the fact that at a certain time rumours from all corners of Russia reached the villagers stating that in the cities Jews were beaten with impunity and people were allowed to rob their property. Here, there, and everywhere peasants appeared from the cities after having taken part in the pillaging during the rioting; they said that the soldiers and the police watched the carnage and did nothing.[2]

For about a year after the initial incidents of anti-government agitation, attacks on Jews, though at times quite savage, were not a critical factor in the revolutionary upheaval. The agitation against the government began in the autumn of 1904, when middle class liberals, appalled by Russia's defeats in the war against Japan, launched a campaign for political reform. Soon the mood of disaffection spread to other social groups, reaching a climax in January 1905 with the procession to the Winter Palace, led by Father Gapon, to petition for economic, social, and political reform. The senseless massacre by soldiers of some 130 peaceful marchers triggered a period of unprecedented unrest — strikes, peasant disorders, middle class appeals for change, demands for autonomy or independence by some of the national minorities — that culminated in the general strike in October 1905, which literally paralyzed the government. To restore calm, the government, then led by Sergei Witte, issued the October Manifesto, which fundamentally changed the political system of the Russian Empire. Tsar Nicholas in effect conceded that he would no longer act as an autocratic ruler in the sense that his word, and his word alone, would be law. He committed himself to the 'unbreakable rule that no law can become effective without the approval of the [elected] State Duma'.[3] At this precarious moment in the revolution, pogroms against the Jews suddenly and unexpectedly erupted into a mass movement of brute force. The government's failure to halt the violence raised questions about the stability of the new order even before it had an opportunity to consolidate itself.

The violence began in many parts of the empire on 18 October, one day after the Tsar had issued the October Manifesto. 'From the centre, the north, the south, from all corners of Russia', the newspaper *Syn otechestva* reported, 'there are telegraphic reports of attacks on demonstrators, of deaths and injuries; in many places exultant mobs are attacking Jewish streets and homes, plundering and demolishing whatever falls into their hands'.[4] Although Jews were the principal focus of the pogroms in October, they were not the only ones to come under attack. The rampaging mobs also targeted the intelligentsia and students — anyone, in fact, who was presumed to have participated in the movement to extract the Manifesto of 17 October or who simply rejoiced in it.

After four days of violence it seemed to one sober commentator that 'complete governmental anarchy' prevailed in Russia. The pogroms continued at high pitch for another three days and then the mobs largely ran out of steam, but sporadic incidents continued until late in November. The attacks on Jews occurred with such frequency that newspapers carried special sections entitled 'Jewish pogroms'; in fact, they told only part of the story. On 23 October, *Rus'* listed eleven serious incidents; on 25 October, thirteen, which took place in eleven towns and cities. On 27 October, *Syn otechestva* reported fifteen pogroms; on 1 November, twenty-six. When none had as yet broken out in a particular city, the Jews lived in dread of an attack. 'The Jews of Moscow', a newspaper account noted on 24 October, 'spent an extremely anxious night expecting a pogrom. Almost no one slept in his apartment; they all hid with Christian acquaintances.'[5] All told, according to the most reliable estimates, 690 anti-Jewish pogroms occurred in those six weeks, primarily in the southwestern provinces; 876 people were killed and between 7,000 and 8,000 injured. In a few cities the Jews lost property estimated overall at more than a million rubles. Altogether, the damage to property during the pogroms has been calculated at 62 million rubles.[6]

There was no single pattern to the disorders. For the most part, they appear to have started when organized gangs attacked demonstrators celebrating victory over the autocracy.[7] Sometimes pogroms erupted after rumours circulated that Jews had perpetrated acts of violence. Thus, on 20 October the Jews of Kiev were accused of having set fire to the Goloseevskaia Monastery and murdering all the monks. A senior military officer, General I. A. Karass, publicly denied that either the massacre or the fire had taken place, but a mob refused to believe him and went on a rampage. The rioters destroyed all the stores in the Jewish bazaar, killed twelve people and injured forty four.[8] In some localities the pretext for a pogrom was the charge that Jews were planning to place one of their co-religionists on the throne.[9]

In accounting for the disorders, critics of the autocracy claimed that the *pogromshchiki* had been organized by reactionaries and abetted by officials at every level of government. Some critics also contended that the government in St. Petersburg had actually planned the violence so as to deal a crushing blow to all who had worked to wrest the October Manifesto from the Tsar.[10] These charges cannot be dismissed out of hand. The reports that the police looked the other way during pogroms are simply too numerous. In Moscow, for example, the police urged janitors — widely used to spy on their tenants — to mobilize 'everyone who was "for the Tsar" '. As for the janitors themselves, 'participation in the demonstrations was obligatory'.[11]

In various localities investigations made shortly after the disorders confirmed that the police had indeed helped foment them. In Kostroma, the police were found to have played a 'leading role' in the assaults on the intelligentsia and students on 19 October. Several witnesses testified that the police had given money to the Black Hundreds and thanked them for their work. Others testified that the governor himself, L. M. Kniazev, had also thanked the *pogromshchiki* for their services. Finally, there was convincing evidence that the police had dragged people from their hiding places and handed them over to the ruffians for beatings.[12]

In Simferopol' (Tauride Guberniia), the city council conducted an especially thorough investigation of disorders that had occurred in October. The commission of inquiry succeeded in interrogating 369 eyewitnesses, despite persistent efforts by the prosecutor and numerous police officials to terrorize them into silence. The commission reached two conclusions: first, that the pogroms had been designed to put a halt to political meetings and strikes; and second, that they had been planned with the participation of the 'chief of the city police, the deputy chief, the colonel of the gendarmes, and the entire police staff, with the connivance or friendly neutrality of the governor'. The commission recommended that a new prosecutor be appointed and that the entire police force of Simferopol' be replaced immediately. The deputy chief of police was actually tried and found guilty of misconduct; the chief of police, however, died before he could be brought to trial.[13] A Bureau of Investigation of the Jewish Pogroms (apparently set up by the government) conducted a general inquiry and concluded that 'in almost every pogrom local authorities participated actively'. Historians of specific pogroms have reached the same conclusion. Information found by this author in the archives of the French Foreign Ministry tends to implicate senior officials in the city of Odessa in the disorders.[14]

That a fair number of local officials tolerated and even abetted the pogroms is therefore beyond dispute. But the question of the culpability of the government in St. Petersburg is more complicated. To be sure, Tsar Nicholas viewed the violence as a natural reaction of loyal citizens to the excesses of the left. On 27 October he wrote his mother that 'the impertinence of the Socialists and revolutionaries has angered the people once more; and because nine-tenths of the troublemakers are Jews, the people's anger turns against them. That's how the pogroms happened. It is amazing how they took place *simultaneously* in all the towns of Russia and Siberia'.[15] But this expression of sympathetic understanding for the pogroms merely confirmed what every official knew, that their ruler despised Jews and opponents of the autocracy and was not likely to be distressed by physical attacks on them. It does not prove that the Court planned or initiated the violence.

The most damaging evidence of complicity by the authorities in St. Petersburg came to light in February 1906. A. A. Lopukhin, Director of the Department of Police in the Ministry of Internal Affairs, informed Witte that in October and November 1905 a secret press in police headquarters in the capital had printed 'thousands of proclamations' urging 'all true Russians to rise and exterminate all foreigners, Jews, Armenians, etc. and all those who were advocates of reform and talked of restricting the autocratic power of the Sovereign'. It also emerged that General D. F. Trepov, the Commandant of the Court who exerted extraordinary influence over the Tsar, had personally made corrections on the proofs of some of the proclamations. After an investigation confirmed the accuracy of Lopukhin's allegations, Prime Minister Witte ordered that the press and the remaining proclamations be destroyed.

Witte later claimed that he had not pressed charges against Captain

M. S. Kommisarov, the officer directly responsible for the printing and distribution of the inflammatory material, because the Tsar had made it clear that he would not allow him to be punished. Kommisarov, it should be noted, had no compunctions about his work. When someone found the press and asked him what kind of work it did, he is said to have replied: 'We can arrange any massacre you like; a massacre of ten or a massacre of twenty thousand.' Apparently, a massacre of 10,000 was planned for Kiev in February 1906 but was averted by action of senior officials in the Ministry of Internal Affairs. However, Nicholas protected Kommisarov because he had done good work in military espionage during the war with Japan. According to the British embassy in St. Petersburg, Witte did request that all the officials involved in running the press be punished, only to be turned down by P. N. Durnovo, the Minister for Internal Affairs, who actually gave them cash awards amounting to 70,000 rubles. The facts of the case were presented to Tsar Nicholas, who promised to 'remove M. Durnovo immediately but expressed his objection to taking any definitive step until the Duma had met'. Some of the details of this sordid affair appeared in the daily press in February 1906 and were not denied by the government.[16]

Significantly, Witte himself, determined to maintain order and to enlist the support of liberals for the government he had formed after the issuance of the October Manifesto, publicly condemned the violence. On 22 October he branded the disorders as harmful to the state and vowed to take the 'most decisive steps' to curb them. In response to a telegram from the Minsk City Council appealing for measures to end the violence there, Witte promised an investigation.[17] In a reply to a similar telegram from lawyers in Kazan' and the city's rabbi, Witte directed officials to 'take energetic measures to stop the destruction and violence' there.[18] Subsequently, two high officials who had brazenly shown their sympathy for the pogroms were punished. P. G. Kurlov, governor of Minsk, and D. M. Neidhardt, the Prefect of Odessa, were dismissed and brought to trial (though both were cleared by the Senate in March 1906).[19] Finally, a report on the violence for official eyes only, prepared at Witte's request, gives no hint of collusion by the central government in the disorders.[20] In truth, the violence was not in Witte's interest since it discredited his government.

Some higher officials in local areas too, did not approve of the pogroms. In Astrakhan and Taganrog, for instance, officials made it clear that they would not tolerate violence, and the cities remained calm.[21] In Saratov the attacks on Jews were initially viewed with benevolent neutrality by the vice-governor, who was in charge during the absence of his superior, Petr A. Stolypin. As soon as he returned, however, Stolypin ordered a halt to the violence, and 'in the course of ten minutes the pogroms were stopped'.[22] On 28 October the governor announced that 'every infringement of the rights of an individual or his property, regardless of his nationality or religion, will be suppressed with the most resolute measures, if necessary with the application of military force'.[23] It seems highly unlikely that Stolypin would have issued such orders had they contravened the directives of the government in St. Petersburg. He surely would not have been promoted to head the government six months later (when he became Chairman of the Council of Ministers) had he done so. By the same token, Stolypin's actions and those of several other officials suggest that without the connivance of local administrators, the *pogromshchiki* could not have engaged in their criminal activities for very long.

One cannot agree, then, with the proposition that the pogroms began in response to a signal from St. Petersburg or that they would not have taken place at all without official inspiration or approval. The random character of the acts of violence by the *pogromshchiki*, the failure of local officials to follow one clearly defined policy, and the absence of evidence incriminating Witte's government argue against this interpretation. Most of the officials found wanting were charged not with instigating the disorders but rather with neglecting to take prompt action to end them.

The causes of the mass violence seem to lie elsewhere. In part, the violence can be traced to the rage of those who feared that the demonstrations applauding the October Manifesto signified the end of a social order in which they enjoyed a certain status that they wished to preserve. As one observer noted, ordinary people who had until October at least been able to take refuge in their superiority to Jews and other social outcasts 'must undoubtedly have felt miserable [in seeing] the streets captured by new people, precisely those people who up to this time had stood outside the law, people against whom everything had been permissible. There are [such] malcontents even among the more solid elements of the population'.[24] In short, to a substantial degree the violence from below late in October was a spontaneous response by various groups determined to crush the opposition and to preserve the old order.

At the same time, there is little doubt that the climate of hatred fostered by right-wing organizations encouraged the outbursts of violence. During the revolutionary period, 200 additional organizations made their appearance, and the most prominent, the Union of the

Russian People, waged a massive campaign to elicit support for right-wing causes and in particular for virulent anti-Semitism.[25] The Black Hundreds, notorious vigilantes loosely aligned with the extremist groups, often took the lead in attacking Jews.

Much of the reckless plundering and beating of innocent civilians was the work of riffraff motivated largely by prejudice and a craving for loot. Peasants, shopkeepers, coachmen, janitors, and even some workers (though apparently not any who belonged to trade unions) also lent a hand, for much the same reasons.[26] For these people, however, another factor played a role. They found unbearable the sight of multitudes of ordinary Russians, among them many Jews and rowdy students, celebrating their victory over the revered Tsar, often by defiling his portrait. For nine months the 'upstarts' had defied authority more or less with impunity; now they had apparently succeeded in bringing down the entire political system, and with it the hierarchical structure on which Russian society had been based. If the autocracy could no longer restrain them, those who yearned to maintain the old order because they felt secure within it would have to take the law into their own hands. To some vigilantes, such conduct may not even have seemed to be a violation of legal norms, for the Tsar's capitulation signified to them that their beloved leader — in their view the only legitimate source of authority — had been under-mined by evil forces, and that they must therefore come to his rescue at all costs.

The prominence of Jews among the upstarts was especially galling to the *pogromshchiki*. For religious, social and economic reasons, hatred of the Jews was deeply rooted among many sectors of the Russian population. Until 1905, the Jewish minority had been legally repressed, denied most of the few rights enjoyed by other citizens of the empire. Now not only was there talk of granting rights of citizenship to Jews; Jews had even assumed positions of responsibility in the political movements that had dealt the Tsar so crushing a blow. Many people, including foreign observers, actually believed that 'Jewish money had been a major mainspring' of the revolutionary movement. The government allegedly possessed incontrovertible evidence that Russian banks had disbursed huge amounts of money received from abroad to members of the Social Democratic and Socialist Revolutionary parties.[27]

The resentment of the *pogromshchiki* revealed itself with telling force in the humiliations they often inflicted on opponents of the Tsar seized during the unrest in October. They would compel Jews and students to kneel in front of pictures of the Tsar or herd Jews into cathedrals to swear their allegiance to him.[28] These rituals — it is hard to think of a better word — were designed to impress upon the opponents of the old order that although the autocracy may have lost a battle, the symbols of authority were still generally venerated and the struggle over the future of Russia was far from ended.

The second major wave of anti-Jewish violence in the first revolution early in June 1906 attracted even more national and international attention than the pogroms in October 1905, in large measure because the State Duma was then in session and deputies elected by the people expressed their outrage at the new acts of barbarism. It had been assumed that after the horrors in the autumn of 1905 and other sporadic incidents, new attacks against members of a defenceless minority would simply not be tolerated.

Once again a pogrom erupted without instigation by high government officials in St. Petersburg. The location this time was Bialystok (Grodno Guberniia), where 60 Jews had been murdered during a rampage by hoodlums on 1 August 1905. During the pogrom in 1906 close to 800 people were killed or wounded and the large Jewish business district was devastated. A major centre of the textile industry with a population of about 44,000 Jews and 21,000 Poles, Bialystok had long been a hotbed of revolutionary activity and an important stronghold of the Bund, the Jewish Marxist organization. The first reports of the pogrom blamed the Jews for having deliberately provoked the violence by throwing a bomb at a Christian religious procession. The governor of Grodno, determined to calm the local population, publicly denied the accuracy of these accounts and in addition dismissed as untrue reports that in a mêlée, Christian children had been trampled upon and that Orthodox as well as Catholic children had been injured. At first the governor's announcement was widely ignored.[29]

Even Western diplomats, who based their assessments on newspaper accounts and on information from senior officials (some of them moderates, such as the Minister of Foreign Affairs, A. P. Izvol'skii), accepted the charges against the Jews at face value. Only after a lapse of a week did they conclude that they had been misled. They then acknowledged that what had occurred in Bialystok was another instance of a brutal attack on Jews which local officials had chosen not to prevent. The German Ambassador went so far as to inform his superiors in Berlin that as a result of the latest pogrom, 'the moral prestige of the ruling classes, who have shamelessly exploited the base instincts of the masses, will decline substantially'.[30] But within the diplomatic corps there was one notable exception. The Austro-

Hungarian Ambassador, Count Aloys Lexa von Aehrenthal, who never missed an opportunity to give vent to his anti-Semitic prejudices, continued to blame the Jews for the disorders in Bialystok. For good measure, he denounced the Jews in Russia and elsewhere for their revolutionary agitation and warned the Russian authorities not to extend equal rights to them. To place the '7–8 million' Jews on an equal footing with the rest of the population, which was 'culturally...on a very low level', would be tantamount to 'delivering the tsarist empire into the hands of the Alliance Israélite. There would then be no point to the Zionist movement; the chosen people would again have its own kingdom.'[31] In Aehrenthal's view, only by crushing the revolution could the Tsar prevent the 'total Judaization' of Russia.[32]

The rapid flow of information from Bialystok, from eyewitnesses, and from outsiders who had rushed to the scene, made it impossible for most diplomats and many others to hold on to their original assessments. Duma deputies, stunned by the initial reports from the city, immediately formed a committee to investigate the matter. On the evening of 2 June, the committeemen — Professor E. N. Shchepkin, a Kadet (member of the liberal Constitutional Democratic Party) from Odessa; M. P. Arakantsev, a Kadet from the Don Military District; and V. R. Iakubson, a Jewish member of the Trudovik, or labour party that favoured democratization of political institutions and the expropriation of privately owned lands from Grodno province — left for Bialystok to gather information on three questions: Who had initiated the pogrom? Why did it take place? How many casualties were there and how much property had been destroyed? The committee was to report back to the Duma within two or three days.[33]

Even before the committee completed its work, major newspapers carried detailed and accurate accounts on the events in Bialystok. At 1:00 p.m. on Thursday, 1 June, a religious procession of Catholics and Orthodox began to pass through the streets of the city, the former to celebrate Corpus Christi and the latter to mark the founding of the Orthodox cathedral. Many of the onlookers were surprised to see soldiers following the procession, interpreting it as an ominous sign. Suddenly revolver shots were heard, and shouts resounded: 'Beat the Jews!' The mêlée began immediately:

> First of all, the thugs flung themselves at Jewish hardware and armoury stores, pillaged them, beat everyone with axes, crowbars, [and] slabs of iron, and right away set out for the jewelry stores. The first blow was struck on Novo-Linsk Street. Here they entered and pillaged virtually all the stores and private homes. They broke the windows and doors, threw the furniture onto the streets; fluff poured out from the feather beds and pillows.

Not a single policeman could be seen, and all the soldiers who had a few minutes earlier filled the streets had vanished.

Within half an hour the plundering spread to other streets. Members of the Jewish self-defence units moved against the thugs with revolvers and knives, initiating a 'life and death' struggle. At this point dragoons appeared and fired ten to fifteen shots at Jews with weapons in their hands. 'The entire city looked like a battlefield.' Emboldened by the support of the soldiers, the *pogromshchiki* moved on to the bazaar in the centre of the city, where they continued to plunder and destroy everything they could lay their hands on. The soldiers and members of the self-defence units continued to exchange shots for much of the day, and toward evening the streets resembled 'a huge cemetery'. According to a newspaper reporter, 'What has happened is beyond comprehension. People have been transformed into wild beasts.' Even the wives of well-to-do gentiles were not ashamed to take part in sorting out the property that had been stolen and amassed in the streets. (To protect their own belongings, gentiles displayed icons in prominent places outside their residences.) 'In many places [in the non-Jewish areas of the city] the mood is festive. In clubs, people are playing cards, singing songs, and eating snacks.'[34] The carnage continued for three days, though the first day was by far the most violent.

It was not until the third day that the Minister of Internal Affairs, Stolypin, sent a telegram to all provincial governors and city mayors reminding them of their duty to suppress pogroms, whether directed at landlords or at Jews, 'with the most decisive measures'. Inaction or official connivance with the marauders would have the 'most serious consequences'.[35] By then Bialystok had been placed under martial law, and substantial military reinforcements had been sent to the city to maintain order. The full extent of the atrocities now became clear. A total of 169 shops and houses had been plundered, among them the largest stores in the city. Whatever merchandise the *pogromshchiki* could not carry off, they had destroyed on the spot. Trampled and scorched merchandise was piled up on the sidewalks. According to final estimates, at least 82 Jews and six non-Jews were killed, and some 700 Jews injured. Eight streets had been 'completely sacked', and total damages amounted to many hundreds of thousands of rubles.[36] Fearful of new outbursts of violence, masses of Jews left the city; by one estimate, three-quarters of the population had left by 6 June. 'At the railway station there are touching, heart-rending scenes. One is ashamed to acknowledge being a Russian. The situation of the poor, ruined people is horrible.'[37] The pain and rage of the Jews of Bialystok are poignantly reflected in the response of one of the widows when some Christians sent wreaths of flowers to be placed on the graves of Jews killed during the pogrom: 'We will not accept any flowers from killers.'[38]

For two weeks after the events in Bialystok, Jews in the surrounding area and in more distant places lived in a state of terror because of constant rumours that further pogroms were imminent. At least three did break out in Grodno province; the most serious was in Starosel'ts, where on 5 June some 50 Jews were murdered. In Saratov the Jewish community pleaded with the governor to take measures to prevent a pogrom. The governor assured a delegation of Jews that he would not allow attacks on them, and if a pogrom broke out, he would immediately stop it. In Brest-Litovsk, Zhitomir and Rostov-on-Don, officials issued special appeals to the population to remain calm and warned that disorders would be quickly quashed.[39]

In the meantime newspapers began to carry articles indicating that local officials and respected citizens in Bialystok had either inflamed the population against the Jews or actually participated in the looting. It turned out that the chief of police, a certain Sheremetev, who was considered the 'boss of the city', had openly denounced the Jews as 'bloodsuckers and robbers' and had urged that they be 'mercilessly exterminated'. Some time before the pogrom the Jews had sent a delegation to the governor of Grodno to request Sheremetev's dismissal. The governor responded that after the assassination of Sheremetev's predecessor, Sheremetev was the only person who could maintain order in the city. The governor had assured the delegation that he trusted the police chief and was confident there would not be a pogrom in Bialystok.[40] Professor Shchepkin told an overflow crowd at the Kadet club in St. Petersburg that he was convinced that low-ranking officials in Bialystok had organized the pogrom and that their superiors had looked the other way during the bloody attacks on Jews.[41] A senior official from the Ministry of Internal Affairs, E. V. Frish, who had also been sent to Bialystok to conduct an investigation, agreed that local bureaucrats and soldiers had indeed taken part in the rampage. Under Frish's directions, searches were conducted of private homes to locate the loot; some of the stolen merchandise was found in the residence of a local priest.[42] In late June a peasant arrested in the small town of Zabludov, not far from Bialystok, confessed that he had fired the shots at the religious procession to provoke the pogrom. He also confessed to having received a substantial sum of money to carry out the criminal act. He had gone to Zabludov to provoke another pogrom but was caught before he could once again carry out his 'dirty tricks'.[43]

The Duma devoted several sessions to the events in Bialystok, (and to other, earlier incidents of unrest), and the deliberations were among the stormiest in the history of the legislature. On 8 June Stolypin felt called upon to present the government's views on the pogrom. In his new position Stolypin was no longer as forceful in denouncing pogroms as he had been as governor of Saratov. To be sure, he tried to persuade the deputies that he would not tolerate illegal violence of any kind, and he conceded that mistakes had been made by local officials and local police officers. But he also insisted that most officials had faithfully carried out their obligations, and that many had 'died at their posts. From October [1905] until 20 April [1906], 288 of them had been killed and 383 injured, and in addition there were 156 unsuccessful attempts on their lives.' To the German Ambassador to St. Petersburg, it seemed that in citing these statistics, Stolypin was appealing to the deputies to be indulgent toward policemen who had sympathized with the *pogromshchiki*. The deputies, however, were not impressed by Stolypin's remarks and interrupted him with shouts of 'Enough' and with so much noise that at one point the Chairman of the Duma, S. A. Muromtsev, called for order. Nor were the deputies impressed by the lesson in political science that Stolypin delivered toward the end of his speech:

> One must not forget that governmental inaction leads to anarchy, that government is not an instrument designed for inaction or ingratiation. Government is an instrument of authority that rests on laws, from which it is clear that a minister should and will demand from his bureaucrats circumspection, caution, and justice, but [also] firm execution of [their] duty and of the law.[44]

One can hardly quarrel with Stolypin's views on the role of government, but in emphasizing this particular point during a debate of official malfeasance, which contributed to the massacre of dozens of innocent citizens, he gave the impression of gross insensitivity. Predictably, not many deputies were persuaded that he would take appropriate measures to prevent such outrages in the future.

As soon as Stolypin left the tribune, Prince S. D. Urusov, Assistant Minister of Internal Affairs for a few months in late 1905 and early 1906 and now a deputy and a member of the Party of Democratic Reform, delivered a speech which, according to the historian Bernard Pares, 'had a greater effect than any other in the First Duma'.[45] Pares did not exaggerate. Urusov, who spoke from firsthand experience, asserted flatly that senior officials, though not necessarily the government itself, played a decisive role in fomenting pogroms throughout 1905 and in the early months of 1906. To buttress his case, he pointed out that each outbreak followed a certain pattern:

> First, the massacre is always preceded by reports of its preparation, accompanied by the issue of inflammatory proclamations, which are uniform both as regards subject-matter and style. Secondly, when the massacre occurs, the facts which are officially stated to be its cause invariably prove to be false. Thirdly, the action of those who take part in the massacre reveals a certain organization, which deprives it of all accidental and elemental characteristics. Those who take part in the massacres act on the assumptions that they have the right to engage in the attacks and that they will not be punished; they continue acting [this way] till the assumptions are shaken; when that moment arrives the massacre ceases swiftly and easily...When the massacre is over, arrests are made, and the authorities who examine the culprits cannot help having the impression that those who have been brought before them are less like criminals than ignorant people who have been misled. Thus we feel that some kind of uniform and widely-planned organization exists.

Urusov went on to warn the deputies that even a government responsible to the Duma could not prevent outbreaks of mass violence unless it purged the entire state administration of the 'dark forces' that would stop at nothing to maintain the old order. 'Herein lies the great danger, and this danger will not disappear so long as in the direction of affairs and in the fortunes of our country we continue to feel the influence of men who have the education of policemen and sergeants, and are *pogromshchiki* on principle.'[46]

In the Duma the speech was received with 'endless and thunderous applause'. Delivered in a calm manner by a man known to be judicious and moderate, the indictment of the entire governmental machinery and the revelations of the brutality of high office-holders could not fail to make a deep impression on the opposition movement. In the words of the liberal newspaper *Russkie vedomosti*:

> After Prince Urusov's speech it has become clear that the question is not what kind of government will triumph, not what kind of policies to support: the question confronting us is the very existence of Russia. So long as power is in the hands of people 'who are policemen and sergeants by training and *pogromshchiki* by principle', no one can be confident that the entire country will not be inundated by blood, that the country will not be sacrificed for the sake of the triumph of police ideals.[47]

Senior officials at the tsarist court were stunned by Urusov's speech and devoted much time to discussing its ramifications.[48] It also made a strong impression in foreign capitals, most notably Berlin, Paris, and London.[49]

Returning to the dais to respond to criticisms leveled at the Ministry of Internal Affairs by Urusov — seconded by other deputies, who demanded that the ministry be thoroughly overhauled — Stolypin made two basic points. First, he had a clear conscience, since the excesses described by Urusov had been committed before he had taken charge of the ministry, and the 'bad' things that had happened would no longer occur, a comment that was interrupted by noise and shouts of: 'And the Bialystok pogrom?' Second, he rejected the notion that it was up to him to change the system of rule. As Stolypin left the chamber there was such an uproar that the Chairman of the Duma ordered a one-hour recess.[50]

Two weeks later, on 22 and 23 June, the Duma Committee of 33, formed to investigate the events in Bialystok after the three deputies returned from the scene of the pogrom, submitted its report. The committee concluded that the police had fostered hostility between the Christian and Jewish communities in Bialystok and had inspired local troops with hostility toward the Jews. Moreover, the committee insisted that the pogrom had been planned, and that the official reports on the violence were inaccurate. There could be no doubt that the 'conduct of the army and civil authorities constituted a clear violation of the law'.[51] The Duma then passed a motion to interpellate the Minister of Internal Affairs on the pogrom, but Stolypin refused to answer any further questions until his subordinates had completed their own investigation.

The Duma soon resumed deliberations on the violence. On 29 June, the Social Democratic deputy from Kutais Province, S. D. Dzhaparidze, introduced one of the more radical proposals for preventing pogroms in the future. The people could only protect their lives and property, Dzhaparidze declared, if they themselves were armed. Accordingly, the Duma should call on the people 'to take the defence of their lives into their own hands'. The Duma should also propose to the organs of local self-government and other public institutions that they help the people achieve that goal.[52] The Kadets, however, opted for a more moderate course, They introduced a resolution, adopted by the Duma on 7 July, demanding that everyone responsible for the violence in Bialystok be brought to justice, and that the government resign.[53] The resolution did not have the desired effect. The military command in Bialystok had already issued a statement (on 25 June) to the troops expressing gratitude to them 'for their glorious service, valour, self-sacrifice, [and] honourable and correct execution of their duty during the Bialystok pogrom'. Moreover, no charges were filed against Sheremetev, the police officer who had instigated the pogrom. He was merely transferred to

St. Petersburg. But in mid-1908, two years after the event the authorities pressed charges against 36 rioters. Several failed to show up in court, and fifteen were acquitted. Of the rest, one received a jail sentence of three years, and thirteen were given lighter sentences, ranging from six months to one year.[54]

One group of particularly zealous participants in the pogrom were made to pay for their crimes almost immediately, but only because of pressure from the local population. It turned out that many employees of the local tram system had been in the forefront of the violent attacks on Jews. The local organization of the Bund, which was very influential in the city, urged citizens to boycott the trams until the guilty men had been punished. On 6 June the trams passed through the city more than half empty, and twelve days later the administration dismissed 27 employees identified as *pogromshchiki*. The Bund then insisted that the names of the 27 be published in a local paper, a request to which the administration also acceded. At that point, on 18 June, the Bund lifted the boycott.[55]

• • •

Anti-Jewish pogroms during the first Russian Revolution were not confined to October 1905 and June 1906, but those two waves of mass violence were the most destructive and attracted the most attention in the press, among the political leadership, and in the international community.[56] Moreover, they evolved in a manner that seemed to be characteristic of all the pogroms. The top leaders of the government — the Tsar and his ministers — did not instigate the violence, though there can be little doubt that the ruler's well-known hostility toward the Jews was interpreted by lower ranking officials and ordinary people as licence for attacks on a group widely held to be an alien element in Russian society. The evidence is conclusive that on the local level officials often played a significant role in planning pogroms and an even more significant role in allowing pogroms to continue for a few days by looking the other way once the violence had started.

But in the last analysis the outbursts of raw passion against the Jews were rooted in profound resentments against a minority that remained unassimilated religiously and culturally and that was seen as a social and political threat during a period of great social and political upheaval. To be sure, many *pogromshchiki* were tempted by the chance to loot with impunity and to destroy the Jewish merchants, who were viewed as exploiters or as economic competitors. Pogroms had, after all, erupted in Russia periodically even during times of relative political calm. But those attacks on Jews were not as widespread, bloody and destructive as the pogroms of 1905 and 1906. The point is that the especially virulent attacks on Jews at the time of the first Russian revolution broke out during periods when the old order was under acute pressure, when, in fact, it seemed to be unable to contain the opposition: first in October 1905, precisely at the moment when the Tsar had been coerced into making his most far-reaching concession to the opposition; second, in June 1906, when the elected Duma, composed overwhelmingly of deputies representing political parties opposed to the autocracy, was making a concerted effort to democratize the country's political system. Moreover, it was widely believed that had that effort succeeded, the Jews would have been granted rights of citizenship equal to those of other citizens of the empire. It was also widely known that Jews, for obvious reasons, strongly supported various liberal and radical parties (in particular the Kadets and the Social Democrats) and this only exacerbated the hatred for them by the defenders of the old regime. In frustration, local officials and ordinary people devoted to the autocracy vented their anger on the Jews, the most inviting target not only because they were defenceless but also because in many minds they had come to symbolize an undesirable and corrosive element in society. It was the first but not the last time in the twentieth century that Jews would come under attack during periods of acute social and political crisis.

NOTES

1. R. Kantor, 'Aleksandr III o evreiskikh pogromakh', *Evreiskaia letopis'*, I (1923), pp. 149–58; Hans Rogger, *Jewish Policies and Right-Wing Politics in Imperial Russia* (Berkeley/Los Angeles: University of California Press, 1986), pp. 29–30; I. Michael Aronson, *Troubled Waters: The Origins of the 1881 Anti-Jewish Pogroms in Russia* (Pittsburgh: University of Pittsburgh Press, 1990).
2. *Agrarnoe dvizhenie v Rossii v 1905–1906 gg.* (St. Petersburg, 1908), Vol. I, pp. 48, 77; Vol. II, p. 290; W. D. Preyer, *Die russische Agrarreform* (Jena: Fischer, 1914), pp. 100–101.
3. Abraham Ascher, *The Revolution of 1905: Russia in Disarray* (Stanford: Stanford University Press, 1988), pp. 43–242. On the first outbreak of anti-Jewish violence, see pp. 130–1.
4. *Syn otechestva*, 23 Oct. 1905, p. 1.
5. Ibid., 24 Oct. 1905, p. 2.
6. Heinz-Dietrich Löwe, *Antisemitismus und reaktionäre Utopie: Russischer Konservatismus im Kampf gegen die Wandel von Staat und Gesellschaft* (Hamburg: Hoffman and Campe, 1978), p. 87. The most comprehensive account of the anti-Jewish pogroms may be found in A. Linden, *Die Judenpogrome in Russland* (Cologne and Leipzig: Jüdischer Verlag GmbH, 1910).
7. For contemporary descriptions of how the pogroms began in various regions, see *Rus'*, 22 Oct. 1905, p. 4; 23 Oct., pp. 1, 2; 28 Oct., p. 1.
8. *Russkie vedomosti*, 22 Oct., 1905, p. 2.
9. L. Martov, P. P. Maslov and A. N. Potresov (eds.), *Obshchestvennoe dvizhenie v Rossii v nachale XX-go veka* (St. Petersburg: Obshchestvennaia pol'za, 1909–14), Vol. II, Part 1, p. 101.

10. This view is also held by some historians. Louis Greenberg, for example, wrote without supporting evidence that 'the emperor and his camarilla had decided to crush the revolutionary spirit by diverting it toward bloody attacks upon the Jews'. Louis Greenberg, *The Jews of Russia* (New Haven: Yale University Press, 1951), Vol. II, p. 76.
11. *Russkie vedomosti*, 22 Oct. 1905, p. 3.
12. *Syn otechestva*, 13 Nov. 1905, p. 5.
13. Ibid., 17 Nov. 1905, p. 4; Löwe, Antisemitismus, p. 92.
14. *Syn otechestva*, 25 Nov. 1905, p. 4; Linden, *Die Judenpogrome*; French Consul in Odessa to Paris, 7 Nov. 1905, Archives du Ministère des Affaires Etrangères. Russie: Direction Politique, nouvelle serie, Paris, Vol. II. For more details on the complicity of senior officials in the pogroms, see Ascher, *Russia in Disarray*, p. 258.
15. Edward J. Bing (ed.), *The Secret Letters of the Last Tsar* (New York, Longmans, Green & Co., 1938), pp. 187–8.
16. British Embassy in St. Petersburg to London, 28 Feb. 1906, British Documents on Foreign Affairs, Public Record Office, London FO 181/869; Howard D. Mehlinger and John M. Thompson, *Count Witte and the Tsarist Government in the 1905 Revolution* (Bloomington: Indiana University Press, 1972), pp. 64, 359; S. Iu. Vitte, *Vospominaniia* (Leningrad: Gosudarstvennoe izdatel'stvo, 1924), Vol. II, pp. 67–70; Maurice Baring, *A Year in Russia* (London: Methuen, 1907), pp. 250–7.
17. *Rus'*, 23 Oct. 1905, p. 1.
18. *Russkie vedomosti*, 2 Oct. 1905, p. 2.
19. Löwe, *Antisemitismus*, pp. 96, 243.
20. Ibid., p. 96.
21. Martov, Obshchestvennoe dvizhenie, p. 104.
22. *Russkie vedomosti*, 22 Oct. 1905, p. 1.
23. *Rus'*, 30 Oct. 1905, p. 1.
24. *Syn otechestva*, 23 Oct., 1905, p. 1.
25. On the right-wing organizations, see Ascher, *Russia in Disarray*, pp. 238–42.
26. Löwe, *Antisemitismus*, p. 90; *Rus'*, 22 Oct. 1905, p. 3.
27. German Consulate in Moscow to Berlin, 8 Nov. 1905, Politisches Archiv des Auswärtigen Amts (PAAA), Abteilung A, Russland, Bonn.
28. Sidney Harcave, *First Blood: The Russian Revolution of 1905* (New York, Macmillan, 1964), p. 205.
29. *Rech'*, 4 June 1906, p. 3.
30. US Embassy in St. Petersburg to Washington, 16 June, 23 June 1906, US Dispatches from US Ministers to Russia, 1808–1906, National Archives, Washington, DC; German Embassy in St. Petersburg to Berlin, 18, 19, 20 June 1906, PAAA; French Foreign Ministry to French Embassy in St. Petersburg, 11 June 1906, Archives du Ministère des Affaires Etrangères. Russie: Direction Politique, nouvelle serie, Paris.
31. The Alliance Israélite Universelle, the first international Jewish organization in modern times for the protection of Jewish rights, was founded in France in 1860. The Alliance set itself the task of defending the rights and honour of Jews everywhere, of improving the cultural and social status of backward Jewish communities and of helping the Jewish population in underdeveloped countries to become more productive.
32. Austro-Hungarian Embassy in St. Petersburg to Vienna, 22 June 1906, Haus-Hof-und-Staatsarchiv, Russland, Berichte, Vienna.
33. *Nasha zhizn'*, 4 June 1906, p. 4.
34. *Rech'*, 6 June 1906, p. 3; *Nasha zhizn'*, 6 June 1906, p. 2.
35. *Russkie vedomosti*, 6 June 1906, p. 2.
36. *American Jewish Year Book* (Philadelphia: Jewish Publication Society of America, 1906–7), pp. 64–5; *Russkie vedomosti*, 6 June 1906, p. 3; 14 June, p. 2; *Rech'*, 6 June 1906, pp. 2, 3; 13 June p. 2; 15 June, p. 3; *Nasha zhizn'*, 15 June 1906, p. 3. There are different estimates of the number of victims; according to some sources, 200 Jews were killed.
37. *Rech'*, 7 June 1906, p. 3.
38. *Rech'*, June 6, 1906, p. 3.
39. *Nasha zhizn'*, 15 June 1906, p. 3; *Rech'*, 6 June 1906, pp. 2, 3; 13 June, p. 2; *Russkie vedomosti*, 14 June 1906, p. 2.

40. *Rech'*, 6 June 1906, p. 3.
41. *Russkie vedomosti*, 10 June 1906, p. 4.
42. *Rech'*, 10 June 1906, p. 2.
43. *Pravo*, 25 June 1906, col. 2250.
44. Gosudarstvennaia Duma, *Stenograficheskie otchety, 1906 god* (St. Petersburg, 1906), Vol. II, pp. 1129–32; German Embassy in St. Petersburg to Berlin, 25 June, PAAA.
45. Bernard Pares, *My Russian Memoirs* (London: J. Cape, 1931), p. 119.
46. Gosudarstvennaia Duma, *Stenograficheskie otchety*, pp. 1129–32. I have used (with some minor emendations) the translation of the speech in Baring, A Year in Russia, pp. 250–7.
47. *Russkie vedomosti*, 9 June 1906, p. 1.
48. *Rech'*, 10 June 1906, p. 3.
49. *Rech'*, 7 June 1906, pp. 3, 4; 11 June, p. 2.
50. Gosudarstvennaia Duma, *Stenograficheskie otchety*, p. 1141.
51. Ibid., p. 1596.
52. Ibid., p. 1825.
53. S. M. Sidel'nikov, *Obrazovanie i deiatel'nost' pervoi Gosudarstvennoi dumy* (Moscow: Moscow University, 1962), pp. 272–3.
54. Gosudarstvennaia Duma, *Stenograficheskie otchety*, p. 1775; Sidel'nikov, Obrazovanie i deiatel'nost', p. 273; German Consul in Kovno to Berlin, 27 June 1908, PAAA.
55. *Rech'*, 18 June 1906, p. 4; *Nasha zhizn'*, 7 June 1906, p. 4; 20 June p. 4.
56. For information on other pogroms in the years from 1905 to 1907, see Ascher, *Russia in Disarray*, pp. 130–1 and Ascher, *The Revolution of 1905: Authority Restored* (Stanford: Stanford University Press, 1992), pp. 327–8; see also Shlomo Lambroza, 'The Pogroms of 1903–1906' in John D. Klier and Shlomo Lambroza (eds.), *Pogroms: Anti-Jewish Violence in Modern Russian History* (Cambridge: Cambridge University Press, 1992), pp. 195–247. This excellent article discusses in detail the pogroms that broke out in the years from 1881 to 1919. Particularly relevant to the theme of this chapter, in addition to Lambroza's article, is Robert Weinberg, 'The Pogrom of 1905 in Odessa: A Case Study', pp. 248–89.

8

Russian Jewry as the 'Little Nation' of the Russian Revolution

JOHN D. KLIER

In 1989 I. R. Shafarevich published an essay, 'Russophobia', which he had written a decade earlier. As a member of the Soviet Academy of Sciences, a world-famous scientist and a respected dissident who had co-edited *From Under the Rubble* with Aleksandr Solzhenitsyn, Shafarevich's views attracted attention. This was even more the case, because his general comments on the enemies of Russian nationalism, the Russophobes, contained a specific attack upon the Jews as the special embodiment of anti-Russian antipathy.

In his writings, Shafarevich borrowed from the 19th century French historian Augustin Cochin the concept of the 'little nation', a self-contained band of intellectuals which is alienated from the broader culture surrounding it, and which serves as a revolutionary ferment within society. In pre-revolutionary France, the 'little nation' comprised the Masonic lodges, which created their own, anti-national culture. They repudiated the foundations of French nationality: the Roman Catholic religion, aristocratic honour, loyalty to the monarchy, pride in the history of France and loyalty to class and family.

Shafarevich contends that the 'little nation' is a universal phenomenon, and identifies analogies throughout modern history: the Puritans in the English Revolution of the 17th century; the Left-Hegelians and 'Young Germany' in post-Napoleonic Germany; the liberal and nihilist movements in pre-revolutionary Russia. The Russophobes are the contemporary 'little nation' in Russia where, 'born émigrés' themselves, they sully the collective Russian soul.[1]

The distinctive aspect of contemporary Russophobes, contends Shafarevich, is their Jewish spirit. This spirit played a disastrous role in

146

Russia's 'great crisis' of 1917. While Shafarevich explicitly denies that the Jews were responsible for the Russian Revolution or its Stalinist aftermath, he marshals his evidence in such a way as to argue this precise claim. Ironically, Shafarevich employs these tactics in an essay in which he complains of the tendentious attacks by some historians and critics against the Russian national character and its messianic pretensions.

Shafarevich concedes that Jews played no part in Russian public life before the 1880s, isolated as they were in their closed religious communities. He argues that at the end of the century, as the traditionalist community began to disintegrate, Jews flooded into Russia's economic, political and cultural life. In numbers quite disproportionate to their size, they played a preponderant role in movements hostile to the existing order, as liberal critics of the autocracy, Marxists or active exponents of revolutionary terrorism. This process accelerated after the revolution, and Shafarevich asserts that Jews were closely involved in the breakdown of Russia's traditions: they commanded the firing squad which executed the last tsar and his family; they dominated the Cheka; they participated in the destruction of the Russian peasantry; they provided the secret police cadres who established the GULAG.[2]

According to Shafarevich, Russian revolutionaries carried a deep love for Russia in their hearts, while the Jewish attitude towards Russia was expressed in the curse 'Rot, damn you!' The contrast is explained by the absence of ties between Jews and the Russian people. The Jews were indifferent to the degradation and destruction of Old Russia. They maintained their feeling of superiority, their sense of being a chosen people, destined to dominate the rest of mankind. The Talmud and the religious traditions of Judaism inculcated in the Jewish mind the belief that gentiles were not even human. The Jews had developed a 'saving hatred' towards the outside world which preserved them as a people for two thousand years, and made them into a relentless and implacable enemy. It is this spirit, contends Shafarevich, which inspires contemporary Russophobia. He concludes, therefore, that the Jewish 'little nation' is unique: it has existed for two millennia, surpassing in durability and malevolence all other variants of this phenomenon.[3]

Shafarevich's allegations offer nothing new: they fit comfortably into a long tradition of accusations that Jews and Judaism are ferments which cause the disintegration of society, wage war against Christian civilization and provide a natural environment for the growth of revolutionary socialism. Some observers have even viewed the alleged propensity of Jews for revolution in a positive light. A good example is

Isaac Deutscher's concept of the 'non-Jewish Jew', the Jew who has abandoned the religious world-view of Judaism — symbolically becoming a heretic to the community of faith while continuing to display the influence of the Jewish tradition. According to Deutscher, Jews in history were always a priori exceptional, because

> they dwelt on the borderlines of various civilizations, religions and national cultures...Their mind matured where the most diverse cultural influences crossed and fertilized each other. They lived on the margins or in the nooks and crannies of their respective nations. Each of them was in society and yet not in it, of it and yet not of it. It was this that enabled them to rise in thought above their societies, above their nations, above their times and generations, and to strike out mentally into wide new horizons and far into the future.[4]

Deutscher contended that revolutionaries of Jewish origin as diverse as Spinoza, Marx, Heine, Trotsky, Rosa Luxemburg and Freud, shared certain features of 'Jewish' thought. They were all determinists who thought in a dialectical manner, because their experience with many nations and societies allowed them to grasp the basic regularities of life, even while life on the periphery revealed to them that society was in a state of flux. The diversity to which they had been witness provided them with an appreciation of the relativity of moral standards. They all agreed that in order for knowledge to be real it must be active. (Compare Spinoza's dictum that 'to be is to do and to know is to do', and Marx's call for philosophers to change, rather than interpret the world.) Finally, all Jewish revolutionaries believe in the ultimate solidarity of man.[5]

The archetype of the non-Jewish Jew is Karl Marx, and an extensive literature exists which links his thought to his Jewishness. As Mikhail Bakunin crudely put it:

> Marx is a Jew by birth. He combines within his person all the advantages and disadvantages of this gifted race. Fearful to the point of cowardice — as some maintain — he is unbelievably vicious, vain, quarrelsome, as intolerant and domineering as the God of his fathers and like him, vengeful to the point of insanity. There is no lie, no treachery, which he would not be capable of using against those who have incurred his jealousy or his hate.[6]

Another Russian, Nikolai Berdiaev, put it more sympathetically:

> Marx was a Jew; he had abandoned the faith of his fathers, but the messianic expectation of Israel remained in his subconsciousness. The subconscious is always stronger than the conscious, and for him the proletariat is the new Israel, God's chosen people, the liberator and builder of an earthly kingdom that is to come. His proletarian communism is a secularized form of ancient Jewish chiliasm.[7]

148

For many, indeed, the atheist Marx remains an 'Old Testament prophet'.

A blend of racism and philosophical flights of fancy are required to explain the activities of revolutionary Jews based on their Jewishness alone. Such explanations contain logical flaws relating both to the general (Judaism) and the specific (the individual revolutionary). First and foremost is the problem of Judaism itself. For example, the dilettantish characterization of Judaism offered by Shafarevich is analogous to a description of 'Christianity' which fails to differentiate between the views of the Early Church Fathers and later Church doctrines, or which ignores differences between the Catholic, Orthodox and Protestant traditions.

Portraying Judaism in the broad and sweeping terms favoured by critics like Shafarevich involves oversimplification and vulgarization of the entire Jewish tradition. Such views assume that the Judaism of the Old Testament, of the Midrash and the Talmud, of the Hasidim and Mitnagdim, of the rabbinic and Karaite traditions, of the Ashkenazi and Sephardi rites, is a uniform system. These critics equate the attitudes of the Jews of Muslim Spain towards their neighbours with those of Jewish victims of Christian Spain's Inquisition. They pretend that there is no difference between Moses, Moses Maimonides and Moses Mendelssohn. In fact, to pose the question of what is 'real', or 'normative' in Judaism is to enter a two-thousand-year-old debate.

Yet complexity does not prevent dilettantes from finding in this vast tradition exactly what they require to serve their polemical needs. Let one example serve for all: that of the 'messianic tradition', so often cited by the likes of Shafarevich, who contends that the idea of 'chosenness' and messianism are the foundations of Judaism — and the State of Israel.[8] Robert Wistrich rightly reminds us that these concepts were often in direct opposition to one another, that 'the universalist thrust of prophetic Judaism always co-existed in a polarized tension with belief in the chosenness of Israel, its particular mission among the nations'.[9]

Shafarevich's sweeping generalizations are likewise unsatisfactory (recalling his earlier efforts in *From Under the Rubble* to demonstrate that the concept of socialism was an expression of the Freudian death wish).[10] He fails to explain why those Jews most closely tied to the Talmud and ritual observance were precisely those who invoked the dictum of *dina demalkhuta dina* (the king's law is law) and supported the regime under which they lived, either through political passivity or outright opposition to secular Jewish activism. Indeed, defenders of the Jews in the nineteenth century argued that, far from bringing something malevolent and 'Jewish' into the revolutionary movement, Jews venturing into the Russian milieu were infected by values that transformed them into assimilationist liberals or revolutionary terrorists.[11]

In fact, we need not rely upon mystical explanations, or invocation of a 'saving hatred', to explain Jewish involvement in the revolutionary movement, especially if we consider the parallel examples of the Poles and Finns. No serious scholar denies that Polish nationalism and political frustration often expressed themselves in dissidence and revolutionary activity (although here too there is much idle talk about 'Polish messianism'). Russian imperial policy transformed the Finns from peaceful subjects into a nation of dissidents, who applauded acts of political terrorism. It is not surprising that *rekhtlozikeyt* (denial of civil rights) or the frustrations felt by Jewish student youth over thwarted careers, gave rise to political dissidence. Tsarist officials certainly thought it did, for they often cited Jewish rightlessness in their analyses of Jewish revolutionary activism.

The revolutionary movement was strongest in urban areas of the empire, where the traumas of modernization and industrialization were most keenly felt. Many of these growth centres were located in the Jewish Pale of Settlement. No great imagination is needed to explain why there were large numbers of Jewish revolutionaries from (as well as in) Odessa, Vilna, Minsk and Warsaw. Nor is it surprising that Russian universities turned out Jewish revolutionaries in the same large numbers as they created their gentile comrades. This comradeship and absence of prejudice among revolutionaries, incidentally, was one of the principal features that drew Jews into the movement, as all the memoir literature attests. The revolutionary movement was the one area of Russian society where Jews were accepted as equals.

Shafarevich complains that Jews played a preponderant role in 'movements hostile to the existing order'. It must be remembered, however, how little choice was open to those discriminated against and excluded from society by the old order which — the 'patriotic' Shafarevich apparently forgets — failed the ultimate test of protecting and preserving the Russian state. (The Russo-Japanese war, which undermined the foundations of the state, was caused not by the revolutionary movement but by a series of diplomatic blunders.) Moreover, it was the strategy of the tsarist Okhrana to lump together all forms of protest, from the liberal 'liberation movement', to the SDs and the SRs, and treat them all as equally hostile to the old order. What other strategy could have made comrades-in-arms of Lenin and Struve?

As for the leadership of the Russian Jewish community — the Gintsburgs, Poliakovs, and Varshavskiis — it was as hostile to movements of dissent within Russian Jewry as to those in society at large. It opposed not only Marxism and populism, but Zionism and bundism as well.

Moreover, how would it have been possible for Jews to participate in the conservative movements assembled to protect the old order? These movements, almost without exception, equated all Jews with socialism and relied upon anti-Jewish pogroms as a weapon of political mobilization. Essential ingredients of the conservative ideology included the fantasy of the 'international Jewish *kahal*', represented by the *Protocols of the Elders of Zion*, as well as the Blood Libel, exemplified by the Beilis Affair.

Why dwell on an essay which must surely be viewed as a polemic, rather than an objective historical study? The problem of such sensationalist works is that they obscure what are in fact a range of legitimate scholarly questions, for we certainly must not disguise the quantitative participation of Jews in oppositionary movements, nor their ideological contribution to such diverse ideologies as labour Zionism, bundism, menshevism and bolshevism. We must not be afraid to ask what factors encouraged the Jews to enter the Russian revolutionary movement. (Some answers to this question have been given above.) What cultural values, what aspects of 'Jewishness' did Jews bring into Russian political life at the end of the nineteenth century? These questions have already produced an extensive scholarly literature in the West. This chapter will briefly survey the state of contemporary research, focusing on the work of three scholars: Erich Haberer, Jonathan Frankel and Robert Brym.

Erich Haberer, in a doctoral dissertation and forthcoming book, has addressed the question of the Jewish contribution to the revolutionary movement in general, and populism in particular (the latter a movement not usually thought to have been receptive to Jews). Haberer, like Shafarevich, takes the disintegration of the traditionalist community as his starting point. He attributes this process to the dual elements of the Haskala, the Jewish version of the European-wide Enlightenment movement, and the socio-economic changes engendered by the Alexandrine reforms. The Haskala challenged the old traditional norms, and sought a goal akin to radical assimilationism. However, Russian society refused to reciprocate, and the process foundered. Consequently, the identity of many young Jews was brought into question, without the existence of a suitable alternative vision. Accompanying this existential dilemma was the secularization and economic change which typified the Reform Era (1856–1881) and made a return to the old ways impossible.

Seeking a common denominator amidst the bewildering welter of ideas offered by a reading of Kant, Pisarev, Belinskii, Mill, Chernyshevskii and others, young Jews, like many of their gentile counterparts, arrived at the fashionable ideas of socialism. This movement provided a new, secular belief system, as well as a sense of purpose. Joining the revolutionary 'church' solved the existential dilemma, and brought them into a brotherhood with 'the cream of the generation, the salt of the earth, the best children Russia ever gave birth to'.[12]

A number of assumptions have been made about the cadres of Jews who entered the revolutionary movement. Foremost is the contention, popularized especially by Lev Deich and accepted by many others, that revolutionaries submerged all trace of their Jewishness in a set of 'universal principles' founded on extreme assimilationism and cosmopolitanism.

Haberer argues to the contrary, that there were distinct Jewish elements in the movement, even in populism, whose peasant-centred romanticism is usually considered not to Jewish tastes. While Haberer concedes that these distinctive Jewish elements were 'set in a populist ideological context and reflected Russian socio-political reality', he nonetheless urges us to recognize their existence, disputing the long-accepted denial by Leonard Schapiro that 'specifically Jewish motives activated these revolutionaries...[whose] whole mode of action and thought became assimilated to a specifically Russian form and tradition'.[13]

Haberer reminds us that even Russian populism was far from being a monolithic ideology, and argues that at least one Jew, Mark Natanson, must be considered one of its 'founding fathers'. Haberer demonstrates the distinctive westernizing influence which Natanson and many of his Jewish comrades brought into the movement: a 'Jewish' cosmopolitanism, a western political sense (that is, respect for German social democracy) and a political minimalism, all of which he contrasts with 'Russian' particularism, romantic peasantism and social revolutionary maximalism.[14] The infiltration of these ideas from the western socialist tradition, argues Haberer, equipped populism for ideological survival, giving it organizational principles which allowed it to propagandize and expand. At the same time, these elements made possible the subsequent evolution of the movement, as well as the gestation within it of adherents of the new, Russian, social democratic movement.

We might explicitly note here the discrepancy between the interpretations of Haberer and Shafarevich. Both acknowledge the impact of the new upon the traditional Jewish community, and both contend that Jews, fleeing the wreckage of the past, carried elements of 'Jewishness' into the revolutionary movement. For Shafarevich the chief element was the Jews' 'saving hatred', which distorted the ideals of the revolution and made it 'Russophobic'. Haberer argues, quite to the contrary, that the Jewish element made the movement less narrow and particularistic, more humane and cosmopolitan.

Jonathan Frankel's magisterial study, *Prophecy and Politics*, also focuses on the crisis of the Jewish community, torn by overpopulation, underemployment, poverty, pogroms and legal discrimination, and massive emigration. In response, the Russian-Jewish intelligentsia created a whole range of post-liberal politics and ideologies. Of course, intellectuals from every ethnic and national community were grappling with the challenges of modernization and change. Jews faced a double challenge, however, because for them change was accompanied by a search for a new, modern Jewish identity. Frankel characterizes this as a 'double alienation' — Russian Jewish intellectuals were both estranged from and drawn to their own nationality, while also attracted to either Russian or universalist political philosophies. This situation produced a whole range of questions touching on ethnic identification, language use, loyalty to nationality/ethnos versus commitment to cosmopolitan ideals. Politically, there was a choice of strategies: revolution or exodus. Even here, every choice provoked a further dilemma: did opting for revolution exclude the need for a Jewish political organization, or discourage the pursuit of specifically national rights? According to what national principles, if any, was the new revolutionary order to be organized?

If exodus was the preferred solution, where was safety to be sought? In Palestine? America? Argentina? Or even Uganda? Did a commitment to emigration logically preclude participation in Russian revolutionary politics?[15]

A multiplicity of questions spawned a multiplicity of responses. This was accentuated because of a unique feature of Jewish life in the Russian empire: a bipolar system with Jewish nationalism at one extreme, and socialist internationalism at the other. In a dialectical fashion, a third force arose, that of Jewish socialism. In all its myriad forms — the Bund, Poalei-Tsion, the Seimisty (SERP), the Zionist Socialists (SS) — Jewish socialism existed in a continuous tension. Depending upon the realities of the moment, it was pulled first in one direction, then in the other. (And even while emphasizing Jewish socialism, another recent study reminds us not to neglect the fledgling Jewish liberal movement, represented by the Union for the Attainment of Full and Equal Rights for the Jews of Russia, as well as the Jewish membership of the Constitutional Democratic Party.)[16] In contrast to Shafarevich, Frankel demonstrates that there was no one 'Jewish' response to the Russian revolution, but a diverse and bewildering variety.

If Haberer and Frankel are primarily concerned with the Jewish influence upon the Russian revolutionary movement, Robert Brym approaches the problem from a sociological point of view. His concern is why, when offered a variety of ideologies, Russian Jews chose to commit themselves to one or another party. He seeks the answer in an analysis of the social conditions underlying the 'ideological directions' taken by Russian-Jewish intellectuals. These directions, he argues, came not from some internal Jewish drive, but in response to socio-economic forces which formed the context of their daily lives.

The starting point is again the disruption of traditional modes of life as emergent capitalism produced greater and more varied contacts between Jews and gentiles. Consequently, Jews began to integrate structurally, and therefore ideologically, into the non-Jewish environment. Brym argues that since these forces were in flux, even Jews from the same family displayed different degrees of 'embeddedness' in the community (that is, varying degrees of Jewish identity). The changing economic environment, and the acidic impact of the Haskala on traditional practice and belief, caused some Jews to become completely estranged from the community (a process Brym calls de-identification). De-identified Jewish intellectuals, in the main, sought to find a place in the Russian middle class (to embed), but were blocked by social and legal obstacles to Jewish upward mobility in tsarist Russia. They responded, Brym contends, by forging concrete social ties with the working class (subject to a wide degree of regional and occupational variation). This produced a re-identification with the working class, seen as the entity best able to give vent to discontent. The degree of Jewish embeddedness, Brym argues, accounts in the main for the tendency to re-embed in the socialist movement along a continuum (Poalei-Tsion, Bund, Menshevik, Bolshevik) moving from more to less Jewish.[17]

Brym himself admits that his analysis may be faulted as over-mechanistic, as 'emphasizing context at the expense of creativity', and it will certainly be familiar to an audience nurtured on dialectical materialism. He justifies himself by the need to provide a corrective to what he sees as the overall neglect of the social context of the Russian intelligentsia. He characterizes his own work as not only a corrective, but as a plea for further research.[18] In light of the fact that the fantasies of Igor Shafarevich, among others, have gained such widespread acceptance, this is an appeal which we ought not ignore.

Perhaps the classic statement of the ambivalence of Russian Jewry towards the revolution appears in Isaak Babel's *Red Cavalry*. The narrator, the archetype of the active Jewish revolutionary, seeks to justify the violence of the revolution to the *shtetl* Jew. '"It cannot do without shooting, Ghedali", I tell the old man, "because it is the Revolution".' Ghedali replies: 'But the Poles, kind Pan, shoot because they were the counter-Revolution. You shoot because you are the Revolution. But surely the Revolution means joy. And joy does not like orphans in the home.'

Ghedali dreams of an International of 'good people'.

> 'I would like every soul to be taken into account and given first- category rations. There, soul, please eat and enjoy life's pleasures. Pan comrade, you don't know what the International is eaten with.'
>
> 'It is eaten with powder', I answered the old man, 'and flavoured with the best blood.'[19]

Who is the authentic voice of Russian Jewry in this exchange? Is it Ghedali whose messianic dreams encompass both Jew and gentile? Can it be Babel's ironic narrator, who proposes a blood-flavoured dish which openly violates the basic tenets of *kashrut*? It is a complex but fundamental question which, not surprisingly, Shafarevich and his acolytes do not even attempt to answer.

NOTES

1. I. R. Shafarevich, *Rusofobiia. Dve dorogi — k odnomu obryvu* (Moscow: Tovarishchestvo russkikh khudozhnikov, 1991), pp. 33–45.
2. Ibid., pp. 71–81.
3. Ibid., pp. 81–90.
4. Isaac Deutscher, *The Non-Jewish Jew and Other Essays* (Oxford: Oxford University Press, 1968), p. 27.
5. Ibid., pp. 35–6.
6. Julius Carlebach, *Karl Marx and the Radical Critique of Judaism* (London: Routledge and Kegan Paul, 1968), pp. 310–33.
7. Robert S. Wistrich, *Revolutionary Jews from Marx to Trotsky* (London: Harrap, 1976), p. 4.
8. Shafarevich, *Rusofobiia*, pp. 57–8. Indeed, we might also note the popularity of the theme of chosenness in official Soviet propaganda.
9. Wistrich, *Revolutionary Jews*, p. 4.
10. M. S. Agurskii, *et al.*, *Iz-pod glyb: sbornik statei* (Paris: YMCA-Press, 1974), pp. 29–72.

11. N. T., 'V kamere prokurora. Rasskaz s natury', *Vestnik Evropy* XII (December, 1880), pp. 494–509.
12. Abe Kahan quoted in Erich E. Haberer, 'The Role of Jews in Russian Revolutionary Populism, 1868–1887', unpublished doctoral diss., Toronto, 1990, p. 691.
13. Leonard Schapiro, 'The Role of the Jews in the Russian Revolutionary Movement', *Slavonic and East European Review*, XL (1961–62), pp. 148–67.
14. Haberer, 'The Role of Jews', p. 462.
15. Jonathan Frankel, *Prophecy and Politics: Socialism, Nationalism, and the Russian Jews, 1862–1917* (Cambridge, Cambridge University Press, 1981), pp. 3–4.
16. Christoph Gassenschmidt, 'Jewish Liberal Politics in Tsarist Russia, 1900–1914: The Modernization of Russian Jewry', unpublished doctoral diss., Oxford, 1993.
17. Robert J. Brym, *The Jewish Intelligentsia and Russian Marxism. A Sociological Study of Intellectual Radicalism and Ideological Divergence* (London: Macmillan, 1978), pp. 73–110.
18. Ibid., p. 117.
19. Isaac Babel, *Red Cavalry.* Trans. John Harland (London: A. A. Knopf, 1929), pp. 47–8.

9

The Doctors' Plot:
The Non-Jewish Response

ALEXANDER LOKSHIN

On 4 April 1953, the USSR Ministry of the Interior released a statement exonerating all physicians accused in the Doctor's Plot. It declared that 'all the charges brought against the medical doctors have been proven false and all the physicians have been fully rehabilitated'.[1] On 6 April *Pravda*'s editorial, entitled 'Soviet Socialist Legality Is Inviolable' pointed out that the Doctors' Plot had been 'designed to fan national animosity'[2] but failed to mention the nationality in question.

These announcements officially put an end to the most vehement anti-Jewish campaign of the Stalin regime — one that might well have become a prelude to the 'final solution of the Jewish question' in the USSR.

The present chapter examines the reaction of various elements of the population at large to the information that the Doctors' Plot had been a fabrication and that all the accused were completely innocent. An examination of this subject will help to convey the social and political atmosphere in which Soviet Jews found themselves in the spring of 1953, immediately prior to and in the first few weeks following Stalin's death.

Recent memoirs contain various information about the reaction of different social groups to the sudden release of the 'doctor-killers'. Notable in this regard are the reminiscences of Yakov Rapoport[3], Ester Markish[4] and Zinovii Sheinis.[5] A fairly typical feature can be found in Sheinis' recollections. On that memorable day, he writes:

> Janitors gathered outside the entrance to our housing complex. A neighbour of mine who lived in the same building...stood in the middle. When she saw me, she started waving a newspaper and said to the janitors in a loud voice so that I could hear her: 'He is a good man. They are all good people.'[6]

Additional sources have now become available. The Interior Ministry statement and the article in the official organ of the Communist Party triggered an avalanche of readers' letters to *Pravda*'s editorial offices. They came from Jews and non-Jews alike. The most typical letters were summarized in the form of digests and, after being signed by *Pravda* editor-in-chief Dmitrii Shepilov and marked 'classified', were dispatched to Nikita Khrushchev personally, at the CPSU Central Committee Secretariat. These digests were intended 'to make the rounds', of the Central Committee secretaries. Signatures of CC secretaries Mikhail Suslov, Petr Pospelov and N. N. Shatalin as well as notes in the margins indicate that they were indeed read.

Two digests of letters concerning the reaction of the population to the closing of the doctors' case are currently accessible to researchers. Dated 9 and 13 April 1953, these digests include full or excerpted texts of letters by the 'working people'. They are housed at the Centre for the Preservation of Contemporary Documents (TsKhSD) created early in 1992 and comprising the archives of the Central Committees of the CPSU and RSFSR apparatus which were previously inaccessible to researchers.

These digests can hardly be regarded as typical examples of the epistolary heritage of the period. The Soviet era and the Stalinist period in particular, produced a special epistolary genre: letters to the editor of central newspapers which usually consisted of programmatic political declarations, incorporating substantial doses of Stalinist mythology. This chapter is mainly devoted to an analysis of the letters written by non-Jews, which the author believes to be of particular interest.

The two digests *Pravda* sent to the CPSU Central Committee were based on 59 letters. The authors' names (many of them are anonymous or collective) and the contents reveal that most of them were written by non-Jews. There are at least 40 letters of this type. Three letters do not lend themselves to any clear-cut attribution.

The letters written by non-Jews may be subdivided into four categories determined by the authors' reactions to the decision of the authorities to rehabilitate the doctors and their attitude toward the Jewish question in general:

In the first group of letters the authors fully subscribe to everything that the 'party has decided'. Their position vacillates in unison with the party line. They wholeheartedly support the decision to rehabilitate the doctors. No reference is made in their letters to the anti-Semitic nature of the case. Some 10 per cent of the letters written by non-Jews belong to this group.

The questions asked by the authors of the second group betray their bewilderment and apprehension over the unexpected re-habilitation. In some cases they express their criticism of the judicial authorities and the State Security and Interior Ministries, and ask for clarification. As a rule, none of them touch on the Jewish question. Letters in this group are the most numerous, making up 40 per cent of the total.

The letters of the third group resolutely support the decision to rehabilitate the physicians and censure the anti-Semitic campaign. They constitute 15 per cent of letters coming from non-Jews.

Representatives of the fourth group resolutely condemn the doctors' rehabilitation, dismiss any doubts about the guilt of the 'murderers in white', declare and argue their anti-Semitic views. Anti-Semitic letters make up 35 per cent of those sent in by non-Jews, second in number to the group of authors keeping a seemingly neutral stand on the Doctors' Plot and ignoring the Jewish issue.

A classic example of a letter from the first group is one from F. I. Budakov of Leningrad:

> Inasmuch as on 4 April 1953, the Presidium of the USSR Supreme Soviet repealed the Decree of 20 January 1953 awarding the Order of Lenin to Doctor Timashuk L. F. as a mistake, in light of the new circumstances, please consider my greetings to Doctor Timashuk, sent via your paper in February, withdrawn.[7]

Another reader, Vavilov from Moscow, writes: 'Like many Soviet people, I am touched by the justice, honesty and humanism of this act of our dear and cherished Government'.[8]

The authors of the second group do not have a clearly defined position. They firmly request further explanations. The following questions are typical of the second group: 'Has everything published in the newspaper of 13 January 1953 not been confirmed or...is some of it valid? In what light should the activities of the Zionist organization Joint be viewed?' (excerpt from the letter sent by Soviet Army Captain A. N. Tonin)[9]. In another letter, signed by Voroshilov Collective Farm chairman Vorontsov, chief bookkeeper of the Vendorozhskoi Machine and Tractor Station (MTS), Busniakov and other members of the staff of the Vendorozhskoi MTS, the hope was expressed that *Pravda's* editor would 'publish detailed information on the reasons for the release of and earlier publications about the doctor-killers'.[10] Readers from this group were anxious to know what considerations and circumstances led the doctors to admit their 'guilt' (letters of M. Murav'ev from Ivanovo[11] and serviceman A. M. Surovitskii[12]). In particular, the readers wanted to know what role Timashuk had played in the Doctors' Plot. Some expressed dissatisfaction over the fact that the State Security and Interior ministries were above criticism. The most outspoken in this respect was M. Seliverov from Leningrad:

> Many officials at the State Security and Interior ministries have become corrupted and have become unsuited for work as *chekisty*...The State Security and Interior ministries are an autonomous republic. Abroad, relatives, lawyers, newsmen, MPs all have access to prisons, interviews are freely granted, there is a free press and there are open rallies. There is nothing of the kind in the USSR. The State Security and Interior ministries are not subject to criticism. No one is allowed beyond the barbed-wire on the pretext of protecting state secrets. Take England, for instance. Could the arrest of twelve professors on patently ridiculous grounds possibly have occurred there? And if such an arrest had been made, would they have been detained for more than 2–3 days? Certainly not. It would have become common knowledge that they were being tortured.[13]

The authors of these letters are trying to understand the reasons for fabricating the Doctors' Plot but virtually none of them, as has already been noted, mention its anti-Semitic nature. It is only S. V. Kainov from Saratov who states that if the charges brought against the doctors are really 'absolutely groundless' he is inclined to see the actions of 'some bunglers from the former Ministry of State Security as a clearly expressed desire...to sow anti-Semitism and ethnic strife'.[14]

Following are a few typical excerpts from letters in the third group. 'Please convey through your newspaper...my deepest contempt and loathing for L. Timashuk, that human scum.' The author of the letter calls Timashuk a 'diplomaed Cheberiachka[15] with a Nazi mentality', a 'loathsome Black Hundred supporter who was on the verge of getting the [country's] highest award, the Order of Lenin' (from A. Chugunov's letter, Moscow).[16] V. Aleksandrov from Moscow writes of the satisfaction with which all progressive people in the Soviet Union received the Interior Ministry's announcement and the editorials which appeared in *Pravda*. He also considers it to be his 'party duty' to draw attention to the '*ostrich-like behaviour of the city party committee*, which on 4 April issued instructions to refrain from commenting on the statement' of the Interior Ministry.[17] He goes on to discuss the unseemly role played by *Pravda* which, instead of demonstrating a class approach to unmasking cosmopolitan ideology, 'set a clearly nationalistic tone'. He continues:

> The struggle against cosmopolitan ravings often boiled down to uncovering pen names in an effort to prove that this or that author was a Semite. *Pravda*...was fostering ethnic animosity. The famous *Pravda* feuilletons brought to mind those of *Novoe vremia* and other Black Hundreds press organs. Many people in our country have been poisoned by chauvinism, including children, which is especially sad.

Aleksandrov suggested that *Pravda* and other mass media start a propaganda campaign on communist morality, specifically targeted to the younger generation. 'People must be reminded openly of what Comrade Stalin wrote,[18] because some people would go so far as to compare Stalin's ideas to the current policy of the party and government'.[19]

An unsigned letter of the Volta Plant workers from Tallinn also expresses the 'great satisfaction' they felt when reading the Interior Ministry statement. The workers suspect that Timashuk was acting as an agent of 'enemy counter-intelligence with the aim of sowing hostility between the Russian and Jewish peoples'. Is it possible that 'state security men have gotten entangled in a net spread by subversive American agents?', the workers ask themselves.[20] The letter from a 'group of communist workers' from Moscow — K. Nikol'skii, A. Panov, Remnikin — shows a less ideological approach. They express their complete mistrust of the *Pravda* editors:

> For two or three years the paper waged a pogrom-like anti-Semitic campaign in its articles and feuilletons, smacking of Jewish names and tried to prove, in the manner of fascist leaflets, that they [the Jews] must get what is coming to them. And now the paper is publishing editorials on the Soviet ideology of friendship among peoples.[21] Who will believe you? You are prostitutes and beasts...Fascists...must be kept out of *Pravda* which our people regard as infallible. Quit before it is too late and surrender your positions to dedicated and honest communists.[22]

There are two more letters that may be put in this group although they are somewhat marginal because they come from relatives of Jews who have first-hand knowledge of the Jewish question. An anonymous letter from Leningrad says that there has been a dramatic change in policy *vis-à-vis* Jews in the city. 'On spurious pretexts and even with no pretext at all, they are being fired, excluded, refused jobs, and harassed openly and in secret.' The author of the letter says he is a Russian. Both my daughters have Jewish husbands, honest workers who spare no effort for the good of the Soviet people's economy.' He also writes that in Leningrad, the 'persecution of Jews' takes place with the tacit consent of the local authorities. 'Our government, our party must intervene without delay...There has been talk about Israel, but that is a capitalist country and I am writing about our Soviet Jews, not about Israeli Jews...Since our beloved leader Iosif Vissarionovich died', the reader concludes, 'Jews have been physically molested in Leningrad.'[23]

There is another letter written by a doctor, E. Iakunina from the small town of Bykovo, near Moscow:

> I can't describe how a mother's heart aches for her sons who have been 'branded' just because their father was Jewish. Just think of the pain and injustice I felt because my children had to be 'ashamed' of their father who lived his life as an honest worker, who came from a family of poor working people, was loyal to his Mother country — the Soviet Union — and gave his life for her at the battle front in 1941.

Iakunina also writes about discrimination against her elder son who had been refused admission to a post-graduate course at Moscow University despite his excellent academic showing. Her younger son was serving in the Navy in the Baltic Fleet, but even there he 'sometimes feels the strain'.

The authors in the final group (in many cases they prefer to remain anonymous yet give their place of work or study; as a rule these are collective letters) resolutely oppose the rehabilitation of the 'doctor-killers'. Their letters are patently anti-Semitic. All contain prevalent stereotypes of Jews: 'Jews are not steel workers, shop hands or unskilled labourers, they shun kolkhozes...they do not work at subway construction sites with pile-drives in their hands or in mines, at the Volga-Don [canal] or do any other arduous labour, they do not study in factory schools' (excerpt from an unsigned letter of the Kirov Plant steelmakers and workers, Leningrad).[24] 'How did it come about that Jewish families enjoy all the good things of life produced by the calloused hands of the workers? Commerce is in the hands of the Jews' (from an unsigned letter from Moscow Region).[25] V. M. Larin from Prokop'evsk writes that all leading posts at the plant where he is working are 'held by people of Jewish nationality...The plant is located in the territory of the RSFSR but is mostly managed by Jews.'[26] 'Jews live off all the other peoples of our country',[27] in the opinion of workers from Kramatorsk (Ukrainian SSSR). The author of an anonymous letter from Moscow believes that Jews are the root of all evil. 'When will this nation relent and stop causing suffering to the Russian people?'[28] '*We have regarded Jews as parasites in the past and will continue to regard them as such*',[29] writes another anonymous author. 'All Jews are rogues and swindlers',[30] insists a Serp i Molot (Hammer and Sickle) factory worker from Moscow.

For the authors of this group of letters, the Doctors' Plot is in essence a 'plot of all Jews'. And since all Jews taken together are guilty, there is no need for any additional proof of the doctors' 'guilt' — all the more so since the 'doctor-killers' confessed. The Interior Ministry statement on rehabilitation and 'impermissible investigation methods strictly forbidden by Soviet law' was met with indignation by almost all authors in this group. The Jews '*have managed to get off scot-free again!*[31] '*Do you really think these professors have been fully rehabilitated? Who is going to believe that?*...Were they subjected to torture like those staunch and true patriots Zoia [Kosmodemianskaia] or Liza Chaikina' (letter from A. Savelev of Moscow).[32] This motif recurs in many letters in this group. 'Even terrible torture did not break the spirit of heroic Komsomol members and did not provide the fascists with the confessions which they sought', students from Yaroslavl wrote.[33] 'And what about our ordinary citizens who stood their ground when stars were being branded on their bodies or parts of their bodies were being amputated. They did not reveal anything'[34] — this from an anonymous author in Moscow.

The rehabilitation of the doctors was seen as the outcome of Jewish influence and penetration into the higher echelons of power. The following conclusions are characteristic of this group: The Interior Ministry statement 'has either been written by a Jew or inspired by a Jew'.[35] 'Now that Stalin is no more, our government is currying favor with the Jews.'[36] Hence the fear and even terror one can discern in some of the letters. 'Stalin is dead, and there is no one to protect the Soviet people', writes an anonymous author from Truskovets.[37] 'After the *Pravda* editorial today we can expect mass arrests of innocent Russians, who are totally defenceless against Jewish slander', wrote a Muscovite, who preferred to remain anonymous.[38] He was asking 'not to destroy the Russian people for the sake of the Jews. We will still prove useful.'[39] To some extent these sentiments are reminiscent of the public mood on the eve of the mass Jewish pogroms in tsarist Russia following the 17 October 1905 Manifesto 'on the granting of rights'.[40]

Many letters, both anti-Semitic ones and those opposed to anti-Semitism, focus on L. Timashuk. For some authors she is still a heroine, a true patriot and — after the Interior Ministry statement — a victim of injustice. For another group, as we have seen in the letters cited above, she is an informer and a criminal. Anti-Semitic authors feel that the powers-that-be have humiliated and insulted them, because their patriotic feelings, personified in Timashuk, have been trampled underfoot. Without beating about the bush, an anonymous author from Moscow asked the CC CPSU 'not to permit citizens' patriotic feelings to be scorned. For this is..."the holy of holies" and not a Jewish bazaar.'[41] Some take the rehabilitation of the doctors as a personal insult. 'I am a young Soviet engineer. After reading in your paper about the release of the saboteur doctors I felt as though I got a slap in the face.'[42]

Apart from expressing their indignation, the authors of a number of letters display readiness to undertake bold protest measures, unprecedented at that time. In their letter, several law students of Lvov University demand that Timashuk come out with a statement in *Pravda*. The students write that 'Jewish nationalists are intensifying their subversive activity in Lvov: spreading rumours that there is going to be a war, that America will help the Jews...Jews will be allowed to engage in private commerce'. These future lawyers declare that unless Timashuk is allowed to speak out they will 'call for a march' in her defence. Doctor Timashuk 'has been awarded the Stalin Order [sic], and Stalin is truth'. The authors of this unsigned letter request that Khrushchev be informed of their demands.[43]

In addition to traditional anti-Semitic clichés, readers' letters of this group contain some new ideas which became part of the anti-Semitic outlook of intellectuals in a later period. An anonymous author, one of the few who appear to be free of Stalinist blinkers, writes:

> Our government has taken a great step: it has made it clear that biased investigation of cases was practised in the past. It has shown the people that it wants to change its domestic policy. *But why did this act of global significance have to begin with exalting a handful of Jews and degrading Russians?* So many victims of the 1933–34 and 1937–38 repressions are still languishing in detention camps; but it is a handful of Jews rather than they who have been rehabilitated first. The Russian people has no use for international prestige which is based on the humiliation and insulting of Russians for the sake of Jews.[44]

Many authors request and even demand that Jews be expelled from various fields of the economy, culture and public life. Addressing the government, an anonymous author from a Moscow suburb writes: 'Remove the Jews from positions of authority...The Russian people are not the block-heads you think they are.'[45] Workers from Kramatorsk urge the government to 'see to it that the doctor-killers and all Jews who sponge off the other peoples of our country get their just desserts'.[46]

Anti-Semitic letters came a close second to those that kept a seemingly neutral stand on the doctors' case and ignored the Jewish issue. An examination of State Security Ministry reports on the mood in the Armed Forces in the spring of 1953 confirms the fact that anti-Semitic letters reflected the views of a considerable part of the population in Stalin's Soviet Union.[47]

An analysis of the digests dispatched to the CC Secretariat shows that readers' letters to *Pravda* in April 1953 reflected public sentiments with a sufficient degree of accuracy and constituted a cross-section of those sentiments. The official statement declaring that the 'murderers in white' were innocent came as a shock to many in the Soviet Union.

'Moscow is buzzing like a bee-hive',[48] one reader wrote. The authorities' unprecedented decision set millions thinking, arguing and doubting. As can be seen from the above, a considerable part of the country's population was not inclined to support the doctors' rehabilitation. Moreover, the rehabilitation announcement provoked mass anti-Semitic sentiments, aggression and fear already triggered by the original announcement of the Doctors' Plot. In the eyes of many people, the declaration that 'the Jews arc innocent' ran counter to a mentality shaped under the influence of traditional anti-Semitic mythology. The letters provide confirmation for the prevailing view in modern historiography[49] that in Russia, traditional anti-Semitism was not bred by the authorities alone, that it was not only state-supported, but found fertile ground in the consciousness of the masses, especially during periods of political and economic upheaval.

At the same time it cannot be ignored that, for all the variety in their assessments of the events, most of the authors appealed for additional information, openness and truth with respect to the Doctors' Plot and the situation of the Jews in general. Indicative is the letter of non-Jewish Komsomol members from Leningrad Secondary School No. 210, addressed both to *Pravda* and the CPSU Central Committee:

> We would greatly appreciate an article on the Jewish Autonomous Republic...Neither our geography teachers nor other teachers give us any information about this republic. Where is it situated? What is its geographical position and population? Who administers the republic and what is the name of its administrative centre? What natural resources and industry does it have? How many Jewish workers, peasants and scientists are there? Is it possible to settle there?[50]

After the fall of Beria in late June 1953, the case of the 'saboteur doctors' was again brought to the forefront of public attention and as before gave rise to a host of questions, rumours and conjectures on the part of the public. This is evident from the information submitted to Khrushchev by N. Mikhailov, Secretary of the Moscow *gorkom* (the city party committee of the CPSU).[51]

As subsequent developments have shown, even during the 'Thaw' the authorities refrained from stressing the anti-Semitic character of the drive against cosmopolitanism and the Doctors' Plot. In his secret speech to the 20th Congress of the CPSU Khrushchev made no mention of the anti-Semitic nature of the Doctors' Plot.

It is possible that Khrushchev was not expressing his personal attitude, but, having just acquired full control of the reins of power, was forced to reckon with public opinion as expressed in the letters which the First Secretary had read and which are now accessible to the public. Launching an unprecedented criticism of the 'personality cult' and fully aware of the attitude of a substantial part of the population to the Jewish question, Khrushchev might have been reluctant to give additional trump cards to his opponents. One thing, however, is indisputable: throughout, the regime tried to adapt itself to the mentality of the masses. It spoke to the people in language which was familiar and comprehensible to them.

NOTES

1. *Pravda*, 4 April 1953; and see Iakov Etinger, 'The Doctors' Plot: Stalin's Solution to the Jewish Question', in this volume.
2. *Pravda*, 6 April 1953.
3. Yakov Rapoport, *The Doctors' Plot of 1953* (Cambridge: Harvard University Press, 1991).
4. Ester Markish, *Stol' dolgoe vozvrashchenie* (Tel Aviv: [Author's edition], 1984).
5. Zinovii Sheinis, *Provokatsiia veka* (Moscow: Pik, 1992).
6. Ibid., p. 117.
7. Tsentr khranenie sovremennykh dokumentov (TsKhSD), fond (f.) 5, opis' (op.) 30, delo (d.) 5, p. 34.
8. Ibid., p. 3.
9. Ibid., pp. 5–6. The reference is to the American Jewish Joint Distribution Committee, so described in the TASS announcement of 13 January.
10. Ibid., p. 6.
11. Ibid., p. 78.
12. Ibid., pp. 37–8.
13. Ibid., p. 38.
14. Ibid., p. 5.
15. The reader is apparently referring to V. Cheberiak, a prostitute, who served as the main witness for the prosecution at the Beilis blood-libel trial in 1913.
16. TsKhSD, f. 5, op. 30, d. 5, p. 8.
17. This and all subsequent emphases were marked on the original text by the only people who read the letters — the staff of the Central Committee Secretariat.
18. The author of the letter is referring to Stalin's reply to a question about anti-Semitism put by the Jewish Telegraphic Agency in 1931: 'Anti-Semitism as an extreme form of racial chauvinism is the most dangerous vestige of cannibalism' — I. V. Stalin, *Sochineniia*, Vol. 13, p. 28.
19. TsKhSD, f. 5, op. 30, d. 5, p. 32.
20. Ibid., p. 35.
21. Ibid., p. 46.
22. Ibid., p. 39.
23. Ibid., p. 4.
24. Ibid., p. 43.
25. Ibid., pp. 44–5.
26. Ibid., p. 42.
27. Ibid., p. 44.
28. Ibid., p. 45.
29. Ibid., p. 14.
30. Ibid., p. 44.
31. Ibid., p. 10.
32. Ibid., p. 9. Kosmodem'ianskaia and Chaikina were partisans who became symbols of Soviet patriotism after being captured by the Germans and executed.
33. Ibid., p. 40.
34. Ibid., p. 12.

35. Ibid., p. 11. Anonymous letter from Moscow.
36. Ibid., p. 44. Serp i Molot Plant worker from Moscow.
37. Ibid., p. 43.
38. Ibid., p. 45.
39. Ibid.
40. See in this volume, Abraham Ascher, 'Anti-Jewish Pogroms in the First Russian Revolution, 1905–1907'.
41. TsKhSD, f. 5, op. 30, d. 5, p. 13.
42. Ibid., p. 11.
43. Ibid., p. 40.
44. Ibid., p. 9.
45. Ibid., p. 45.
46. Ibid., p. 44.
47. See documents on Stalin's fatal illness from USSR State Security Ministry reports on the mood in the Soviet Armed Forces in the spring of 1953 in V. Lazarev, *Neizvestnaia Rossiia*, Vol. 2 (Moscow, 1992), pp. 253–60.
48. TsKhSD, f. 5, op. 30, d. 5, p. 39.
49. See Shlomo Lambroza and John Klier, (eds.), *Pogroms: Anti-Jewish Violence in Modern Russian History* (Cambridge: Cambridge University Press, 1992).
50. TsKhSD, f. 5, op. 30, d. 5, p. 42. For Birobidzhan, which was an autonomous *oblast'*, not republic, see Robert Weinberg, 'Jews into Peasants? Solving the Jewish Question in Birobidzhan', in this volume.
51. TsKhSD, f. 5, op. 30, d. 4.

IV

WORLD WAR II AND ITS AFTERMATH

10

The Unique Features of the Holocaust in the Soviet Union

MORDECHAI ALTSHULER

Throughout the history of modern man, with all its carnage and butchery, the Holocaust remains unparalleled for its human barbarism.[1] However, while killing has usually been the means to an end, whether the acquisition of territory or the destruction of a political enemy, the annihilation of the Jewish people was an end unto itself. Jews were condemned to death not because of their activities, behaviour or way of life, but for the sole reason that they were born of Jewish parents. The resources of one of Europe's most advanced nations were harnessed to destroy the Jewish people. This country had at its command an efficient bureaucracy which carried out directions smoothly and accurately, a sophisticated communications network, a well-oiled propaganda machine and a highly trained cadre of troops to implement its policies. All this was set in motion to destroy a peaceful population with no organized physical power. It is no wonder, there-fore, that the Holocaust presents a compelling challenge to scholars of religion, philosophy, psychology and literature. Even more important, however, the Holocaust is first and foremost an integral part of Jewish history, since it is an outgrowth of the uniqueness of this history and has changed the face of the Jewish people for generations to come.

Despite the shared experience of the Holocaust in the Nazi-occupied countries, there were many variations in form, swiftness and, in part, results. Even the reaction of the local populace, and, to some extent, of the Jewish community, were not uniform in every country. Reactions were influenced, at least partially, by the historical attitude of the surrounding population toward the Jews and by the political and social reality of the times. Even the Jewish reaction, by its nature very limited, was profoundly influenced by the condition of the Jewish communities on the eve of the Holocaust.

Over the years, the Holocaust has commanded increasing interest. In the last decade, barely a day went by without the appearance of a new book, publication or article dealing in one way or another with the Holocaust. As a result of prevailing conditions in the Soviet Union, however, literature, both Jewish and non-Jewish, has persistently ignored this topic.[2] The Holocaust did not exist as a subject of research, historical or otherwise, in the Soviet Union, and Jews were rarely mentioned, directly or indirectly, in connection with German cruelty. Even Holocaust research in the West concerned itself very little with the Jews of the Soviet Union. When it did deal with this region, the primary focus was on the Baltic states and on Polish territory annexed by the Soviet Union, namely, western Belorussia and the western Ukraine. Despite the thousands of volumes of memoirs and testimony relating to the Holocaust, the Jews living within the 1939 borders of the Soviet Union were nearly forgotten, since they were unable to relate their experiences during the terrible years of Nazi occupation.[3]

It is only recently that several books have been published, whose main object is to commemorate the slaughter of Jews in certain towns.[4] Moreover, once the archives were made available, several collections of documents came to light which enabled serious and comprehensive research of the subject.[5] This article is not a summary of research, but rather, an attempt to delineate the uniqueness of the Holocaust in the Nazi-occupied areas of the Soviet Union from three aspects: genocide; the local populace; Jewish resistance.

GENOCIDE

As previously stated, Nazi Germany's ultimate goal was the physical destruction of the Jews of Europe, but the practical application of this objective went through several stages. During the first stage, they sought to 'purify' Germany and Austria from the Jewish race and, accordingly, put pressure on Jews to emigrate through confiscation of property and wealth.

With the swift occupation of Poland, millions of Jews came under Nazi rule, and deportation was out of the question for such large numbers of people. Even in the first stage, the Nazis learned that the world was not prepared to absorb the Jews of Germany and Austria, to say nothing of the millions of Polish Jews. Consequently, the second stage of Nazi anti-Jewish policy now began. The main objective at this point was to isolate the Jews from the general population by exploiting their property and their ability to work for the war effort. Toward this end, proposals were put forward to concentrate Jews in 'reservations' near Lublin or Madagascar. The object of this was to bring about the slow physical destruction of the Jewish population through degradation, depression and inhuman living conditions, which would result in a high mortality rate and prolonged, collective misery. The plans for Jewish 'reservations' were never implemented, but the ghettos in which the Jews were ultimately imprisoned were designed to achieve the same result.

With the invasion of the Soviet Union on 22 June 1941, the Nazis embarked upon a new stage in their anti-Jewish policy: the immediate physical destruction of the Jews.

In all phases of the Nazi plan, the final goal remained the same: the complete physical annihilation of the Jews. Nevertheless, the differences in method and in speed of accomplishment are of some historical significance. The Wannsee Conference, held at the end of January 1942, is regarded as the beginning of the third stage of Nazi Germany's policy toward the Jews, which they termed the 'Final Solution'. However, within the 1939 borders of the Soviet Union, the Final Solution had been implemented even before the Wannsee Conference and was actually put into effect from the outbreak of the war between Germany and the Soviet Union.

The war against the Soviet Union was perceived as a total war between two world views and two regimes which could never coexist: bolshevism, a natural outgrowth of Judaism, and the Aryan philosophy. The latter could flourish only if the former were eradicated. In other words, the Jews, in whose spirit and image bolshevism was conceived, must be destroyed.

In Hitler's speech at the Nazi Party Congress on 13 March 1937, he emphasized that Jewish world domination 'derived from the Jewish Bolshevik authorities in Moscow'.

On 12 September 1941, General Keitel pointed out that 'the struggle against bolshevism calls for drastic and merciless measures primarily against the Jews, as the main champions of bolshevism'.[6]

It is thus easy to understand that one of the objectives of the war was to exterminate the Jews as quickly as possible. This can also be seen in a directive issued by the headquarters of the Wehrmacht on 19 May 1941, in which it was stated:

> Bolshevism is the mortal enemy of German National Socialism and, consequently, Germany must fight this destructive ideology and its proponents. This war requires strong and decisive measures against the Bolshevik propagandists, partisans, saboteurs and Jews.[7]

This directive already reflects the basic distinction drawn between Jews and other people. Regarding others, the army is commanded to take steps against activists — Bolshevik propagandists, partisans and saboteurs — but in relation to Jews, against all without exception. One can deduce from this that the order to destroy Bolshevik commissars[8] was easily applied to Jews, regardless of sex or age, since Jews were considered to be Bolshevik by nature.

A similar inference may be drawn from the following order relating to behaviour in the occupied zone of the Soviet Union, given by Reinhard Heydrich, chief of the Reich Security Administration and of the SS in the occupied territories, on 2 July 1941:

> The following people are to be put to death:
> Comintern activists and active professional communists;
> middle and upper echelon personnel of the [Communist] party and particularly active personnel from the lower echelons — that is, personnel from the central committee and district and regional committees;
> peoples' commissars;
> Jews — members of the [Communist] party, and state workers.[9]

Regarding the general population, Heydrich did not speak of executing the lower echelon party members who were not particularly active, nor the party's rank and file. However, he ordered the execution of all Jews who belonged to the party, as well as those who worked for the state. Since the entire Soviet economy was controlled by the state, and all workers were considered state workers in one way or another, this was actually an order to kill the entire adult Jewish population. Bolshevism, moreover, was regarded as an inherently Jewish concept and, as a result, even Jewish children were potential Bolsheviks and should, therefore, suffer the same fate: death.

The Nazi authorities saw a particular urgency in exterminating Jews within the pre-World War II borders of the Soviet Union, as seen in the testimony of Otto Ohlendorf, chief of Einsatzgruppen D, before the international tribunal in Nuremberg. On the eve of the German invasion of the Soviet Union, Ohlendorf gave the command to destroy 'Jews and political commissars...in the Russian territories [that is, the pre-war territory of the Soviet Union]'.[10]

This differentiation between the original and the annexed territories is evident in the timetable for liquidating Jews. For example, during the period between the two world wars, part of the historical *guberniia* of Volhynia was located in independent Poland and part (the Zhitomir Oblast) in the Soviet Union. In the Polish sector of the district, the ghettos were destroyed at the end of 1942, while in Soviet territory proper, the Jews from the ghettos were killed at the end of 1941 and the beginning of 1942.[11] This means that part of the Jewish population in the Polish areas of the district of Volhynia survived a full year longer than the Jews in the Soviet areas. From a list of twenty-two ghettos in occupied Soviet territory, it appears that in five cities, all the Jews were killed within an average of twenty-three days following the Nazi occupation. In nine cities, they were killed within ninety-nine days, and in eight cities, in an average of two hundred and ninety five days after the Nazis occupied the area.[12] Thus, in the original Soviet areas, as opposed to the annexed territory (the ghettos in Vilna and Bialystok were destroyed in September 1943, and in Lvov, in June and July of the same year), it took a relatively short time from the invasion of the Nazis to the killing of the majority of those Jews who were unable to escape further inland.[13] Although extensive research has yet to be done in this area, the facts seem to indicate that the Nazi authorities viewed the annihilation of the Jews within the USSR's original boundaries with particular urgency, since they regarded them as the mainstay of the Bolshevik regime.

The massacre of Jews in the occupied zone of the Soviet Union was accomplished through four principal methods or a combination of them. Following their occupation of a city, the Nazis would appoint a man, sometimes referred to as the 'Jewish elder' (*starosta*), or several men, mentioned in the documentation as a 'Jewish committee' and/or *kehila*. To a certain degree, this institution was similar to the *Judenrat*, which the Nazis established in other occupied countries, but in Soviet territory it differed in its make-up and even its function. In other Nazi-occupied areas, including those annexed to the Soviet Union during the war, *Judenrat* appointees were mainly pre-war leaders of the *kehila* and other Jewish bodies.[14] In the original territory of the Soviet Union, there were no Jewish organizations before the Nazi occupation, and those concerned with Soviet-Jewish culture were, for the most part, thoroughly communist in nature. Consequently, appointees to the *Judenrat* were selected either from among Jews who knew German or Jews whom the German authorities chose at random. They were doctors, engineers and, sometimes, craftsmen whom the German administration came upon by chance.[15] One cannot speak, therefore, of a Jewish leadership as is customary regarding the *Judenrats* in other Nazi-occupied countries. According to available testimony, the members of these bodies did not appear to enjoy any privileges and were killed along with the rest of the Jewish population.

Even the function of these institutions differed, to a great extent, from those in other countries. One of their primary tasks, and, at times, the only one, was to compile a list of the Jewish population. In many towns Jews were ordered to register. This was not at all difficult, since nationality was indicated on Soviet identity cards. Indeed, most of the Jews registered voluntarily. Upon doing so, they were required to wear a prominent identifying symbol, whether in the form of a yellow patch or a white patch with a Jewish star, to distinguish them from the general populace even from a distance. In certain cities, Jews were concentrated in a separate neighbourhood or in a number of abandoned buildings far from the city. It was a kind of ghetto, although it was not always guarded or surrounded by a fence, and it was intended as a preliminary step to the mass killing of the Jews in the area. From these ghetto-like areas, young men were taken out for hard labour in conditions of starvation and brutality. In many cases, the Germans would first kill the young men and women to minimize resistance during the massacre of the entire Jewish population. In other areas, Jews were gathered in places resembling concentration camps — in abandoned factories and shacks, or a field that was guarded and surrounded by a fence.[16] In some of the towns, particularly in small villages, where most of the inhabitants knew the Jews, a *Judenrat* was not established. A list of Jews was drawn up, and they would be killed immediately.[17] The guards were mostly members of auxiliary units and local policemen. Various methods of killing were sometimes employed in the same town at different times. The main purpose was to expedite and facilitate the killing, which was implemented soon after the area was occupied.

The Nazis tried to conceal their true intentions until the last moment, telling their Jewish victims that they would be transferred to a workplace where they could live peacefully, or spreading rumours that Jews were to be transported to Palestine. In the city of Rostov, they insisted that the transfer of the Jewish population was intended to protect it from the wrath of the city's inhabitants.[18] The assembled Jews were requested to take with them only necessary clothing and enough food for a few days, ostensibly for the duration of the trip. They were even required to hand over the keys to their homes with the address clearly written. However, after the Jews had gathered in the appointed place, they were transported by foot and in trucks to areas near the town and then murdered.

Most of the mass killing of the Jews in the Soviet Union was accomplished by machine gun. Despite their cruelty, the men who pulled the trigger could not always bear the horror, and they would be supplied with alcoholic drinks to help them get through the job, as indicated by one of the participants: 'They gave alcohol to the Russian police; otherwise, it was questionable whether they would have been able to carry out this difficult task.'[19]

The Einsatzgruppen units, trained and prepared for this type of assignment, almost always took charge of the mass killings. They were aided by Wehrmacht units, police units and the local populace. The Jews were shot in anti-tank ditches, in ditches dug specifically for the mass killings and in ravines near the towns. As a result, the Nazis could not hide their deeds from the people living in the vicinity, as is evident from the description of the killing in Borisov, Belorussia:

> It is possible that they wanted to carry out this operation [the killing of the Jews] in secret, but it would have been impossible, since people lived on the other side of the street and on the side streets.[20]

Indeed, some of the area's inhabitants were eyewitnesses to the slaughter, and most could at least hear the sounds of the mass murder of their Jewish neighbours, who had lived among them for so many generations.

THE LOCAL POPULACE AND THE JEWS

The attitude of the local populace toward the Jews during the Holocaust is a complex and emotionally-charged issue with far-ranging political ramifications. At times there is a tendency to make sweeping generalizations, and these blur the historical picture.

Police and Nazi auxiliary units drafted from the local population took an active part in the slaughter of the Jews. The members of these units did not only come from the fringes of society, as some would make it seem. They were drawn from all classes, and among them were men who fulfilled certain functions in the Soviet regime. The reasons for joining these units were many and varied — money, sympathy with the Nazi regime (a feeling held by many Soviet citizens), hatred of the Soviet government and, sometimes, even nationalist aspirations. It is also possible that they killed Jews out of a strong desire for revenge for all the years of suffering under the Soviet government which, in common with the line followed by Nazi propaganda, they regarded as a Jewish-Bolshevik regime. The cruelty of these units toward the Jews measured up to that of the Nazis and, at times, surpassed it. In addition, they were more effective in hunting down Jews who had hidden during the mass killing operations. However, the units that participated in the actual killing of Jews constituted only a small percentage of the millions of inhabitants who lived in the areas of the Soviet Union occupied by the Nazis.

There were also not a few people who, either out of greed or a deep hatred of Jews, were happy to turn Jews over to the Nazis, knowing well that this meant certain death. They themselves, however, may have been incapable of killing the victims with their own hands.[21] This is illustrated in the following account of a survivor to a friend:

> My husband, Andrei, deserted from the Red Army and passionately despised the Soviet regime and the Jews who established it. I am afraid that he informed on you.[22]

Indeed, at times, informers assumed a monstrous form, as seen in the following description of a Kiev orphanage:

> The children told me that a short time ago the Germans took all the Jewish children and killed them. Four Jewish children, ten and eleven years old, were hung two days ago in the orphanage yard. A woman doctor who worked in the orphanage informed on them.[23]

Although informers again constituted a small minority within the general population, they were, apparently, more numerous than those who cooperated in the organized killing of the Jews.

Given the poverty of the Soviet people and the popular image of affluent Jews living at the expense of the rest of the populace, many participated in looting Jewish property. Some were happy to do it, while others justified their actions by claiming they had no choice. One witness from the town of Gorodok (Vitebsk Oblast) stated:

> The Germans walked around with the police and entered the homes of the more affluent Jews. They took the household goods out to the street to show the Russians the Jewish wealth and told them to take it for themselves...This influenced large numbers of people who became wealthy at the expense of the Jews. Nevertheless, many Russians still refused to take part in the looting, and the Germans had to threaten them with weapons. When they took the property, some of these Russians asked forgiveness from the Jews ('I don't need your possessions,' 'Forgive me, I am taking it, but what else can I do?' and more in the same vein).[24]

All expressions of hostility toward Jews mentioned so far have been active and direct, but extremely large numbers of people contributed indirectly to the murder of the Jews, taking a position somewhere between active participation and passive acquiescence. Many of them did not inform on the Jews who lived in their buildings or neighbourhoods, but whenever they could purge themselves of Jews, they did so. If Nazis appeared in the yard or near their house and asked where the Jews lived, they would gladly point out their homes.[25] Broad strata of the population who did not collaborate directly with the Nazis felt compelled by a desire to 'rid' themselves of the Jews, which derived from a historical enmity toward them. This tradition had not lessened during the Soviet regime and had been nourished by Nazi propaganda claiming that the Bolshevik regime was really a Jewish one. Thus, they rejoiced at Jewish misery, as expressed by an inhabitant of the city of Borisov: 'So they'll die — they've caused us enough harm.'[26]

According to a German report, the town of Shmelenk in Belorussia held a special prayer of thanksgiving on becoming *judenrein* (free of Jews).[27] Apparently, this feeling of deliverance was experienced by the majority of the surrounding population.

However, when many of these same people who hated Jews saw the terrible slaughter, they recoiled for a moment or even expressed pity for the innocent victims, as recounted by one of the participants:

> [The inhabitants'] eyes expressed either complete indifference or horror, since what was happening was monstrous. If in the evening, before they took the Jews out to kill them, the non-Jews thought that the Jews deserved a fate such as this, in the morning, [upon seeing the slaughter] they cried, 'Who gave the order for this? How is it possible to destroy 6,500 Jews at once? Today it is the Jews, but when will it be our turn? [What wrongs] did these poor Jews commit?'[28]

Apparently, the reaction of most of the local population to the mass killings varied from joy at their fate, through indifference, to passive identification with the victims. All these feelings, contradictory as they might be, could be experienced by the same people in different situations and at different times. These people were not collaborators, and most were unable to withstand the scenes of mass murder but, indirectly, they aided in the slaughter of the Jews.

The aid given to the Jews also varied both in form and degree. It went from a simple woman who brought milk to Jewish children in the Polotsk Ghetto, which was not yet walled-in,[29] and the offer of food or lodging to a Jew who escaped the mass killing, to hiding Jews at the risk of the lives of those who took them in.

In all their directives, the Nazis emphasized that anyone hiding a Jew would be killed. It is therefore no wonder that only a very few risked their lives in this manner.[30] There is no way to evaluate the complex motives that drove people to hide Jews, but apparently some were motivated by their Christianity, particularly when children were involved.[31] Indeed, throughout Nazi-occupied Europe, thousands of Jewish children were hidden in monasteries. This did not occur within the original borders of the Soviet Union, however, since the Soviet authorities had destroyed all religious institutions before the war. Those who hid Jews at the risk of their own lives were, according to available testimony, mostly simple people who acted independently and had to be on their guard with their neighbours and friends.[32]

A chapter unique to the Soviet Union, more than any other country in East Europe, is the relationship of gentile spouses to their Jewish husbands and wives in life or death situations. In most East European countries, intermarriage was marginal, but in the Soviet Union it was quite substantial. According to statistics, in 1937 in Belorussia, 16.5 per cent of Jewish men and 15 per cent of Jewish women intermarried; in the Soviet Ukraine in 1938, 18 per cent of Jewish men married gentile women, and approximately 17 per cent of Jewish women married non-Jewish men.[33]

Many Jewish women sought to free their gentile husbands from their fate, but according to testimony in our possession, the husbands did all in their power to actually save their spouses, as expressed by a simple railroad worker in Kiev when he said to his wife: 'As long as I am still alive, you will also live.'[34]

In Kharkov, a non-Jewish husband went with his wife to the ghetto. He agreed to leave it only after she had promised to escape with him.[35] There were also instances, although not many, in which non-Jewish spouses shared the fate of their Jewish partners and they were killed together.[36] At times, a non-Jewish spouse had to act not only against neighbours and society, but also against family members, whose primary interest was to protect their own flesh and blood.[37] However, while most family members understood the crisis and rescued the Jewish spouse, there were also innumerable instances when non-Jewish parents gave over their Jewish daughter- or son-in-law to the Nazis.[38] Undoubtedly, the behaviour of non-Jewish family members toward the Jews in their family depended, to a great extent, on relationships within the family, the personalities involved, and so on. During normal times, these things were not always given expression, but during the Holocaust, they decided a person's fate.

Many intermarried couples had children, and Nazi policy relating to them in the occupied Soviet Union differed from policy in Germany. According to their twisted race theory, the Nazis ostensibly believed that the children of mixed marriages in other countries had Aryan blood in their veins, but in Soviet territory they had a mixture of inferior Jewish and Slavic blood. Consequently, they ordered the children of mixed marriages to be killed like the Jews.[39] Non-Jewish parents and grandparents were thus faced with the challenge of rescuing their children and grandchildren. Indeed, available testimony indicates that, in most cases, the non-Jewish parent and/or grandparents attempted to save the lives of the children. At times, they had to do this through trickery, so that it would not become known to neighbours and friends.[40] However, there were also cases where relatives refused to save their grandchildren, who were then killed along with their Jewish mothers.

Apparently, there were many who informed on the presence of children of a mixed marriage. According to an account of events in the town of Chausy in Belorussia:

> In this provincial town lived a girl renowned for her beauty, Ira Gubnykh, eighteen years old, tall, blonde, with big eyes that were always smiling. Her mother worked until the war as a pharmacist, and her father was a doctor. Her grandfather was Jewish. All the inhabitants of...Chausy accompanied Ira on her last, sorrowful journey. The girl walked in the middle of the road, surrounded by dozens of small children, whose only crime was that their fathers or mothers were Jewish. The young children cried, and the girl with the bright hair consoled them, 'Don't cry! We must not let the hangmen see that we are afraid of them. We will be avenged!'

Dozens of these children were killed a short time after the Jewish adults of the town had been taken away to be shot on the banks of the River Pronia.[41]

Any generalizations concerning the attitude of the local population, that itself was exposed to cruel conditions and threats of death, and the concomitant attribution of actual political significance, are necessarily imprecise historically. Nevertheless, it seems that few participated in the actual killing of Jews and some even risked their lives to save them.

JEWISH RESISTANCE UNDER OCCUPATION

Two prime factors figured in the Jews' response to the inhuman conditions forced on them during the Nazi occupation of the Soviet Union: the short time span that elapsed from the onset of the occupation until the actual killing; the state of the Jewish population on the eve of occupation.

For the Jews, as for most of their countrymen, the Nazi occupation came as a complete surprise. There had been a widely-held belief that the Soviet Army was sufficiently powerful to stave off a German invasion. In response to the attack, a massive draft was instituted throughout the Soviet Union, and Jewish families, like all others, were left without their men. This fact further stymied possibilities for Jews to escape the bitter fate awaiting them.

The rapid chain of events from occupation to obliteration of the majority of the Jewish population seriously impeded attempts at escape, and moreover, thwarted efforts to organize resistance. In towns where ghettos were set up, they existed for so brief a period that it was impossible to form a resistance movement within the ghetto itself or, alternatively, organize attempts for escaping into the forests. The only Jewish settlement where this activity did take place was the Minsk Ghetto,[42] which, as mentioned previously, lasted a comparatively long time. Even cases of sporadic flight to the forests or joining the partisans were relatively rare.

A Jewish partisan organization *per se* did not exist anywhere. However, according to partial figures, in the partisan movement in all of Eastern Europe there were an estimated 20-30,000 Jews, and some of them fought in units that were entirely or mostly comprised of Jews. For the most part, young Jewish men and women who could bear firearms were apt to join established partisan movements.[43] However, this usually depended on two requisites: the existence of a partisan group in the area, and the group's willingness to accept Jews. With regard to the Soviet Union, significant partisan organizations could be found only in Belorussia, the northern Ukraine and certain parts of Russia. It is thus clear that partisan groups were not present in every locale, and this fact alone could have curtailed the possibility of Jews joining up. However, the crucial point was the willingness or refusal of the group to accept Jews.

In the Balkan states — Yugoslavia, Bulgaria and Greece — Jews were admitted into partisan ranks on an equal footing. It was very different in the Soviet Union, where the groups were reluctant to admit Jews until mid-1942, when there was a basic change in approach.

Although even the early stages of the German-Soviet war could be seen as a partisan struggle, the Soviet partisan movement was an outgrowth of sporadic organization. It included various groups of fighters who had separated from their units, people from the Soviet rank and file, communist activists who had been unable to escape and Soviet *apparatchiki* who had been left behind in order to operate against the Germans. The first groups to organize were prepared to accept, first and foremost, fighters, weapon-owners and people who were well acquainted with the area. They were hesitant to accept Jews. And indeed, we know of numerous cases where Jews were turned away because they did not own weapons and had not been adequately trained to fight. A literary rendition of this recurring event can be found in the work of Peretz Markish who wrote about Naomi, a Jewish girl who fled the tides of death and made her way to the partisans. She was rejected by them because, 'Naomi did not have a weapon/ She had only a badge'. Dejected, she returned to the ghetto.[44] It can be said, then, that not all Jews who sought to joint partisan movements and managed to find them in the forests, succeeded in getting accepted into them.

It is only natural, therefore, that at that time partisan groups began to appear, which were made up mostly, or even totally, of Jewish fighters. These groups pursued two objectives. Like all other partisan groups, they joined the fight against the Germans, but unlike the others, they admitted Jews and/or helped them to flee, albeit with limited success. Consequently, a unique phenomenon began to appear in the Jewish partisan movement — 'family camps' in the forest. One of these camps was organized by Shalom Zorin, a carpenter by profession, who was born in Minsk in 1902. During the Civil War, he had fought with the Reds. Following the Nazi occupation of Minsk, he befriended Semen Gonzenko, a prisoner from the Red Army, and they both went into the forests. Together, they built a partisan unit called Parkhomenko. According to Zorin's perception, one goal of the unit was to save Jews. This activity was not viewed with favour by the other partisans, including Gonzenko, and there were growing instances of distinct anti-Semitic expressions. The Jewish fighters left Parkhomenko and organized their own group, officially called 106, but actually referred to as 'Zorin's unit'. Nearly all the fighters in Zorin's unit were Jewish, and they saw to it that entire families were brought into the forest. Thus, a camp of some 800–1000 people was established. Although the residents of the camp performed numerous services for the partisan groups, many commanders did not approve of it. It continued to exist primarily due to the tenacity of Shalom Zorin.[45] In this camp, like the few others in territories annexed by the Soviet Union, there was a school in which the language of instruction was Yiddish and, sometimes Hebrew as well. Social activities were conducted along the lines of those in the Polish ghettos. Small as the numbers may have been, it is imperative to mention this phenomenon as an example of how a rescue operation could and did save lives, but ultimately it amounted to no more than a drop in the ocean of the hundreds of thousands killed.

From mid-1942, there was a marked change in attitude regarding Jewish participation among the partisans. The movement became organized and maintained regular contact with Moscow and a number of other smaller settlements, like the town, Luninets, which still had a ghetto in 1943. Sometimes, groups even initiated actions to rescue Jews.[46] However, the change of heart came too late for most Jews in the Soviet Union. As far as the Jews were concerned, the partisan movement was largely ineffective in offering resistance, rescuing them or fighting to protect the majority of the population.

In most of the countries conquered by the Germans, there were Jewish societal frameworks that gave the individual a feeling of belonging to the community. This was not so in the Soviet Union where atomization of Jewish society had taken place prior to the war. There were no Jewish youth groups, not even communist ones, which could provide the impetus for any kind of organization. Given the time constraints and the cruel and inhuman conditions in which they were placed, the Jews, who had hitherto seen themselves as part and parcel of the Soviet population, were patently unable to adjust to the new reality and create their own leadership.

Every individual and family faced the brutal facts alone, with no feeling of kinship or group support and with no sense of leadership. Each family raced against the clock in an effort to decide which of the limited avenues of escape it should risk taking. Flight was made even more precarious by the Soviet policy of registering nationality on identity cards and all official documentation. The apathy or overt hostility of the surrounding population must obviously be added to the list of obstacles faced by the Jews. We can, therefore, understand that according to all information at our disposal from the Soviet Union proper there is no evidence of Jewish organization in any settlement other than Minsk. At most, we can speak about sporadic and isolated responses of Jews in the occupied areas of the Soviet Union.

If we do not restrict the definition of resistance to armed response, and we include every action taken or not taken in contradiction to Nazi orders or wishes, then there are many instances of resistance that can be cited. Thousands of Soviet Jews hid, refusing to report to concentration points, and the hunt for them lasted months. There were also thousands who tried, not always successfully, to change their identity by using forged documents and pretending to belong to another nationality. In almost every city, there were stories of Jews captured in their hiding places or in possession of false papers. There were also those Jews, and not just a few, who refused to fall into Nazi hands and instead, took their own lives as free men. Many families in the town of Berezin, as well as in other cities, chose this route.[47]

Resistance continued for some as they stood on the precipice of death; each person in his own way. There were religious Jews who bore on their lips a prayer to the Creator of the Universe until their last second on earth, thus expressing their resistance to the enemy who sought to transform them into subhuman creatures. A witness at Babii Iar described one such case:

> Next to me walked an old man with a long beard. He was wrapped in a *tallit* [prayer-shawl] and *tefillin* [phylacteries]. He was whispering. He prayed exactly as my father did when I was a small child.[48]

While the Nazis attempted to equate Jews with lowly pestilence, some responded by increasing their piety, as recorded in this testimony:

> My father arose in the morning to pray to his God and said, 'Wife, bring me clean underwear. If it is our fate to die, I will go clean to the next world.'[49]

In his poem, 'Milhome' ('War'), Peretz Markish presents a literary blend of spiritual-religious and physical resistance. He describes a man of eighty enveloped in his *tallit*, being led to his death on the eve of Yom Kippur. The guard orders him to dig his own grave after most of the town's Jews have been killed in the adjoining pits. At that moment, the sun was about to set and in the synagogue it was time for the recitation of 'Kol Nidre'. This Jew also began to pray, and while praying, struck the head of the Nazi with a spade.[50] And there were Jews who stood on the edge of the pit of death and spat at or slapped the faces of their oppressors; shouted that their sons would avenge their blood or died with the words 'Long live Stalin' on their lips. All these Jews drank from the sources of human pride and were personal examples of resistance. And thus, even in the Soviet Union, where, for the most part, the murder of Jews took the population by surprise, where it followed closely upon the heels of occupation, and where there was no organized Jewish life, the Jews did not go like sheep to the slaughter. Many resisted to the utmost of their ability within the limitations they faced.

Three major characteristics, then, typified the Holocaust within the pre-war borders of the Soviet Union: the murder of the Jews just a short time after the occupation; their extermination in close proximity to their homes; and the absence of organized Jewish public life, that was the result of Soviet policy in the two decades preceding the war. To a great extent, these factors dictated the character of Jewish resistance, which was determined by these unique circumstances and was carried out against a backdrop of general apathy and hostility and, in some cases, active collaboration on the part of the local population.

NOTES

1. This article focuses on the areas of the Soviet Union that were occupied by the German Nazis and does not cover Romanian-occupied Transdnistria.
2. For the Holocaust in the Soviet Union in literature, see S. Holavski, 'Ha-shoah ve ha-lekhimah be-Belorussia ba-sifrut ha-sovietit ve-hugei ha-mehagrim ba-ma'arav', in Y. Gutman and G. Greif (eds.), *Ha-shoah be-historiografiah* (Jerusalem: Yad Vashem, 1987), pp. 255–71; B. Pinkus, *The Soviet Government and the Jews, 1948–1967* (New York: Cambridge University Press, 1984), pp. 387–420.

3. See Yitshak Arad, 'Ha-shoah be-historiografiah ha-sovietit', in Gutman and Greif, pp. 139–65; Mordechai Altshuler, 'Lehimah yehudit ve lohamat yehudim bi-Vrit ha-Mo'atsot be-historiografiah ha-sovietit veha-ma'aravit', in Gutman and Greif, pp. 167–85; Zvi Gitelman, 'Soviet Reaction to the Holocaust, 1945–1991', in L. Dobroszycki and J. Gurock (eds.), *The Holocaust in the Soviet Union* (New York: M. E. Sharpe, 1993), p. 27; L. Hirszowicz, 'Holocaust in the Soviet Mirror', in Dobroszycki and Gurock, pp. 29–59, 421–38.

4. See Iu. M. Liakhovitskii, *Poprannaia mezuza — kniga Drobitskogo iara* (Kharkov: KhGU, 1991); G. Gubenko, *Kniga pechali* (Simferopol': Krymskoe upravlenie po pechati, 1991); S. Ia. Elisavetskii, *Berdichevskaia tragediia* (Kiev: Ukr. NIINTU, 1991). D. Romanovskii, 'Chasniki', in *Vestnik evreiskogo universiteta v Moskve*, 1 (1992), pp. 157–99; D. Romanovskii and A. Zel'tser, 'Unichtozhenie evreev v Vitebske v 1941 godu', in *Vestnik evreiskogo universiteta v Moskve* 4 (1993), pp. 198–228.

5. Yitshak Arad (ed.), *Unichtozhenie evreev SSSR v gody nemetskoi okkupatsii 1941–1944: Sbornik dokumentov i materialov* (Jerusalem: Yad Vashem, 1991); I. Altman and Sh. Krakovskii (eds.), *Neizvestnaia chernaia kniga* (Jerusalem: Yad Vashem, 1993); Mordechai Altshuler, Y. Arad, Sh. Krakovskii (eds.), *Sovetskie evrei pishut Il'e Erenburgu*, (Jerusalem: Yad Vashem and Centre for Research and Documentation of East European Jewry, 1993).

6. Arad, *Unichtozhenie evreev*, p. 50.

7. Ibid., p. 37.

8. For this order of 6 June, 1941, see ibid., p. 38.

9. Yad Vashem Archives, 0–4/53–1.

10. *Niurnbergskii protsess* (Moscow: Gosiurizdat, 1959), Vol. 4, p. 627.

11. Cf. Sh. Spector, *Shoat yehudei Vohlin 1941–1944*, (Jerusalem: Yad Vashem, 1986), pp. 286–7; V. Ohrbach, 'Hashmadat ha-yehudim be-shithei Brit ha-Mo'atsot ha-kvushim al yadei ha-Germanim', *Yalkut Moreshet* (June 1975) Vol. 19, pp. 142–58.

12. Based on the article by Sh. Spector in note 15.

13. On escape and evacuation, see Mordechai Altshuler, 'Escape and Evacuation of Soviet Jews at the Time of the Nazi Invasion — Policies and Realities', in Dobroszycki and Gurock, pp. 77–104.

14. In the Nazi orders establishing a *Judenrat*, issued in 1939, reference is always to the appointment of rabbis and heads of the community — see I. Trunk, *Judenrat* (New York: Macmillan, 1972), pp. 1–13.

15. For other *Judenrat* appointments in Polotsk, Rostov, Smolensk, Kharkov, Mariupol, Essentuki, Evpatoriia, Sevastopol', Khmel'nik, see Arad, *Unichtozhenie evreev*, pp. 129, 220, 231; Altman and Krakovskii, *Neizvestnaia chernaia kniga*, pp. 86, 212, 222, 389; Gubenko, *Kniga pechali*, pp. 12, 31; see also Sh. Spector, 'Getaot ve-yudenratim be-shithei ha-kibush ha-natsi be-Vrit Ha-Mo'atsot, *Shvut* 15 (1992), p. 270, Testimony of Avraham Becker, Il'ia Erenburg Collection, Yad Vashem Archives.

16. In addition to the ghettos mentioned in Spector's article, there were also those in the towns of Gorodok, Polotsk (Vitebsk Oblast') Borisov and Nemirov — Arad, *Unichtozhenie evreev*, pp. 126, 128, 137, 229.

17. See ibid., pp. 100–101, 115; also Romanovskii and Zel'tser, 'Unichtozhenie evreev v Vitebske'; cf. S. Holavsky, *Ba-sufot ha-kilaion: yahadut Belorussiya ha-mizrahit be-milhemet ha-olam ha-shniya*, (Tel Aviv: Sifriat Poalim., 1988), pp. 179–205.

18. The Einsatzgruppen D commander testified regarding the transport order at the Nuremberg trials of Nazi war criminals in Jan. 1946. In Polotsk notice was given that the Jews were going to be transported to the Land of Israel — Arad, *Unichtozhenie evreev*, pp. 69, 129, 220. In the city of Kislovodsk it was announced that the Jews were about to be moved to the Ukraine — *Dokumenty obviniaiut* Vol. 2, (Moscow: OGIZ, 1945), pp. 140–4. In Kharkov it was said that the Jews would be moved to the western Ukraine — Liakhovitskii, *Poprannaia mezuza*, p. 52.

19. See Arad, *Unichtozhenie evreev*, pp. 140.

20. Ibid. p. 138. In the report of the German Army commander on the mass killing of the Jews of Zhitomir, he noted that next to the murder site, 'there was a large civilian population, including women and children' — *Prestupnye tseli — prestupnye sredstva; Dokumenty ob okkupatsionnoi politike fashistskoi Germanii na territorii SSSR*

(Moscow: Izd-vo politcheskoi literatury, 1968), p. 109.

21. Altman and Krakovskii, *Neizvestnaia chernaia kniga*, pp. 66, 397. For example a Jewish woman who had fled the carnage in Chimielnik, went back to her own town and vandalized home and wrote: 'And on 12 January 1942, three days after the mass murder of the village's Jews, the wife of Kurt who had gone off to loot, kept an eye on me and turned me in to the police' — ibid., pp. 146–7. Thus, for example, a woman from Zhitomir informed on a young Jewish townswoman because the latter refused to relinquish her last coat — ibid., p. 53.

22. Arad, *Unichtozhenie evreev*, p. 112.

23. Altman and Krakovskii, *Neizvestnaia chernaia kniga*, p. 63.

24. Arad, *Unichtozhenie evreev*, pp. 124–5.

25. Ibid., pp. 38–9, 51, 54. For example, a survivor from Kiev writes: 'I was in Kiev for only one month when the Germans arrived, and then the neighbours informed on me. I had lived with these same neighbours in a house for many years. Until Hitler [the Germans] came we were the closest of friends, and in ten days they informed on me and brought the Gestapo to my house' — ibid., p. 51. See also Arad, *Unichtozhenie evreev*, pp. 125, 138.

26. Ibid, p. 138. A woman who had escaped from Kiev and was walking to Zhitomir, met a resident of Kiev going in the same direction en route to get his two sons released from German custody. While talking, the woman asked the man, 'Are you satisfied that they killed so many Jews?' He smiled with contentment and quickly responded, 'I am extremely happy about this' — ibid., p. 62.

27. Ibid., p. 102.

28. Ibid., pp. 138–9.

29. Ibid., p. 128.

30. For two and a half years a family hid an 11-year-old girl who had escaped from the death pit in the town Khashchevatoe — ibid., p. 192. In Simferopol' (Crimea), a Russian woman, who was a mathematics teacher, hid the bibliographer, Evsei Gopshtein for years — Gubenko, *Kniga pechali*, p. 18. After the Babii Iar massacre, Jews who had been hiding in non-Jewish homes were taken out and killed along with their protectors. Altman and Krakovskii, *Neizvestnaia chernaia kniga*, p. 49. During the liquidation of the Minsk Ghetto, a Russian woman rescued a 12-year-old boy who had been a friend of her son's. She gave him one of her own children's birth certificates and set him up in a neighbouring village where she visited him from time to time until the liberation of Belorussia — Arad, *Unichtozhenie evreev*, pp. 319–21. On the rescue of Jews, see Ohrbach, 'Hashmadat ha-yehudim be-shithei Brit ha-Mo'atsot', p. 125, and particularly footnote 82.

31. For instance, the priest Glagolov hid a Jewish woman and her 10-year-old daughter, endangering his own life and the lives of his family. Arad, *Unichtozhenie evreev*, pp. 109–13. One of the priests in Kremenchug cooperated with the Ukrainian mayor in baptizing Jews and giving them forged papers that saved their lives — ibid., p. 322.

32. For a Ukrainian family from a small village that hid a Jewish woman and her son, see Altshuler, *Sovetskie evrei pishut Il'e Erenburgu*, pp. 165–6.

33. Rossiiskii gosudarstvennyi arkhiv ekonokmiki, fond 1562, opis' 20, delo 101, p. 151.

34. Altman and Krakovskii, *Neizvestnaia chernaia kniga*, p. 43. Feliks Giterman, born in 1906, an artist and decorator, wanted to join the Jews of Kiev who were brought to Babii Iar, but his wife objected. After she realized the fate of the Jews, she hid her husband with the help of her father, and he was saved — ibid., pp. 45–50. A Jewish engineer from Kharkov — Krivorechko — was hidden by his non-Jewish wife and was thus saved — ibid., pp. 86–9. A Ukrainian engineer from Dnepropetrovsk, who escaped together with his Jewish wife was humiliated and beaten and, nevertheless, continued to share her fate. When she was in mortal danger in one of her hiding places, he placed her in a sack and carried her on his back to another location — ibid., pp. 201–2. In the village Nem-Adargin, a Greek woman was arrested and tortured because she refused to reveal her husband's hiding place — Arad, *Unichtozhenie evreev*, p. 186. For more on Jewish men and women who were saved by their spouses in Simferopol', see Gubenko, *Kniga pechali*, p. 18.

35. Altman and Krakovskii, *Neizvestnaia chernaia kniga*, pp. 92–6.

36. One example was Petr Mikhailov, a lecturer in the Pedagogic Institute in Simferopol', who was killed together with his Jewish wife while he was holding their five-month-old baby in his arms — Gubenko, *Kniga pechali*, p. 18.
37. Altman and Krakovskii, *Neizvestnaia chernaia kniga*, p. 36.
38. Ibid., p. 94.
39. An announcement published in Rostov stated: 'All Jews of both sexes and all ages and all children of mixed marriages of Jews and non-Jews must report on Tuesday, 11 Aug. 1942 at 8:00 in the morning at the appropriate point', Arad, *Unichtozhenie evreev*, p. 220.
40. Altman and Krakovskii, *Neizvestnaia chernaia kniga*, pp. 37. A custodian in Kiev claimed that since the mother of one of the chidren who lived in the house was Jewish, he had to be turned over to the Germans — ibid., p. 39.
41. Ibid., p. 272.
42. There is, relatively, an extensive amount of literature on the Minsk Ghetto and underground. Only a few will be cited here: Holavski, *Be-sufat ha-kilaion*, (Jerusalem: Institute of Contemporary Jewry, 1988), pp. 87–176; Y. Greenstein, *Ud mi-kikar-bayovel*, (Tel Aviv: Hakibbutz Hameuhad, 1963); H. Smoliar, *Fun Minsker geto*, (Moscow: Der Emes, 1946); H. Smoliar, *Yehudim soviietim meahorei gderot ha-geto*, (Tel Aviv: Sifriat Poalim, 1984).
43. Regarding Jews in the partisan movement in the Soviet Union, see Moshe Kaganovich, *Der yidisher onteil in der partizaner-bavegung fun sovet-rusland* (Rome: Central Historical Commission at the Union of Partisans in Italy, 1948). The entire subject is still awaiting thorough research.
44. Perets Markish, *Milhome* (New York: Ykuf-Farlag, 1956), Vol. 1, pp. 291–4.
45. David Hanegbi (ed.), *Sefer ha-partizanim ha-yehudim* (Tel Aviv: Sifriat Poalim, 1959), Vol. 1, pp. 445–6, 461–2, 525–37; Shlomo Even-Shoshan (ed.), *Minsk ir va-em* (Jerusalem: Kiryat sefer, 1985), Vol. 2, *passim*.
46. *Vsenarodnoe partizanskoe dvizhenie v Belorussii v gody Velikoi otechestvennoi voiny* (Minsk: Belarusiia, 1975), Vol. 2, Part 1, p. 456.
47. Arad, *Unichtozhenie evreev*, p. 139. Altman and Krakovskii, *Neizvestnaia chernaia kniga*, pp. 57, 161, 202, 390.
48. Arad, *Unichtozhenie evreev*, p. 108. Another witness spoke about the massacre at Babii Iar and wrote, 'Elderly Jews prayed to God and shouted, "Shema Yisrael, Adonai Alohenu, Adonai Ehad".' In the town of Chudnov, 'the old man, Shmuel-Dovid, donned his prayer clothes [*tallit* and *tefillin*] and without waiting to be called, walked to the pit in the public garden'. Altman and Krakovskii, *Neizvestnaia chernaia kniga*, pp. 56, 159.
49. Ibid., p. 168.
50. Markish, *Milhome*, pp. 100–8.

11

Revival, Reconstruction or Rejection: Soviet Jewry in the Postwar Years, 1944–48

ALLAN L. KAGEDAN

Throughout its seventy-four-year existence, the Soviet government vowed to eliminate differences between nationalities and classes and replace them with a classless, socialist society. To this end, Soviet leaders devised a system of partial recognition of nationality differences tied to territorial units. These units, they hoped, would provide nationalities with a comfortable framework in which social and economic processes could dissolve distinct identities.[1]

By the beginning of the Second World War, Jews in the USSR realized that this nationalities policy had failed them. Despite colonization efforts in Crimea, Birobidzhan and elsewhere, the Jews lacked the settled territorial base needed to win even minimal respect for their ethnic rights. Paradoxically, in the chaos and destruction of the Second World War, uprooted Jews dreamed of finally integrating — as a national group — into the Soviet territorial system. The more modest hope of most Jews was for a return to their pre-war lives. But even the latter goal proved too ambitious — the immediate postwar years brought no revival, and equal measures of reconstruction and rejection.

In 1939, the Soviet Jewish population numbered approximately 3,000,000. Some 2,160,000 Jews lived in the territories that fell under Nazi control after June 1941. Of these, 1,533,000 were in the Ukraine, 350,000 in Belorussia, 200,000 in the RSFSR and 50,000 in Crimea. How many of these Jews were killed by the Nazis? Raul Hilberg put the number at 700,000; Willa Orbach estimated the total higher, at 1,000,000. In sum, about one-third of the pre-war Soviet Jewish population perished in the Holocaust. Of the remaining two million, one-half resided in areas not occupied by the Germans; the other half, joined by tens of thousands of Jews from Eastern Europe, fled ahead of the Nazi advance into the Soviet interior.[2]

At the war's end, returning home seemed a natural choice for those Jews who had evacuated into the interior. But the road there proved to be bumpy. Wartime circumstances had stimulated latent anti-Jewish sentiment in the Soviet occupied and unoccupied populations. On the one hand, Nazi propaganda articulated and glorified traditional anti-Semitic notions of Jews as parasites and evil-doers. On the other, local populations had every reason to resist the reintroduction of Jews, partly out of guilt over their own actions and possible retribution against them; and partly because they were concerned about the property and positions which they had seized when the Jews had fled.[3] The politics of scarcity — that is, the relations among individuals and groups conditioned by a lack of housing and consumer goods which had long characterized Soviet life — affected the Jews negatively.

A report from the Ukrainian SSR describes the hostile reception returning Jews received: physical assaults, court battles over property, the rejection of Jewish applicants for entrance into a school of management, and verbal attacks on Jews serving in the army.[4] Similarly, an engineer who returned to Kuibyshev told of pervasive anti-Jewish remarks in public places; the death of several Jewish families under suspicious circumstances; and the resulting efforts by many Jews to conceal their identity by changing their names.[5]

War-weary Jews received little support from local and union republic authorities for restoration of their cultural institutions. Jewish schools in the Ukrainian and Belorussian SSRs, closed after 1939, did not reopen after the Soviet victory over the Nazis. Nor did Yiddish-language publishing resume. Between 1946 and 1948, the presses of the Ukrainian and Belorussian SSRs published only one Yiddish-language publication each — a precipitous decline from the 1930s. Yiddish-language cultural activities were reduced almost entirely to Moscow, where 17 Yiddish books were published in 1946, 47 in 1947 and 46 in 1948.[6]

Jewish refugees from Poland and from areas annexed by the USSR during the war, who had fled their homes ahead of the advancing Nazis, also faced obstructions on the road back. In 1945, a group of Jewish refugees from Lithuania, Bessarabia and Bukovina applied to the Soviet authorities for relief from their status as *spetspereselentsye* (special migrants). Confined to small villages, the Jewish refugees were forced to report regularly to the internal security agencies. Though permitted to work at a nearby mine, some Jewish refugees were forbidden to reunite with their families.[7]

Returning Baltic Jews also faced a cultural downgrading, hinted at even before the Nazi invasion. Soon after the Soviets seized the Baltic states in June-July 1940, a prominent Jewish writer, Zelik Aksel'rod, who visited the region, warned local Jewish leaders of the Kremlin's decision to close Jewish institutions. Aksel'rod was subsequently imprisoned and executed by the Soviet authorities. The war interrupted Moscow's plans to squelch Jewish culture in the Baltics. When Soviet troops reconquered Vilnius, however, the authorities permitted only one Jewish school to open, and only those who spoke Yiddish better than any other language were permitted to attend. The school only went up to the fourth grade and its graduates had to pursue further study at Russian or Lithuanian-language schools. The Kremlin rejected appeals for a policy change from well-known Soviet Jewish writers and poets and Vilnius' Jews did not gain permission to publish in Yiddish.

Decimated in body and spirit, harassed by anti-Jewish sentiments, denied their property, and thwarted in their efforts to rebuild their culture, the predicament of Soviet Jews seemed to have reached a nadir. At the same time, this was the hour of approaching victory against nazism. In this dissonant atmosphere of tragedy and triumph, members of the Jewish Anti-fascist Committee (JAC) appealed to the Soviet leadership to make a categorical statement against fascism and nazism by granting Soviet Jews a viable autonomous republic.[8]

The Jews pinned their hopes on four war-related phenomena: a relaxation of political orthodoxy, moderation towards nationalities (with a few obvious exceptions), an anti-Nazi ideological stance, and improved relations with the West. Comparative political laxity was prompted by the exigencies of war: to win, the communist ideologues had to take a back seat to professional military men and even managers. Between 1941 and 1945, a streamlined government structure, the State Defence Committee (GOKO), ruled the USSR. Its initial membership was: Kaganovich, Beria, Voroshilov, Malenkov and Molotov. Aiding the Defence Committee was an informal 'managerial group', consisting of Kosygin, Planning Chairman N. A. Voznesenskii, Foreign Trade Commissar Mikoian, P. A. Rodionov, and Eugen Varga, a reformist economist, who was Jewish.[9]

Moderation was also the watchword in nationalities policy, with the notable exception of the wholesale deportations of the Volga Germans in 1941, the Crimean Tatars and a number of Caucasian groups from

1944–45. Despite, for instance, the collaboration of some Ukrainians with the German invaders, and the continued presence in the western Ukraine of anti-Soviet guerrilla groups, including the Organization of Ukrainian Nationalists, Moscow enhanced the republic's status. Early in 1944, the Soviet government granted the Ukrainian SSR its own foreign and defence commissariats and subsequently enlarged the republic's territory with lands taken from Romania and Czechoslovakia. In November 1944, Politburo member Nikita Khrushchev laid a wreath at the grave site of the Greek Uniate, Metropolitan Sheptitskii, a Ukrainian leader who had stood up to the Nazis.[10] These gestures were part of Stalin's ultimately successful campaign to win recognition for the Ukraine as an 'independent' state, meriting a seat in the United Nations. Another positive sign for the Jews was the good relationship between the Kremlin and the West; they realized that this would help their cause. Since America had a large Jewish population, the USSR could win political points with the US government if it created a Soviet Jewish republic. Much benefit in foreign aid could also be garnered. However, if Soviet-American relations soured, then the prospect for American financial or political assistance disappeared and the fact of the large American Jewish community would become a liability for Soviet Jews.

In 1944 Soviet Jewish hopes for positive relations with America were not entirely fanciful. Toward the end of the war and its aftermath, the Soviets did not see the West as a prime enemy. The USSR had joined the United States and its allies in the war against Hitler; they now shared a common foe — resurgent nationalist and fascist groups in Eastern and Western Europe. In 1945 at Yalta, Molotov promised the US future Soviet purchases of American goods totalling six billion dollars. Americans and Soviets collaborated on de-Nazification plans.[11]

Why not deepen this friendship by holding out the prospect of a Jewish Crimea? As in the 1920s, the Soviet leadership in the mid-1940s regarded notions of a Soviet Jewish republic as a useful foreign policy ploy. In 1944–45 three scenarios were possible in Palestine. First, the Zionist enterprise there could fail; if so, then the Soviet Jewish republic would indeed be the first and only Jewish national home. Second, a Jewish state in Palestine might become the subject of prolonged negotiations and conflict. In that case, a Soviet Jewish alternative could serve to goad the Western powers into reaching a solution. Third, a Jewish state could rise in Palestine and maintain close relations with the US and/or Britain. In this event, a rival Soviet Jewish republic would compete with Palestine for the money and political support of the world Jewish community.

It is not surprising that some Jews positively assessed their chances for a republic as World War II drew to a close. The Jews' wartime credentials were impeccable. Unlike other Soviet nationalities, the Jews had been steadfast anti-fascists and indeed had suffered severe blows at the hands of the Nazis; this should have raised their stature among the Soviet leadership. Il'ia Erenburg had personally delivered broadcasts to Soviet forces impelling them to victory.[12]

The proponents of a Soviet Jewish republic were the leaders of the (JAC). The Soviet government had created the JAC in 1942 to raise funds and secure support from foreign, particularly American, Jews. As the war came to a close, the JAC sought a new role. At its second plenum, held on the heels of the Battle of Stalingrad, the members decided to focus their efforts on refugee resettlement, Holocaust documentation and combating anti-Semitism. However, they differed over whether the organization should restrict itself to propaganda work, or whether it should engage in self-help efforts.[13]

In the public sessions of the JAC's third plenum in April 1944, the 3,000 participants reiterated their desire to preserve the memory of Holocaust victims, while two leaders, Solomon Mikhoels and Itsik Fefer, focused on the need to reduce anti-Semitic sentiment among the Soviet population. In private, JAC leaders discussed the notion of forming a Jewish republic in the Crimea or in the former Volga German ASSR. These sites would provide a real alternative to the failed Birobidzhan project.[14]

The JAC leaders were aware that the ideas they were discussing carried risks. After all, Birobidzhan was a functioning part of the Soviet Union; the revival of the Crimean plan underscored Birobidzhan's failure to become a viable Jewish autonomous region. Worse, Soviet Jews and Soviet officials had debated the relative merits of Birobidzhan and Crimea in the 1920s and a decision had been taken in favour of the Far Eastern option. The Crimea advocates had won a consolation prize: two Jewish nationality districts (*raiony*) were formed in the Crimea and another three in neighbouring south Ukraine.[15]

The JAC leadership, schooled in the practices of the Kremlin, sought to interest top leaders in their idea of a new Crimean plan. One conduit was Polina Zhemchuzhina, a friend of Solomon Mikhoels, who was married to Foreign Minister Molotov. The JAC also approached Lazar Kaganovich, the sole surviving Jew on the Politburo, and Solomon Lozovskii, who had long been active in communist party activities in foreign countries, especially the United States. Lozovskii was a Deputy Foreign Minister and, during the war, had been the Head of Sovinformburo (the Soviet agency responsible for servicing foreign correspondents) to which the JAC was subordinated.[16]

Contacts and connections notwithstanding, if the JAC's proposal were to succeed, it would have to be approved on domestic policy grounds. The solution was to draft a policy memorandum. The document began by providing facts about the dislocation of the Jewish population caused by the war. Over one million Jews had been killed, and many of the survivors were scattered around the USSR, in Central Asia, Siberia and the interior of the RSFSR. The dispersed Jews, the authors stated, wanted to return home, but they were hamstrung; moreover, many of the Polish Jewish refugees had become Soviet citizens; and Jewish homes and property had been seized by local residents.[17]

The memorandum warned that it would be dangerous to ignore the Jews because, already, these displaced individuals were falling prey to 'harmful elements', a veiled reference to Zionists and capitalists. These negative influences on Jews would impede 'further economic recovery and the revival of Soviet Jewish culture'. In addition, the dislocated Jews faced 'new outbursts of anti-Semitism', resulting from 'an intensification of certain capitalist vestiges in the psyche of the population...[and] fascist propaganda'. Completing the dialectic, anti-Semitism fed Jewish fears and evoked among Jews 'nationalistic and chauvinistic feelings'. Here, the JAC writers took a leaf from Stalin, who, in the early days of Soviet rule, had noted that nationalism fed nationalism.[18]

But this line of argumentation begged the question that if nationalism was the enemy of socialism, why address the concerns of particular ethnic groups at all? The JAC's response mirrored the Soviet reply of the 1920s: 'we must fight fire with fire. By giving the Jews some national relief and recognition, we can inoculate them against nationalism'.

This answer, however, had already been given in the form of the Jewish Autonomous Region in Birobidzhan. Conceding that Birobidzhan held the 'prospect of transforming it[self] into a Soviet Jewish republic, thus granting the Jewish people a normative and legal status...[which] equalized its position in the family of fraternal peoples', the JAC claimed that the region simply did not attract enough Jews to 'produce the desired effect'. In comparison, the Ukrainian and Crimean districts had been more successful both economically and culturally. Therefore, the Soviet government should include the issue of a Jewish republic on the agenda of postwar problems with the aim of resolving it 'once and for all...in a Bolshevik manner'.

The JAC noted that a plan for a viable Jewish republic would win foreign financial and political support. American Jews in particular would 'offer us essential help', a reference to the extensive involvement of the American Jewish Joint Distribution Committee in Soviet Jewish colonization efforts in the 1920s and 1930s. The memorandum concluded that among Soviet Jews, the idea of a Jewish republic 'enjoys unusual popularity'.

Since the plan for a revived Jewish republic never came to fruition, it is impossible to test these propositions, but both claims — American Jewish and broad Soviet Jewish support — seem dubious. American Jews had been chastened by their brush with Stalinism and the ravages of Hitler, and a new investment in the Soviet Union would have drawn less support than before, in particular, because of the considerable rise in the appeal of Zionism. In addition, wealthy American Jews who had previously sent money to the USSR were opposed to Jewish national politics — in Palestine as in the Soviet Union. In the 1920s and 1930s, the American Jews had acted as philanthropists; but the JAC's plan was clearly political. As for Soviet Jews, they too were affected by Stalinism and Hitler, and may have preferred to lay low rather than launch on a new political venture in search of an elusive Soviet Jewish republic.

The JAC memorandum never achieved its goal. Indeed, it brought tragic results. In July 1952, a group of Jewish writers and political figures were tried before the Military Collegium of the Soviet Union Supreme Court. A key charge against the group was that it had planned an armed insurrection with the aim of severing the Crimean region from the USSR and establishing there a Jewish bourgeois and Zionist republic that would serve as a base for American imperialism. After a week of deliberations, thirteen of the defendants were sentenced to death.[19]

The unlucky authors of the proposal were victims of a pendulum swing in Kremlin policy, counterbalancing the one that had opened the door to talk of a Jewish republic: the arrival of *zhdanovshchina*. Stalin signalled a return to hard-line attitudes in a February 1946 speech which placed the Second World War in a Marxist-Leninist framework. 'It would be a mistake', Stalin said,

> to consider that the Second World War broke out by accident or as a result of the errors of one statesman or another...Essentially, the war broke out as an inevitable result of the development of the world's economic and political forces on the basis of contemporary monopoly capitalism.[20]

During the course of *zhdanovshchina*, all the factors that had encouraged the JAC to propose a Soviet Jewish republic became irrelevant. The party once again subordinated the managerial class; the censors reimposed a full measure of control over culture; the West was again the enemy; and nationalities were mistrusted anew. In the case of the Ukrainians, for instance, this shift was translated into a ban on the Ukrainian Uniate Church, accused of collaboration with the Nazis, and a press campaign condemning nationalism.[21]

As for Jews, between 1946–48 the government clarified the main lines of policy: not obstructing the return of hundreds of thousands of Jews to the areas formerly occupied by the Germans; condemning Jewish nationalism; refusing to reconstitute Jewish cultural institutions eliminated before or during the War; and encouraging Jews to further assimilate, linguistically and culturally.

Statistical evidence bears out the party efforts to reintegrate Jews. In the March 1946 election campaign in the Ukrainian SSR, 47 Jews won seats to the 569-member Supreme Soviet, the nominal parliament. Thirty-two Jews were elected to the Soviet of the Union, and fifteen to the Soviet of Nationalities — increases from 1939, despite a much reduced Jewish population. A Soviet list of honours to 'workers in industry, agriculture, science, culture and art in the Ukrainian SSR', published in January 1948, included a significant number of Jewish names. And, as if to underscore the point that Birobidzhan was alive and well, and would not be abandoned or bettered, between January and March 1948, 300 Jewish families arrived in the Autonomous Region from the reconstituted Jewish settlements in the Ukraine and the Crimea. Althogether, between 1946 and 1948, some 10,000 Jews emigrated to the Jewish Autonomous Region.[22]

In spite of local discrimination and hostility, Soviet Jews moved back to the Ukraine and Belorussia during the late 1940s. By 1946, Kharkov's Jewish population numbered 30,000; Odessa's 80,000; and Chernovtsy's, 60,000. By 1959, the Ukrainian Jewish population had reached 840,000, the Belorussian 150,000, and that of the RSFSR, 875,000. Only 67,000 Jews remained in the Kazakh, Uzbek and Turkmen SSRs.[23] Moreover, a repatriation agreement permitted Polish Jewish refugees in the USSR to return to Poland.[24]

The paths home were many and varied. A Leningrad resident fled to Kirgiziia to escape the Nazis at the beginning of the war, and remained there until 1944. Returning to Leningrad in 1945, she found her apartment ransacked, but she was able to reoccupy it. A former Odessa citizen was less fortunate: her apartment had been occupied by the custodian. Luckily her brother-in-law was a major and drove a car. She explains: 'He drove to the house in uniform and told them to clear out or he'd give them something to remember.' Jews who had been exiled during the purges of the 1930s had a harder time returning to their native cities. But an overwhelming number of Jews did return to the western Soviet Union, if not to their exact pre-war residences.[25]

The ambiguous reception that returning Jews received in the early postwar period is illustrated by the fortunes of the Kiev Yiddish theatre company, which spent the war in the Kazakh and Uzbek SSRs.[26] In 1944, the local authorities rejected its application to return to Kiev on the grounds that its building had burnt down. After months of pleading, the Ukrainian authorities permitted the company to relocate in Chernovtsy. From its new base, the theatre troupe made further appeals to the Ukrainian and central authorities for leave to return to Kiev, and they received this, finally, in June 1945. But their return permit was valid for one month only.

After one of the theatre troupe's performances, Solomon Mikhoels, chairman of the JAC and director of the Moscow Yiddish Theatre (Goset), made a moving presentation of crystal vases to several of the actors. Mikhoels urged them to fill the vases with earth from Babii Iar, the site of the massacre of Kiev Jewry. 'Water [the vases] each day,' Mikhoels implored,

> and soon you will see...how that earth will bring forth flowers — a sign and symbol of the blossoming of the Jewish people whose adversaries wished to exterminate it. But the Jewish people will never be destroyed.[27]

In the immediate postwar years, Soviet Jews sought greater recognition as a distinct ethnic group, but the Soviet regime was unwilling to comply. For the Kremlin, the destruction of Jewish cultural institutions was, in effect, a progressive step on the path to assimilation. Jews remained a Soviet nationality in theory and would suffer discrimination on that account. But in practice the Soviet regime, insofar as it defended the rights of Jews, did so on an individual level. After 1948, even this modest form of postwar reconstruction would face severe tests.

NOTES

1. *The Program of the Communist Party of the Soviet Union: A New Edition* (Moscow, 1981), pp. 47–8.
2. Solomon M. Shvarts, *Evrei v Sovetskom Soiuze s nachala Vtoroi mirovoi voiny, 1939–1965* (Syracuse: Syracuse, 1966), p. 182; Willa Orbach, 'The Destruction of the Jews in the Nazi-Occupied Territories of the USSR', *Soviet Jewish Affairs* 6, 2 (1976), p. 23.
3. For both Nazi propaganda and its effect, and the attitude of the local population to their Jewish neighbours, see Mordechai Altshuler's 'The Unique Features of the Holocaust in the Soviet Union', in this volume.
4. Shvarts, *Evrei v Sovetskom Soiuze*, p. 197.

5. Mordechai Altshuler, 'The Jewish Anti-fascist Committee in the USSR in Light of New Documentation', in Jonathan Frankel (ed.), *Studies In Contemporary Jewry* (Bloomington, 1984), pp. 271–4 (document 7), 275–77 (document 8) and 278–80 (document 10).
6. Shaul Esh (ed.), *Jewish Literature in the Soviet Union during and following the Holocaust Period* (Jerusalem, 1960), p. 32; *Pirsumim yehudiim bi-Vrit ha-Mo'atsot, 1917–1960* (Jerusalem: Ha-Hevra ha-historit ha-yisraelit, 1961), Introduction, p. 99.
7. Altshuler, 'The Jewish Anti-fascist Committee', pp. 274–5.
8. Esh, pp. 15–16.
9. William O. McCagg, Jr., *Stalin Embattled, 1943–1948* (Detroit: Wayne State University Press, 1978), pp. 16–17.
10. Alexander Nekrich, *The Punished Peoples,* trans. George Saunders (New York: W. W. Norton, 1978); McCagg, *Stalin Embattled*, pp. 127–8.
11. McCagg, *Stalin Embattled*, p. 153.
12. Ibid., p. 105.
13. Shimon Redlich, *Propaganda and Nationalism in Wartime Russia* (New York: Columbia University Press, 1982), p. 44.
14. Ibid., pp. 51–2; for Birobidzhan see Robert Weinberg, 'Jews into Peasants? The Agrarianization of Soviet Jewry and Solving the Jewish Question in Birobidzhan', in this volume.
15. Allan L. Kagedan, 'Soviet Jewish Territorial Units and Ukrainian-Jewish Relations', *Harvard Ukrainian Studies* IX, 112 (June 1985), pp. 118–32.
16. Redlich, *Propaganda and Nationalism*, p. 44.
17. Mordechai Altshuler, 'The Jewish Anti-fascist Committee', pp. 271–80.
18. *Dvenadtsatyi sezd RKP(b), 17–25 Aprelia, Stenograficheskii otchet 1923 g.* (Moscow, 1968), pp. 447–9.
19. Benjamin Pinkus, *The Jews of the Soviet Union* (Cambridge: Cambridge University Press 1988), p. 176.
20. Shvarts, *Evrei v Sovetskom Soiuze*, p. 186.
21. McCagg, *Stalin Embattled*, pp. 127–8.
22. Shvarts, *Evrei v Sovetskom Soiuze*, pp. 186–92.
23. Salo W. Baron, *The Russian Jew under Tsars and Soviets* (New York: Macmillan, 1964), pp. 329–30.
24. *American Jewish Year Book, 1947* (Philadelphia: Jewish Publication Society of America, 1947), pp. 520–1.
25. Sylvia Rothchild, *A Special Legacy* (New York: Simon and Shuster, 1985), pp. 85–92.
26. Benjamin West, *Struggles of a Generation* (Tel Aviv: Massada, 1959), pp. 210–6.
27. Ibid., p. 116.

V

CULTURAL EXPRESSIONS
OF THE SOVIET JEWISH ANOMALY

12

The Re-education of Der Nister, 1922–1929

DAVID G. ROSKIES

> Stand up, my teacher and students. I deserve what was done to me. I brought you to shame, and you turned me to ash.
>
> Der Nister, 1929

Der Nister, born Pinkhes Kahanovitsh, was at the pinnacle of his career in 1922, and if anyone believed that stories would suture the wounds of the world, it was he. His fantastical tales, written in a poetic-hypnotic style, were appearing simultaneously in Moscow, Berlin, and New York, and a two-volume collection with the enigmatic title of *Gedakht* (*Imagined*) had just been published in Berlin.[1] Proclaiming that the World War and the Bolshevik Revolution had given rise to a 'modern myth', a new apocalyptic vision, Yiddish literary critic Shmuel Niger placed Der Nister at the centre of its pantheon.[2] Mark and Rachel Wischnitzer, meanwhile, recruited Der Nister and his good friend Dovid Bergelson as the literary editors of *Milgroym*, the most lavishly illustrated journal of Jewish arts and letters ever produced. In Berlin, the Mecca of Yiddish high culture, Der Nister might have found the only *Gemeinschaft* willing to support his élitist, uncompromising, and utopian art. In a sacred fellowship of Yiddish utopian dreamers, Der Nister would have officiated as High Priest.

What happened in fact was quite a different story. The critical reception of Der Nister's fantastical tales was stillborn. Except for Marc Chagall, in 1917, Jewish artists ignored them altogether. None of Der Nister's verse for children was ever set to music. After 1929, it was impossible to find his fantasies for grown-ups anywhere but in a private or specialized library. Tales that so brilliantly refashioned the Yiddish folk- and fairy tale were never channeled back to the folk. They were either discarded as so much decadent trash or simply forgotten.

These dreams of a literary-cultural renaissance came to an end when Bergelson and Der Nister quit the editorial board of *Milgroym* after the first issue (1922) and threw in their lot with the Bolsheviks. Later that same year the Moscow-based *Shtrom* carried this one-sentence letter to its editors that arrived just as the issue was going to press:[3]

> We wish to inform our colleagues, whom we had invited by word of mouth or in writing to collaborate in *Milgroym,* that we no longer have any connection to the Editorial Board of this journal and are no longer contributors thereto
> D. Bergelson
> Der Nister

Der Nister made a cleaner break still with his petty-bourgeois and nationalistic past in 1923. Under his joint editorship, an anthology titled *Geyendik* was published by the Jewish Section at the Commissariat for Public Education in Berlin, with an opening dedication to *Shtrom*, and featuring Der Nister's most programmatic tale, 'Naygayst' ('New Spirit'). This story, dated 'Moscow-Malakhovka, Summer 1920', ended with an ecstatic vision of the rising East, and there could be no doubt whatsoever that this 'Holy East' was the site of Lenin's great experiment.[4] Der Nister and his fellow pilgrims were not quite ready to set out for the New Jerusalem on foot, as the title of their journal suggested, but their trajectory was already set by the Red Star above.

Pinkhes Kahanovitsh came from priestly stock that did not abide any compromise. His father, Menahem-Mendl, once lost himself so completely in a talmudic tractate that he remained oblivious to the civil war raging in the streets outside. Aaron Kahanovitsh, his older brother, became a Bratslav Hasid and cut himself off from the world. Max, the sculptor, was off and away in Paris. And Pinye, who sculpted each word; who was the harshest critic of his own work and discarded whatever struck him as inferior; who absorbed the style and structure of Reb Nahman of Bratslav's *Tales*, dreamed of redemption-through-art.[5]

Pinkhes Kahanovitsh means Phineas, Son-of-the-Priest, or Kohen. It was unmistakably the name of a Russian Jew But the writer who called himself *Der Nister,* a pen name so redolent with kabbala and Jewish esoteric traditions, served notice from the very outset that he belonged to the world; to the cosmos. For all that this 'hidden One' probed the depths of purity and danger and wrote an almost liturgical prose, he had no intention of placing the Jewish perspective at the centre of consciousness. Unlike previous Yiddish writers who had tried to pass themselves off as preachers, pietists or folk philosophers, but whose real concerns were decidedly secular and this-worldly, Der Nister donned the cloak of a Jewish mystic, high priest, or prophet, the better to explore the universal reaches of creation, revelation and redemption. He delighted, moreover, in mixing poetry and prose, cosmology and folklore, and made religious syncretism into the gospel of a new, idealistic religion. The name for Der Nister's new faith was Symbolism, as practised in Russia in the first decade of the twentieth century Its central credo was the ability of art to literally transform mankind.

Just about everything in Der Nister's method — the attempt to go beyond the denotative limits of language and achieve pure musicality through repetition, connotative sound relationships, word inversions; his preference for myth, the occult and the demonic; not to speak of his view of the poet as prophet — were inspired by the teachings of Vladimir Solov'ev and the poetry and prose of Andrei Belyi. Like them, Der Nister communed with the spirit of E. T. A. Hoffmann, master of the supernatural rendered in realistic manner. If fellow Symbolist Aleksei Remizov was moved to write for children, so too was Der Nister. And if the Russian poets and storytellers mined the Eastern Orthodox Church for underground traditions and still potent Christian myths, Der Nister sought access to Jewish mystical traditions.[6]

World War I and the Bolshevik Revolution strengthened Der Nister's faith in the marriage of art and reality. From his perspective, the collapse of the old order in Russia presaged the rise of a new holy community composed of wandering writers, graphic artists, and teachers. When he first moved to Kiev with his wife and three-year-old daughter in the winter of 1916, the 32-year-old paterfamilias had little to show for himself except for the coveted 'white ticket' exempting him from active service. He hated the thought of tutoring Hebrew as he had done before and hoped instead to make his living as a translator.[7] The stories of Hans Christian Andersen were his initial project.[8] A year later Der Nister published his first original *Tales in Verse* for children with stark and striking illustrations by Marc Chagall.[9] Active as well in the newly-organized network of Yiddish secular schools, Der Nister by war's end had come to view education as the front line in the aesthetic revolution.

Never was Der Nister more explicit about his own utopian ambitions than in 'New Spirit', his ecstatic manifesto of 1920 [10] Here and here alone he reconciled his élitism and esoteric knowledge with the demands of the collective. 'Your calling is to be below', Ishmael the High Priest prophesies to young Phineas the Priest as both are seated in heaven, 'and with others, and with *your kind* to build a *new* tabernacle there...Because people there have long grown unaccustomed to a tabernacle, and because for long now and for quite some time God's word and the Spirit's voice have not been heard among the Priests'.[11] Following through, young Phineas, son of Menahem the Priest (whose name, like everything else in this story, cries out to be identified with the author), joins with other priests in a mountain cave down below, where they commune in sacred fellowship to redeem what is left of the world. While the Mountain Spirit dreams and prophesies the imminent redemption, with imagery borrowed from the Gospels, the Revelation of John and Reb Nahman's 'Master of Prayer',[12] our young hero addresses an impassioned plea to his 'brothers and friends', who belong 'to a single generation and a single idea': That which existed in a disparate state before must now be brought together and distributed among the folk, for the priests possess the spark and spirit that everyone else has lost.[13] Then all emerge from the cave and face the East, rising from its slumber.

Though written in the heat of apocalyptic events, in the summer of 1920, when he and other Yiddish writers from war-torn Kiev had fled to Moscow and among other escape routes, were seriously considering America, Der Nister thought highly enough of this messianic manifesto to publish it three times, each time under Soviet auspices and in the Soviet-Yiddish orthography.[14] That he addressed his most public and propagandistic story to the radical pro-Soviet fellowship alone, means that he did not choose that route by default, however few viable alternatives were open to him.

'New Spirit' gave voice to Der Nister's most personal and cherished dreams. From Berlin he wrote repeatedly to critic Shmuel Niger in New York (whom he had never met and would never meet) of the need for a central forum that would express 'all our accumulated seriousness, our growth and awareness', and would unite the best and greatest talents, now dispersed throughout the world.[15] Yet given the rootlessness of Yiddish cultural life in German exile, he despaired of such a centre ever taking shape. 'A whole generation of ours will die without making a final confession', he wrote in a brilliant turn of religious phrase (*A gantser dor undzerer vet shtarbn on vide*).[16]

Where would one create such a centre if Der Nister himself had just broken off with both his publishers, in Warsaw and Berlin, and had the most disparaging things to say about the Yiddish press and literary periodicals in New York? How did he expect Abraham Lyessin, editor of the literary monthly *Di tsukunft* in New York, to continue publishing his stories when the cover letter inveighed against 'your American ignoramuses'? 'They don't understand [my stories]?' he raged. 'So they'll learn to understand. In any event, it's not my mistake but their disgrace.' (*Bekhol-oyfn iz dos nisht mayn feler, nor zeyer bezoyen*).[17] The Soviet Union beckoned precisely because everything there had been destroyed by war and revolution, so there was still a chance of starting over from scratch, of recreating the centre in one's own uncompromising image. Or as Dovid Bergelson put it in his programmatic essay on the 'three centres' of Yiddish culture — America, Poland, and the USSR — 'socioeconomic conditions' in the Soviet Republic had destroyed the rotten foundations of the Jewish petit bourgeoisie, leaving the field open for an organic bond to be forged between the Yiddish intellectuals and the Jewish labouring masses.[18] In 1926, the year of Bergelson's essay, Der Nister returned to the USSR, as did Peretz Markish and Dovid Hofshteyn — to rebuild the tabernacle of Yiddish culture 'down below'

Der Nister was given only three years, 1927–29, in which to adapt his personal style to the demands of the 'collective' or give up story-telling altogether. During that period (which marked the end of NEP), the guardians of proletarian culture mounted ever fiercer attacks against him for his decadence, aestheticism, indeed, for his *nisterizm.*[19] As a result, Der Nister's game of hide-and-seek took on a desperate urgency.

In his priestly fictions, Der Nister had maintained a hierarchy of values and a strict separation between good and evil, spirit and matter, fantastical story and everyday life. In his political fictions, written in the Soviet Ukraine, everything became the antithesis of everything else, victim turned tyrant, the hero's quest collapsed into a maze of self-betrayal, suicide, drunkenness, miscegeny, promiscuity and greed, and the ravenous bears (Mother Russia? the Soviet State?) stood ready to tear his heart out. It was as if the guilt of Der Nister's betrayal weighed so heavily upon him that he turned the vicious attacks upon him inward; as if the possibilities of dialogue and true discipleship had now been reduced to one long monologue, soliloquy and confession; as if the art he had fashioned with so much care and hope had been abandoned by his fellow priests, leaving only *Der Nister aleyn* — Der Nister himself, by himself.

Abandoned though he was, he did not go down without a fight. Pulling out the stops, Der Nister delivered a catalogue of blasphemies aimed at all that he once held sacred The vehemence and vulgarity of

'A Tale of an Imp, of a Mouse, and of Der Nister Himself' (1929) can take one's breath away, so great is the stench that emanates from all the copulating, pissing, farting, defecating and fat producing that goes on there.[20] Its menagerie of rodents, insects, and lascivious demons, makes this sequel to Kafka's 'Metamorphosis' and precursor of Art Spiegelman's *Maus* the first X-rated Yiddish fantasy. Like 'Der Nister Himself', the story's Pied Piper and parodic autobiographer, the reader is torn between laughter and revulsion.

This story takes place in two different lands, one inhabited by people of glass whose only fleshy part is their navel, and so they cannot eat, sleep or copulate; and the other, a fleshy country where *all* people do is eat, sleep and copulate. Der Nister visits both, and great healer that he is, restores the first to passion by making their navel grow and grow, and inspires the second land to abstinence, only to discover that one country is the mirror of the other This last image was most subversive: Der Nister's revelation that the land of capitalist pigs, with the fat literally oozing from their bodies, was the same as the land of glass where there was nothing to eat and people were robbed of all desire. In the modern world, in postwar Europe, west or east, there was no longer any difference, any choice to be made, between spirit and matter.

Der Nister was forced to give up writing symbolist tales one year before the terror-famine began that claimed the lives of some ten million peasants in his native Ukraine, and seven years before the show trials of the Great Terror. But judging from what little he did write between 1927–29, he could have produced a Yiddish storytelling corpus commensurate with the Stalinist horrors. His years of training and mastery did not fail him. Moreover, the immediate and painful experience of trying to conform to party dictates suggested to him a higher, universal level of struggle which he then recast into the language of Yiddish fantasy. To do this, the settings necessarily became more crowded, urban, noisy, smelly, venal and hazardous. No more leisurely strolls through the forest or desert; in fact, there were no more quests at all, only senseless trials and tribulations. In 'Under a Fence: A Revue' (1929), the last will and confession of Der Nister as a storyteller, the main event was a trial-within-a-trial, culminating in an auto-da-fé.[21] If Der Nister had warned Shmuel Niger back in 1923 that their generation would 'die without confession', here was the writer's last chance to do penance for betraying his artistic mission. In so doing, Der Nister unwittingly wrote the forced confessions of the many writers — Jews and gentiles — who would soon perish without a trace.

Der Nister offers several clues that 'Under a Fence' is to be read as his final and most personal statement — perhaps even as an answer to 'New Spirit', his utopian manifesto of 1920. It is the most modern of all his stories, the most overtly psychological, and the most openly derivative of *European* literary sources. The subtitle, 'A Revue', already points to the contemporary world of the cabaret, or in this case, of the circus. The story's outer frame is similarly grounded in reality: a scholarly type, someone with proper bourgeois credentials, is rejected by a circus lady. He gets drunk, is awakened by a cop, goes home to sleep it off and is awakened sometime later by his daughter to whom he tries to tell the whole story 'Under a Fence' is thus a variation on the theme of Heinrich Mann's *Professor Unrat*, better known in its unforgettable screen version with Marlene Dietrich, *The Blue Angel*.[22] Here the artiste is played by Lili, a distant relative of the arch-seductress of Jewish lore, Lilith. Otherwise, the only identifiable character is the monk Medardus, hero of E. T. A. Hoffmann's *The Devil's Elixir*, a novel that also features a double trial.[23]

The 'revue' is also a 're-view', that is, a transcript of what the groggy, guilt-ridden professor says to his daughter the morning after. As his opening line, 'I am sick to death with grief', attests, the burden is great and there is much to work through. Here is a man obsessed with his own guilt. Because of that, his confession follows a psychological, rather than logical sequence.[24] After confessing his love for the circus performer and imagining himself as a circus rider, dressed in flesh-coloured tights and with a whip in his hand, and guilty as well for his daughter's fall in the circus ring, the vision turns surrealistic: the walls of his study crack open and begin pelting father-and-daughter with stones. He manages to protect her, but one stone hits him in the head and knocks him out cold.

Therein begins his trial and formal confession. Thus far the dreams and hallucinations developed his sense of guilt that was tremendously egotistical. From now on he is referred to as a *nozir*, a hermit, as he stands accused before his teacher and fellow monks of betraying the faith.[25] 'I feel like a turtle without a shell', he confesses, 'completely naked'.[26] This was not the seductive nakedness of skin-tight leotards, the nakedness that casts its illusory spell on the crowd, but the nakedness of a hermit who has spent his whole life within the stone tower of his monastery and has left it, and his habit, forever.

How could a person move from one such home to another? The tower was built for permanence as a repository of eternal truth. It supported a monastic, ascetic life that was run according to a strict and exclusive hierarchy.[27] In his initial defence, the hermit blames the fallen state of things inside the tower: it is hollow, cold and dark; the light has gone out The world outside considers it a museum piece, while inside there is no love; straw children suckle from (male) breasts of straw. He even blames Medardus, his teacher: 'You should have foreseen it, Medardus, my teacher, and told us to abandon the house.' The hermit defected because he lost faith in his own convictions, because of public opinion, because of financial pressures, and because of — the Dustman. Dustman is to the tower what Lili was to the circus: the id, the seducer. Dustman convinces the hermit to burn the monastery down. Dustman makes his straw-baby come alive and then leads her and her father to a lucrative job in the circus. There, in the circus, Dustman stages a mock trial of the monks, to the hysterical delight of the crowd, at which the *nozir* outdoes the rest in ridicule: 'And I mocked more than any of them, and when I told the monks off, I was wittier than anyone. And finally the sentence was pronounced: dirt and garbage that had to be burned.'[28] Lili, meanwhile, is jealous of the monk's daughter and plots her downfall. Because he could foresee what would happen and did nothing to stop it, the father accepts responsibility for her accident, and for everything else:

> And it is my fault, my judges. This is what happened to me after I left our house. I betrayed my teachers and made my only daughter a cripple And it all came about in the course of time because the corners of our house were broken up, and dustmen and those who lived off our mold got control of us, and we were good for nothing and completely unprepared for the outside world, and they took over and led us where dustmen have to lead us, to the street and the marketplace, to tricks and the circus and to giving up the shirt off our backs, the eyes in our heads, and the daughter of our loins, for a piece of bread Sentence me and do what you want with me. Deny me, just as I denied you, and just as I injured my daughter, do me injury too, and carry out your sentence on me [29]

That is not all he is ready to confess, for abruptly the circus act changes and it is he, once more, who stands in the dock, with Medardus and his students playing the judges. Since the crux of his defence is that the Dustman made him do it, he must now confess that 'dustmen and similar creatures are not persons or living creatures at all, but only illusions, born in the sick minds of hermits, and to allow oneself to be led by them and do as they do is a disgrace'. He is therefore burned at the stake for believing in witchcraft, and rising from the ashes he says: 'Stand up, my teachers and students. I deserved what was done to me. I brought you to shame, and you turned me to ash (*Un ikh hob aykh tsu bezoyen gebrakht, un ir mikh tsu ash*).'[30] Then he wakes up with his head under a fence — the place, according to Jewish custom, where suicides are buried.

The worlds of the monastic tower and the circus tent are mutually exclusive Therefore he is torn apart. The first is a world of religious faith in which the artist served God through traditional means. Medardus embodies that sacred trust, the old literary traditions that once had worth. But in the secular world, it is each man for himself. Here the Dustman takes over: the artist ready to sell himself and the con-artist who can make straw babies come to life. Whosoever betrays his artistic mission by allowing it to be identified with the idolatry, the witchcraft that is political ideology, can only end in guilt, condemnation and self-annihilation.

'Under a Fence' is, of course, open, to other, equally ominous readings. It can be read, for example, as a statement on assimilation into European society. The hermit's conversion to the circus is real, but Lili's acceptance of him is not. Agnon developed this theme in his Nisterian parables written during the Holocaust. Yet Der Nister did not labour so long and hard in the forbidding stone tower of his utopian art in order to agonize over the fate of the Jews. However profoundly he grieved over betraying his messianic calling, he remained as surely a disciple of Hoffmann as of Nahman. Even at the point when the State apparatus was conspiring to rob the Jewish writer of his Judaism *and* of his art, Der Nister produced a universal parable on the fate and function of art in the modern world.

'Under a Fence' marked the end of Jewish fantasy, and for all intents and purposes, of Jewish messianic dreams, in the vast Soviet Empire. Yet despite the horrible strictures of that time and place, the High Priest was able to bid farewell to Yiddish fantasy not in a programmed confession of error, but in an amazing symbolist tale in which he did penance for having made the wrong political choice six long years before.

NOTES

1. Der Nister, *Gedakht*, 2 vols. (Berlin: Literarisher farlag, 1922–23).
2. Sh. Niger, 'Moderner mitos', *Dos naye lebn* 1 (1923), pp. 22–31. The essay begins with a quotation from Russian symbolist writer Aleksei Remizov.
3. *Shtrom* 3 (1922), appended to p. 83.
4. See Dov Sadan, 'Der shtern fun derleyzung', *Toyern un tirn* (Tel Aviv: Yisroel-bukh, 1979), pp. 56–7.
5. Portrait of his father: Yankev Lvovski, 'Der Nister in zayne yugnt-yorn', *Sovetish heymland* (March 1963), p. 106; on brother Aaron see Khone Shmeruk, 'Der Nister, hayyav ve-yetsirotav', Intro. to Der Nister, *Ha-nazir ve-bagdiyah: sippurim, shirim, ma'amarim*, trans. Dov Sadan (Jerusalem: Bialik Institute, 1963), pp. 9–10; and on brother Max see Kh. Shmeruk, 'Der Nister's "Under a Fence": Tribulations of a Soviet Yiddish Symbolist', *The Field of Yiddish, Second Collection* (The Hague: Mouton, 1965) pp. 285–6.

The major and indispensable source on Der Nister's personal life are his letters to critic Shmuel Niger from 1907–23, now published and annotated by Abraham Novershtern. See 'Igrotav shel Der Nister el Shmuel Niger', *Huliyot* 1 (Winter 1992) pp. 169–206. In his introduction (pp. 159–68), Novershtern points out the astonishing fact — unique in the annals of Yiddish literature — that Der Nister never republished anything of his that first appeared in the Yiddish press before 1913.

6. The Symbolist influence on Der Nister's writing has been dealt with by Shmeruk, in 'Der Nister's "Under a Fence"'; by Delphine Bechtel, in her unrevised dissertation, 'Der Nister's Work 1907–1929: A Study of a Yiddish Symbolist' (Berne: Peter Lang, 1990), pp. 35–44; and, most recently, by Daniella Mantovan, 'Der Nister and his Symbolist Short Stories (1913–1929): Patterns of Imagination', Ph.D. diss. (Columbia University, 1993).

7. This new information on Der Nister's activities during World War I is gleaned from letter No. 26 to Shmuel Niger, from Nov.–Dec. 1916.

8. *Andersons mayselekh*, Der Nister, trans. (Kiev, 1919).

9. Der Nister, *Mayselekh: A mayse mit a hon, Dos tsigele*, illus. Mark Chagall (Petrograd: Kletskin, 1917); facsimile ed. (Jerusalem, 1983); 2nd ed. (Kiev: Kiever farlag, 1919); 3rd ed. (Warsaw: Kultur-lige, 1921). The Warsaw edition has only two anaemic drawings by Chagall. The 4th ed. published by Shveln (Berlin, 1923) has none at all.

10. Der Nister, 'Naygayst', in Der Nister, L. Kvitko, M. Lifhshits (eds.), *Geyendik* (Berlin: Jewish Section at the Commissariat for Popular Education, 1923), pp. 5–30. Published simultaneously in *Shtrom* 4 (1923) pp. 8–30 and reprinted in *Fun mayne giter* (Kharkov: Melukhe-farlag fun der USSR, 1928), pp. 7–40.

11. *Geyendik*, p. 13.

12. Some of these New Testament allusions have been identified by Sadan, 'Der shtern fun derleyzung', and Mantovan, Ch. 4.

13. *Geyendik*, p. 23.

14. See Khone Shmeruk, 'Azivat sofrei yidish et Brit ha-Mo'atsot ve-shuvam eleha le-or iggeret bilti-yadu'a shel Der Nister', *Bein Yisrael le-umot* [Festschrift for Shmuel Ettinger] (Jerusalem: Zalman Shazar Center, 1987), pp. 297–305. The quote is on p. 303.

15. Letter No. 31, summer 1922.

16. Letter No. 34, mid-1923.

17. Undated letter to Lyessin, YIVO Archive, quoted by Novershtern, n. 100. On Der Nister's break with the Kultur-lige (relocated in Warsaw), which published his translations of Hans Christian Andersen, see letter No. 32 of November 1922. In letter No. 34 of mid-1923, Der Nister accused the Berlin-based Literarisher farlag of making excessive changes in his text. He therefore decided to publish volume three of *Gedakht* elsewhere (which, in fact, he never did).

18. D[ovid] B[ergelson], 'Dray tsentern', *In shpan* 1 (April 1926) pp. 84–96.

19. Shmeruk, 'Der Nister's "Unter a ployt"'; Bechtel, 'Der Nister's Work', pp. 17–21.

20. Der Nister, 'A mayse fun a lets, fun a moyz, un fun Dem Nister aleyn', *Fun mayne giter*, pp. 43–80.

21. Der Nister, 'Unter a ployt (revyu)', in *A shpigl oyf a shteyn*, pp. 186–217. After first appearing in *Di royte velt* (Kharkov), 7 (1929), the story was reprinted at the end of the Kiev edition of *Gedakht*, replacing 'A Bove-mayse' The English translation is by Seymour Levitan, in Irving Howe and Eliezer Greenberg (eds.), *A Treasury of Yiddish Stories*, 2nd rev. ed. (New York: Penguin Books, 1989), pp. 574–96.

22. For a comparison between the two, see Mantovan, 'Der Nister and his Symbolist Short Stories', Ch. 6.

23. On this connection, see Shmeruk, 'Der Nister's "Under a Fence"', p. 281, and Bechtel, 'Der Nister's Work', pp. 223–6.

24. I owe the psychological reading of the story to lecture notes of Dan Miron's course, 'Yiddish Fiction in the Twentieth Century: Continuity and Revolt after the Classicists (1900–1918)', Max Weinreich Center, New York, Fall 1976.

25. Levitan, in an otherwise admirable translation, consistently renders *nozir* as 'scholar', thus eliminating the religious dimension of the story.

26. Der Nister, 'Unter a ployt', pp. 194–5; in English, S. Levitan, trans. in Howe and Greenberg (eds.), *A Treasury of Yiddish Stories*, p. 580.
27. For a parallel use and probable source of this tower image, see Vladimir E. Alexandrov, *Andrei Bely: The Major Symbolist Fiction* (Cambridge: Harvard University Press, 1985), p. 17.
28. Der Nister, 'Unter a ployt', p. 211; Levitan, p. 591.
29. Der Nister, 'Unter a ployt', pp. 213–14; Levitan, p. 593.
30. Der Nister, 'Unter a ployt', p. 215; Levitan, p. 595.

13

Vasilii Grossman and the Holocaust on Soviet Soil

JOHN GARRARD

Fifty years ago and two years before Allied armies had liberated concentration camps in Germany, Vasilii Grossman discovered the first evidence of what has become known in English as the 'Holocaust'.* As both a front-line special correspondent for *Krasnaia zvezda*, the influential daily newspaper of the Armed Forces and a creative writer, Grossman faced the dual dilemma that continues to bedevil all of us today: How are the facts to be recorded so that the memory will never be lost? And how can the facts be presented so that Jew and non-Jew alike, separated by time and space, can learn the appropriate lessons? As Nietzsche said, 'There are no facts in themselves. For a fact to exist, we must first introduce meaning.'[1]

The genocide against the Jews was all the more traumatic for Grossman because he feared that his mother, Ekaterina Savel'evna, had been one of the victims at Berdichev, a small town southwest of Kiev, where he himself had been born and had grown up. In several letters to his father from the front soon after the German attack (his parents had long been divorced and his father lived in Moscow), Grossman expressed the fear that both his mother and his daughter Katia from a previous marriage had been caught in the German net. On 8 August 1941 he wrote:

> I am troubled constantly by Mama's fate; where is she, what has happened? If you find out, write to me at once. Have you tried to check with the Evacuation Administration?[2]

* The author owes a special debt to Carol Garrard for setting aside her own work in order to read an initial draft of this chapter and make valuable suggestions for its improvement. Gratitude is also due to the Memorial Foundation for Jewish Culture in New York City and the Foreign Travel Committee of the University of Arizona for providing funds that enabled the author to attend the Moscow Conference.

Fortunately, he soon learned that Katia had been evacuated with her Ukrainian mother to Tashkent. But 'now I feel doubly concerned for Mama', he wrote on 1 October 1941. The long-feared news arrived in May of 1942. On the last day of that month Grossman wrote to his father from Chistopol' (where he was on leave writing *The People Immortal* (*Narod bessmerten*) which was to become the first Soviet war novel) that the Evacuation Administration had written to say that his mother's name was not on the list of those people removed from the war zone: 'I knew myself that she had not got away, but my heart sank when I read those sad lines.'

Following the decisive Soviet victories at Stalingrad and Kursk in 1943, Grossman advanced with the Red Army across Ukraine. He saw firsthand the mass atrocities the Germans had been committing since the summer of 1941. Some of the ruined towns and shattered villages he entered had been well known to him before the war. He had attended school in Berdichev and Kiev before moving to Moscow. He had often returned to visit his mother and other relatives elsewhere in Ukraine, and to vacation on the Black Sea coast. Like both his parents he considered himself Russian. But every metre of ground abandoned by the German army brought fresh evidence that the Wehrmacht and SS considered him and every member of his family as Jews. All human characteristics other than this were ignored: Jews were to be butchered whether assimilated or not.

It was in the full bitterness of this family tragedy that Grossman wrote two pieces about the genocide against Soviet Jewry in the crucial year of 1943. The first, 'The Old Schoolteacher' ('Staryi uchitel'') is a fictionalized account of the events leading up to the mass murder of Jews in a small Ukrainian town; it was published in *Znamia*. [3] The second, 'Ukraine without Jews' ('Ukraina bez evreev'), is a documentary report of the German effort to murder all Jews in occupied Ukraine; it appeared (in a Yiddish translation) in the 25 November and 2 December 1943 issues of the newspaper *Eynikeyt*, published by the Jewish Anti-fascist Committee (JAC), which Grossman joined in the spring of 1944.[4] These two 1943 publications prefigure the strategies he would employ in order to shape the material for his documentary record *The Black Book* (*Chernaia kniga*), which he edited and helped to compile, and his fictional masterpiece *Life and Fate* (*Zhizn' i sud'ba*). Both reveal Grossman's awareness that the meaning, in the Nietzschean sense, of these horrific events must be communicated through art, and that art has its own laws. Raw facts must submit to these laws if they are to be gathered, to use Yeats' phrase, 'into the artifice of eternity'.

In 'Ukraine without Jews' Grossman begins by relating that he visited many Ukrainian villages, where the few survivors told of German brutality. But there were other places where he saw no survivors, no tear-stained cheeks, and heard no crying, indeed, no noise at all. Where were the inhabitants? Where had they gone? He answers his own questions:

> There are no Jews in Ukraine. Nowhere — Poltava, Kharkov, Kremenchug, Borispol', Iagotin — in none of the cities, hundreds of towns, or thousands of villages will you see the black, tear-filled eyes of little girls, you will not hear the sad voice of an old woman, you will not see the dark face of a hungry baby
>
> All is silence. Everything is still. A whole people have been brutally murdered.

To demonstrate that a whole people were destroyed, as well as their 'homes, families, books, beliefs', Grossman presents a list of people with their various occupations, each preceded by the same refrain, *ubityi* (murdered). Then he differentiates people by their personality and appearance: some women were faithful and devoted wives, others were frivolous; some girls were pretty, others were plain; but all were *ubity*. Grossman ends with mothers and even suckling babies — again all preceded by the word *ubityi* The repetition of *ubityi* has the monotony of a metronome, signalling one by one the death-knell of the countless numbers of Jews murdered by the Germans and their allies in occupied Ukraine, 1941–43. Eventually, Grossman stops this painful repetition by admitting defeat. It is impossible to list all the occupations and characteristics of the victims, just as it is physically impossible to give all their names.[5] It is even impossible to name all the perpetrators, the officers and soldiers who committed or collaborated in these crimes.

In 'Ukraine without Jews' Grossman demonstrates his awareness of the dimension of the human and artistic problems involved in presenting the facts of the Holocaust. He says that the human mind possesses a special quality that makes it inconceivable for us to fully comprehend horrors of this magnitude:

> This limitation is a fortunate characteristic of the human consciousness, which protects people from moral torment and madness. This limitation is at the same time a malevolent characteristic of our consciousness, because it makes us thoughtless, permitting us to forget (if only for a moment) the greatest crime in world history

However, insists Grossman, we must remember:

> It seems to me that, in the cruel and terrible time in which our generation has been condemned to live on this earth, we must never make peace

with evil We must never become indifferent and undemanding either of
ourselves or of others.

Even before he compiled and edited eyewitness accounts for *The
Black Book*, Grossman knew that documenting the record was not
enough. The Holocaust places demands on us that extend beyond the
skill of a given writer who marshals and presents the evidence to his
readers. The truth of what happened is not simply a matter of fixing
the guilt of the perpetrators and their accomplices. As Grossman
shows in 'The Old Schoolteacher', the very enormity of the crime
committed destroys any hope of adequately covering what happened.
Therefore, the writer must select in order to shape the material in a
compelling way The crimes of the Holocaust were so horrific that the
story does not tell itself. To merely list the facts is to risk repelling the
very audience of later generations who must be reminded of what
took place.

Boris Isaakovich Rozental' lives in the reader's memory as
unique — one of those teachers mentioned as having been *ubit* in
'Ukraine without Jews' The narrator does not name the town, but
Rozental' is described in detail, physically and emotionally He is 82,
old and frail. He had taught algebra and geometry for fifty years, but
now is retired on a small pension. He loves books; he receives letters
from former students; he had an unhappy love affair that has affected
him for the past sixty years of his lonely life. Rozental' behaves just as
he did before the Germans arrived He alone of all the inhabitants
remains unaffected by the virus that has spread over the town, in-
fecting it with evil. The Germans' approach summons forth wicked-
ness, 'just as in the folk-tale the magic spell evokes evil spirits'. Rozental' is destined to be shot with the other Jews of his town. The firing
squad is made up only of volunteers; no German soldier was forced to
carry out this grisly task As the column of doomed people reaches the
killing ground, a scuffle arises: one of the Jewish men strikes a German
guard. A little girl named Katia Vaisman loses touch with her mother
and grandmother. She holds on to Rozental', who picks her up and
wonders: 'How can I calm her fears, how can I deceive her?' Rozental'
watches as the first fifteen victims are marched to the lip of the ravine.
Once again, as in 'Ukraine without Jews', Grossman stresses that each
victim is different, unique, and thus irreplaceable.

Awaiting death, Rozental' finds himself longing for a word of
comfort, 'the word he yearned so much to hear all his life, more than
all the wisdom of books about the great ideas and actions of mankind'.
In a poignant triumph of the human spirit over evil, at the moment of
his death Rozental' is comforted by Katia, whose father has already

been killed at the front. The little girl turns her calm face to Rozental' with sympathy and compassion: '"Teacher", she said, "don't look that way, you will be frightened." And like a mother she closed his eyes with her palms.' The narrator leaves them at that moment, forcing our imagination to hear the gunshots that will end their lives.

Similarly, in *Life and Fate* Grossman declines to describe the physical details of death inside the gas chamber. That horror of smashed brains and congealed blood he portrays only in his documentary article 'The Hell of Treblinka', published at the end of 1944.[6] Instead, throughout the gas chamber scene in his novel we are inside the consciousness of an unmarried doctor, Sof'ia Levinton, who cradles the orphan David in her arms at the moment of death, just as Rozental' befriends Katia. In 'The Old Schoolteacher', the little girl's name recalls that of Grossman's own daughter (perhaps a projection of his nightmare that she could have shared his mother's fate). Katia's gesture — made 'like a mother' — suggests Grossman's mother, as does Sof'ia Levinton's final thought before she too dies: 'I have become a mother.' The fictional schoolteacher's fate reflects what Grossman imagined must have been the last moments of Ekaterina Savel'evna, who was also a frail and lonely retired schoolteacher.

Considering the facts that both 'Ukraine without Jews' and 'The Old Schoolteacher' were published under wartime censorship and that Grossman was obliged, or chose, to give his story an upbeat ending, he managed to deal with a remarkable number of sensitive subjects. These included desertion by Soviet soldiers and glances at Ukrainian collaboration in the shooting of Jews. Some of the local Ukrainians eagerly awaited the Germans' arrival, having (as Grossman can only hint) suffered Soviet repression during collectivization a decade earlier.

While by this time Grossman understood how Einsatzgruppe massacres were organized in Ukraine, it seems that he did not yet know the technical means of murder in the 'Operation Reinhard' death camps of Poland. When the Gestapo chief in 'The Old Schoolteacher' discusses with the Wehrmacht commander problems involved in murdering such a large number of Jews, he laments that they must 'operate in field conditions'; it is very different in Poland, where 'we had broader possibilities of employing more energetic methods'. It was only in 1944, when the Red Army entered Poland and he witnessed the liberation of Majdanek and talked to survivors of the destroyed death camp at Treblinka, that Grossman could move beyond the vague 'energetic methods' to a detailed account of the gassing and burning in 'The Hell of Treblinka'.

'Ukraine without Jews' and 'The Old Schoolteacher' illustrate the fact that documentary and fiction are not airtight genres. In 'Ukraine without Jews' Grossman employs his skills as a creative writer to give flesh and blood to the nameless victims. Using Rozental' as a mouthpiece in 'The Old Schoolteacher' Grossman introduces the metaphor of a 'vast ladder of oppression' to explain the way in which Nazi racism ranked all the subject peoples of occupied Europe. At the top of the ladder are the Danes, then the Dutch, the French, the Czechs, Greeks, Serbs, Poles, and beneath them the Ukrainians and the Russians: 'The lower down, the more blood, slavery, sweat'. Beneath the ladder yawns the vast chasm reserved especially for the Jews, the *only* people condemned to annihilation.[7] Thus all the subject peoples on the ladder must behave circumspectly to avoid the Jews' fate The schoolteacher makes the important historical point that this structure results from a cold-blooded plan, from 'the simple arithmetic of bestiality, not impassioned hatred'.

In both works Grossman stresses the vital and, given official Soviet policies then and later, ideologically suspect fact that the Jews had been marked for liquidation as a people His determination to press home this point was demonstrated by his participation in the Jewish Anti-fascist Committee's efforts to document the Holocaust. From the spring of 1944 he served as a member of the JAC's Literary Commission, which had the responsibility of collecting and editing eye-witness accounts for *The Black Book* He took over as chairman of the Commission after Il'ia Erenburg's resignation.

It is clear from the transcript of the Literary Commission's meeting on 13 October 1944 that Erenburg understood the political scene and the difficulty of getting *The Black Book* approved. For example, he insisted that the word 'Ukrainian' should be replaced with the word '*politsiia*'; he called this a political question that brooked no argument. Grossman responded that the word '*politsiia*' should be avoided altogether. Why not use instead 'villain', 'traitor', 'murderer', and even 'Judas'. Grossman appears to have grown impatient. He went on to object to spending so much time on accounts of those who escaped the genocide:

> All the materials in our possession are accounts by people who managed to escape death by some miracle But we also have the responsibility of speaking on behalf of those who lie in the earth and cannot speak for themselves We must shed light on what happened to the 99 per cent of those led off to Babii Iar, and not to the five people who escaped from Babii Iar.[8]

Such frank comments suggest that the optimistic ending to 'The Old Schoolteacher' was probably imposed by the censors. However, as chairman of the Literary Commission, Grossman found he had to compromise with Glavlit (the Chief Directorate for the Protection of State Secrets in Publications) if he hoped to get *The Black Book* published as quickly as possible. To this end he inserted the obligatory quotation from Stalin in his Foreword — a remark made fifteen years earlier (on 12 January 1931) in answer to a question from the Jewish Telegraphic Agency in America on the subject of anti-Semitism.[9] In the Foreword, Grossman posits 'Soviet humanism' as not only the wartime enemy but also the ideological adversary of nazism By introducing what Russians used to call this 'locomotive' of correct ideology, Grossman succeeded in persuading the ever-watchful censors to pass the work for publication. However, all his efforts were in vain.

Grossman saw the manuscript through to completion and even to the proof stage, as can be seen from a letter he wrote to his father on 14 August, 1946 (probably from Peredelkino, the retreat of the Writers' Union outside Moscow):

> I am still working hard. And now in addition to my personal writing I have the job of checking the proofs of *The Black Book* Things seem to be going pretty well with *The Black Book*. The director of the publishing house thinks that it should be published by the winter.

Ironically, on this same day — 14 August — the Central Committee of the CPSU approved the decree 'The Journals *Zvezda* and *Leningrad*'. The decree was published in the newspaper *Kul'tura i zhizn'* on 20 August 1946 and marked the beginning of *zhdanovshchina* — the savage postwar repression of Soviet intellectual and creative life named after Central Committee Secretary for Ideology Andrei Zhdanov, that led to the arrest and re-arrest of countless innocent persons, the 'anti-cosmopolitan' campaign, and eventually the Doctors' Plot The decree spelled doom for *The Black Book* and almost for Grossman himself.[10] Only Stalin's death saved his life.

With the end of hopes to publish a documentary account of the Holocaust, Grossman turned his attention to the second horn of the dilemma posed in 1943: how to recast the basic facts of the Holocaust into an artistically valid presentation to give them meaning for later generations. The results of this effort are best seen by juxtaposing his account of the murder of the Jews in his home town Berdichev, which he wrote (at Erenburg's request) for *The Black Book*, against his fictionalized account of the same crime which appears in *Life and Fate*.

In 'The Murder of the Jews in Berdichev' ('Ubiistvo evreev v Berdicheve'), Grossman lays out shocking details of a specific instance of this genocide, called by Churchill a 'crime without a name' Not only names, but also dates and places are given. When Grossman mentions acts of kindness toward Jews, he names the people involved. But he does not hesitate to mention collaboration in planning and carrying out the massacre of Jews by 'the chairman of the town council Reder (a Russified German who had been a POW in World War I)' and 'the police chief Koroliuk'. Grossman calls the latter 'a traitor' — thus following his own suggestion at the 13 October 1944 meeting of the Literary Commission, quoted above. Even though Grossman was obliged to use the term '*politsiia*' he clarifies that these were Ukrainian volunteers For example, when it is discovered on the morning after the massacre that many victims had crawled out of the pits and some were still alive, we are told: 'The next morning the Germans and the police picked up the bodies, killed those still breathing, and buried them again.' But just a couple of pages later Grossman tells us that 50 Jews with special skills were kept alive until the Soviet counter-offensive: 'they were put in jail and forced to work on behalf of the Gestapo and the Ukrainian police'.

Throughout 'The Murder of the Jews in Berdichev' Grossman holds nothing back. He describes each German *Aktion*, carefully designed to dehumanize the victims by treating them as animals The Germans laugh as they kill. At first they force Jews to jump in the acid vats located in the leather-curing factory. Grossman reports that the Germans made a joke of this: 'they said they were curing the skins of Jews'. He relates another German 'joke': an officer ordered an elderly kosher butcher to ritually kill a neighbour's two small children. When he refused, the officer killed him with the knife.

Grossman explains exactly how 12,000 people were shot on just one day.[11] He spells out the sickening details that he learned from eyewitness accounts in 1944:

> The pits were filled with blood since the clay soil could no longer absorb any more, and the blood spilled over the edges, forming enormous puddles and flowing in rivulets into low-lying areas. The boots of the executioners were soaked in blood.

Grossman does not mention that his mother was one of the victims.

When the time came to distil the essence of what had happened at Berdichev into his novel *Life and Fate*, Grossman made two crucial decisions: he would portray only those events leading up to the massacre, just as he had in the earlier fictional treatment, 'The Old Schoolteacher'; and, he would filter the facts through the eyes of Viktor Shtrum's mother — who was quite obviously based on Ekaterina Savel'evna, just as Shtrum is an *alter ego* of Grossman himself. Both decisions are embodied in the device of a letter, which

Anna Shtrum has smuggled to her son outside the ghetto by means of a friendly courier. Grossman himself never received such a letter from Ekaterina Savel'evna; this is his own version of what his mother might have written during her last days. The narrator of 'The Old Schoolteacher' breaks off before the gunshots. Anna's letter ceases at an earlier moment as the Jews await their fate in the temporary ghetto

What Grossman kept from *The Black Book* and what he changed for Anna's letter represents a remarkable example *in situ* of the writer transmuting fact into art Ekaterina Savel'evna was a French teacher; Grossman makes the fictional Anna Shtrum an eye doctor but, penned in the ghetto and no longer able to practise medicine, she passes the time and earns money by giving the ghetto children French lessons. In his letters to his father, after learning that his mother had not been evacuated, Grossman wrote that he had dreamed she was alive. In the novel he transfers his own emotions to Anna Shtrum, who says that *she* has dreamed of her own mother. Her dreams are a release from the horror of her situation; when she awakens she remembers that 'there are Germans here, and I am a leper; I had not fallen asleep, but on the contrary had woken up'. By transferring to Anna his own dreams, Grossman leaps time and space to be, even if only briefly, psychologically united with his mother.

Anna's letter functions as a narrative from beyond the grave. Thus, as Grossman said at the 1944 meeting of the JAC Literary Commission, it speaks for those who 'lie in the earth and cannot speak for themselves' Grossman forges a living connection between his created text of Anna's letter, and the historical events that occurred in Berdichev from 7 July until shortly before 15 September 1941, the day when Ekaterina Savel'evna was most probably shot by members of Einsatzgruppe C and Ukrainian collaborators. Berdichev is present in the narrative, but the name of the town is never given; instead Anna writes that Germans entered the town on 7 July [1941] — the date Berdichev fell to von Kleist's XI Panzer division.[12] Anna's letter reads as unmediated fact — she naturally would not know the designations of military units. That 'truth' can be found in a history book. What Anna knows is the kind of people the Germans are: 'That morning I was reminded of a fact that I had forgotten over the years of Soviet rule, the fact that I was a Jew. Some Germans drove past on a lorry, shouting out: *"Juden kaput"*'[13] This incident, drawn directly from Grossman's article about Berdichev in *The Black Book* is now given substance by being put in the mouth of a 'real' person.

Some incidents are considerably changed when reworked in the novel. It is significant that many changes involved the degree of

Ukrainian collusion. In *The Black Book* Grossman reports that when Jews had been declared outside the law, non-Jews had been so incensed that they went to the German commandant's office to protest. However, the protesters were chased away. Anna's letter shows us an entirely different account of what is discernibly the same event She writes that a Ukrainian woman had ordered her out of her own room: '"You are outside the law", she said in such a way as to suggest that this was to her advantage But her daughter Alenushka sat with me all evening and I read stories to her.' The city's Ukrainians are far from petitioning the German commandant to redress the Jews' wrongs. Anna relates that there was a meeting between the German commandant and the Ukrainian citizenry, but it was called by the commandant. There a long-time friend of Anna's stood up and denounced the Jews in vile language that Anna had previously associated only with the Black Hundreds of the late tsarist period. The supposed documentary record of *The Black Book* must yield to the truth found in the fictional *Life and Fate*.[14]

When Grossman transmuted events from *The Black Book* to *Life and Fate*, he performed the creative miracle of breathing life into facts. The Jews in Anna's ghetto are varied; some are good, some are bad, and some are indifferent as people, as she herself relates: 'My dear Viktor, I have seen many bad people here — grasping, cowardly, cunning, some even ready to turn traitor' She has also seen examples of kindness and goodness from the people she would have least expected to show compassion. It is the man she thought callous who carries her bundle to the ghetto, gives her 300 rubles and promises to help. Anna's letter begins with an admission straight from the heart, 'Viktor, it is hard to really get to understand people.'

Viktor resurrects his mother's phrase in the short section that immediately follows her letter. As a scientist he tries to categorize and define the ideologies of the two warring states. Both nazism and 'Soviet humanism' are inhuman, precisely because they have arrogantly proclaimed that their ideology does 'understand people'. Each ends by reducing the infinite variety of human beings either to races or classes Each has a lowest common denominator, whether it be called 'Jew' or 'enemy of the people'. Thus the Nazi and Soviet ideologies are merely two faces of the same Janus of hatred and exclusion, not bitter enemies, as had been stated in Grossman's Foreword to *The Black Book*.

Viktor uses words hauntingly similar to those in Anna's letter: 'Never before the war had Shtrum thought of himself as a Jew, or thought of his mother as a Jew.' Then Viktor segues into the themes

Grossman adumbrated in his Foreword to *The Black Book* but without Miltonic 'Forc'd Hallelujahs' to Stalin and the Red Army. Here he offers a more searching analysis of the Nazi virus first mentioned in 'The Old Schoolteacher' The physics terminology is entirely appropriate to Viktor's professional background, but also serves to set nazism into the general intellectual and political frame of reference:

> The century of Einstein and Planck was also the century of Hitler...There is a terrible similarity between the principles of fascism and those of contemporary physics.
>
> Fascism has rejected the concept of a separate individuality, the concept of 'a man', and operates only with vast aggregates. Contemporary physics speaks of the greater or lesser probability of occurrences within this or that aggregate of individual particles. And are not the terrible mechanics of Fascism founded on the principle of quantum politics, or political probability?[15]

Grossman, who held a degree in chemistry from Moscow University, understood that the behaviour of a quantum, a discrete bundle of energy, cannot be pinpointed exactly, but only estimated, using probability theory. He draws a parallel with nazism, which claimed to embrace a kind of *political* probability — the idea that the elimination of certain social strata would result in a higher probability of a desired occurrence. By exterminating the Jews, an entire 'quantum' of society, Hitler believed it was probable that a super-race would emerge.

Viktor does not live under nazism, but the inference is clear: Stalin's Soviet Union also eliminates whole 'quanta' of people — bourgeoisie, capitalists, kulaks, Mensheviks, 'rootless cosmopolitans' National Socialism's 'racism of the blood' is paralleled by Soviet socialism's 'racism of class'. Both deny the uniqueness of each individual.[16] Anna Shtrum echoes Grossman's own simple theme: she is not a 'beast without rights' (a phrase which subliminally recalls the butchering of Jews in *The Black Book*), but an 'unfortunate human being'.[17]

Thus we see that *Life and Fate* concerns more than the Holocaust; it represents a sustained fictional analysis of the nature of German nazism and of 'Soviet humanism' — which in his censored Foreword to *The Black Book* Grossman had defined as a worthy opponent to nazism. The documentary record of the Holocaust on Soviet soil needs creative reworking in fiction. Indeed, the two genres must exist in a symbiotic relationship if the full story is to be told and its 'meaning' is to be grasped.

Grossman had ended his Foreword to *The Black Book* with a plea:

> May the memory of the sufferings and fearful deaths of millions of murdered children, women, and old people never be forgotten. May the

radiant memory of those brutally murdered people become a terrifying guardian of good. May the ashes of the crematoria flow in the hearts of the living, calling for a brotherhood of people and nations.[18]

Grossman acted out that imperative in his own lifetime In 1950 and again on the twentieth anniversary of his mother's death in 1961, he wrote her a letter — answers to the one she could not send in real life.[19] He also dedicated *Life and Fate* to her, not to her memory, but as though she were alive — as he had promised in his second letter. For him, the wound of her brutal murder would not heal.

As the tormented twentieth century draws to a close, both Nazi and communist ideologies have been discredited. But the Holocaust cannot be packed away as an historical event that is over and done with. Given the enormity of the crimes, which depended upon thousands of active collaborators and millions who gave their consent through silence, it could be argued that the Holocaust's 'meaning' is that human beings are an evil species. Grossman tries to draw a different conclusion. He asks us to love one another without the distorting lens of racism and intolerance. His message of the consequences that will flow when humans 'make peace with evil' endures for our own time.

NOTES

1. Cited in James E. Young, 'Interpreting Literary Testimony: A Preface to Rereading Holocaust Diaries and Memoirs', *New Literary History* 18, 2 (Winter 1987) For a judicious review of the peculiar relationship between art and horror, see Lawrence L. Langer, *The Holocaust and the Literary Imagination* (New Haven: Yale University Press, 1975).
   The opening of two Holocaust museums in the United States in 1993 — the Wiesenthal Center's Museum of Tolerance in Los Angeles on 8 Feb. and the US Holocaust Memorial Museum in Washington, DC, on 22 April — has helped focus the debate over the ways in which the memory should be preserved and the lessons learned. See Herbert Muschamp, 'Shaping a Monument to Memory', *New York Times*, 11 April 1993; Yossi Klein Halevi, 'Who Owns the Memory', *Jerusalem Report*, 25 Feb. 1993.
2. Unpublished correspondence The author is grateful to Ekaterina Vasil'evna Zabolotskaia for making this correspondence available. The original copies, which she deposited in the Central State Archive for Literature (Tsentral'nyi Gosudarstvennyi arkhiv literatury i iskusstv — TsGALI), have been closed to researchers by Grossman's stepson Fedor Guber
3. *Znamia*, 7–8, 1943.
4. This author has not seen either Grossman's original Russian (which may no longer exist) or the published *Eynikeit* version (25 Nov. and 2 Dec. 1943), but 'Ukraina bez evreev' — retranslated back into Russian — is included by Shimon Markish in his *Vasilii Grossman: Na evreiskie temy* (Jerusalem: Biblioteka-Alia, 1985), II, 333–40.
   It is possible that Grossman had originally intended the material in 'Ukraina bez evreev' to be part of his long article 'Ukraina', published in *Krasnaia zvezda*, 12 Oct. 1943 The original version of 'Ukraina' excludes the ending that appeared in a collection of Grossman's wartime writings, *Gody voiny* (Moscow, 1945), which was

translated into English as *The Years of War, 1941–1945* (Moscow, 1946). This later version ends with the statement of refugees from Kiev that the Germans had massacred 50,000 Jews at Babii Iar in Sept. 1941 (the actual number of victims was in fact much higher) and that they were now frantically digging up the corpses and burning them in an effort to conceal the evidence of their crime.

5. In the United States, B'nai B'rith has coordinated a national project to have volunteers read aloud the names of victims. The project is entitled 'Unto Every Person There Is a Name' The reading takes place on Holocaust Memorial Day. In 1993 names were read in 120 communities, including the steps of the Capitol in Washington, DC. The reading occupies volunteers for the entire day. However long the list, B'nai B'rith admits that their record is still incomplete, for the names of all the victims are still a mystery, just as the exact number of victims can only be rounded off to the nearest tens of thousands. See 'Victims Recalled' in *New York Times*, 10 April 1993.

6. Grossman's 'Treblinskii ad', *Znamia* 11 (1944) was the first documentary account of a death camp to attract attention not only in the Soviet Union, but further afield; it was translated and used at the Nuremberg Trials of leading Nazi war criminals.

7. In fact, the gypsies were a second group condemned to total annihilation, although there were far fewer in number than Jews It may be that Grossman was unaware of this fact at the time.

8. Stenogramma zasedaniia literaturnoi komissii Antifashistskogo Evreiskogo Komiteta (13-go oktiabria 1944 goda). Il'ia Al'tman kindly gave me a copy of the typed notes of this meeting, and also of the Protokol zasedaniia prezidiuma EAK (ot 25 aprelia 1946 goda). For an excellent English translation and commentary, see Ilya Altman, 'Toward the History of *The Black Book*', *Yad Vashem Studies*, Vol. XXI (Jerusalem, 1991).

9. Vasilii Grossman, 'Predislovie' in *Chernaia kniga* (Jerusalem: Tarbut, 1980), pp. 5–6. English translation taken from *The Black Book* (New York: Holocaust Publications, 1981) This version is based on a copy of the proofs that Vasilii Grossman gave to Irina Erenburg (the writer's daughter) for safekeeping once he realized that the Soviet authorities were going to destroy the project, and most members of the JAC as well. One wonders whether Stalin's American correspondents were happy with the statement that 'active anti-Semites' were executed according to Soviet law. It is worth pausing to consider that Stalin at this time was ordering the mass famine in Ukraine, which resulted in the deaths of several million innocent men, women and children — and indeed in cannibalism among the starving population.

10. In late 1993 a more complete version of *The Black Book* was published: *Chernaia kniga* (Vilnius: Yad, 1993). This version is also based on a copy of the proofs mentioned in note 9, above. In 1993 Yad Vashem in Israel and the State Archive of the Russian Federation (Gosudarstvennyi arkhiv Rossiskoi Federatsii — GARF) — formerly the October Revolution Archive, TsGAOR — published in Jerusalem and Moscow the unedited documentary evidence which the JAC was planning, initially with official approval, to publish as a second volume of *The Black Book: Neizvestnaia chernaia kniga*, with an introduction by Yitshak Arad, and an essay by Il'ia Al'tman outlining the tragic history of the project and of the fate of leading members of the JAC.

11. For eyewitness accounts of the massacres at Berdichev, drawn from KGB archives, see S. Elisavetskii, *Berdichevskaia tragediia (Dokumental'noe povestvovanie)* (Kiev, 1991). The documents suggest that a total of 18,640 people were shot in mid-September of 1941, not 12,000. Grossman was evidently using a rough estimate from witnesses.

12. There is some disagreement about the actual date of the fall of Berdichev. Alan Clark states, in *Barbarossa: The Russian-German Conflict 1941–45* (New York: Morrow, 1965), p. 132, that Panzers entered both Berdichev and Kazatin (connected by a vital twenty-mile stretch of railway) 'on the night of 15th–16th July' But John Erickson, in *The Road to Stalingrad* (Boulder, CO : Westview Press, 1984), p. 168, states categorically that the 11th Panzer Division took Berdichev 'on 7 July [1941]' My inference is that Erickson (and Grossman) were working from the same Soviet source while Clark was using a German record. It seems probable that Grossman's personal interviews with eyewitnesses would be more reliable.

13. For Anna Shtrum's letter see Vasilii Grossman, *Zhizn' i sud'ba* (Moscow: Knizhnaia palata, 1989), pp. 63–71. This is the complete edition, based on Grossman's own

corrected manuscript, which had been hidden for a generation by an old school friend and his wife. The manuscript contains a dedication: 'Posviashchaetsia moei materi Ekaterine Savel'evne Grossman'.

14. In this matter we are of course dealing with a specifically Soviet obstacle to providing a complete documentary record of the Holocaust, and that is Soviet censorship.
   The whole subject of Ukrainian collaboration was *verboten* after the war; it might raise embarrassing questions. In his 'secret speech at the Twentieth Party Congress, Khrushchev said that Stalin did not deport the Ukrainians for the simple reason that there were too many of them.

15. Vasilii Grossman, *Zhizn' i sud'ba* (Moscow, 1989), p. 72. The English translation from *Life and Fate*, trans. Robert Chandler (New York: Harper and Row, 1985), p. 94. This translation was made from an earlier, incomplete manuscript of the novel.

16. Viacheslav Kondrat'ev, praising a documentary on Soviet penal companies and battalions, notes that Grossman was the first to make this 'amazing parallel' between Hitler's Germany and Stalin's Russia. See 'Parii voiny: shtrafnye roty v obektive kinokamery', *Literaturnaia gazeta*, 31 Jan. 1990.

17. Grossman returned to this same theme at the end of his life, in his brilliant memoir, *Dobro vam!*, an account of his two-month visit to Armenia in the winter of 1961–62. See the present writer's article, 'Palomnichestvo neveruiushchego: Dobro vam! Vasiliia Grossmana', in Boris Averin and Elizabeth Neatrour (eds.) *Russkaia literatura XX veka: issledovaniia amerikanskikh uchenykh*, (St. Petersburg: Petro-Rif Publishers, 1993), pp. 458–75.

18. In the meetings of the Literary Commission of the Jewish Anti-fascist Committee, Grossman always insisted on referring to the victims of the Holocaust as 'people' and 'human beings' — not Jews. His idea was to focus on the Jews as people, like everyone else, so that readers would feel more involved in their fate.

19. The two letters are reproduced in 'Pis'ma materi. Pis'ma k materi...', *Nedelia* 47 (1988), p. 18.

14

Institutionalized Jewish Culture from the 1960s to the mid-1980s

VELVEL CHERNIN

Official Soviet doctrine regarding culture which was 'national in form and socialist in content' permitted Soviet Jews to maintain certain features of their culture until their ultimate 'natural assimilation'.* True, Soviet doctrine excluded any forms of national-cultural autonomy that were not connected with a nationality's territorial concentration. Lenin's dictum censuring the Bund on this issue was part of the curriculum at all levels of education beyond primary school. Yet, given their status, or perhaps, in order to give them status as a Soviet people, the Jews had been officially granted territorial autonomy — in the Jewish Autonomous Region in Birobidzhan.[1]

By the early 1950s, however, the Jewish Autonomous Region, had suffered a second round of purges and cultural repression. As a result, it was unable to provide conditions for exercising this right even to its own Jewish population, which constituted only a small fraction of Soviet Jews.[2] The newspaper *Birobidzhaner shtern* preserved its sluggish existence as the sole relic of the past. Apart from the language, it had no specifically Jewish content and up to 1974 was not circulated nationwide. Thus, in practice, throughout the 1950s Soviet Jews were denied the right to maintain their culture in any form. Alone

---

* The author was on the editorial staff of *Sovetish heymland* from 1983-1988. During that time he worked closely with editor-in-chief Aron Vergelis. For a year he served as Moscow correspondent for *Birobidzhaner stern*. He also taught Yiddish and wrote texts for the two Moscow-based Yiddish theatre troupes. Unattributed information in this chapter is based on the author's personal experiences in those capacities.

of all Soviet national cultures — except for those of the 'punished peoples' deported by Stalin from their national territories — Jewish culture had been outlawed *in toto*.[3]

Only toward the end of the decade, for 1959 was the hundredth anniversary of the birth of Sholem Aleichem, did a major cultural event in Soviet Jewish life take place, with the publication of a volume of Sholem Aleichem's collected works in the original Yiddish.[4] It was the first book published in the USSR in Yiddish from the time Der Emes publishing house in Moscow was closed in 1948. In the course of liquidating the press, all the Yiddish type was destroyed. As a result, preparing the Sholem Aleichem volume for print posed serious typographic problems. The book was finally set in newspaper type which had miraculously escaped destruction. It is significant that the traditional Soviet orthography of Yiddish was used in the edition.

Foreign factors also played an important role in shaping Soviet policy toward Jewish culture in the Khrushchev period. The presence of numerous Jewish communities abroad, whose influence on the policies of Western countries was often overestimated by the Soviet *apparatchiki*, the existence of the State of Israel, with which the USSR maintained diplomatic relations up to June 1967; an erroneous appraisal about the status of Yiddish there and in the major Diaspora communities — all these figured powerfully in the decision to establish the Yiddish-language *Sovetish heymland* as an organ of the USSR Writers' Union. The journal initially appeared bimonthly and then on a monthly basis.[5]

It is significant that beginning with the first issue of *Sovetish heymland*, which appeared in mid-1961, the magazine discarded the traditional Soviet Yiddish orthography still used by the *Birobidzhaner shtern* and came considerably closer to the norms accepted in the West and in Israel. It thus restored final consonants while maintaining phonetic spelling in words of Semitic origin.

The poet Aron Vergelis was the chief editor of *Sovetish heymland* for three decades. In the postwar period he had headed Radio Moscow's Yiddish department which broadcast for listeners outside the Soviet Union. He remained in the post until 1949 when Yiddish broadcasting was discontinued.[6]

Like other colleagues and writers in the new journal, Vergelis belonged to the generation of the Jewish men-of-letters who had matured as creative personalities prior to the annihilation of Soviet Jewish culture in 1948. The very title, *Sovetish heymland*, combining the names of two almanacs from the 1940s — *Sovetish* and *Heymland* — implied continuity in the cultural and social life of Soviet Jews.[7]

To the degree that this was tolerated by the Soviet regime at the time, the magazine sought to serve as an *ersatz* semi-official organ of national-cultural autonomy. In its day, the Jewish Anti-fascist Committee and its newspaper, *Eynikeyt,* had attempted to fulfil this same role.

Practically all Jewish cultural and public undertakings in the period from the 1960s to the mid-1980s, which were initiated, or at least, permitted by the Soviet authorities, were connected in one way or another with *Sovetish heymland* and its permanent editor-in-chief. Vergelis subsequently became the unofficial censor of all Yiddish-language literature and the chief Central Committee consultant on matters relating to Soviet Jews and, to an extent, even to Jewish communities outside the USSR.[8]

In 1962, the Moscow Jewish Theatre Ensemble was created. Most of its leading actors had been with Mikhoels' Goset (the Moscow Yiddish State Theatre) which was closed in 1949. The ensemble, under the administration of Moskontsert, toured cities all over the USSR.[9] It should be noted that at a time when the publication of literature in Yiddish was a losing venture — appearing in editions of no more than several thousand (and not all of these were sold), the Moscow Jewish Theatre Ensemble was a box-office success, playing to full houses.

According to the 1959 USSR population census, the number of Jews who claimed Yiddish as their native tongue was a little over 20 per cent of the number of people registered as Jews.[10] This percentage fell consistently from census to census. It should be noted, however, that these figures did not fully reflect the actual situation, because responses were influenced by non-linguistic considerations. In many cases the respondent named the language in which he could read and write, and not the language which he had spoken in his parents' home. Sometimes Yiddish was claimed as a native tongue by people who had either no command or very poor command of the language but had a keen urge for national self-identification. It was clear that the number of Jews who knew spoken Yiddish (even if only passive knowledge) by far exceeded the number of those who could read it, because since the 1930s the vast majority of Soviet Jewish school-children were studying in non-Jewish schools. Yiddish theatre, unlike Yiddish literature, offered a form of national self-identification accessible even to Jews who had no command of Yiddish whatsoever. No simultaneous translation facilities were available during the performances of the Moscow Jewish Dramatic Ensemble, but there were always people who understood Yiddish (usually the older generation) and they would whisper translations of the essential passages to those who did not know the language.

The ensemble's first director, Binyomin Shvartser, had received his training as an actor at the school attached to Goset. He sought to preserve its theatrical traditions and repertoire under new conditions. This situation continued, with small variations, until 1980, when Shvartser was replaced by Yakov Gubenko, a director belonging to the younger generation, who knew hardly any Yiddish. At that point, a new generation of actors took over. This altered both the repertoire and the spirit of the theatre. After the death of the ensemble's 'star', Zinovii Kaminskii, Sholem Aleichem's classic work *The Enchanted Tailor* was dropped from the repertoire. Although Yiddish remained the language of the stage, Russian became the theatre's working language. Most of the young actors did not know any Yiddish and would mechanically learn their parts from texts transliterated into Cyrillic letters.

Yiddish-speaking actors were becoming scarce and in the mid-1980s Yakov Gubenko made repeated attempts to create a bilingual, and even a Russian-language, Jewish theatre in which Yiddish would have a purely ornamental function.[11] This turning point in the theatre's development brought about a clash between Gubenko and Vergelis. Vergelis had initially supported the ensemble, interceding with various administrative bodies on its behalf and trying to become its playwright-in-residence. In contrast to Gubenko, however, Vergelis stubbornly supported a Yiddish theatre which performed exclusively in Yiddish.

The amateur theatres that existed in three Soviet cities during the period under discussion — Vilnius, Kaunas and Birobidzhan — had much weaker links with *Sovetish heymland*. Attempts were also made to establish Yiddish artistic collectives in other cities — Tallinn, Kishinev, Chernovtsy and Leningrad — but they met with only limited and temporary success.

The oldest registered drama group was the Vilnius Jewish Amateur Theatre established in 1956, following the 20th Party Congress. In 1965, it was given the official status of Amateur (*Narodnyi*) Theatre. It comprised several groups of performers, who were divided by genre, and in practice it constituted the Lithuanian capital's Jewish cultural centre. In its prime it included as many as 150 amateur artists, many of whom attained the level of professionals. The Palace of the Lithuanian Trade Unions served as premises for rehearsals. The theatre performed exclusively in Yiddish, which was only natural considering the comparatively low level of language assimilation of Lithuanian Jews.[12]

The theatre's dramatic company was headed by a professional director, Emil' Khersonskii, who was born in Ukraine and moved to Lithuania after the Second World War.

The theatre staged over 40 productions during the period under review. Its repertoire consisted mainly of original Yiddish plays and contemporary prose works adapted for the stage. These included *200,000, Dos groise gevins* (*The Grand Prize*), *Tuvye der milkhiker* (*Tevye the Milkman*), *Mazl Tov* and *Di blodznde shtern* (*Wandering Stars*) by Sholem Aleichem, *Masoes Binyomin hashlishi* (*The Travels of Benjamin III*) by Mendele Moikher-Seforim, *Boitre* by Moishe Kulbak, *Hershele Ostropoler* and *Di Khelmer khakhomim* (*The Wise Men of Chelm*) by Moishe Gershenzon, *Kreitzers sonate* by Yakov Gordin, *Freilekhs* by Zalman Shneur-Okun, and others. There were only two modern plays — *Komendantskii chas* (*Curfew*) by Grigorii Kanovich (translated from Russian) and *Fun himl falt gornisht nit arop* (*There Are No Miracles*) by Buzi Miller.

In the late 1960s and early 1970s, many of the actors of the Vilnius Jewish Theatre emigrated to Israel. The theatre suffered a crisis but continued its work.[13] At the end of the 1970s and the beginning of the 1980s, a vocal-instrumental folk music group called Feyerlekh, was also formed in Vilnius. Like the Vilnius Jewish Theatre, its fame extended beyond the borders of Lithuania. The ensemble was directed by Vladimir Glushkov (a Russian who had a Jewish wife), with the popular performer Iakov Magid as its lead singer.

In 1960 a Jewish amateur troupe was organized in Kaunas, Lithuania's second largest city, and from 1962 it rehearsed and performed at the Kaunas Trade Union Palace of Culture alongside the Polish artistic collective. The Kaunas Jewish group was headed by Iakov Bel'tser. As in Vilnius, Yiddish was the language of both the stage and the rehearsals. There were far fewer Jews in Kaunas than in Vilnius and the Kaunas group was no match for the Vilnius Theatre either in size or versatility. Yet, in the first years of its activity the Kaunas troupe played a prominent part in the city's cultural life. It disbanded in 1970 as a result of the large-scale emigration to Israel, but in 1972 Jewish amateur performances were resumed on the initiative of Yudl Ronder, Itzhok Iones and Bentsion Shlom, who became chairman of the Kaunas Jewish Amateur Artistic Council. Still, the level of the founding company was never paralleled.

In 1968, a Jewish amateur theatre was established in Birobidzhan. It was intended to fill the vacuum created after the Kaganovich Birobidzhan State Jewish Theatre was liquidated in 1948. The theatre's first director was Moishe Bengel'sdorf and the actors were mostly members of the older generation, who had a fluent command of Yiddish.

After Bengel'sdorf's death in 1971, Berta Shil'man took up the post of director. Like her predecessor, she resided in Birobidzhan. At that time amateur actors of the younger generation, whose native tongue was not Yiddish, began joining the company. At the beginning of the 1980s, the theatre fell into decline even though it enjoyed the backing of the regional authorities, who saw 'ideological importance' in the existence of a Jewish theatre in the Jewish Autonomous Region.

The theatre's repertoire included classical plays by Sholem Aleichem, Avrom Goldfaden and Moishe Gershenzon, plays by a Birobidzhan playwright and member of the *Sovetish heymland* editorial board, Buzi Miller, and translations from Russian. In 1984, as part of the celebration of the Jewish Autonomous Region's 50th anniversary, the theatre staged *Temnaia zavesa* (*The Shroud*), an anti-Zionist propaganda play (written in Russian) based on a book by Tsezar Solodar', notorious member of the Anti-Zionist Committee.[14]

These three collectives (in Vilnius, Kaunas and Birobidzhan) were the only long-standing Jewish theatrical troupes. For the most part, Jewish amateur activity had solely local significance. The chief exception was the Vilnius Jewish Amateur Theatre which gave guest performances in Moscow, Riga, Tallinn, Kishinev and Leningrad. As of the late 1970s, the work of this theatre too was essentially confined to Lithuania due to the opposition of the Soviet authorities.[15] Moreover, there was practically no coordination or collaboration between the various theatre companies, aside from the joint soirées of the Vilnius and Kaunas amateur troupes to commemorate the Warsaw Ghetto uprising.

In this period, particularly from the 1960s to the early 1970s, prominent singers with Yiddish repertoire appeared on the Soviet stage. Among these were Anna Guzik, Nehama Lifshitsaite, Sidi Tal, Emil Gorovets and Polina Ainbinder. In the 1960s, the national Melodiya recording studio began to put out recordings of these artists. Most of these performers left for Israel or the US in the early 1970s.

'Officially sanctioned' Soviet cultural activity encountered increasing difficulties over the years. Jewish culture fell into the trap laid by the authorities. Yiddish was not taught, and no Yiddish textbooks were published. The foreign Yiddish alphabet prevented many people who could still speak the language from actually reading it. There was hardly any demand for fiction in Yiddish. A few volumes were printed in small unprofitable editions by the Moscow-based publishing house Sovetskii pisatel' Soviet Yiddish culture was becoming the exclusive fare of the older generation, which had been socialized under entirely different circumstances. On the other hand, the creation of Russian-language Jewish culture was not encouraged as it did not fit into the 'national in form and socialist in content' formula.[16] It can be assumed that the Soviet authorities regarded culture of this kind as a threat to the natural assimilation' of Soviet Jews, inasmuch as it presupposed the preservation of peculiarly national traits even without a national language.

At the same time, Yiddish books translated into Russian and other languages of Soviet peoples were published on a regular basis. The publishing policy with respect to Russian translations of Yiddish literary works was largely controlled by Aron Vergelis (at least those books published by Sovetskii pisatel'). There were several printings of Russian translations of books by three pre-revolutionary Jewish writers — Mendele Moikher-Seforim, Itzhok-Leibush Peretz and Sholem Aleichem. Collected works by Sholem Aleichem appeared in several volumes. Nevertheless, while his writings enjoyed the greatest popularity in the Soviet Union among the classics of Jewish literature and he was regarded as the symbol of Jewish culture, some of his works never appeared in the Soviet Union. Soviet Jews knew practically nothing about *Der Koisl* (*The Wailing Wall*), *Farvos darfn yidn a land* (*Why Jews Need a Country of Their Own*), *Ugandiade*, and *Biografie fun Teodor Herzl*, which indicate the author's sympathy for Zionism. They appeared inside the Soviet Union in Russian for the first time in Jewish *samizdat* at the end of the 1980s. On the other hand, books by contemporary Yiddish writers regularly appeared in Russian translation. Just a few of them attracted public attention, such as poems for children by Leib Kvitko and Ovsei (Sheyke) Driz, and Aron Vergelis' travel notes *Raizes* (translated into Russian as *16 stran, vkliuchaia Monako*).

Aron Vergelis, the Soviet Union's de facto 'chief Jew', fully realized the severity of the language problem that Jewish culture in the USSR was facing. In recurrent polemics with his 'ideological opponents', he reiterated the thesis that Jewish schools were unnecessary in the USSR and that assimilation was a completely natural process. Nevertheless, in the late 1960s, he launched a new column in his magazine, 'Di shmuesn vegn yidish' ('Chatting about Yiddish'), which was later followed by 'Far di, vos lernen yidish' ('For Those Learning Yiddish'). In the 1980s, on his and his colleagues' initiative, work was started on a Yiddish primer (ostensibly for use in Birobidzhan schools) and a Yiddish-Russian dictionary. The primer was prepared for publication by poet Haim Beider, *Sovetish heymland*'s deputy editor-in-chief, while philologist Moiny Shulman, a columnist and a long-standing member of the magazine's staff, took an active part in compiling the dictionary.

In 1981 Aron Vergelis initiated a Yiddish program as part of the Advanced Literature Program of the Gorky Literary Institute in Moscow. All five students[17] (four of whom now live in Israel) were admitted on Vergelis' recommedation. This class had its first graduates in 1983. All of them immediately became involved in various forms of official Jewish cultural activities, although these are beyond the scope of this chapter.

Since the mid-1980s, the following trends gained momentum in Soviet Jewish cultural life:
- the legalization of 'informal', unofficial Jewish organizations;
- the 'sudden' appearance of a legalized Russian-language Jewish culture;
- the appearance of numerous Jewish theatrical and variety troupes, some of which were actively supported by the authorities 'out of ideological considerations'. Among them was the Jewish Repertory Musical Theatre headed by Yuri Sherling — later succeeded by Mikhail Gluz — which was formally a Birobidzhan theatre, but in fact was Moscow-based.
- the rise of alternative centres of Jewish *ersatz* national-cultural autonomy unconnected with *Sovetish heymland* or Aron Vergelis. A case in point was the abortive attempt at creating state-wide Jewish representative bodies such as the Anti-Zionist Committee headed by David Dragunskii and Samuil' Zivs.
- efforts to turn Birobidzhan into a genuine Jewish centre, which were most evident when Leonid Shkolnik was the editor-in-chief of *Birobidzhaner shtern*. Later he was elected deputy of the USSR Congress of People's Deputies, where he remained until he emigrated in 1991. He currently works for a Russian-language newspaper in Israel.

As a result of all these changes, *Sovetish heymland* lost its supreme position in Soviet Jewish culture; the boundary between 'official' and 'informal' or 'unofficial' (as a rule, pro-Zionist) instruments of Jewish cultural activity in the USSR were obliterated, and the Yiddish language was pushed to the periphery of Jewish cultural life.

The ethno-cultural development of Soviet Jews in the period under review reveals certain features that were analogous to processes in the Jewish Diaspora in the West. It should be emphasized that Soviet Jewry was isolated for decades from world Jewry, not only from the Jewish communities in the West and from the State of Israel, but from communities in the communist bloc as well Romania, Poland, Czechoslovakia, Hungary, Bulgaria and the GDR permitted a curtailed form of Jewish cultural-national autonomy, which orthodox Soviet ideology viewed as seditious.

Like the broad masses of Western Jewry, the Soviet Ashkenazi Jews were dispersed among an ethnically alien population. Distinct, relatively compact groups, which had survived the Holocaust and which inhabited traditional enclaves of East European Ashkenazi Jewry (the Ukraine, Belorussia, Moldavia, Lithuania), were in a steady state of decline. As in the Jewish Diaspora in the West, the Yiddish language fell into disuse in the USSR and became mainly an ethnic symbol. The great majority of its custodians consisted of members of the older generation.

The political realities of the USSR left their imprint on the ethno-cultural processes taking place within Soviet Jewry at that time[18], endowing them with certain features which distinguished them from similar processes in the West. On the one hand, the lack of Jewish education and organized community life (apart from religious communities, whose activities were heavily restricted) led to an almost complete loss of any cultural-linguistic distinctiveness among Soviet Jews. This was noticeable too, although to a lesser degree, in the Western countries of the Jewish Diaspora. On the other hand, state support for specific Jewish cultural activities (which without exception were associated with the Yiddish language) placed Soviet Jews in a privileged position: they were spared from having to seek sources of financing, cutting expenses, or being forced to compete with non-Yiddish forms of cultural expression.

State involvement in Yiddish cultural activity, combined with the steady linguistic assimilation of the Soviet Jewish population which was accelerated by the total lack of formal instruction in this language up to 1981, led the vast majority of middle-aged and younger Jews increasingly to avoid any active or passive participation in Jewish cultural life. This situation seemed to affirm the premises of Soviet ideology regarding the 'natural assimilation of Jews'.

It should be noted that the practice of publishing Russian translations of Yiddish literature can generally be viewed as a specifically Jewish domain of cultural activity, since Russian-speaking Jews constituted a significant portion, if not the majority of the market for such books. The practice of translating literature from the 'languages of the peoples of the USSR' into Russian was regulated from above and applied to all national literatures of the USSR. The volume of translations from a given language was, in theory, proportionally determined, that is, according to the size of the nationality. It did not take into account, however, the number of Russian-speakers of the nationality in question who might be interested in becoming familiar with their own national literature through its translation into Russian.

Only toward the end of the period under review did more realistic tendencies toward increasing the role of the Russian language in strictly Jewish cultural activity (theatre, literature and press), become evident. These were not welcomed by representatives of the traditional Yiddish cultural élite.

The cultural policy toward Jews was dependent, to a certain extent not only on central, but also on local organs of power. Thus, for example, in the Baltic Republics, particularly in Lithuania, this policy was distinguished by greater liberalism. The existence of a nominal Jewish national-territorial autonomy, in the form of the Jewish Autonomous Region, also allowed for certain forms of Jewish cultural activity, absent in other regions of the USSR. At the same time, in spite of attempts to connect this or that manifestation of Jewish cultural life with the Jewish Autonomous Region (for example, Jewish Musical Theatre, the Freylekh show company, and others) Moscow was the real centre of officially sanctioned Jewish cultural activity throughout the years under discussion.

NOTES

1. For more on Birobidzhan, see Robert Weinberg, 'Jews into Peasants? Solving the Jewish Question in Birobidzhan', in this volume.
2. For the closing down of the Jewish Autonomous Region's (JAR) cultural institutions in 1948–49, see Benjamin Pinkus, *The Soviet Government and the Jews 1948–1967. A Documentary Study* (Cambridge: Cambridge Univ. Press, 1984), pp. 372–3, 379–80. The first round of purges in Birobidzhan had coincided with the Great Purge of 1937–38.
3. For the 'punished peoples' see Igor Krupnik, 'Soviet Cultural and Ethnic Policies towards Jews: A Legacy Reassessed', in this volume; for the outlawing of Jewish culture, see Yaacov Ro'i, *Soviet Decision Making in Practice. The USSR and Israel, 1957–54* (New Brunswick: Transaction, 1980), Ch. 7.
4. Sholem Aleichem, *Oysgeveylte verk* (Moscow: Melukhe farlag, 1959). One other book also appeared in 1959, Mendele Moikher Seforim's *Masoes Binyomin hashlishi/Fishke der krumer* — see Chone Shmeruk (ed.), *Jewish Publications in the Soviet Union, 1917–1960* (Jerusalem: The Historical Society of Israel, 1965), p. 194.
5. For *Sovetish heymland*, see Chone Shmeruk, 'Twenty-five Years of Sovetish heymland: Impressions and Criticism' in Yaacov Ro'i and A. Beker (eds.) *Jewish Culture and Identity in the Soviet Union* (New York: NYU Press, 1991), pp. 191–207; for the effect of Jewish pressure in the West on Moscow to improve the situation of Jewish culture in the Soviet Union, see Yaacov Ro'i, *The Struggle for Soviet Jewish Emigration 1948–1967* (Cambridge: Cambridge University Press, 1991), Chs. 4, 5, and 6 (passim).
6. A. Vergelis to the author, oral communication; for Yiddish Broadcasting, see Ro'i, *Soviet Decision Making*, index entry Radio Moscow, in Yiddish.

7. *Sovetish*, a literary almanac, was the organ of the Association of Moscow Yiddish Soviet Writers of the USSR Writers' Union and was published from 1934–41; *Heymland — a Literary-Artistic Almanac* was the Yiddish organ of the USSR Writers' Union and appeared from 1947–48.

8. A. Vergelis to the author, oral communication.

9. Every theatre or troupe, indeed every artist, was affiliated with a municipal, regional or union republic organization which fixed and supervised the number of performances for a given year, as well as the place and content of each performance.

10. Actually, 21.5 per cent said their native tongue was a Jewish language; yet, this included Jews of the USSR's non-Ashkenazi communities who spoke Judaeo-Tat and Judaeo-Tadzhik — Mordechai Altshuler, *Soviet Jewry since the Second World War* (Westport, CT: Greenwood Press, 1987), Ch. 7.

11. V. Tshernin, 'Dialogen vegn der yidishe kultur in FSSR'. Appendix to *Sovetish beymland*, 11 (1986), pp. 3–4.

12. Ibid., pp. 5–8. This held generally for the 'Western Territories' i.e., those areas annexed by the USSR during World War II, see Altshuler, *Soviet Jewry*, p. 188.

13. V. Tshernin, 'Dialogen', pp. 9–10.

14. Ibid., pp. 21–2.

15. The Birobidzhan Jewish National Theatre gave occasional performances outside the Jewish Autonomous Region but only in the Far East, in Khabarovsk and Vladivostok. The Vilnius and Kaunas companies performed in Druskenniki and other Lithuanian resorts to Jewish audiences from all over the USSR.

16. The first reference to the concept of 'Russian-language Jewish culture' in the official Soviet Jewish press of this period was in V. Tshernin, 'Ven der bukh iz durkhgeheyent', *Birobidzhaner shtern*, 29 Sept. 1985. For a discussion of this genre and the problems it entailed, see, e.g., Shimon Markish, 'The Role of Officially Published Russian Literature in the Reevalution of Jewish National Consciousness (1953–1970)', in Ro'i and Beker, *Jewish Culture and Identity*, pp. 208–31.

17. Chone Shmeruk, 'A Half-Century of *Sovetish beymland* — Comments and Assessments', in David Prital (ed.), *Yehudei Brit-ha-Mo'atsot*, (Jerusalem: Zur-Ot, 1988), No. 11, pp 63–9.

18. For a further discussion of these processes and their impact on Soviet Jewish policy, see Igor Krupnik, 'Soviet Cultural and Ethnic Policies', in this volume.

15

Russian and Hebrew Literature in Cross Mirrors

DIMITRI SEGAL

This chapter examines the relative position of Hebrew and Russian literature as reflected in mutual borrowings, in each one's view of itself and the other, and perhaps, most significantly, in the cross-fertilization of literary and cultural paradigms. For the purposes of this chapter both Hebrew and Russian literature are viewed across the entire chronological span of the existence of each literary tradition. Thus, the beginnings of this literary encounter necessarily encompass the reception by Russian culture of the Hebrew Bible (including the Apochryphal books that never entered into the Jewish canon), even though it was always viewed through the prism of Christian religion and culture. These Biblical texts became available in Russian only gradually, over a long period of adaptation and assimilation which lasted until the appearance in the fifteenth century of the first complete translation of the entire Hebrew Bible into Old Russian.

These first contacts between the nascent Russian literary tradition and the ancient, rich, powerful and exotic Hebrew culture did not necessarily lead to any understanding or appreciation on the part of the recipient; indeed, it was the older tradition which opened up before the younger one. This must be emphasized in spite of the current intellectual vogue of stressing the early, very tenuous and historically questionable connections between the newly Christianized eastern Slavs and their Jewish or Jewish Khazar neighbours or adversaries. The same is true of the much vaunted, allegedly direct, Old Russian translations from the Hebrew. Neither of these fleeting encounters, if indeed they ever took place at all, left any awareness of Jewish or Hebrew culture within Russian literature. Perhaps this lack of early traces of immediate contacts between the Russians and the Jews in 'high' Old Russian literature may be partly responsible for the relative scarcity in the latter of the type of openly anti-Jewish works which abound in Czech, Polish or German medieval literary traditions.

On the other hand, it appears that the Russian oral folk tradition, especially that aspect of it which occupied itself with questions of faith, religion and devotion, did gain access to Jewish wisdom. Definite traces of familiarity with certain midrashic tales (in particular, those dealing with *ma'ase bereshit* — the Creation, the stories of Adam giving names to animals, birds and objects) can be discerned in the Old Russian apocryphal and sectarian oral religious literature (sacred legends and *dukhovnye stikhi*, for example). Variants of well-known *midrashim* about King Solomon can be found in Russian narrative lore. It is quite significant that this enrichment of the Russian spiritual heritage with specifically Jewish motifs occurred at the 'lowest' cultural level (in the sociological sense). It can be said that to a very significant degree this remains true almost to this very day: the most tangible evidence of Russian-Jewish — including specifically Hebrew — 'literary' contacts are Jewish anecdotes and jokes as well as gems of the Russian thieves' argot (such as *musor* 'policeman' from the Yiddish/Hebrew *mosser* 'police informer') or modern Hebrew profanities (e.g. the ubiquitous Israeli curse *kebenemat*).

True, Old Russian religious literature did include, almost from its very inception, a certain mirror-image of the Jewish tradition and the Jews, which it inherited from the giants of the patristic tradition, in particular, Basil the Great and John Chrysostom. This view was significantly enhanced in the *Vita Constantini*, which related the story of the Christianization of the Slavs in expressly anti-Semitic terms and was canonized, after Metropolitan Hillarion, in his twelfth century 'Sermon on Law and Grace', had contrasted the 'inferior' law of the Jews with the 'higher' notion of grace which he ascribed to Christianity. At the same time, as we have pointed out above, the lack of tangible contacts between Russians and Jews during most of the Middle Ages (which lasted in Russia until the seventeenth century) left Russian literature generally devoid of any reference to Jewish individuals.

With the incorporation of sizable Jewish populations into the Russian empire after the dismemberment of Poland, the situation changed. Gradually, the impact of Russia's contacts with its new neighbours found expression in Russian literature — from the anti-Semitism of Gogol or the early Leskov to the slowly emerging philo-Semitism of the very same Leskov in the later years of his life. But the aim here is not to trace the history of the Jewish *themes* in Russian literature, although this by itself is a fascinating subject which deserves further study. Rather, it is to establish a deeper *paradigmatic* influence of one literature upon the other. Therefore, we will begin with the case of modern Hebrew literature where this impact seems to be much more pronounced.

To be sure, Russian literature entered the Jewish world almost a millennium after the first contacts between the Russians and the Jews, and at a point when the Russian culture, at least its literary, urban, Westernized version, shed its traditional ecclesiastic form and content and opened itself to people of other faiths who were ready to absorb its message The earliest documented instance of actual contact between Jewish and Russian letters was Yitshak-Ber Levinson's masterful translation into Hebrew of several poetic evocations of Russian landscape and climate by Kheraskov, published in *Ha-Mevasser* in the 1820s. Henceforward, Russian literature became a constant presence in Hebrew letters, first in the writings of the Haskala and later in the ever-growing body of emerging modern Hebrew literature. To fathom this truly remarkable phenomenon one must pause to consider some of the relevant traits of both literatures.

First, it should be stressed that early on, Jewish thought (and later the Jewish soul) opened to the charms of Russian, and more generally, eastern Slavic culture: some traces of this predominantly spiritual influence can be discerned in the writings of the famous talmudic scholar, Moses of Kiev.[1] Second, and probably much more significantly in the context of later powerful Russian literary influences, were the young nineteenth century Jews who so eagerly embraced Russian literature. They emerged from a traditional Jewish milieu that came to appreciate Slavic folk music, dance and the written word.[2] Once again, it was the more traditional and lower-class circles which initiated and maintained this contact.

However, such contact alone could not and did not produce the outstanding phenomenon of 'russianness' in early modern Hebrew literature. This can only be explained by a unique combination of factors. In the first place, early Hebrew literature was certainly not searching for purely literary 'models' and 'patterns', nor was it seeking any linguistic inspiration and sophistication — this notwithstanding the fact that in both respects Hebrew Literature was sorely in need of ready-made models. While German was a well-established and prestigious language of high-level cultural communication among educated Russian Jews, Russian literature, especially prose, did have a very high international reputation in the second half of the nineteenth century. Nascent Hebrew literature was desperately looking for a kindred spirit, a fellow-revolutionary, and among all others only

Russian literature could and did provide this spiritual sustenance While portraying basically familiar surroundings, Russian literature embodied in the foreign language it represented, lofty values inherent in the Jewish tradition itself, which the rebellious young Hebrew writers rejected in its ritual aspects, but certainly not in terms of its human existential drive.

In the second place, having found a worthy source of support for their own revolution, the young Hebrew writers discovered that Russian literature was remarkably free from any national-revolutionary impulses of its own. In other words, unlike other significant prose traditions of the last decades of the nineteenth century which were probably known to aspiring Hebrew writers in Poland and Germany, Russian literature could direct its revolutionary fervour towards the liberation of man and not be preoccupied with specifically Russian national problems. This enabled Hebrew writers to concentrate on the universal messages of Russian literature while ignoring those aspects which were, or could be construed as, anti-Semitic. Such anti-Semitism could then be written off as 'immaturity' rather than an authentic expression of the Russian idea.

Thus, while Polish literature, to take just one example, was permanently obsessed with the Polish question (the famous *sprawa polska*) and the fate of Poland, and consequently demanded of its readers complete identification with this spirit of *polskosc*, Russian literature taught its readers how to rebel, how to feel, behave, suffer and rejoice in revolution *per se*. And the Jews in Russia experienced infinitely more suffering and repression than even the most oppressed Russian peasant. The young Jews felt very keenly that Russian literature was *their* literature, because it rebelled against any and all injustice, not just injustice against the Russians. This *sovestlivost'* (spirit of consciousness) of Russian literature was what made it so special.

The young Jews who lived in the Pale were on the whole very traditional, but they rebelled against the institutionalized persecution of the Jews which was pursued so scrupulously by the tsarist regime. Their reception of Russian literature was aptly summarized by Berl Katznelson in an introductory article which he wrote for the collected works of his friend Moshe Beilinson:

> Russian literature, so great and profound, was his [Beilinson's] art. Descended from generations of Lithuanian Torah scholars, he inherited from his forefathers a legacy of strong character and spiritual power, but not the twenty-two letters of the holy tongue. He imbibed Russian culture from his early childhood, and it was the foundation of his spiritual world. It can be said about him that he was at home in all the nooks and crannies

of Russian poetry, thought and social life. Some of the basic features of his character, his lifestyle and literary work grew directly out of this Russian soil. And without attempting to define it in all its depth and complexity, certain general features can be noted: the reign of conscience; being harsh on oneself; unmasking lies on a social and personal level; lashing out at self-deception; despising 'those who do not practise what they preach'; disdain for all philistinism...a view of man as the centre of the universe; personal responsibility for the suffering of others; genuine concern for the wretched and down-trodden...unwillingness to separate between personal ethics and those of society.[3]

This view of Russian literature — which, incidentally, is not very far removed from the way Russian literature views itself to this very day[4] — with its highly complimentary concept of the values inherent in the culture of the Russian intelligentsia, was so completely assimilated by the emerging Hebrew culture that it can be said that even those Hebrew writers who, like Shmuel Yosef Agnon, appear to be largely independent of Russian influences, do relate to this complex of values. They may even be described in terms of typological affinity to Russian models which they ignored or which existed in another time-space (in Agnon's case, those of Leo Tolstoy and Andrei Platonov). The latest example of the preoccupation of Hebrew literature with its Russian 'model' is Meir Shalev's *Russian Romance*.[5] Its Hebrew title preserves the double-entendre of romance and novel (*roman*).

One must admit that the extreme russification of early modern Hebrew prose, and somewhat later, of much of modern Hebrew poetry by authors such as Alexander Penn, Avraham Shlonsky, Rahel and Natan Alterman, not only led to a very understandable reaction of rejection in younger generations of Israelis, but presented a picture of Russian literature which was very far removed from its actual historical development. On the other hand, Russian literary-cultural models within Hebrew literature produced semiotic results quite unlike those models evoked in the Russian context.

Thus, a Russian reader would find within the Hebrew literary-cultural system a very homogenized and largely idealized reflection of certain trends and aspects of Russian literature, mainly from the nineteenth century, but also from selected domains of Russian twentieth century literature. The selection was made largely along lines which emphasized civic and populist collective values or the depths of psychological and emotional insight into the soul of a man forced to examine those values against the vicissitudes of history. What was left outside the modern Hebrew picture of Russian literature was not only all that related to pre-nineteenth century history, but also the problematics of the profound gap between Westernized modern

Russian culture and the timeless culture of the peasants. More individualistic, modernist and politically conservative thinkers and writers, such as the poets Fedor Tiutchev and Innokentii Annenskii, the writer-philosophers Vasilii Rozanov and Andrei Belyi and many others, remained outside the scope of interest of the new Hebrew culture. In our own times Hebrew belles-lettres are largely unaware of the prolific and highly seminal heritage of Russian, Soviet, anti-Soviet and post-Soviet avant-garde and experimental literature.

However, these omissions probably served some purpose, because, at least as of today, Hebrew culture seems to be remarkably free of the specifically Russian social features which characterized the flowering of literature in Russian, and later Soviet, society: inflation of the social role of literature at the expense of more practical socio-cultural mechanisms, clannishness and disdain of the outsider (although this feature becomes more familiar the more one comes to know the Hebrew *literati*). In short, Russian literature, with its highly developed sense of social and cultural borders, niches, alienations, individualistic anarchisms and mystic idiosyncrasies was transformed into a vehicle for moulding a new Hebrew society where all these signs and symptoms of class, niche, group or (in the words of one of the ideologists and historians of the Russian intelligentsia, Pavel Miliukov) 'mystic civic order', were simply discarded in favour of equality and popular appeal.

As for the way in which Russian literature viewed its Hebrew counterpart, it must be stated that during its entire history, Russian literature was and remains completely unaware of the existence of Hebrew literature. In other words, there is no Hebrew reflection in the mirror of Russian literature. To be sure, there were isolated courageous attempts to make Hebrew poetry accessible to the Russian reader — for example, Vladislav Khodaseevich's translations of Tchernikhovsky, Shneur and other Hebrew poets. However, there are virtually no translations of Hebrew literature into Russian and all existing translations (originating both in Russia and in Israel) from the Bible onwards are inadequate in one way or the other. This inadequacy stems from the fact that Russian still tackles Hebrew through the intervening medium of Greek and Old Church Slavonic. The basic features of conciseness and economy in Hebrew, coupled with the language's paradoxic combination of antiquity and modernity, still eludes translators.

Russian literature never knew periods of authentic interest and passion for the Old Testament common to all other European literatures: English with the King James Bible and Milton; German with translations of the psalms by Luther; Italian with Dante's visions of Biblical heroes in *Commedia Divina*. There is a tangible gap between the way the Russian language deals with biblical and ancient Hebrew subjects and its approach to modern everyday Jews. True, in the short history of Russian-Jewish literature there were attempts by Jewish writers who wrote in Russian to find a suitable modern Russian idiom for the world of ancient Hebrew glory [6] However, these paradigms were quickly forgotten by the emerging Soviet culture that was inimical to all sorts of national Jewish, and especially Hebrew, expression. On the other hand, the living Jewish-Yiddish idiom slowly but surely began to trickle into mainstream Russian literature from the time that the first Jewish anecdotes and jokes reached the pages of the Russian newspapers and the stage of Russian metropolitan and provincial theatres sometime in the 1880s.

It was at this point that certain Jewish stereotypes began to take shape in Russian literature. They were remarkably similar for both anti-Semitic and philo-Semitic Russian writers. The evaluation of them and their hierarchical position varied depending on the writer's attitude to the Jews, but the inventory was the same: the ability of the Jews to combine the tragic and the comic, their love for self-deprecating humour, their extreme attachment to their families, their wit and wisdom, thorough knowledge of the material and commercial world and perceived ability to use this knowledge, their suffering, their disdain for external aesthetics and their incomprehensible faith and religiosity In this respect, Jewish topics, traits and features could be observed in the work of such purely Russian writers as Leonid Andreev,[7] Aleksandr Kuprin, Vladimir Korolenko, as well as Russian writers of Jewish origin, such as the playwrights Solomon Iushkevich, Osip Dymov and David Aizman, whose work was very popular on the Russian stage at the beginning of the twentieth century. Jewish stereotypes permeated virtually all Russian writing on Jewish themes in later years, beginning with Isaak Babel up to contemporary writers such as Anatolii Rybakov and Grigorii Kanovich.

It appears then, that each literature, due to circumstances and preconceived notions, developed its own mirror of the other, and one might venture to say, projected its own notion of itself onto the literary paradigm of the other. However, since the 1970s something has happened which has disturbed this asymmetric mirror image: new works in Russian and in Hebrew have appeared in Israel, which may demonstrate the ability of Israeli culture to transcend these historical constraints. It seems that in large part we owe this breakthrough, directly or indirectly, to the pioneering linguistic and literary work of

Vladimir Nabokov. It is important to emphasize the Israeli venue of this momentous change, for Russian literature in Russia still remains shackled by its well-worn Jewish-stereotyped treatment of all Jewish material, be it of native Russian or even Israeli origin.

The work of two writers, Dan Tsalka, the Israeli Hebrew prose writer, and Mikhail Gendelev, an Israeli poet writing in Russian, opens up perspectives for a new and richer mutual contemplation of the two literary traditions In 1991, the Hebrew publishing house Am Oved published two volumes of Dan Tsalka's new epic work *Elef levavot* (*A Thousand Hearts*). At first glance it would seem that Tsalka's novel bears no relation at all to the problem of Russian literary-cultural models in Hebrew literature. His biographic roots are in Poland and his literary background betrays deep and detailed knowledge of such diverse literary and cultural traditions that Russian seems only one of the many gems in this extremely colourful mosaic. However, the very fact that much of the novel's plot is concerned with Russia, the Soviet Union, its history and immense space, its people and their vicissitudes and aspirations makes *Elef levavot* part and parcel of the great Russian epic tradition.

It is no exaggeration to say that in this respect Tsalka's novel is closer to the tradition of Tolstoy than any other novel, Russian or non-Russian, that has appeared since *War and Peace*. The author's masterful power of evocation of the spirit of time and space and his control and insight into the inner soul of the hundreds of figures who populate this immense and vibrant literary world, his consummate skill in capturing the texture and colour, smell and feel, movement and shape of the details of the real world in which his characters dwell, are reminiscent of Tolstoy — a Tolstoy of our times, more interested in people and things than in moralizing or presenting and defending some dialectic position. In Tsalka's novel the tradition of Tolstoy is enriched and enhanced by the fact that it is transplanted into the new and unknown territories of the East (Central Asia, Palestine, and later, Israel) and into the West (Italy, Germany and Poland). Suddenly we realize that the great narrative epic tradition is not irretrievably lost or antiquated but can, in fact, flourish in unfamiliar circumstances.

Another literary paradigm of Russian provenance extremely important for Tsalka is that of Nabokov. Tsalka's narrative is definitely very modern in terms of his style and composition, which are as removed from the classic linear and homogeneous plot of Tolstoy as any avant-garde prose. Nabokov's evocation of the potency of literary imagination, his belief in the power of language hold a strong sway over Tsalka. In this sense, the world depicted in his novel has the same enchanted and fantastic quality as the world of Nabokov. However, one basic Nabokovian quality — his overpowering nostalgia for the lost world of his youth and for the Russia which existed in those irretrievably lost years — is absent from Tsalka's world. In fact, all of the novel's heroes and passing characters, its landscapes and streets, its summers and winters are suffused by an opposite passion: the yearning for Zion. *Elef levavot* is thrust into the future, and that future is always Zion. All the heroes of the novel, the young Polish-Jewish *wunderkind* Alek, Ezra Marinsky, the talented architect from Simferopol' in the pre-revolutionary Russian empire, Rieti, an Italian-Jewish Israeli, and many others embody this sweeping movement towards Zion that appears rising from the waters of the Mediterranean in the form of old Jaffa with its mixture of Arab and Jew. The extraordinary freedom with which Tsalka moves from place to place and from time to time, his total mastery of the Hebrew idiom acquires, under his pen, the virtuosity of an epic tradition, which hitherto was unknown in Hebrew letters.

The achievement belongs both to Hebrew and Russian literature, because it shows that Hebrew can truly claim the status of a language completely suited for modern, highly developed and sophisticated prose, and because it presents Russian literature with a paradigm of a contemporary Jewish novel which supersedes not only all previous achievements of Jewish prose in Russian, but epitomizes the ideal Russian novel written in Hebrew. Thus, the picture of Russian literature in the Hebrew mirror of Dan Tsalka's novel is one of beauty, delight and promise, the qualities which — like the ascent to Zion in *Elef levavot* — lie always ahead of us...

The second inter-literary event of great importance for both literatures was the appearance in 1993 in Jerusalem of *Prazdnik. Stikhotvoreniia i poemy* (*The Feast. Poems*) by Mikhail Gendelev. Gendelev belongs to a generation that immigrated to Israel in the 1970s. A medical doctor by profession, he has brought into his Russian poetry an acute awareness of the magic of the human body. Gendelev's collection of poems is very much in the tradition of the Russian Silver Age. The most obvious influence seems to be that of Velimir Khlebnikov, the idiosyncratic genius of Russian futurism, from whom Gendelev learned to appreciate the extreme suppleness and hidden exotic possibilities of the Russian language. However, while, Khlebnikov experimented with Russian morphology, endlessly creating new and fascinating words in the fashion of the existing derivational models, like *smekhachi* (laughers — people whose function or occupation is to laugh), Gendelev attacks Russian syntax which he moulds and re-moulds until it begins to resemble some fantastic non-existent idiom, in this case, Hebrew. Thus Gendelev's Russian is, in fact, a Hebrew of sorts. This linguistic 'possession' (and Gendelev is truly possessed in these poems) makes his work extremely difficult to translate and imposes quite stringent demands upon his readers, who are expected to know both Russian and English. One short poem by Gendelev will, perhaps, illustrate some of these points:

Pamiatnik

Nad lysym cherepom liubvi
Soorudim iz pal'tsev 'V'

A Monument

Right above the bald skull of love
Let our fingers form a 'V'

In this particular case the linguistic dialogue, on the face of it, is not with Hebrew but with English: there is no rhyme if the 'V' is pronounced in any but the English fashion. However 'the bald skull' immediately evokes images of the Crucifixion: *Golgotha* [Aram. 'bald skull'] the hill in Jerusalem upon which Christ was crucified and hence of Jerusalem, inhabited by heroes of Gendelev's poetry — all of whom experienced the trauma of the Lebanon War to which the ironic 'V' refers.

Gendelev never uses direct calques from the Hebrew. He creates a poetic impression of Hebrew by purely Russian means. In this case a special syntactic ellipsis creates the impression of a Hebrew nominal phrase: in another case it is the use of the *figura etymoligica*, then it is the evocation of biblical laconism. Gendelev is fascinated by the crypto-palindromic qualities of Hebrew viewed through the prism of a Russian and the Russian received back from the mouth of the Hebrew poet who reminds one of Gendelev himself. The palindromic structure is evident in Gendelev's love of butterflies (again a motif from Nabokov).

The image of Hebrew poetry one obtains from Gendelev's poems is unlike any actual Hebrew poem. It is its Platonic idea expressed in language: the more potent it is, the greater the gap between it and the actual Russian or Hebrew. The image of a butterfly seems especially apt because it refers not only to the butterfly's shape, but to the tortuous process of discovering one language within the other, like a butterfly emerging from a cocoon.

Close scrutiny of the works of Dan Tsalka and Mikhail Gendelev reveals something deeper about the process of mutual cultural discovery between Russian and Hebrew literatures. It is a fact that both writers approached their respective models (Russian in the case of Tsalka and Hebrew in the case of Gendelev) not intuitively, nor existentially as writers and poets are expected to do, but on a much deeper level, as scholars. This opens new vistas before Hebrew and Russian culture, especially the latter. In Tsalka's novel there are signs of quite intensive research into certain aspects of contemporary Russian history that have been generally neglected by scholars, both Western and Russian, like the evacuation of the civilian population into Central Asia during World War II. But, as we have already said, it is the Russian history of literature and culture that still has to discover the world of Hebrew culture. Serious research into this field has not even begun in Russia. Unless this ignorance is dispelled there is very little future for any cultural contacts between the two countries and peoples.

NOTES

1. The author is grateful to Prof. Moshe Idel of the Hebrew University, who related this information.
2. In this respect see the famous Habad devotional song in Russian, 'Ne boius' ia nikogo krome Boga odnogo!'
3. Berl Katznelson, 'Im Ha-kerekh ha-rishon', (Introduction to the writings of M. Beilinson) in *Kitvei Berl Katznelson*, Vol. X (Tel Aviv: Mifleget poalei Eretz Yisrael, 1950), p. 154.
4. The accuracy of this description was questioned by some more insightful Russian writers such as Vasilii Rozanov.
5. Meir Shalev, *Roman rusi* (Tel Aviv: Am oved, 1988).
6. Notable in this respect were poems on Jewish national themes written by the well-known Russian, Yiddish and Hebrew poet Semen (Shimon) Frug.
7. Compare his Jewish mystical play *Anathema*, which was very popular in the 1910s, in the famous production by the Moscow Art Theatre with the great actor Vasilii Kachalov in the leading role of the poor Jew Leizer.

VI

THE JEWISH RELIGION UNDER THE SOVIET HEEL

16

Judaism in the USSR, 1917–1930: The Fate of Religious Education

DAVID E. FISHMAN

THE ASSAULT ON RELIGIOUS SCHOOLING

Between 1921 and 1923 the Jewish section of the RCP(b), the *evsektsiia*, waged an intense anti-religious campaign in which the drive to eradicate Jewish religious education was particularly fierce.[1] Most features of Jewish religious life, such as the Sabbath, holidays, dietary laws and circumcision, were vehemently attacked in the Yiddish press and at public meetings and demonstrations, but they were not proscribed by law or suppressed by executive measures. The *heder* and *yeshiva*, the organs of Jewish education, however, were banned by virtue of the law separating church and school, and subjected to tough police and administrative actions; they were closed, and instructors and students were arrested, tried and imprisoned.

Although hundreds of synagogues and Jewish houses of prayer were forcibly converted into hostels and clubs during those years, the synagogue as an institution did not suffer as traumatic a blow as the *heder* and *yeshiva*. According to frequently cited statistics, 646 synagogues were seized by the Soviets between 1917 and 1929. But even after a full decade of closures, there were still approximately 500 legally constituted synagogues in Belorussia and 934 in the Ukraine, and public houses of prayer continued to exist in every city and town with a sizable Jewish population. The same could not be said for religious schools.[2] In the struggle for the hearts and minds of the younger generation, the *evsektsiia* refused to adopt a posture of patient gradualism plus public propaganda, as it did in its treatment of religious worship and practice by adults.

The singularly harsh policy toward Jewish religious education was underscored by Rabbi Moshe Eisenstadt, the Crown Rabbi of St. Petersburg/Leningrad,[3] in a confidential memorandum to the American Jewish Joint Distribution Committee (JDC) in 1926:

> The impression that the authorities in Soviet Russia forbid us to pray or circumcise our children etc., is not correct. We are permitted to have our synagogues, we are permitted to pray, we are permitted to circumcise our children, we may eat kosher meat...No one hinders us in that...The discrimination against us consists, however, in the interference with the religious education of our children...When [the 'evseki'] discovered a religious school where three or more children were taught, the teachers were immediately arrested...Our younger generation is being torn from us by force...It is our duty to call the attention of American Jewry to this terrible injustice.[4]

Eisenstadt contended that religious instruction was being hounded more forcefully among Jews than among Christians, and attributed this discrimination to the fanatical zeal of the *evsektsiia*.

Be that as it may, there can be no doubt that it was education, more than any other matter, which provoked dramatic, and even violent, confrontations between traditionalists and the *evsektsiia*: the mock trial of the *heder* in Vitebsk in 1921 sparked a popular riot against the local 'evseki', which was eventually put down through a massive show of military force. The efforts of Rabbi Mordechai Barishanskii of Gomel' to defend the *heder* against its attackers led to his arrest and public trial for engaging in counter-revolutionary activity.[5]

But despite heroic efforts at resistance, the traditionalists were clearly on the defensive and in retreat against the overwhelming forces of the party and state. One reflection of this was the decision by several famous heads of talmudic academies to emigrate to Poland, taking along with them groups of students. Rabbi Moshe Soloveitchik (of the Volozhin Yeshiva dynasty), Rabbi Israel Meyer Kagan (the Hafetz Hayyim), Rabbi Barukh Ber Levovitz, and Rabbi Isser Zalman Meltzer all left Soviet territory between 1921 and 1923, in reaction to communist pressure. The students of the Novogrudek (Novar'dok) *musar yeshivot*, who waged an aggressive recruiting effort among irreligious Jewish youths in the face of communist threats and persecution, likewise surrendered in 1922. The instructors and students of the *yeshivot* smuggled themselves across the border to Poland, taking with them as many Jewish youngsters as they could entice to leave their parents and families behind.[6]

By the end of 1923, observers in most places would have agreed with a correspondent from Zhitomir to *Der Emes*, who reported that *haderim* and *yeshivot* had been liquidated throughout the entire province, except for one or two in remote provincial towns. The task now facing Jewish communist activists, he wrote, was the rapid expansion of the Soviet Yiddish school system, to absorb the thousands of displaced former *heder* students.[7]

On the surface, this conclusion would have appeared correct. As one religious activist, Rabbi Shlomo Yosef Zevin of Novozivkov, wrote a few years later:

> People belonging both to our camp and to that of our opponents frequently state that the authentic Judaism, which transmitted and preserved eternal values has expired in the Soviet Union. And it is no wonder that the superficial observer reaches such a conclusion...Only he who does not restrict himself to superficial observations...and who attempts to examine the life of Soviet Jewry more intently will reach a different conclusion.[8]

In fact, as Zevin went on to report, Jewish religious education had not been 'liquidated', but had been driven underground. And in its subterranean form, the *heder* and *yeshiva* actually underwent a process of consolidation and growth during the mid and late 1920s.

THE COMMITTEE OF RABBIS OF THE USSR

The agency which was responsible for effecting this underground resurgence was the Committee of Rabbis of the USSR (*Va'ad Rabbanei SSSR*), a clandestine organization founded and headed by the Lubavitcher Rebbe, R. Joseph Isaac Schneerson, and which existed from late 1922 until spring 1930. Although dominated by Schneerson, the Committee of Rabbis was not a Lubavitch 'front-organization'. Besides Schneerson, its leadership council consisted of the chief rabbis of the capital cities of Russia, Belorussia and the Ukraine; Rabbis Shmuel Rabinovitz (of Moscow), Menahem Mendl Gluskin (of Minsk) and Eliya Aaron Mileikovskii (of Kharkov). The former two were non-Hasidic, 'Lithuanian' rabbis of the old school, and the latter was a religious Zionist.[9]

Schneerson conceived of the Committee of Rabbis as more than an occasional forum for discussion and consultation. He envisioned it as the supervisory agency for all of Jewish religious life in the Soviet Union. His goal was to unite all religious communities and institutions in a tightly-knit network with a strong centralized leadership. In isolation, the individual religious Jew, rabbi, synagogue, *mikva* or *heder* would never be able to withstand the overwhelming forces of the communist party and its state organs. A central organization could funnel the necessary funds, offer moral support, tactical advice, legal defence and political intervention. It could also dispatch to the localities religious professionals, books and supplies.

This was a new model for the social organization of Jewish religious life. For hundreds of years, Judaism had flourished in Eastern Europe on a decentralized basis, with each individual community caring for its own religious affairs. Russian Jewry had never had a chief rabbi, central consistory, or even a real nation-wide rabbinical assembly or union of synagogues. In part, Schneerson drew his inspiration for this centralized structure from his own Hasidic milieu. In Hasidic communal life, the Rebbe supervised the religious affairs of geographically dispersed conventicles — appointing rabbis and *shohetim* (ritual slaughterers), disbursing funds, corresponding with his followers and offering them worldly and spiritual guidance. Schneerson sought to adapt this system to meet the difficult needs of Jewish religious life in the Soviet Union, with himself, as chairman of the Committee of Rabbis, at its apex.[10]

But the new structure differed from Hasidic communal life in that it needed to be conducted on a clandestine basis. In this respect, Schneerson borrowed many of the techniques of the Russian revolutionary movement, and its Jewish arm, the Bund. Effective underground work required tightly-knit organization and aggressive propaganda, or as Schneerson called them, *histadrut ve-ta'amulah*. Among the tools which he borrowed from the revolutionary movement were the covert channeling of funds from abroad, and the use of secret emissaries, who inspired Jews to engage in religious activity. Schneerson referred to the latter as *arumforer* (travelers), as well as by a more revelatory term — *agitatorn* (agitators).[11]

The Committee of Rabbis engaged in a wide range of activities, but its highest priority was the effort to protect, finance, and expand a network of underground *haderim* and *yeshivot* in the USSR.

The Committee's first organized activity after its establishment in late 1922 was a campaign to improve the legal and political status of the *heder*. The Committee's secretary, Rabbi Shlomo Yosef Zevin of Novozivkov, submitted an ostensibly private inquiry to the Central Legal Consultation Office of the Soviet Bar Association of the Russian Republic asking whether private instruction of religion outside of school, at home, to a group of five or six children, was permissible by Soviet law. The Consultation Office replied that small-scale, informal religious instruction at home did not violate the law on the separation of church and school. The Committee's office then proceeded to dispatch notarized copies of this opinion to Jewish communities across the USSR, where it was a source of encouragement to frightened and demoralized *melamdim*. If they ran afoul of the local authorities, they used the Consultation Office's ruling to argue that they were engaged in legal activity; if they were arrested and tried, it served as the basis for their defence. Five years after its issuance, the Committee of Rabbis' office still processed requests for notarized copies.[12]

When, in 1923, the People's Commissariat of Justice proposed modifying the Soviet Criminal Statute so as to prohibit private instruction of religion, the Committee of Rabbis worked behind the scenes to lobby against the amendment. It organized petitions in Kiev, Minsk, and several smaller towns, and collected 4,934 signatures to protest the unjust persecution of Jewish religious instructors. The Committee of Rabbis then persuaded one of the elders of the Moscow synagogue, Professor David Shor, to submit the petitions and an accompanying memorandum to Lev Kamenev, chairman of the All-Union Executive Committee (VTsIK). At a meeting with Shor on 22 July 1923, Kamenev expressed his total agreement with the memorandum, and passed it on to Deputy General Prosecutor N. V. Kirilenko. At a subsequent convening of the VTsIK, Kirilenko announced that the Commissariat of Justice had decided to withdraw its amendment. The reversal was seen by the Committee of Rabbis as a political victory. Notarized copies of the minutes of the VTsIK meeting were once again dispatched to the communities.[13]

FUNDING THE UNDERGROUND EDUCATIONAL NETWORK

In 1924, Schneerson developed ties with the Moscow representative of the American Jewish Joint Distribution Committee (JDC), Dr. Joseph Rosen. Although the JDC's official mandate for operation in the USSR was limited to economic relief and reconstruction, Rosen and the JDC leadership in New York agreed to divert some of their funds to support 'cultural work' among Zionists and religious Jews. In 1925 the Committee of Rabbis received $18,000 from the JDC, in 1926 — $24,000, and in 1927 — over $25,000. This was 40 per cent of the JDC's overall budget for 'cultural work' in Russia.[14] With these funds in hand, the Committee functioned as a funding agency for underground *haderim* and *yeshivot*. There is no comprehensive statistical information on the size of the Committee's religious educational network between 1925 and 1927; retrospective reports by Schneerson and Zevin speak of these years as a time of growth and expansion. This is corroborated by figures from Minsk, which report 273 children in Committee-supported *haderim* in 1926, and 324 children in 1928.[15] The first comprehensive figures are from the Committee's 1928 report:

the Committee provided regular, monthly support to *haderim* in 22 communities, with a total enrolment of 3,480 children. In addition, *haderim* in 44 other communities received occasional, irregular assistance, though no enrolment figures were kept for those schools.[16]

In its reports and budget requests, the Committee of Rabbis contended that it could easily expand its network of *haderim* if additional funds were made available by the JDC. In 1928 it proposed incorporating 161 additional communities into its educational network, and increasing the total enrolment of its affiliated *haderim* to 8,700. Schneerson estimated at the time that there were at least 20,000 Jewish children in the USSR whose parents were eager to give them a religious education. If this estimate is correct — and the statistical information at the Committee of Rabbis' disposal was astonishingly detailed and comprehensive — it represented slightly less than 5 per cent of Jewish school-age children in the USSR in 1928.[17]

According to its 1928 report, the Committee funded *yeshivot* in 12 cities, with a total of 620 students. The *yeshivot* received considerably more support than the *haderim*; whereas the latter were allocated roughly 5 rubles per month per student, *yeshivot* got 25 rubles.[18] There were, to be sure, practical reasons for this higher level of funding. Parents were willing to pay some tuition for their child's elementary religious education, but were not willing or accustomed to pay for advanced studies in a *yeshiva*. Costs were also higher, since many *yeshiva* students were not the sons of local families, and required room and board. But there were also ideological motives for the disproportionate allocation of funds to the *yeshivot*. The Committee of Rabbis viewed the *yeshivot* as the linchpin of all Jewish religious life; without them and their students, the synagogue, and religious observance as a whole, would soon wither and die. One Committee report expressed this outlook in the following terms:

> The *yeshiva* is the spiritual centre, which generates hope for the recovery of the broken Jewish spirit. The student usually devotes his activity afterwards to one of the religious professions, such as becoming an instructor of Torah for children...a slaughterer of kosher meat...and last but not least, a rabbi of a community...Even if the *yeshiva* student chooses to devote himself to the crafts, trade or something else, he will remain a devoted religious layman, who observes the laws of family purity, and the Sabbath...He will stand beside the rabbi and fight the holy battle with great dedication...The *yeshiva* student is the spiritual strength of Israel, its heart and its eyes. And therefore maintaining these institutions and supporting them is for us the holiest of holies.[19]

At the apex of its educational system, the Committee of Rabbis established the Seminary for Rabbis and *Shohetim* (*Bet midrash le-rabbanim ve-shohetim*) in Nevel', Belorussia. Unlike the *yeshivot*, this institution was exclusively geared toward the training of religious professionals, and was an independent, non-sectarian institution unaffiliated with any one orthodox group or orientation. The seminary was a national institution whose sole source of funding was the Committee of Rabbis, which allocated 50 rubles per month for each student. Enrolment varied between 35 and 40 students in most years. Associated with the seminary was a professional placement bureau, which corresponded with communities in need of rabbis, *shohetim*, and religious instructors. Between 1925 and 1928, the Nevel' Seminary placed 48 of its graduates in positions as communal rabbis and *shohetim*.[20]

DISSENSION AND DECLINE

As chairman of the Committee of Rabbis, Schneerson enjoyed extensive freedom in deciding which *haderim* and *yeshivot* would receive Committee funding. Although the Committee's Leadership Council met annually to review the past year's activities and set guidelines for the future, there was no real supervision over Schneerson's disbursements between one meeting and the next.

Soon after the Committee began receiving JDC funds, some of its members started complaining that Schneerson was showing partiality toward Lubavitch institutions. Schneerson himself later recalled a meeting with Dr. Rosen in 1925 which he reports as follows:

> He had received many letters [...] claiming that all my work had been for Hasidim, and Habad Hasidim in particular...I also received information from the bureau in New York that many letters were arriving [...] stating that they were dissatisfied with my activity, which contradicted decisions adopted at the meeting [of the Committee of Rabbis].[21]

The suspicions and resentments were not totally misplaced. Schneerson did not make a clear distinction between his roles as Lubavitcher Rebbe and chairman of the Committee of Rabbis. The Committee's staff of secretaries and secret emissaries consisted of young Lubavitch Hasidim, for whom it was difficult to differentiate between Judaism and Habad Hasidism. In addition, Schneerson's control over the purse-strings served to strengthen his personal influence and prestige. The Mitnagdic *yeshivot* of Minsk and Slutsk came to him with fawning requests that they be included in the list of institutions receiving regular monthly allocations and, in their desperation, they felt a need to profess admiration for Lubavitch Hasidism and deprecate the Mitnagdic traditions of talmudism and *musar.* The *yeshivot* even offered to incorporate the study of Hasidism into their curricula.[22]

Certain religious communities, such as that of Odessa, refused to participate in the Committee of Rabbis and received funds from the JDC through other channels. As a result, Odessa's underground *haderim* did not belong to the Committee's educational network. The Minsk community briefly seceded from the Committee in 1926, apparently due to dissatisfaction over its allocation practices.[23] Because of these divisions, as well as the Committee's lack of adequate funding, its instructional network never encompassed the entire universe of Jewish religious education in the Soviet Union. But it certainly did constitute its largest and best-organized part.

Much to the chagrin of the *evsektsiia*, this small religious educational network proved to be remarkably durable and resilient until the end of the 1920s. Communist Yiddish periodicals railed against the counter-revolutionary Schneerson, but even after his arrest and subsequent exile from the Soviet Union in September 1927, its activities did not cease. The Committee of Rabbis continued to function with Rabbi Zevin, its secretary, and Rabbi Jacob Klemes, the chief rabbi of Moscow, assuming additional responsibilities.[24]

The underground *yeshivot* suffered their first major setbacks in the winter of 1928–29, when the Seminary for Rabbis and *Shohetim* was discovered and closed down by the authorities, and its inspirational leader, Rabbi Shmuel Levitan, arrested and exiled to Siberia. Two of the twelve *yeshivot* supported by the Committee, in Nevel' and Polotsk, were closed down shortly thereafter.[25] But the Committee seemed to take these losses in its stride. A report on its activities written in 1929 struck a heroic and confident tone:

> The attacks that are made on the Yeshivoth, no matter how hard they are, have not broken the spirit of the yeshivoth students and their deans. Although ten were imprisoned as a result of this, the Yeshivoth are not destroyed. When the evsektsiia starts oppressing a Yeshiva, [it] moves to another city, and breaks up into several divisions, and continues studies. With the destruction of the Nevel Yeshivah,[...]the boys have gone to other cities and are studying in groups of fifteen or ten.[26]

As late as May 1929, a letter signed by Zevin, Klemes, and a hundred lesser-known rabbis and 'active workers in Orthodox Jewry' called upon Western Jewry to continue its material support for the *yeshivot* and other religious institutions.[27]

THE DEMISE

The situation took a dramatic turn for the worse in the early months of 1930, when an unprecedented government campaign was launched against religious functionaries. Numerous practising rabbis in Belorussia and the Ukraine were stripped of their civil rights and branded as *lishentsy* (disenfranchised people).[28] Their homes were confiscated by the state and they were unable to find legal housing. Rabbis were levied with excessive taxes, which forced them to sell off their personal belongings, or face arrest and deportation.

The crack-down sent shock-waves throughout the rabbinate, which was the conduit through which the Committee distributed its funds. Numerous rabbis resigned from their posts — many doing so publicly in the press in order to free themselves from the exorbitant taxes. Others left their communities for distant locales where they would not be known and could attempt to evade the legal status of *lishentsy*.[29]

An anonymous plea for help entitled 'Are we doomed to perish?' offered a bleak depiction of the situation:

> In the Vitebsk region, not a single rabbi is to be found in his city. They have all left for places where they are not recognized, lest they be destroyed or prosecuted on account of the taxes. Thus, almost all of the men of Torah have gone into exile; their lips rustle with the question, 'Are we doomed to perish?' (Num. 17:28)[30]

With the disintegration and dispersion of the rabbinate, the Committee of Rabbis had no mechanism for disbursing its funds to the *haderim*. The crack-down also led to the discovery of several more underground *yeshivot* (in Kremenchug, Kharkov and Vitebsk), and culminated in the arrest of fourteen rabbis, preachers and synagogue elders in Minsk in March 1930.

The Minsk arrests were a particularly traumatic blow to the Committee. Among those seized was Rabbi Menahem Gluskin, the city's chief rabbi and a member of the Committee's leadership council, who had been intimately involved in its internal affairs. He and his colleagues were formally charged with counter-revolutionary activity, an offense then punishable by death. Most ominous was the announcement by the authorities that they had discovered 'correspondence with Jewish associations abroad...a hectograph machine, and documents proving that the community had engaged in counter-revolutionary activity, by transferring information to the [foreign] associations'. There could be little doubt that the correspondence and documents had been prepared by the Committee of Rabbis for the JDC.[31]

The announcement had a chilling effect on Rabbis Klemes and Zevin, who were in charge of the Committee's operations, and who were personally implicated by the uncovered documents. Correspondence with Schneerson in Riga and the JDC in New York was discontinued. Rosen in Moscow was no less traumatized. He immediately stopped disbursing funds for religious activity, expressing the fear that the recipients of JDC funds would be placed in grave danger. Rosen must also have worried that any continued funding of religious activity would jeopardize the agency's operation in the USSR altogether, now that the authorities had discovered documents related to its clandestine activity.[32]

Gluskin and his colleagues were released after two weeks of detention, thanks to a public outcry in the West, and were never tried for their alleged offense. Instead, they were required to sign a statement denying the existence of anti-religious persecution in the Soviet Union, and protesting against the anti-Soviet propaganda being spread by Western Jewish organizations. But the repercussions of their arrest and the anti-clerical campaign of 1930 were long lasting. As one JDC official reported, 'rabbis and teachers go around in constant danger of arrest, and have given up most of their religious activity'.[33]

The JDC itself concluded that the allocation of funds for religious activity in Russia would cause more harm than good. In the wake of the stock market crash of November 1929 and the deepening Depression, the JDC could not afford to expend its scarce resources on such a futile and counter-productive endeavour, and it decided to eliminate its budget for 'cultural work' in Russia. The decision was the final nail in the coffin of the Committee of Rabbis of the USSR and its network of underground educational institutions.[34]

CONCLUSION

Jewish religious education in the USSR persisted as a clandestine minority enterprise for considerably longer than has been presumed. The educational underground functioned with remarkable resourcefulness and resilience throughout the 1920s, and Schneerson and his colleagues were convinced that it would guarantee the survival and perpetuation of Judaism in the USSR. Their efforts and their hopes were crushed, with great force and finality, by the anti-clerical campaign of 1930.

NOTES

1. See Zvi Gitelman, *Jewish Nationality and Soviet Politics: The Jewish Sections of the CPSU 1917–1930* (Princeton: Princeton University Press, 1972), pp. 291–318; Mordechai Altshuler, *Ha-Yevsektsia be-Vrit ha-Mo'atsot* (Tel Aviv: Moreshet and Sifriat Poalim, 1980), pp. 292–303; Benjamin Pinkus, *The Jews of the Soviet Union: A History of a National Minority* (Cambridge: Cambridge University Press, 1988), pp. 98–105.
2. Gitelman, *Jewish Nationality and Soviet Politics*, p. 314. More than 1,000 *haderim* were forcibly closed in 1922–23 alone; ibid. p. 305.
3. The Crown Rabbi was a rabbinic functionary officially recognized by the tsarist Russian government (Eisenstadt was appointed to his post prior to the 1917 Revolution).
4. 'Jewish Religious Education in Soviet Russia', JDC Archives, USSR File No. 472, pp. 1–3.
5. On traditionalist resistance in Vitebsk, see A. A. Gershuni, *Yahadut be-Rusiya ha-sovyetit* (Jerusalem: Mosad Harav Kook, 1961), pp. 26–36, 215–36; on Gomel', see Altshuler, 'The Rabbi of Homel's Trial in 1922', *Michael* 6 (1980), pp. 9–61.
6. Professor Haym Soloveitchik, oral communication, 20 Oct. 1990; Moshe M. Yosher, *Ha-Hafets Hayim: hayav ve-po'alo* (Tel Aviv: Netzah, 1958), Vol. I, pp. 430–6; S. K. Mirsky (ed.), *Mosdot tora be-Eropa be-binyanam uve-hurbanam* (New York: Histadruth Ivrith of America, 1956), pp. 152, 233, 314–16, 261–6 On the Novar'dok *musar yeshivot* see also Dov Katz, *Tenuat ha-musar*, Vol. 4 (Tel Aviv: Avraham Tzioni, 1963), pp 227–8; Y. Shayn, 'Ha-yeshiva ha-merkazit bi-Mezrits, *Kol Yisrael* (Jerusalem), 26 April 1946; David E. Fishman, 'The Musar Movement in Interwar Poland', in Y. Gutmann *et al.* (eds.), *The Jews of Poland between Two World Wars* (Concord, NH: University Press of New England, 1989), pp. 247–71.
7. Jacob Leshchinski, *Dos sovetishe yidntum: zayn fargangenhayt un kegnvart* (New York: Yidisher Kemfer, 1941), p. 320 (a letter from the town of Glukhov to *Der Emes* makes the same point as the one from Zhitomir).
8. 'Doklad o deiatel'nosti ravvinskogo komiteta v SSSR', JDC Archives, File No. 473, p. 1; for a Hebrew version of this document see Joseph Isaac Schneerson, *Igrot kodesh Mahariits* [Moreni ha-Rav Yosef Yitshak] (Brooklyn, 1982), pp. 569–85.
9. Rabinowitz died in 1925, and was succeeded by R. Jacob Klemes. Gluskin joined the Leadership Council in 1926. See *Igrot kodesh*, Vol. 1, p. 527; Vol. 11, pp. 44f., 73f.; Vol. 13, p. 120, 124; Sholem Duber Levin, *Toldot Habad be-Rusiya ha-sovyetit* (Brooklyn: Kehot Publication Society, 1989), pp. 18–19. For a broader treatment of the Committee's history and activities, see David Fishman, 'Preserving Tradition in the Land of Revolution: The Religious Leadership of Soviet Jewry 1917–1930', in Jack Wertheimer (ed.), *The Uses of Tradition: Jewish Continuity in the Modern Era* (New York: Jewish Theological Seminary of America, 1992), pp. 85–118.
10. Schneerson's vision for the Committee's operation is best encapsuled in Zevin's 1927 report, cited in note 7.
11. Schneerson's clandestine modes of operation are presented very vividly in his retrospective letter, written in Riga in Sept. 1927; *Igrot kodesh*, Vol. 1, pp. 616–37 He refers to the *arumforer/agitatorn* on pp. 623, 629.
12. *Igrot kodesh*, Vol. 1, Letter 319.
13. Levin, *Toldot Habad be-Rusiya ha-sovyetit*, pp. 22–31. As of 1923, the Commissariat of Justice ruled that religious study could be carried out in groups of not more than three children.
14. *Igrot kodesh*, Vol. 1, pp. 619, 624, 630; 'Budget for Cultural and Religious Work in Russia, Sept. 1925 to Aug. 1, 1926', JDC Archives, File No. 472. The Committee also received sizable JDC allocations for Passover relief, or as it was referred to in official documents, 'Passover cultural work'.
15. *Igrot kodesh*, Vol. 1, pp. 519–25 (Zevin's report, written in spring 1927), and pp. 616–37 (Schneerson's retrospective, written in Riga, Oct. 1927). Minsk figures for 1926: 'Survey of the Religious and Cultural Work with the Sums Offered by the Joint Distribution Committee in USSR by Means of the Rabbins' [sic] Committee in USSR', JDC Archives, USSR File No. 473, p. 3 (also in Hebrew); Minsk figures for 1928: 'Report

of the Accomplishments of the Rabbinical Board in Russia During 5688', File No. 476, p. 3.

16. 'Budget Proposal for Torah Study in Russia, Oct. 1928–Oct. 1929', dated June 1928, *Igrot kodesh*, Vol. 13, p. 170; list of 44 other communities — 'Report of the Accomplishments' (as in n. 15 above), pp. 1–2.
17. *Igrot kodesh*, Vol. 13, pp. 160–5; 176. In 1928, there were 411,711 Jewish children enroled in school in the Soviet Union. Of these, approximately 120,000 attended Soviet Yiddish schools — Pinkus, *The Jews of the Soviet Union*, p. 109.
18. Levin, *Toldot Habad*, p. 292.
19. *Igrot kodesh*, Vol. 13, pp. 171–2.
20. Levin, *Toldot Habad* 266f.; *Igrot kodesh*, Vol. 1, p. 578; 'Dokladnaia zapiska pravlenia seminara "Bet Yosef", Nevel' ', Dec 1926, JDC Archives File No. 473. The placement figure is from the 'Report of the Accomplishments' (as in note 14), p. 17.
21. *Igrot kodesh*, Vol. 1, p. 620. The bracketed ellipses are found in the published version of the letter, and indicate passages which were excluded/censored by the editors.
22. *Igrot kodesh*, Vol. 2, pp. 101–3.
23. Odessa is absent from the lists of communities whose *hederim* received support from the Committee of Rabbis. e.g., *Igrot kodesh*, Vol. 13, pp. 160–1. It is known to have supported plans for a congress of Jewish religious communities which were vigorously opposed by Schneerson and the Committee of Rabbis — *Igrot*, Vol. 1, pp. 610ff. and 628. In the spring of 1926, Rabbi Menahem Gluskin of Minsk attempted to establish a separate, direct relationship between his own organization, the Union of Congregants of Synagogues and Prayer Houses in Minsk, and the JDC, thereby circumventing the Committee of Rabbis. The conflict between Gluskin and the Committee was apparently resolved in the late summer, when he was appointed to its leadership council. See Gluskin's letter to the Leaders of World Jewry, 24 Nisan 5686, and to James Rosenberg and Bernard Kahn of the JDC, 1 Sivan 5686, Central Relief Committee collection, Yeshiva University Archives, 117/21, and *Toldot Habad*, p. 18.
24. For a contemporaneous account of Schneerson's arrest, exile and departure from the USSR, see *Di yisurim fun lubavitcher rebn* (Riga, 1930). For evidence of Zevin's and Klemes' expanded roles after 1927, see Levin, *Toldot Habad*, pp. 125–6; letter from Committee of Rabbis to JDC, May 1928, JDC Archives, USSR File No. 475.
25. Levin, *Toldot Habad*, pp. 268–71, 274–6.
26. 'Report on the Accomplishments of the Rabbinical Board in Russia during 5688', JDC Archives, USSR File No. 476, p. 12.
27. 'An Open Statement', Iyyar 5689, JDC Archives, USSR File No. 476.
28. Not only Jewish clergy were deprived of their civil rights. See Dimitry V Pospielovsky, *Soviet Anti-religious Campaigns and Their Authors* (New York: Macmillan, 1988), pp. 61 ff.
29. Levin, *Toldot Habad*, p. 200 f.; Gershuni, *Yahadut be-Rusiya ha-sovyetit*, pp. 71–3.
30. 'Ha'im tamnu ligvo'a?' (anonymous undated declaration), JDC Archives, USSR File No. 477
31. Meir Hildesheimer, 'Parashat rabanei Minsk ve ma'asaro shel Rabi Yehezkel Abramski, *Ha-Ma'ayan* 17/2 (1977), pp. 4–12.
32. Correspondence between Rosen, Cyrus Adler (Chairman of the JDC's Cultural Committee), and Joseph Hyman (President of the JDC), JDC Archives, USSR File No. 477.
33. Hildesheimer, 'The Affair of the Minsk Rabbis'; the quote is from a letter by Cyrus Adler to Rabbi Samarius Gourary, 28 Feb. 1930, JDC Archives, USSR File No. 477.
34. Based on memoranda and correspondence in the JDC Archives, USSR File No. 477; especially the memorandum by Evelyn Morrissey, 12 March 1930, and letter from Cyrus Adler to Leo Jung, 13 March 1930. Adler, who was one of the strongest supporters of religious aid to the USSR in the 1920s, radically altered his position in light of the new circumstances, and opposed such aid in the 1930s.

17

The Jewish Religion in the Soviet Union after World War II

YAACOV RO'I

The end of World War II found the survivors of the Soviet Jewish population traumatized by the Holocaust, the tribulations of evacuation and the losses and havoc of the war. Gradually, they sought to reconstruct their lives in the cities and townships of a devastated country. Many had lost their entire families; many returned to find their homes destroyed, confiscated or simply occupied; many were war invalids or in bad physical condition. At the same time, the war years had reawakened the Jews' national identity and consciousness. The awareness of their common fate created a sense of solidarity and a desire to be together. In these circumstances, a natural role seemed to be carved out for the synagogue and the community around it, especially given the fact that hardly any other Jewish institutions had survived the vicissitudes of the first decades of 'the building of communism', during which the vast majority of synagogues, too, had been closed down and sequestrated.

As the Soviet armed forces reconquered the territories that had been under German occupation, Jews started returning and quickly began thinking about reopening synagogues. In the years 1944–46 this was a feasible line of conduct. During World War II, as the Soviet leadership sought to mobilize its citizenry for the war effort, it had shown an unusual readiness to compromise with a number of institutions and social forces it had earlier repressed and opposed, the most important of which was probably the Russian Orthodox Church. As a result, and in view, perhaps of the inevitable growth of religiosity in the difficult conditions of World War II, there was a marked increase in the religious activity of believers of all faiths.[1] In order to implement the new *modus vivendi*, even *modus operandi*, with the religious

263

establishment, and to implement effective supervision and control over it, a Council for the Affairs of the Russian Orthodox Church and a Council for the Affairs of the Religious Cults (*Sovet po delam religioznykh kul'tov* — CARC) were set up, subordinated directly to the government. The latter council dealt with all recognized religions other than the Russian Orthodox Church: the various Christian sects and denominations, Islam, Buddhism and Judaism.[2]

In the pre-war period, Soviet policy toward the Jewish religion had not been inherently different from policy toward other faiths, nor had the situation of the Jewish religion been fundamentally distinct from that of other creeds. Yet, while policy toward religion seemed even now to be basically uniform, the Jewish religion did not benefit from some of the concessions awarded other creeds, perhaps because the Jews had no alternative but to harness themselves to the war effort against Nazi Germany and so did not need to be lured or cajoled into giving their full support. Whereas during the war some religions were given the possibility to create an all-union umbrella organization that supervised the activities of their believers, notably the Moscow Patriarchate of the Russian Orthodox Church, or institutions that coordinated the activities of the clergy of major regions of the country, such as the four Muslim spiritual boards or administrations, each Jewish community had perforce to function on its own.[3] There was no chief rabbi or board of synagogues or any other central organization that brought together or enabled cooperation between different rabbis either on the national or on the republican level. Moreover, although some religions were allowed to open religious seminaries, for example the Russian Orthodox Church and Islam, and also the Roman Catholic, Greek Catholic and Armenian churches, no such permission was given for Judaism.

The protocols, reports and resolutions of CARC, on which much of this paper is based, give interesting glimpses of the peculiar features of Judaism and Jewish life, admittedly, as seen through the eyes of government officials who did not share the view of the Jews that the synagogue or community should indeed play a role in their endeavour to return to a normal existence. In this connection it might be well to make a methodological observation: On the face of it there could perhaps be no better informed source than the documentation of the Soviet establishment itself. Yet, there is a distinct possibility that, since the Soviet authorities were clearly concerned about the considerable activity being conducted in and around the synagogues and therefore sought pretexts to curtail it, some of the innuendoes and connotations of this activity may have been exaggerated and coloured.[4]

In the first period after the restoration of Soviet rule in the territories that had been occupied by the Germans, one of the major issues before the council was the registration and/or reopening of prayer houses. Nor was this question limited to the area which the Germans had controlled or to prayer houses destroyed as a result of the war. Applications were received from wherever the new policy of relative openness or moderation toward religion bred the hope or belief that some of the prayer houses confiscated or closed by the authorities in the 1920s and 1930s might now be reopened or returned to their original function. Side by side with the purely procedural registration of prayer houses that were in fact active, believers of all faiths, and the Jews among them, thus approached the council and its local representatives with requests to be allowed to retrieve their former properties and to reactivate them as houses of worship. In the years 1944–48, the council dealt with hundreds of such requests, including many from Jews who asked to reopen synagogues in the various parts of the country, in the RSFSR, the Ukraine, the Western territories that had been annexed in the course of the war, the Caucasus and Central Asia. The council authorized the opening of no less than 33 synagogues in the first three years of its existence (summer 1944–summer 1947). In this same period, however, it turned down a total of 235 applications, usually on the grounds of their rejection by the local *gorispolkom* or *raiispolkom* (the municipal or district executive committee), which contended that the building in question was being used for other purposes.[5] There were also other criteria for not permitting the opening of a prayer house, such as the poor condition of the building and its unsuitability for use by would-be worshippers, or, especially as time went on, the 'political inexpediency' of opening a synagogue in a particular city or township. By summer 1947 the instructions received by CARC stipulated that, whereas prayer houses might be opened for certain religions in areas where there were none, or where the opening or construction of a prayer house might be expedient, Roman Catholic, Lutheran, sectarian and Jewish prayer houses were to be opened only in extraordinary cases.[6] The number of applications to open new synagogues, which presumably reflected the chances the Jews believed they had to succeed, diminished accordingly. If in 1946 and 1947 there were 197 and 188 respectively, by 1948 there were 75, in 1949 just 37 and in 1950 a mere 10.[7]

In the late 1940s approximately 200 synagogues actually operated in the Soviet Union. According to one report, there were as many as 217 in mid-1947, including 47 that operated in practice, but had not registered.[8] From this time the number seems to have steadily decreased. By the end of the Stalin period it was down to approximately 130. Those closed down undoubtedly included all that had not managed to register officially. Of the 189 synagogues listed by CARC as having operated at the end of 1947, 38 were in the RSFSR, 79 in the Ukraine, 31 in Georgia, 14 in Moldavia, 10 in Uzbekistan, and from one to five in each of eight other republics (three republics had none: Turkmenia, Armenia and the Karelo-Finnish SSR).[9] One hundred twenty five of these synagogues had operated before the council began its activity in June 1944. Most of the 35 actually opened after permission was given by CARC were communities which had in fact conducted prayer meetings prior to the granting of permission, but had neither a building nor a rabbi.[10]

As early as summer 1945, CARC chairman Polianskii noted that the Jews were particularly active in presenting applications to open prayer houses, 'doggedly demanding' the opening of synagogues in Moscow, Kharkov, Kiev, Rostov, Dnepropetrovsk, Odessa and other cities.[11] In addition to their zealousness in pressing their applications, the Jews were prepared to spend unusually large sums to restore synagogues. Some of these were actually opened without permission, for example in the Ukrainian towns of Belaia Tserkov' and Cherkassy.[12]

There were even occasional attempts by Jewish communities to actually build synagogues without permission from CARC.[13] In Samarkand, for instance, a group of Bukharan Jews reached an understanding with the local *raikomkhoz*, and proceeded to build four additional buildings in the courtyard of their synagogue, equip them with the necessary furnishings, and operate all four as separate synagogues, each with its own minister of religion and congregation. In the words of the report delivered to the council in Moscow, to all intents and purposes they had set up a 'miniature *kahal*'. (The *kahal*, or *kehila*, was the Jewish communal organization whose existence had been officially prohibited by the Bolsheviks in the early stages of their rule.) In the RSFSR itself, in Roslavl' (Smolensk Oblast), the leaders of the unregistered local community received permission through the *gorsovet* (city council) to obtain a plot of land for the construction of a house under a false name. The plot they chose was the very same one where the synagogue had stood before it was destroyed during the Nazi occupation, and they were stopped only when the council's representative in the *oblast'* discovered 'this deception'.[14]

One of the concomitants of this activity that attracted the attention of the authorities was that in order to raise the necessary funds, the rounds were made of the entire Jewish population of the city or town in question,[15] the funds at the disposal of 'believers' alone being apparently insufficient.[16]

The social composition of the believers in Kiev Oblast in the immediate postwar period was said to be heterogeneous: 'artisans, workers, tradesmen, employees of soviet and cooperative organizations'. Yet, on Jewish holidays, 'people whom one could hardly call believers' attended synagogue, 'army officers, leaders of soviet organizations and even representatives of the world of learning (*uchennogo mira*)'. Perhaps no less insidious from the point of view of the authorities was that senior ranking officials 'of Jewish nationality' took advantage of their position to help 'of course clandestinely' in the restoration of synagogues and in resolving a number of the religious communities' administrative and economic problems.[17] In 1949 and 1950 officers and soldiers still attended synagogue services, presumably on Jewish holidays in particular, as did the wives of communists, and even occasionally communists and members of the Komsomol.[18]

Some, but far from all, synagogues had rabbis and a few also had other religious personnel: *mohelim* (circumcisers), *shohetim* (ritual slaughterers), and an occasional cantor. A cantor might be invited for the holidays, sometimes even with a choir, to give the synagogue service a festive air; in such an event the entire Jewish population would be notified, among other reasons, to attract worshippers to the synagogue.[19] A number of synagogues had facilities for baking *matzot*, the unleavened bread eaten on the Passover, and a ritual bath (*mikva*). The Kiev synagogue had sought in 1945 to build its own oven.[20] One of the problems that concerned the Jewish religious communities and their rabbis throughout the period under discussion was the dearth of personnel to fulfil the tasks that a Jewish community had by tradition to implement and of facilities for training new 'cadres'. A large number of the officiating rabbis were in their seventies and eighties by the end of the 1940s — at this time in the entire RSFSR there was not a single rabbi in an officially registered community under the age of fifty — and a significant percentage even of these had had no religious training at all, let alone any religious authorization to act as rabbis.[21] Another problem was the dearth of religious articles. Already in this period Rabbi Shlifer of Moscow's Choral Synagogue was asking permission to publish a *siddur* (prayer book) in 5–10,000 copies in view of the believers' great need for one.[22]

In addition to the synagogues, in a number of cities and smaller towns there were *minyanim*, that is non-registered, unofficial, and therefore, from the point of view of the authorities, illegal, groups of believers.[23] These groups met to pray in private apartments on the sabbath or, more often, on Jewish holidays. CARC pointed out in spring 1948 that the situation regarding Judaism was noteworthy not for its officially registered prayer houses but for 'the large-scale spontaneity of the religious movement. In many cities where Jews live, whether they have or do not have registered synagogues for believers, there are so-called *minyanim*.'[24] According to a report of the council in early 1949, *minyanim* existed in 'practically every city with a Jewish population'. Official policy was to liquidate these *minyanim*. Yet, for various reasons, this policy was not always implemented, although the authorities usually knew at least the addresses of the apartments and even the names of the central figures of the *minyan* in question. They were aware even that in some instances *minyanim*, in their attempt to evade trouble, changed their meeting place from one occasion to the next.[25]

The *minyanim*, by their very nature as unregistered associations, were a considerable thorn in the side of the authorities, whether they existed in places where there was also a functioning synagogue or in those where no synagogue had been allowed to open. In the words of a council survey of the Jewish religion, these *minyanim* provided 'fertile ground for all kinds of operators, rascals and other dubious characters'. In Kiev some of these *minyanim* were run by people who were 'dissatisfied' with the activity of the clergy in the city's official synagogue. One of them, when summoned to the local CARC representative, refused to heed the order to close his prayer meeting (*sobranie*), insisting that the 1936 Stalin Constitution entitled him to open prayer premises.[26] One of the methods used to bring about the closure of *minyanim* was the imposition of taxes. In Kiev a tax of no less than 9,000 rubles (a sum equivalent to six or seven average monthly salaries) was imposed on a person who had put his apartment at the disposal of a *minyan*, upon which the other *minyanim* in the city terminated their existence of their own accord.[27] Despite these draconic measures, many *minyanim* continued operating. In 1948 over twenty were said to exist in Leningrad, with a similar situation pertaining in Moscow, Kiev, Tashkent and other cities; in Gorkii, with its 6,000 believing Jews, there were purported to be no fewer than 40 *minyanim*. In Vinnitsa Oblast there were also said to be 40.[28] In 1950, 11 were still operating in Zhitomir Oblast, while in other Ukrainian towns, where they had almost stopped operating, they were revived for the fall holidays.[29] In the same year there were several dozen in Bobruisk after the official synagogue was closed down, while *minyanim* functioned in the outskirts of Minsk, in Pinsk, Gomel', Mozyr', Polotsk and Baranovich (all in Belorussia); 12 *minyanim* were also functioning in Moscow and another thirteen in Moscow Oblast, eleven in Leningrad, some of which stopped functioning in that year with the arrest of their leading figures (1950 was a year of large-scale arrests of Jews in Leningrad).[30]

In some places, too, a registered synagogue and/or rabbi endeavoured to take on functions that the Soviet authorities considered extraneous to the strictly ceremonial rites, which, according to Soviet law, were within the jurisdiction of a religious community. Although the Jewish religion had no centre, each community existing independently, a CARC report of early 1947 pointed out that

> a characteristic trait of the Jewish communities is a distinctly expressed tendency to revive the communal-*kahal* system and to turn the synagogue into a centre of Jewish social activity (*obshchestvennost'*). The tragic sacrifices suffered by the Jewish people during the war led to a manifest growth of a nationalist frame of mind. A specific 'Soviet' Zionism has developed (*uyros*) whose representatives, not wishing to see the ways and forms (*videt' puti i formy*) of the so-called Jewish question, which has long ago been settled in the USSR, have stated that 'the synagogue is the only place of national concentration (*natsional'noi kontsentratsii*) and the only centre (*ochag*) of national culture'[31]

These nationalist tendencies of the Jewish religious communities were the second distinguishing trait of Judaism (in addition to the spontaneity of the Jewish religious movement) that demanded CARC's constant attention. In

> the majority of the major Jewish religious centres (Moscow, Leningrad, Lvov, Chernovtsy, Zhitomir, etc.) nationalist clerical elements, playing upon the feelings of the most backward, believing Jewish masses, and taking advantage of the Jewish religion in which religious rites are perpetually interwoven with national motifs, seek to turn the synagogue into a national-social organization.

Representatives of these communities, as a rule speaking in the name of the entire Jewish people, sought to develop an extensive charity on a general Jewish scale, collect money among the entire Jewish population to lay out cemeteries, show initiative in setting up memorials to the Jewish heroes and victims of the Great Fatherland War, establish contact between communities within the USSR and abroad, and strive to subordinate to the influence of the religious community as many Jews as possible, irrespective of their religious convictions.[32]

Another report spoke in the same vein of how the religious community took advantage of the 'specifics of the Jewish religion, the intricacies of its dogma and its abundance of rites and customs' to develop 'charity with national traits' to revive 'national-religious festivals (Purim, Hanukka, Tishebeov, Lagboimer, and so on); and take every measure to attract to the synagogue the largest possible number of believers'.[33]

Religious propaganda was said to be prevalent in the late 1940s; the Soviet constitution authorized only anti-religious propaganda. Its main goal was to attract non-believers, especially young people, its chief forms — religious lessons in groups (*gruppovoe obuchenie*), individual conversations and offering material aid. The first form was practised by Muslims, Jews and certain Roman Catholic priests. The CARC representative in Georgia, one Kuridze, reported one religious official (*sluzhitel' kul'ta*) conducting lessons in the synagogue 'under the guise of prayer-meetings, and prior to the beginning of those meetings he posts an observer outside'.[34] CARC officials said that the leaders of Jewish religious communities did not mostly ask official permission to open religious schools — the *heder*, for children up to thirteen — as they know a priori that the answer would be a negative one. 'Nonetheless, such schools are illegally set up and fall into the Council's line of vision, or that of its representatives, quite accidentally.' One such *heder* operated after the war for about two years in Novgorod-Rodynsk with some twenty children. The teacher was an 86-year old man, who had in the past been a 'professional Jewish teacher'. At first, studies were conducted in the teacher's home, but were later 'transferred' to the apartments of parents.[35]

The council's representative in the Belorussian SSR stated that community leaders resorted to a variety of methods in order to 'deploy religious propaganda, retain their influence on the masses of the believer population and replenish the ranks of the believers...Prayer meetings are conducted wherever Jews live and where the authorities are not sufficiently watchful.' The 'assertiveness of these groups' was especially manifest prior to the fall festivals, when, despite steps taken by the authorities, Jews came together to conduct religious rites in all places with a Jewish population.[36] Sometimes, for lack of facilities for holding services, they were held under the open sky.[37] In the period prior to the Jewish holidays the synagogues would be redecorated. More important, their spiritual leaders (*dukhovenstvo*) and 'active religionists (*religiozniki*) launched an extensive agitation concerning the necessity for all Jews to attend synagogue on the holidays'. In a number of synagogues, notably in Moscow, they pointed out in sermons and in private conversations that the synagogue was 'the only place where Jews can congregate and maintain contact'. In some communities they even made the rounds of believers' apartments reminding them of the approaching holidays and inviting them to attend synagogue.[38]

Material assistance to the needy was also prevalent among Jewish religious communities. In Riga the community president thought it his specific task to give expression to the Jewish tradition of mutual assistance.[39] In Chernovtsy, too, the Jewish religious community established a fund for helping the needy. To this end, the synagogue mounted paid concerts and lectures by leading clerics (*klerikaly*). In Kharkov attempts to help needy Jews included plans to build a home for the aged and for homeless single people.[40] In Nikolaev, the synagogue leaders (*rukovoditeli*) collected money from Jews in order to organize help to 'sick and "needy" Jews'.[41] Other towns where the community engaged in charitable activity included Moscow, Leningrad, Kiev, Irkutsk, Tambov, Zhitomir, Vinnitsa and Berdichev. Needless to say, charity would not be confined to believers.[42]

These aberrations were especially evident in the areas annexed by the Soviet Union during or in the wake of World War II, where the tradition of the Soviet repression of religion had not made its mark as profoundly as in areas where it had prevailed for thirty years. In Lvov the Jewish community sought to open a second synagogue. In the charter that was drawn up it was decided to call the new community

> a voluntary association — the Jewish community of Lvov This same document declared that 'the Jewish community in Lvov...sees as its basic goal: a. the national-cultural and religious unity (*obedinenie*) of the Jewish population of Lvov city and Oblast; b. raising the political, national and cultural consciousness of the Jewish population; c. implementing various...measures to improve the material living conditions of the Jewish population of Lvov city and Oblast.

The community's funds, it was laid down, were to be composed of 'voluntary payments and donations by members of the community, income (*postupleniia*) from lectures, concerts, etc., and from contributions in parcels and money from abroad'. The president of the community told the CARC representative that he was not personally religious and his chief interest was to procure material help for Jews from America and to organize *arteli* through the 'voluntary association'.[43] In Moldavia some of the rabbis, such as Rabbi Sholom Epel'baum in Kishinev and Rabbi Averbukh in Bel'tsy, entertained ideas that stood in stark contradiction to those of the authorities: they wanted to open schools for Jewish children at the synagogue (for supplementary Jewish studies),[44] since, they maintained, Jews were forgetting both their language and their customs. They also asked to be permitted to hold Jewish concerts at the synagogue in the absence of any Jewish theatre and to publish books and calendars in Yiddish. Perhaps worst of all, from the point of view of the representatives of

CARC, they sought to set up a chief rabbinate of Moldavia, that would speak in the name of all that republic's Jews, not only believers and not only the members of their respective communities. Rabbi Averbukh even suggested that Jews be excused from work during the 1947 fall festivals. The council, which could in no way condone what it considered 'extremist nationalist tendencies', had little option but to remove these rabbis.[45]

Yet religious practice also increased in the immediate postwar years in areas that had been part of the Soviet Union prior to 1939. Rites that had been all but dropped in the pre-war period and whose observance the council did not consider to be an integral part of religious ritual, reappeared in all parts of the country. A council report on religious practices noted that circumcision, for example, which before had been observed by only 'the most backward fanatic religious Jews', was now conducted by all believing Jews and even some non-believers. In every city and township with Jewish inhabitants there was 'a special *operator*, a so-called *mohel*, who carries out this operation'. In the course of just three months 150 circumcisions had been undertaken in Leningrad. Nor was it possible to estimate exactly the number of operations, since mostly they were conducted in private homes. 'Clerically and nationalistically minded elements' were suggesting that 'a Jew upon whom the rite of circumcision had not been performed, could not consider himself a Jew'; among 'reactionary Jews' one could often hear that circumcision was 'not so much a religious rite as a solely nationalist one'. In the Ukrainian towns of Olevsk and Kerosten' a number of people had been expelled from the party 'because of circumcision' (presumably for circumcising their sons) and in Zhitomir circumcision took on a 'mass character'.[46]

Another of the customs 'long obsolescent and forgotten even among believers themselves',[47] the sale of kosher meat, had also been revived. Indeed, in 1947, *Tsentrosoiuz* (the central consumers' organization) had permitted the sale of kosher meat by cooperative commercial organizations and by early 1949 it was sold in nearly all cities. In principle, the authorities were prepared to countenance the sale of kosher meat in the regular official stores upon agreement with the local consumer organizations (*oblpotrebsoiuz*), but not on synagogue precincts.[48] The baking of *matza*, which for many years before the war had been a major bone of contention between rabbis and Jewish communities, on the one side, and the authorities, on the other, now became somewhat easier, although it was not always conducted in strict accordance with Jewish law and in some places, at least, Jews continued to bake *matza* clandestinely in private homes.[49]

In a letter to Deputy Chairman of the Council of Ministers Kliment Voroshilov in mid-1947, CARC chairman Polianskii noted that the council had received petitions from Rabbi Shlifer in Moscow, as well as from believers in Vilnius, Kharkov, Kiev, Odessa, Kuibyshev, Orel, Penza and other places concerning the need to make kosher meat and *matza* available to Jews.[50] The use of the ritual bath or *mikva* was likewise said to have acquired broader dimensions in this period;[51] according to the council, nearly every synagogue had its own. At the same time, the communities were said to be concealing the number of women availing themselves of this facility in order to hide from the financial organs details of the resulting income.[52] Those practices, however, which were inherently financial, such as charity or the sale of the honour of being called to the Torah reading (the *aliya*) and of places in the synagogue, were forbidden by the authorities and had more or less been abandoned.[53] Nonetheless, the council was of the opinion that both were still being carried on by the synagogues in 'disguised' and roundabout forms.[54] At one of his periodical meetings with CARC officials in 1949, Rabbi Shlifer complained that the restrictions imposed by the authorities on collecting moneys for the synagogue in traditional fashion led it to being in severe financial straits.[55]

In spite of the constraints imposed by CARC, on the one hand, and the rabbi's complaints on the other, the Choral Synagogue was said to be still the scene of business meetings and dealings. One of these dealings concerned the sale of a 14-page Jewish calendar.[56]

The council's officials reported that in communities where the synagogues were not under the influence of 'nationalist elements', the numbers of believers and the extent of community activities were diminishing toward the end of the 1940s. It was not stated what the reason was, or was thought to be: the increasingly evident disapproval of the authorities; or a waning of the intense feeling and enhanced Jewish identity that had characterized the immediate postwar period; or the large-scale Jewish internal migration of these years that left many of the smaller towns in Ukraine and Belorussia, to which Jews had returned following the re-establishment of Soviet rule, with an ever-diminishing Jewish population. Thus, the council noted that in Birobidzhan, for instance, the religious community had lost its influence: whereas in 1947 not only older people, but even young girls had abandoned work and gone to the synagogue on the fall festivals,[57] in 1948, except for some 'old inveterate fanatics' no one had gone to the synagogue, going instead to the Jewish theatre or the cinema.[58] A few communities were reported to have disbanded altogether.[59]

The enhanced tendency of community leaders to 'impart to the synagogue a social and national character', had been worrying the authorities since the end of the war. A CARC circular to council representatives in 1945 pointed out that the heads of communities were saying that communities need not necessarily have rabbis. This request was thought to have a hidden reason, namely 'to give the community not so much a religious as a social and, specifically, a national character'.[60] In December 1945 Polianskii wrote to Deputy Premier Molotov:

> The most characteristic trait of the Jewish religious communities lies in a clearly expressed desire to lend them significance less as religious than as socio-political organizations, as spokesmen and vehicles for the national interests of the entire Jewish population.

Some presentations or applications to open synagogues state specifically that the actual applicants 'as well as those whom they represent, are far from religion', yet seek the formation of religious communities 'purely as form of national association' (*obedinenie*). The attempts of certain leaders of religious communities, Polianskii went on, to lend to the synagogues a totally religious character, met with stringent opposition on the part of nationalist-minded elements who accused them of implementing 'the assimilation of Jewry and in fact wiping it out as a nationality'.[61] Interestingly, for this very reason CARC appealed to Molotov to open a Jewish all-union religious centre and choose a chief rabbi; this centre would be not only a 'religious-consultative' one, 'in accordance with Judaism's centuries-old tradition', but 'above all an administrative-religious' one. Such a centre would be recognized by Jewish religious leaders who appraised the situation correctly and would deprive the communities of their political and nationalist hue.[62]

In the same year, CARC's representative in Zhitomir Oblast reported that one could sense among the Jews 'a certain exclusiveness, perhaps even a totally unconcealed nationalism; they are very close to each other'.[63] Five years later religious communities of the same *oblast'* were described as trying to direct their activity above all to 'strengthening those tenets (*dogmatik iudaizma*) that most vividly express Jewish exclusiveness, instilling believers with the idea that Jews are "God's chosen people"' Thus in 1950, in Zhitomir, parents 'submitted their children who had married non-Jews' to a 'curse' at public prayers (*na obshchestvennykh molebstviiakh*). In the same year, Odessa's Rabbi Dimont said in a sermon that the Jews were above all other peoples.[64]

Some community leaders were said even to be non-believers,

people, often intelligentsia, who sought to implement their 'narrow nationalist' aspirations through the synagogues, which were an appropriate forum for this purpose, and to impose their views on the community at large. Indeed, the community's spate of activities in this period was often connected not so much with the rabbi as with its president. This secular functionary, who had no parallel in other religions in the Soviet Union, was concerned primarily with the synagogue's administrative affairs, the collection of funds for a variety of purposes, the procuring and sale of kosher meat, the baking of *matzot*, and the various other activities that required funds and also brought in a certain income. The community president was, indeed, often suspect in the eyes of the authorities of seeking every feasible means, including illegal ones, of enhancing the community's income. One of these spheres of activity was the burial service. Most communities had their own *hevra kadisha*, or burial fraternity, which exercised control over the Jewish cemetery, sold burial plots and conducted funerals in accordance with Jewish ritual, whether the deceased's relatives wished this or not. In the Caucasian town of Nal'chik the Jewish religious community, having declared its ownership of the Jewish cemetery, sold burial plots to community members to grow vegetables.[65] In one instance at least, in Riga, the president of the community was asked by the CARC representative to resign his post. The justification for this demand was the president's open declaration to the CARC representative that he was not a believer, and, moreover, that he specifically perceived his task as providing assistance to other Jews (see above).[66]

Such testimonies certainly demonstrate that as a result of the war and/or the annexation of new territories with a considerable Jewish population, new life was being injected into the community in the second half of the 1940s. In the Ukrainian town of Berdichev, for instance, in the immediate postwar period, the community collected money to conduct major repairs at the synagogue. Since all Jews, not just those who defined themselves as believers, were willing to contribute, no less than 100,000 rubles were collected for that purpose.[67] The idea was actually broached to hold a meeting at the synagogue for the purpose and to publicize it in the local press to inform the city's Jewish population, but this was categorically prohibited.[68] These nonbelievers, who told the synagogue representatives, 'We will not pray, you pray for us', also came to the synagogue on the Day of Atonement, the day on which all Jews, even party members, felt themselves to be Jews. The community received authority from the relevant municipal organization to slaughter four heads of cattle per week and organized trade in kosher meat. It called in a 'specialist in circumcision' from nearby Shepetovka and provided for him, introduced new amenities at the Jewish cemetery, planned the construction of a monument to the victims of fascism buried at the city airport,[69] conducted charitable activity and helped Jewish families returning from evacuation.

Not a few communities organized activities in connection with commemorating the Holocaust. The general fast proclaimed by the Palestinian Chief Rabbinate just two months before the end of the war was the occasion of a major gathering at Moscow's Choral Synagogue. News of the event caused such a stir among Moscow's Jews including those who had little or no affiliation to the Jewish community, that the synagogue authorities decided to sell tickets for the ceremony to limit the numbers of those entering the building. Thousands stood in the street outside and the service was relayed to them over loudspeakers. In the words of one observer, this service drew the attention of the city's Jews to the synagogue as a centre of Jewish activity and expression and provided a new, legitimate context — the condemnation of fascism — that enabled them to attend the synagogue without apprehension. The Jewish wife of Foreign Minister Molotov, Polina Zhemchuzhina, occupied the seat of honour, next to the Ark, at the above-mentioned service. A number of Jews had approached the CARC representative in Zhitomir Oblast to officially recognize the occasion as a day of mourning and prayer in memory of the Jews killed in the war throughout the Soviet Union, on which they could go to the cemeteries. But he had turned down their request after discussing it with the *obkom* party secretary, for they believed this would turn into 'a political demonstration of the Jewish population'.[70]

In the following year, 1946, the Jewish community of Simferopol' in the Crimea, organized a ceremonial meeting on the anniversary of Victory Day and the liberation of the Crimea from Nazi occupation. The meeting took place at the restaurant of the NKVD *Spetstorg*, which was rented for the occasion. Among the participants were community members, including Krymchaks, the Crimea's indigenous Jewish population, and a number of Russians; it was specifically noted that some of those present were party members. A similar meeting with banquet was organized by the Jewish community in the Belorussian town of Mozyr', and attended by representatives of the town's soviet and its institutions. In Dnepropetrovsk, one of the synagogue's activists convinced a group of Jewish artists to hold a performance as part of his effort to collect funds for the monument he sought to set up in that town. The director of the local Shevchenko Theatre agreed to the theatre being used for the purpose.

Holding secular concerts and 'evenings' at synagogues was thought to be a way of attracting non-believers. In Leningrad such events were held in late 1946 and Jewish national songs performed and alcoholic beverages drunk on Simhat Torah and the Sunday of Hanukka. (The report of these events just gives the dates, without mentioning the fact that these were Jewish festivals.) The Irkutsk Jewish community asked permission (which was denied) for a visiting troupe called Muzkomediia, most of whose artists were Jewish, to perform at the synagogue.[71]

This extension of the community's activities beyond the limits of ritual practice as determined by the authorities appears, then, not to have been an unusual phenomenon in these first postwar years. The holding of special prayer meetings at the synagogue or even elsewhere under the community's auspices, made it possible to include in religious services speeches, reminiscences, and sometimes an artistic program. Moreover, these occasions were attended not merely by the synagogue's regular congregation, but by all the Jews of the city or township. As late as 1948, Kharkov's non-believer intelligentsia were said to be drawn to the synagogue out of love for their nation and to be aspiring to dominate the community.

These nationalist tendencies grew in connection with the establishment of Israel in May 1948.[72] In June of that year the Moscow Choral Synagogue held a ceremonial service to celebrate the event. Over 10,000 people participated, filling the building and almost the entire street outside. The synagogue was decorated with Star of David, greenery, a broad blue ribbon, and two placards, one announcing that 'On 14 May the State of Israel was declared' and the other — in Hebrew — 'Am Yisrael hai' ('The people of Israel are alive'). At the end of the service, the synagogue president read out three telegrams, sent in the name of 'the believers' to Stalin, Chaim Weizmann and Israeli Chief Rabbi Herzog.[73]

In the Ukraine a number of communities sought to hold similar ceremonies. So-called 'nationalist elements' in Chernovtsy made contact with like-minded groups in other Ukrainian cities with this end in view. The very attempt to establish contact between different Jewish communities, each of which was supposed to operate in limbo, was, as we have seen, a violation of the terms of reference stipulated by the Soviet authorities for Jewish religious institutions. In Lvov a service was held in May, which was said to have served as a signal (provodnik) for other communities. In Chernovtsy itself a service was held in June with the participation of 1,000 people, at the end of which a prayer was recited for those killed 'in Jerusalem', that is, in Israel's War of Independence. In Odessa the community asked the council representative for permission to hold such a service, but the request was turned down, while in Kiev feelers to this effect led the community to understand that permission would not be given and the idea was dropped.[74]

Nor did the synagogue communities satisfy themselves with holding religious ceremonies. Some of them considered giving concrete assistance to Israel's war effort, as was being done by other Jews throughout the USSR in groups and individually. The president of the Leningrad synagogue asked the local council representative about the possibility of Jews in the Soviet Union organizing help for the Jews fighting in Palestine and setting up a Jewish Anti-fascist committee at the synagogue. In Uzhgorod in Transcarpathia, the community secretary said that Jewish believers would ask permission to form military units, obviously to take part in Israel's war of independence. The council's representative in Uzbekistan reported that among that republic's believers there was frequent talk of the likelihood, in view of the USSR's recognition of Israel and the exchange of diplomatic missions, of Moscow even allowing Jews to emigrate to Israel.

Polianskii reported personally to Molotov on the first visit to the Choral Synagogue of the Israeli diplomatic staff on the sabbath following Mrs. Meyerson's presentation of credentials. At the end of the service Mrs. Meyerson had gone into the synagogue's main hall — during the service she had been in the women's gallery — greeted the rabbi ceremoniously in Hebrew and burst into tears. As she and her companions passed between the worshippers on their way out, they had been greeted by applause.

Twice in the week following the Jewish New Year in early October 1948, Rabbi Shlifer was received by Polianskii. He reported on the visit to the Choral Synagogue of the Israeli Minister and her staff, telling the CARC chairman that the synagogue, the courtyard and the alley in which it was situated were simply packed; he estimated those present at 10,000. Mrs. Meyerson's appearance had been greeted with applause and when he asked one of the synagogue board members to try to stop the applause, people retorted: 'We've been awaiting this event for 2,000 years. How can you prohibit us displaying our feelings?' There were many tears during the service and one worshipper called to the Torah reading made a special prayer for his children who were fighting in Palestine. Rabbi Shlifer described the throng that surrounded Mrs. Meyerson as she left the synagogue in order to see her from close up and greet her personally and suggested that in the future if such visits recurred, special security measures should be taken. Polianskii was against this on the grounds that it would draw even greater attention to the Israeli diplomats He told the rabbi to relate to them as ordinary foreigners and not to give any emphasis to their visits to the synagogue 'as if they had a special significance for the USSR's Jewish citizens'. The rabbi was also told not to hold a special ceremony upon receipt of the Torah scroll the legation had brought his synagogue from Israel, an instruction about which he was clearly displeased, saying it would be difficult to implement.

The main points of the above conversation were transmitted to Molotov, including CARC's recommendations to Rabbi Shlifer, which had already been agreed upon with the Foreign Ministry. These were basically that the rabbi should not extend his authority as rabbi in his contacts with the Israelis, not entering into any personal relationship with them. He should therefore refuse Mrs. Meyerson's invitation to him to visit the legation, at first on the pretext that he had recently been severely ill, but later on letting it be understood that a personal visit would be 'possible from a religious point of view only under exceptional circumstances'. Polianskii explained that in his view, were the Torah scroll to be presented at a special ceremony, this would turn into 'a demonstration with elements of political Zionism'. The day after he wrote the letter to Molotov, Polianskii was informed that the foreign minister agreed with his recommendations.[75]

Some communities were in actual contact with the Israeli legation in Moscow, admittedly on the latter's initiative. The legation sent one of its bulletins to the Uman' community; appearing in Russian, the bulletin discussed both the international situation and Israel's domestic scene. The Chernigov and Tbilisi communities received a five-page letter with Israel's official stamp, which told of the country's activities, of the massive influx of immigrants from all countries and the financial assistance to Israel of Jews from all over the world. Presumably in the wake of this communication, the Chernigov rabbi tried to organize the collection of funds for Israel. In Dnepropetrovsk, a synagogue activist got the agreement of the town's lecture office to hold a lecture on Palestine in one of Dnepropetrovsk's theatres or clubs.[76] CARC inspector M. I. Birman contended that the rabbi in Kuibyshev had received an unofficial communication from one of the Israeli representatives in Moscow in which Jews were invited 'to evacuate to Israel from the USSR' The letter had indicated that 20,000 Jews were supposed to be thus evacuated during 1949.[77]

Israel's diplomats, although not always the minister in person, continued attending synagogue in the capital, at least on major holidays. Following the 1952 fall festivals, Rabbi Shlifer reported to CARC that on the Feast of Tabernacles these diplomats had not conducted themselves with decorum, giving out Israeli chocolates to worshippers. He was severely reprimanded for having connived with the Israelis by treating them with unseemly deference, thus encouraging them to behave with undue freedom and impunity. Although he had told a member of the synagogue's inspection commission to keep an eye on the Israelis, this was clearly not sufficient and Rabbi Shlifer was told he must be more determined in keeping them in check. Otherwise, today they give presents, 'tomorrow they may actually give a speech'.[78]

'Nationalist' or 'political' activity was not only evident in connection with Israel. In a sermon in May 1950, Leningrad's Rabbi Lubanov insisted that people who were preoccupied with worldly affairs and not Torah, the sole source of freedom, were in fact slaves. Only those who studied Torah regularly could be free men.[79] The Omsk and other Jewish communities informed the religious community of Irkutsk when exactly the echelons bringing Jewish settlers to Birobidzhan would be passing through their town, and the Jews of Irkutsk collected money, food and other items, which they brought to the railway station for distribution among the migrants.[80]

The link between different Jewish communities had other expressions as well. To quote CARC:

> In the person of its Rabbi Shlifer, the Moscow Choral Synagogue aspires to be a Jewish religious centre. Thus, for instance, not a single application to open a Jewish religious community (wherever it might be) comes through without the applicants holding a preliminary consultation with Rabbi Shlifer.

Not infrequently, too, Rabbi Shlifer intervened with CARC in matters concerning other synagogues.[81] On a more local level, the executive organ of the Nikolaev religious community sent a member of its board to Voznesensk, where he organized a *dvadtsatka* (the nucleus of twenty people who undertook responsibility before the authorities for the activity of a religious community) and composed an official application to open up a synagogue. The Irkutsk synagogue board supplied scrolls of the law to the religious communities of Ulan-Ude, Birobidzhan and 'other cities'. When the Dnepropetrovsk synagogue was opened, a notice board was displayed in the Riga synagogue noting the names of the president and two of the members of the Dnepropetrovsk synagogue who had shown particular energy in achieving this. The Kishinev community had sought to organize a second community parallel to the existing one; and so on.[82]

Other 'activist' efforts at certain synagogues were of concern to CARC. In certain communities there were 'activists' who were far more occupied on behalf of the community than its official *aktiv*. The Odessa community had only to decide that the synagogue needed to be repainted, and the job was immediately done with the best quality paint, or that it be lit with electricity for the synagogue to be better lit within two or three days than any Soviet institution in Odessa. Within two weeks, moreover, the synagogue was furnished in a way that any government institution in Odessa might envy. The synagogue *aktiv*, 85 per cent of whom were over seventy, was so weak that the community should have disintegrated; but this did not happen due to tendencies of 'so-called national "solidarity"'. On the contrary, during the 1948 fall festivals, 6–8,000 people filled not only the synagogue and its courtyard but the street outside for 2–3 blocks. The crowd included young people, army officers and people who arrived in government cars. As one person explained: 'not a religious but a national sentiment motivates many of those present'.[83]

Yet a further instance of Jewish religious communities violating the law was the organization in synagogues (in Odessa, Dnepropetrovsk, Kharkov, Kiev) of study circles, to learn '*mishnais*, that is, Talmud or, to be more precise *hevra-mishnais*, a form of fraternity'. This method of study, among others, was condemned by the authorities since it brought material profit to those heading these circles, each of which had at least ten participants, who paid 20–25 rubles apiece for every course. In Odessa the rabbi employed a special teacher for the study of *mishnais*, who received a monthly salary of 500 rubles, apparently from the approximately 20,000 rubles collected by the rabbi from the sale of *matzot* before the Passover. Since these circles, like every fraternity, exceeded the parameters laid down in the law on religion (*kanon religii*) and their organization was intended solely to make profit, they were ordered to disband.[84]

A CARC report on the situation of the religions under its jurisdiction for the year 1951 noted that the size of the Jewish congregations had not changed noticeably over recent years. On both the Passover and the Day of Atonement there were violations of labour discipline. In Kiev 'many commercial enterprises' had simply not functioned on the latter date; in the single *raion* of Podol, 34 such enterprises had been closed, their employees being in the synagogue; in Odessa, 38 'stores and *arteli* had not opened, and in Zhitomir 24; in Chernigov, 33 general repair services had not worked at all and 50 had worked only part of the day; in Chernovtsy, too, 33 of these had been closed.

Even as late as 1951, the synagogues were being castigated for trying to rally 'all Jews, irrespective of their religiosity'. The Odessa rabbi was said, in one of his fall festival sermons, to have called upon 'Jews who did not come to synagogue', to 'come to their senses and fulfil their obligations as Jews'. In Kiev the rabbi had been asked, presumably by the local CARC representative, whether all the Jews who had come to synagogue for the fall festivals were believers. He had replied: 'No, not all are believers, but they come to synagogue out of national custom (*obychai*).' Jews who frequented the synagogue said that a Jew cannot be a non-believer. Sometimes, moreover, one could hear conversations at the synagogue about the State of Israel. The president of the Transcarpathian community of Beregovo said: 'it is our opinion that the State of Israel was created thanks to our prayers, that God has given it to us. Our Jews are ready to set off for Israel, even tomorrow'.

Finally, the synagogue remained a place where Jews came together not only for purposes of prayer but also to settle a whole lot of matters, 'commercial, family and other', that were quite irrelevant to religious practice.[85]

• • •

In conclusion, then, the situation of the Jewish religion in the immediate postwar years was an unusual one. The heightened sense of Jewish identity and solidarity as a result of the war and the Holocaust, the relatively concessionary attitude of the authorities to religion as a whole in the context of the war, the terrible plight of the survivors and the lack of other Jewish institutions in most cities and townships — although there were still a few theatres and cultural organizations — created circumstances which gave the synagogue and the religious community a new role. This social or nationalist role, as it was described by the organizations responsible for supervising synagogue activity, epitomized a new Jewish sense of solidarity that had not been in evidence in the pre-war period, and was inevitably looked upon askance by the Soviet authorities.[86] It may well have contributed to the virulence of anti-Jewish policy in Stalin's last years. There was a clear conflict between the desire of the authorities to limit the actual number, membership and activity of functioning synagogues (at least as of July 1947), and what they saw as a constant endeavour by the communities themselves to open new prayer-houses, to reach and attract as many Jews as possible and to extend their operations beyond the performance of religious rites permitted by Soviet law, to include the traditional services rendered by the synagogue and community to the individual Jew. The flourishing of the synagogue was given concrete expression in the financial and philanthropic activity which, although specifically forbidden by law, accompanied the resuscitation of the community. It was also manifest in the return of rites and ceremonies that had all but disappeared before the war (circumcision, the sale of kosher meat and the baking of *matzot*) which further antagonized the powers-that-be. By the end of the 1940s, religious activity was being limited once more and the short revival of the immediate postwar period was being curtailed, although actual attendance in the synagogues on the major festivals does not seem to have diminished until the early 1950s.[87]

NOTES

1. This was noted by the chairman of the Council for the Affairs of the Religious Cults, I. V. Polianskii, in a letter to chairman of the RCP(b) Central Committee's Propaganda and Agitation Administration (*upravlenie*) G. F. Aleksandrov, 31 Aug. 1945, Rossiiskii tsentr khraneniia i izucheniia dokumentov noveishei istorii (RTsKhIDNI), fond (f.) 17, opis' (op.) 125, delo (d.) 313. For the concern of the party leadership over misinterpretations on the part of the population of concessions made to the Russian Orthodox Church, as if the party had, or was having, second thoughts regarding its earlier, principled anti-religious position, see G. F. Aleksandrov and P. N. Fedoseev, also of the Central Committee's Propaganda and Agitation Administration, to Andrei Zhdanov, the Secretary responsible for ideology and propaganda, undated, RTsKhIDNI, f. 17, op. 125, d. 242, pp. 61–9.
2. For the May 1944 decree on establishing the latter council, see Gosudarstvennyi arkhiv Rossiiskoi Federatsii (GARF), f. 6991, op. 1, d. 1. The decree defined its task as the maintenance of ties between the government and the leaders of the various religious groups (*obedineniia*) apart from the Russian Orthodox Church. The reason for establishing two separate councils seems to have been twofold: in the first place, the Russian Orthodox Church was a distinctly Russian religion, which had its home base, as it were, in Russia. It served, therefore, to propagate Soviet influence abroad through its various affiliated organizations, whereas most of the other religions originated either in the West or in the Middle East. In retaining their confessional affinity to their 'analogous religious associations' outside the USSR, they served as instruments rather for the penetration of the influence of these associations into the Soviet Union. Secondly, the Russian Orthodox Church was historically dependent on the attitude of the state toward it, and if that attitude was negative or failing, it was prone to split or languish. The 'structural and doctrinal characteristics' of the other religions enabled them to be vital and flexible even in adverse conditions. Finally, the Russian Orthodox Church's more consummate (*sovershennaia*) hierarchy made it easier to control and regulate than the clergy of other faiths. Indeed, in the immediate postwar period, the Russian Orthodox Church was believed to be 'completely loyal' to the point of regarding itself a 'participant in the construction of socialism' — Report by the CARC to G. F. Aleksandrov on the work of the council, 1 July 1947, RTsKhIDNI, f. 17. op. 125, d. 506. For the work of CARC, see also Polianskii to Aleksandrov, 31 Aug. 1945.
3. The Roman Catholic and Lutheran churches also had no centre in the Soviet Union.
4. E.g., their comments regarding the repairs at the Odessa synagogue, see text p.281; It should be noted that this chapter is not based on the entire plethora of archival material, but on those lists of files (*opisi*) that were first opened and a sample of further material.
5. Altogether, the council sanctioned the opening of 320 prayer houses of various faiths and rejected 1963 in these three years — Report to Aleksandrov, 1 July 1947, RTsKhIDNI, f. 17. op 125, d. 506. For the tribulations of one community whose application was rejected, that of Bobruisk, which applied in 1946 to open a

synagogue, see I. V. Polianskii to A. A. Zhdanov, 22 July 1947, Report on Distortions and Violations of the Legislation Concerning Religious Cults, RTsKhIDNI, f. 17, op. 125, d. 506.

6. These instructions read as follows:
   1. To proceed to each instance of opening new synagogues with special attentiveness and heightened exaction, counsidering the current number to be the uppermost limit.
   2. To continue the line of limiting and effectively regulating the activity of the communities solely to the implementation of ritual (*kul'ta*), depriving them of functions not intrinsic to religious organizations. To elaborate and give the Council's representatives practical instructions on these questions.
   3. To reject applications concerning the formation of an all-union centre of Judaism in Moscow and publication of a prayer-book and religious calendar.
   Unsigned, and without indication of the source of these instructions, July 1947, RTsKhIDNI, f. 17, op. 125, d. 506. It is perhaps worth noting that in six places, Jewish prayer houses were nonetheless given permission to open and/or register at this time: in Ulan-Ude (Buryat-Mongolian ASSR), Bobruisk, Boguslav, Zaporozhe, Stanislav and Krivoi-Rog — ibid.
   These instructions, as other documents make clear, were just the beginning. The atmsophere prevailing in some of the synagogues in the late 1940s–early 1950s has been recorded by eyewitnesses, e.g., Mordecai Namir, *Shlihut be-Moskva* (Tel Aviv: Am Oved, 1971), *passim*; Barukh Vaisman, *Yoman mahteret ivri* (Ramat Gan: Massada,1973), pp. 178–223.
7. Information concerning the number of prayer houses and the Commission of Religious Rites, signed by CARC Vice-Chairman Gostev, undated, RTsKhIDNI, f. 17, op. 132, d. 285, pp. 202–17.
8. Altogether, there were at this time 1536 unregistered religious communities in the religions subordinated to CARC. The reasons for their not registering were: the local soviet or its executive committee refused to return the property of the former prayer house for the functioning of the 'cult', and therefore it functioned in unsanctioned places; the lack of a minister of religion, without whom a community could not register; insufficient activity on the part of the religious community in question, in which case it often preferred to remain informal; and the local authorities, too, in order not to spoil the image of the *oblast'*, sometimes preferred an amorphous religious movement to one functioning officially within the framework of the law, which, moreover, alleviated the community's activities — CARC to Aleksandrov on the work of the council, 1 July 1947, RTsKhIDNI, f. 17. op. 125, d. 506.
9. Survey of the Jewish Religion in 1948, 18 March 1949, GARF, f. 6991, op'. 4, d. 23, pp. 19–360.
10. There are some discrepancies and unclear points in the documentation, as a result of which the figures are not absolutely final. For example, CARC's Survey of the Jewish Religion in 1948 talks of 181 synagogues as having been in operation on 1 Jan. 1949, whereas the table included in the document shows just 179. Nor is there any categorization of the synagogues closed during the past year. Nor is it clear how the 189 are composed, specifically the 29 not included in the two categories, those which had operated prior to June 1944 and those opened by permission. Nineteen of the 29 seem to have been the synagogues of Transcarpathia, which was only annexed officially by the USSR after this date, in June 1945.
11. Polianskii to Aleksandrov, 31 Aug. 1945, RTsKhIDNI, f. 17, op. 125, d. 313.
12. Information concerning the meeting of CARC's representatives in the Ukraine, (undated) — GARF, f. 6991, op. 3, d. 13, p. 7. In Minsk in 1945 Rabbi V. E. Rozentsvi, with the permission of the *oblispolkom*, opened a synagogue that had not functioned since 1914 and organized regular services there. He also initiated activity with the purpose of a 'large-scale' opening of synagogues in Pinsk Oblast and in other areas of Belorussia and then left for Poland. Report to Polianskii of the CARC representative in Belorussia for the 2nd quarter of 1945, (undated) — GARF, f. 6991, op. 3, d. 29, p. 35. (The document was received on 13 July 1945).

13. A draft resolution of Dec. 1945, signed by Deputy Premier Viacheslav Molotov and *Sovnarkom* administrative secretary (*upravliaiushchii delami*) Ia. Chadaev, established that the construction of new prayer houses might be allowed 'in individual cases through the efforts and means of the believers, with permission from CARC' — GARF, f. 6991, op. 3, d. 10, pp. 106–7.

14. A Short Survey of the Jewish Religion in 1948, GARF, f. 6991, op. 4, d. 23. Similar attempts to build without permission were noted in Belorussia — in Polotsk, Kalinkovichi and Zhlobin — I. V. Polianskii to A. A. Zhdanov, 22 July 1947, RTsKhIDNI, f. 17, op. 125, d. 506.

15. Polianskii to Zhdanov, ibid.

16. The distinction made between 'believers' and the general Jewish population is clearly important for the unfolding of our story of CARC, i.e., Soviet official policy toward the Jewish religion and the synagogue. Those who were not 'believers' evidently did not fall under the jurisdiction of the religious community, and any activity conducted by it among them was an unauthorized over-extension of the prerogatives of the religious community and its officials. The actual use of the term 'believer' varies in Soviet sources; here, presumably, it means those who went, or would have liked to go, to synagogue on major Jewish festivals, except perhaps Yom Kippur — see below.

The 1929 Laws on Religious Associations stipulated specifically: 'The members of the groups of believers and religious societies may pool money in the prayer building or premises and outside it by voluntary collections and donations, but only among the members of the given religious association and only for the purpose of covering the expenses for the maintenance of prayer building[s] or premises and religious property, and for the salary of the clergy and activities of the executive bodies' (Article 54). Article 11 of the same Laws laid down the precise uses for which religious associations were authorized to collect funds. They were permitted to make contractual agreements hiring persons to fulfil certain jobs connected with guarding, repairing or procuring church property or materials connected with its preservation, but not for the purpose of commercial or industrial operations, such as leasing candle-making plants or printing-shops to produce religious books — Dimitry V. Pospielovsky, *A History of Marxist-Leninist Atheism and Soviet Anti-Religious Policies*, (London: Macmillan, 1987), p. 145.

17. Report of the CARC representative of Kiev city and Oblast, Zaretskii, to Polianskii for the period March–Nov. 1945, 20 Nov. 1945, GARF, f. 6991, op. 3, d. 28, pp. 116–7.

18. A Short Survey of the Jewish Religion in 1950, signed L. A. Prikhod'ko and Abushaev, CARC member and inspector respectively, 18 May 1951 — GARF, F. 6991, op. 3, d. 73. Soldiers and officers were among the worshippers in Riga; in Kherson there were workers of both the sea and river ports and the railways; in Birobidzhan on Yom Kippur a militiaman actually prayed with prayer book in hand. Communists' wives drew attention in Chernigov, and communists, party candidate members and *komsomol'tsy* in Novgorod-Severskii in Chernigov Oblast.

19. Report of the CARC representative for Kiev Oblast for the period July–Sept. 1945 to Polianskii, undated, GARF, f. 6991, op. 3, d. 28, p. 98. Those who attended synagogue on the Jewish New Year in 1945 included many young people, particularly girls, soldiers (two officers were actually identified by name), war invalids, and some soldiers from the Czechoslovak army; The practice of inviting cantors was followed in not a few synagogues in subsequent years as well — A Short Survey of the Jewish Religion in 1950, pp. 32–3.

20. Report to Polianskii of the CARC representative for Kiev city and Oblast for the period March–Nov. 1945, 20 Nov. 1945 — GARF, f. 6991, op. 3, d. 28, pp. 116–7.

21. See list of functioning registered synagogues, 1 July 1950 — with amendments updating it to 1952 — including details of the rabbis and other para-clerics who officiated in them, GARF, f. 6991, op. 4, d. 27.

22. Report of conversation between Rabbi Shlifer and CARC official L. A. Prikhod'ko, 5 Sept. 1951 — GARF, f. 6991, op. 3, d. 8, pp. 256–57. Rabbi Shlifer was told to present an official statement in writing. The prayer book eventually appeared in late 1956 in an edition of 3,000 copies.

23. See., e.g., G. Vrachev and Uzkov, both CARC officials to I. V. Polianskii, 29 Nov. 1946, RTsKhIDNI, f. 15, op. 125, d. 405, p. 102. Again, this was not a peculiarly Jewish phenomenon. A letter sent to Deputy Chairman of the Council of Ministers Kliment Voroshilov in early 1950 by the chairman of CARC on the topic of the council's struggle against such groups claimed that according to the data at its disposal, which were 'far from complete', there were no less than 2000 in the country (841 of these belonged to the Evangelical Christian Baptists and 647 to the Muslims) — I. V. Polianskii to K. E. Voroshilov, 4 Feb. 1950; RTsKhIDNI, f. 17, op. 137, d. 285, pp. 21–3.
24. Report of CARC's activity for 1947 and the 1st quarter of 1948, 9 June 1948, GARF, f. 6991, op. 3, d. 53, p. 30.
25. Survey of Jewish Religion in 1948.
26. Report of CARC's representative in Kiev city and Oblast, Zaretskii to Polianskii for the period March–Nov. 1945, 20 Nov. 1945, GARF, f. 6991, op. 3, d. 28, pp. 116–7. Article 124 of the constitution said: 'Freedom of religious worship...is recognized for all citizens.'
27. This information was provided by CARC inspector M. I. Birman at a CARC meeting in Jan. 1948 (the meeting took place on 23 Jan., yet Birman's testimony is dated 31 Jan.; it is not clear whether the meeting had more than one session or whether the date refers to the time he signed the document), GARF f. 6991, op. 4, d. 22, p.74, 31 Jan. 1948; a similar tactic was employed in Kharkov, where a tax of 3,000 rubles was imposed on one of the people who had made his apartment available for a *minyan* — ibid.
28. Survey of the Jewish Religion in 1948. N. Morozov, secretary for propaganda of the Gorkii *obkom* (party *oblast'* committee), to Comrade Zaborskii of the party's Central Committee Propaganda and Agitation Administration, 6 April 1948, RTsKhIDNI, f. 17, op. 125, d. 593; Report of CARC activity for 1947 and the 1st quarter of 1948, 9 June 1948, GARF, f. 6991, op. 3, d. 53, p. 30.
29. A Short Survey of the Jewish Religion in 1950.
30. Report of CARC activity for 1947 and the 1st quarter of 1948, as in n. 24; and A Short Survey of the Jewish Religion in 1950.
31. CARC report of the situation as of 1 Jan. 1947, GARF, f. 6991, op. 3, d. 47, p. 63. The CARC report of its activity in 1947 and the 1st quarter of 1948 also stressed that 'Jewish bourgeois-nationalist elements are trying to turn the synagogues into centres of Jewish social activity' — Report of CARC activity for 1947 and the 1st quarter of 1948, 9 June 1948, GARF, f. 6991, op. 3, d. 53, p. 30. For the alleged solution of the 'Jewish problem' in the USSR see Igor Krupnik, 'Soviet Cultural and Ethnic Policies towards Jews: A Legacy Reassessed', in this volume.
32. Report of CARC activity for 1947 and the 1st quarter of 1948, 9 June 1948, GARF, f. 6991, op. 3, d. 53, p. 30.
33. Survey of the Jewish Religion in 1948.
34. I. V. Polianskii in a secret letter to CARC representatives (Letter of instructions, No. 7), Appendix 3 to protocol No. 15, CARC meeting of 24–25 Aug. 1948, GARF f. 6991, op. 4, d. 22, pp. 20–21. For the activity conducted in Georgian synagogues in this period, see Lili Baazova, 'Synagogues and Synagogue Life in Georgia in the Postwar Era', in this volume.
35. Report of CARC activity for 1947 and the 1st quarter of 1948, 9 June 1948, GARF, f. 6991, op. 3, d. 53, p. 30.
36. Survey of the Jewish Religion in 1948.
37. E.g., in 1950 in Nikolaev, Korosten' and Zhitomir — A Short Survey of the Jewish Religion in 1950.
38. Ibid.
39. Testimony of the CARC representative in Latvia, V. Ia. Sheshken, at a CARC meeting, 21 Dec. 1946, GARF f. 6991, op. 4, d. 15, p. 116.
40. Survey of the Jewish Religion in 1948, p. 31. Needless to say, the very idea of special institutions for citizens of any one nationality was anathema to the Soviet authorities.
41. A Short Survey of the Jewish Religion in 1950.
42. Report by V. I. Polianskii to A. A. Zhdanov, On the Forms and Methods of Religious Propaganda, 7 July 1947, RTsKhIDNI, f. 17, op. 125, d. 506, p. 149; for Berdichev, see below. For the charity practised by Rabbi Shlomo Shlifer in Moscow, see Imanuel

Mikhlin, *Ha-gahelet* (Jerusalem: Shamir, 1986), pp. 110–12.

43. Report of the activity of the CARC representative in Ukraine, July–Sept. 1945 — GARF, f. 6991, op. 3, d. 28, p. 349.
44. In Chernovtsy, too, 'special children's groups' were reported to be functioning in the synagogues in 1945, to study Jewish religious songs and Talmud under the aegis of the rabbi — V. I. Polianskii to G. F. Aleksandrov, 31 Aug. 1945, RTsKhIDNI, f. 17, op. 125, d. 313.
45. Report of the CARC representative in Moldavia, S. K. Desiatnikov, on the situation and activity of the religious cults in Moldavia, 23 Jan. 1948, GARF, f. 6991, op. 4, d. 22.
46. M. Birman, A Short Report (*spravka*) on the Jewish Religion, undated, GARF, f. 6991, op. 3, d. 61, pp. 153–65 (the document was received on 1 Dec. 1949); and A Short Survey of the Jewish Religion in 1950.
47. Survey of the Jewish Religion in 1948.
48. Circular No. 45 to CARC representatives, signed I. V. Polianskii, 30 Aug. 1948, GARF, f. 6991, op. 3, d. 55, p. 17. Kosher meat was sold and poultry slaughtered according to ritual law, for instance, in the courtyard of the Leningrad synagogue in 1947 — I. V. Polianskii to A. A. Zhdanov, 22 July 1947, RTsKhIDNI, f. 17, op. 125, d. 506.
49. For the history of *matza*-baking under the Soviet regime, see Yaacov Ro'i, '*Hag ha-pesah mul ha-mishtar ha-sovieti*', Bar Ilan, 24–5, (1989), pp. 173–95.
50. I. V. Polianskii to K. E. Voroshilov, 21 Aug. 1947 — GARF, f. 6991, op. 3, d. 48, pp. 20–1. See p. 267 and note 20.
51. The Kharkov community had signed an agreement for the construction of a *mikva* at the city bath-house — Polianskii to Zhdanov, 22 July 1947, Report on Distortions and Violations, RTsKhIDNI, f. 17, op. 125, d. 506.
52. All three activities, the sale of kosher meat and *matza* and running a *mikva*, were condemned by the authorities as financial transactions. Thus, Polianskii's 22 July report to Zhdanov, discussing the commercial activities of the Kharkov community that CARC considered violations of the law, referred to the agreement concluded with the municipal public bath and laundry trust for building a *mikva*, the sale of kosher meat at the market, and an agreement for baking *matza*. While it paid 9 rubles per kilogram of *matzot*, the report noted, the community sold this same quantity at 16 rubles; moreover, an article in the agreement stipulated: 'In order better to serve the poor Jewish population, the *artel'* obligated itself to provide three tons of *matzot* at cost price.'
53. However, for the 1946 fall festivals, seats in the Leningrad synagogue were sold, in the words of a CARC report, at box-offices, as in a theater — ibid.
54. Survey of the Jewish Religion in 1948.
55. Minutes of a meeting between Rabbi Shlifer, CARC Chairman Polianskii and Inspector M. I. Birman, 3 Sept. 1949 — GARF, f. 6991, op. 3, d. 8, pp. 190–1.
56. A Short Survey of the Jewish Religion in 1950.
57. This appears to have been the year the synagogue was opened — Dominik Horodynski, *Syberia inaczej*. Warszawa, 1959, p. 70, quoted in Yaacov Levavi (Babitsky), *Ha-hityashvut ha-yehudit be-Birobijan* (Jerusalem: Ha-hevra ha-historit ha-yisraelit, 5728), p. 251 — and it was clearly an attraction. Moreover, if the synagogue was opened, this meant that it had the authorities' sanction, so it could be safely visited.
58. In Birobidzhan 43 people had remained out of some 300 believers. In Sumy Oblast the numbers of believers had diminished considerably since 1946–7: in Romny — there had been 132 believers in 1946, whereas in 1948 there were only 54 (our source talks of Romny being in Smolensk Oblast while in fact it is in Sumy Oblast); in Konotop, where there had been about 300, only 70 remained — Survey of the Jewish Religion in 1948.
59. Ibid.
60. Letter of instructions to all council representatives, Oct. 1945 — GARF, f. 6991, op. 3, d. 23, p. 74.
61. I. V. Polianskii to V. Molotov, 7 Dec. 1945 — GARF, f. 6991, op. 3, d. 10, pp. 140–1.
62. Ibid.
63. Report to Polianskii of the CARC representative for Zhitomir Oblast for 1945 (with

copies to P. A. Vil'khov, CARC representative in Ukraine and to the *obkom* party secretary), GARF, f. 6991, op. 3, d. 28, p. 227.

64. A Short Survey of the Jewish Religion in 1950.

65. I. V. Polianskii to A. A. Zhdanov, 22 July 1947 Report on Distortions and Violations, RTsKhIDNI, f. 17, op. 125, d. 506.

66. Testimony of CARC representative in Latvia, V. Ia. Sheshken, 21 Dec. 1946, Garf, f. 6991, op. 4, d. 15, p. 120.

67. A similar sum was collected by the Jews of Bobruisk to renovate and reopen their synagogue — V. I. Polianskii to A. A. Zhdanov, July 22, 1947, Report on Distortions and Violations of the Legislation Concerning Religious Cults, RTsKhIDNI, f. 17, op. 125, d. 506.

68. GARF, f. 6991, op. 4, d. 23, p. 31. A Survey of the Jewish Religon for 1948.

69. For the 'action' at Berdichev airport, where 12,000 Jews were killed on 15 Sept. 1941, see *Ha-sefer ha-shahor.* (Tel Aviv: Am Oved, 1991), pp. 36–43.

70. Mikhlin, *Hagahelet*, pp. 94–6. This was the same day the Jews of Zhitomir had not been allowed to mark as a day of prayer and fasting — Report to Polianskii (as in note 63).

71. I. V. Polianskii to A. A. Zhdanov, 7 July 1947.

72. In the CARC survey of the Jewish Religion in 1950, the authors note that the prayer with which the Yom Kippur service finishes "'*Leshana habaah bi-Yerushalayim*" (To next year in Jerusalem) was, prior to Israel's establishment, generally perceived by believers as a prayer, but is presently used by Jewish clergy for nationalist purposes'.

73. Survey of the Jewish Religion in 1948. For an account of this service, based on Jewish sources, see Y. Ro'i, *The Struggle for Soviet Jewish Emigration, 1948–1967* (Cambridge: Cambridge University Press, 1991), p. 25.

74. Survey of the Jewish Religion in 1948.

75. Notes on conversations between Polianskii and Rabbi Shlifer, 6 and 8 Oct. 1948 — GARF, f. 6991, op. 3, d. 8, pp. 168–9; I. V. Polianskii to V. M. Molotov, 6 Oct. 1948 — GARF, f. 6991, op. 3, d. 54, pp. 194–6. Molotov's acceptance of the recommendations was noted in handwriting on the document.

76. Survey of the Jewish Religion in 1948; Memorandum of CARC's work for 1948 and the first quarter of 1949 signed by Polianskii and sent to Malenkov and Voroshilov, RTsKhIDNI, f. 17, op. 132, d. 111. According to the latter source the letter sent by the Israeli legation to Chernigov and Tbilisi was ten pages long, not five.

77. M. Birman, A Short Report (*spravka*) on the Jewish Religion, (undated), GARF, 6991, op. 3, d. 61, pp. 153–65. This documentation was confiscated by the Council's representatives and the community presidents warned that any future communications should immediately be brought to the attention of the relevant officials. CARC also informed the Soviet Ministry of Foreign Affairs, see I. V. Polianskii to Deputy Foreign Minister V. A. Zorin, 19 Feb. 1949, GARF, f. 6991, op. 3, d. 58, p. 45.

78. Reception by Polianskii of Rabbi Shlifer, 23 Oct. 1952 — GARF, f. 6991, op. 3, d. 8, pp. 290–1. Also present were CARC deputy chairman V. I. Gostev and the representative for Moscow Oblast, S. Ia. Barshaposhnikov.

79. A Short Survey of the Jewish Religion in 1950; Within a few months the 72-year-old Lubanov was arrested and imprisoned.

80. A Short Survey of the Jewish Religion in 1948, p. 35.

81. A Short Survey of the Jewish Religion in 1950.

82. M. Birman, A Short Report on the Jewish Religion, as in n. 46.

83. A Short Survey of the Jewish Religion in 1948, p. 30.

84. Ibid., pp. 36–7.

85. Information concerning the Activity of the Religious Cults in the USSR for 1951, (undated and unsigned), RTsKhIDNI, f. 17, op. 132, d. 497, pp. 58–61.

86. Polianskii's report to Aleksandrov of 1 July 1947 (as in note 2), but special stress was laid on the growth of activity of Jewish religious communities and clerics.

87. Information concerning the number of prayer houses (as in note 7). According to this source, attendance at the fall festivals in Irkutsk had been 300 in 1946, 500 in 1948 and was up to 5000 in 1950; in Riga, it rose in the same period from 3000 to 6000, and in Leningrad from 5000 to 7000. Only in one city of the five mentioned in this report, in Rostov-on-Don, had the number risen from 2000 in 1946 to 3500 in 1948 and then dropped again, to 2500, in 1950. According to another source (Prikhod'ko and Abushaev's Short Report on the Jewish Religion in 1950, GARF, f. 6991, op. 3, d. 73, pp 30–41), 1949 seems to have been a peak year, with 10,000 attending Moscow's Choral synagogue on the major holidays, 9,000 the synagogue in Odessa, 8,000 in both Leningrad and Kiev and 5,000 in Kishinev.

18

Synagogues and Synagogue Life in Georgia in the Postwar Era

LILI BAAZOVA

Jewish houses of prayer in Georgia have a long history, which according to legend can be traced to the first millennium B.C.E. From time immemorial Georgian Jews lived in tightly-knit groups all over Georgia, predominantly in the countryside and in separate urban neighbourhoods and every community had its own synagogue. For the Jewish population in Georgia, the synagogue has always been more than a house of prayer. It has been a temple of hope, which has helped to preserve Jewish national consciousness and Judaism in its virtually primordial state. This is borne out if only by the fact that no rabbinical-talmudic movement arose in Georgia, while the influence of the conservative clergy over the believers has been absolute up to the present time.

Today, many Georgian Jewish communities have ceased to exist. There are no longer any religious communities in western and eastern Georgia, in Lailashi, Sukhumi or Tskhinvali. This situation is due primarily to rapid social change in the territory of the former USSR. However, the process of decline, the primary fracture in the socio-political stability of the Georgian Jewish community, began long before the disintegration of the USSR.

Immediately after the Second World War, the Soviet leadership began 'putting things in order' in religious communities all over the Soviet Union. This meant the establishment of full control over all religious groups throughout the country, including Georgian Jewish communities. In 1946, the classified List and Card Catalogue of All Functioning, Registered Synagogues in the Georgian SSR was compiled and systematized.[1] From then on, Jewish religious communities all over Georgia had to submit detailed information on the activities of synagogues and religious communities to the representative of the Council for the Affairs of Religious Cults (CARC) in Georgia.

The information included statistics on the incomes and expenditures of each synagogue, the number of worshippers on weekdays and holidays, and the number of believers, broken down by sex and age and religious rites performed. Of course, information on the disposition of the congregation was of primary interest to the authorities. Special state security departments monitored the situation, assigning an agent to each synagogue. Religious Jews became accustomed to seeing in the courtyard or inside the synagogue, the familiar plainclothesman, who matter-of-factly probed into all the details of their social and personal lives. There was also a network of secret informers recruited from among members of the religious communities.[2]

In 1946, 27 functioning synagogues were registered in Georgia. In all, well over 6,000 people attended synagogue during that year (See Appendix 18-1).

In the late 1940s to early 1950s a massive anti-Jewish campaign took place. It consisted of various political manipulations and provocations, arrests, assassinations and charges of 'criminal activity' along the lines of the show trials of 1937–38. The repressions that swept across the entire country did not bypass Georgia. Tens of leaders of Jewish religious communities and believers were arrested, thrown into the state security prison dungeons and tortured.

In 1951 the synagogue of the Iranian Jews was closed down in Tbilisi and permission was granted to turn the building into a cultural and educational centre.[3]

In October of the same year the Sukhumi synagogue was destroyed.[4] In February 1952 the Sukhumi Jewish religious community filed a complaint with the CARC representative in Georgia, D. Shalutashvili. Soon afterwards, complaints started pouring in to the Georgian Council of Ministers which demanded explanations from Shalutashvili. He submitted the following explanatory statement to his superiors:

> The Executive Committee of the Soviet of the Working People's Deputies in Sukhumi [gorispolkom] closed down and demolished the functioning synagogue without the permission of the Council for Affairs of Religious Cults of the USSR Council of Ministers. This is a gross violation of Art. 1 of the Decree of the USSR Council of People's Commissars of 28 January 1946, 'On the Prayer Houses of Religious Communities'...In view of the violation of the Soviet legislation on cults by the Sukhumi gorispolkom on 26 March 1952, the Council for Religious Affairs of Cults of the USSR Council of Ministers decided to relocate the above-mentioned religious community. However, this decision has been ignored. Moreover, according to representatives of the religious community, Riginashvili, Boterashvili, and Efremashvili, certain officials forbid Jewish believers to perform their religious rites in a private house rented for that purpose.[5]

The affair of the demolished synagogue did not end there. On the contrary, it made considerable waves and the bureaucratic paperwork connected with it snowballed. Disturbed by the fact that Sukhumi Jews were stubbornly upholding their right to worship, CARC Chairman I.V. Polianskii asked his Tbilisi representative for detailed information on the matter. Shalutashvili informed his chief without delay:

> I told the president of the Jewish religious community in Sukhumi, Riginashvili: 'The Sukhumi authorities demolished the building of the former synagogue because it was required for urban development; there is no possibility to offer an alternative location and the religious society has the right to rent premises on a private basis to use as a house of prayer...Riginashvili and the other religious activists concerned do not find this acceptable. To my mind, it would be expedient to ignore all future complaints of the Sukhumi religious community pertaining to this matter.'6

The Sukhumi Jews wrote to Prime Minister Malenkov in May 1953, following Stalin's death:

> In 1951, without any legal justification or grounds whatsoever, the Secretary of the Abkhazian Committee [obkom] of the Georgian CP, A. I. Mgeladze razed the synagogue to the ground in a matter of three hours.

> For over three years now the prayer house on Kuibyshev St. has been lying in ruins, nothing is being built on the site, and the remains of the demolished house have been taken away to an unknown destination. All this gives us grounds to believe that the destruction of the prayer house was part of a criminal plot instigated by Mgeladze in order to incite national strife and was very much similar to the anti-Semitic pogroms in tsarist Russia.7

While the Sukhumi Jews were engaged in a dialogue with the Soviet authorities, the offensive against the synagogues was proceeding unabated everywhere, including in Georgia.

In western Georgia, in the village of Kulashi, where Jews had lived for centuries, there were five prayer houses, each with its own congregation. One of the synagogues had become dilapidated, and in 1944 the congregation began to build a new one on the same site. They notified the local authorities (sel'sovet) and were issued building materials and charged accordingly. In May 1948 the prayer house was almost completed, with the exception of the roof. All of a sudden, the Kulashi village soviet suspended construction on the pretext that there were no more building materials. Without the roof the building began to decay. For three years running the believers petitioned the authorities for permission to complete the building. Receiving no reply, they sent an appeal to Stalin, which was returned to the CARC representative in Georgia. In this connection, Sh. Sikharulidze, Chairman of the Samtredia District Executive Committee (raiispolkom), wrote to the Deputy Chairman of the Georgian Council of Ministers:

'As you know, with your approval the unfinished edifice of Synagogue No.4, unregistered and liquidated in accordance with the decision of the Samtredia *raiispolkom* of 5 July 1951, was given to the Samtredia District Cooperative Council to be completed for subsequent use.'

In reply, Shalutashvili ordered chairman of the Samtredia District Executive Committee to summon the leaders of the religious community, Batashvili and Elishagashvili, and tell them that their complaint had been rejected.[8]

On 20 October 1950, the local authorities closed synagogues in the town of Akhaltsikhe. In early September 1952, after fruitless visits to various-level administrative bodies, 120 local Jews sent a complaint to CARC. They wrote:

> This is an outright farce. After issuing an order to confiscate the synagogue and give it to the club on 20 November 1951, less than a month later, on 15 December, the Akhaltsikhe Executive Committee demanded that the community pay the insurance, and on 23 February 1952, received 163 rubles and 67 kopecks in insurance payment.[9]

The decision written in the upper right-hand corner of the complaint in bold script reads, 'Give a negative response through the Council Representative. 3 Sept. 1952.'[10]

Meanwhile officials in Moscow, were 'perfecting' the mechanism of absolute control over Soviet Jewry. In this connection, Shalutashvili received the following instructions (signed by CARC Deputy Chairman Gostev):

> The Council ... requests you to submit no later than 1 August 1952, a list of the registered synagogues in the Georgian SSR on the attached form. When compiling the list please see to it that columns...are filled out accurately. These data shall be final and will be changed only in exceptional circumstances. All subsequent alterations in the list are to be submitted to the Council in quarterly information reports.[11]

In the same year, 1952, all synagogues were closed down in the city of Kutaisi. This triggered a most painful reaction within the Jewish community. There are many witnesses still alive today, who remember how the Jewish population literally flooded the streets in front of the synagogues, and women mourned for several days. 'The Kutaisi episode' became famous all over Georgia. The massive opposition of the Jewish population impelled the authorities to reopen the synagogues.[12]

On 12 February 1953, on the order of Polianskii, the synagogues of the Akhaltsikhe and Tskhinvali religious communities in Tbilisi were closed down. Shalutashvili informed Chairman of the Tbilisi City Soviet (*gorsovet*) G. Dzhavakhishvili:

> On the orders of the highest authorities the synagogue of the Akhaltsikhe Georgian Jews...and of the Tskhinvali Georgian Jews...have been closed down as of today, and their religious communities have been declared dissolved. The synagogue buildings are now coming under your jurisdiction, and may possibly be used as premises for cultural and educational institutions.[13]

The closed synagogues were pillaged. Hoodlums, possibly instigated by the authorities, broke into the prayer houses, looted them, smashed valuable religious articles and threw many of them out into the street. The remaining religious books were damaged to such an extent that in May 1953, when the Akhaltsikhe synagogue in Tbilisi was reopened, the community sent synagogue official Davitashvili to Rostov-on-Don to bring a specialist to restore the books.[14]

The Jewish religious communities did their best to have the synagogues returned. After Stalin's death, they intensified their efforts. Much was done by rabbis such as A. Dzhindzhikhashvili, K. Paltagashvili, I. Mordukhiashvili from Tbilisi and others, but in vain.[15] Then some prominent black marketeers intervened. They collected what was, at the time, a huge sum of money. According to rumours, a high-ranking official in Moscow was bribed by an important member of the Tbilisi religious community. In May that same year the doors of the Akhaltsikhe community synagogue were opened to the congregation.

After Stalin's death in 1953, repressions against Jewish religious communities in the USSR, including Georgia, continued.

At the end of December 1958 observant Georgian Jews from the town of Zestafoni sent an appeal to the Central Committee of the Georgian Communist Party and the republic's Council of Ministers. Signed by M. Torikashvili and D. Dzhanashvili, it pointed out that some 70 Jewish families lived in Zestafoni, and for 40 years religious Jews had been renting a room where they gathered for prayers. Having learned that all prayer houses, large and small, had to be registered, the Zestafoni community had applied to Shalutashvili for registration. The letter read as follows:

> Shalutashvili got in touch with the State Security department in Zestafoni and ordered the local [K]GB to abolish our constitutional right to a prayer house. Chief of the Zestafoni [K]GB Kamkamidze summoned me [Torikashvili] as head of the synagogue and told me to suspend the activities of the prayer house until it was duly registered. However, Shalutashvili would not let us register the synagogue. We turned to First Secretary of the Zestafoni District Committee of the Communist Party

> Khuskivadze but he turned us out, saying: 'First get it registered, and then pray.' We are appealing for help.

The Georgian Council of Ministers forwarded this complaint against Shalutashvili to the very same Shalutashvili for his consideration.[16]

In that same year, 1958, the synagogue of the religious community in Batumi was expropriated. Shalutashvili notified Moscow that the building was being handed over to the Batumi City Soviet. He continued to insist, nonetheless, that the rights of the Jewish community in Batumi were not being violated.[17]

In 1962, the synagogue in the town of Tskhakaia (now Senaki), where some 300 families lived, was closed down. The local authorities alleged that they needed the site for urban development. The religious community was given an old building elsewhere which it renovated at its own expense. Soon, however, the new premises were taken away as well and a movie theatre was opened there. The community was given yet another location, less suitable for the purpose and requiring considerably larger outlays for restoration. Still, the local Jews undertook the job and effectively remodelled the premises. After the renovated building was ready and had assumed the appearance of a prayer house, some thugs set fire to it. It burned down, together with the Scrolls of the Law kept there.[18] Jews from all over Georgia lent a helping hand to their brethren in Tskhakaia. It was decided to build a new synagogue. However, when it was completed in 1969, it was also destroyed by the authorities, its contents were appropriated, and the ruins together with the site were turned over to a soft drink factory.

In an appeal written on 16 December 1969 on behalf of all the observant Jews of Tskhakaia, the chairman of the local religious community I. Sepiashvili declared: 'How can a Jew live in a place where there is no synagogue!'[19]

These words, uttered in an outburst of despair reflected the the most characteristic trait of the religious and social life of Georgian Jewry — the traditional and intimate link between Jewish religious principles and the spiritual and social life of the Jewish population.

For Georgian Jews, the synagogue was a kind of 'little homeland' that made them feel they belonged to the world of their brethren outside the USSR. There, the words of the ancient language, passed from generation to generation, came alive for them. Georgian Jews were interested in every scrap of information about Israel that they could obtain. This feeling became especially acute in the 1960s and 1970s, which proved to be a turning point in the modern history of Georgian Jewry. The emergence of the State of Israel and the Six-Day

War gave a powerful impetus to the development of a Georgian Jewish social movement which evolved into an essentially political one. Zionism, suppressed in the 1920s, again re-emerged in Georgia. Suddenly, clandestine Zionist circles were active all across Georgia. Their members were mostly young people who disseminated illicit publications and information about Israel. It was then that the Jewish spirit and awareness of belonging to the Jewish people, correctly interpreted by the Soviet authorities as an expression of opposition to Soviet ideology, manifested itself in vigils and protracted hunger strikes outside the Central Post Office in Moscow, in the 'letter of the eighteen families' and other well-known actions. Mass *aliya* from Georgia was one of the immediate and tangible results of this movement. The Soviet authorities were very much perturbed by this turn of events. The 'Jewish problem in Georgia' became a thorn in the side of many Soviet administrative and political bodies. Among other things, OVIR (the Department of Visas and Registration of the Ministry of the Interior) in Georgia was ordered to collect information on all Georgian Jews who had submitted requests for permission to leave for Israel. Synagogues and religious communities again found themselves the focus of attention.

In 1971, Georgian city, town and regional executive committees were directed to send the representative of the Council of Religious Affairs[20] detailed information about all members of the religious communities. Special attention was devoted to whether or not any of them were pro-Israeli and wanted to leave for Israel.[21]

These were attempts to thwart *aliya*. The veteran and experienced head of the Council for Religious Affairs, Shalutashvili, went to Moscow for instructions. On his return to Tbilisi, he got down to implementing the plans outlined in Moscow. In March 1971 he sent a detailed report to Moscow on the measures he had taken to step up control over synagogue activities and gauge the mood of the people.[22]

Shalutashvili wrote that, as planned, all chairmen of the executive bodies of the religious communities had been briefed regarding the strict observation of religious legislation. From then on, implementation of regulations on religious gatherings and observance of religious rites was to be more severe. Believers were categorically forbidden to congregate outside the synagogue grounds or even inside the synagogue courtyards before or after religious services. The chairman of the executive body of the Tbilisi religious community was told to take measures to prevent car owners from parking their cars in front of the synagogue.

The religious community's spokesmen tried to explain that the worshippers usually went out into the courtyard during breaks in the service. Nevertheless, they were told it was their duty to prevent people from milling in the synagogue courtyard or in the street outside, and the authorities were vigilant about enforcing this decision.

On 24 June 1972, Shalutashvili reported to Moscow:

> The plan for the first half of the year provided for our informing you of the supervision exercised over the activities of the religious communities and measures to check undesirable tendencies in the synagogues of the Georgian SSR.
>
> Please find enclosed the required information.[23]

The text of the relevant information provides documentary evidence of the period and its history and therefore is quoted almost in full.

> In principle, there are three undesirable trends in the synagogues of the Georgian Jews: 1. Pro-Israeli sentiments; 2. Violations of Soviet legislation on religious cults; 3. Religious activity:
>
> 1. Pro-Israeli sentiments find expression in sympathy for Israel and the desire of most Jews to settle there. Over three thousand Jews have already emigrated to Israel. Georgian Jews live, work and study in Georgia like people of other nationalities living in the republic and there are no special circumstances that might account for their aspiration to emigrate. Still this aspiration persists.
>
> The main reason for this situation lies in the religious fanaticism of the Georgian Jews.
>
> For truly observant Jews — they constitute a majority of Georgian Jews — the Passover refrain 'Next year in Jerusalem' is not just words. All this, as well as the external ritual aspect of the believers' lives, which is thoroughly sustained by the synagogue, allow those who would implant and support Jewish nationalism, to use religion for this purpose. Religious ministers enjoy enormous prestige among Georgian Jewish believers. They control the life of the synagogues and even regulate believers' lives to some extent...
>
> One of the major factors making for stronger pro-Israeli sentiments is Zionist propaganda in the press and in radio broadcasts [materials brought to Georgia from abroad and *samizdat*]. Representatives of the Jewish intelligentsia [family names specified] often publish articles in the [Georgian] press exposing the lies of Israeli propaganda. Their articles abound with current material and are very convincing and timely.
>
> Of late, commissions assisting in supervising the observance of legislation by the religious cults of the town and district soviets in Gori, Kutaisi and the Kirov Oblast soviet in Tbilisi have stepped up their activity. There are already some results, albeit modest — M[...] from Gori refused to take a parcel, the A[...] family from Kutaisi refused a visa.
>
> 2. Violations of the law on religious cults take the form of material aid to needy members of religious communities and improper financial transactions...

3. The immediate result of the religious communities' activities is the involvement of children and young people. Religious traditions have a strong impact on the younger as well as the older generations. Most young Jews observe such rites as *bar mitzva*, marriage and burial, adhering strictly to the religious canons. Many take a direct part in religious services. Many teenagers and even children attending the synagogue have a good command of Hebrew, are well acquainted with religious customs and follow them meticulously. We still do not know where, when and from whom young people acquire religious knowledge.[24]

In March 1972, regional sessions of chairmen of the commissions supervising the implementation of legislation on religious cults were held in Georgia. New lists of believers were compiled with detailed information about each of them. All synagogues had to submit reports on their annual income and expenditures, attendance on weekdays and on holidays, in the mornings and the evenings, ratios of male and female worshippers and the extent of donations.[25]

In May 1973, Moscow informed its representative in Georgia that another commission had been established. Its task was to expose all tendencies among the Jewish population which were incompatible with Soviet ideology. Apparently, this struggle was not very successful, because on 24 November 1975, as a follow-up to the above-mentioned ruling, another resolution was adopted by the Central Committee of the Georgian Communist Party: 'On Measures to Intensify the Struggle against Harmful Traditions and Customs'.[26]

One of the reports compiled for the Council for Religious Affairs in Moscow contained the following information about the Georgian Jewish community:

There were 27 functioning synagogues in Georgia, one of them, in Zestafoni, unregistered. Five synagogues have discontinued their activities as a result of the disintegration of religious communities and emigration of Georgian Jews: two in the village of Bandza, Gegechkori District, one in Sachkhere, one in the village of Sujuna, Abasha District, one in Lailashi, Tsageri District.

The number of Jewish clergy has dwindled by half over the last two or three years. There are now 14 of them, and many synagogues are in acute need of ministers and are looking for them all over the country.[27]

The social and religious self-awareness of the Jewish community in Georgia travelled a complex and difficult path before acquiring new content and expressing itself as a mature national consciousness. At the same time, the struggle for *aliya* was intimately linked with the activities of the religious communities, and in the 1970s, it became one of the most vivid manifestations of Georgian Jewish identity.

NOTES

1. Arkhiv Oktiabr'skoi Revoliutsii (AOR), Tbilisi, fond (f.) R-1880, opis' (op.) I, delo (d.) 1, pp. 3–4.
2. AOR, f. R-1880, op. I, d. 161, pp. 5–8, 18.
3. Jews of Turkish and Iranian origin used to assemble in this synagogue. Many locals recall that Akiva Moshe-Ogly, brought to Georgia from Turkey as a child, was the much revered leader of this small and unique congregation.
4. AOR, f. R-1880, op. I, d. No. 23, pp. 1–5.
5. Ibid.
6. Ibid., p. 14.
7. Ibid., p. 22.
8. AOR, f. R-1880, op. I, d. 23, pp. 11–12.
9. Ibid., p. 18.
10. Ibid.
11. Ibid., p. 26.
12. By the latter half of the 19th century, when Jews began to settle in Tbilisi, Kutaisi already had two synagogues. A third was built in the late 19th century. In 1897, the city had a population of 32,492, of which 3,464 were Jews. *Kavkazskii kalendar'* (Caucasian Yearbook), 1898, No. 6; see also Arie Eliav, *Between Hammer and Sickle* (New York: New American Library, 1969), pp. 157–9.
13. AOR, f. R-1880, op. I, d. 7, pp. 1–12.
14. AOR, f. R-1880, op. I, d. 30, p. 6.
15. AOR, f. R-1880, op. I, d. 23, pp. 2–3.
16. AOR, f. R-1880, op. I, d. 30, pp. 7–9.
17. Ibid., p. 4.
18. AOR, f. R-1880, op. I, d. 140. p. 1.
19. AOR, f. R-1880, op. I, d. 148. pp. 1–2.
20. In 1965 the two Councils, CARC and the Council for the Affairs of the Russian Orthodox Church, merged into a single Council for Religious Affairs.
21. AOR, f. R-1880, op. I, d. 173, pp. 18–34, 64–6.
22. AOR, f. R-1880, op. I, d. 270, p. 26.
23. Ibid., pp. 1–2.
24. Ibid., pp. 33–5.
25. AOR, f. R-1880, op. I, d. 147, p. 6.
26. Ibid., pp. 34–6.
27. AOR, f. R-1880, op. I, d. 148, p. 12.

APPENDIX 18-1 Data on Georgian Synagogues for 1946

TBILISI:
1. Akhaltsikhe religious community.[a] Active since 1885. Attendance — 817[b]
2. Tskhinvali religious community. Active since 1922. Attendance — 265
3. Synagogue of Iranian Jews. Built in 1922. Attendance — 35
4. Ashkenazi synagogue. Built in 1864. Attendance — 924[c]

AKHALTSIKHE:
5. Synagogue built in 1880. Attendance — 140
6. Synagogue built in 1860. Attendance — 180[d]

KUTAISI:
7. Built in late 18th — early 19th cent. Attendance on weekdays — 200, on holidays — 400
8. Built in 1835. Attendance on holidays — 200
9. Built in 1886. Attendance on weekdays — 300, on holidays — 800

KULASHI:
10. Synagogue No. 1 built in 1862. Attendance — 270
11. Synagogue No. 2 built in 1902. Attendance — 180
12. Synagogue No. 3 built in 1910. Attendance — 150
(Synagogue No. 4 see text)
13. Synagogue No. 5 built in 1905. Attendance — 140

BANDZA, GEGECHKORI DISTRICT:
14. Sepiashvili synagogue, active since 1910. Attendance — 100
15. Adzhiashvili synagogue, active since 1916. Attendance — 140
16. Kveda Vani, Vani District, active since 1911
17. Sujuna, Abasha District, active since 1822. [Another list indicates the construction was completed in 1819] Attendance — 100
18. Zugdidi — active since 1944
19. Oni — built in 1895, active throughout. Attendance — 200
20. Kareli, Kareli District. Attendance — 150
21. Surami, Khashuri District. Built in 1915, attendance — 300[e]
22. Staliniri (now Tskhinvali). Breti prayer house. Year of etablishment unknown. Attendance — 245
23. Gori. Built in 1944. Attendance — 103[f]
24. Tskhakaia. Built in 1880. Attendance — 120
25. Sachkhere. Year of establishment unknown. Attendance — 160
26. Sachkhere. Built in 1903. Attendance — 150
27. Lailashi, Tsageri District. Built in 1880. Attendance — 120

A noteworthy addition appears on the 1952 List of Functioning Registered Synagogues: Abkhaz ASSR: according to official assessments, 'there is no synagogue in Sukhumi, the believers assemble in private homes'. Attendance — 70-180[g]

a. Addresses of synagogues, included in the original document, have been deleted.
b. AOR, fond R-1880, op. I, d. 7, pp. 1–46. Here and below the number of people attending on holidays is given.
c. Ibid., p. 1.
d. Ibid., p. 26.
e. Ibid., pp. 7–86.
f. Ibid., pp. 1–100.
g. AOR, F. R-1880, op. I, d. 24, pp. 5–6.

Sources: Arkhiv Oktiabr'skoi Revoliutsii, fond R-1880, opis' I, dela 7, 24.

VII

SOVIET JEWRY
AND THE INTERNATIONAL ARENA

19

The Soviet Position on the Establishment of the State of Israel

IURII STRIZHOV

On 14 May 1948 a new entity appeared on the political map of the world — the State of Israel. The history of the creation of the State of Israel was long and complex. Its concluding stage was closely linked with the Second World War and the Nazi genocide.

The war and its outcome created historically unique preconditions for a successful resolution to the Jews' vigorous struggle for a sovereign state of their own in Palestine. In the words of former US Under-Secretary of State Sumner Welles:

> When the Second World War broke out, the chances for the establishment of a Jewish Commonwealth in the Holy Land seemed indeed to have vanished. Yet, the forces that the war had brought into being had a determining effect in arousing world public opinion to the imperative need of finding a solution for the Palestinian problem.[1]

From the first days of the war, David Ben-Gurion, one of the leaders of this struggle, noted: 'The question that absorbed us was Palestine's future after the war. I was certain that we had to exert ourselves to set up a Jewish State.'[2]

Other plans, however, for creating a Jewish state were being worked out during the war. Thus, on 20 February 1945, the Third European Division of the USSR People's Commissariat for Foreign Affairs (NKID) sent a memorandum to Deputy People's Commissar for Foreign Affairs V. G. Dekanozov. It informed him that the Soviet Embassy in Italy had forwarded two letters to the NKID, one addressed to I. V. Stalin, the other to V. M. Molotov, from the Rome-based Jewish Committee of the International Union of Emigrants and Refugees. Enclosed with the letters was a proposal for creating an independent Jewish state on German territory and a map of Germany where the prospective state was delineated.

In the letter to Stalin, dated 11 November 1944, the Jewish Committee expressed the hope that after Germany's defeat, everything would be done to expedite the establishment of an independent Jewish state on German territory. It also noted that the governments of all the European Allied states, the United States and the Soviet Union had been advised of its decisions, and that Professor Albert Einstein had been entrusted with the task of forming a provisional government for the Jewish state.[3]

During, and especially after the war, the Palestine problem was a central issue of Great Power rivalry — in particular between the United States and Great Britain.[4] At that time the situation in Palestine and its surroundings was deteriorating and demanded an urgent solution. In preparation for Soviet participation in a settlement of the problem, the Foreign Ministry was at work formulating the Soviet stand.

On 27 July 1945 M. M. Litvinov, Chairman of the Committee on Preparing Peace Treaties and the Postwar Order set up by the NKID, sent a memorandum entitled 'The Palestine Question' to Stalin, Molotov and the Deputy Ministers of Foreign Affairs. Its conclusion read:

1. No matter how hard the British may try to prove that their present policy in Palestine conforms to the Balfour Declaration, it is obvious that they have failed to live up to the mandate entrusted to them. This was admitted in the...statements by high-ranking British statesmen. This is sufficient justification for taking the Palestine mandate away from the British.

2. The Palestine question cannot be duly settled without impinging upon the wishes and rights of Jews or Arabs, or perhaps both. The British government is in equal measure subject to the influence of the Arab states and world Jewry. Hence its difficulties in choosing the correct means to settle the Palestine problem.

3. The US government is subject to the same influences. While British Palestine policy is necessarily affected mainly by orientation towards Arab interests, the American government is subject in the first place to the influence of the powerful US Jewry. It should be recalled that at the latest presidential elections both the Democratic and the Republican parties felt compelled to issue declarations on their attitude to Palestine, demanding unrestricted immigration of Jews and unrestricted rights for Jews to their own land. At the same time, the US government would hardly choose to quarrel with the Arabs, in view of the fact that the oil pipeline from Saudi Arabia in which they have a stake will run through hundreds of kilometres of Arab territory. That would put the US government in as difficult a position regarding Palestine as the British government.

4. The USSR, free from either Arab or Jewish influence, would be in a better position to tackle the Palestine issue. This at least entitles it to request a temporary trusteeship over Palestine until a more radical solution is found.

5. The British attach to Palestine, which guards the approaches to the Suez Canal and has an outlet for Iraqi oil on its territory, too much importance for us to expect them to consent even to a temporary transfer of Palestine to the hands of another state, particularly, the USSR.

6. In the event that the Soviet request is rejected the following solution suggests itself: transfer of Palestine to the collective trusteeship of three states — the USSR, USA and Britain. These three powers will be able to take the requisite decisions collectively, paying less tribute to the opinion of the Arab or the Jewish population than either the American or British government acting on its own would feel obliged to do.

7. The provisions of collective trusteeship shall be bound neither by the Balfour Declaration nor by any promises Britain has earlier given as the mandatary power, so that the new collective administration could tackle the Palestine problem in all fairness, in accordance with the interests of the entire population and the new imperatives of political realities and general security.5

In December 1945 an Anglo-American Committee was set up to investigate the situation in Palestine. It was entrusted with a wide range of tasks connected with the Palestine problem as a whole. The Committee's report was made public in April 1946 and 'was met with an outburst of violent recriminations throughout the Arab states and with bitter disappointment on the part of the Jews'.6

A memorandum entitled 'The Palestine Question', based on the results of the Litvinov Committee, was compiled by the Middle East Department of the USSR Foreign Ministry7 and on 15 May 1946 was sent to Dekanozov. It read:

Attempts by Britain and the US jointly to continue the British mandate outside the framework of the UN reveal their aspiration to prevent the interference of other countries in the settlement of the Palestine question until Palestine is fully under the control of the US and Britain.

Our silence on the Palestine issue might be interpreted by the US, Britain, Arabs and Jews as the Soviet Union's partial approval of the proposals put forth by the committee. Bearing this in mind and in view of the fact that official and unofficial representatives of both Arab states and Jewish organizations are turning to the Soviet Union in order to have the Palestine problem settled it would be expedient to set forth the Soviet point of view on the Palestine problem in two or three articles to be published in the press. Later our diplomatic representatives may refer to these articles in private conversations if they are approached by Arab or Jewish representatives in connection with the Palestine question.

Presumably, our position on the Palestine question should be as follows:

1. The Anglo-American committee set up to study the Palestine question without the participation of the UN was not competent to discuss...and tackle the Palestine problem without the participation of the parties directly concerned.

2. The Jewish question in Europe cannot be solved through Jewish immigration to Palestine, inasmuch as only complete eradication of fascism and the democratization of European countries can create normal conditions for the existence of the Jewish masses.

3. The British mandate in Palestine should be abrogated since it is impeding a radical solution of the Palestine question and jeopardizing security in the Middle East. All foreign troops should be withdrawn from Palestine.

4. Palestine should be placed under the trusteeship of the UN which within a certain period of time will lay the groundwork for a sovereign and democratic Palestine.

We must not submit the Palestine question for consideration by the UN. It should be raised by the Arab UN members themselves. We should only voice our opinion and uphold it.

It would be expedient to postpone the publication of articles on the Palestine question until the session of the Council of Foreign Ministers has completed its deliberations.[8]

On 20 May 1946 Dekanozov sent this document to Molotov, with the following recommendation: 'I think the proposals are on the whole acceptable.'[9]

With the evident connivance of the Soviet Foreign Ministry, the weekly *Novoe vremia* published the article 'A Seat of Unrest in the Middle East',[10] giving a detailed analysis of the work of the Anglo-American committee and its results, consonant with the above-mentioned memorandum.

On 12 July 1946 the Soviet Ambassador to Poland V. Z. Lebedev sent a letter to Deputy Foreign Minister A. Ia. Vyshinskii, saying:

Last May, a delegation of leaders of Jewish democratic parties in Palestine came to Poland to get acquainted with the position of the Jews in Europe and organize relief and resettlement of a portion of them in Palestine.

The delegation was headed by Central Committee members of the Palestine-USSR Friendship League L. Levite, M. Erem (of the left-wing Poalei-Tsion) and Y. Barzilai (Hashomer-Hatsair workers' party). Through [Jacob] Berman and other democratic Polish leaders they insisted on meeting me. At my request they were received by [Vladimir] Iakovlev.

In the course of the discussion it became clear that the Palestine delegation had come to Poland in the hope...of arranging a visit to the USSR through the Soviet Embassy so they could inform the Soviet leadership about the situation in Palestine and obtain the Soviet government's support for the organization of independent life and statehood of the Jewish population there.

From his talk with them, Iakovlev established that both the left-wing representatives of Poalei-Tsion (Levite, Erem) and of Hashomer-Hatsair (Barzilai) are fighting for the preservation of the remnants of the Jewish population in Europe and Jewish immigration to Palestine. While the Poalei-Tsion group advocates the creation of an exclusively Jewish independent state in Palestine, Hashomer-Hatsair, taking account of the fact that Arabs constitute half the population there, favours a federative Arab-Jewish state with two national chambers. That is the main point of difference in their approaches to the state system in Palestine.

The delegates of both orientations represent parties consistently advocating friendship with the USSR. Levite and Barzilai told Iakovlev that they were worried by the British aspiration to turn Palestine into a Middle East military base of British imperialism and attempts to draw the leadership of the Arab states into the orbit of Britain's adventurist policy.

Iakovlev treated their request for a visit to the Soviet Union with reserve and asked them to file an appropriate application for visas (Barzilai had done so even prior to meeting Iakovlev and his request was turned down by the USSR Foreign Ministry).[11]

Further joint attempts by the British and the US to find a solution to the Palestine problem in the latter half of 1946 were also unproductive. The Palestine problem had 'clearly become a challenge that must be met by the United Nations',[12] according to Sumner Welles, who hoped that 'the United States...would immediately assume leadership within the United Nations in having the Organization accept the responsibility for finding a permanent and just solution of the Palestine issues.'[13]

In mid-February 1947 the British government officially admitted that since it was unable to find a solution to the Palestine problem, it was going to ask the United Nations to recommend one.[14]

In 1947–48 the Palestine question was the subject of spirited debate in the UN, during which the USSR assumed a clearcut and consistent stand aimed at establishing an independent Jewish state in Palestine. This is borne out by the documents cited below, which are preserved in Russia's Foreign Policy Archives and published for the first time. It must be noted that Jewish circles counted heavily on the support of the USSR in the creation of a Jewish state. Menahem Begin related:

> Early in 1946, we analysed the relations between our people and the USSR...We wrote...'we say with absolute confidence that Russia too will help in making Eretz Israel a Jewish state. How? Though she continued to oppose the concentration of the Jewish people in its homeland, Russia, which is capable of exploiting the events in Indonesia and the demands of Syria and Lebanon, wants the fight of the Jewish people against the British Mandatory. The Jewish State will arise only as a result of our struggle against the British rule in Eretz Israel, and in this struggle we shall be helped by the Soviet Union.'[15]

On 5 March 1947 the Middle East Department of the USSR Foreign Ministry sent Vyshinskii a memorandum entitled 'The Palestine Problem (October 1946–February 1947)'. It stated that in the event that Britain relegated the Palestine question to the UN, the Soviet position would be based on points 2 and 3 of the May 1946 memorandum. Moreover, the UN would prepare the ground for the creation of a united, independent and democratic Palestine which would ensure equal national and democratic rights to the peoples inhabiting it.[16]

On 6 March Soviet UN delegation member Boris Shtein sent a further memorandum to Vyshinskii. It outlined the USSR's tentative position as follows:

> Up until now the USSR has refrained from formulating its stand on the Palestine question. However, the upcoming discussion of the issue by the UN impels us to formulate our position.
>
> First of all, the USSR must come out resolutely for the abrogation of Britain's Palestine mandate. Britain has not coped with its responsibilities as the mandatary power. Throughout the duration of the mandate...Britain has not succeeded in establishing order in the country and preventing almost unintermittent bloodshed. Substituting British trusteeship for the mandate is also out of the question. The change of signboard will not change anything. What could be considered is collective trusteeship over Palestine by the UN as an organization or by several nations (in effect, permanent Security Council members). However, this possibility is excluded by the fact that the population of the country, both Arabs and Jews, are mature enough for independence. Neither Arabs nor Jews would agree to any trusteeship whatsoever and want complete independence.
>
> The Soviet Union cannot but support the demand for full independence for Palestine...The withdrawal of British troops from the country should be the first and obligatory precondition for the independence of Palestine.
>
> Still, granting independence to Palestine would not take the edge off Arab-Jewish contradictions in the country. The Soviet Union cannot see any way of settling them other than by democratic means. Thus, alongside independence, Palestine should obtain a democratic statute ensuring full and genuine equality (civil, political and national) for the population of Palestine as a whole. The statute is to be worked out by the UN Organization, which is subsequently to become a guarantor of its implementation.
>
> The fact that Britain has relegated the Palestine question to the United Nations for discussion, enables the USSR for the first time not only to voice its views on the issue but also to take an active part in Palestine's fate.[17]

On 14 May 1947 in an address to the Special Session of the UN General Assembly devoted to the Palestine issue, Gromyko pointed out that 'the mandate administration established in Palestine in 1922 has not proved itself'. Moreover, he went on to say:

> As is known, the aspirations of a considerable portion of the Jewish people hinge on Palestine and its future statehood.

Gromyko continued by relating the Jewish people's 'unprecedented' suffering at the hands of the Germans during the last war 'that defy description'. The Jewish population in the territories occupied by the Nazis was 'almost completely exterminated', the total number of those killed being 'estimated at about six million. Only some one and a half million Jews in Western Europe survived'. Of these, 'vast numbers' were homeless and without means of subsistence.

> Hundreds of thousands of Jews are wandering all over Europe in search of a livelihood and shelter. Many of them are in displaced persons camps where they are still suffering hardships.
>
> The fact that not a single West European state has succeeded in protecting the elementary rights of the Jewish people and shielding them from the violence of the fascist butchers makes the Jewish striving to create a state of their own understandable. It would be unfair to ignore this and deny the Jewish people the right to realize such aspirations.

Gromyko pointed out that neither 'past history' nor 'the conditions now obtaining in Palestine' justified a 'one-sided settlement of the Palestine question' that ignored 'the legitimate rights' of both the Arab and Jewish populations. The Soviet delegation had come to the conclusion that the legitimate interests of both the Jewish and the Arab peoples of Palestine could be safeguarded only if an 'integral Arab-Jewish democratic state' were established. If this variant proved 'un-attainable' due to the deterioration of Arab-Jewish relations, then it would be necessary to consider the second variant, which had gained currency in Palestine: the partition of Palestine into two independent sovereign states — one Jewish and one Arab.[18]

Gromyko's speech, an Israeli diplomat commented many years later, 'was in complete contradiction to the explicitly anti-Zionist attitude which both communist ideologists and practical politicians had expressed repeatedly and consistently over several decades...[and] therefore came as a great surprise'.[19]

At its concluding plenary meeting on 15 May 1947, the special UN General Assembly session endorsed the composition, functions and terms of reference of the United Nations Special Committee on Palestine (UNSCOP). The report compiled by this committee was submitted for consideration by the 2nd Regular Session of the General Assembly. On 13 October 1947, during discussion of the above-mentioned report in the ad hoc committee on Palestine set up by this session, Soviet representative S. K. Tsarapkin pointed out that the Jews' desire to create their own state was understandable, and 'it would be unjust to deny the Jewish people the right to realize these aspirations. The creation of a Jewish state has become a ripe and urgent issue'.

Having supported 'in principle the recommendations submitted by a majority in the special committee' for the partition of Palestine, he declared:

> If this session of the General Assembly decides to establish a Jewish and

an Arab state, it would be a big stride forward in the settlement of the Palestine question as a whole.[20]

On 25 November 1947 the ad hoc committee adopted the proposal for the partition of Palestine into two states, one Arab and one Jewish. The Soviet, Ukrainian and Belorussian delegates all voted for the proposal.

The Partition Plan was considered and put to the vote at the General Assembly plenary sessions held between 26–29 November 1947. The session's proceedings were marked by heated debate.

On 26 November 1947 Gromyko addressed the plenary session. His speech was devoted to a detailed substantiation and defence of the Partition Plan:

> The resolution of the question of Palestine on the basis of its partition into two independent states will have great historic significance inasmuch as it meets the legitimate demands of the Jewish people...
>
> In the opinion of the Soviet delegation, the plan for the settlement in Palestine submitted by the committee and stipulating that the Security Council is to be entrusted with its practical implementation, fully coincides with the interests of maintaining and strengthening international peace and the promotion of inter-state cooperation. Therefore the Soviet delegation supports the recommendation for the partition of Palestine.
>
> Unlike some other delegations, the Soviet delegation has from the very outset taken a clearcut and unambiguous stand on this question and is consistently upholding it. It will not engage in manoeuvring or manipulations with votes as is regrettably the case at the Assembly, in particular in connection with the debates on the Palestine issue.[21]

On 29 November 1947 the General Assembly adopted the well-known Resolution 181(II) on the partition of Palestine into two states. This decision, to which the Soviet Union contributed significantly, preordained the establishment of the State of Israel.

Resolution 181(II) provided for the establishment of a special UN commission to supervise preparations for the creation of the Arab and the Jewish states. In January 1948 the commission was formed and got down to work. From the very outset it encountered active opposition from the British colonial administration. The work of the commission generated acrimonious debate and differences in the UN Security Council which was to ensure the implementation of the resolution.

At the Security Council meeting on 19 March 1948 the United States representative Warren Austin submitted a proposal for convening the 2nd Special Session of the General Assembly 'to establish UN trusteeship over Palestine', claiming that 'it is allegedly impossible to carry out the Palestine partition program...by peaceful means'. In reply, Soviet representative Gromyko declared that the US stand had nothing in common with the General Assembly resolution and that the Soviet Union could not agree with that position.[22]

On 30 March 1948 when two US resolutions providing for an immediate truce between the Arabs and the Jews and the convocation of a special General Assembly session to reconsider the earlier decision on partition were submitted to the Security Council, Gromyko criticized the US trusteeship plan, characterizing the partition of Palestine as a just solution and insisting that US allegations about the impossibility of effecting the partition by peaceful means were groundless. He said the Palestine Commission should continue its work in order to carry out the partition 'so long as the General Assembly decisions remained in force'.[23]

On 1 April 1948 the Security Council, by nine votes, with representatives of the Soviet Union and Ukraine abstaining, accepted the US proposal on the convocation of a special General Assembly session to reconsider the future administration of Palestine.[24]

The Special Session of the UN General Assembly on Palestine opened on 16 April 1948. Speaking in the 1st Committee of the UN General Assembly on 20 April, Gromyko severely censured the stand assumed by the US and Britain.

> They are out to torpedo the partition decision and impose on the United Nations their decision on Palestine's future, prompted by the self-seeking interests of the US ruling circles, which have put forward new...proposals to establish trusteeship over Palestine.

He stressed that following comprehensive study of several variants, the UN had arrived at the conclusion that the partition of Palestine into two states would be the most just solution and that such a settlement of the Palestine question would coincide with the legitimate aspirations of the Jewish people to establish a state of their own in Palestine with which they had 'close and long-standing bonds'.

In conclusion, Gromyko declared that the Soviet delegation believed, as before, that the new US proposals were unacceptable and would vote against them. He asserted that the decision on the partition of Palestine was the correct one and that the United Nations should take 'efficacious steps' to carry it out.[25]

On 3 May 1948 Tsarapkin, addressing the 1st Committee, rejected the US attempts 'to impose a trusteeship regime on the peoples of Palestine'. He said:

> The high level of cultural, social, political and economic development of the Jewish people is indisputable. Such a people should not be put under trusteeship. Such a people has every right to a sovereign state of its own. Any attempts to impose trusteeship on such a people will only discredit

the main idea and essence of trusteeship. And are the Palestinian Arabs less deserving of independent existence in their own state than Arabs living outside Palestine? Certainly not. Both the Jewish and the Arab people in Palestine have undoubtedly reached such a stage of political, economic and social development that placing them under trusteeship of any kind is out of the question.

The US proposal for establishing trusteeship over Palestine, Tsarapkin said in conclusion, should be rejected as running counter to a major UN principle providing for the right of peoples to self-determination, the right of peoples to an independent existence within their own state.[26]

At the 1st Committee Session on 4 May 1948, Gromyko called on the General Assembly to admit that partition was in fact being implemented. This, he said, was clear from a statement made by a representative of the UN Secretariat, from reports of the Jewish Agency and publications in the US and elsewhere. 'While the General Assembly is engaged in discussions, the Jewish state will become a reality despite the efforts of some UN members to create all kinds of obstacles', he asserted.[27]

On 14 May 1948 the Special Session of the UN General Assembly ended, for on that day the establishment of the State of Israel was proclaimed in Tel Aviv. *Pravda* commented:

> Developments at the Special Session of the General Assembly showed that the US, on whose initiative it had been convened, suffered a fiasco. The initial plans of the US were frustrated. The US delegation did not even dare to put its proposal for establishing a trusteeship regime over the whole of Palestine to the vote.
>
> The General Assembly also rejected the British proposal for a provisional regime for Palestine. This proposal, amounting to trusteeship but presented in a disguised form, was criticized by the delegation of the USSR and some other countries.
>
> In the course of the debate on the Palestine issue, the USSR pursued a consistent policy, upholding the decision on the partition of Palestine and exposing all scheming with respect to Palestine.[28]

On 16 May 1948 Moshe Shertok (later Sharett), Foreign Minister of the Provisional Government of Israel, sent a cable to Molotov:

> I am honoured to inform you and request to pass this information on to your Government that the National Council of the Jewish State, consisting of members of elected representative organizations of Palestinian Jews, met in session yesterday, on 14 May, in connection with the expiration of the term of the British mandate and, guided by the UN General Assembly resolution of 29 November 1947, proclaimed the establishment of an independent Jewish state in Palestine to be known as the State of Israel.
>
> On behalf of the Provisional Government of Israel, I request the Government of the Union of Soviet Socialist Republics to extend official

recognition to the State of Israel and its Provisional Government. I hope that the recognition of the State of Israel will take place at an early date and am confident that it will strengthen the friendship between the Soviet Union and its peoples, on the one hand, and the Jewish people of Palestine, on the other, and serve the cause of peace and justice in international relations generally.

I am taking this opportunity to express the feelings of immense gratitude the Jewish people of Palestine and Jews all over the world have towards you for the firm stand the USSR delegation took in the UN on the question of the establishment of a sovereign and independent Jewish state in Palestine and its consistent support of this position in the face of all difficulties; for expressing sincere sympathy for the suffering the Jewish people went through in Europe under the heel of the fascist butchers and for backing the principle that Palestinian Jews are a nation which has the right to sovereignty and independence.[29]

In a telegram to Shertok of 17 May 1948 Molotov replied:

This is to inform you that the Government of the USSR has decided to extend official recognition to the State of Israel and its Provisional Government.

The Soviet Government believes that the creation by the Jewish people of its sovereign state will serve the cause of strengthening peace and security in Palestine and the Middle East and expresses confidence that friendly relations between the USSR and the State of Israel will develop successfully.[30]

Shertok sent a second cable to Molotov on 24 May 1948, saying:

I am honoured to express to you the profound satisfaction with which my Government received the information about the official recognition of the State of Israel by the Government of the USSR...The Government of the State of Israel fully shares the wishes you expressed so magnanimously and reaffirms its unshakeable belief, based on the developments that have brought about the creation of our Government, that most friendly relations can be established between the State of Israel and the Soviet Union. In pursuance of these goals we would respectfully suggest that you communicate your consent to the immediate establishment of an Israeli Mission in Moscow composed of an Envoy or Chargé d'Affaires and Consul-General and to the simultaneous establishment of a Soviet Mission of the same rank in Tel Aviv.[31]

On 25 May 1948 Molotov replied to Shertok:

I am honoured to inform you that the Soviet Government agrees to the establishment of a Mission of the State of Israel in Moscow headed by an Envoy or Chargé d'Affaires, and including discharge of consular functions, and on its part is ready to establish a Soviet Mission in Tel Aviv.[32]

A month later, on 26 June 1948, *Izvestiia* announced officially the appointments of P. I. Ershov 'USSR Envoy Extraordinary and Plenipotentiary in the State of Israel' and Mrs. Golda Meyerson 'Envoy Extraordinary and Minister Plenipotentiary of the State of Israel in the USSR'.[33]

On 7 September 1948 Golda Meyerson, who had already arrived in Moscow, was received by Molotov. After presenting her credentials, she said that her government had instructed her to take the first opportunity to express to Molotov the gratitude of the people and Government of the State of Israel for the help rendered by the Soviet Union in the United Nations.[34]

The Soviet Government, Molotov replied, regarded this 'as its duty, all the more so in that it was fully in keeping with Soviet USSR policy *vis-à-vis* other peoples'.[35]

In his talk with Meyerson, Molotov pointed out that the State of Israel was off to a good start and that there was a basis for the creation of a viable state.[36] On 15 September 1948, while on a protocol visit to I. N. Bakulin, head of the Middle East Department of the USSR Foreign Ministry, Meyerson declared: 'The State of Israel will become viable when its population increases severalfold'.[37] Bakulin, like Deputy Foreign Ministers V. A. Zorin and F. T. Guseev to whom Meyerson also paid her respects on 15 and 17 September, respectively, made it clear that this immigration would have to come solely from the capitalist countries and that Israel could not even cope with all the repressed and persecuted Jews from these countries.[38]

NOTES

1. Sumner Welles, *We Need Not Fail* (Boston: Houghton-Mifflin, 1948), p. 17.
2. David Ben-Gurion. *Israel: Years of Challenge* (Tel Aviv: Massadah-PEC Press, 1963), p. 17.
3. Arkhiv vneshnei politiki MID SSSR (AVP), fond (f.) 05, opis' (op.) 4, papka (pk.) 18, delo (d.) 115, p. 77.
4. For the international treatment of the Palestine question at the end of the war, see Michael Cohen, *Palestine and the Great Powers, 1945–48* (Princeton, NJ: Princeton University Press, 1982).
5. AVP, f. 07, op. 12a, pk. 42, d. 6, pp. 36–8.
6. Welles, p. 36.
7. In March 1946 the Sovnarkom, the Council of People's Commissars, had become the Council of Ministers.
8. AVP, f. 06, op. 08, pk. 42, d. 694, pp. 2–4.
9. Ibid., p. 1.
10. *Novoe vremia*, 11 (1946), pp. 14–17.
11. AVP, f. 07, op. 12a, pk. 42, d. 6, pp. 42–3.
12. Welles, *We Need Not Fail*, p. 41.
13. Ibid.
14. Ibid.
15. Menachem Begin. *The Revolt* (Tel Aviv: Steimatzky, 1951) p. 197.
16. AVP, f. 07, op. 12, pk. 42, d. 6, p. 133.
17. AVP, f. 07, op. 12, pk. 42, d. 6, pp. 140–1.
18. *Izvestiia*, 16 May 1947.
19. Avigdor Dagan, *Moscow and Jerusalem* (London: Abelard-Schuman, 1970), pp. 19–20.
20. *Pravda*, 16 October 1947.
21. *Vneshnaia politika Sovetskogo Soiuza* (Moscow, 1948), pp. 240–2, 244–5.

22. *Pravda*, 21 March 1948.
23. *Pravda*, 1 April 1948.
24. *Pravda*, 3 April 1948.
25. *Izvestiia*, 23 April 1948.
26. *Izvestiia*, 6 May 1948.
27. *Izvestiia*, 7 May 1948.
28. *Pravda*, 16 May 1948.
29. *Pravda*, 18 May 1948.
30. Ibid.
31. *Pravda*, 26 May 1948.
32. Ibid.
33. *Izvestiia*, 26 June 1948; Meyerson later changed her surname to Meir.
34. AVP, f. 06, op. 10, pk. 46, d. 623, p. 1.
35. Ibid.
36. Ibid., p.4
37. AVP, f. 06, op. 10, pk. 46, d. 624, p. 1.
38. G. Meyerson to M. Shertok, 24 Sep. 1948, *Medinat Yisrael. Te'udot li-medinyut ha-butz shel Medinat Yisrael, mai–september 1948* (Jerusalem: Ha-madpis ha-memshalti, 1981), pp. 595, 638; Mordecai Namir, *Shlibut be-Moskva* (Tel Aviv: Am Oved, 1971), pp. 52–6.

20

Soviet Diplomacy and the Issue of Jewish Immigration to Israel, 1946–1953

NINA SEMENTCHENKO and SERGEI MIROKHIN

For well-known reasons, the academic study of Soviet-Israeli relations was long avoided in the USSR. Virtually all Soviet scholars on Israel and problems of the Middle East refrained from discussing the development of relations between the Soviet Union and Israel. Even monographs especially devoted to Israel did not deal with that subject.

The brochure, *The Palestine Problem*, written by a prominent Arab and Middle East scholar, V. B. Lutskii and published in 1946, is representative of the attitude towards the issue at that time. Lutskii echoed a harsh variant of the official view that 'the Anglo-American imperialists and their Zionist agents artificially link the Jewish question in Western Europe with the question of Palestine. The latter is an important, independent problem.'[1] The author of the brochure does not actually dwell on the issue of Jewish immigration. Describing the country and its population, he notes that

> As a result of immigration, the average density of Palestine's population currently exceeds 70 people per square km. In other words, it is four times larger than the population density of the US, 10–15 times more than that of Argentina or Brazil. And if one takes into consideration the fact that a third of the country is generally unfit for habitation, and another third can be settled only sparsely, and that as a result, the bulk of the population is concentrated in an area of some eight thousand square kms., Palestine must be regarded as one of the most overpopulated countries in the world.[2]

Soviet diplomats who visited Palestine at the time reacted in a peculiar manner to the comments of the Palestine communists regarding Lutskii's work. The communists drew their attention to the 'inaccuracies' in the brochure, which referred to Palestine as an Arab country. They pointed out that Palestine had become a bi-national country. To this the diplomats replied, 'If that is your opinion, don't distribute the brochure. No problem.'[3]

Another brochure under the same title was published in Moscow in 1948. It was written by I. A. Genin in a much more restrained tone than the above-mentioned work. Genin's brochure is one of the few Soviet publications which describes in a rather detailed manner the USSR's stand on the Palestine question and the creation of the State of Israel. The brochure, for example, cites excerpts from the speech of Andrei Gromyko, the Soviet representative at the UN during the special session of the General Assembly in May 1947.

Like Lutskii, Genin does not deal with the problem of immigration and only states that 'from 1919 until 1939, 323,000 Jews immigrated to Palestine. Between 1940 and 1945, another 50,000 entered the country'.[4]

Neither did subsequent studies, including works published after 1967, touch upon the history of relations between the USSR and Israel, let alone the question of the emigration of Soviet Jews. Even in the 1980s there was an obvious tendency to avoid the question. Only after the re-establishment of diplomatic relations in 1989 did Russian studies and publications begin to deal earnestly with the subject of Soviet-Israeli relations.

The immigration to Israel of Soviet Jews has occupied a special place in the history of the relations between the Soviet Union and Israel. It is an issue which has traditionally had a direct bearing not only on the political interests of each of these countries, but also on their ideological platforms.

G. S. Nikitina expressed the attitude of the Soviet state to Jewish emigration from the USSR when she stated in her monograph 'The State of Israel' that 'theories' on the 'ingathering of the Diaspora' and the return of Jews to the 'land of [their] forefathers...are intentionally turned into an ideological weapon by those who flagrantly slander the USSR and the entire socialist camp'.[5]

Israeli sovietologists paid special attention to the problem of Jewish emigration from the USSR as an important factor in the development of relations between the two states. The question of Jewish emigration was tackled both independently and within the framework of the problem of the status of Jews in the Soviet Union and the campaign of the Soviet leadership against Zionism.

In his book *Soviet Decision Making in Practice. The USSR and Israel 1947–1954*, Yaacov Ro'i states that the official Soviet stand 'was based on two tenets: a) that since a Jewish problem existed only in capitalist states, Israel had come into existence as a refuge for their

Jews and immigration would naturally come from these states, and b) that since Israel could not absorb even all the Jews inhabiting the capitalist world, the Jewish state had to promote the struggle of the forces of progress there, and there was no sense in seeking emigration from parts of the world where there was no Jewish problem', that is, the Soviet Union and the People's Democracies.[6]

At the very first stage after the establishment of diplomatic relations, Israel tried to make the Soviet side realize that it regarded the issue of Jewish immigration as a central challenge of its foreign policy.[7]

Nonetheless, the issue of the emigration of Soviet Jews was not immediately raised at meetings with Soviet representatives. In its talks with Moscow, the Israeli leadership preferred to focus exclusively on emigration from the East European countries. Knowing the Soviet stand, Israeli leaders were afraid that discussion of the emigration of Soviet Jews might negatively affect the continuation of emigration from the People's Democracies which was favourably regarded by the Soviet Union.[8]

The Soviet position *vis-à-vis* Jewish emigration emanated from the state's attitude toward the emigration of Soviet citizens in general. In principle, the authorities excluded the possibility of any citizen leaving the country. Moreover, the emigration of citizens on the basis of nationality could never be justified, because it was officially held that the national question had been fully resolved in the Soviet Union, and there were no reasons for Soviet citizens of any minority, including Jews, to emigrate.

Moreover, the Soviet authorities were not inclined to create a precedent by allowing Jews to leave the Soviet Union, even when there were sufficiently weighty justifications for doing so. As Moshe Zak maintains in his book *Israel and the Soviet Union — A Forty Year Dialogue*, Soviet Foreign Minister Andrei Vyshinskii explained at his meeting with Israeli Foreign Minister Moshe Sharett in November 1950 that the Soviet Union was not interested in creating a precedent of Jewish emigration which could be used by other peoples.[9]

The Soviet stand on Jewish emigration was actually formulated before the establishment of the State of Israel, at the time of the discussion of the Palestine question by the world community. Its position was reflected, *inter alia,* in the draft of the main points of Gromyko's 14 May 1947 speech prepared by the Foreign Ministry. The document states that 'the Palestine question should not be linked with the Jewish question as a whole. The proposition that a solution to the Jewish question in Western Europe allegedly depends on resolving the problem of permitting broad-scale Jewish emigration to Palestine does not stand up under scrutiny. Palestine alone would not be able to receive all Jews suffering from fascist persecution'.[10]

The Soviet leadership was justifiably of the opinion that 'the significance of the Jewish question is much broader'. But it maintained that the Jewish question had no relevance to the Soviet Union and 'should be resolved in the West European countries and, above all, in the territories that had been under Nazi rule, by decisively destroying all roots of fascism'. In the opinion of the Soviet leadership there was only one way to resolve that question: 'Jews should be given equal political and economic rights [in these countries], treated on an equal footing with people of other nationalities. Linking a solution of the Jewish question to settling of Jews in Palestine can only intensify anti-Semitism in the countries of Europe, where democratic principles still need to be established on a broad basis.'[11]

The Israeli diplomat, Yosef Govrin, has pointed out that even after the first meeting between the Israeli representatives in Moscow and their counterparts in the Soviet Ministry of Foreign Affairs, it was apparent that the Soviet Union approved of Jewish emigration from the Western countries only, and that emigration from the USSR had been completely ruled out.[12]

Several minor documents also testify to the negative approach of the Soviet foreign ministry officials to the problem of the emigration of Jews to Palestine. Thus, for instance, in December 1945, a cable addressed to Stalin was received from an international congress of Jewish political émigrés held in Rome. It contained a request to the Soviet Union to support its demand for free immigration to Palestine and the creation of a Jewish state. In the cover letter addressed to Deputy People's Commissar for Foreign Affairs V. G. Dekanozov, the Chief of the Middle East Department of the People's Commissariat for Foreign Affairs I. Samylovskii suggested not to send any reply to the cable.[13] It seems that a message sent to Stalin on 15 November 1945 by Swedish Jews requesting assistance in resolving the question of the return of Jews to Palestine, met with a similar response.[14]

Despite its reservations over Soviet Jewish emigration, the USSR made a profound contribution to the decision to establish a Jewish State. The Soviet leadership evidently expected that the formation of the State of Israel would deliver a blow to British imperialism in the Middle East. In accordance with Moscow's blueprint, the young Jewish state would head the national-liberation movement throughout that region.

Soon after the declaration of the State of Israel, Gromyko, speaking at the UN regarding Israel's War of Independence, stated that

319

the delegation of the USSR cannot but express its surprise at the stand of the Arab states *vis-à-vis* the Palestine question, and particularly at the fact that these states...resorted to such actions as sending troops to Palestine and military operations aimed at the suppression of the national liberation movement in Palestine.[15]

The exchange of envoys between the USSR and Israel in 1948 was an important event in the development of relations between the two countries. Golda Meir, in her book *My Life* and Mordecai Namir in his *Shlihut be-Moskva* (Mission in Moscow) recounted their first impressions upon arriving in Moscow. The first Soviet diplomats in Israel did not leave any memoirs, but reports and other documents may give some insight into their perceptions of events at that time.

Thus, for instance, the first Soviet minister to Israel, Pavel Ershov, wrote in 1950:

> The Soviet Union's stand on the Palestine question at the UN, which played an important role in the establishment of the state of Israel, the official recognition of Israel on the third day of its existence and the establishment of normal diplomatic relations and the subsequent arrival in Tel Aviv of the Soviet Mission, the first diplomatic mission [to be set up in the country], evoked general approval and the growth of fraternal sentiments among the working masses of Israel.[16]

It should be noted that in the initial stage of its relations with Israel, Soviet diplomats, representatives of Soviet political circles and the press characterized the 1948–49 war as 'an aggression of the Arab countries against Israel', and as a struggle against the forces of the Arab feudal lords supported by British imperialism'.[17] Gradually, the attitude to that war underwent a profound change.

There were other issues, such as the status of Jews in the Soviet Union and, in particular, the question of Jewish emigration, on which their position remained firm. In his report for the period from May 1948 up to December 1949, Ershov wrote:

> In an effort to slanderously depict the struggle against cosmopolitanism in the USSR as a new form of anti-Semitism and the liquidation of Jewish culture, Israel's ruling circles have launched, with full-force, a broad scale campaign of nationalist propaganda inside and outside their country.
>
> Meanwhile, all political movements in Israel, with the exception of the communist party, are conducting a systematic attack on the People's Democracies such as Romania and Hungary, for obstructing Jewish emigration.[18]

In the initial stage, as noted above, Israel did not want to raise the question of direct Jewish emigration from the USSR. In a meeting with Vyshinskii on 14 April 1949 (on the eve of her departure from the USSR), Golda Meyerson said that in accordance with the instructions of her government, she was requesting that the Soviet government support the appeal addressed to the governments of Romania and Hungary, to facilitate the departure to Israel of Jews living in these countries and wishing to leave.[19]

It appeared, however, that Israel's demands would not be directed only at the People's Democracies for long. In his report for 1949, Ershov pointed out that 'in its practical activities the [Israeli] government puts the main stress regarding immigration on the People's Democracies but has in mind, as the most significant potential source of immigration — the Soviet Union'.[20]

Though the Soviet leadership and diplomats strove to restrict the discussion of the question of Jewish immigration during their talks with Israel's representatives, their interest in that question and everything that pertained to the conditions of immigrants was considerable. In a message of 15 October 1949, Ivan Bakulin, Head of the Department of the Middle and Near Eastern Countries at the USSR Ministry of Foreign Affairs, informed M. L. Mukhin, the Soviet Chargé d'Affaires in Israel that in accordance with the Department's work plan for the second half of 1949 which had been approved by the ministry, one of the two reports to be prepared by the Soviet Mission in Israel should deal with 'Jewish immigration to Israel'. Bakulin's instructions to Mukhin contained the recommendation that the report examine the 'social structure of Jewish immigration , its main causes and dynamics, the immigration policy of the Zionist organizations and the government of Israel, the legal, economic and political situation of immigrants in Israel and their impact on Israel's economy'.[21]

The mission fulfilled its assignment and continued to pay great attention to that question. It showed interest in the fate of immigrants who had come to Israel from various countries. The data on their hardships and their difficulties in adjusting were used for anti-Israeli propaganda inside the Soviet Union.[22]

In his political report for 1950, Ershov stressed that the USSR's popularity was given a major boost by the arrival of the Soviet Mission to Tel Aviv. 'But', he wrote,

> even then the government of Israel was using friendly relations with the USSR for its selfish Zionist purposes. It assumed that the recognition of Israel by the Soviet Union would automatically mean the recognition of Zionism, and it expected to be able to conduct Zionist propaganda side by side with subsequent immigration to Israel of Jews from the USSR...Only after the publication in Pravda of the well-known article by I. Erenburg and the measures adopted by the USSR Ministry of Foreign Affairs to prevent Zionist activities by the Israeli Mission in Moscow, did it become clear to the government of Israel, that its plans were doomed to

failure and that the USSR, having recognized the State of Israel, had reverted to regarding Zionism as a reactionary bourgeois ideology.[23]

Soviet ambassadors' reports reflected, as a rule, the stand of the Foreign Ministry and of the Soviet state and party leadership as a whole. In their annual and quarterly reports, ambassadors tried to evaluate all events, first and foremost, and sometimes exclusively, in the context of the confrontation between the two socio-political systems existing at that time, the 'socialist' or communist — and the capitalist.

Ershov, pointed out in his report for the year 1951 that,

> the consolidation of a pro-American orientation on the part of Israel's government has affected, above all, Israel's relations with the Soviet Union and the People's Democracies...Repeated anti-Soviet statements by members of the government and persistent anti-Soviet campaigns in the Israeli press testify to the fact that the government of Israel does not at present need the USSR's political support for resolving issues concerning Israel, as it did in the past, and that it is intentionally exacerbating relations with the Soviet Union. The question of Jewish immigration from the USSR to Israel arises with increasing frequency, and it is quite possible that this question will become the criterion for future relations between Israel and the USSR.[24]

In the conclusion of this report, Ershov wrote that

> the attitude of the government of Israel toward the Soviet Union in 1951 was one of greater hostility, as is manifest in a number of anti-Soviet pronouncements by government members, the systematic anti-Soviet campaign of the reactionary Israeli press, the refusal to comply with the USSR's legitimate demands regarding the transfer of property [that is, the property of the Russian Palestine Society, the former Russian Imperial Government, and some land registered in the name of Grand Duke Sergei Aleksandrovich] and the restrictions on the dissemination of Soviet literature in Israel. The hostile attitude of the Israeli government to the USSR will intensify in future, and it cannot be ruled out that the Israelis may be prepared to engage in a political conflict with us using the question of Jewish emigration from the USSR to Israel as a pretext.[25]

Assessing the situation in this way, Ershov recommended that Moscow consider the following measures in its relations with Israel:

1. Discontinuing all support of Israel on issues under consideration at the UN and its various bodies.
2. Cutting off Jewish immigration to Israel from the People's Democracies, since the immigration broadened Israel's potential options[26]

The question remains: to what extent were these recommendations taken into account by the Kremlin in pursuing its foreign policy course? The opinion on the political report of the USSR Mission in Israel for 1951 expressed by Aleksandr Shchiborin, Acting Head of the

Department of the Middle and Near East of the USSR Ministry of Foreign Affairs, testifies to the fact that the stand of the heads of that department was less categorical. 'Regarding the proposals of the mission contained in the report', Shchiborin writes:

1. The proposal to discontinue all political support for Israel on issues discussed at the UN and its organs, was formulated in the report in a general manner, without relating to the particular nature of individual questions. The USSR's position on issues discussed at the UN is determined, as is well-known, in each individual case on the basis of the USSR's own policy, and bearing in mind the international situation.

2. The suggestion to halt immigration to Israel of Jews from the People's Democracies has been presented in general terms, without sufficient justification. In particular, it is not accompanied by any factual data or analysis of Jewish immigration from the People's Democracies. This question may be considered only if the mission submits detailed information and a serious analysis of the issues which it raises'.[27]

Interestingly, in his assessment of the political report, Shchiborin emphasized that 'Comrade Ershov has not given an evaluation of the policy of the [Israeli] Communist Party regarding immigration to Israel and only remarked that its stand on that issue "is puzzling"'.[28] Confusion was apparently aroused by the fact that the Israeli Communist Party (Maki) did not come out at the time as forcefully against the demands of the Israeli government as the Soviet leadership would have liked.

The assessment by Soviet diplomats of the 'Prague events' in November 1952 reveals the extent of their knowledge regarding all the subtleties of their leadership's foreign policy. In another of his regular reports Ershov stressed that 'the trial of a group of traitors of the Czecho-Slovak people conducted in Prague in November, 1952, exposed the role of the Ben-Gurion Government in the espionage network of the American intelligence service and showed that Israel has long ago become a centre of US espionage against the countries of the socialist camp'.[29]

And he continued: 'This entire torrent of vicious slander and accusations was necessary to disguise the acts of espionage and sabotage in the People's Democracies.'[30]

The analysis of the assessment by Soviet diplomats in Israel of the Israeli response to the 'situation of the Jews in the People's Democracies' makes it clear that they did not question the correctness of Soviet policy. Dwelling on the Doctors' Plot and the 'anti-Soviet hysteria' which had broken out in Israel in January 1953, Soviet Minister Ershov wrote:

The aims of this new anti-Soviet campaign are 1) to show the USA and, in particular, the new government of the Republican Party that Israel's government is firmly on the side of the USA and that it may fully rely on Israeli support while implementing its own aggressive plans in the Near and Middle East and use Israel, as before, as a centre of espionage for operations in the countries of the Socialist camp. 2) To enhance the activity of American Jews in collecting funds and rendering other assistance to Israel. The advancement of the demand for Jewish emigration from the USSR, when immigration has decreased considerably as a result of economic considerations, is demagoguery designed to strengthen Israeli requests for 'aid'.[31]

Analysis of the position of the Soviet diplomats in Israel as expressed in their political reports and other communications, allows us to assert that they were characterized by a simplistic approach to the national question in general and the Jewish question in particular.

Further evidence of such an approach can be found in the explanation of the causes of Jewish immigration from the People's Democracies in the late 1940s. In the opinion of the Soviet Mission, that mass immigration was due to the fact that the

nationalistic propaganda of the Zionists, conducted in those countries in the first half of the twentieth century, found fertile ground in view of the large-scale spread of anti-Semitism. In addition, German fascism, aside from annihilating a tremendous part of the Jewish population of those countries, confiscated the property of the surviving Jews, who engaged mainly in trade and handicrafts. These Jews, brought up on nationalist Zionist ideology, are trying, after the establishment of the bourgeois Israeli state, to emigrate there and resume their former occupations.[32]

The over-simplified nature of the approach of Soviet diplomacy is seen also from the attempt to directly link the demand of free Jewish immigration from the Soviet Union with the pro-American course of the Israeli government.

Thus, for instance, the Soviet Chargé d'Affaires *ad interim*, Aleksandr Abramov described the situation existing in the middle of 1952 in the following way:

Complete submission to the American diktat determines Israel's relations with the USSR. The latest official pronouncements by Ben-Gurion and Sharett testify to the desire of the Israeli government to cause a further deterioration in Soviet-Israeli relations. The question of the emigration of Jews from the USSR, which continues to be a subject of Israeli demagoguery in an effort to essentially halt immigration to Israel, and which, in accordance with US demands, has been introduced to explain the unwillingness of the USSR and the People's Democracies to permit the departure of Jews, is being used as a pretext for anti-Soviet declarations.[33]

The first Soviet diplomats in Israel (in the period from 1948–53) found themselves in a very complex situation. The events in the region developed rapidly and adjustments in the Soviet line on the Middle East had to be made accordingly.

Soviet diplomats at that time were practically unable to exert meaningful influence on the shaping of the Soviet Union's foreign policy course *vis-à-vis* Israel. Moreover, their reports and opinions were not always made known to the political leadership of the country. Thus, for instance, it was felt in the Near and Middle East Department of the Foreign Ministry that 'as a result of flaws', the reports of the Soviet Mission in Israel for the 3rd quarter of 1951, the Annual Report for 1951 and the 2nd quarter of 1952 should not be sent to the Central Committee of the RCP(b).[34] Ershov's report for the 3rd quarter of 1952 was also criticized. According to the evaluation of the Deputy Foreign Minister Georgii Pushkin, the fundamental flaw in that report was that it was compiled on the basis of newspaper reports.

This did not mean that the position of the diplomats in Israel differed from the general line of Soviet policy. It had necessarily to be in line with the Soviet stand as a whole and, among others, on the issue of immigration. Indeed, the position of the diplomats in Israel not only coincided with the general Soviet approach to the question of emigration, but actually served as a basis for the disinclination of the Soviet Foreign Ministry to engage in talks with the Israeli side on questions of the emigration of Soviet Jews.

The reports and proposals of Soviet diplomats in Israel were geared toward the demands of Soviet propaganda, and their position was used to demonstrate the 'correctness' of the Soviet course. Soviet diplomats, directly or indirectly, affected the moulding of public opinion within the Soviet Union. Thus, for example, in later years, members of the staff of the Ministry of Foreign Affairs were directly involved in the preparation of the book *The State of Israel* by Ivanov and Sheinis.[35]

On the eve of the establishment of the State of Israel and in the first years of Israel's existence, Soviet diplomacy fully reflected the Soviet leadership's attitude to the Palestine question, to the young state and to one of the major issues of Israel's foreign policy — the issue of the immigration of Soviet Jews. The changes that occurred in the Soviet stand at various stages and as a result of a variety of circumstances were also reflected in the activity and reports of Moscow's diplomats. From there it was clear that as long as the problem of Soviet Jewish emigration remained on the agenda of Soviet-Israeli relations, there was little hope of normalizing bilateral relations between the two states.

NOTES

1. V. B. Lutskii, *Palestinskaia problema* (Moscow: Pravda, 1946), p. 31 — verbatim report of a public lecture delivered on 9 Aug. 1946, at the Gorky Central Park of Culture and Rest in Moscow.
2. Ibid. p. 5.
3. *Arakhim* 4 (1993), p. 16. Meir Vilner's interview with the Director of the Heikhal Ha-atsmaut Museum, on the occasion of the 45th anniversary of the establishment of the State of Israel.
4. I. A. Genin, *Palestinskaia problema* (Moscow: Pravda, 1948), p. 6. Verbatim report of a public lecture delivered at the Central Lecture Hall of the Society for the Dissemination of Political and Scientific Knowledge in Moscow.
5. G. S. Nikitina, *Gosudarstvo Izrail'* (Moscow: Nauka, 1965), p. 224. Nikitina also referred to 'Western reactionary circles' who 'in all sorts of ways exaggerate the "Jewish Question" in the Soviet Union and invent various unfounded fabrications'.
6. Yaacov Ro'i, *Soviet Decision Making in Practice. The USSR and Israel 1947–1954.* (Transaction Books: New Brunswick/London, 1980), pp. 141–2.
7. Ibid; and see Iurii Strizhov, 'The Soviet Positon on the Establishment of the State of Israel', in this volume.
8 Ro'i, *Soviet Decision Making*, pp. 142–8, 203–6, 344.
9. Moshe Zak, *Arba'im shnot du-siah im Moskva* (Ma'ariv: Tel Aviv, 1988), p. 447.
10. Arkhiv vneshnei politiki MID SSSR (AVP), fond (f.) 118, opis' (op.) 5, delo (d.) 1, papka (pk.) 3, p. 14. Draft outline of Gromyko's speech on the Palestine problem.
11. Ibid.
12. Govrin, *Yahasei Yisrael Brit ha-Mo'atsot* (Magnes: Jerusalem, 1990), p. 128.
13. AVP, f. 87, op. 4, d. 60, pk. 8. Zionism and the Palestine problem. Relations of the Arab countries, the USA, England, France and the USSR toward the Palestine problem. For an earlier letter from the Jewish Committee of the International Union of Emigrants and Refugees, based in Rome, see Iurii Strizhov, 'The Soviet Position on the Establishment of the State of Israel', in this volume.
14. Ibid.
15. AVP, f. 89, op. 9/a, d. 2, pk. 16, pp. 63–4.
16. AVP, f. 089, op. 3, d. 8, pk. 6, pp. 211–2.
17. AVP, f. 089, op. 3, d. 8, pk. 6, p. 103.
18. Ibid., pp. 101–2.
19. AVP, f. 089, op. 2, d. 4, pk. 3, p. 10.
20. AVP, f. 89, op. 3, d. 8, pk. 6, p. 102.
21. AVP, f. 089, op. 2, d. 3, pk. 3, p. 41.
22. AVP, f. 089, op. 3, d. 8, pk. 6, pp. 207–8.
23. AVP, f. 4, d. 60, pk. 8.
24. AVP, f. 089, op. 5, d. 9, pk. 12, p. 186. Report of the Soviet Mission in Israel for the year 1951, compiled by P. Ershov.
25. Ibid., pp. 249–50.
26. Ibid., p. 250.
27. AVP, f. 089, op. 5, d. 9, pk. 12, pp. 268–9. Conclusion of the political report of the USSR Mission in Israel in 1951, signed by A. Shchiborin.
28. Ibid., p. 267.
29. AVP, f. 089, op. 6, d. 8, pk. 15. Poltical-economic report of the USSR Mission in Israel for the Fourth Quarter of 1952, compiled by P. Ershov.
30. Ibid., p. 33.
31. Ibid., pp. 33–5.
32. AVP, f. 089, op. 4, d. 9, pk. 9, p. 68. Report of the USSR Mission in Israel for 1950.
33. AVP, f. 089, op. 5, d. 9, pk. 12, p. 339. Political-Economic Report of the USSR Mission in Israel for the Third Quarter of 1952, compiled by A. Abramov.
34. AVP, f. 089, op. 5, d. 9, pk. 12, concerning conclusions of the Report for the Third Quarter of 1951, pp. 1–8; for the report of 1951, pp. 252–69; Letter of S. T. Bazarov to a member of the Foreign Ministry Collegium, A. A. Arutiunian, p. 339.
35. AVP, f. 089, op. 12, d. 5, pk. 26. Political report for the first half of 1959, compiled by Ambassador M. Bodrov. The reference is to Konstantin Ivanov, Zinovii Sheinis, *Gosudarstvo Izrail'* (Moscow: Gospolitizdat, 1958).

21

The Beginnings of the Struggle
for Soviet Jewish Emigration and
Its Impact on Israel-Soviet Relations

YOSEF GOVRIN

The struggle on behalf of Soviet Jewish rights consisted of the demand that Soviet Jews be permitted to emigrate to Israel, that they be accorded equal rights in religion, education, and culture, and that there be an end to manifestations of anti-Semitism. Three stages are discernible in the development of this struggle.

First, Israel's need for *aliya* was made clear to the Soviet foreign minister and high-ranking diplomats by Israeli envoys, immediately following the establishment of diplomatic relations between the two countries. The Soviet response was extremely chilly. The USSR favoured *aliya*, but only from capitalist countries. *Aliya* from the Soviet Union was not on the cards, while the question of *aliya* from the East European People's Democracies, which was the main focus of discussion, required careful study.[1] Almost two years passed from the time the matter was first broached at the diplomatic level until David Ben-Gurion, then Prime Minister of Israel, issued an urgent public appeal to the USSR (in May, 1950) to allow any Jew within its borders who so wished to emigrate to Israel and 'join those building the country'.[2] In December 1951 Israel made this demand for the first time in an official note to the USSR, maintaining that 'the return of the Jews to their historical homeland is the paramount mission of the State of Israel', and 'the Government of Israel believes that this desire is in complete accord with Soviet policy, which is based on national equality and the right to self-determination of every people'.[3]

The demand was based on two fundamental principles: first, the historical connection of the Jewish people to Palestine, which was recognized by Gromyko at the UN General Assembly on 14 May and 26 November 1947; and second, the right of the Jews to immigrate to the State of Israel, which was established with the help of the Soviet Union and which received that country's immediate and full recognition.

The second stage in the struggle followed the anti-Semitic campaign in the Soviet Union and Eastern Europe in late 1952-early 1953. This stage, epitomzed by the Slansky trial in Prague[4] and the disclosure of the Doctors' Plot in Moscow, elevated the demand for *aliya* from the bilateral to the international arena. The demand was explicitly expressed for the first time by Israeli leaders both from the Knesset podium[5] and in the United Nations,[6] and was coupled with fierce criticism of the repressive Soviet regime and its anti-Semitic policies. Following this verbal attack and the explosion of a bomb at the Soviet diplomatic mission in Tel Aviv, the Soviet government informed the government of Israel that it was severing diplomatic relations.[7]

In addition to the attack on its Tel Aviv mission, Moscow cited statements made by Israeli government officials, including Foreign Minister Moshe Sharett himself, following the 'exposure' of the Doctors' Plot libel.[8] These statements, they claimed, overtly incited hostility towards their country.

Representatives of parties in the Israeli government had publicly criticized the USSR, which they had previously refrained from doing in any official forum. Now they castigated the Soviet regime for plotting 'spiritual extermination and national repression', condemned its anti-Semitic policies, and accused it of preparing the masses to carry out pogroms against the Jews. They vehemently insisted that the rights of Soviet Jewry be restored and that Jews be permitted to settle in Israel. They charged that the Soviet legal system was based on terror and deceit. They appealed to public opinion in the West in an attempt to shake it from its apathy and induce it to take immediate steps to prevent disaster. They resolved to bring up the matter as an urgent problem on the agenda of the United Nations.

These criticisms, demands, and warnings were voiced publicly not only for the sake of Knesset debate but also as a show of Jewish solidarity and as a plan of governmental action to oppose the anti-Jewish policies of the Soviet Union. For the first time, Israeli leaders exposed the criminal aspects of Soviet policy in the domestic arena in general and toward the Jews in particular. The State of Israel had become the 'spokesperson' for Soviet and world Jewry and had overtly taken a stand against the Soviet Union. It is reasonable to assume that the response of representatives of the coalition parties in the Knesset, especially that of the foreign minister, its scale, ferocity and main objective — the mobilization of world public opinion to have the libel of the Doctors' Plot nullified and to improve conditions for Soviet Jews — seemed to the Soviets sufficient grounds for severing relations.

The critical attitude of Ben-Gurion, Sharett and their colleagues toward the methods of terror practised by the communist regimes in Eastern Europe and their hostility toward the Jews, Zionism and Israel was nothing new. The difference lay in the decision to embark on an ideological and political struggle against communist hostility as personified by Stalin. Israel's leaders sensed that Soviet Jewry was on the threshold of a physical and spiritual holocaust. Israel believed it its national and moral duty to mobilize to rescue Soviet Jewry with the only weapon that it could take up against a superpower: enlightened public opinion in the West.

From Israel's standpoint, the severance of relations was seen as the price that it had to pay for its struggle for Soviet Jewry, which began in the aftermath of the Doctors' Plot and continued through the days of perestroika and glasnost.

Public opinion in the Western world sided with Israel, and preliminary arrangements were made to raise the problem at an international Jewish conference to be held in Zurich in March, at the United States Congress[9], and at the United Nations.

The Israeli government decided to send Minister of Labour Golda Meyerson (later Meir) to the UN to wage the battle. Her status as a member of the government, as well as her previous tenure in Moscow, added a large measure of credibility and weight to Israel's stand. In her remarks in the 1st Committee of the UN on 13 April 1953, following Stalin's death in early March and the public dismissal of charges against the doctors,[10] she noted that groundless accusations and libels in Prague and Moscow about a world Jewish conspiracy were inconsistent with the goals of peace and friendship between nations, and that Israel viewed with profound concern the anti-Jewish incitements that were an integral part of these charges. The revival of anti-Semitism by Soviet and East European governments as a means of attaining political objectives should also be worrisome to the United Nations, she said. Israel welcomed the Soviet announcement that the charges against the Jewish physicians had been found groundless, and was satisfied with the Soviet denunciation of the libel in sharper terms than those used by the Israel foreign minister on 19 January 1953; his remarks had thereby been endorsed, in effect, by the Soviet government. Meyerson expressed the hope that, following retraction of the libel, all anti-Jewish manifestations would be condemned, discrimination against Jews prohibited, and propaganda against them halted. Israel would continue to monitor the conditions of the Jewish communities in the USSR and Eastern Europe. The best way to guarantee the prevention of problems, she said, would be to grant the Jews of Eastern Europe the right to self-determination in their cultural and community life and the freedom to settle in Israel if they so chose. The problem should be considered in the broad conduct of international relations, peace between nations and respect for human rights.[11]

The labour minister's speech at the UN was accompanied by similar utterances by representatives of delegations from Panama, the Netherlands, the Dominican Republic, Nationalist China, Cuba, the United States and Uruguay.[12] It was an impressive demonstration of international condemnation of anti-Semitism in the Eastern bloc and a warning that persecution of Jews in these countries would constitute a grave obstacle to East-West relations. Israel's first campaign on the international stage was a success, and the problem took on an international dimension. Israel learned that it was indeed possible to engage Western public opinion in the struggle against Soviet anti-Semitism and for improvement of the situation of Soviet Jews[13]; and the Soviets presumably learned that this fact would be worth taking into account in the future.

After the Soviet Union announced that the charges in the Doctors' Plot had been dropped and the doctors had been released from prison, and after it resumed diplomatic relations with Israel in July 1953 and a new style of 'peaceful coexistence' began to typify East-West relations, the public campaign for Soviet Jewry ebbed for a few years. It surfaced again when the murder of the Jewish writers in Stalin's last years became widely known, and when Khrushchev revealed Stalin's crimes in his speech at the 20th Congress of the Soviet Communist Party in February 1956 — ignoring totally the Jewish aspect of the Doctors' Plot. The former event revealed the magnitude of physical terror that Soviet Jewry had faced in Stalin's last days. In view of the openness that became visible in Khrushchev's policy towards the West, the latter event triggered hope that vigorous action on behalf of Soviet Jewry would pay off. It also indicated, however, that de-Stalinization did not necessarily apply to the Jews. This period marked the beginning of the third stage: consolidation of the struggle.

A major turning point in Israeli tactics came about in the early 1960s, with intensification of the demand for free emigration and equal rights for Soviet Jews. It could be seen primarily in the frequent talks conducted by Israeli representatives with the senior echelons of the Soviet Foreign Ministry and with Soviet envoys throughout the world; in statements by the country's leaders in the Knesset or in public appearances, including interviews with Israeli and foreign media; in statements by Israeli representatives at the UN Human Rights Commission; in statements at world Jewish forums and at an international conference, the first of its kind, convened for this purpose in Paris in 1960; and in direct written appeals to Soviet leaders.[14]

This activity attested to the Israeli government's determination to persist in its demand that Soviet Jews be allowed to emigrate to Israel. It met with understanding and support from Western governments, including that of the United States, and from leftist circles around the world. Prime Minister Levi Eshkol no doubt took this fact into account in his forceful public appearances on behalf of *aliya* from the USSR. On the other side of the divide, Soviet Prime Minister Kosygin had this in mind when he told journalists in Paris on 3 December 1966:

> Regarding family reunification, if families wish to leave the Soviet Union or meet their families abroad, the Soviet Union will do everything in its power to open the gates for them. No question of principle is or will be involved.[15]

Kosygin's statement took on historic significance, for it aroused new hopes among Soviet Jews that they would be able to emigrate to Israel. Israeli Foreign Minister Abba Eban welcomed it.[16]

The declaration did not lead to a swift change in the number of emigrants (although prior to the Six-Day War, the number of exit permits issued by the Soviet authorities to Jews who wished to leave for Israel was slightly higher than in previous years).[17] However, the statement did attest to a new trend of thought in Soviet policy-making on this issue. This trend, which would subsequently leave its imprint, namely recognition of *aliya* as an issue, and the need to resolve it in response to internal and external pressure, was a watershed in Soviet attitudes toward the emigration of its Jews to Israel.

Several factors may explain this. In the first place, there was a certain Soviet sensitivity to public opinion in the West, where its response to the demand that Jews be allowed to leave for Israel was used as a litmus test of Soviet respect for human rights. In addition, communist parties in the West considered the demand for Jewish minority rights justified. On more than one occasion they interceded with the Soviet authorities to solve the Jewish question within the framework of Marxist-Leninist theory. The USSR undoubtedly also needed the support and sympathy of the West in its confrontation with China. More Soviet openness toward Western Europe was an additional factor. Beginning in the mid-1950s, the Soviet Union increased its political, economic and scientific activity in Western Europe. Soviet leaders visited Western capitals, and Western figures visited the Soviet Union fairly often. In most of the encounters, Western leaders raised the issue of Soviet Jewish *aliya*. The fact that Soviet Premier Kosygin made his statement concerning permission to leave the USSR while on a visit to Paris hints at concern over West European public opinion. Finally, the Soviet authorities were displaying a slightly more liberal attitude toward minorities, including Jews, particularly in the cultural field. It was this relative liberalization that made possible the Jewish national awakening, and the resulting pressure by Soviet Jews wishing to emigrate to Israel

These developments were unthinkable in Stalin's time. The increase in the number of exit permits proved that the struggle for *aliya* had been worthwhile and that the Soviets could be influenced.

The first official Israeli memorandum on the status of Soviet Jewry reached Soviet leaders via the Prime Minister of Burma, U Nu, in October 1955. U Nu was asked to bring up the matter of Soviet Jews in his talks with Soviet leaders during his visit to Moscow. In the memorandum, Sharett, now prime minister, reviewed the plight of Soviet Jewry, stressing the danger of cultural extinction that Soviet Jews faced. Cut off from Diaspora Jewry and Israel, they could not even maintain a community framework of their own to safeguard Jewish values and educate the younger generation. This was not the result of an anti-Jewish policy set by the Soviet government, but a consequence of the impact of the Soviet regime on Jewish community life. Other minorities in the Soviet Union, the memorandum asserted, could conduct a national life of their own in the USSR; the Jews could not. Accordingly, the Soviet government was asked to permit the Jews within the country's borders to do three things: live Jewish lives in keeping with the Jewish historical tradition; settle in Israel if they so desired; and associate freely with world Jewry.

Although Sharett used relatively restrained language toward the Soviet Union, refraining from accusing it of a deliberate anti-Jewish policy, the Soviet leaders responded to the memorandum with rage.[18]

On 25 April 1956, the leaders of the World Jewish Congress (WJC) presented an official memorandum (the first of its kind) to the Soviet leadership, on the occasion of the state visit to Britain of Nikita Khrushchev and Premier Nikolai Bulganin.[19] This was the first trip by top Soviet leaders to Britain, and it was intended to demonstrate the desire of the Soviet Union for peaceful coexistence with the Western powers. In Israel, it was felt that if the British hosts, Jewish organizations, and

British public opinion were to bring up the issue of Soviet Jewry, it would be an opportunity to show that true peace between East and West was inconceivable unless the matter of Soviet Jewry was solved. The demands made in the WJC memorandum were analagous to the principles set forth by Sharett in his own memorandum.

Similar appeals were presented to Soviet envoys in the West by heads of state, parliaments, parliamentarians, authors, and Jewish and non-Jewish organizations. Over time, *aliya* became the central demand, rather than just 'family reunification'; moreover, the USSR was asked to put an end to its campaign of anti-Semitism, manifested in anti-Jewish propaganda literature in the Soviet Union, the 1960 blood libel in Dagestan, and the economic trials held in the USSR in the early 1960s.[20]

Three basic principles were set forth from the start in the strategy of struggle: avoidance of inciting the West against the Soviet Union; separation of this issue from the inter-bloc confrontation; concealing Israel's role as sponsor and orchestrator of the struggle. The third principle was somewhat mitigated when, beginning in 1962, Israel abandoned its circumspection and increasingly emerged as the spearhead of the struggle.

From the very outset the struggle on behalf of Soviet Jewry in the post-Stalin period consisted of:

- mobilization of the world Jewish community for extensive, systematic action, with Israel's active role in this initiative concealed; the intent being to arouse anxiety among world Jewry concerning the fate of Soviet Jews and to recognize the urgent need to take action to rescue them
- arousing world public opinion (through the media), *inter alia*, by publicizing anti-Jewish manifestations and distributing information connected with the plight of Soviet Jewry
- lobbying organizations (both Jewish and non-Jewish), parliamentarians, socialist party activists, and other politicians and statesmen to press Soviet leaders to grant rights to the Jewish minority in their land and to express concern over their fate; the aim was to emphasize that the problem angered public opinion, was an obstacle to rapprochement between East and West, and that friends of the Soviet Union in Western countries were particularly bothered. From 1960 on official statements by delegates from member countries of the UN, high-ranking officials and international organizations became frequent; these included a resolution by the Socialist International,[21] Bertrand Russell's correspondence with Khrushchev,[22] a declaration by the President of the United States on 28 October 1964,[23] and the discussion and resolution by the Council of Europe in early 1965.[24]
- embarrassing Soviet leaders and putting them on the defensive by forcing them to recognize the existence of the problem and the need for a solution.[25]

These policy measures created continual pressure from as many quarters as possible to catalyze the situation of Soviet Jewry, especially when the right political atmosphere seemed conducive there to get things moving in a positive direction.

The Soviet government, for its part, responded to the Israeli campaign on various levels: at the UN, in the media, in diplomatic circles. When Israel began to complain openly about discrimination against Soviet Jews, Soviet delegates to the UN Human Rights Commission responded by attacking Israel for discriminating against, oppressing and humiliating its Arab minority. As early as 1965 the Soviet Union attempted to link condemnation of Zionism with that of nazism in the Third (Social and Humanitarian) Committee of the UN General Assembly.[26] The attempt initially failed, but it succeeded a decade later. In 1975 Zionism was equated in the international arena with anti-Semitism, nazism and other racist movements.

At home, the Soviet Union launched a systematic and unremitting campaign to blacken Israel's image in the media, citing the abuses of its social system (exploitation, poverty, famine), the imposition of religious law on its citizens, the ethnic divide, militarism, nationalist chauvinism, and hostility toward immigrants.[27] While the intention was to deter Jews from fostering illusions about Israel, the campaign also reflected Soviet hostility toward Israel, perhaps more than toward any other country in the Western camp.

In response to activities by the Israel Embassy in Moscow among Soviet Jewry, the Soviets voiced sharp, and even threatening, protestations to the Israeli ambassadors, expelled Israeli diplomats as *personae non gratae*, and disparaged Israeli diplomats in the Soviet press.[28]

This reaction, in both the domestic and the international arena, gradually led to a considerable deterioration of relations between the USSR and Israel. Israel tried to ignore the Soviet moves and continue with business as usual, knowing that this was the price it had to pay for efforts on behalf of Soviet Jewry. However, the Soviets ignored Israeli overtures and their hostility toward Israel intensified, with sharp denunciations and repeated warnings on the harm Israeli activity was causing to their mutual relations.

In 1966, the USSR's position toward Israel became more extreme. Cultural ties were severed, although it would be a while before the Soviet Union would break its diplomatic ties with Israel following the Six-Day War.[29] There can be no doubt that the struggle for Soviet Jews was an important factor, together with Middle East policy considerations, in the Soviet decision to sever ties for the second time in the history of the two countries.

The 'balance sheet' of efforts on behalf of Soviet Jewry (until ties were broken off in 1967) was as follows:

Unquestionably, the growing national consciousness among Soviet Jewry fed the worldwide struggle on their behalf and provided an ethical basis for pursuing it. At the same time, this struggle also served to strengthen Jewish national consciousness. The goals set at the start had been achieved: the world became aware of the problems of Soviet Jewry, the issue was placed on the permanent agenda of talks between Western diplomats and the Soviet Union, and it became an international problem. The status of Soviet Jews changed somewhat, with the publication of the Yiddish journal *Sovetish heymland*; the organization of recitals of Jewish songs; and the publication of Jewish classics and contemporary works.[30] Anti-Semitism was officially denounced; the economic trials against Jews ceased; baking of *matza* was allowed; the number of Soviet immigrants to Israel rose gradually; and the Soviet prime minister expressed his government's willingness to permit 'family reunification', the practical expression of which was the somewhat increased number of exit visas issued to those who wanted to emigrate to Israel.

On the other hand, there was no improvement whatsoever in the status of Jewish education or religion. The isolation from the Jewish world continued. A Jewish professional theatre was not revived. No nationwide Jewish representative body was established. The anti-Israeli-Jewish-Zionist campaign intensified and placed considerable strain on Israel-USSR relations. Israeli policies toward the Arab sector were condemned in UN institutions, and political, social and economic discrimination against the Arabs was highlighted. There was an attempt in UN institutions to condemn the Zionist movement along with anti-Semitism and fascism. Zionism was depicted as 'the enemy of humanity', and Israel's policy regarding Soviet Jewry was presented as a factor hindering East-West rapprochement.

Despite the pressure of world public opinion, the changes in the status of the Jewish people were merely cosmetic. The USSR did not alter its basic policy, which was to assimilate the Jews among the Soviet peoples.[31] Moreover, the USSR's intensive condemnation of Zionism and Israel earned it the gratitude of the Arab nations.

Nationalist fervour grew among the Jews, forcing the Soviet Union to issue more exit permits to Israel. However, its attitude toward the Jews had a deleterious effect on its status in the international arena. Just over a month after Stalin's death, the Kremlin was forced to defend its policy concerning Jews in the UN. It continued to be badgered in the international community and its image was tarnished.[32]

Prime Minister Moshe Sharett remarked prophetically at the Zionist General Council on 23 August 1955:

> It is our heartfelt wish that with the opening of a new era in the relations between the nations, a new dawn will also break for the Jews of Soviet Russia, and that as a result of the easing of international tensions and greater facility for mutual contact between the two Blocs, the ties between that great Jewry, which has suffered so sorely, and the remainder of the Jewish people will be restored, and the right of every Jew to settle in this country will be afforded full recognition.[33]

This vision has come about in our lifetime.

NOTES

1. Mordecai Namir, *Shlihut be-Moskva* (Tel Aviv: Am Oved, 1971), p. 52; Yaacov Ro'i, *The Struggle for Soviet Jewish Emigration* (Cambridge: Cambridge University Press, 1991), p. 35 and Ch. 1, n. 104; Medinat Yisrael, *Teudot li-medinut ha-hutz shel Medinat Yisrael*, Vol. 2, Oct. 1948–April 1949 (Jerusalem: Ha-madpis ha-memshalti, 1984), pp. 288–91; see also Iurii Strizhov, 'The Soviet Position on the Establishment of the State of Israel', in this volume.
2. *Davar*, 23 May 1950.
3. The Note was read by David Ben-Gurion in the Knesset Plenum on 27 Feb. 1952 — *Divrei ha-kneset*, Vol. 11, p. 1465, 27 Feb. 1952.
4. *Pravda*, 8 Dec. 1952.
5. *Divrei ha-kneset*, Vol. 13, pp. 130–1, 156–78, 22 Feb. 1952; pp. 481–7, 19 Jan. 1953; pp. 820–1, 25 Feb. 1953.
6. UN General Assembly 7th Session, 1st Committee 587th Meeting, 25 March 1953; 596th Meeting, 10 April 1953; 597th Meeting, 13 April 1953; see also Ro'i, *The Struggle*, p. 99; and below.
7. *Izvestiia*, 12 Feb. 1953.
8. *Divrei ha-kneset*, Vol. 13, p. 493.
9. See Ro'i, *The Struggle*, p. 96; and Special Report, No. 1 and No. 2 on treatment of Jews by the Soviets. Seventh Interim Report of Hearings before the Select Committee on Communist Aggression, House of Representatives, 83rd Congress, 2nd Session, 22–24 Sept. 1954.
10. *Pravda*, 4 April 1953.
11. UN Gen. Ass. 1st Committee, 597th Meeting, 13 April 1953.
12. Ibid. 597–98th, 600–602nd Meetings, 13–15 April 1953.
13. In early 1953 Shaul Avigur, acting on behalf of the Israeli government, initiated the establishment of a small group to deal specifically with the issue of Soviet Jewry — see Ro'i, *The Struggle*, pp. 101–5.
14. Yosef Govrin, *Yahasei Yisrael Brit ha-Mo'atsot* (Jerusalem: Magnes Press, 1990), pp. 130–7.
15. *Le Monde*, 4 Dec. 1966; full details in *Jews in Eastern Europe* 3, 8 (1967), p. 15.
16. *Kol ha'am*, 22 Dec. 1966.
17. Up to the outbreak of the Six-Day War, 1162 Jews actually left, versus 1892 who had left in 1966 — Ro'i, *The Struggle*, p. 328. A larger number of visas, however, seems to have been issued as there were a considerable number of Jews whose departure was prevented by the war and subsequent developments.
18. Moshe Sharett, *Yoman ishi*, Vol. 6. (Tel Aviv: Maariv, 1978), p. 1712.

19. The memorandum was signed by Israel Sieff, Chairman of the WJC's European Executive and by Alex L. Easterman, WJC Political Sector; see also Ro'i, *The Struggle*, p. 113.
20. On the Blood Libel in Dagestan, *Divrei ha-kneset*, Vol. 30, p. 344, 29 Nov. 1964; on the Economic Trials, see *Jews in Eastern Europe*, 11, 2 (1963).
21. *Jewish Chronicle*, 13 May 1966.
22. Ro'i, *The Struggle*, pp. 162–4.
23. President Lyndon Johnson's letter was read out at a New York Conference on Soviet Jewry which took place on 28 Oct. 1964 — Ro'i, *The Struggle*, p. 190.
24. Resolution 295 (1965), Dec. 1912, Strasbourg, 6 May 1965; Ro'i, *The Struggle*, pp. 182–4; *The Council of Europe on the Jews of the Soviet Union* (London: WJC, July 1965); *Jewish Chronicle*, 7 May 1965.
25. E.g., when *Izvestiia* editor Aleksei Adzhubei, who was Khrushchev's son-in-law, came to Paris in April 1964, in the midst of the consternation created by Trofim Kichko's book 'Judaism without Embellishment' — see *Jews in Eastern Europe* 5 II (1964), pp. 34–60.
26. UN Gen. Assembly Document A/6181, 20 Oct. 1965.
27. See Ro'i, *The Struggle*, Index under *Soviet Union; Relations with and policy toward Israel; anti-Israel propaganda*.
28. Govrin, 'Peilutam shel diplomatim yisraelim be-kerev yehudei Brit ha-Mo'atsot bi-re'i ha-itonut ha-sovyetit ba-shanim 1964–1966', *Shvut*, (1981), pp. 68–70.
29. Govrin, *Yahasei Yisrael Brit ha-Mo'atsot*, pp. 185–6.
30. For official Yiddish culture in the 1960s, see Velvel Chernin, 'Institutionalized Jewish Culture in the USSR from the 1960s to the mid-1980s', in this volume.
31. For Soviet policy toward the Jews in the post-Stalin period, see Igor Krupnik, 'Soviet Cultural and Ethnic Policies towards Jews: A Legacy Reassessed', in this volume.
32. Ibid. pp. 186–7.
33. Greetings of the Israeli Government to the Sixth Session after the 23rd Congress of the Zionist General Council, Jerusalem, 23–31 Aug. 1955.

22

United States Policy and Soviet Jewish Emigration from Nixon to Bush

MINTON F. GOLDMAN

Soviet Jewish emigration became a problem for US-Soviet relations at the end of the 1960s. Increasing numbers of Soviet Jews wanted to leave the Soviet Union. For example, the number of Jews obtaining exit visas increased from 229 in 1968 to 2,979 in 1970, though, of course, the number of exit visas granted, nowhere near reflected the number of Jews wanting to emigrate.[1]

The swift and decisive Israeli victory in the 1967 Arab-Israeli War stirred pride in many Soviet Jews and probably inspired some to make the decision to emigrate to Israel. Also, many Soviet Jews wanted to join relatives who already had settled in Israel and other countries in the West in the wake of the Holocaust. But, the primary reason for Jews wanting to emigrate was to escape an increase in officially sanctioned and pervasive discrimination in almost all walks of Soviet life — education, employment, and in the practice of their religious and cultural life — which under the Brezhnev regime (1964–82) was particularly harsh. At that time, officials criticized what they termed 'the over-concentration of Jews in the scientific and academic professions' and restricted the admission of Jews to universities. The number of Jews entering universities declined from 112,000 in 1968 to 105,000 in 1970, 88,500 in 1972, and an estimated 50,000 in 1980.[2] Finally, many Soviet Jews had become pessimistic about the future. They were convinced that discrimination at home would be permanent and that there was little they could do to improve their situation in the Soviet Union except to emigrate.[3]

Extreme anti-Semitism certainly existed prior to the Brezhnev regime. The deeply-rooted Russian variant of anti-Semitism was based on bigotry inherited from the tsarist era and fed by Russian patriotism.

Russian nationalism discouraged conciliatory gestures toward minorities. During the Soviet era, with a diminishing proportion of ethnic Russians in the Soviet population and with Russian nationalism linked to Soviet nationalism, anti-Semitism intensified. Moreover, Marxist-Leninist doctrine was relentlessly hostile to a separate Jewish identity in the Soviet state. But discrimination became worse in the 1960s. Soviet officialdom blamed Jews for the apparent explosion of dissident challenges to communist party rule in Poland and Czechoslovakia in 1968 and in Poland and Hungary a decade earlier.[4]

Yet, when Soviet Jews faced with this hostility tried to emigrate, the regime put up insurmountable barriers, despite its acceptance of the Human Rights Convention concluded at Helsinki in 1975 which guaranteed everyone the right to leave his country and to return to it.[5] Soviet Jews who applied for exit visas were often punished. The Soviet authorities imposed exit fees on emigrants and required that emigrants produce foreign invitations in order to leave the Soviet Union. Many highly educated and experienced Jewish professionals in scientific and technical areas who requested to leave were prevented from doing so on the grounds that they might take 'secrets' with them. Jews and other emigrants who did leave were prohibited from returning to the Soviet Union.

Behind this restrictive policy was a line of Soviet thinking about emigration — both Jewish and other — that Americans could not understand and never accepted. According to a widely held view throughout Soviet society as well as officialdom, emigration was a betrayal of the motherland. Why in the world, Soviet officials asked, would Soviet citizens want to leave the land of their birth when it provided them with the best standard of living it possibly could, one that was superior to that in capitalist societies, where there was exploitation and no guarantee of material well-being or even survival for ordinary people. For the Soviet government emigration was also an embarrassment because it seemed to be a message to the outside world that Soviet society was anathema to many of its members.[6]

Brezhnev refused to allow unrestricted emigration of Soviet Jews also for reasons of foreign policy. He did not want to antagonize the USSR's Arab friends in the Middle East who opposed Jews going to Israel, enlarging its population, enriching its economy with their technological skills, and thereby increasing Israel's strategic advantage in its ongoing conflict with them. This concern was especially important to the Kremlin when it lost influence in Egypt in the aftermath of the expulsion of an estimated 15,000 Soviet military personnel in the summer of 1972. It was also vital following the Soviet invasion of

Afghanistan at the end of 1979, when the Soviets wanted to win back the favour of Arab countries, which angrily denounced the USSR on in January 1980 at meetings of the Islamic Conference Organization.

Despite this policy the Kremlin never completely barred Jewish emigration. On the contrary, in the early 1970s it allowed an increasing number of Soviet Jews to emigrate, with figures reaching an all time high of 34,733 in 1973.[7]

The Soviets had reasons to allow some Jewish emigration. They wanted to ease a potentially explosive internal situation exacerbated by a growing number of disaffected and alienated Jews, who were becoming increasingly depressed by the pervasive and officially sanctioned discrimination in education and employment. The Kremlin also wanted to avoid provoking the West, where public opinion was sensitive to the limits imposed on emigration from the Soviet Union. Brezhnev did not want to jeopardize *détente* and the prospect of concessions from the West in arms control and trade.[8]

DETERMINANTS OF US POLICY

As a consequence of Brezhnev's restrictive policies, the United States under Presidents Richard Nixon, Gerald Ford, Jimmy Carter, and Ronald Reagan were concerned about Soviet Jewish emigration. Soviet restrictions on Jewish emigration were a highly visible issue — one that US citizens could identify with and support — in contrast with the more extensive official internal discrimination against Jews that was an integral part of the Soviet political and social fabric, difficult to identify, and even more difficult for outsiders to remedy.

Moreover, pushing the US Government to confront the Kremlin on its policy toward emigration were influential groups committed to the interests of American and world Jewry such as B'nai B'rith International, the Conference of Presidents of Major Jewish Organizations, the National Council on Soviet Jewry and Congressional Wives for Soviet Jewry. These groups as well as influential Jewish members of Congress such as New York Republican Senator Jacob Javits and Senator Abraham Ribicoff, Democrat from Connecticut, lobbied aggressively on behalf of the well being of the Jewish community in the Soviet Union.

American sensitivity to Soviet emigration policy was also a logical outgrowth of a traditional and deep dislike of the Soviet communist system as well as of Soviet human rights violations, including discrimination against Jews and restrictions on their right to emigrate. The 1975 Helsinki Agreement signed by the Soviet Union, guaranteeing free emigration, gave Washington a strong legal as well as moral basis for challenging Soviet restrictions on emigration. In the period following the Helsinki Agreement, American leaders regularly accused the Soviets of violating pledges they had made in the Helsinki Agreement, especially regarding emigration.

THE NIXON ADMINISTRATION

President Richard Nixon had to cope with the problem of Soviet restrictions on Jewish emigration in the early stages of his first administration (1968–72) when a small group of Soviets Jews — desperate to leave the Soviet Union but denied exit visas — planned to hijack a plane in Leningrad. They were promptly arrested, tried and convicted, and two of them were actually sentenced to death. This punishment provoked an explosion of criticism abroad, especially in the United States. Congress was outraged. The harsh Soviet punishment of the Leningrad Jews accused of the highjacking encouraged Congress to explore the whole issue of discrimination against Jews in the Soviet Union in hearings held in November 1971.[9]

The Administration, however, which was bent on promoting *détente* with the Soviet Union and persuading it to make concessions with regard to its support of North Vietnam, was reluctant to openly confront the Soviets on issues of human rights. It did little to further the cause of Soviet Jewish emigration, despite the sympathy for Soviet Jews both in the country and in Congress, until forced to do so by the so-called Jackson-Vanik amendment to the new treaty on US-Soviet trade presented to Congress in July 1972. This treaty grew out of informal understandings between Nixon and Brezhnev at their May 1972 summit in Moscow where Nixon held out to Brezhnev the prospect of 'more favourable conditions' for commerce based on 'mutual benefit'. Nixon and Brezhnev had in mind a trade treaty in which Washington would give Soviet trade most favoured nation status (MFN). Nixon and his National Security Advisor Henry Kissinger hoped that this would help inspire the Soviets to accept the American understanding of *détente* involving superpower restraint in the competition for strategic advantage in Europe and the Third World and induce a more cooperative Soviet position with regard to influencing the North Vietnamese in negotiations to end the Vietnam war.[10]

The Nixon-Kissinger strategy, however, suffered a setback when in August 1972 the Soviet government announced the imposition of a head tax on all emigrants with higher education. The tax may have been aimed at recouping some of the cost of advanced academic training of people who now wanted to leave the country in order to help the Kremlin purchase expensive Western technology. It may also have been intended to discourage a 'brain drain' from the Soviet Union.[11]

The head, or diploma, tax produced an explosion of anger in the US Senate from anti-communist conservatives and human rights liberals, neither of whom had much use for Nixon, and even less for his policy of conciliating the Kremlin. It led directly to the proposal of an amendment to the Administration's trade treaty by Democratic Senator Henry Jackson, the spokesman for a group of conservative senators from both the Republican and Democratic Parties hostile to Soviet communism and deeply suspicious of *détente*. The amendment was co-authored by Congressman Charles Vanik. The Jackson-Vanik amendment linked the award of MFN status for Soviet trade with the Kremlin's willingness to give assurances regarding unrestricted Soviet Jewish emigration.[12]

The Administration now took up the issue of Soviet-Jewish emigration in earnest, focusing on the controversial head tax. Kissinger thought that the best way of approaching the Soviets on this highly sensitive issue, which the USSR considered a matter of internal policy, was through 'quiet diplomacy'. Kissinger wanted unpublicized meetings between US and Soviet officials in which the Soviet side might be persuaded to make concessions unobtrusively that they had so far refused to make in public. Administration officials also went to Moscow to explain that Congress, which had to approve the treaty, was not likely to do so without some assurances from Moscow regarding a liberalization of Soviet emigration policy.

Nixon and Kissinger had reason to believe the Kremlin would agree to easing restrictions on Jewish emigration in return for desired benefits, such as granting MFN to Soviet trade. The essential marginality of the Soviet Jewish emigration problem for the Kremlin was critical in their reasoning. After all, most Soviet Jews sought no major alteration of the Soviet political system — they were not advocating democratization — all they wanted was the right to leave the Soviet Union. It also was not unreasonable for Washington to assume that the internal security apparatus might well be in favour of letting more Jewish activists, who had been refused exit visas and were now referred to as 'refuseniks', leave the country to be rid of at least one source of dissidence.

Furthermore, while the Kremlin opposed a formal linking of MFN to adjustments in Soviet internal policy, it apparently was so eager for congressional approval of the trade treaty that it went out of its way to compromise. Brezhnev told then Secretary of the Treasury George Shultz in a meeting in Moscow in March 1973, that the head tax had been the consequence of a bureaucratic bungle in Moscow. In that same month the Soviet government allowed 44 Jews who had obtained higher education in the USSR to leave without paying the head tax and Victor Louis, a Soviet journalist whom the Kremlin often used as a mouthpiece for official leaks, wrote in the Israeli paper *Yedi'ot aharonot* that the tax would no longer be enforced. And in early May 1973, Kissinger himself went to Moscow to urge Brezhnev to help improve the prospects for congressional approval of the trade treaty by allowing 1,000 Jewish emigrants to leave. Brezhnev said he would look into the matter and that the USSR would allow annually between 36,000 and 40,000 Soviet Jews to emigrate.[13]

The Administration's efforts with the Soviets, however, failed to assuage Senator Jackson. Indeed, the more the Soviets gave the more he wanted. He began speaking of explicit Soviet assurances of an annual emigration rate of 60,000. He made a very persuasive defence of his amendment to Congress and the public when he asserted that the United States 'ought to use its vast economic power to help bring freedom and dignity to thousands of individuals who were seen willing to stand up and fight for their right to leave Russia'.[14]

Moreover, Jackson, Vanik, and others continued to insist that increasing the number of emigrants was not enough. The Soviets had to take concrete steps to eliminate the harassment and other obstacles to Jewish applications for emigration. Also, conservatives in Congress who strongly supported Jackson did little to conceal their belief that Nixon was a traitor to their cause and that under the subversive influence of Kissinger, the Administration was trying to conciliate an historic and hated enemy. Senator Adlai E. Stevenson IV, a Democrat from Illinois, proposed an amendment to the Export-Import Bank bill extending the life of the bank. The Stevenson amendment set a ceiling of 300 million dollars on credit that the bank could extend to the Soviet Union, prohibited the use of American funds for the production of Soviet gas and oil, and stipulated that congressional as well as executive approval would be needed to override the ceiling.[15]

The Administration's battle to get the trade treaty ratified without the Jackson amendment quickly became a lost cause. In mid-December 1973 the House of Representatives approved the treaty with the Jackson amendment by a vote of 272 to 140.

The Administration continued to try for withdrawal of the amendment in 1974 but failed. Although in early 1974 the Kremlin reportedly pledged to suspend the head tax on Soviet Jewish emigrants over 55 years of age, to reduce it for others according to certain criteria, and to allow 45,000 Jews to emigrate in 1975, Jackson refused to withdraw his amendment to the trade treaty.[16] Jackson's hardline approach to the Soviet Union was popular throughout the country and in Congress. Indeed, it is possible to argue that Jackson's position was influenced as much by politics as principle — he knew he had taken a popular stand, and he was determined to get as much political benefit from it as possible. Another reason for Nixon's failure was the way in which the emigration issue provided the president's numerous political enemies in Washington an opportunity to support a position on the USSR about which they had strong ideological sentiments while simultaneously denying Nixon a political victory. Finally, the Nixon Administration was gradually losing credibility as a result of the unfolding Watergate scandal and the prospect of the president's impeachment.

The Soviets were upset by the unwillingness of Congress to approve MFN without linkage; they were angered by the failure of their concessions to influence Congress and in particular by the Stevenson amendment ceilings on credit to the Soviet state; and they greatly resented the intrusiveness of American policy. Indeed, Kissinger subsequently admitted to American Jewish leaders that 'no country could allow its domestic regulations to be dictated as we were pushing the Soviets to do'. In January 1975, the Soviet government repudiated the trade treaty.[17]

THE FORD ADMINISTRATION

No less committed to *détente* with the Soviet Union than President Nixon, President Gerald Ford, who succeeded Nixon in August 1974, seemed more supportive of the cause of Jewish emigration than his predecessor. He apparently reassured Senators Javits and Ribicoff as well as Senator Jackson that he would confront the Soviets on their illiberal emigration policy. He had some leverage over the Kremlin, given its eagerness for further reductions of strategic arms evident at the Ford-Brezhnev summit meeting in Vladivostok in November 1974.

Ford also overcame opposition from conservatives to the convening of a conference of European countries sought by the Kremlin to approve the post-World War II Soviet-influenced territorial status quo in Eastern Europe. Conservatives opposed such a conference for the very reason the Soviets wanted it — that it would strengthen Soviet-dominated communist regimes in Eastern Europe. Ford supported the conference as an opportunity to get the Soviets and their allies to sign a treaty, not only resolving international political and economic issues in which they were interested, but also providing guarantees of human rights, including freedom of emigration. These were issues in which they had no interest and, indeed, wanted to avoid.[18]

Like Nixon, Ford wanted to avoid confrontation with the Kremlin and tried to get Congress to pass the trade treaty without the Jackson amendment. But, Jackson and his supporters were too strong for Ford. He was no more able than Nixon to conciliate the Soviets as a means of persuading them to fully and permanently liberalize their emigration procedures.

Nevertheless, he did succeed in encouraging the Soviets to keep the doors to emigration open, despite Kremlin disappointment over the unwillingness of Congress to approve the trade treaty except with the Jackson-Vanik amendment. In 1975, 13,221 Soviet Jews emigrated, 14,261 in 1976, and 16,736 in 1977.[19]

THE CARTER ADMINISTRATION

The Carter Administration also tried to get the Soviets to ease restrictions on Jewish emigration as part of its larger strategy of raising human rights issues with communist countries. In part, Carter pursued a direct approach through an aggressive propaganda and diplomatic campaign. Although he shared Nixon's commitment to *détente*, he was more willing than Nixon and Ford to make a public issue of Soviet human rights violations now that the USSR was a signatory of the Helsinki agreement. He was sending an obvious message to the Soviets when, at the White House, he interviewed Vladimir Bukovskii, a noted Soviet dissident recently released from prison. His lecturing tone infuriated the Soviets and prompted a sharp response from Brezhnev in a speech to the Supreme Soviet in early March 1977. Brezhnev pointedly advised President Carter not to tell the Soviet government how to run its country.[20]

Carter also tried a conciliatory approach. He responded to the fact that the Soviet government was allowing an increased number of Jews to emigrate in the late 1970s, with emigration peaking at 51,320 for 1979.[21] The most plausible explanation of this unusually high level of Jewish emigration was the expectation of obtaining concessions from Carter on trade and arms control. Moreover, the Soviets seemed more flexible when they were able to yield voluntarily rather than in response to embarrassing and potentially humiliating external pressures of the kind Senator Jackson and others were inclined to exert on the Kremlin.

In any event Carter consulted congressional leaders as well as Jewish groups in 1979, to find out if they would approve a waiver of the Jackson Amendment and grant the Soviet Union MFN and renewed access to Export-Import Bank credits. Congressman Vanik was sympathetic to a waiver, saying the amendment had outlived its usefulness and Senator Stevenson made a proposal that would allow the president to grant MFN to the Soviets after making a determination about the acceptability of emigration levels. Hyman Bookbinder, of the American Jewish Committee, also thought a waiver was appropriate in light of the level of Soviet Jewish emigration in the late 1970s.[22]

Yet, Carter met opposition to conciliating the Kremlin. There was Jackson's own opposition to a waiver of his amendment. Jackson's position may have been partly emotional: he could never forget entering the German concentration camps at the end of World War II. Jackson also was influenced by the fact that Jewish advocacy groups continued to oppose a waiver of the amendment. Some of them, together with strong anti-communists in Congress, believed that by conciliating the Kremlin, the Carter Administration would encourage it to renege and slow down the rate of Jewish emigration.[23]

This was not an implausible position, given the Brezhnev regime's intensified harassment of Soviet dissidents, including Jewish 'refuseniks' demanding to emigrate. Indeed, as early as May 1979, there seemed to be a reversal of Soviet policy with new restrictions on emigration in response, not only to the Carter Administration's outspokenness on human rights but also its conciliatory gestures toward China. US recognition of the Chinese communist government in January 1979 enraged Brezhnev.[24]

On the other hand, it could be argued that the inflexibility of Jackson and his supporters among the Jewish organizations was a mistake: the increase in Soviet Jewish emigration in the late 1970s, despite the uproar over the Jackson amendment, offered the United States an opportunity to make a conciliatory gesture of its own that could have enabled the Soviets to act reciprocally without appearing to have bowed to US policy.[25]

Carter's tactic failed also because of developments that had nothing to do with Jewish emigration. Throughout the US government there was growing anger over perceived Soviet expansionism in what National Security Adviser Zbigniew Brzezinski called the 'arc of crisis', a region stretching from Angola and the Horn of Africa to Afghanistan. In the late 1970s the Americans saw the Brezhnev regime aggressively expanding Soviet political and military influence in the countries lying within this arc. The Soviet invasion of Afghanistan in particular aggravated President Carter, as well as Congress, where anyway there was little interest in giving the Kremlin the 'benefit of the doubt', so to speak, on the issue of Jewish emigration.

THE REAGAN ADMINISTRATION

President Reagan also took up the cause of Soviet Jewish emigration. In the early 1980s there was a radical decline in Jewish emigration from the Soviet Union, from a high of 51,320 in 1979 to 21,471 the following year and then to 9,447 in 1981, 2,688, in 1982, 1,314 in 1983, and only 896 in 1984.[26]

This decline coincided with, and probably was influenced by the Brezhnev regime's crackdown on dissidents. It also most likely reflected the indignation of Brezhnev and his successors over trade sanctions instituted by the US in response to the Soviet invasion of Afghanistan. Relations between the United States and the Soviet Union remained severely strained in the early 1980s as a result of deepening Soviet military involvement in Afghanistan. Also, at this time the Soviets were cultivating the Arab countries in the Middle East to defuse their opposition to the Soviet military presence in Afghanistan.

In his strong condemnation of Soviet human rights violations in the early 1980s, Reagan responded to the immediate issue of toughened Soviet restrictions on the granting of exit visas to Jews in violation of the Helsinki Agreement. In part his goal was to embarrass and under-mine the Soviet regime in the international community. Driving this strategy was Reagan's long-standing, visceral hostility to Soviet com-munism, which he knew was shared by many Americans, especially his most ardent supporters in the 1980 presidential campaign.

The Reagan Administration took concrete steps to underscore its concern with Soviet human rights violations and with the newly toughened position on Soviet-Jewish emigration. Despite Soviet pro-tests, Reagan met with Iosif Mendelevich, a former Jewish prisoner of Zion, who had participated in the 1970 plane-hijacking plan, and with Avital Shcharansky, wife of the imprisoned Anatolii (Natan) Shcharansky. These meetings were intended to signal to the Kremlin that the Administration would continue vocal and visible support for Soviet-Jewish emigration. Indeed, Reagan said publicly in February 1983, that

> the issue of Soviet Jewry is of high priority to the Administration. We have repeatedly stated that our concern for human rights in general and Soviet Jewry in particular is integral to our national interests and remains a major focus of our foreign policy.[27]

347

The Reagan Administration pursued other tactics to further the cause of Soviet Jewish emigration. According to Secretary of State George H. Shultz, the US Embassy in Moscow and the US consulate in Leningrad maintained contact with individual Jewish 'refuseniks'. And US officials in Washington and Moscow made numerous representations on behalf of Soviet citizens who were denied permission to emigrate.[28]

These representations were not without some effect. Toward the end of 1985 the Soviet government began approving a very small number of exit visas for Russians with links to the United States who were on a published list drawn up by the State Department. At the same time the Soviet bureaucracy frequently denied exit visas to some members of a family while granting them to others, presumably to underscore the fact that there had been no official departure from the highly restrictive policy in place since the beginning of the decade.[29]

In Reagan's second administration (1985–89) Gorbachev's political ascendancy seemed to improve the opportunities for Soviet Jewish emigration. By the end of 1985, the Soviet government was approving exit visas for Russian Jews, whose names appeared on the State Department list. Other Soviet Jews were allowed to leave, including 'refuseniks'. In the spring of 1986, in a symbolic gesture, the Soviet government released Anatolii Shcharansky, imprisoned in 1977 for his human rights activism, and approved his emigration to Israel. By the end of 1987 over 8,000 Soviet Jews had been allowed to emigrate, up from 914 in 1986. And in the first nine months of 1988, Soviet Jewish emigration hit an eight-year high of 11,815. In March 1989 alone, 4,000 Jews emigrated. By the end of 1989 the number of Jewish emigrants from the Soviet Union for that year had reached 71,196 (see Appendix 22-1). Deputy Foreign Minister Anatolii Adamishin told American Jewish leaders in late December 1989 at the first national congress of Soviet Jews in over 70 years that most of the estimated 100 remaining 'refuseniks' would be allowed to emigrate.[30]

Gorbachev's liberalization of emigration procedures was partly a result of his willingness to go to great lengths to strengthen relations with the United States. Gorbachev's new policies of perestroika and glasnost were predicated on improved relations with the United States. He knew the US would not offer the economic, financial, and technical assistance he needed to make a success of perestroika without a discernible improvement in Soviet-American relations. This, in turn, required concessions on important aspects of Soviet domestic policy, such as Jewish emigration, as well as in foreign policy (that is, a reduction of Soviet support for the radical so-called 'front-line' states that advocated a militant opposition to Israel, notably Syria, Iraq, and Libya).[31]

In addition, Gorbachev was more willing than his predecessors to pay the ideological and political costs of strengthening Soviet ties with the United States and to go along with the United States on human rights issues, *inter alia,* with regard to easing restrictions on Jewish emigration and on the promotion of Jewish cultural life. Gorbachev was prepared to override the resistance of conservative (and frequently bigoted) party bureaucrats who had little sympathy for a liberal emigration policy, especially when applied to Jews.

While the Reagan Administration welcomed the new Kremlin policy, the easing of Soviet restrictions on Jewish emigration produced a problem for Washington. Soviet Jewish emigration jumped from 8,155 in 1987 to 18,965 in 1988. But, about 70 per cent of Soviet Jewish emigrants who received Israeli visas never went to Israel. They switched their destinations in Vienna, a transit station, and came to the United States as refugees, who were entitled to admission. It was estimated in 1990 that perhaps 750,000 of the USSR's Jewish population of 1.8 million wanted to leave the Soviet Union, with a majority seeking entry into the United States.[32]

Washington was in a quandary. Should it cooperate with Israeli policy by encouraging Soviet Jews to go to Israel by a more restrictive definition of 'refugee' status and thus risk complicating Soviet Jewish emigration, which was running at 2,000 emigrants a month by October 1988? Or should it ignore Israeli policy for the sake of facilitating Soviet Jewish emigration and risk antagonizing Jerusalem and inviting a flood of Jewish émigrés to the United States? Furthermore, if the US accepted waves of Jewish emigrants as 'refugees', it also risked undercutting its support for Gorbachev. By calling Jewish emigrants 'refugees', the US would in effect be saying that they were fleeing oppression in Gorbachev's Soviet Union, thus questioning the validity of Soviet political liberalization that was said to signal a real change for the better in the Western view of Soviet domestic behaviour?

Toward the end of 1988 the Reagan Administration retreated from Washington's historic commitment to facilitate Soviet Jewish emigration, and from the traditional 'open door' policy on the admission of political refugees. It redefined 'refugee status' by saying that people who claimed to be refugees from the Soviet Union must demonstrate 'a well-founded fear of persecution'. On this basis US immigration officials denied refugee status to about 175 Soviet Jews in the last few months of 1988.[33]

THE BUSH ADMINISTRATION

President Bush continued this new turn in American policy toward Soviet Jewish emigration. He was at least as determined as Reagan had become to strengthen US-Soviet relations in response to and as a means of encouraging Gorbachev's reform program and in particular Gorbachev's own resolve to strengthen relations between the super-powers. Moreover, Bush's Administration coincided with the development of growing political strife inside the USSR that threatened both Gorbachev's leadership and the continuation of perestroika.

In September 1989, taking up where the Reagan Administration had left off in restricting the entry of Soviet Jewish emigrants into the United States, the Bush Administration announced that the United States would admit no more than 50,000 emigrants from the Soviet Union as refugees, effectively closing the door to thousands of Soviet Jewish emigrants seeking entry. In addition, the Bush Administration shifted the processing of Soviet refugees from the US embassies in Vienna and Rome to its Moscow embassy, ostensibly for reasons of managerial expediency. The practical effect of this action was to further reduce the number of Soviet Jews seeking refugee status because they feared retribution if they told their stories of persecution while still in Moscow within arm's reach of the Soviet authorities.[34]

What factors account for the change in US policy? Senator Allen K. Simpson, Republican of Wyoming, provided one explanation when he said in an interview in 1987 that 'we must distinguish between the right to leave the Soviet Union and the right to enter the United States'.[35] He complained about the way in which the US refugee law had been 'manipulated' by emigrants seeking immediate entry into the US. Instead of going through the very time-consuming and restricted process of applying for an American visa, they were simply claiming persecution in their home country and demanding 'refugee status' at a time when there seemed to be a significant liberalization of the political environment, including emigration. For example, Simpson observed, Gorbachev had already diminished official discrimination against Soviet Jews and had allowed a revival of their religious and cultural life. He publicly condemned anti-Semitic gestures when they appeared, even though they were allowed in the new openness of the social environment brought about by glasnost. Gorbachev also provided for the establishment of a Jewish cultural centre in Moscow in February 1989 and the opening of a *yeshiva* to train rabbis, and he allowed public instruction of the Hebrew language and the publication of Yiddish newspapers.[36]

Deputy Secretary of State Lawrence Eagleberger declared that the decision to process the requests of Soviet refugees in Moscow rather than in Rome was logistical. In Rome there was a backlog of more than 14,000 Jewish refugees to be processed. The situation for many of them, especially those ultimately denied refugee status, was becoming intolerable. They felt stranded. They could not easily return to the Soviet Union though legally they were now permitted to do so. Their only option was to go to Israel, which many did not want to do.[37]

The growing number of applicants for visas to the United States was becoming not only an embarrassment for Washington, but also a financial hardship. According to US immigration officials the expense of caring for Soviet Jews in Italy reached about $34 million in 1989.[38]

But there were still other reasons for the change in US policy on receiving Soviet Jewish emigrants. The Bush Administration wanted to give the Gorbachev leadership credit for implementing a dramatic political liberalization as well as for revolutionary changes in Soviet economic life. Bush did not want to do anything that might undermine these fundamental changes.

US policy was also an expression of support for the Israeli desire to have more of the Jewish emigrants come to Israel. Israeli officials presumably reasoned that more Soviet Jewish emigrants would strengthen the country economically and socially. The Administration pointed out that unlike emigrants from other places, Soviet Jews denied the refugee status they needed to come to the United States, could always go to Israel.[39]

Finally, the Bush Administration may have been sensitive to Gorbachev's complaint that emigration from the Soviet Union of its most talented people threatened an unacceptable 'brain drain'. From the Soviet perspective the Americans had been encouraging this drain of Soviet talent by allowing well-educated and trained Soviet émigrés to easily claim refugee status and thereby gain immediate entry into the United States. These émigrés were the very people Gorbachev most needed for the success of perestroika. Georgii Arbatov, head of the Institute for the Study of the United States and Canada of the Soviet Academy of Sciences, said that the Soviet Union did not want to train people at public expense only to see them leave for the West. The Administration, therefore, had been under some subtle pressure from the Kremlin to modify its open-door policy on receiving Soviet refugees.[40]

American Jewish organizations, in particular the Hebrew Immigrant Aid Society (HIAS), were understandably upset by the shift in American policy. They knew what the Administration must have

351

known prior to the shift, namely, that despite all Gorbachev's reforms in the political sphere, there was continuing harassment of Jews in the Soviet Union. Quotas continued to limit the number of young Soviet Jews accepted to prestigious institutions of higher education. Opportunities for Jews to make a career in the army, the security apparatus and the foreign service remained slim or non-existent. Under Gorbachev there was an explosion of anti-Semitic propaganda in the Soviet media as it enjoyed unprecedented freedom from censorship. Finally, though more Soviet Jews were allowed to emigrate than in past years, many others ran up against a bureaucracy which could not process all the requests for exit visas. Many Jews were still afraid to initiate a request to emigrate lest they be punished. Jews in the late 1980s still had every reason to want to emigrate.[41]

Nevertheless, Jewish organizations recognized the obvious change in Gorbachev's policy and, like the new Bush Administration, wanted to encourage the Soviet leader to follow through with pledges Soviet officials had been making in the late 1980s of a new permanent law liberalizing the procedures for emigration. Emigration did not exist as a right in the Soviet Union, which meant that the rate of emigration could sharply change for the worse depending on the inclination of the leader in power at the time. They thought the time had come for the US government to acknowledge the new situation and proposed a one-year suspension of the restrictions on Soviet trade in the Jackson amendment if a new emigration law codifying recent liberalization of Soviet emigration policy were passed by the Soviet parliament.[42]

By the early 1990s the Bush Administration was looking at the issue of Soviet Jewish emigration in the context of Gorbachev's decline as well as in the context of long-range US policy. Acknowledging the obvious relaxation in Soviet policy on emigration, Bush was ready to make concessions to the Soviets on trade, not only to reward the Kremlin for an unprecedented liberalization of past Soviet restrictions on Jewish emigration, despite its failure to come up with a permanent law transforming emigration from a privilege to a right. He was also interested in making a conciliatory gesture to Gorbachev as his political situation in Moscow steadily deteriorated in 1990 and 1991. On 29 July 1991, during his summit meeting with Gorbachev in Moscow, Bush promised that he would seek to put the Soviet Union on an equal footing with the United States' other trading partners as soon as possible, and declared that he would ask Congress to approve a new trade treaty granting the Soviet Union MFN status that the two powers had signed in 1990. In September 1991, the Administration presented Congress with that treaty.[43]

The Bush Administration's willingness to grant the Soviet Union MFN status without evidence that the living and working conditions of Soviet Jews had really improved, along with the continuing insistence that Jewish emigrants could not automatically claim refugee status and obtain entry visas to the United States as had been the case earlier, suggest that Washington, to all intents and purposes, no longer considered Soviet Jewish emigration an issue in its relations with Moscow.

Indeed, this change in US policy coincided with increasing fears of Soviet Jews about their personal security and safety in a newly emancipated political environment in Russia and Ukraine where the majority of Soviet Jews lived. It also coincided with, if it did not in fact contribute to, a decline in Soviet Jewish emigration, from a peak in 1990 of 181,802 to 108,292 two years later in 1992.[44]

This policy of Bush certainly gave the Kremlin little incentive to push through the Soviet parliament a new emigration bill codifying recent changes in emigration policy that had greatly eased past restrictions on leaving the Soviet Union. Indeed, this bill, which was still far from making emigration a right for all citizens in 1993 (it restricts emigration of citizens in possession of state 'secrets'), had not been enacted into law by the Supreme Soviet of the Russian Republic by the end of this institution's life in September 1993. It remains to be seen whether its successor under the new Russian constitution, the State Duma, will pass it into law.[45]

ACHIEVEMENTS OF AMERICAN POLICY

The Nixon, Ford, and Carter Administrations overestimated the willingness of the Soviets to improve relations with the United States. Despite the enormous advantages the Soviet Union stood to gain from good relations with the United States, Brezhnev would not go beyond a certain point. No matter how much Moscow wanted Western technology, official treatment of Soviet citizens, in particular the imposition of restrictions on emigration, was a prerogative not to be bartered away.

Moreover, the belligerence of American politicians such as Senator Jackson backfired. Soviet leaders were sensitive to any perceived foreign interference in the USSR's internal affairs, especially by the Americans, who had been lecturing the Kremlin on the wrongness and evils of the Soviet system since the Bolshevik Revolution. Invariably, an aggressive American approach to the Soviets on Jewish emigration or on Afghanistan simply made matters worse for Washington by encouraging Soviet stubbornness, rigidity, toughness and a siege-mentality.

Indeed, the strong US emphasis on the whole emigration problem may have given some in the Soviet political establishment a reason to resist changing Soviet emigration policy or reducing discrimination. Resentment over US pressure on the Soviet government to acknowledge and do something about official discrimination against Jews may have strengthened the inclination of some bureaucrats to continue to make life difficult for Jews in education and employment. University administrators could tell themselves that they were justified in discriminating against Jewish students because they eventually would leave the country. Employers could refuse to hire Jews for sensitive positions with the excuse that someday they would leave the country and take with them Soviet 'secrets'.

Moreover, American hardliners were not responsive to measures the Kremlin did take to increase the number of Jewish emigrants in the 1970s. Those who pushed for Soviet Jewish emigration missed this opportunity to encourage the Kremlin to increase still further the number of Jews allowed to leave. The hardliners underestimated the accommodation the Kremlin was willing to make to the Americans for the sake of improving superpower relations, as well as the ideological and other costs of making an exception for Soviet Jews to the restrictive policy on emigration.

With the severe deterioration of US-Soviet relations in the early 1980s — marked by American opposition to Soviet policy in Afghanistan, the development of new American political and military links with China, and the harsh treatment of dissidents by the Brezhnev regime — Washington lost whatever slight leverage it might have had over the Kremlin in the area of human rights and Soviet Jewish emigration. *Détente* with the United States, which had not only worked to the advantage of Soviet dissidents, especially in the sphere of Soviet Jewish emigration, but also had been beneficial to Soviet economic and global strategic interests, was almost dead. The failure of the US Senate to ratify the SALT II agreement, as well as the Carter Administration's sanctions policy, convinced the Soviets that they had little to gain from easing restrictions on Jewish emigration. Later, the ill-concealed vehemence of Reagan's anti-communism made it difficult if not impossible for his administration to exert any influence on Soviet policy regarding Jewish emigration until the advent of Gorbachev.

American presidents from Nixon to Bush at some point in their administrations wanted to strengthen US-Soviet relations with a view to resolving outstanding issues, like Soviet Jewish emigration and ending confrontation and achieving a genuine reconciliation between the superpowers. But they were always limited in what they could do because of strong domestic support for a hard line. This support consisted of a coalition of very powerful constituencies inside and outside the US political establishment (especially in Congress), which were responsive to influential Jewish advocacy groups as well as to the views of those legislators who had a special interest in the issue of Soviet Jewish emigration and whom no president could ignore.

Indeed, throughout the 1970s and 1980s there was a running conflict between the White House and Congress over how to deal with the Kremlin on the issue of Soviet restrictions on Jewish emigration. The president tended to view the emigration issue in the larger context of US-Soviet relations. Members of Congress tended to focus on those grievances against the USSR which were the concern of specific interest groups within their constituencies. Moreover, inside Congress there were always influential members ready, willing, and able to challenge the president in his handling of the Soviet Union for narrow political and ideological reasons.

Change in official Soviet policy came only with the development of a completely new political situation in Moscow, that is, Gorbachev's ascendancy and the inauguration of his program of sweeping reforms known as perestroika. They, more than any other development, were responsible for the easing of restrictions on Jewish emigration and for the significant improvement in Jewish cultural and religious life in the late 1980s and early 1990s. Gorbachev was pragmatic and flexible on both doctrinal and practical issues of government and could compromise where Brezhnev either could not or would not.

At best, the United States seems to have been a kind of catalyst in encouraging continued Soviet Jewish emigration and in particular the Gorbachevian reform program that led to a marked easing of restrictions on emigration. At worst, it could be argued that the confrontational approach in American policy toward Soviet Jewish emigration provoked the Soviets and gave them an excuse to continue severe limitations on Jewish emigration at a time when daily living conditions for many Jews were becoming increasingly difficult and unpleasant.

Throughout this period the United States never really achieved a discreet balance between coercion and conciliation to influence Soviet policy on Jewish emigration. This balance would have meant judicious use of power to make a point to. the Kremlin without provoking a backlash. It also would have meant making concessions to take advantage of Soviet interests in strengthening relations with the United

States. This balance seemed to elude American leaders, no doubt because of the complexity of the US-Soviet relationship, because of the way in which the issue of Soviet Jewish emigration was linked closely to a variety of other difficult issues between the two countries, and because of strong differences within the US government over the best way of dealing with the Soviet Union.

NOTES

1. Robert B. Cullen, 'Soviet Jewry', *Foreign Affairs* 65 (Winter, 1986–87), p. 260.
2. An extensive history of discrimination against Jews living in the Soviet Union appears in House of Representatives, 92nd Congress, First Session, Committee on Foreign Affairs, Subcommittee on Europe, *Hearings* (9 and 10 Nov. 1971), pp. 14–75, hereafter cited as *Hearings*, etc.; see also William Korey, 'Brezhnev and Soviet Anti-Semitism', in Robert O. Freedman (ed.), *Soviet Jewry in the Decisive Decade, 1971–1980* (Durham: Duke University Press, 1984), Chapter 3, pp. 29–37; Yoram Gorlizki, 'Jews', in Graham Smith (ed.), *The Nationalities Question in the Soviet Union* (New York: Longman, 1990), pp. 339–44; the beginnings of Soviet Jewish emigration in the 1950s and 1960s are discussed extensively in Yaacov Ro'i, *The Struggle for Soviet Jewish Emigration* (Cambridge: Cambridge University Press, 1991), especially Ch. 5, pp. 145–54 and Ch. 6, pp. 185–212, which cover official and private American concerns about the plight of Soviet Jews in the Khrushchev and early Brezhnev eras.
3. Ro'i, *The Struggle*, p. 128.
4. See Maurice Friedberg, 'The Plight of Soviet Jews', *Problems of Communism* XIX, 6 (Nov -Dec., 1970), pp. 17–26; Zvi Gitelman, 'Moscow and the Soviet Jews: A Parting of the Ways', *Problems of Communism* XXIX, 1 (Jan.-Feb. 1980), pp. 20–31.
5. Principle VII of the Agreement committed the participating states including the Soviet Union to act in conformity with the Universal Declaration of Human Rights (UDHR) and to fulfil their obligations set forth in the International Covenant on Human and Political Rights (ICHPR). Both the UDHR and the ICHPR state: 'Everyone has the right to leave any country including his own.' See House of Representatives, 99th Congress, First Session, Committee on Foreign Affairs, Subcommittee on Europe and the Middle East and on Human Rights and International Organizations, *Hearings* (11 Sept. 1985) (Washington, DC: US Government Printing Office, 1985), p. 41.
6. Georgii Arbatov, 'America Also Needs Perestroika', Stephen F. Cohen and Katrina vanden Heuvel (eds.), *Voices of Glasnost: Interviews with Gorbachev's Reformers* (New York: Norton, 1989), p. 320.
7. Cullen, 'Soviet Jewry', p. 260.
8. William Korey, 'The Future of Soviet Jewry: Emigration and Assimilation', *Foreign Affairs* 58 (Fall, 1979), pp. 74–5; for a more detailed analysis of this aspect of Soviet policy see Korey, 'Soviet Decision-Making and the Problems of Soviet Jewish Emigration', *Survey* 22 (Winter, 1976), pp. 117–8.
9. See *Hearings* (9 and 10 Nov. 1971), *passim*.
10. Raymond L. Garthoff, *Détente and Confrontation: American-Soviet Relations from Nixon to Reagan* (Washington DC: Brookings Institution, 1985), pp. 304–5.
11. Yevgeny Velikhov, 'Chernobyl Remains on Our Mind', Cohen and vanden Heuvel (eds.), *Voices of Glasnost*, p. 170; Robert O. Freedman, 'Soviet Jewry and Soviet-American Relations: A Historical Analysis', in Freedman, *Soviet Jewry in the Decisive Decade*, p. 44; Garthoff, *Détente and Confrontation*, p. 309.
12. Garthoff, *Détente and Confrontation*, pp. 309–10; Freedman, 'Soviet Jewry and Soviet-American Relations', p. 45.
13. Garthoff, *Détente and Confrontation*, pp. 325, 327; Korey, 'Soviet Decision-Making', p. 125; Freedman, 'Soviet Jewry and Soviet-American Relations', p. 45.

14. Marshall Goldman, 'Soviet-American Trade and Soviet Jewish Emigration: Should a Policy Change Be Made by the American Jewish Community', in Robert O. Freedman (ed.), *Soviet Jewry in the 1980s: The Politics of Anti-Semitism and Emigration and the Dynamics of Resettlement* (Durham: Duke University Press, 1989) p. 149; Korey, 'Soviet Decision-Making', p. 126.
15. Garthoff, *Détente and Confrontation* , pp. 327, 404, 412; Freedman, 'Soviet Jewry and Soviet-American Relations', p. 46; Korey, 'The Future of Soviet Jewry', p. 76.
16. Korey, 'Soviet Decision-Making', p. 127; Freedman, 'Soviet Jewry and Soviet-American Relations', p. 45.
17. Garthoff, *Détente and Confrontation*, p. 460; a thorough analysis of the Jackson Amendment appears in William Korey, 'The Story of the Jackson Amendment', *Midstream* 21 (March, 1975), pp. 7–36.
18. Freedman, 'Soviet Jewry and Soviet-American Relations', pp. 467–70; Garthoff, *Détente and Confrontation*, pp. 453–4.
19. Cullen, 'Soviet Jewry', p. 260.
20. Minton F. Goldman, 'President Carter and the Soviet Union: The Influence of American Policy on the Kremlin's Decision to Intervene in Afghanistan', in R. Gordon Hoxie (ed.), *The Presidency and National Security Policy* (New York: Center for the Study of the Presidency, 1984), pp. 225–6.
21. Cullen, 'Soviet Jewry', p. 260.
22. Garthoff, *Détente and Confrontation*, p. 730; Cullen, 'Soviet Jewry', p. 261; Goldman, 'Soviet-American Trade and Soviet Jewish Emigration', p. 155.
23. Cullen, 'Soviet Jewry', p. 261; Goldman, 'Soviet-American Trade and Soviet Jewish Emigration', pp. 152–3, 155.
24. A. Petrov, 'Concerning Teng Hsiao Ping's Interview', *Pravda*, 1 Feb. 1979, in *Current Digest of the Soviet Press* XXXI, 28 Feb. 1979, pp. 1–2; 'On the American-Chinese Meeting', *Pravda* 4 Feb. 1979, in *Current Digest*, pp. 3–4.
25. Goldman, 'Soviet-American Trade and Soviet Jewish Emigration', p. 154.
26. Laurie Salitan, *Politics and Nationality in Soviet Jewish Emigration, 1968–1989* (New York: St. Martin's Press, 1992), p. 108, Table 1.
27. House of Representatives, 98th Congress, First Session, Committee on Foreign Affairs, Subcommittee on Human Rights and International Organizations, and Commission on Security and Cooperation in Europe, Subcommittee, *Hearing and Markup on H. Con. Res. 63* (23 and 28 June 1983) (Washington, DC: US Government Printing Office, 1984), pp. 47–8.
28. Secretary Shultz, 'Soviet Jewry and US-Soviet Relations', *Department of State Bulletin* (Dec., 1984), pp. 11–12.
29. 'Soviet Affirms That Spouses Will Go', Philip Taubman, 'Russians with Kin Are Leaving', 'Soviet Bars a Daughter's Emigration', *New York Times*, 6, 27, 31 Dec. 1985, respectively.
30. 'Soviets Reportedly Vow to Free Most Refuseniks', *Boston Globe*, 22 Dec. 1989.
31. See Natan Shcharansky, 'Jews' Summit Message to Gorbachev', *New York Times*, 30 Nov. 1987.
32. Michael R. Gordon, 'Shultz Holds Off on Soviet Emigrés', Robert Cullen, 'For A Quiet Deal On Soviet Emigrants', *New York Times*, 22 July 1988 and 30 Nov. 1988, respectively; see also Leon P. Baradat, *Soviet Political Society* (Englewood Cliffs, NJ: Prentice Hall, 1992), p. 364.
33. Robert Pear, 'US Bars Soviet Jews and Armenians as Refugees', *New York Times*, 3 Dec. 1988.
34. Robert Pear, 'Emigrés' Stooped Ceiling', *New York Times*, 14 Sept. 1989.
35. Ibid. In the article, Pear refers back to an interview from the previous year.
36. Ibid.
37. Robert Pear, 'Why US Closed the Door Halfway on Soviet Jews', *New York Times*, 24 Sept. 1989.
38. Ibid.
39. Pear, 'Emigrés' Stooped Ceiling'; 'Why US Closed the Door'.
40. Robert Cullen, 'For a Quiet Deal on Soviet Emigrants', *New York Times*, 30 Nov. 1988; Arbatov, 'America Also Needs Perestroika', p. 322.

41. Felicity Barringer, 'For Soviet Jews Emigration Poses a Decisive Dilemma', Michael Gordon, 'US Faces Flood of Soviet Emigrés', Robert Pear, 'US Bars Some Soviet Jews and Armenians as Refugees', *New York Times*, 6 Dec. 1987, 10 Nov. 1988 and 3 Dec. 1988, respectively; Steve Erlanger, 'Trying to Get Out: Soviet Jews Who Attempt to Emigrate Face Loss of Jobs, Prison', Betsy Glidwitz, 'The New Openness Excludes the Jews', *Boston Globe*, 11 March 1986 and 8 Feb. 1987, respectively; see also Gorlizki, 'Jews', pp. 344–7.
42. Pear, 'Emigrés' Stooped Ceiling'.
43. R. W. Apple, 'Bush Vows to Put Soviets in Group Favored in Trade', Keith Bradsher, 'Soviet Trade Pact Sent to Congress', *New York Times*, 31 July 1991 and 12 Sept. 1991, respectively.
44. This statistical information comes from the Action for Soviet Jewry, 24 Crescent Street, Waltham, Massachusetts.
45. United States Department of State, Office of Language Service, 'Draft Law of the USSR on the Procedures for Leaving and Entering the USSR for Citizens of the USSR', Xeroxed copy, LSN 135101 — Russia, pp. 1–17, especially Article 7, p. 7.

APPENDIX 22-1

SOVIET JEWISH EMIGRATION

May 1954-1994 = 976,481

Year	Total Number Emigrating	
1954	53	
1955	105	
1956	454	
1957	149	
1958	12	
1959	3	
	(776)	= Total for
1960	60	Decade Above
1961	202	
1962	184	
1963	305	
1964	537	
1965	891	
1966	2,047	
1967	1,406	
1968	229	
1969	2,979	
	(8,840)	
1970	1,027	
1971	13,022	
1972	31,681	
1973	34,733	
1974	20,628	
1975	13,221	
1976	14,261	
1977	16,736	
1978	28,865	
1979	51,320	
	(225,494)	
1980	21,471	
1981	9,447	
1982	2,688	
1983	1,315	
1984	896	
1985	1,139	
1986	914	
1987	8,155	
1988	18,919	
1989	71,196	
	(136,140)	
1990	181,802	
1991	178,566	
1992	108,292	
1993	102,134	
1994 (May)	34,437	
	(605,231)	

SOURCE: ACTION FOR POST-SOVIET JEWRY
Suite 306, 24 Crescent   Street, Waltham, MA 02154, U.S.A.

APPENDIX 22-2

SOVIET JEWISH EMIGRATION
MONTHLY TOTALS

YEAR	JAN	FEB	MAR	APR	MAY	JUN	JUL	AUG	SEP	OCT	NOV	DEC
1979	3722	3837	4418	4296	4163	4358	4068	4711	4663	4746	4193	4145
1980	2803	3023	3049	2469	1976	1767	1205	770	1307	1424	789	889
1981	850	1407	1249	1155	1141	866	779	430	405	368	363	434
1982	290	283	289	288	205	182	186	238	246	168	137	158
1983	81	125	101	114	116	102	167	130	135	91	56	97
1984	88	90	51	74	109	72	85	83	69	29	55	91
1985	61	88	97	166	51	36	174	29	92	124	128	92
1986	79	86	47	72	49	55	31	88	126	104	102	77
1987	98	146	470	717	877	790	819	787	724	912	910	899
1988	682	690	949	1017	1047	1385	1370	1780	2051	2068	2228	3652
1989	2796	2425	4240	4557	3779	4354	4537	6756	8442	9450	11170	8690
ISRAEL												
1990*	4700	5749	7300	10500	10202	11015	15283	17494	18725	20324	25186	34000
1991	13360	7164	13336	16286	16048	20473	10325	8688	9877	9845	8090	10359
1992	6237	4233	4913	4696	3361	3890	4872	5009	6725	6058	6250	6745
1993	6016	4324	6120	4060	4910	5512	3939	6113	6207	6187	6574	6591
1994	4750	3848	3933	4585	4581							
US												
1990	4846	5801	7257	4131	4176	822	413	414	617	294	967	2186
1991	1313	1790	2484	2212	2424	3228	2247	3269	4163	3891	3344	4350
1992	4353	3849	3498	3011	3608	2940	2941	4684	6073	3406	2896	4044
1993	3880	2424	2979	3379	2494	2846	2250	3364	2846	2781	2961	3377
1994	2782	2306	2768	2389	2405							

* 1990 onward lists figures for Israel and the U.S. separately. U.S. allows 40,000 Soviet Jews per year, or 3,333 per month. 1990 fell short of the quota and an additional 11,000 were to be allowed in in fiscal year 1991-1992.

Source: Action for Post-Soviet Jewry
Suite 306, 24 Crescent Street, Waltham, MA 02154, U.S.A.

APPENDIX 22-3 SOVIET JEWISH EMIGRATION TO ISRAEL AND THE UNITED STATES
JANUARY 1990–MAY 1994

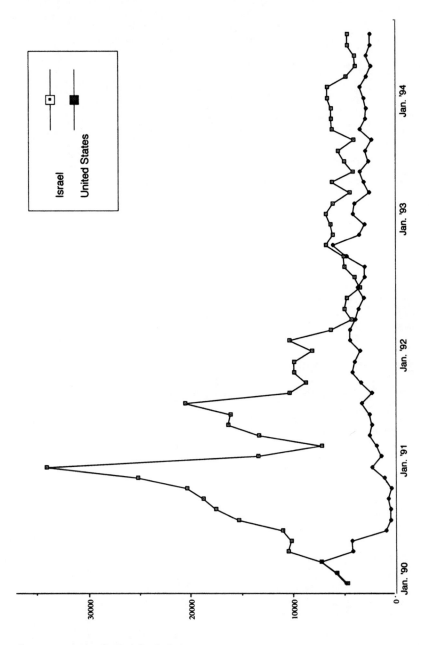

Source: Action for Post-Soviet Jewry
           See Table 22-2

VIII

DEMOGRAPHY AND EMIGRATION:
PAST TRENDS AND PROSPECTS

23

Trends in Soviet Jewish Demography since the Second World War

MARK TOLTS

Today's Jews of the former Soviet Union are a striking example of demographic decline.* The demographic evolution of the Soviet Jewish population is characterized by accelerated erosion over a long period: deaths increasingly exceeding births, dramatic aging, unbalanced sex ratios, and more intermarriage than inmarriage. As of the 1970s these phenomena were accompanied by large-scale emigration from the USSR.

Prior to the period of glasnost the relevant statistical data on Jewish demography in the USSR were mostly kept secret. Nevertheless, voluminous demographic information on Soviet Jewry was collected by population censuses and vital statistics. Whereas vital statistics are

* This paper is part of a broader research project being carried out by the author at the Division of Jewish Demography and Statistics, the Institute of Contemporary Jewry, the Hebrew University of Jerusalem. The project is being supported by the Israel Ministry of Immigrant Absorption. Sections of the paper are based on adaptations and updatings of Mark Tolts, 'The Balance of Births and Deaths among Soviet Jewry', *Jews and Jewish Topics in the Soviet Union and Eastern Europe* 2, 18 (1992) and 'Changes in the Composition of the Jewish Population of the USSR: Aging and the Marriage Market', paper presented at the Third Canada-CIS Academic Dialogue on Jewish Themes, 22—25 December 1992, Jerusalem (forthcoming in *Yahadut zmanenu* 9, 1994).

The author wishes to express his appreciation to Prof. Sergio DellaPergola for his advice. Dr. Evgeny Andreev, Mr. Dmitry Bogoiavlensky and Dr. Leonid Darsky offered some important data for this chapter. The author is grateful to Prof. Sidney Goldstein and other colleagues for their comments and to Mrs. Judith Even for reading and editing an earlier draft. Responsibility for the content of the paper is, of course, the author's alone.

based on legal ethnic status and the census is dependent on self-declaration, the two sources can be used together. A majority of scholars agree that the Soviet census figures on Jewish ethnic nationality (adults only) correspond very closely with 'legal' ethnic nationality as recorded in internal passports.

DECLINE AND CRISIS OF THE JEWISH POPULATION

According to official censuses, between 1959 and 1989 the Jewish population of the USSR fell from 2,267,814 to 1,450,511. (These data as all others in the text include Ashkenazi Jews, Georgian Jews, Mountain Jews, Central Asian (Bukharan) Jews and Krymchaks, but not Karaites). Within this period the percentage of Jews in the total population of the country declined from 1.1 to 0.5 per cent.

As already stated, these numbers are based entirely on self-declaration of persons in the censuses. Conceptually, they correspond to what has been defined as the 'core Jewish population'.[1] By definition, the 'core' population does not include persons of Jewish origin who reported another ethnic nationality in the census. The alternative definition of the 'enlarged Jewish population' includes Jews and their non-Jewish family members, and this group may be significantly larger than the 'core' Jewish population (see below).

Before the 1970s almost the entire decrease in the USSR's Jewish population was caused by internal processes: the balance of births and deaths, and assimilation. Between the 1970 and 1989 censuses, more than 290,000 Soviet Jews (and their non-Jewish family members) left the USSR. Significantly, however, this large emigration caused only about 42 per cent of the decrease of the Jewish population in this period; most of the decline in numbers (approximately 58 per cent) was still due to internal processes.[2]

Over the three decades from 1959 to 1989 the number of births to Jewish mothers fell dramatically by 65 per cent. During the same period, the total number of births to at least one Jewish parent fell by 53 per cent — even if we assume the number of children born to non-Jewish mothers and Jewish fathers to be twice that born to Jewish mothers and non-Jewish fathers. On the other hand, the number of Jewish deaths rose by 39 per cent despite the fact that the population of Soviet Jewry fell by a third (Table 23-1).

Over the period from 1958 to the late 1960s, the ratio of Jewish deaths to births worsened, from 1:1.37 to more than 1:1. In 1989 Jewish deaths in the USSR exceeded births by a ratio of approximately 3:1; in the RFSFR it reached roughly 4:1 (Table 23-2).

TABLE 23–1 Jewish Population, Births and Deaths in the USSR, 1959 and 1989

	1959	1989	1989 as % of 1959	% of total pop./events 1959	% of total pop./events 1989
Number of Jewish population	2,267,814	1,450,511	64	1.09	0.51
Number of children born to:					
endogamous Jewish couples	22,567	5,507	24	0.43	0.11
Jewish mothers	27,854	9,699	35	0.53	0.19
at least one Jewish parent:[a]					
equality hypothesis	33,100	13,900	42	0.63	0.27
two-fold hypothesis	38,400	18,100	47	0.73	0.36
Number of Jewish deaths	21,686	30,196	139	1.35	1.05

a. See note to Table 7.

Sources: TsSU SSSR, *Naselenie SSSR, 1973: Statisticheskii sbornik* (Moscow: Statistika, 1975), pp. 37, 69; Goskomstat SSSR, *Demograficheskii ezhegodnik SSSR, 1990 g.* (Moscow: Finansy i statistika, 1990), p. 91; Goskomstat SSSR, *Natsional'nyi sostav naseleniia SSSR: Po dannym vsesoiuznoi perepisi naseleniia 1989 g.* (Moscow: Finansy i statistika, 1991), pp. 20–26; and unpublished data of the former Soviet Central Statistical Administration.

TABLE 23–2 Evolution of the Vital Index[a] of the Jewish Population, 1958–1989

Republic	1958	1968	1978	1988	1989
USSR	137	..	..	37	32
RSFSR	100	56	40	27	24
West					
Ukraine	127	59	41	30	26
Belorussia	224	91	77	52	40
Moldavia	244	94c	75	49	42
Baltic					
Latvia	179	73	62	..	29
Lithuania	192b	100	69	46	40
Transcaucasia					
Azerbaidzhan	208	116	122d	..	89
Georgia	260	199	(135)	79e	..
Central Asia					
Uzbekistan	289	181c	136d	128	118
Tadzhikistan	390	276	264	191	160
Kazakhstan	218	93c	60	59	45

a. Percent ratio of the number of all children born to Jewish mothers to the number of Jewish deaths.
b. 1959.
c. 1967.
d. 1977.
e. 1987.

Source: Unpublished data of the former Soviet Central Statistical Administration.

The data indicate that an unfavourable balance of births and deaths first occurred in the RFSFR in the 1950s, and in other European republics in the 1960s, before the large-scale emigration of the 1970s. On the eve of the great exodus, the balance was positive only in the Asiatic republics (Tadzhikistan and Uzbekistan).

The data also clearly show that the vital crisis of Soviet Jewry is not linked to levels of longevity, but rather to the decline in fertility. The longevity of the Jewish population is at present among the highest in the former USSR. Life expectancy at birth for the Soviet Jews in 1988/89 was 70.1 for males and 73.7 for females.[3]

The fertility of Soviet Jews has for a long time been too low to ensure replacement. Total Jewish fertility in Russia has not exceeded 1.6 children per woman, at least in the generations born since the beginning of the 20th century.[4] According to data from the census of 1989, the average number of children ever born to Jewish women aged 45–49 in the RFSFR was 1.3. The main cause appears to be low marital fertility. Soviet Jewry did not experience a postwar baby boom like that of many Western, including Jewish, populations.[5]

AGE/SEX STRUCTURAL CORRELATES OF DEMOGRAPHIC EROSION

Since World War II the age structure of the Soviet Jewish population has become substantially older, a fact which is linked to the fertility decline discussed above. According to data from the 1989 census of Jews in the USSR, the population aged 65 and over reached 24 per cent of the total, or approximately 2.7 times more than in 1959 (Table 23-3).

Today's ex-Soviet Jewish population is very aged. According to data from the 1989 census, the median age was 49.7, more than ten years older then three decades ago, and nineteen years older than the median of the total Soviet population.

Soviet Jewry is one of the most aged Jewish populations in the world: in 1990 the median age of American Jewry was 37.3 and that of Israeli Jews was 28.4. On the eve of the great exodus, Soviet Jewry included 153,513 persons aged 75 and over. At the end of 1988 in Israel, with a total Jewish population 2.5 times the size of USSR Jewry, the number of Jews in this age group was only 155,200.[6]

There is considerable differentiation of aging among Jews of the former union republics. Russian Jewry is the most aged Jewish population of the former USSR. The data on age composition show that by 1970 Russian Jewry had already reached what has been defined as the 'terminal stage' of demographic evolution, when the proportion of those under 15 fell to 10 per cent.[7] Ukrainian Jewry had by 1979 also reached this stage of demographic evolution.

TABLE 23–3 Jews in the USSR, USA and Israel, and Total Population in the USSR, by Age Group, Late 1950s–1989/90, Per Cent

Population group and year	All ages	0–14	15–64	65+	Thereof 75+	Median age
USSR – Jews						
1959[a]	100.0	17.0	74.2	8.8	2.3	39.2
1970	100.0	13.7	71.1	15.2	4.0	43.1
1979	100.0	11.3	66.8	21.9	7.0	46.6
1989	100.0	11.6	64.8	23.6	10.6	49.7
USSR – Total						
1959	100.0	29.6	64.2	6.2	2.1	26.6
1970	100.0	29.0	63.2	7.8	..	29.3
1979	100.0	24.8	65.7	9.5	3.1	29.1
1989	100.0	25.8	65.2	9.0	3.8	30.7
USA – Jews						
1957	100.0	23	68	10	..	36.7
1970	100.0	21.2	66.8	12.0	3.9	35.5
1980	100.0	16.2	68.3	15.5	5.6	34.8
1990	100.0	19.0	63.9	17.2	8	37.3
Israel – Jews						
1960	100.0	34.8	60.1	5.1	1.5	25.6
1970	100.0	30.0	62.8	7.2	2.0	24.7
1980	100.0	30.5	59.8	9.7	3.1	26.8
1990	100.0	28.7	60.8	10.5	4.4	28.4

a. Ashkenazi Jews (the data cover the RSFSR, the Ukraine, Belorussia, Lithuania, Latvia, Estonia, Moldavia and Azerbaidzhan).

Sources:
S. Goldstein, 'American Jewry, 1970: A Demographic Profile', *American Jewish Year Book*, Vol. 72 (1971), p. 58; Goldstein, 'Profile of American Jewry: Insights from the 1990 National Jewish Population Survey', *American Jewish Year Book*, Vol. 92 (1992), pp. 105, 155; *Statistical Abstract of Israel, 1992* (Jerusalem: Central Bureau of Statistics, 1992), p. 87; U. O. Schmelz and S. DellaPergola, 'The Demographic Consequences of US Jewish Population Trends, *American Jewish Year Book*, Vol. 83 (1983), p. 144–5; Goskomstat SSSR, *Naselenie SSSR, 1987: Statisticheskii sbornik* (Moscow: Finansy i statistika, 1988), p. 48; Goskomstat SSSR, *Demograficheskii ezhegodnik SSSR, 1990*, p. 27; and unpublished data of the former Soviet Central Statistical Administration.

In 1970 the Jews of the RFSFR and all the European republics had a median age of over 40 (except Lithuania with 39.5 years). The Jewish population of the Asiatic republics was younger with a median age of 30–32 (Table 23-4).

TABLE 23–4 Jews in Union Republics, by Age Group, According to the 1970 Census, Per Cent[a]

Republic	All ages	0–14	15–29	30–44	45–64	65+	Median age
USSR	100.0	13.7	16.8	22.6	31.7	15.2	43.1
RSFSR	100.0	10.3	15.7	23.1	33.9	17.0	45.5
West							
Ukraine	100.0	12.6	15.7	22.3	33.0	16.4	44.7
Belorussia	100.0	16.5	18.3	24.3	27.7	13.2	40.1
Moldavia	100.0	15.8	19.9	20.9	31.2	12.2	40.8
Baltic							
Estonia	100.0	10.2	17.1	25.4	34.3	13.0	43.6
Latvia	100.0	13.2	20.3	21.0	33.9	11.6	42.2
Lithuania	100.0	15.2	23.4	20.2	31.9	9.3	39.5
Transcaucasia							
Azerbaidzhan	100.0	28.5	18.2	20.3	21.8	11.2	32.2
Georgia	100.0	28.6	21.2	22.6	19.7	7.9	30.1
Central Asia							
Uzbekistan	100.0	26.6	20.2	21.9	21.5	9.8	31.9

a. Population of known age.

Source: Unpublished data of the former Soviet Central Statistical Administration.

In the period between the 1970 and 1989 censuses, only the age group 75 and above increased steadily in absolute numbers in all republics, with the exception of Georgia. During the same period, in the RFSFR, Estonia and Latvia, the number of Jews of this age group actually doubled. In most of the republics the number of Jews aged 65 and above also increased. The number of Jews in all the age groups under 65 decreased in all the republics.[8]

In 1989 more than 20 per cent of the Jews were aged 65 and above in the RFSFR and all the European republics, and that age group outnumbered children under 15. The differentiation between republics had grown. In the RFSFR and the Ukraine the median age reached 52.3 and 51.6, respectively, whereas in Tadzhikistan and Uzbekistan it was only 30 and 32.6 (Table 23-5).

TABLE 23–5 Jews in Union Republics, by Age Group, according to the 1989 census, per cent[a]

Republic	All ages	0–14	15–29	30–44	45–64	65+	Median age
USSR	100.0	11.6	13.0	20.2	31.6	23.6	49.7
RSFSR	100.0	8.4	11.4	19.5	33.8	26.9	52.3
West							
Ukraine	100.0	9.7	12.0	19.8	33.2	25.3	51.6
Belorussia	100.0	12.5	13.7	21.8	31.8	20.2	47.0
Moldavia	100.0	16.4	13.5	23.9	26.0	20.2	42.7
Baltic							
Estonia	100.0	11.3	11.7	23.0	31.4	22.6	48.7
Latvia	100.0	12.4	12.7	22.8	28.8	23.3	47.1
Lithuania	100.0	15.1	13.7	24.0	26.1	21.1	43.4
Transcaucasia							
Azerbaidzhan	100.0	22.3	20.7	19.4	23.8	13.8	34.5
Georgia	100.0	20.0	20.3	20.9	26.1	12.7	36.5
Central Asia							
Uzbekistan	100.0	25.4	20.6	20.2	22.5	11.3	32.6
Tadzhikistan	100.0	28.9	21.1	20.2	21.3	8.5	30.0

a. Population of known age.
Source: Unpublished data of the former Soviet Central Statistical Administration.

A distinctive feature of the age structure of the Soviet Jewish population in the postwar period is its 'regressive' nature, that is, younger generations tend to be consistently less numerous.

MIXED MARRIAGE AND ITS CONSEQUENCES

An examination of the ratio of females to males in the relevant age groups shows the limited possibilities for Soviet Jewish males to select a suitable marriage partner from their own ethnic group. The shortage of potential partners has been very pronounced. In 1989, for example, the number of Jewish males aged 25–29 exceeded by almost one-third the corresponding number of females aged 20–24. The opposite situation exists within the total urban population: in most instances, there is a shortage of potential male marriage partners.[9] Partly as a result of this situation of imbalance, many Jewish males found wives outside the Jewish group.

In the postwar period one of the most characteristic features of Soviet Jewry was the great rise in mixed marriages. This increase was a continuation of a process which had already begun between the two world wars.[10] In 1988 in the USSR as a whole, among Jews who married, 58.3 per cent of males and 47.6 per cent of females entered into mixed marriages. Ethnically mixed marriages were widespread in the former USSR, and Jews were no exception among the relatively small and widely dispersed ethnic groups.[11]

Among Jews, the leading place in mixed marriage was held by the Jewish population of the RFSFR. In 1988 the frequency of mixed marriages among all marriages involving Jews in the RFSFR was 73.2 per cent for Jewish men and 62.8 per cent for Jewish women — a relative increase of 23 per cent and 46 per cent respectively, as compared to 1978. Within Russian Jewry mixed marriages became more prevalent especially among those males and females marrying under the age of 20, although not many Jewish males married early (Table 23-6).

TABLE 23–6 Percentage of mixed marriages among all Jewish marriages In RSFSR, Ukraine and Belorussia, by age group, 1978 and 1988, according to marriage registration statistics

Sex and age group	RSFSR		Ukraine		Belorussia	
	1978	1988	1978	1988	1978	1988
Males						
Total	59.3	73.2	44.7	54.1	38.3	48.3
under 20	69.6	84.4	55.0	70.1	59.0	63.6
20–24	57.8	73.6	45.0	53.4	38.2	51.4
25–29	53.6	69.1	42.5	55.4	37.3	48.6
30–34	64.8	72.6	49.1	57.4	41.7	42.5
35–39	67.2	75.3	56.7	56.0	41.1	60.9
40–44	66.0	77.5	56.9	59.1	53.7	45.7
45–49	68.4	78.6	44.8	61.2	55.6	68.6
50–54	70.5	77.7	48.0	57.4	32.1	55.2
55+	50.8	69.9	33.4	43.5	23.9	33.1
Females						
Total	43.0	62.8	34.2	44.7	26.1	39.9
under 20	41.8	71.3	35.2	50.9	31.3	49.1
20–24	42.8	61.1	33.9	49.5	21.3	39.4
25–29	43.7	67.1	38.7	46.8	33.1	40.1
30–34	51.4	69.5	39.4	50.8	41.6	47.1
35–39	48.7	64.7	41.2	51.6	48.6	49.2
40–44	53.6	68.4	40.9	44.8	27.3	42.9
45–49	47.7	59.6	43.0	37.9	33.3	55.6
50–54	38.1	57.9	28.9	34.5	17.9	16.0
55+	27.0	20.9	20.9	19.8	8.9	18.4

Source: Computed from data in Goskomstat SSSR, *Naselenie SSSR, 1988: Statisticheskii ezhegodnik* (Moscow: Finansy i statistika, 1989), pp. 212–3.

The higher frequency of mixed marriages among men reflects the already mentioned peculiarities of the Jewish population structure, namely the 'shortage' of women. A more balanced Jewish age-sex structure, as for example in the US, would probably be associated with a more similar ratio of mixed marriage by sex of spouses.[12]

In the postwar period rising intermarriage was accompanied by a great increase in the proportion of children born to mixed couples. The percentage of these children among all children born to Jewish mothers in 1989 in the USSR reached 43 per cent, or 2.3 times more than in 1959. However, approximately twice as many Jewish men were currently married to non-Jewish women in the USSR as Jewish women currently married to non-Jewish men.[13] Hence, the proportion of children born to mixed couples as a whole among all newborn children with at least one Jewish parent was probably about 40 per cent in the late 1950s and may have approached 70 per cent in the late 1980s (Table 23-7).

TABLE 23–7 Percentage of children of mixed origin, 1959 and 1989

| Republic | Among all children born to Jewish mothers | | Among all children born to at least one Jewish parent | | | |
| | | | Equality hypothesis | | Two-fold hypothesis | |
	1959	1989	1959	1989	1959	1989
USSR	19.0	43.2	32	60	41	70
RSFSR	26.6	59.2	42	74	52	81
West						
Ukraine	17.5	46.8	30	64	39	73
Belorussia	14.0	37.8	25	55	33	65
Moldavia	7.0	20.6	13	34	19	44
Baltic						
Latvia	16.9	37.1	29	54	38	64
Lithuania	12.7	30.0	23	46	30	56
Transcaucasia						
Azerbaidzhan	15.2	30.9	26	47	35	57
Georgia	8.7	34.9	16	52	22	62
Central Asia						
Uzbekistan	10.4	13.3	19	24	26	32
Tadzhikistan	14.6	14.1	25	25	34	33
Kazakhstan	40.5	52.1	58	69	67	77

Note: According to the equality hypothesis, the number of children born to non-Jewish mothers and Jewish fathers was equal to the number of children born to Jewish mothers and non-Jewish fathers. According to the two-fold hypothesis, the number of children born to non-Jewish mothers and Jewish fathers was twice the number born to Jewish mothers and non-Jewish fathers.

Sources: M. Tolts, 'The Balance of Births and Deaths among Soviet Jewry', *Jews and Jewish Topics in the Soviet Union and Eastern Europe* 2, 18 (1992), pp. 19, 26; Tolts, 'Jews in the Russian Republic since the Second World War: The Dynamics of Demographic Erosion', *International Population Conference, Montreal 1993: Proceedings*, Vol. 3, p. 106; and unpublished data of the former Soviet Central Statistical Administration.

There is considerable differentiation in the level of this indicator between Jews of the former union republics. It can be assumed that in the RFSFR the proportion of children born to mixed couples as a whole among all newborn children with at least one Jewish parent perhaps even approached 80 per cent on the eve of the great exodus. However, this proportion was only between a quarter to one-third in Uzbekistan and Tadzhikistan.

All data on the offspring of mixed couples in the Soviet Union show a clear preference for the national affiliation of the non-Jewish spouse. This preference was even greater among couples where the wife was Jewish.[14] A comparison of vital statistics and census data shows that in the RFSFR only between 17 and 26 per cent of children born to mixed couples in 1988 were reported as Jews in the 1989 census. However, the proportion of children born to mixed couples out of all children less than one year old who were reported as Jews in the 1989 census in the RFSFR was rather high: 42 per cent. In the USSR as a whole this proportion was 31 per cent (Table 23-8).

TABLE 23–8 Children of mixed origin reported Jewish, under one year of age, in the 1989 census[a]

Republic	Percentage of children of mixed origin among all children reported as Jewish	Percentage of children reported Jewish among all children of mixed origin born 1988[b]	
		Equality hypothesis	Two-fold hypothesis
USSR	31	..	..
RSFSR	42	26	17
West			
Ukraine	22	19	13
Belorussia	17	18	12
Moldavia	22	..	..
Baltic			
Latvia	29	44	29
Lithuania	42	..	..
Transcaucasia			
Azerbaidzhan	36	51	34
Central Asia			
Uzbekistan	26	..	..
Tadzhikistan	29	..	..

a. Estimate based on comparison of vital statistics and census data.
b. See note to Table 7.

Sources: Tolts, 'The Balance of Births and Deaths among Soviet Jewry', pp. 16–17; Tolts, 'Jews in the Russian Republic since the Second World War', pp. 106–7; and unpublished data of the former Soviet Central Statistical Administration.

THE BALANCE OF BIRTHS AND DEATHS

Based on the different sources of data available and alternative assumptions, we can construct various birth and death balances for Soviet Jewry. The estimates of all births of children of Jewish parentage show the total results of Jewish fertility. 'Effectively Jewish' fertility, or the number of newborns who are identified as Jews,[15] has here been estimated according to census data on children under one year old. Moreover, one can estimate the extent to which offspring of mixed couples were declared as Jewish and the number of children of Jewish parentage who were brought up as Jews. Mortality data utilized to draw up the several Jewish population balances are based on available statistics of Jewish deaths (Table 23-9).

TABLE 23–9 Balances of Crude Birth and Death Rates in the USSR Per 1,000 Jews, 1958/59 and 1988/89

	1958/59	1988/89
1. Endogamous crude birth rate	9.9	4.3
2. Crude birth rate of Jewish mothers	12.3	7.3
3. Crude birth rate of Jewish parents:[a]		
a. Equality hypothesis	14.6	10.4
b. Two-fold hypothesis	17.0	13.5
4. 'Effectively Jewish' crude birth rate	9.4[b]	6.8[c]
5. Crude death rate	9.3	21.3
6. Balance of endogamous crude birth rate and crude death rate [(6)=(1)-(5)]	0.6	-17.0
7. Balance of crude birth rate of Jewish mothers and crude death rate [(7)=(2)-(5)]	3.0	-14.0
8. Balance of crude birth rate of Jewish parents and crude death rate:		
a. Equality hypothesis [(8a)=(3a)-(5)]	5.3	-10.9
b. Two-fold hypothesis [(8b)=(3b)-(5)]	7.7	-7.8
9. Balance of 'effectively Jewish' crude birth rate and crude death rate [(9)=(4)-(5)]	0.1	-14.5

a. See note to Table 7.
b. According to 1959 census data on number of children under one year old who were reported as Jewish, for Ashkenazi Jews (the data cover the RSFSR, the Ukraine, Belorussia, Lithuania, Latvia, Estonia, Moldavia and Azerbaidzhan).
c. According to 1989 census data on number of children under one year old who were reported as Jewish.

Sources: Tolts, 'The Balance of Births and Deaths among Soviet Jewry', pp. 18, 20, 23; and unpublished data of the former Soviet Central Statistical Administration.

The balances of Jewish population change reported here relate to quantitatively different aspects of internal processes among the Jewish population in the USSR. All balances presented here indicate a sufficiently consistent picture, which in various ways reveals a decline in the capacity of the Soviet Jewish population to replace itself. During the three decades from 1958–59 to 1988–89 there was a radical change in these balances. By the end of the 1980s, all of them were decidedly negative.

On the eve of the great exodus, for the Jews of the RFSFR and all the European republics, even balances of the crude birth rate to Jewish parents (regardless of Jewish identification of the new-born) and the crude Jewish death rate were negative (Table 23-10).

TABLE 23–10 Balances of Crude Birth Rate of Jewish Parents and Crude Death Rate, Per 1,000 Jews, 1958/59 and 1988/89

Republic	Birth rate of Jewish parents[a]		Death rate		Balance	
	1958/59	1988/89	1958/59	1988/89	1958/59	1988/89
USSR	17.0	13.5	9.3	21.3	7.7	-7.8
RSFSR	15.6	13.6	10.2	24.4	5.4	-10.8
West						
Ukraine	15.2	12.4	9.4	23.4	5.8	-11.0
Belorussia	19.8	13.5	7.4	17.9	12.4	-4.4
Moldavia	15.1	10.7	6.0	17.1	9.1	-6.4
Baltic						
Latvia	15.6	11.7	6.9	18.3	8.7	-6.6
Lithuania	14.0	12.2	6.0[b]	17.8	8.0	-5.6
Transcaucasia						
Azerbaidzhan	30.0	22.1	9.6	13.8[c]	20.4	8.3
Georgia	27.4	..	9.2	..	18.2	..
Central Asia						
Uzbekistan	27.1	16.9	8.6	10.9	18.5	6.0
Tadzhikistan	29.8	19.1	6.1	8.4	23.7	10.7
Kazakhstan	26.0	16.6	7.9	16.6	18.1	0.0

a. According to the two-fold hypothesis (see note to Table 7).
b. 1959.
c. 1989.

Sources: Tolts, 'The Balance of Births and Deaths among Soviet Jewry', p. 18; Tolts, 'Jews in the Russian Republic since the Second World War', p. 107; and unpublished data of the former Soviet Central Statistical Administration.

HOUSEHOLD COMPOSITION:
'CORE' AND 'ENLARGED' JEWISH POPULATION

Soviet censuses recorded data on the number of ethnically homo-geneous (uninational) Jewish family (versus non-family) households. Soviet statistics provide no data on the number of multinational (mixed) Jewish family households, but this lacuna can be overcome.[16]

We computed estimates based on the average size of uninational Jewish family households and on the percentages living in family households among the total urban population in the respective former union republics and the USSR as a whole. According to our estimates, in the RSFSR between 1979 and 1989, the total number of Jewish family households fell by 11–13 per cent. During the same period, the decline in the number of Jewish uninational family households reached 30 per cent (Table 23-11).

TABLE 23–11 Jewish uninational and multinational family households, Russia, 1979 and 1989, and the USSR, 1989

	Russia 1979	Russia 1989	USSR 1989	Russia as % of USSR 1989
Number of Jewish uninational family households	127,281	88,608	280,100	32
Number of Jewish multinational family households				
minimum estimate	124,700	130,900	223,750	59
maximum estimate	236,948	235,552	447,500	53
Total number of family households with Jewish presence				
minimum estimate	251,981	219,508	503,850	44
maximum estimate	364,229	324,160	727,600	45
Percentage of multinational family households among total number of family households with Jewish presence				
minimum estimate	49	60	44	..
maximum estimate	65	73	62	..

Note: Minimum estimate based on assumption that there was only one non-Jew in each Jewish multinational family household. Maximum estimate based on assumption that there was only one Jew in each Jewish multinational family household.

Sources: Goskomstat SSSR, *Sem'ia v SSSR: po dannym vsesoiuznoi perepisi naseleniia 1989 g.* (Moscow: Finansy i statistika, 1990), p. 14; A. Sinel'nikov, 'Nekotorye demo-graficheskie posledstviia assimiliatsii evreev v SSSR', *Vestnik Evreiskogo Universiteta v Moskve*, 1, 5 (1994) p. 91; Tolts, 'Jews in the Russian Republic since the Second World War', p. 108.

In other Slavic republics the decline in the number of Jewish uninational family households was not quite as great: 28 per cent in the Ukraine and 23 per cent in Belorussia.

Between 1979 and 1989, the proportion of Jews living in ethnically heterogeneous households among all Russian Jews living in family households rose from 39 to 49 per cent. During the same period, the corresponding proportions in the Ukraine and Belorussia rose from 23 to 31 per cent, and from 16 to 25 per cent, respectively. These comparisons emphasize Russian Jewry's more advanced stage of ethnic assimilation.

In 1989, 32 per cent of all the USSR's Jewish uninational family households were in the RSFSR, whereas more than half of the Jewish multinational family households were there.

As noted above, the 'enlarged' Jewish population is the total aggregate of all Jews and their non-Jewish family members.[17] Theoretically, stagnation or decline of a 'core' Jewish population can occur concomitantly with the growth of the respective 'enlarged' Jewish population, as has been shown by American Jewry.[18]

To estimate the 'enlarged' Jewish population, we must add to the known 'core' Jewish population living in uninational family units, or outside any family households, all members of Jewish multinational family households. The latter group may be estimated by multiplying the number of such multinational households by the average size of Jewish family households.

Based on these assumptions, in the late 1980s the ratio of 'core' to 'enlarged' Jewish population in the RFSFR was roughly 1:1.8, and in the USSR as a whole about 1:1.6 (Table 23-12). We estimated that in 1989 the 'enlarged' Jewish population in the USSR was 2,345,500. In that year 38 per cent of the 'core' Jewish population of the Soviet Union, and 42 per cent of the 'enlarged' Soviet Jewish population, lived in the RSFSR.

According to our estimates based on the dynamics of family households, not only the 'core' but also the 'enlarged' Jewish population in the RSFSR in the 1980s was decreasing. Calculations based on vital statistics data for 1988/89 confirm this decline. A similar situation existed in the Ukraine.

By the eve of the recent great exodus, Soviet Jewry as a whole had reached a stage of extreme demographic erosion.

TABLE 23–12 'Enlarged' Jewish population,[a] by components, Russia, 1979 and 1989, and the USSR, 1989

	Russia 1979	Russia 1989	USSR 1989	Russa as % of USSR 1989
Jews living outside family households	94,588	65,905	174,100	38
Jews living in uninational family households[b]	369,115	249,590	828,900[c]	30
Jews living in multinational family households	236,948	235,552	447,500	53
'Core' Jewish population[b]	700,651	551,047	1,450,500	38
Non-Jewish members of multinational family households w/Jewish presence[d]	450,200	424,000	895,000	47
'Enlarged' Jewish population	1,150,851	975,047	2,345,500	42

a. Maximum estimate
b. Census figure
c. The result of slight adjustments which compensated for 2 per cent who lived in Armenia, Kazakhstan, Kirgiziia and Turkmenia
d. Excluding persons living in households without 'core' Jews

Source: See sources to Table 23–1 and 23–11

RECENT TRENDS

Up until the late 1980s the main factor in Jewish population decrease in the Soviet Union, as delineated above, was the negative balance of births and deaths. Since 1989, the situation has been changing dramatically due to the great Jewish exodus from the USSR. In 1989–93 alone, more than 700,000 Jews (and their non-Jewish family members) emigrated. By the end of 1992 the number of Jews in the former Soviet Union had fallen to 890,000,[19] and we may assume that by early 1994, this figure dropped to less than 800,000. By this time the 'enlarged' Jewish population, which includes non-Jewish members of Jewish families fell to a roughly estimated one and a half million. The main factor in Jewish population decrease in the former USSR as a whole has become emigration.

At the same time, the vital crisis of (ex-)Soviet Jewry is rapidly intensifying. One of the main reasons for this is the selective character of emigration, which has considerably intensified the aging of the Jewish population in the former USSR.

As result, by 1990 the ratio of Jewish deaths to births by Jewish mothers in the USSR had increased to 4:1 (the data did not cover Georgia). In the RFSFR this ratio in 1990 was 5.4:1; in 1991 it was 7.2:1, and in 1992, 8.3:1. In 1990 even in Uzbekistan Jewish deaths exceeded births to Jewish mothers.

In the short period between 1989 and 1991 in the RFSFR, the number of births to Jewish mothers fell by 44 per cent. During this same time span, the total number of births to at least one Jewish parent fell by 40 per cent, even if we again assume the number of children born to non-Jewish mothers and Jewish fathers to be twice that born to Jewish mothers and non-Jewish fathers. However, the number of Jewish deaths fell by only 2 per cent, despite the fact that the number of Jews in the RFSFR had, by the end of 1991, fallen by 22 per cent.[20]

The situation became so unbalanced that in 1991 in the RFSFR, the number of births to Jewish mothers was only 4 per 1,000 Jews and the number of Jewish deaths exceeded these births by 24 per 1,000.

These processes have been accompanied by a continuing increase in the proportion of children born to mixed couples. In 1990, the percentage of such children among all children born to Jewish mothers in the USSR (excluding Georgia) reached 48 per cent, but in the RFSFR this percentage was 63 per cent and in 1991–92 it was as high as 67–68 per cent.

In 1992 in the RFSFR only 472 children were born to endogamous Jewish couples, a drop of 64 per cent from the 1989 figure. The percentage of such children among all children born to at least one Jewish parent had fallen to 14–19 per cent. In the former USSR as a whole for 1993, the total number of children born to endogamous Jewish couples can be estimated at about one thousand.

A discussion of the policy implications of the latest demographic trends among (ex-)Soviet Jewry is beyond the scope of the present paper.[21] It will suffice here to note the direct demographic consequences such as aging and the growth of mixed marriages.

The incidence of mixed marriages among (ex-)Soviet Jews, which, in general, reflected the growing cultural and social assimilation of the Jewish population, has become more acute due to the development of a severe age-sex imbalance among Jews of marriageable age. The recent great exodus can only intensify the erosion of the Jewish marriage market in the former USSR and this will, of necessity, lead to a further increase in mixed marriages and in the percentage of children born to mixed couples. In turn, the emigration of young people, many of whom are of mixed origin, intensifies the shrinkage of the 'enlarged' Jewish population.

TRENDS IN SOVIET JEWISH DEMOGRAPHY

From all the above, we may conclude that the demographic basis of (ex-)Soviet Jewry has been undermined, and it definitively lacks the demographic forces required for self-renewal.

NOTES

1. See U. O. Schmelz and Sergio DellaPergola, 'World Jewish Population, 1992', *American Jewish Year Book, 1994* (Philadelphia: Jewish Publication Society of America, 1994).
2. Y. Florsheim, 'Yetziat ha-yehudim mi-Brit ha-Mo'atsot be-shanim 1979–1988 ve-hashpa'ata al yahadut Brit ha-Mo'atsot', *Yahadut zmanenu* 6 (1990), p. 309 ; and V. Konstantinov, 'Jewish Population of the USSR on the Eve of the Great Exodus', *Jews and Jewish Topics in the Soviet Union and Eastern Europe* 3, 16 (1991), p. 6.
3. E. M. Andreev, V. M. Dobrovol'skaia and K. Iu. Shaburov, 'Etnicheskaia differentsiatsiia smertnosti', *Sotsiologicheskie issledovaniia* 7 (1992), p. 45.
4. Mark Tolts, 'The Balance of Births and Deaths among Soviet Jewry', *Jews and Jewish Topics in the Soviet Union and Eastern Europe* 2, 18 (1992) p. 24.
5. See G. Bondarskaia and L. Darskii, 'Etnicheskaia differentsiatsiia rozhdaemosti v SSSR', *Vestnik statistiki* 12 (1988), p. 20.
6. *Statistical Abstract of Israel 1989* (Jerusalem: Central Bureau of Statistics, 1989), p. 78.
7. Sergio DellaPergola, 'Major Demographic Trends of World Jewry: The Last Hundred Years', in B. Bonne-Tamir and A. Adam (eds.), *Genetic Diversity among Jews* (New York: Oxford University Press, 1992), p. 26.
8. See Mark Tolts, 'Changes in the Composition of the Jewish Population of the USSR: Aging and the Marriage Market', paper presented at the Third Canada-CIS Academic Dialogue on Jewish Themes, 22–25 December 1992, The Hebrew University, Jerusalem.
9. Mark Tolts, 'Jewish Marriages in the USSR: A Demographic Analysis', *East European Jewish Affairs* 2 (1992), p. 4.
10. Mordechai Altshuler, 'Nesuei-ta'arovet be-kerev yehudei Brit ha-Mo'atsot bein milhamot ha-olam', *Shvut* 13 (1988), pp. 31–40; Mark Kupovetsky, 'Mi-toshavei ayarot le-integratsia ironit — ha-yehudim bi-Vrit ha-Mo'atsot bein shtei milhamot ha-olam', paper presented at the conference From Revolution to Revolution: The Soviet Jews under the Soviet Regime, 28–29 December 1992, Jerusalem, pp. 2–3.
11. See A. A. Susokolov, *Natsional'no-smeshannye braki i sem'i v SSSR*, Part 1 (Moscow: Institute of Ethnography, USSR Academy of Sciences, 1990) pp. 97–9.
12. See Sergio DellaPergola, 'New Data on Demography and Identification among Jews in the US: Trends, Inconsistencies and Disagreements', paper delivered to the Institute for Advanced Studies, Hebrew University, Jerusalem, December 1991, p. 12.
13. A. Volkov, 'Etnicheski smeshannye sem'i i mezhnatsional'nye braki', in A. G. Vishnevskii (ed.) *Sem'ia i semeinaia politika* (Moscow: Institute for Socioeconomic Studies of Population, USSR Academy of Sciences, 1991), p. 85.
14. Tolts, 'The Balance of Births and Deaths', pp. 21–2; A. Volkov, 'Etnicheski smeshannye sem'i v SSSR: Dinamika i sostav', *Vestnik statistiki* 8 (1989), p. 18.
15. U. O. Schmelz, 'Jewish Survival: The Demographic Factors', *American Jewish Year Book, 1981*, (Philadelphia: Jewish Publication Society of America, 1981), pp. 70–1.
16. See M. Altshuler, *Soviet Jewry since the Second World War: Population and Social Structure* (New York: Greenwood Press, 1987), p. 37–8.
17. Sergio DellaPergola, 'Jewish Demography', in Jack Wertheimer, (ed.), *The Modern Jewish Experience* (New York: NYU Press, 1993), p. 277.
18. DellaPergola, 'New Data on Demography and Identification among Jews in the US', p. 3; S. Goldstein, 'Profile of American Jewry: Insights from the 1990 National Jewish Population Survey, *American Jewish Year Book, 1992*, (Philadelphia: Jewish Publication Society of America, 1992), p. 92.

19. U. O. Schmelz and S. DellaPergola, 'World Jewish Population 1992'.
20. M. Tolts, 'Jews in the Russian Republic since the Second World War: The Dynamics of Demographic Erosion. *International Population Conference, Montreal 1993: Proceedings*, Vol. 3, p. 101.
21. On this question see, for example, Zvi Gitelman, 'Recent Demographic and Migratory Trends among Soviet Jews: Implications for Policy', *Post-Soviet Geography* 3 (1992), pp. 143–5.

24

Russia's Economic Future:
The Calculus of Jewish Emigration

STEVEN ROSEFIELDE

Economic factors often have a significant influence on people's locational preferences. When individuals contemplate emigrating for whatever reason, they usually try to assess the material ramifications of their choice. They consider national economic prospects, as well as special opportunities and risks that might affect them.

This chapter attempts to evaluate how informed Jews might appraise the economic costs and benefits of emigrating from Russia. It examines basic macroeconomic trends that are apt to shape Russian material welfare in the years ahead, and describes how various institutional reforms are likely to shape material aspects of Jewish life in the former RSFSR.

The analysis is restricted to the Russian future, without a parallel consideration of trends in Israel and the West because it is implicitly assumed that material conditions in developed countries will continue to advance more or less as they have in the recent past, affording a superior standard of living. This assumption obviously can be challenged, and of course it goes without saying that non-material factors may easily dominate economic concerns. Subject to these reservations it will be shown that Russian economic prospects for the remainder of the decade are bleak, but opportunities might be brighter for Jewish entrepreneurs and the Jewish community at large insofar as they are intertwined. Academics, scholars, *institutniki* and blue collar workers will be especially hard hit, and should accordingly account for the majority of Jewish emigrants.

SECULAR ECONOMIC DECAY

Economic conditions in the USSR had been deteriorating for decades, judging from official statistics and personal testimony. The deterioration manifested itself in three distinct ways. Economic growth reflected in the USSR's real gross national product (GNP adjusted for inflation) began to decline steadily after 1968,[1] degenerating into a period of stagnation, followed by an agonizing collapse. For illustrative purposes, if the true growth rate between 1970 and 1990 was 2 per cent, and GNP statistics thereafter are accurate, current Russian national income has fallen back to the level of the early seventies.[2] The situation is far worse if viewed from the standpoint of personal consumption, because the population of the RSFSR grew 0.65 per cent annually between 1970 and 1990, increasing by 18 million people.[3]

Prices have followed a similar pattern. Repressed inflation gradually increased during the Brezhnev years, accompanied by other forms of price distortion. Overt inflation for this period was low, but escalated rapidly, culminating in hyperinflation. The inflation rate for 1992 was 2,900 per cent per annum,[4] it abated to 800 per cent in 1993, and if Prime Minister Viktor Chernomyrdin is to be believed, will fall to under 200 per cent in 1994.[5]

On a more subtle level, the correlation between society's material desires and the goods actually supplied diminished continuously from the late sixties onward as Soviet products became increasingly obsolete relative to consumption standards set in the West. Although, the volume of output rose uninterruptedly until 1989, the worth of these goods in the public's eyes declined steadily, causing considerable discontent.[6]

The crux of the matter then, lies in the fact that the Soviet economy has been degenerating for decades, and although the catastrophic decline of the nineties has some special causes, it is also an artifact of a more enduring process that may not soon disappear (see Table 24-1).

CATASTROIKA

The secular decay of the Russian economy is attributable to the fundamental deficiencies of administrative command planning. The command model, as it is commonly known, rests on the unstated premise that economic welfare can be optimized by preventing private demand from directly influencing factor allocation, production and distribution. Supply in all its aspects is seen as the proper

TABLE 24-1 Aggregate Indicators of Soviet Economic Performance: Growth, Unemployment and Inflation 1975-1994 (per cent)

	GNP GROWTH	UNEMPLOYMENT	INFLATION
1975-1980	4.8	0	0.7
1980-1985	3.7	0	1.0
1985-1990	2.4	-1.0	2.8
1990-1991	-11.0	..	92.7
1992-1993	-20.0	..	2900
1992-1993	-12.0	..	800
1993-1994	-14.8	..	735

Source: *Narodnoe khoziaistvo SSSR*, 1990, pp. 8, 166. *Narodnoe khoziaistvo SSSR*, 1989, p. 47; *Narodnoe khoziaistvo SSSR za 70 let*, p. 482; *Narodnoe khoziaistvo SSSR, 1985*, p. 478; *Ekonomika sodruzhestva nezavisimykh gosudarstv* (Moscow, 1992), pp. 81, 85; Anders Aslund, 'Prospects for a Successful Change of Economic System in Russia,' *Stockholm Institute of Soviet and East European Economics*, 60 (November 1992), p. 16; Emil Ershov, Director of the Research Institute of the Russian State Statistical Committee (Goskomstat), interview October 13, 1992; *Russia 1994*, Center for Economic Conjuncture, Russian Federation, Number 1, (Moscow, 1994), p. 1.

GNP (*valovoi natsional'nyi produkt*) is measured in comparable prices, which many believe overstate growth due to the over-pricing of new and special order goods.

Unemployment: until 1989, official Soviet statistics denied the existence of any unemployment. The 1989 edition of Narkhoz states that there were 4 million transitorily, or seasonally unemployed workers, plus invalids and those who preferred to loaf (mostly in Azerbaidzhan and Central Asia). Using American definitions this probably implies an unemployment rate of less than 2 per cent, none of which is attributable to deficient aggregate effective demand.

Inflation: the statistics reported above refer to retail prices. Many believe they understate inflation because the value added of new goods is exaggerated.

For a more detailed critique of Soviet GNP statistics, see Steven Rosefielde, 'The Illusion of Material Progress: The Analytics of Soviet Economic Growth Revisited,' *Soviet Studies*, Vol. XXXIII, 2 (July 1991), pp. 597-611. The figures for 1994 have been extrapolated from Russian economic performance in the first quarter of 1994 compared with the same quarter in 1993.

responsibility of the state, not the market. Supporters of this approach generally argue that command economies are extremely productive because planners direct resources to their best social use, promote rapid growth through the state's mobilization of resources, and place the common good over individual interest.

Whatever the truth of these assertions, such strategies necessarily create conditions of intense and pervasive disequilibrium because supply at all levels is deliberately rendered unresponsive to consumer demand. This means that the economy may generate great quantities of goods, but little that people desire.

Under some circumstances such as war, the benefits of command resource mobilization may outweigh the costs. But an economy cannot be energized for long by unfulfilled promises of prosperity. Sooner or later the leadership's ability to mobilize community effort diminishes, and the deficiencies of administrative command planning predominate. The negative aspects of controlled economies are easily understood. The unresponsiveness of supply to private demand necessarily means that enormous volumes of resources are squandered by producing goods according to expedient technical norms, the serendipity of accounting incentives and arbitrary directives. This waste not only affects consumer goods, but capital stock as well, causing productivity and social welfare to stagnate or decline even though the capital stock measured in accounting prices rises. Productivity, understood as the utility generated from the employment of a given amount of capital and labour is impaired further as shifting government priorities disorganize established routines and workers reserve their labour in response to their meagre compensation. These formidable degenerative forces which are apt to overwhelm the system, manifest themselves initially in growth retardation, followed in stages by stagnation, decline and in the worst case, mass destitution. The process is best conceived as a strong tendency rather than an iron law. Administrative command planning, buttressed by ideological fervour, technological progress, improved regulation, coercion and terror could plausibly endure, but as Soviet experience and the collapse of East European communism vividly testify, the odds are against it. The evidence suggests that however configured, command systems are prone to degenerate,[7] prompting those who can to emigrate.

These shortcomings were greatly exacerbated under Gorbachev and his successors by policies designed to liberate enterprises from state planning controls, before a properly functioning market could be installed to take their place. Most enterprise managers whether in state or 'collectively' privatized firms, as a consequence, now find themselves in an untenable position where they remain dependent on shrinking state orders, and constrained by excess regulation without being able to offset these impediments by diverting sufficient productive capabilities toward the free market. This schizophrenic liberalization has predictably spawned 'catastroika', a situation in which destructively inconsistent reforms cause an economic implosion; a sudden and drastic contraction in gross national product. The phenomenon may be accompanied by hyperinflation and/or mass involuntary unemployment. It may be triggered and/or exacerbated by civil strife and political disintegration, but whatever its precise etiology, the root cause is a colossal policy blunder, not the normal sclerotic decay of administrative command planning.

The good news implied by this diagnosis is that the policy can be reversed or modified by the political leadership. The bad news is that they are unlikely to do so for a very long time. The reasons are elementary. Russian President Boris Eltsin and a parliamentary majority do not want to reinstall the command economy, but are unwilling either to abandon misregulation or pay for the enormous structural adjustment costs of transition. They are content to fob responsibility off onto the shoulders of enterprise directors by pretending that the formal abolition of central state planning is tantamount to the creation of a competitive market. This enables them to eliminate subsidies, and cut state orders to prod self-sufficiency, while ignoring the fact that managers are paralyzed by a welter of state restrictions, and do not have the financial resources to retool obsolete capital, retrain labour and redesign their products to satisfy private demand.

Various factions have attempted to skirt this impasse through credit expansion, state purchases of unbudgeted goods and endless appeals to entrepreneurial initiative, all to no avail. Hyperinflation, unbudgeted state purchases and the allure of entrepreneurial gain no doubt may have prevented aggregate effective demand from falling even further than it has, but they have not raised capacity utilization rates to normal levels, nor are they likely to do so anytime soon. Expedients of these kinds are palliatives, and no sustained recovery can be expected until the political leadership either abandons stultifying economic controls, or restores much of the old order before proceeding with a sound program that restricts the pace of transition to a structurally sustainable rate.

Neither technical solution is in the political cards. Students of Russian and Soviet economic history know that politics usually are in command, and that economic welfare can be sacrificed for decades on the altar of ideology and dogma. Perhaps things will now be different, but it would be unwise to count on it. Russia could mount a successful recovery soon, at least to the pre-Eltsin level, but the more likely outcome is for more of the same. The reformers will continue to seek quick results by cutting state orders, and the beneficiaries of the new mutated variant of administrative command planning will respond by providing a few privileged managers with extravagant credits, which are nothing less than disguised, lavishly profitable state contracts. Aggregate production consequently will continue to languish, while inflation drives millions into destitution. The outlook, in short, is extremely bleak.

KLEPTOCRATS, CRIMINALS AND ENTREPRENEURS

Social revolutions, like the fall of communism in the former Soviet Union and Eastern Europe, and the economic chaos often associated with them generate legions of victims, and a handful of victors. The French Marxist scholar Charles Bettleheim has vividly described the mélange of opportunists, careerists, speculators and criminals who prospered during War Communism and NEP, subverting communism and precipitating a state capitalist counter-revolution.[8] Regardless of how one appraises Bettleheim's characterization, the parallels between the situations in the aftermath of the Bolshevik and Eltsinist revolutions are striking. In both instances the idealistic initiators of change were not its principal beneficiaries. The bureaucrats, party officials and other state functionaries, castigated as conservative obstructionists by the partisans of perestroika, have not only managed to enhance their power by adapting administrative command planning to the new political realities, but have enriched themselves by appropriating state assets. This stratum, which includes managers locked in a co-dependent relationship with the state sector, can be conveniently described as 'kleptocrats'. Although they own important segments of the means of production and desire to augment their wealth, they are opposed to free enterprise and market competition, which threaten the monopoly rents garnered through their control of the system, and access to foreign assistance. Criminal elements, commonly referred to as the mafia likewise have prospered from the licentious conditions of the times, but they too hardly serve as agents of progress.

The only pro-market victors prodding the system toward free enterprise are a small band of successful entrepreneurs, managers, cooperators and other businessmen servicing the nascent private market without state largesse. It is possible that they may grow in numbers and wealth under post-communist arrangements, profiting from the gaps in the supply system, even though the economy as a whole remains mired in acute depression.

The outlook for the rest of society is unpromising. The wages of workers and state administrative employees are being ravaged by inflation. State demand for the services of the intelligentsia has declined markedly, and those who are still employed receive a pittance. Professors, teachers, and *institutniki* are being treated in the same manner. This trend may be slightly ameliorated by dividends paid to workers as inside shareholders and to the public for its voucher equity. It is also possible that people will augment their incomes materially through petty trade and real estate speculation, but it would be unreasonable to suppose that supplements of these sorts will significantly alleviate the plight of the vast majority, whose lives will be materially blighted for years to come.

CIVIL STRIFE

The economic hardships forecast might well foment civil strife which could have dire consequences for Russia's Jews. They could easily become embroiled in revolutionary insurrections, civil and/or inter-Commonwealth hostilities. Moreover, they could become victims of ultra-nationalist persecution either at the hands of the state, or other demagogues riding the tide of popular resentment against their immiseration. A return to vicious authoritarianism cannot be ruled out, much wishful thinking to the contrary notwithstanding. These dangers are broadly understood in Russia, by Jews and non-Jews alike, and could easily have a powerful impact on attitudes toward emigration. Although they are not economic threats in a narrow sense, the correlation between economic distress and civil disorder is sufficiently plain that this economically-induced spectre should be taken explicitly into account in gauging the near-term prospects for Russian Jewish emigration.

JEWISH EMIGRATION

From the foregoing analysis it may be concluded that economic factors will strongly incline Jews to emigrate from Russia at least until the year 2000. Pressure will be especially severe on Jewish intellectuals, academics, *institutniki*, professionals in wage-controlled occupations, and workers. The enormous possibilities for personal enrichment open to Jewish kleptocrats, criminals, and successful businessmen provide some counterweight to mass emigration. The broad impact of these phenomena is difficult to calibrate, but it is easy to see that if the success of these groups expresses itself in demand for private services which may be provided by the Jewish community, including displaced intellectuals, economic pressures for emigration could be significantly dampened. But, of course, should the Jewish community prosper amid more general destitution, intensified anti-Semitism could well prompt a mass exodus. A serious analysis of this possibility, however, lies beyond the author's self-imposed mandate. Insofar as material considerations determine rational choice, Jewish emigration should be high in the years ahead, mitigated only to the extent that any prosperity enjoyed by a small Jewish commercial and/or kleptocratic élite nourishes the rest of the Jewish community victimized by catastroika.

NOTES

1. *Narodnoe khoziaistvo SSSR, 1969*, p. 39; *Narodnoe khoziaistvo SSSR za 70 let*, p. 5.
2. According to Emil Ershov, Director of the Research Institute of the Russian State Statistical Committee (Goskomstat), real GNP fell 40 per cent from 1989 through Aug. 1992. For the full period through Dec. 1992, GNP probably fell another 5 per cent. GNP would have grown 48.6 per cent between 1970 and 1990 at a 2 per cent compound annual rate.
3. *Narodnoe khoziaistvo SSSR 1990*, p. 67. The standard of living in Russia today measured on a per capita basis could easily be at a level last experienced in the early sixties under Nikita Khrushchev.
4. Anders Aslund, 'Prospects for a Successful Change of Economic System in Russia', *Stockholm Institute of Soviet and East European Economics*, 60 (Nov. 1992), p. 16. The myth that hyperinflation occurs when prices rise 50 per cent per month has crept into the literature. There is no scientific basis for this concept.
5. Prime Minister Chernomyrdin predicted that inflation would fall to eight per cent by the end of 1994. BBC, May 16, 1994.
6. Steven Rosefielde, 'The Illusion of Material Progress: The Analytics of Soviet Economic Growth Revisited', *Soviet Studies*, 43, 4 (1991), pp. 597–611.
7. Steven Rosefielde and R.W. Pfouts, 'Egalitarianism and the Economic Potential of the Post-Communist East', draft, 1993; 'A communist legitimation crisis of substantial dimensions seems to be in the making as a direct consequence of a one-sided success (in mass weapons production), and if the world survives, it will be fascinating to observe whether communist idealism can really triumph over the destructive logos of Stalinism.' — Steven Rosefielde (ed.), *World Communism at the Crossroads* (Boston: Martinus Nijhoff, 1980) p. 323.
8. Charles Bettleheim, *Class Struggles in the USSR: Second Period 1923–1930*, (New York: Monthly Review Press, 1978), p. 8.

25

Conflicting Values among the Jewish Population of Moscow, Kiev and Minsk

ROZALINA RYVKINA

Soviet Jews are known to have strongly identified with the USSR, the policies of the CPSU and communist ideology. Since 1985 four factors, which have emerged against the backdrop of the new political and economic situation, have changed the conditions of Jewish life. The first factor is the upsurge of anti-Jewish activity: the accusation of the 'national-patriots' that the Jews aided and abetted the Bolsheviks; in exploitation of the 'Jewish card' in the struggle against the democratic movement in the CIS; in increasing anti-Jewish propaganda in the press; and in anti-Jewish slogans displayed at mass demonstrations. The second factor is the normalization of relations between the CIS member-states and Israel: the declarations by the governments of Russia, Ukraine and Belarus of their commitment to their Jewish populations; promulgation of the Entry and Exit Law providing for unobstructed emigration; and the massive emigration of Jews in the late 1980s to early 1990s. The third factor is the impact of market-oriented economic reforms: the dramatic slackening of centralized state regulation, greater economic freedom for industry, and the emergence of the private sector. The final factor is political instability.

These factors have had a multifaceted effect on the status and disposition of the Jewish population. Some of them amplify the Jews' sense of alienation from their countries of residence and encourage their emigration. Such is the effect of the first factor — an abundance of anti-Jewish activities of the 'national patriots', and of the fourth factor — political instability. In contrast, the third factor — development of the market in the CIS — has had a stabilizing effect on the Jewish population, inasmuch as it gives the Jews new opportunities for self-fulfilment. The second factor — democratization — works in conflicting directions. On the one hand, a healthier political situation improves the Jews' attitude toward their countries of residence while, on the other hand, greater political freedom facilitates and thus stimulates emigration.

All this creates new challenges for Jewish sociological research into the complex of new social orientations that reflect the anomalous position of CIS Jewry.[1]

This chapter will probe some aspects of these challenges. In particular it will describe the attitude of the Jews of Moscow, Kiev and Minsk toward Jewish national culture, their jobs and emigration. It is based on a survey of the social orientations of 1,000 Jews in Moscow, Kiev and Minsk (333 persons in each city) collected by the Russian Centre for Public Opinion Studies in April–May 1993. These three cities were chosen because they are the capitals of the three Slav CIS countries. The sample in these countries is typical both of the corresponding states (Moscow of Russia, Kiev of Ukraine, Minsk of Belarus) and of the major cities of the former Soviet Union in general, where most Jews live.

NATIONAL COMPOSITION OF THE RESPONDENTS

The Jewish composition of the aggregate sample was to be ensured by choosing individual interviewees from families with Jewish surnames. The families and individual members to be polled were chosen from a list of Jewish households, generated by computer on the basis of 405 of the most common Jewish surnames in Russia, Ukraine and Belarus.[2]

Interviewees were considered eligible for the survey if they met any of the following criteria: were registered as Jews in their internal passports; had one or more Jewish parent (registered as a Jew in his or her internal passport); identified themselves as Jews. Jews having two Jewish parents and a Jewish spouse made up 62 per cent of the respondents; the children of mixed marriages — 18 per cent. Table 25-1 compares the respondents' answers about the nationality registered in their passport with their feeling of national affiliation.

TABLE 25-1 WHAT IS YOUR NATIONALITY? (IN PERCENTAGES)

	By Passport	Personal Identification
Russian	19	13
Ukrainian	6	4
Belorussian	2	1
Jewish	73	63
Jewish and another nationality	—	13
No response	—	6
TOTAL	100	100

It can be seen that the share of those considering themselves Russians, Ukrainians and Belorussians is smaller than the percentage of these national groups as registered in the passports. The number of people who feel they are Russians, Ukrainians or Belorussians is, respectively, 6 per cent, 4 per cent and 1 per cent less than the number of those who are registered as such in their passports. The number of those feeling Jewish is 10 per cent less than those registered as Jews in their passports. Presumably this discrepancy can be explained by the fact that some people consider themselves members of two ethnic groups — 13 per cent of those polled feel they are Jewish but also belong to another nationality. These 13 per cent can be described as national marginals who cannot be classified either as Jews or as members of the other nationality to which they feel they belong. This may be seen as a microcosm of the 'de-judaisation' or assimilation process which began with the inception of the Soviet state or perhaps even earlier and, which has been described in detail in demographic studies.

Thus, 27 per cent of the aggregate sample chosen from a list of families with Jewish family names turned out to be non-Jewish 'by passport' while 37 per cent did not identify themselves as Jews. Still, the sample will be referred to hereafter as 'Jewish' even though, strictly speaking, this is not absolutely the case.

ATTITUDES OF THE JEWS OF MOSCOW, KIEV AND MINSK
TO JEWISH NATIONAL CULTURE

The attitudes of Jews toward Jewish national culture can be discussed on two levels: the first is that of national self-identification as revealed in the attitudes toward selection of a spouse, Jewish religion and languages and actual patterns of behaviour; the other level surfaces when respondents are asked whether Jewish culture should be promoted in Russia, what is checking its development, and what conditions must be established in order to foster it. In the latter instance they take on an altogether different role — that of experts on the state of Jewish culture in their country of residence.

In the course of the interviews, information was collected on both aspects of the sample's attitude to Jewish national culture: the respondents' personal identification, and their opinion on the present state of Jewish culture and its prospects in their countries.

The question 'Were you involved in Jewish culture as a child? Was this involvement strong, moderate, weak or non-existent?' was very elucidating for characterizing the respondents' national composition.

The responses can be broken down in the following manner (in percentages):

Involvement was:
Strong | 3
Moderate | 10
Weak | 28
Non-existent | 57
No response | 2

It would appear that 28 per cent of the interviewees had some links with Jewish culture in their childhood, albeit weak ones, while 13 per cent had rather close ties.

That was the situation in the past. But what is the current situation? To what extent did the respondents have a sense of involvement in Jewish culture at the time the poll was taken? To what extent were they objectively integrated? How was this integration manifested?

In order to clarify these points, a series of questions were asked about involvement in Jewish cultural activities.

The questions were addressed only to people who knew at least some Hebrew or Yiddish. Eleven per cent of the sample knew some Hebrew and 26 per cent knew some Yiddish. A small percentage of respondents knew both languages. Thus, of 1,000 interviewees, 300 responded to these questions. (See Table 25-2)

TABLE 25-2 INVOLVEMENT IN JEWISH NATIONAL CULTURE

	Regularly, often	Sometimes	Never	No response
Attend synagogue	1	32	65	2
Read Jewish Press (in Russian)	5	41	53	1
Speak Hebrew or Yiddish at home	4	30	58	8
Speak Hebrew or Yiddish w/friends	3	28	61	8
Speak Hebrew or Yiddish w/Israelis	4	19	67	10
Speak Hebrew or Yiddish in the synagogue	3	19	68	10

Of the 300 respondents, from one half to two-thirds never attend synagogue, never read the Jewish press or speak Yiddish or Hebrew with relatives, friends or Israelis. That is, most of them do not use their knowledge actively. Between 1 and 5 per cent regularly use Jewish languages.

Membership in Jewish organizations and participation in their activities are an important indicator of attitudes towards Jewishness. Our study shows considerable inertia in this respect. Only 5 to 8 per cent of the interviewees are involved in the work of such organizations.

To verify our conclusions we asked the respondents: 'How do you assess your involvement in Jewish culture?' Here are the replies (in percentages):

Involvement is sufficient	19
Insufficient	62
No response	19

Does 'involvement is insufficient' mean that the person regrets his or her weak ties to Jewish culture? Or is it a simple statement of fact, that is, that insufficient opportunities are available? Perhaps, indeed, the latter is the case if only because the percentage that think this way (62 per cent) is practically the same as that of people not involved in Jewish culture (57 per cent). (see Table 25-3).

TABLE 25-3 ATTITUDE TOWARD JEWISH ORGANIZATIONS

	Yes	No	No Response
Are you a member of any Jewish organization (cultural, religious, political or other)?	5	93	2
Do you participate in the work of Jewish organizations?	8	90	2

As already noted, the attitude towards Jewish national culture has two aspects: a personal one, and a more general one, which could be described as an objective approach. An examination of the first aspect has shown that Jews of Moscow, Kiev and Minsk are far removed from Jewish national culture. The replies to questions about the necessity and possibility of a Jewish cultural revival in the country (Russia, Ukraine, Belarus) reveal an altogether different picture. In the latter case, the respondents were not evaluating their own activity but an objective situation; they assumed the role of 'experts' on the status of Jewish culture in their countries.

Table 25-4 presents a series of such questions. While only 23 per cent of those polled said they belong to the Jewish community, between 62 and 86 per cent think Jewish culture and religion should be revived in their country, although only 39 per cent believe the pre-conditions for this exist.

TABLE 25-4 ATTITUDE TOWARD JEWISH COMMUNITY, CULTURE, RELIGION

	Yes	No	No Response
Is there a Jewish community in your country?	77	7	16
Do you feel you belong to the Jewish community?	23	47	30
Is it necessary to revive Jewish culture in your country?	86	4	10
Is it necessary to revive Jewish religion?	62	16	22
Do conditions exist for a genuine revival of Jewish culture in your country?	39	38	23

If the respondents genuinely wanted to see a revival of Jewish culture, their behaviour might be expected to correspond with this goal. However, they seem to have no intention of taking steps in this direction. Only 17 per cent of those polled plan to study Hebrew or Yiddish, 54 per cent do not intend to study these languages and 29 per cent are still undecided. Only 28 per cent think that Jews should not intermarry; for 68 per cent it is immaterial. A mere 15 per cent raise their children in the spirit of the Jewish tradition.

The respondents' attitude towards Jewish national culture is clearly ambiguous. On the one hand, they are removed from, rather than involved with, this culture and have no profound connection to it. On the other hand, many of them would like to see a revival of Jewish national, cultural and religious life in their countries. In other words, Jews of Moscow, Kiev and Minsk favour a revival of Jewish culture as a matter of principle but are indifferent to it in their everyday lives, when it requires investing time and effort.

SELF-FULFILLMENT IN THE PROFESSIONAL SPHERE

The attitude of Jews with regard to their work is one of relative satisfaction: 73 per cent of those employed[3] are satisfied with their jobs and have no intention of looking for another job; 84 per cent do not intend to change their professions.

Under conditions of market-oriented reforms involving a restructuring of the economy, different causes may lie behind attitudes toward employment: either 1) the respondents' present occupation fully accords with their professional or personal inclinations; 2) there are no established programs in the country for retraining and change of profession; or 3) there are other reasons for the respondents' reluctance to change jobs and professions. Additional information is needed to explain these orientations.

Thirteen per cent of the sample work full-time at non-state, including privately-owned firms, and 3 per cent are self-employed businessmen. These numbers correspond roughly to the percentage of the general population employed in the non-state sector in Russia and other CIS states. In addition, a considerable percentage of people, as many as 8 per cent, hold two jobs — one in the state, the other in the non-state sector. This indicates that the Jewish population is availing itself of the new opportunities offered by the market-oriented economic reforms. Finally, 75 per cent of working Jews are employed solely in the state sector. This is how the answers to the question 'What is more important to you — that is, what would you prefer — work in the state sector, in the private sector or in both at the same time?' Responses were distributed (in percentages) as follows:

Work is more important:
in the state sector	23
in the private sector	28
in both at the same time	46
no response	3

The conclusion is that the working Jews of Moscow, Kiev and Minsk are already making good use, and hope to make even better use in the near future, of at least two aspects of the expanding economic liberalization: the right to free enterprise and the right to hold more than one job. This self-fulfillment in work stems from the position and professional pattern of the sample. Only 8 per cent of those employed in the state sector are clerks without specialized education and only 9 per cent are manual labourers. The rest are scientists (6 per cent), engineers (33 per cent), teachers, doctors, lawyers (17 per cent), creative intelligentsia (6 per cent) and managers (5 per cent). In reply to the question 'What position do you occupy?', 24 per cent of the those polled indicated that they were directors, deputy directors and department heads of enterprises or institutions.

Although nearly three-quarters of those polled are satisfied with their jobs, their evaluations of different aspects of their work vary significantly.

TABLE 25-5 JOB SATISFACTION

	Satisfied	Dissatisfied	No Response
Position	74	12	14
Salary	26	69	5
Relations with management	13	77	10
Relations with co-workers	90	4	6
Opportunities for advancement	44	32	24
Working conditions	64	30	6

The three aspects viewed with the highest measure of satisfaction (74–90 per cent) are the position occupied, relations with colleagues and employment conditions. Salary and relations with management got the highest share of 'dissatisfied' answers — 77 per cent and 69 per cent, respectively. It is worth mentioning that the situation as regards relations with colleagues is just the opposite: here 90 per cent said they were satisfied. Lastly, opinions vary greatly with regard to promotion and advancement opportunities — 44 per cent are satisfied with the way things are, 32 per cent are not satisfied, and 24 per cent chose not to evaluate the situation.

On the whole, participants in the poll evidently set much store by their jobs. Jews have retained their traditional occupations, and they feel a sense of loyalty to the organizations in which they work and to their colleagues. The replies demonstrate that the respondents value what they have in hand, and express dissatisfaction only when the situation is patently unfavourable.

One interesting trait is evident: the Jews polled revealed little drive for advancement, that is, for occupying higher positions in the hierarchy of production and power. When asked whether they were satisfied with their social status or would prefer to be on a higher or lower rung of the social ladder, 45 per cent said they were satisfied, 40 per cent would like to occupy a higher position and 15 per cent did not respond. Thus, on the one hand, they would prefer a higher status. Yet, on the other hand, when asked 'Is it important to you to be a leader?' 'Is it important to you to take part in making important decisions?', 70 per cent and 48 per cent, respectively, said it was immaterial to them. Judging from these responses, the respondents' motivation to 'achieve' is weak. There are many explanations for this phenomenon, but given the current situation in the CIS, the main reasons seem to be the myths concerning 'Jewish domination' in the former USSR and the 'Zionist nature' of the post-Soviet Russian government. Today the opposition is promulgating a number of anti-Jewish provocations, in particular, that the 1917 revolution was carried out by Jewish Bolsheviks; the claim that Jewish Bolsheviks are to blame for all Russia's misfortunes; and that the present democrats who have 'ruined the country' are Jews. In the opinion of this opposition, Eltsin and his team are under the influence of 'Zionism'. It is understandable that the virulent propagation of these myths does not encourage Jews to seek higher, more prestigious positions in the production and power hierarchies.

ATTITUDES TOWARD EMIGRATION

Replies to the question 'Do you plan to emigrate from the country?' were divided in the following manner: yes — 33 per cent, no — 52 per cent, undecided — 15 per cent. Those who responded affirmatively were asked to specify reasons (one or more) for wanting to leave. The replies were as follows:

> For the sake of the children's future — 64
> To achieve a higher living standard — 42
> I do not believe the situation in the country will improve — 40
> Fear of anti-Semitic pogroms — 31
> To join my family — 24
> Fear of violence and assault — 1

This would indicate that three groups of reasons are pushing people to emigrate: 1) familial (fear for the children and desire to reunite with relatives), 2) political (instability, threat of pogroms and violence), and 3) economic (dissatisfaction with one's financial situation). Only 18 per cent are satisfied with their material situation while 74 per cent are not satisfied, and 8 per cent did not respond.

Emigration depends in great measure on people's attitude to the country of their residence. Therefore, in an effort to learn more about the social mechanism of emigration, we asked those not intending to emigrate: 'What ties you to the country in which you live?' We wanted to find out what prevents people from leaving the country, or in other words, what causes people to stay. The respondents gave one or more reasons, broken down (in percentages) as follows:

> I am used to living here — 73
> I feel a connection to this country's culture — 40
> I do not want to leave my relatives — 36
> I do not want to part from my friends — 30
> I hope the political situation in the country will stabilize — 13
> I have a good job — 12
> My prospects for raising my living standard are good here — 8
> I hope to succeed in business — 6
> I am too old — my health is poor — 19

Whereas the desire to emigrate was prompted by family, political and material considerations, pragmatic considerations took a back seat to more subtle psychological motives in deciding to stay; these included attachment to the country of residence, affinity with its culture, reluctance to sever, not only family, but also social ties.

If we compare our model of motives for emigration with the one for remaining in the country, then the following picture emerges:

TABLE 25-6 MOTIVATION

Rank (in descending order)	For leaving the country	For staying
I	Preserving the family, children's future	Familiarity with the country
II	Desire to increase standard of living	Personal relationships
III	Fear of political instability, anti-Semitism	Cultural affinity

It may be deduced that the motivation to stay in the country is primarily emotional and subjective, while that for emigrating is of a more pragmatic nature. The main point, however, is that the motives for staying or leaving relate to different aspects of the life of the Jews polled. Concern for family and children, considerations of survival and self-preservation impel people to emigrate. But the motivations for staying in the country are equally profound. This would seem to indicate that if the countries of residence were to satisfy the pragmatic requirements of Jews, the share of those planning to emigrate would be much smaller. In principle this is self-evident. What is new, however, is that Jews have maintained their strong attachment to their countries of residence, first and foremost to Russia, in spite of the fact that in the latter half of the 1980s and the first half of the 1990s they have lived with the threat of possible pogroms.

In this light, it is worth noting the opinion of the sample regarding the prospects for emigration. In reply to the question 'How many Jews will ultimately emigrate from your country?', 54 per cent believed that the majority would leave. This forecast seems to betray pessimism about the future of Russia, Ukraine and Belarus. The questionnaire also included two questions about how Jews view the political future of their country of residence and their own personal future.

What political system will govern your country a year or two from now? (in percentages):

The country will be freer	13
Less free	24
Will remain as it is today	36
Undecided	27

Are you confident about your own future?

Yes	15
No	72
Undecided	13

If we want to understand the mechanism of emigration, it is also important to understand the attitude of CIS Jews to the countries of destination, in particular to Israel, the intended destination of 31 per cent of those (33 per cent) who said they were planning to emigrate. When asked what kind of country Israel is and what they think about it, only one-fifth of the sample said it was their historic homeland.[4] About one-third knew nothing about Israel, about 50 per cent considered it one of the developed countries. So the respondents do not feel 'the irresistible call of the homeland'. Those who did not name Israel among possible countries of destination were asked to give one or more reasons why they did not want to emigrate to Israel. The answers (in percentages) show a patently unfavourable attitude towards emigration to Israel:

> I will not find a sufficiently good job in Israel — 76
> I have too few close relatives and friends there — 53
> It is difficult to live in a purely Jewish milieu — 45
> I am afraid of the Arab-Israeli conflict and a possible war — 39
> The Hebrew language is too difficult — 31

VALUE CONFLICTS

The analysis of the attitude of 1,000 Jews of Moscow, Kiev and Minsk to their work, to Jewish national culture and to emigration shows that there are deeply conflicting values in both their consciousness and behaviour. These consist of individual conflicts in various spheres of life (family, work, culture, migration, etc.); and conflicts of a more general nature.

In the course of the study two profound value conflicts in the cultural sphere have come to light. The first is between the revival of Jewish national self awareness, on the one hand, and the lack of models for expressing this identity, on the other. The second conflict is between the weak framework for attachment to Jewish national culture and the desire to see more vibrant Jewish cultural and religious activity in Russia, Ukraine and Belarus. This is a conflict between individual motivation in the sphere of national culture and general evaluation of the prospects for this culture in the country. The value orientation of the respondent is: 'I, personally, do not possess this culture but in principle it should be developed in my country.'

In the sphere of work, the value conflicts are between satisfaction with work in general and dissatisfaction over the lack of opportunities for promotion. Here two values clash: the importance attributed to the work place as a collective and to working relationships versus actual prospects of moving ahead in one's professional career.

Finally, the most common value conflict revealed by the study is between the traditional attachment of Jews to Russia or other countries of the former USSR, and the existence of conditions there which stimulate emigration. Here, again, two values clash: on the one hand, deep-rooted personal and family ties with Russia, Ukraine, or Belarus, and on the other hand, consideration of factors such as family health and well-being, and personal safety.

The next few years will tell which trend will prevail and how these conflicts will be resolved.

NOTES

1. Different aspects of this problem were probed by earlier research: in 1990–92 Lev Gudkov and Aleksei Levinson of the Russian Center for Public Opinion and Market Research made a study of ten republics of the former USSR; cf. *Sotsiologicheskie issledovaniia* 12 (1992), pp. 108-11; in May 1992 Vladimir Shapiro and Valerii Cherviakov polled the leaders of 320 Jewish communities from the CIS states. The results of the survey on which this chapter is based do not contradict the results of those polls. A book based on the results of our study is to appear shortly under the title *Between East and West. Survey of the Jews of Moscow, Kiev and Minsk* by Robert J. Brym with the assistance of Rozalina Ryvkina (London: Macmillan and the Institute of Jewish Affairs, 1994).
2. In order to create the sample, the list was produced by linguists and specialists on surnames and then checked against lists of registered citizens in the cities in question. Only family members above the age of 18 were included in the sample.
3. The sample's composition by employment: 65 per cent — employed; 20 per cent — pensioners; 6 per cent — students; 4 per cent — housewives; 4 per cent — unemployed and 1 per cent did not respond.
4. All the respondents answered the question 'What do you think about Israel?'

26

Emigration, Immigration and Cultural Change: Towards a Trans-national 'Russian' Jewish Community?

FRAN MARKOWITZ

Like the Soviet Union, Soviet Jews are no longer a political fact or a juridical category.[1] However, without an agreed-upon categorical grouping for hundreds of thousands of people who lived at least part of their lives in what was formerly the Soviet Union, it becomes difficult, if not impossible, to discuss their 'identity'.

The lack of a politically appropriate, historically correct label is not the only obstacle that hampers a study of this issue. Even years before the dissolution of the USSR, the usefulness of such an encompassing term 'Soviet Jews' had been challenged but used nonetheless. Besides the problem of the ethno-geographical divide among, as Zvi Gitelman calls them, '*Zapadniki*, heartlanders and Central Asian and Georgian Jews',[2] one can also point to the varied experiences of the 'Soviet Jews' under the Soviet regime: some lived through only a few events of the Soviet period, while others passed through them all — World War II, Stalinism, 'the thaw' under Khrushchev, the Brezhnev years, as well as the transformations of glasnost and perestroika. The term 'Russian Jews' is considered inappropriate too, because by definition it excludes the several hundreds of thousands of Jews, Russian-speaking or otherwise, outside the Russian republic, and also because it is more generally used as a descriptive label for Jews in the pre-revolutionary Russian empire. To add to the confusion, hundreds and thousands of 'Soviet Jews' have become residents, if not long-term citizens, of Israel and the United States. As a result of emigration and immigration, as well as political changes from within, former Soviet Jews now span the globe and make their homes in dozens of independent countries.

While discussions of questions of identity among Soviet Jews suffered in the past from lack of information and difficulty of access, the problem today is constrained by a new, double bind: the first results from the dissolution of the Soviet Union, and the second from the variety of experiences that have reshaped the contours of Soviet Jewry. This double bind compels Sovietologists to search for a fitting way of labelling themselves, as well as 'Soviet Jews', and more broadly, forces anthropologists to break with old models as they confront the challenge of working with peoples who migrate, disperse, regroup and change the cultural construction and modes of reproduction of their group identity. Arjun Appadurai justly points out that 'the landscapes of group identity — the ethnoscapes — around the world are no longer familiar anthropological objects insofar as groups are no longer tightly territorialized, spatially bounded, historically unselfconscious, or culturally homogeneous'.[3] Soviet Jews, like hundreds of late twentieth-century peoples, do not in the least conform to tidy definitions of an 'ethnic unit'[4] or 'ethnos',[5] to say nothing of 'nation',[6] and thus they demand the development of new methods and genres for analyzing and writing about dispersed and variegated groups that somehow see themselves — and are seen by others — as linked together into a community by a common past and a shared future.[7]

The aim of this chapter is to tackle these problems by reviewing how the group identity of Soviet Jews has been represented over the past three decades: first, as a unified whole, and then — after emigration, confrontations with other Jewish (and non-Jewish) groups and the dismantling of the USSR — as fragmented. Some tentative conclusions will be drawn about what might be viewed as the re-consolidation of 'Soviet Jewish' — or rather now 'Russian Jewish' — identity from this post-modern variety of post-Soviet Jewish experience. Finally, the significance of a trans-national 'Russian Jewish' community in light of the dissolution of the Soviet Union, will be discussed.

SOVIET JEWRY AND ITS PLIGHT

In the 1960s Elie Wiesel, a survivor of the Nazi death camps, shook the Western Jewish world by alerting it to the tragic situation of Soviet Jewry.[8] At the height of the Cold War and in the aftermath of World War II, Wiesel revealed a haunting contradiction in the position of Jews in the Soviet Union: in all official documents they were demarcated by their Jewish identity but in practice they were denied the right to build social institutions or cultural facilities to support this identity. Equally important was the fact that the stigma attached to their Jewish 'nationality' barred them from full participation in Soviet society. Wiesel's compelling portrait of 'the Jews of silence' — millions of Russian-speaking men and women imbued with an emotionally strong Jewish identity but denied any legitimate means for its expression and vilified just because of their Jewish parentage — became the definitive statement of Soviet Jews and their plight. Indeed, it ignited and intensified movements to free Soviet Jewry,[9] to stop the ethnocide — or cultural denudation — of this people. Noisy demonstrations at Soviet consulates and embassies in major North American and European cities were directed at the right of Soviet Jews to *be* Jews — that is, to practice Judaism, have links to world Jewry, learn Hebrew, display emblems, symbols and ritual items unique to Jews — not simply to be (negatively) labelled as such. And if this were not to be possible in the USSR, then Soviet Jews should be allowed to emigrate to Israel, their historic homeland. In the 1960s and 1970s, emigration — at least in the eyes of Israeli and North American Jewish activists, as well as of thousands of Jews in the USSR — became the logical end result of the Soviet Jews' struggle for their Jewish identity.[10]

Equally, Israel's unanticipated victory in the 1967 Six-Day War could also be seen as the initial spark that inspired Soviet Jews to wage their own fight against ethnocide and to campaign for emigration. However, no matter where the emphasis is laid — on America's campaign to Free Soviet Jewry[11] or on the internal movement of Soviet Jews to free themselves — in the US, Israel, Britain, Canada and Russia itself, Soviet Jews have been depicted as a people resolutely struggling to maintain a positive, historically-imbued and future-oriented Jewish identity under the onslaught of a political system that had given them a legally-constituted, stigmatized Jewish badge of identity but had denied them the right to realize it.[12]

It is interesting to ponder if Soviet Jews actually saw themselves in this same light. While it is difficult to even estimate what proportion of the Soviet Jewish population overtly fought to give positive substance to their Jewish identity, an examination of written works by, and interviews with, immigrants to Israel and the United States gives some clues. Early publications, which featured articles by Alexander Voronel and other members of study circles of Jewish refuseniks in Moscow and Leningrad,[13] perpetuated the idea that Soviet Jewish immigrants, frustrated by their silence, challenged the Soviet system and took pride in learning Hebrew, and studying their religion and heritage. Many Soviet Jews interviewed by this author in New York, Israel and

Chicago, however, denied being modern-day Jewish heroes. They maintained that they had really been striving for assimilation in the USSR and had only left when they — or their children — encountered unbridgeable obstacles in their path. Others, primarily from places in the USSR with a large Jewish population and a long history of Jewish settlement, were puzzled by their portrayal as 'Jews of silence' or as a 'shadow people'.[14] Dora, from Vilnius, spoke of the Israeli folk dance troupe and Jewish singing ensemble in which she was an active participant during her childhood in the 1950s, and Boris, from Odessa, described his father's role as the *gabbai* and *matza*-baker for the synagogue. He concluded:

> Of course my family went to synagogue, and they celebrated all the holidays. As for me, I simply didn't care about this at all. I went to synagogue a few times in my life, but I didn't like it...I just wasn't interested...I always knew I was Jewish, but I didn't think about it one way or the other.

Despite these differences, virtually all agreed that it was difficult for them to delineate tangible cultural traits or religious practices that constituted Jewish identity. Rather than a traditionally-imbued, religiously-motivated, backward-looking Jewish orientation, during the 1970s and 1980s Soviet Jews stressed as their distinguishing characteristics a high degree of intellectualism, cosmopolitanism and a strong drive to achieve, against a backdrop of anti-Semitism.[15] Although these qualities were quite different from those attributed to Soviet Jews by most Western analysts, both the insider and outsider (or emic and etic) views of Soviet Jewish identity shared one feature in common: they tended to be based on a monolithic model or ideal type. In other words, there was agreement that Soviet Jewry — whether described by Israelis, Americans, Odessans, Muscovites or Kievans — comprised one definable unit, a distinct social group with a certain world-view and a tangible group identity based on a common history and destiny. It was only with the onset of Soviet Jewish emigration and resettlement in Israel and North America, that challenges to both ideas of group unity arose.

CONFRONTATIONS WITH JEWISH OTHERS: IDENTITY UNRAVELS

The Western image of 'the Jews of silence' became transformed during the 1970s into *Shcharansky: Hero of Our Times*.[16] Suddenly Soviet Jews were emerging from their hidden recesses, breaking their silence and announcing their intention to emigrate by presenting petitions, forms, documents and requests to the Office of Visas and Registration

(OVIR). Such acts of defiance often resulted in job loss and then the possibility of arrest for parasitism if an exit visa was not issued speedily. Between 1968 and 1980, as hundreds, then thousands, and eventually hundreds of thousands turned in their documents and obtained rail and plane tickets for the one-way trip out, the cowering, almost de-Judaized 'Jews of silence' took on a new cast: now they were courageous men and women risking everything for the opportunity to live as Jews in the Free World.

Only with the arrival of some 220,000 Soviet *olim* to Israel and 100,000 Soviet Jewish refugees to the United States (this is the official terminology used by the Israeli and US governments, respectively) did the hegemony of this encompassing identity begin to crumble. Israelis and American Jews were at first puzzled and then outraged by what they saw as the greater concern of Soviet Jews for their own personal welfare — learning a new language, finding jobs commensurate with their education and economic aspirations, making new homes, finding good schools for their children, and receiving recognition of their status and achievements — than for the broader mission of reunification with the Jewish people. In Israel, long-term residents joked that when 'the Russians' gave the double 'V' for Victory sign as they disembarked at Lod Airport, they were really signalling their wish for a 'Villa and a Volvo'. In America, where well-meaning activists had formed strong lobby groups to 'Free Soviet Jewry', disseminating images of them as 'Jews of silence', prominent refuseniks and Prisoners of Zion, they were surprised and dismayed to find that many Soviet Jews were coming to their own shores and not to Israel. Communal service workers at Jewish social welfare organizations — as well as a significant proportion of the American Jewish public — tossed out their old definitions of Soviet Jewry and came to re-label the newcomers as 'Russians' who were simply not 'Jewish enough'.[17]

In the meantime, former Soviet Jews — now immigrants in new lands — confronted an array of oddities that challenged their own views of Jewish identity. The semi-hostile, or even politely friendly, Jewish resettlement workers and government clerks they dealt with upset their scheme of things (that is, that bureaucracy is *always* antagonistic), and the new immigrants often restored the balance by equating them with Soviet bureaucrats. As they battled against their own (Jewish) people for material assistance and government benefits, the kinship ethic that had existed to unite Jews against a common enemy broke down before their eyes.[18] Second, and perhaps more shocking, they confronted and were confounded by Jews both within and outside their migration cohort who were not only engineers, lawyers, administrators, scientists, journalists, professors, musicians and teachers, but also taxi-drivers, dockworkers, hairdressers, drug-dealers, prostitutes and ne'er-do-wells. In America they found that many of their Jewish neighbours were liberal democrats who scoffed at their fears of communism and their desire for law and order,[19] and in Israel they discovered that some segments of the population — best represented by the 'Black Panthers', a group of young, mainly second-generation Moroccan Jews who loudly and sometimes violently staged demonstrations to bring attention to the plight of Israel's poor — resented their presence.[20] The monolithic meaning of Jewish identity had cracked and was beginning to shatter.

This process of fragmentation was further accelerated by changes that were occurring within the immigrant groups. In both Israel and the United States thousands of newcomers entered the work force, and while social analysts commented on the rapidity of their economic adaptation,[21] individuals re-established themselves in their professions at uneven rates. Indeed, many never did, and while they may now be earning a decent living as manicurists, draftsmen, drivers, janitors and clerks, those who experienced downward social mobility while their friends and relatives either transferred their professions or even increased their status, caused a shake-up in the ethos of sharing that had sustained a value system and common Jewish identity. The friendship and kinship system that had linked Jews together in a place where people had 'nothing but their ideas', fell apart when people could now earn money, buy things, and thus have something to lose.[22]

While Soviet Jewish immigrants on two continents were experimenting with new lifestyles, standards of behaviour, consumer items and definitions of self outside their migration cohort, they also felt compelled to turn inward toward fellow immigrants for com-panionship, relaxation in their Russian language and with their native cuisine, and — most important — for assurances that their old, as well as their new, lives had meaning and merit. As they came together to compare, contrast and re-group themselves, the immigrants recast questions of their identity. Indeed, these new experiences not only caused them to mull over the changes that had occurred in their ideas of what constitutes being a Jew, but they also became acutely aware of another element that they had always taken for granted: just as they were Jews, they were also Russians — despite having been denied an official identity as such in the USSR. Their Russianness, once subsumed under their Jewish identity in the Russian-speaking Soviet Union, only now, after immigration, had begun to take on a life of its own.

At the outset, Soviet Jewish immigrants were surprised and hurt by being dubbed 'Russians' and responded by rejecting this label outright.[23] However, as time went on and they became citizens of the US and Israel, they began referring to themselves as 'Russians' as well, but as 'Russians' in a totally different context and with a completely different significance than that attributed to this term in their old 'Soviet' lives. In the USSR, the designation 'Jew' subsumed a taken-for-granted Russianness, although Russian and Jewish identities (that is, state-approved nationality categories) were mutually exclusive. Now in Israel and in the US, the term 'Russian', includes a taken-for-granted Jewishness. Only through their contacts with other ways of inter-preting ethnicity and nationality as well as with other individuals, Jewish or not, have Soviet Jewish immigrants become aware that being Jewish *and* Russian is not a contradiction in terms.

The untangling of these Soviet, Russian and Jewish strands of identity, while interweaving Israeliness or Americanness into an even more complex and sometimes contradictory self- and group-image, continues to this day. Indeed, in the late 1980s when a new wave of glasnost/perestroika Soviet Jews arrived on Israel's and America's shores the process started all over again, but with a new twist.

At the same time that the first 300,000 and then the second group of Soviet Jews began to leave the USSR and became newcomers else-where, their emigration exerted an impact on those — the majority — who stayed behind. First, the letters, photographs and packages that arrived alerted Soviet Jews to an alternate reality that lay beyond their country's borders. Second, delayed effects of the original under-ground, illegal Jewish study groups and *aliya* activities suddenly re-emerged in the mushrooming of legally-sanctioned Jewish cultural centres, schools and *yeshivot*, and their administrative unification through the *Va'ad*,[24] during the glasnost era. Soviet Jews could and did give voice to their newfound ability for ethnic expression. But again, as in the 1970s, the majority will probably remain quiet, hoping for a renewed opportunity for assimilation.

Now in the 1990s, as the new states of the former Soviet Union confront economic turmoil and political upheavals while reformulating and revitalizing their national languages and cultures, those million[25] to 3 million (formerly) 'Soviet' Jews[26] who remain in the land of their birth face a new ontological and existential problem: they must re-think who they are, what they can be and where they might go — and act accordingly. Like that of their former compatriots who resettled in Israel and the US, their 'Soviet Jewish' identity as a legal fact is no more. While being a Jew during the 1970s in the Soviet Union was not always fruitful or easy, it was predictable. It was an identity that they understood, knew how to manipulate, deal with and live with. Now, without the Soviet Union they must recast their fate much as the émigrés did before. However, this time they must do so without moving, and learn what it means to be Jews in a newly-constituted Russia, Ukraine, Latvia, Georgia, etc., or perhaps simply to become Russians, Ukrainians, Latvians or Georgians. On the other hand, they might decide to take the step they may not have considered before and leave, tying their fate to that of Israel — or the US, Canada, Germany or Australia.

TOWARDS A TRANS-NATIONAL 'RUSSIAN-JEWISH' COMMUNITY?

Already deracinated from a traditional, religiously-based, linguistically distinct and geographically-bound Jewish community, Soviet Jews in the latter part of the 20th century were a quintessentially modern people. With their values of cosmopolitanism and progress, they had staked everything on knowledge and technology and their professions, and ironic as it seems, on their doubts regarding an all-encompassing political system that mandated the Truth. They knew, more or less, who they were, having amended and re-invented their Jewish identity, first, during the 'century of ambivalence' prior to the Revolution,[27] and then in the seventy or so years afterwards. They had witnessed the crumbling of their faith in two doctrines — Judaism and communism — and had become cynical in the wide world. They had learned how to manipulate rules of social behaviour in the Soviet Union and to phrase the 'truth' within the idiom of 'science'. What they did not know, at least in the 1970s, was that alternate lifestyles, cultural meanings and social universes would alter their own views of themselves, especially as regards their identity as Jews.

With their emigration and confrontation with new worlds, Soviet Jewish immigrants not only faced the problem of re-adjusting their self- and group-identity but also challenged their neighbours to alter their perceptions of them. These Jewish immigrants from the USSR, now dubbed 'Russians' by their hosts, became conscious of their Russianness as they thought about and experimented with their Jewishness. And, along the way, they became Israelis and Americans as well. Their Russian language is now tinged with Hebrew or English, their diet, clothing choices, daily routine and mannerisms have all been altered as a result of living and participating in Israeli and American society. Indeed, when the newest emigrants from the Soviet Union began arriving in New York and Tel Aviv, they, as well as the veteran immigrants, were often surprised to find that their old friends and family members were quite different from the people they remembered.[28]

It could thus be argued that people who were once Soviet Jews have been and are now refashioning themselves into a number of distinct Jewish groups that reflect the particular meaning of Jewishness — and Russianness — in the countries in which they are now living, including the successor states of the Soviet Union. It is also possible to contend, however, that the Jews of the former Soviet Union now scattered throughout the world, are united into a trans-national community. This community, unimagined,[29] unintended, and obviously without a bounded territory, rests on a social base of kinship and friendship ties across the continents, and on an emotional base of a common understanding of what it was like to have lived as Jews in the USSR. In addition, it is bonded by a strong value for Russian high culture and the Russian language, an orientation toward intellectualism and professionalism, and an awareness of the necessity of adjusting these values, beliefs and life patterns to a different, non-Soviet reality. With the recently expanded potential for international exchanges of information as well as trans-national travel, the theoretical idea of such a worldwide community has been converted into a reality.

Since the onset of glasnost, a profusion of Russian and Russian-Jewish musicians, theatrical troupes, satirists, poets and comics has been making performance tours in the West. Films and videotapes freely cross borders, linking émigrés to their native country both linguistically and through cultural updates. At the same time, former Soviet Jews from Israel and America have been permitted to visit their old home, and ordinary Soviet citizens have come to New York and Tel Aviv to see what kind of life America and Israel have to offer. Emigré authors give readings in Moscow and St. Petersburg, where they sell or distribute their previously banned books and journals to be read by the home crowd. In addition, the Israeli and Jewish cultural centres that now span the territory of the former Soviet Union serve as attractive meeting places for the Jews of each region. Since they are usually equipped with reading material and videos from Israeli and American Jewish organizations, they also serve as forums for discussing Jewish life outside the USSR and even as launch pads for emigration.

Former Soviet Jews on three continents have become acutely aware that their identity is in flux. As they assess, play out, test and adjust the contours of their Jewishness, and their Russianness, in new socio-political domains, they share the knowledge that they have gained from these experiences with others, both within and beyond their national boundaries. 'Soviet Jews' thus live on in altered identities as 'Russians', 'Russian Jews' or 'Russian-speaking Jews' — abroad and in successor state populations. The post-Soviet trans-national Russian Jewish community that they now comprise both maintains continuity with a past that was not without merits, and provides an arena for consolidating ideas for charting a predictable, comprehensive and satisfying future.

NOTES

1. Any review and analysis of the issue of identity among what have been termed 'Russian-speaking Jews', 'Russian Jews', 'Soviet Jews' and 'Jews in or from the former Soviet Union', is inundated with a flood of problems, not the least of which is this crisis of representations.
2. Zvi Gitelman, *Assimilation, Acculturation and National Consciousness among Soviet Jews.* (NY: Synagogue Council of America, 1973).
3. Arjun Appadurai, 'Global Ethnoscapes: Notes and Queries for a Transnational Anthropology', in Richard G. Fox (ed.), *Recapturing Anthropology: Working in the Present*, (Santa Fe: School of American Research Press, 1991), pp. 191–210.
4. Raoul Narroll, 'Ethnic Unit Classification', *Current Anthropology* 5 (1964), pp. 282–312.
5. Iulian V. Bromley, 'The Term "Ethnos" and Its Definition', in I. R. Grigulevich and S. Y. Koslov (eds.), *Races and Peoples: Contemporary Ethnic and Racial Problems* (Moscow: Progress Publishers, 1974) pp. 17–44.
6. Joseph Stalin, *Marxism and the National-Colonial Question* (San Francisco: Proletarian Publishers, 1975).
7. See Michael M. Fischer, 'Ethnicity and the Post-Modern Arts of Memory', in James Clifford and George E. Marcus (eds.), *Writing Culture: The Poetics and Politics of Ethnography* (Berkeley: University of California Press, 1986), pp. 194–233.
8. Eli Weisel, *The Jews of Silence.* (London: Valentine and Mitchell, 1969).
9. This is not to say that Weisel's book began the movement — see Yaacov Ro'i, *The Struggle for Soviet Jewish Emigration* (Cambridge: Cambridge University Press, 1991).
10. Emigration had been the logical end result for Soviet Jews even earlier, but it was given only indirect expression — ibid. See also Joseph Schechtman, 'Soviet Russia, Zionism, and Israel', in G. Aronson (ed.), *Russian Jewry 1917–1967* (New York: Thomas Yoseloff, 1969); Viktor Zaslavsky and Robert J. Brym *Soviet-Jewish Emigration and Soviet Nationality Policy,* (New York: St. Martin's Press, 1983).
11. William Orbach, *The American Movement to Aid Soviet Jews* (Amherst: University of Massachusetts Press, 1979)
12. See Salo Baron, *The Russian Jew Under Tsars and Soviets* (NY: Macmillan, 1964); Benjamin Fain and Mervyn F. Verbit, *Jewishness in the Soviet Union* (Jerusalem: Jerusalem Center for Public Affairs, 1984); Martin Gilbert, *The Jews of Hope: The Plight of Soviet Jewry Today* (NY: Viking, 1984); Zvi Gitelman, *The Jewish Religion in the USSR* (NY: Synagogue Council of America, 1971); Ze'ev Katz, 'After the Six-Day War', in Lionel Kochan (ed.), *The Jews in Soviet Russia since 1917,* (London: Oxford University Press, 1972) pp. 321–36; William Korey, 'The Legal Position of the Jewish Community of the Soviet Union', in Erich Goldhagen (ed.), *Ethnic Minorities in the Soviet Union* (New York: Praeger, 1968), pp. 315–50; Paul Panish, *Exit Visa: The Emigration of the Soviet Jews* (NY: Coward, McCann & Geohegan, 1981); Sylvia Rothchild, *A Special Legacy: An Oral History of Soviet Jewish Emigres in the United States* (NY: Simon & Schuster, 1985); Solomon Schwarz, *The Jews in the Soviet Union,* (NY: Arno Press, 1972); Boris Smolar, *Soviet Jewry Today and Tomorrow* (NY: Macmillan, 1971).

13. See Alexander Voronel and Viktor Yakhot (eds.) *I Am a Jew: Essay on Jewish Identity in the Soviet Union* (NY: Academic Committee on Soviet Jewry and Anti-Defamation League, 1973).
14. Ben Ami [Arie Eliav], *Between Hammer and Sickle* (Philadelphia: Jewish Publication Society of America, 1967), p. 24.
15. See Fran Markowitz, *A Community in Spite of Itself: Soviet Jewish Emigrés in New York* (Washington, DC: Smithsonian Institution Press, 1993) and Gitelman, 'The Evolution of Jewish Culture and Identity in the Soviet Union', in Yaacov Ro'i and Avi Beker (eds.) *Jewish Culture and Identity in the Soviet Union* (NY: NY University Press, 1991), pp. 3–24.
16. Martin Gilbert, *Shcharansky: Hero of Our Time* (London: Viking, 1986).
17. Zvi Gitelman, 'Soviet-Jewish Immigrants to the United States: Profile, Problems, Prospects', in Robert O. Freedman (ed.), *Soviet Jewry in the Decisive Decade, 1971–80* (Durham: Duke University Press, 1984), p. 97; Markowitz, 'Jewish in the USSR, Russian in the USA', in Walter P. Zenner (ed.) *Persistence and Flexibility: Anthropological Studies of American Jewry* (Albany: SUNY Press, 1988), pp. 79–95.
18. Markowitz, 'Jewish in the USSR'.
19. Markowitz, *A Community In Spite of Itself*, pp. 164–76.
20. See Erik Cohen, 'The Black Panthers and Israeli Society', in Ernest Krausz (ed.), *Studies of Israeli Society*, Vol. 1, (New Brunswick: Transaction Books, 1980), pp. 147–64.
21. See especially Gur Ofer, Aron Vinokur and Y. Bar-Haim, *The Absorption and Economic Contributions to Israel of Immigrants from the Soviet Union* (Jersualem: The Falk Institute Press, 1980); Rita J. Simon and Julian L. Simon, *The Soviet Jews' Adjustment to the United States* (NY: Council of Jewish Federations, 1982).
22. See Markowitz, '*Russkaia Druzhba*: Soviet Patterns of Friendship in American and Israeli Context', *Slavic Review* 50, 36 (1991), pp. 637–45.
23. See, for example, Uri Farago, 'The Ethnic Identity of Russian Immigrant Students in Israel', *The Jewish Journal of Sociology* 20, 2 (1978), pp. 115–28; Simon and Simon, *The Soviet Jews' Adjustment to the United States*; Federation of Jewish Philanthropies of New York, *Jewish Identification and Affiliation among Soviet Jewish Immigrants in New York — A Needs Assessment and Planning Study* (NY, 1985).
24. The *Va'ad* was established in late 1989 as a sort of all-union Jewish umbrella organization.
25. See Mark Tolts, 'Trends in Soviet Jewish Demography since the Second World War', in this volume.
26. Alex Benifand, 'Jewish Emigration from the USSR in the 1990s', in Tanya Basok and Robert J. Brym (eds.) *Soviet-Jewish Emigration and Resettlement in the 1990s* (Toronto: York Lanes Press, 1992), pp. 35–52.
27. Zvi Gitelman, *A Century of Ambivalence* (NY: Schocken Press, 1988).
28. Markowitz, 'Responding to Events From Afar: Soviet Jewish Refugees Reassess Their Identity', in Linda Camino and R. Krulfeld, *Reconstructing Lives, Recapturing Meaning: Refugee Identity, Gender, and Culture Change* (London: Gordon & Breach, 1994).
29. Cf. Bendeict Anderson, *Imagined Communities: Reflections on the Origin and Spread of Nationalism* (London: Verso Editions, 1983).

Notes on Contributors

ABRAHAM ASCHER is Distinguished Professor of History at the Graduate Center, City University of New York. He has published extensively, including *The Revolution of 1905: Russia in Disarray* (1988) and *The Revolution of 1905: Authority Restored* (1992).

MORDECHAI ALTSHULER is Professor of Soviet and East European Jewry at the Institute of Contemporary Jewry, Hebrew University of Jerusalem. He is also Director of the Centre for Research and Documentation of East European Jewry at the Hebrew University. His numerous works on Jews in Russia and the Soviet Union include *The History of the Mountain Jews in the Caucasus from the Beginning of the 19th Century* (Hebrew, 1990), which was awarded the Bialik Prize for Jewish scholarship.

LILI BAAZOVA is a Researcher at the Cummings Center, Tel Aviv University. A specialist in Iran and Afghanistan, she was a Fellow of the Oriental Institute of the Georgian Academy of Sciences from 1975 until her immigration to Israel.

NAOMI BLANK teaches at Bar-Ilan University. She is the co-author of *Underground for the Sake of Rescue* (Hebrew, 1993). Her current research focuses on changes in the ideological approach of the USSR towards the State of Israel and Zionism between 1948 and the Gorbachev era.

VELVL CHERNIN teaches Yiddish literature at Bar-Ilan University. He is the author of several articles on the ethnography of oriental Jewish communities and on Yiddish literature in the USSR.

IAKOV ETINGER was a Professor at the Institute of World Economics and International Relations at the Russian Academy of Sciences until his retirement in 1989. He is the author of ten books and several hundred articles on international politics, and is currently working on a book dealing with Stalin's anti-Semitism after the war and the Doctors' Plot.

415

DAVID E. FISHMAN is Assistant Professor of Jewish History at the Jewish Theological Seminary of America, and Research Associate at the YIVO Institute for Jewish Research. He is the author of several studies on rabbinic responses to modernity in Eastern Europe, and the book *Russia's First Modern Jews: The Jews of Shklov 1772–1812* (forthcoming).

JOHN GARRARD is Professor of Russian Literature at the University of Arizona. He is co-author of *Inside the Soviet Writers' Union* (1990) and *Stepson in the Motherland: Vasily Grossman and the Holocaust* (1995), as well as co-editor of *World War Two and the Soviet People* (1993).

MINTON GOLDMAN is Associate Professor of Political Science at Northeastern University. He is a specialist on Soviet international behaviour and US-Soviet relations and has contributed articles on these topics to *East European Quarterly, Asian Thought and Society* and *Comparative Strategy.*

YOSEF GOVRIN is a professional diplomat, who is currently serving as Israeli Ambassador to Austria. His previous posts included Deputy Director General for Central/East Europe and the CIS, Ambassador to Romania from 1985–89 and First Secretary in Moscow from 1964–67. He is the author of several publications, including the book *Israel-Soviet Relations 1953–1967* (Hebrew, 1990).

ALLAN L. KAGEDAN is Adjunct Professor of Russian and East European Studies at Carleton University in Ottawa. He is the author of *Soviet Zion: The Quest for a Russian Jewish Homeland* (1994) and editor of *Ethnicity and the Soviet Future* (1991).

JOHN D. KLIER is Corob Reader in Modern Jewish History and Head of the Department of Hebrew and Jewish Studies at University College London. Among his publications is the book *Imperial Russia's Jewish Question, 1855–1881* (1994). He is also co-editor of *Pogroms: Anti-Jewish Violence in Modern Russian History* (1991).

IGOR KRUPNIK is a Research Anthropologist at the Smithsonian Institution in Washington, DC. He has published widely on ethnicities and ethnic policies in the former Soviet Union and Jewish communities and cultural resources in Russia. His most recent publication is *Arctic Adaptations* (1994).

ELI LEDERHENDLER is Lecturer in American Jewish History at the Institute of Contemporary Jewry of the Hebrew University, Jerusalem. He is the author of *The Road to Modern Jewish Politics* (1989) and *Jewish Responses to Modernity* (1994).

ALEXANDER LOKSHIN teaches Russian and Soviet Jewish History at the Jewish University in Moscow. He is also a Senior Researcher at the Institute of Oriental Studies of the Russian Academy of Sciences.

FRAN MARKOWITZ is Lecturer in Anthropology at the Department of Behavioral Sciences, Ben-Gurion University, Israel. She is the author of *A Community in Spite of Itself: Soviet Jewish Emigrés in New York* (1993), and several articles about identity, community and family dynamics among Soviet Jews.

SERGEI MIROKHIN is a fellow in the Sector for Arab Countries at the Oriental Institute of the Russian Academy of Sciences. His most recent publications include The Role of the "National Unity" Government in the Formulation of Israeli Middle East Policy' and `The Israeli Position in Light of New Realities in the Middle East'.

YAACOV RO'I is a Senior Fellow of the Cummings Center and Professor of History at Tel Aviv University. He is the author of numerous works, among them *Soviet Decision Making in Practice. The USSR and Israel 1947–54* (1980), *The Struggle for Soviet Jewish Emigration 1948–1967* (1991), and co-editor of *Soviet Jewish Culture and Identity* (1991).

STEVEN ROSEFIELDE is Professor of Economics at the University of North Carolina. He has published widely on the Soviet and post Soviet economy. His most recent work is *Efficiency and the Economic Recovery Potential of the Former Soviet Union* (forthcoming).

DAVID G. ROSKIES is Professor of Jewish Literature at the Jewish Theological Seminary of America. He is co-founder and editor of *Prooftexts: A Journal of Jewish Literary History*, and author of *Against the Apocalypse: Responses to Catastrophe in Modern Jewish Culture* (1984), *The Literature of Destruction* (1989) and *The Lost Art of Yiddish Storytelling* (forthcoming).

ROZALINA RYVKINA is Head of the Socio-Economic Laboratory at the Russian Center for Public Opinion and Market Research (VTsIOM) of the Russian Academy of Sciences. She has published 12 monographs and over 200 articles.

NINA SEMENTCHENKO has been a Fellow at the Oriental Institute of the Russian Academy of Sciences since 1971 and since 1985 in the sector for Israeli Studies. She specializes in Russian Soviet relations with Israel, Israeli domestic politics and the Arab-Israeli conflict.

SHAUL STAMPFER is a Senior Lecturer in the Department of Jewish History at the Hebrew University of Jerusalem. He specializes in large-scale studies of demographic, economic and communal developments among East European Jewry and Jewish education in Russia.

IURII STRIZHOV is Senior Counsellor of the Historical Documents Division at the Foreign Ministry of the Russian Federation. He has served in USSR Missions in Egypt, Burundi, Canada and Lesotho.

MARK TOLTS is a Research Associate at the Institute of Contemporary Jewry, Hebrew University of Jerusalem. He has written widely on the demography of ex-Soviet Jewry, as well as on the general demography of the former USSR.

ROBERT WEINBERG is Associate Professor of History at Swarthmore College. He is author of *The Revolution of 1905 in Odessa: Blood on the Steps* (1993). His current research focuses on the history of the Jewish Autonomous Region.

Glossary

aliya	immigration to Israel
CC	Central Committee of the Communist Party of the Soviet Union
Cheka (ChK)	colloquial name for the All-Russian Extraordinary Commission for Fighting Counter-Revolution and Sabotage, which existed from 1917–22
Council of People's Commissars	name given the Soviet cabinet (government) before 1946, when it became the Council of Ministers; also known by Russian acronym Sovnarkom
CPSU	Communist Party of the Soviet Union
evsektsiia	the Jewish Section of the Central Committee founded in 1918; operated alongside other national sections — German, Polish, Yugoslav, Lithuanian, Estonian, Czech and Hungarian. Abolished in 1930.
GARF	Gosudarstvennyi arkhiv Rossiiskoi Federatsii, State Archive of the Russian Federation
gorispolkom	municipal executive committee
gorsovet	municipal council of deputies
guberniia (pl. *gubernii*)	administrative territorial unit established by Peter the Great; in 1917 there were 79; abolished in 1929
Gulag	Glavnoe upravlenie ispravitel'no-trudovykh lagerei, Chief Administration of the Corrective Labour Camps — organ responsible for supervising the forced labour camps 1934–60
beder (pl. *badarim*)	religious school for children up to the age of 13
kabal (or *kebila*)	Jewish communal organization whose existence had been officially prohibited by the Bolsheviks in the early stages of their rule
krai	administrative territorial unit usually including at least one autonomous *oblast'*
matza, (pl. *matzot*)	unleavened bread eaten at the Passover
MGB	Ministerstvo gosudarstvennoi bezopasnosti (Ministry of State Security); existed from 1946–53; succeeded by KGB
mikva	Jewish ritual bath

minyan (pl. *minyanim*)	quorum of ten men without whom, according to Jewish law, no public prayer can be held
Narkomnats	Narodnyi komissariat po delam natsional'nostei, People's Commissariat for Nationality Affairs.
NKID	Narodnyi komissariat innostrannykh del, People's Commissariat for Foreign Affairs. Succeeded by MVD.
NKVD	Narodnyi komissariat vnutrennykh del, People's Commissariat for Internal Affairs; existed from 1934–46. Succeeded by MID.
obkom	*oblastnoi komitet, oblast'* party committee
oblast'	the main administrative territorial unit after the union republic; corresponds roughly to the former *guberniia*
olim	immigrants to Israel
OVIR	Otdel viz i registratsii, Visa and Registration Department, Soviet Ministry of the Interior
raiispolkom	*raion* executive committee
raion (pl. *raiony*)	an administrative unit in the USSR; a subdivision of an *oblast'*
RCP(b)	Russian Communist Party (of Bolsheviks); name of Soviet Communist Party from 1919-25 when it was changed to the All-Union Communist Party (of Bolsheviks) and finally to CPSU in 1952
RTsKhIDNI	Rossiiskii tsentr khraneniia i izucheniia dokumentov noveishei istorii, Russian Center for the Preservation and Study of Documents of Contemporary History
TsKhSD	Tsentr khraneniia sovremennykh dokumentov, Center for the Preservation of Contemporary Documents
uezd (pl. *uezdy*)	an administrative unit in the USSR forming part of a *guberniia*; in 1917 there were 777; by 1929 all were abolished; *uezdy* were retained in the Baltic Republics until 1949-50
VTsIK	Vserossiiskii tsentral'nyi ispolnitel'nyi komitet, All-Russian Central Executive Committee; the highest state body of the RSFSR from 1917–37, when it was succeeded by the Presidium of the Supreme Soviet
yeshiva, (pl. *yeshivot*)	a school for advanced talmudic study

Index

Judaism (*see* religion, Jewish)
Judenrat, 175–6, 186n

Kabbalah, 202
Kagan, Rabbi Israel Meyer, 252
Kaganovich, Lazar, 120, 191, 193
kahal, 18, 22, 151, 266, 269
Kahanovitsh, Pinhes (*see* Der Nister)
Kalinin, Mikhail, 64n, 75, 90
Kalmyks, 81, 83n, 84n
Kanovich, Grigorii, 230, 243
Karachai-Cherkess, 83n
Karass, I.A., 130
Karelo-Finnish SSR, 83n, 266
Karpai, S.E., 114, 115, 123n
kashrut (*see also shobetim*), 155, 252,
  272–3, 275, 276, 283, 287n
Katznelson, Berl, 240–1
Kaunas, Yiddish theatre in, 229, 230, 231,
  236n
Kazan', 132
kehila (*see kahal*)
Kerosten', 272
KGB (*see also* Cheka, '*chekisty*', NKVD,
  MGB, MVD), 294; archives of, 107, 109,
  115, 224n
Khabarovsk, 92, 97, 236n
Khabarovsk Krai, 88, 97
Kharetskaia, M.P., 106
Kharkov, 128, 180, 186n, 187n, 196, 214,
  253, 259; Jewish religious life in, 266, 271,
  273, 277, 281, 286n, 287n
Khavinson, Ia.S., 118
Khlebnikov, Velimir, 245
Khodaseevich, Vladislav, 242
Khrushchev, Nikita (*see also* Thaw, the,
  CPSU - 20th Party Congress of), 57, 58, 59,
  61–2, 65n, 330, 356n, 390; and Doctors'
  Plot, 114, 117, 118, 122–3, 124n, 158, 164,
  165, 166; policies toward Jews, 227, 332;
  on Stalin's anti-Semitism, 103; on Stalin's
  death, 119; and Ukrainian collaboration
  with Nazis, 192, 225n
Khuskivadze, 295
Kiev, 23, 118, 203, 204, 406; attitudes of
  contemporary Jews of, 391–402;
  Holocaust in (*see also* Babii Iar), 178, 180,
  187n, 188n; pre-revolutionary Jewish
  demography of 22, *31, 32, 35, 36, 41,*
  44n; pogroms in, 130, 132; religious life
  in, 22, 255, 266, 267, 268, 271, 273, 278,
  281, 282, 289n; Yiddish theatre in, 80, 197
Kiev Oblast, 267
Kirgiziia, *196*

Kirov Oblast, 112, 114, 297
Kirov, Sergei, 105
Kishinev, 280, 289n; Yiddish theatre in 229,
  231, 271,
Kissinger, Henry, 341–4
Kniazev, L.M., 130
Kogan, Boris, 112, 113
Kolyma, 111, 112
Kommissarov, M.S., 132
Komsomol, 163, 165, 267, 285n
Komzet (Commission for the Settlement of
  Jewish Toilers on the Land), 89, 90, 91–2,
  94, 96, 97, 100n, 102n
korenizatsiia (*see* nativization)
Korolenko, Vladimir, 243
kosher (*see kashrut*)
Kostroma, 130
Kosygin, Aleksei, 191, 331
Kreizer, Iakov, 119
Kremenchug, 187n, 259
Krymchaks, 276, 366
Kuibyshev, 190, 273, 279
Kulashi, 292–3, *300*
Kuprin, Aleksandr, 243
Kuridze, 270
Kurlov, P.G., 132
Kursk, 128, 213
Kutaisi, 293, 297, 299n, *300*

Lailashi, 290, 298, *300*
land colonization, Jewish (*see*
  agrarianization)
Landsmannschaften, 40, 46n
Latvia (*see also* Riga), 75, 410; demography
  of Jews in, *317,* 370, *370, 373, 374, 376*
Lebanon, 246, 307
Lebedev, V.Z., 306–7
Left-Hegelians, 146
Lenin, Vladimir Il'ich, 58, 103, 150, 201; on
  nationality and the Jewish question, 2–3,
  4, 51–55, 57, 64n, 75, 88, 226
Leningrad (*see also* St. Petersburg), 18, 159,
  196, 341, 348; Jewish culture and theatre
  in, 80, 86n, 229, 231; Jewish religious
  activity in 252, 268, 269, 271, 272, 278,
  287n, 289n, refuseniks in, 405
Leninism, 51, 52, 53
Leskov, Nikolai, 238
Levanda, Lev, 24
Levitan, Rabbi Shmuel, 258
Levite, Lev, 306
Levovitz, Rabbi Barukh Ber, 252
Libya, 349
literature (*see also* Yiddish, literature,

Mukhin, Mikhail, 321
Muromtsev, S.D., 139
MVD (Ministry of Internal Affairs) (*see also* OVIR), 119–122

Nahman of Bratslav, 202, 204, 209
Nal'chik, 275
Namir, Mordecai, 320
Narkomnats (Commissariat of Nationality Affairs), 54, 75
Natanson, Mark, 152
nationalities policy (*see also* deported peoples, emigration, Narkomnats, nativization), 25, 67–86, 176, 184, 189, 226, 286, 318; Jews and (*see also* aliya, Birobidzhan, Doctors' Plot, *evkom*, *evsektsiia*, JAC, Jewish Question), 8, 52–54, 60, 63–4, 64n, 78–82, 193, 197, 274, 405, 409–10; and national literature, 234–5
nativization, 68
Nazi Germany (*see also* Nuremberg Trials), 82, 160, 160, 192, 319, 404; collaborators with, 5, 177-9, 185, 192, 193, 196, 216, 218–19, 225; and destruction of European Jewry (*see also* Holocaust) 174; Jewish resistance to 181–5; linked to Zionism in Soviet propaganda, 61, 334; occupation of USSR by, 4–6, 171, 172, 189, 192; and Soviet Jewry (*see also* JAC), 99, 106, 171–88, 189–91, 193, 196, 264, 266, 276
Neidhardt, D.M., 132
Neo-nazism, in post Soviet Russia, 123
NEP (New Economic Policy), 205, 388
Netherlands, 330
Nevel', 257, 258, 317
Nezlin, S.E., 114
Nezlin, V.E., 114
Nicholas II, 88, 127–47 *passim*
Nikitina, G.S., 326n
Nikolaev, 271, 280, 286n
NKVD, 83, 98, 102n, 276;
Novar'dok (*see* Novogrudek)
Novikov, 116
Novogrudek, 252
Nuremberg Trials, 174, 186n, 224n

Odessa, 18, 22, 150, 196; migration to, 29, 34, 38, 43, 44n, 46n; pogroms in, 131, 132, 136; religious life in, 258, 262, 273, 278, 281, 282, 283, 406; synagogues in, 266, 289
Ogol'tsov, S.I., 109, 120, 121
Ohlendorf, Otto, 174
Okhrana (tsarist secret police), 150
Olevsk, 272
olim (*see* aliya)
Ordzhonikidze, Grigorii (Sergo), 105

Orel, 128, 273
OVIR (Visa and Registration Dept.), 296, 406
Ozet (Association for the Settlement of Jewish Toilers on the Land), 65n, 89, 90, 94, 100n

Pale of Settlement, 3, 18–19, 22, 26, 88, 91, 99, 150, 240; migration from, 29, 38, 42
Palestine (*see also*, aliya, emigration, Israel, Jewish question - Palestine as solution to), 9, 176, 278, 279, 316–20, 325, 326n, 327; Soviet position on establishment of Jewish state in 303–326
The Palestine Problem, 316–17
Paltagashvili, K., 294
Pares, Bernard, 139
partisans (World War II), 77, 166; Jewish, 173–4, 182–4, 188n
Passover (*see also* matza), 261n, 281, 297
peaceful coexistence (*see détente*)
Pegov, Nikolai, 117
perestroika, 63, 329, 348–9, 350, 351, 355, 388, 403, 409
Peretz, I.L., 232
Pieck, Wilhelm, 105
Platonov, Andrei, 241
Poalei-Tsion (*see* Jewish Social Democratic Party), 153, 154, 306
Podol, 281
Podolia, *31, 32,* 34, *35, 36, 41*
pogroms, 2, 127–45, 163, 151, 153, 292; CIS Jews fear of, 399, 400; and Jewish migration, 42; Lenin on, 64n; under Soviet regime, 118, 329
Poland (*see also* Lodz, Warsaw), 240; and Jewish migration, 28, 30, 44n; Jews of, 1, 4, 16–20 *passim*, 24, 88, 172, 174–5, 238, 240; on Palestine question, 306–7; Yiddish culture in 205;
Polianskii, I.V., 266, 273, 274, 278–9, 283nn, 284nn, 285nn, 286nn, 287nn, 288nn, 292, 293–4
Polotsk, 179, 186nn, 258, 268, 285n
Poltava, 128, 214; migration of Jews to and from, *31, 32, 35, 36, 41*
populism, 151
Poskrebyshev, A.N., 116
Pospelov, Petr, 158
privatization, 85n, 386, 388, 390, 391, 397,
productivization, 89, 90
Protocols of the Elders of Zion, 151
punished peoples (*see* deported peoples)
Purim, 123, 269
Pushkin, Georgii, 325

428

Togliatti, Palmiro, 105
Torah, 78, 240, 256, 259, 273, 277, 278, 279, 280
Torikashvili, M., 294
Transcarpathia, 278, 282, 284n
Trepov, D.F., 131
Trotsky, Leon, 89, 103, 148
Trotskyism, 103
Tsageri, 298, *300*
Tsalka, Dan, 244–5, 246–7
Tsarapkin, Semen, 309, 311–2
Tskhakaia, 295, *300*
Tskhinvali (Stalinari), 290, 293–4, *300*
Tula, 128
Turkmeniia, 266

Ukraine (*see also*, Berdichev, Borispol', Cherkassy, Chernigov, Chernovtsy, Dnepropetrovsk, Iagotin, Kerosten, Kharkov, Kiev, Kremenchug, Lvov, Nikolaev, Odessa, Poltava, Uman', Vinnitsa, Zhitomir), 192, 206, 224n, 311; Jews of, 1, 5, 46n, 84nn, 89, 94, 97, 180, 193, 196, 253, 259, 277, 284n, 353; Jews under Nazi occupation, 5, 172, 182, 186n, 189, 212–25; Jews in pre-revolutionary, 17, 18, 20, 24, 29; Jewish attitudes in post-Soviet, 391–402; demography of Jews of Soviet Ukraine, *367*, 370, *370, 371, 373, 374*, 378; post-Soviet, 410; synagogues in 251, 265, 266, 284n
Uman', 279
Union for the Attainment of Full and Equal Rights for the Jews of Russia, 154
Union of the Russian People, 133–4
Union of Soviet Socialist Republics (*see* Soviet Union)
United Nations, 192, 303–328 *passim*, 329–30; condemnation of Israel, 334, 335; Gromyko speech to Special Session of Gen. Assembly, 317; Soviet support for Israel in, 319–20, 322, 323
United Nations Human Rights Commission, 331, 334
United Nations Special Committee on Palestine (UNSCOP), 309
United States (*see also* emigration - US policy on), 9, 25, 192, 193; and Doctors' Plot, 329; and Palestine, 192, 304–7, 310–2; Russian Jewish emigration to, 1, 28, 37, 40, 46n; Soviet Jewish emigration to, 231, 403, 405–412
urbanization, 8, 21, 28–47
Urusov, Prince S.D., 139–41
Uzbekistan (*see also* Bukhara, Samarkand,

Tashkent), 266, 278; demography of Jews of, *367*, 368, 370, *370, 373*, 374, *374*, 380

Va'ad, the (*see* Committee for Soviet Jewry)
va'ad arb'a aratsot, 17
va'ad medinat Lita, 17
Vanik, Charles (*see also* Jackson-Vanik Amendment), 342, 343, 346
Varga, Eugen, 191
Vasilenko, V.Kh., 115
Viktorova, R.K., 106, 107, 112–3
Vil'k, N.L., 114
Vilnius (Vilna), 191; Jewish life in, 18, 22, 23, 150, 175, 191, 229, 230, 236n, 273; pre-revolutionary migration to and from, *31, 32, 35, 36, 41*, 46n
Vilnius Jewish Amateur Theatre, 229–30, 231
Vinnitsa, 268, 271
Vinogradov, V.N., 110, 111, 112, 115, 116
Vitebsk, 22, 178, 252, 259, 261n
Vladivostok, Jews in, 97, 236n; Ford-Brezhnev summit in, 344
Vlasik, N.S., 115
Volga Germans, 76, 81, 191, 193
Vol'fson, M., 55, 65n
Voronel, Alexander, 405
Voronezh, 128
Voroshilov, Kliment, 191, 273, 286n, 288n
Vovsi, M.S., 105, 111, 112
Voznesensk, 280
Voznesenskii, N.A., 191
Vyshinskii, Andrei, 306–8, 318, 320

Wannsee Conference, 173
Warsaw, 22, 23, 24, 27n, 150, 204; migration of Jews to and from, *31, 32*, 34, *35, 36*, 38, *41*, 46n
Warsaw Ghetto uprising, 231
Wehrmacht, 173, 177, 213, 216
Weizmann, Chaim, 277
Western territories (*see also*, Bessarabia, Bukovina, Estonia, Latvia, Lithuania, Transylvania, Nazi Germany - occupation of USSR), 4, 236n, 265
White Russia (*see* Belorussia, Belarus)
Wiesel, Elie, 412n
Wistrich, Robert, 149
Witte, Count Sergei, 128, 131–2
World War I, 20, 203
World War II (*see also* ghettos, Holocaust, Nazi Germany), 4, 8, 189, 247, 263; and creation of State of Israel, 303; religion in USSR during, 263, 271; and Soviet Jewish identity, 82; Stalin on, 195

Printed in the United States
60987LVS00003B/5-16

9 780714 641492